A
WILLIAM FAULKNER
ENCYCLOPEDIA

A

WILLIAM FAULKNER
ENCYCLOPEDIA

Edited by
Robert W. Hamblin
and
Charles A. Peek

Greenwood Press
Westport, Connecticut • London

Library of Congress Cataloging-in-Publication Data

A William Faulkner encyclopedia / edited by Robert W. Hamblin and
  Charles A. Peek.
    p.   cm.
  Includes bibliographical references and index.
  ISBN 0–313–29851–3 (alk. paper)
    1. Faulkner, William, 1897–1962—Encyclopedias. 2. Novelists,
American—20th century—Biography—Encyclopedias. 3. Yoknapatawpha
County (Imaginary place)—Encyclopedias. 4. Mississippi—In
literature—Encyclopedias. I. Hamblin, Robert W. II. Peek,
Charles A.
PS3511.A86Z459   1999
813'.52—dc21   99–17857

British Library Cataloguing in Publication Data is available.

Library of Congress Catalog Card Number: 99–17857
ISBN: 0–313–29851–3

First published in 1999

Greenwood Press, 88 Post Road West, Westport, CT 06881
An imprint of Greenwood Publishing Group, Inc.
www.greenwood.com

Printed in the United States of America

The paper used in this book complies with the
Permanent Paper Standard issued by the National
Information Standards Organization (Z39.48–1984).

10 9 8 7 6 5 4 3 2

To the Memory of
EVANS HARRINGTON
(1925–1997)
Teacher, Writer, Scholar, Citizen, Gentleman, Friend

Contents

Preface   ix

Abbreviations   xiii

The Encyclopedia   1

Selected Bibliography   449

Index   461

About the Contributors   485

Preface

William Faulkner is sometimes called "the American Shakespeare."¹ The recent centennial of his birth—September 25, 1997—was celebrated not only in his native Mississippi, where a life-size bronze statue of the famous author was placed on his hometown square, but also across the nation and even in such distant places as Paris, Beijing, Moscow, Tokyo, and Venice. Another measure of Faulkner's worldwide success and acclaim is that since his winning of the Nobel Prize for Literature in 1950 the annual Modern Language Association Bibliography has listed almost 5,000 scholarly books and articles devoted to his works—on average, more than 100 per year. Among his contemporaries, only James Joyce has received as much critical attention.

Despite Faulkner's international fame and ongoing critical repute, there has not been until now an encyclopedia of his life and work. Previous overviews such as Dorothy Tuck's *Crowell's Handbook of Faulkner* (1964), Edmond L. Volpe's *A Reader's Guide to William Faulkner* (1964), and Walter K. Everett's *Faulkner's Art and Characters* (1969)—all highly useful books in their time— employed a much more restricted focus than the present work. Moreover, these books (when they can still be found) now appear quite dated, written as they were before the posthumous publication of a number of Faulkner texts and before the advent of deconstructionist approaches that have redefined Faulkner's handling of race, class, and gender issues.

Terry Eagleton has argued that any great writer's so-called universal appeal and stature result not so much from a worldwide or even national consensus regarding an absolute and timeless set of values as on the continuing relevance of that writer's texts to the shifting needs and emphases of successive generations of readers. Faulkner represents, and has benefited from, both sides of this question. Certainly he gave expression on numerous occasions to his belief in universality, what he termed "the old verities of the human heart"; and great numbers of readers, both in the United States and around the world, have found in his books a poignant and accurate rendering of the ageless human condition. At the same time, there can be little doubt that a great deal of the challenge and attraction of Faulkner's texts has resulted from their relevance to changing times and conditions. Just as Faulkner's individual texts communicate through the differing voices of multiple narrators, so also do his texts as a whole speak in various ways to succeeding generations of readers. Early reviewers found Faulkner's work to be, for both better and worse, the epitome of modernist art— experimental, willfully complex and obscure, subjective, and antitraditional. These early readers similarly debated whether Faulkner's writings were moral or immoral, decent or indecent, uplifting or depressing. By the 1940s and 1950s, literary and artistic considerations gave way to cultural approaches: Faulkner's works were now interpreted as a compendium of the American South, both past and present, and were frequently offered as guidebooks to social and racial reform of the region. From the 1960s onward Faulkner has increasingly become the focus of race, class, and gender critics who have repackaged his texts as statements (or silences) regarding the evolving roles of blacks, women, gays, and other minorities in contemporary culture. Concurrent with all of the above approaches, there has been a growing international interest in Faulkner, quite independent of ''American'' or ''Southern'' concerns.

Given the multiple voices of both Faulkner's texts and the critics who read and interpret those texts, it seemed not merely appropriate but necessary that the contents of this encyclopedia represent a multiplicity of approaches to Faulkner's work. We are pleased that more than fifty contributors have supplied material for this volume; many of these are well-known and highly respected Faulkner scholars, but happily a number of contributors are younger scholars or others only recently coming to the study of Faulkner. Contributors include representatives of research institutions, four-year colleges, community colleges, and secondary schools; of regional, national, and global perspectives; and of various races, origins, and genders. In sum, the volume reflects a variety of critical approaches—textual, biographical, historical/cultural, modernist, formalist, mythic, psychoanalytic, materialist, humanistic, deconstructionist, comparative. While as editors we have been required to seek a degree of consistency in style and format, we have neither sought nor desired to have all contributors write or think alike. To have done so, we believe, would not only have violated the very concept of an *encyclopedia*; it would also, we feel quite sure, have caused the ghost of Faulkner to rise up in protest.

Arranged alphabetically, the topics in this volume include Faulkner's works and major characters and themes, as well as the literary and cultural contexts in which the works were conceived, written, and published. There are also entries on relatives, friends, and other persons important to Faulkner's biography; on historical events, personages, and places; on social and cultural developments; on literary and philosophical terms and movements. Despite its range of topics, the volume does not purport to be a gallery of Faulkner's characters, a glossary of his times, or a reference guide to individual works. Our intended goal is to apprise an already literate reader of what constitutes the main body of Faulkner's work and to demonstrate why the critical estimation of that work is so secure and still growing. While we have sought to ensure that all entries meet scholarly standards of reason, accuracy, and thoroughness and prove to be both interesting and useful to academics, we also hope that the book will assist those as yet unversed in reading and appreciating Faulkner's work. Ideally, the volume will encourage in all its users further exploration of the varied issues and circumstances that situate Faulkner's work for readers at the beginning of the twenty-first century.

To assist in this ongoing exploration, we have appended topic-specific references for further reading to many of the individual entries, as well as provided a selected bibliography of Faulkner sources at the end of the book. In order to save space and avoid redundancies, we have not, except in essential cases, duplicated titles in these bibliographies. When duplication has been deemed necessary, we have used truncated formats in the entries and full treatment in the selected bibliography. Certain approaches to the study of Faulkner, at this point in time, must be accepted as axioms. Readers interested in Faulkner's short stories, for example, should consult the books by Carothers, Skei, Ferguson, and Jones; those seeking biographical information must utilize the biographies by Blotner, Minter, Karl, Oates, Williamson, and Gray; those desiring to critique Faulkner's characterizations of women should read Page, Roberts, Clarke, Gwin, and Williams; those wishing to know more about Faulkner and Hollywood will benefit from the works of Kawin, Phillips, and Brodsky and Hamblin; those interested in the evolution of Faulkner's texts should examine the forty-four-volume Garland facsimile edition of Faulkner's manuscripts, edited by Blotner et al. Since such associations are givens in the study of Faulkner, there seemed no real reason to repeat those titles over and over again in this volume.

We have also sought, both to facilitate reading and to conserve space, to keep internal citations to a minimum, both in number and in wording. Moreover, because as yet there is no definitive edition of Faulkner's texts (the ''corrected texts'' project presently under way is far from finished), we have elected not to include page references to particular Faulkner editions. Readers interested in locating particular quotations in Faulkner's works are referred to the helpful series of *Faulkner Concordances* issued by UMI Research Press. When we have employed internal citations, they refer to works listed either at the foot of the individual entry or at the end of the book. Only works not listed in either of those places are given detailed internal treatment. Throughout, a number of frequently cited titles are abbreviated; a list of those abbreviations may be found at the front of the volume. With such devices, we have attempted to limit scholarly apparatus and jargon and make the book as reader-friendly as possible.

As editors, we are deeply grateful to Greenwood Publishing Group for proposing this project and for entrusting it to us. We owe a special debt of gratitude to George F. Butler, Greenwood's Associate Editor for Acquisitions, for his great kindness and indispensable advice and counsel from start to finish, and to

Gillian Beebe and Lisa Webber, Production Editors, and Susan E. Badger, Copy-editor, for their expert assistance. We also want to acknowledge and express appreciation for the support of our respective institutions, Southeast Missouri State University and the University of Nebraska at Kearney, each of which provided financial assistance, clerical help, and released time to ensure the completion of the work. We especially want to thank (at Southeast) Carol Scates, Chair of the Department of English; Michael Hogan, Professor of English and Director of the Graduate Assistant Program; Martin Jones, Dean of the College of Liberal Arts; Charles Kupchella, Provost; and the Grants and Research Funding Committee; and (at Nebraska–Kearney) Robert Luscher, Chair of the English Department; Ken Nikels, Dean of the Office of Graduate Studies and Research; and the Research Services Council. We also sincerely thank the succession of research assistants who provided essential help at various stages of the project: Rebecca Humphrey, Darcy Schultz, Dawn Pearson, Betsy Baker, Mary Pyron, Jessica Hesse, Douglas Howard, Charlotte Grider, Andrew Mebane, Michelle Slinkard, and Wendy Talliaferro.

All of the material support acknowledged above would have been insufficient without the emotional support of family, colleagues, and friends. We are particularly indebted to our colleagues in English at Southeast and Kearney, and we express our warmest love and gratitude to Kaye Hamblin and Nancy Peek for allowing us the time and space for this undertaking.

We save our final words of thanks for our contributors, the ones who made the book, and our readers, the ones who will use it. To the former we are grateful for your hard work, patience, and cooperation; your efforts have validated for us once more the immense joy and satisfaction to be found in the collaborative acts of scholarship, teaching, and learning. To the latter we are grateful for your curiosity about, interest in, or passion for Faulkner that has led you to these pages. If in any way this volume proves useful to you in your quest to know more about the small man who became the giant of twentieth-century American literature, then the efforts of all of us—editors and contributors—will have been amply rewarded.

Robert W. Hamblin

Charles A. Peek

Abbreviations

EPP	*William Faulkner: Early Prose and Poetry*, edited by Carvel Collins
ESPL	*Essays, Speeches & Public Letters by William Faulkner*, edited by James B. Meriwether
FAB	*Faulkner: A Biography*, by Joseph Blotner
FCF	*The Faulkner-Cowley File*, by Malcolm Cowley
FIU	*Faulkner in the University*, edited by Frederick L. Gwynn and Joseph L. Blotner
FR	*The Faulkner Reader*
FWP	*Faulkner at West Point*, edited by Joseph L. Fant and Robert Ashley
LIG	*Lion in the Garden: Interviews with William Faulkner*, edited by James B. Meriwether and Michael Millgate
PF	*The Portable Faulkner*, edited by Malcolm Cowley
SL	*Selected Letters of William Faulkner*, edited by Joseph Blotner

A

ABSALOM, ABSALOM!, Faulkner's eighth novel, published in 1936, is generally recognized as one of the greatest American novels ever written. Different elements and techniques for what was to become *Absalom* apparently were on Faulkner's mind as early as the late 1920s, when he finished his stories "Mistral," with its shared narration, and "The Big Shot," with a character who somewhat resembles Thomas Sutpen. At the source of the novel stood, more directly, two short stories of the early 1930s: "Evangeline," which introduces Colonel Sutpen and Henry, the son who kills his sister Judith's husband to prevent the consummation of a marriage that would have meant bigamy, miscegenation, and (in the mind of a narrator who foreshadows Quentin Compson) incest; and "Wash," which concerns the murder of Thomas Sutpen by Wash Jones for the abuse of the latter's granddaughter Milly.

In early 1934 Faulkner began combining these stories into a manuscript that he initially entitled *Dark House*. "Roughly," he wrote to his publisher Harrison Smith, "the theme is a man who outraged the land, and the land then turned and destroyed the man's family." He had decided that Quentin Compson, his protagonist from *The Sound and the Fury*, would be his main and final narrator. As he further explained to Smith: "I use him because it is just before he is to commit suicide because of his sister, and I use his bitterness which he has projected on the South in the form of hatred of it and its people to get more out of the story itself than a historical novel would be" (*SL* 79).

By August 1934 Faulkner had decided on a different title, *Absalom, Absalom!*, shifting the attention from the house and its darkness to the relationship between a father and a son of mixed blood, as in the biblical story of David and Absalom (2 Samuel 13). Faulkner worked on the novel off and on while employed by Twentieth Century–Fox in Hollywood as a scriptwriter, finishing it after much difficulty in early 1936. After the book was published by Random House in

October of that year, Faulkner reportedly said: "I think it's the best novel yet written by an American" (Gray 204).

Not everyone, however, was of this opinion. Although the New York *Herald Tribune* called the author "a Southern Orestes" and the *Nation* named him "a lyric poet," others considered the work boring, unnecessarily complicated, even unreadable. Mary-Carter Roberts in the Washington *Evening Star* saw Faulkner "fighting with his own prose like a man slashing his way through a forest of falling velvet curtains armed only with a dull knife." Receiving little attention even in the South, the novel had earned Faulkner only about $3,000 after four years. It is, of course, as all reviewers agreed, a difficult novel to read, with each of its different narrators seriously disturbing the chronology of the original events and bringing in his or her own experiences, interpretations, prejudices, and motivations; and it has continued to puzzle and exasperate readers over the years.

Dirk Kuyk, Jr.'s *Sutpen's Design* categorizes the types of difficulties that readers of *Absalom, Absalom!* have encountered, as well as the solutions that they have found—for instance, in focusing on "narrative form," "allusion," "historical analysis," or "foreign" theories like those of Roland Barthes, Jacques Derrida, and Sigmund Freud to make sense of the work. Kuyk warns that such approaches have led to oversimplification and an underappreciation of the uniqueness of the work. One such simplification concerns the denial by some critics of any form of external reality in the narrative.

Richard Gray calls the novel "Faulkner's greatest historical novel, in the sense that it investigates the meanings of history." He views it as "a version of Einstein's theory of relativity or Heisenberg's formulation of the indeterminacy principle" (205–206). Nevertheless, he stresses that even if the stories of the different narrators are necessarily untrustworthy, this does not mean that the historical account they try to relate does not exist. As Gray puts it: All of the novel's narrators—Rosa Coldfield, Jason Compson, Quentin Compson, and Shreve McCannon—create "the idea of yesterday" in terms of their own "unfinished business of today" (225). Thus the novel may be called historical as well as psychological.

Absalom, Absalom! is, indeed, one of Faulkner's great "psychological novels," and it can be seen as one long answer to the most worrying questions that an outsider can ask a Southerner: *"What's it like there. What do they do there. Why do they live there. Why do they live at all?"* In an attempt to answer these questions, for himself as much as for his Canadian friend Shreve, Quentin Compson draws on a mixture of fact and fiction concerning the legendary Thomas Sutpen and his family, former inhabitants of his own hometown. But Quentin cannot answer the questions satisfactorily, not even for himself, and the imaginative re-creation of Sutpen's life and downfall that the two friends engage in only moves Quentin closer to his ultimate suicide, for which he is preparing himself in *The Sound and the Fury*. If *Absalom* is read in close connection with the earlier novel, as Estella Schoenberg and others have convincingly argued, it clearly provides more complex reasons behind Quentin's suicide than his problematic desire for his sister Caddy.

The story of Thomas Sutpen, as constructed by the two friends, presents itself as a classic Gothic frame story—John Irwin compares it to Poe's "The Fall of the House of Usher"—with its different levels of narration and, at its core, the young Sutpen's devastating experience of being sent to the back door of the planter's house by a "monkey nigger." In an attempt to redress this insult, Sutpen puts into place his "design," promising himself not to rest before he has established his own dynasty. As Faulkner explained in an interview, "[Sutpen] said, I'm going to be the one that lives in the big house, I'm going to establish a dynasty, I don't care how, and he violated all the rules of decency and honor and pity and compassion" (*FIU* 35).

Thus he feels compelled to reject his first wife and newborn son because of the drop of black blood they supposedly possess; he alienates his second wife, their children Henry and Judith, and the rest of the family, especially his wife's younger sister Rosa Coldfield, by whom he hopes to father a new heir outside marriage. As John Longley states, Sutpen "has not only isolated himself from all human commitments, he has committed the worse sin of violating the sanctity of the individual human heart" (216). It is this flaw that makes him unable to accomplish the design by which he would have managed to "undo" the insult of his early experience and that ultimately causes the collapse of the dynasty he had wanted to establish, leaving nothing behind but the "haunted" mansion with the name Sutpen's Hundred.

Critics have recognized the theme of the rejected child in the core story, as well as its parallel in the story of Charles Bon, Sutpen's mulatto son, who, in turn, is rejected and comes to haunt his father by threatening to marry Judith. Pretending not to know that she is his half sister, he seeks desperately to force his father to tell him, to prevent the sin of incest, and thus to acknowledge him as his son. Fewer critics have given due attention, however, to the personal parallels created by Quentin's own "unfinished business" around this theme. In *The Sound and the Fury*, Quentin, after all, pretends to have committed incest with his sister to force his own father into acknowledging his despair. In *Absalom*, Quentin's despair is clear when he finally answers the last of his friend's questions, "Why do you hate the South?" by insisting, "I dont hate it . . . I dont hate it."

In an interview with Sally Wolff, Faulkner's nephew Jimmy Faulkner argues that the love-hate feelings that Quentin Compson expresses here were not Faulkner's own. As he puts it: "Brother Will didn't hate it; he loved it" (Wolff and Watkins 173). Yet it is clear, as demonstrated in the essay "Mississippi," that Faulkner could imagine such a love-hate relationship with his native South. The novel combines many of the most sensitive taboo issues of the South, and most of these are issues that might well induce feelings of both love and hate.

The intimate view of the Southern people that the novel presents exposes the very roots of Southern myths, among them the aristocracy myth: the belief that

the real Southerner had sprung from the most honorable of English Cavaliers, which sets Thomas Sutpen apart as a brute among them; the myth of the Great Southern Heart, which justifies the way people are classified and subsequently treated in the South; and above all, the myth of the purity of the Southern white woman, perpetuator of white supremacy and symbol of the South, which goes far to explain the impact of incest and miscegenation at the heart of the novel.
See also **Gothic**.

FURTHER READING

Bloom, Harold, ed. *Modern Critical Interpretations of William Faulkner's* Absalom, Absalom! New York: Chelsea House, 1987.

Goldman, Arnold, ed. *Twentieth Century Interpretations of* Absalom, Absalom! Englewood Cliffs, N.J.: Prentice-Hall, 1971.

Kinney, Arthur F. *Critical Essays on William Faulkner: The Sutpen Family*. Boston: G. K. Hall, 1996.

Kuyk, Dirk, Jr. *Sutpen's Design: Interpreting Faulkner's* Absalom, Absalom! Charlottesville: University Press of Virginia, 1990.

Montauzon, Christine D. *Faulkner's* Absalom, Absalom! *and Interpretability: The Inexplicable Unseen*. Berne, Switzerland: Peter Lang, 1985.

Parker, Robert Dale. Absalom, Absalom!: *The Questioning of Fictions*. New York: Twayne, 1991.

Ragan, David Paul. *Annotations to William Faulkner's* Absalom, Absalom! New York: Garland, 1991.

———. *William Faulkner's* Absalom, Absalom!: *A Critical Study*. Ann Arbor, Mich.: UMI Research Press, 1987.

Schoenberg, Estella. *Old Tales and Talking. Quentin Compson in William Faulkner's* Absalom, Absalom! *and Related Works*. Jackson: University Press of Mississippi, 1977.

Ineke Bockting

"ABSOLUTION, AN." *See* **"Fire and the Hearth, The."**

"AD ASTRA," a short story by Faulkner, first collected in *These 13* (1931) and included in *Collected Stories*. Written in 1918, "Ad Astra" reflects Faulkner's thoughts about World War I, expressed through the speeches of a philosophically minded Indian "subadar," a chief native officer in the British Indian Army, who describes his Western companions as "robbed of all save the impotence and the need." The story also shows Faulkner's ability to write fiction with an international cast of characters. That loss of identity is a central concern is made clear in the opening paragraph: "I don't know what we were. With the exception of Comyn, we had started out Americans, but after three years, in our British tunics and British wings and here and there a ribbon, I dont suppose we had even bothered in three years to wonder what we were, to think, or to remember." American Southerners remain much in evidence, although as the evening's drunkenness continues, they are joined by Frenchmen, an Irishman, a

German prisoner, and the Indian subadar who remains cold sober through it all and comments tellingly on the personal disintegrations that give the story's title, "Ad Astra" (To the Stars), its darkly ironic twist.

"Ad Astra" is essentially a mood piece, one that captures the wasteland of war and the aimless drinking it occasions, as well as the necessary illusions that individual aviators mount against their psychic destruction. Bland, for example, drunkenly insists that he has a wife stateside, although his companions are well aware that he is not married. Mentions of this illusionary person, however, in effect, frame the story, suggesting a measure of just how sterile the landscape has in fact become. Comyn, a drunken Irishman, insists on fighting a man named Monaghan and proudly boasts that he is willing to give him a shilling for the privilege. Meanwhile, Monaghan has a German prisoner in tow whom he intends to take back to America as a living trophy/souvenir of his war experience. Unlike Bland, however, the German really does have a wife and son waiting for him back in Beyreuth. Even more important is the German's tragicomic rendering of his family history and the tangled ways it has led to a sense of national doom: "Defeat will be good for us. Defeat iss good for art; victory, it iss not good." Comyn makes much the same point from an Irish perspective.

The story itself moves by slow inches until the assembled crew of disaffected Americans, along with Comyn and the enigmatic subadar, reach a French watering hole in Amiens, where the motley crew swells in number with one mission in common—to drink themselves into oblivion. As the subadar puts it: "What is your destiny except to be dead? It is unfortunate that your generation had to be the one. It is unfortunate that for the better of your days you will walk the earth a spirit." Faulkner's subject, then, is the war's destruction of values as exemplified through a representative sampling of world-weary soldiers who exemplify what the subadar—and Faulkner himself—calls the "pitiableness of man."

"Ad Astra" has received scant critical attention. The bulk of the commentary either points out the influence of Elliot White Springs (*War Birds*) or suggests the ways that Faulkner's early portrayal of aviators culminates in *Pylon*. Other possibilities, however, are surely closer at hand, because with the story's introduction of Bayard Sartoris and the death of his twin brother, John, there are intimations of the tragic destiny that Faulkner would develop more richly in *Flags in the Dust/Sartoris*.

FURTHER READING

Collins, Carvel. " 'Ad Astra' Through New Haven: Some Biographical Sources of Faulkner's War Fiction." *Faulkner and the Short Story*, ed. Harrington and Abadie. 108–127.

Dillon, Richard T. "Some Sources for Faulkner's Version of the First Air War." *American Literature* 44 (1973): 629–637.

MacMillan, Duane. "*Pylon*: From Short Stories to Major Work." *Mosaic* 7 (Fall 1973): 185–212.

Sanford Pinsker

"ADOLESCENCE," an early short story by Faulkner. According to Faulkner, this story was composed in the early 1920s. Although he probably tried to sell the story, no record confirms such efforts, and it was not published until *Uncollected Stories* (1979). Concurrent with the changes from "her flat body" to the development of her "hard little breasts," Juliet Bunden's response to her world changes from defiance to despair. Leaving is the one certainty Juliet knows, and her response to most leave-taking is, Good riddance. Yet when her friend Lee Hollowell leaves without a good-bye, and her eleven-year-old brother Bud sets out on his own, she turns her weeping eyes to the "sharp earth." Juliet's infirm grandmother, the one stable influence in her short life, will soon leave her, too.

Diane Brown Jones

AFRICAN AMERICAN history and culture influenced Faulkner as a person and as an artist. Growing up, he heard the drums from the Negro cabins; he attended dances played by W. C. Handy and visited jukes in the Delta; and later his exposure to the greater world afforded him acquaintance with African Americans of diverse personalities, views, and attainments. While it is hard to determine if he had read African American authors such as Paul Laurence Dunbar, Charles Waddell Chestnutt, and James Weldon Johnson, he acknowledged that he read some of those contemporary to him, especially Richard Wright, with whom he corresponded about *Native Son* and *Black Boy*.

Faulkner's own influence on African American writers was felt and often acknowledged. Ralph Ellison, Ernest Gaines, and Albert Murray come immediately to mind. John Duvall believes, "Toni Morrison's fiction . . . suggests particular resonances between her writing and that of . . . Faulkner" (Kolmerten, Ross, and Wittenberg 5).

Significant elements of spirituals, jazz, and blues can be traced in Faulkner's fiction. Thadious Davis shows how, during the period of "reverse acculturation" that "positioned blacks as referential structures for whites," Faulkner developed two bases for black characterization. The less positive (drawn from examples from *Soldiers' Pay*) is a configuration from jazz that features "encounter between blacks and whites . . . meanings of amassed emotion and rhythm that . . . discourage individuation, and forward comic portraiture" (Fowler and Abadie, *Faulkner and Race* 71, 81). However, the more significant and positive is a configuration from blues from which Faulkner derived a "structure of emotion" that gave blacks "autonomous knowing" and authentic "folk tradition" and gave his portraits of them "meaning that is both personal and communal" (86, 82, 90). Here, Davis focuses on Rider's characterization in "Pantaloon in Black." Jazz, blues, and their cultural backgrounds may also have been the sources for Faulkner's attraction to some aspects of primitivism and, though they transcend race, his acquaintance with figures such as the Trickster and Rover Man.

Clearly, something must have challenged the upbringing Blyden Jackson describes as "designed to present Negroes in a most unfavorable light." As he notes, Faulkner's fictional Negroes are not confined to the only types he was brought up to accept: the "incorrigibly childlike" or the "degraded . . . brutal . . . danger to the social order of America and . . . stench in the nostrils of every right-thinking human being" (59). In Jackson's view there are "in Faulkner . . . two fictive Negroes, the Negro before Yoknapatawpha and the Negro as he developed . . . after Yoknapatawpha preempted Faulkner's art" (62). In general he praises Faulkner for "freeing himself from the dominance of other authors and from a total subjection to the attitudes toward Negroes expected of him" (63). Jackson saw Faulkner as asking, as Twain before him, "If slavery had not been the institution that accounted most for the ostracism of Negroes from American democracy, what institution had, and still did?" (65). Faulkner answers, as seen especially in "The Bear" and "Delta Autumn": "It was because of color caste." Thus, Jackson concludes, "Faulkner would not have [Negroes] judged without a due admission of the external circumstances that have surrounded and degraded them" (68–69).

Not all African American estimates of Faulkner are so admiring. Noting "the myth about race that Faulkner grew up hearing, believing, and having ingrained into him," Margaret Walker finds, "In Faulkner we see for the first time the southern white writer rising above time and place, struggling beyond the racist limitations of his society" (119). While Faulkner rejected "the idea that all Negroes are lazy, steal, are nasty, and . . . always raping white people," nevertheless she notes, "He maintains most of the sexual stereotypes . . . clings to the plantation ideas . . . of the faithful old retainer . . . and . . . either knows no educated blacks or has no respect for them" (117). She finds Faulkner to be a racist but notes that racism touches "the whole of American society" and that Faulkner at least knew he was racist and never used it as an excuse for himself (107).

Were Faulkner's aesthetic aims strong enough to overcome the pathology of racism? Darwin T. Turner grants that Faulkner "was no conventional conveyer of that plantation myth which romanticizes" the white South and that Faulkner came "to understand he did not know [blacks] as well as he once thought he had" (Harrington and Abadie, The South . . . 64). To Turner, however, Faulkner's most conspicuous sins are those of omission: of "any picture of physical brutality" in "Faulkner's depiction of slavery"; of any "mentions [of] Reconstruction Black politicians of . . . quality." He notes that even when Faulkner "defends Blacks . . . his defense is not one that a knowledgeable Black person would use" (69, 79, 80). Turner also believes blacks would have difficulty "sharing the optimism that Faulkner expresses through [Gavin] Stevens" and that their preference "to gain total freedom of opportunity [rather] than to establish . . . interracial harmony" (74, 75) would be at odds with Faulkner's assumptions.

Blyden Jackson notes, moreover, that, for all the variety of Negroes in Faulkner's fiction, "none of them is a member of that most beleaguered and maligned class in all America, the black bourgeoisie'' (Fowler and Abadie, *Faulkner and Race* 62). And despite tracing his borrowing two structures of characterization from the blues, Thadious Davis maintains that neither of these ''obviates racially biased views in [Faulkner's] texts'' (91). Her harshest statements about Faulkner come in the wake of the Compson Appendix where she finds his ''attempt to define his own privileged condition'' comes at the expense of further marginalizing the African Americans of *The Sound and the Fury* (Kartiganer and Abadie, *Faulkner and Ideology* 242).

Some African American views of Faulkner, therefore, are in agreement with Lee Jenkins's charge that, in Faulkner's creation of Dilsey as an ''honorable commendation of the life of Mammy Caroline,'' the reader ''sees the arrogant self-indulgence of Faulkner's application of the dicta of his private obsessions'' (165). Harsher still are the views of James Baldwin. Here the critic as essayist confronts the novelist as public speaker. Taking to task Faulkner's views on the race issue, Baldwin sees ''the squire of Oxford'' as being ''guilty of great emotional and intellectual dishonesty.'' This, he claims, is not because Faulkner doesn't mean what he says but precisely because he does. ''Faulkner means everything he says, means them all at once, and with very nearly the same intensity'' (*Nobody Knows My Name* [Dial Press, 1961] 121). Baldwin's concern is the effect the force of Faulkner's personal mythology of race could have on open public discourse. In this view, Faulkner ''concedes the madness and moral wrongness of the South but at the same time . . . raises it to the level of a mystique which makes it somehow unjust to discuss Southern society in the same terms in which one would discuss any other society'' (118).

Such harsh views hold their own in the critical debate over Faulkner; many of them point up real weaknesses in his attempts to come to grips with the many black characters he includes in Yoknapatawpha. Some bring a new sensibility to that gray area between asking an author's intent and finding it in the views his characters express. Some apply an Afrocentric protocol that denies what some Eurocentric protocols (New Criticism, for example) see as irony in Faulkner's texts. Even his staunchest defenders would grant James Snead's point that ''Faulkner [is not] primarily concerned with the suffering of blacks'' (Fowler and Abadie, *Faulkner and Race* 152).

Yet among his staunchest defenders are African American scholars, including Snead himself. Snead notes, ''Faulkner's narratives utter a truth of merging across social boundaries that his contemporaries found unspeakable'' (152). He sees Faulkner as opposing ''large-scale ideological concepts encoded in the form of rhetorical narratives,'' exposing the ''effects of these classifications on human sensibilities'' (154, 155). Basing his analysis on Faulkner's insights into how racism's ''normative recipe'' demands ''omission and concealment,'' Snead offers an African American basis for reading irony in Faulkner, particularly in *Light in August*. He concludes that ''Faulkner's narratives dismember figures of division at their weakest joint, the 'purity' notion that seems the requirement for white supremacist logic'' (156).

Thus, just as Faulkner may "run . . . the gamut to traditional and nontraditional treatment of black characters" (Harrington and Abadie, *The Maker and the Myth* 116), so African American response runs the gamut of critical stances. One of its contributions is the exploration of important issues, such as whether Faulkner exposes racism or merely "gives us the choice to be racists in a very cunning way" (Fowler and Abadie, *Faulkner and Race* 157), or whether the African American writer should be an artist first, as Faulkner thought Ellison was, or a Negro first, as he felt Wright had become. Over such critical questions there is no more reason to expect African Americans to speak with one voice than there is to expect it of any other readers, writers, and critics.

Overall, it would seem fair to say that although an increasing diversity of acquaintance with African Americans helped reconstruct the racial views into which he was bred, these acquaintances did not come soon enough in his life to overcome completely his origins or to render even his later fictional portraits of African Americans complete. However, whatever his virtues and liabilities in depicting African Americans and their world, Faulkner would have welcomed one African American judgment of his failure. Blyden Jackson charged: "[Faulkner] had seen an autumn in the Delta. He failed to foresee there the imminence of spring" (Fowler and Abadie, *Faulkner and Race* 69). But was Jackson himself overly optimistic? For the century of and immediately before Faulkner's life, Lafayette County, Mississippi was—like a microcosm of America—a contested territory. Nearly forty years after Faulkner's death, it still is.

See also **Race**.

FURTHER READING

Davis. *Faulkner's "Negro."*
Kolmerten, Carol, Stephen M. Ross, and Judith Bryant Wittenberg, eds. *Unflinching Gaze: Morrison and Faulkner Re-Envisioned*. Jackson: University Press of Mississippi, 1997.
Peters. *William Faulkner*.
Werner, Craig. "Tell Old Pharoah: The Afro-American Response to Faulkner." *Southern Review* 19 (1983): 711–735.

Charles Fort and Charles A. Peek

"AFTERNOON OF A COW," one of Faulkner's slighter and lesser-known short stories. Written in 1937, "one afternoon when I felt rotten with a terrible hangover, with no thought of publication" (*SL* 245), the story first appeared in a French translation in 1943, in *Fontaine*; its first appearance in English was in a 1947 issue of *Furioso*. The story is now conveniently available in *Uncollected Stories*. A jeu d'esprit, written in an ornate, pleonastic, Johnsonian style, "Afternoon" recounts an adventure of a character named "William Faulkner" and his amanuensis, unnamed in the story but referred to elsewhere by Faulkner as "Ernest V. Trueblood." The story's premise is that Trueblood, a prudish, censorious man, is the true author of Faulkner's fiction, the topics of which are assigned to him each afternoon by Faulkner himself. Interrupted in receiving such an assignment by a fire accidentally set in a pasture, Trueblood joins Faulkner and a black servant in attempting to rescue a cow named Beulah, who has retreated from the fire into a ravine. The attempt ends ingloriously, as Beulah slips back down the slope of the ravine onto "Mr. Faulkner," who receives "the full discharge of the poor creature's afternoon of anguish and despair." The humor of the story derives largely from the contrast between its barnyard subject matter and Trueblood's inflated diction and censorious manner. The title reaches back to Faulkner's first published poem, "L'Apres-Midi d'un Faune," while the content anticipates the encounter between Ike Snopes and the cow in *The Hamlet*. Despite its slightness, the story offers some insight into Faulkner's understanding of the creative process, in both its social and psychological dimensions.

FURTHER READING

Grimwood, Michael. " 'Mr. Faulkner' and 'Ernest V. Trueblood.' " *Southern Review* 21
     (1985): 361–371.

Karl F. Zender

AIR FORCE, a Warner Bros. film released in 1943, directed by Howard Hawks. Although he received no screen credit, Faulkner rewrote two scenes for this movie. One is minor, in which a soldier offers a Faulknerian complaint against California weather. The other is a crucial death scene, where Captain Quincannon, surrounded by his crew in a base hospital, imagines that he is about to "take off" into the sky while the music score suggests the sound of an airplane engine. The death of the captain solidifies the crew.

Joseph R. Urgo

ALCOHOLISM. Young Billy Falkner's early awareness of the consequences of heavy drinking occurred in Memphis on trips his mother Maud engineered to sober up his father Murry. Ironically, Faulkner himself died not so far away at Wright's Sanitarium in Byhalia twenty-six years after he had first been hospitalized there. Of course, *alcoholism* was not the label Faulkner used for his drinking. To him, it was part of a way of life, a part of living normally; and if he could not live normally, he would rather be dead. He had begun imbibing this way of life early on, learning, as he put it, "the medicinal value of . . . liquor" (1974 *FAB* 179) at his grandfather's bank and from his Aunt Willie Medora. His mother Maud detested liquor, but her opposition was not strong enough to overcome both the genetic and cultural predisposition toward alcohol. These influences were abetted by Faulkner's associations of drunkenness with the poetic tradition he felt heir to (Baudelaire, Verlaine, Swinburne) and his Bohemian repudiation of middle-class values.

It was, in part, his drinking that led to his contacts with the bootlegging underworld, which ranged from New Orleans to Memphis' Mulberry and Gay-

oso Street establishments and to Delta locations like Clarksdale. In such places
he met Reno De Vaux, Slim, and Walter Bates and from these contacts created
legends of himself as a bootlegger. Some of his drinking occurred, of course,
in the more normal circumstances in which it is usually found: sporting outings,
such as baseball trips to Starkville; cocktails at home with Estelle; social gatherings; offices where he worked; and the hunting camps. The geography of his
drinking was prodigious. Even a short list would include the offices of *The
Double Dealer* in New Orleans or in its Latin Quarter with Spratling and Saxon;
in New York with Ben Wasson; at the Bennett Cerfs' among writers and publishers; in California at the Musso & Frank Grill with Frank Gruber and Max
Brand or fishing with them at Big Bear Lake; with Clark Gable or Buzz Bezzerides in Hollywood; at the Roosevelt Hotel reciting Shakespeare with Edmund
Kohn; with William C. Odiorne at the Dome in Paris; at the Hotel Commodore
with a journalist covering the National Book Awards or behind a curtain at
those awards with journalist Paul Flowers; at the Excelsior or St. George's in
St. Moritz with Humphrey Bogart and Lauren Bacall; at the Metropolitan Club
with the People-to-People crowd; in the Grande Bretagne in Athens or the Hotel
Bolivar in Lima, Peru; on board the *Jeannetta* in the Aegean or the *Henry R.
Mallory* off Virginia's Atlantic coast.

Along the way, he was often able to treat his problem with humor. This
tendency, too, was part of the family tradition: For example, after throwing a
brick from his car through the bank window, J.W.T. Faulkner reportedly gave
the justification that it is "my Buick, my brick, and my bank" (1974 *FAB* 134).
In a similarly humorous vein Bill told friends in Hollywood, "There's a lot of
nourishment in an acre of corn" (928). The alcohol not only eased awkward
social situations and helped him cope with publishing and financial pressures
but also gave him a way to avoid talking about his work. Clearly, too, drinking
helped him create the many personal fictions he was to design, adopt, and incarnate, including his early persona as a flight cadet.

Both romanticism and humor, however, ultimately give way to that other list
of sites associated with his drinking—those institutions in which he had to be
hospitalized for treatment: Cedars of Lebanon, Baptist Hospital in New Orleans,
the Clinique Remy de Gourmont in Paris, the Gartley-Ramsay Hospital in Memphis, the Westhill Sanitarium in the Bronx, Charles B. Towne's private hospital
and Doctor's Hospital in Manhattan, the Anglo-American Hospital in Cairo,
Baptist Hospital in Memphis, the University of Virginia Hospital, and the Tucker
Neurological and Psychiatric Hospital in Richmond. Predictably, Faulkner often
resented the fees billed for his rehabilitation.

On the way to these institutions, his drinking brought increasingly horrid
consequences. Early on, according to his recollection, drinking while flying had
ended in his crashing a plane into a hangar and hanging upside down. The
frequency of his bouts increased, and he experienced collapse at their close.
Long bouts of the hiccups were joined by badly burning his back on a radiator
at the Algonquin, having life-threatening kidney seizures in the hunting camp,

vomiting blood, enduring electroshock therapy, and experiencing an increasing number of general injuries, falls from horses, and respiratory and urinary tract infections. He also experienced increasing losses of memory, which experts in the treatment of alcoholism would recognize as alcoholic blackouts.

Worse than these physical results were those that Faulkner must have hated even more: being so debilitated he was forced to dictate his work; barely able to last through a screen meeting with Hal Wallis before he collapsed; reduced to autographing all of Bezzerides's copies of his novels in return, he hoped, for a drink; needing to drink by 7:30 in the morning; drinking while on Seconal; and endangering embassy and information service staff jobs by his behavior on world tours. Perhaps most unfortunately for his admirers, throughout the course of his drinking there grew a marked tendency toward violence between him and Estelle and toward a meanness to others uncharacteristic of an otherwise gentle man. These debilitations became more and more public, especially as he faced the stresses of addressing the racial situation, culminating in his often-quoted statement about taking to the streets armed if necessary and prompting his own excuse that his were statements "no sober man would make, nor, it seems to me, any sane man believe" (1601).

Faulkner's growing sense of his own condition makes all the more poignant his reply when asked regarding his last trip there if he would like to go to Byhalia. Presciently he replied, "I want to go home" (1836).

FURTHER READING

Dardis, Tom. "Faulkner." In *The Thirsty Muse: Alcohol and the American Writer*. New York: Ticknor and Fields, 1989. 23–95.

Charles A. Peek

"AL JACKSON," a tall tale by Faulkner, based on humorous exchanges, both verbal and written, with Sherwood Anderson in New Orleans in 1925. Narrated in two letters to Anderson that Joseph Blotner includes in his edition of *Uncollected Stories*, the story tells of a descendant of Andrew Jackson who never recovered from a boyhood fever brought on by memorizing a thousand Bible verses and who, as an adult, experiments with raising sheep in the Louisiana swamps. The venture fails, however, when both the sheep and his son Claude evolve into sea creatures. Jackson's financial circumstance is considerably improved with the advent of Prohibition.

Robert W. Hamblin

"ALL THE DEAD PILOTS," a World War I short story by Faulkner. This story first appeared in *These 13* (1931) and was revised somewhat for *Collected Stories*. The theme of the story concerns the fine line between courage and recklessness in the young men who go to war—a theme that Faulkner would also utilize in *Sartoris, Light in August*, and *A Fable*. Spoomer, the corps commander's nephew, and Johnny Sartoris vie first for the attentions of "Kit"—so

called because she has as many soldiers as Lord Kitchener—and then of
'Toinette. After Spoomer arranges to have Sartoris's flying schedule altered,
Sartoris strikes back by stealing Spoomer's clothes while he is otherwise engaged. Later, Spoomer must face his superiors dressed in a woman's skirt and
shawl. He is sent back to England to command a ground school, and Sartoris
is killed in combat.

FURTHER READING

Bradford, Melvin E. "The Anomaly of Faulkner's World War I Stories." *Mississippi
     Quarterly* 36 (1983): 243–261.
Day, Douglas. "The War Stories of William Faulkner." *Georgia Review* 15 (1961): 385–
     394.
Jones, Ann Goodwyn. "Male Fantasies?: Faulkner's War Stories and the Construction
     of Gender." *Faulkner and Psychology*, ed. Kartiganer and Abadie. 21–55.

Larry Wharton

"AMBUSCADE," the first chapter of Faulkner's *The Unvanquished*, was originally published in the September 29, 1934 issue of the *Saturday Evening Post*
as the first of a series of short stories about the Sartoris family during the Civil
War. The story revolves around the juvenile Bayard Sartoris and his black playmate, Ringo, whose war games take a serious turn when they use a real musket
to defend their home from what they perceive to be invading Union troops. The
story, particularly as revised for the novel, reveals in miniature the South's
headstrong embrace of war with little consideration of its consequences.

FURTHER READING

Donaldson, Susan V. "Dismantling the *Saturday Evening Post* Reader: The Unvan-
     quished and Changing 'Horizons of Expectations.' " *Faulkner and Popular Cul-
     ture*, ed. Fowler and Abadie. 179–195.

John B. Padgett

AMERICAN RENAISSANCE. To broach the subject of William Faulkner and
the writers associated with the American Renaissance requires care. Faulkner's
formal education was limited, so one cannot assume Faulkner's knowledge of
these writers individually or as grouped under such a rubric. In his adult years,
some influences did lead Faulkner to encounters with his literary predecessors.
Phil Stone was a guiding influence; also the New Orleans enclave was rich with
talk of writers. Records of gift books may also suggest a growing acquaintance,
if not familiarity, with previous writers. Eventually his library held volumes by
all of these writers. Moreover, Faulkner's own growing reputation may have
encouraged him to learn more about those writers with whom he was often
compared. One's knowledge of this background should restrain expectations of
connectedness.

    This caution notwithstanding, Faulkner's rank among American writers compels comparisons of his work with the great flourishing of American literature in the period of the American Renaissance. F. O. Matthiessen, in his seminal work *American Renaissance* (Oxford University Press, 1941), applied this name to the period of literary productivity from 1850 to 1855. Matthiessen discussed Ralph Waldo Emerson, Nathaniel Hawthorne, Herman Melville, Henry David Thoreau, and Walt Whitman. Since Matthiessen's study, the list of writers associated with the American Renaissance has been expanded; nevertheless, as the comparative questions prevail, the original focus group remains fairly tightly intact. Questions of Faulkner's connections with the American Renaissance revolve around what Faulkner knew of these writers and their works, what specific influences can be deduced from comparisons of texts, and what generalized assessments may be offered linking Faulkner's prevailing concerns with those of particular writers of the American Renaissance.

Faulkner's infrequent comments about the people of the American Renaissance are scattered throughout letters, speeches, and interviews. He regularly identified Herman Melville as a major influence, specifically mentioning *Moby Dick*, which on numerous occasions Faulkner identified as the greatest novel in American literature. In one lecture, however, he added that it "was still an attempt that didn't quite come off" (*FIU* 15). On another occasion Faulkner compared three men who represented a "trinity of conscience" in *Moby Dick* with a similar trinity in *A Fable* (*LIG* 247). In 1940, when daughter Jill was a mere seven years old, Faulkner read *Moby Dick* to her. Much later, when Faulkner set up residence in Virginia and compiled a library for that home, *Moby Dick* was a specific request.

The other American Renaissance writer with whom Faulkner expressed some familiarity was Nathaniel Hawthorne. In truth, if the quality and kind of references are a measure, his familiarity with Hawthorne grew over the years. Faulkner's use of the title *The Marble Faun*, however, apparently does not represent a young writer's tribute to a master: Phil Stone said that he, and not Faulkner, suggested Faulkner's title. When Lemuel Oldham, Estelle Faulkner's father, questioned the wisdom of an already-used title, Faulkner responded, true or not, that he had not heard of Hawthorne (1974 *FAB* 379). Stone stated that Faulkner had read some Hawthorne but not much. Stone remarked, "The truth is, I don't think he is extremely well read in anything" (Brodsky and Hamblin II: 184). Much later in Faulkner's life, during an interview in Japan, Faulkner stated that Hawthorne was not an influence (*LIG* 95). In subsequent statements, Faulkner reiterated his claim that Hawthorne wrote in the European tradition (*LIG* 168). In 1958 when Faulkner advised his audience in "A Word to Young Writers" to study masters, among those he identified were both Hawthorne and Melville (*ESPL* 163).

Over the years, Faulkner seemed to expand his knowledge of the other writers associated with the American Renaissance. Of Whitman, Faulkner cited the poet's claim that a great audience is required to foster great poets (1974 *FAB* 390). Other published comments on Whitman are limited, although Faulkner occasionally included Whitman as one of the poets able to articulate truth (*FIU* 145). In 1938 Faulkner returned home from a trip to New York with several books, among them a Whitman volume (1974 *FAB* 1003). Several years later, at home in Oxford, Faulkner advised a local African American poet, Joe C. Brown, to read, among several poets, Whitman (1974 *FAB* 1182). In 1955 Faulkner named Whitman as the first writer who wrote in the American tradition, but Faulkner qualified the remark by suggesting that Whitman experimented with the notion of American literature and that Mark Twain first manifested it (*LIG* 137).

Faulkner apparently paid almost no attention to Emerson or Thoreau. Few references to Emerson exist, so it is difficult to determine what Faulkner might have known or read of Emerson. For Christmas 1945 Faulkner received *The Complete Writings of Ralph Waldo Emerson* as a gift. If Faulkner discussed Thoreau, it was not in a public or published forum.

Faulkner's comments about writers of the American Renaissance, of course, are not the only source for determining connectedness. Literary critics have sought, through comparative analysis, to track general influence and specific intertextuality. As Michael Millgate has noted, Faulkner's use of Gothic elements aligns him with Melville and Hawthorne, although they do not possess an exclusive use of Gothic (*Achievement* 162). Faulkner himself commented on the Gothic elements in Melville's work (*FIU* 56). Frederick Karl suggests that Faulkner is the only twentieth-century American writer who sustained a dark vision comparable to those of Melville and Hawthorne (312). Specific comparative analyses link *Absalom, Absalom!* to *Moby Dick* and *Billy Budd*, connections ranging from theme to character to style. Isaac McCaslin, for example, is profitably compared to Melville's Ishmael through initiation themes.

One of the early critics of Faulkner's work, George Marion O'Donnell, related Faulkner not to the naturalists, who were his immediate predecessors and to whom numerous links were possible, but rather to the Romantics, specifically Hawthorne. Since that critical assessment, others have continued to pursue Hawthorne-Faulkner correspondences, looking often at both authors' need to tell stories of family and region. Specific comparison of the writers' respective works has produced some interesting results: for example, comparison of *As I Lay Dying* to *The Scarlet Letter* and *Absalom, Absalom!* to *The House of the Seven Gables*.

In addition to specific influences from one text to another, there are overarching similarities between the American Renaissance writers and Faulkner. Faulkner shared with the American Renaissance writers a notion that the atmosphere in America was not supportive of its artists, once remarking that artists in America did not receive appropriate recognition and respect (*ESPL* 70). Nevertheless, Faulkner felt that such neglect did not relieve the artist of the responsibility to speak. Like his nineteenth-century predecessors, Faulkner embraced individualism and directed much of that concern for the individual in society to a specifically national vision. Further, Faulkner viewed the artist's responsibility as nothing less than ''to save man's humanity'' (*FIU* 245). He echoes, in fact, the voices of the American Renaissance when he states that the artist must ''save the individual from anonymity before it is too late and humanity has vanished from the animal called man. And who better to save man's humanity than the writer, the poet, the artist, since who should fear the loss of it more since the humanity of man is the artist's life blood'' (*ESPL* 165).

FURTHER READING

O'Donnell, George Marion. ''Faulkner's Mythology.'' *Kenyon Review* 1 (Spring 1939): 285–299.

Diane Brown Jones

AMES, DALTON, the lover of Caddy Compson in Faulkner's novel *The Sound and the Fury*, is also the obsessive focus of her brother Quentin's erotic fantasies and ruminations. In one sense, Quentin identifies with Ames as the handsome and virile lover of his sister; in another sense, Quentin identifies with Caddy and so assumes, in fantasy, her erotic position with respect to Ames. And in still another sense, Quentin attempts to protect the honor of his sister by giving Ames ''until sundown to leave town.'' In this role of what his friend Spoade sarcastically calls the ''champion of dames,'' Quentin fails ludicrously. Twice attempting to hit Ames in the face, Quentin passes out ''like a girl'' when Ames grabs both his wrists in one hand. Dalton Ames is persistently fused in Quentin's mind with the figure of his antagonistic Harvard classmate Gerald Bland.

FURTHER READING

Duvall, John N. ''Contextualizing *The Sound and the Fury*: Sex, Gender, and Community in Modern American Fiction.'' *Approaches to Teaching Faulkner's* The Sound and the Fury. Ed. Stephen Hahn and Arthur F. Kinney. New York: MLA, 1996. 101–107.

Michael Zeitlin

ANDERSON, SHERWOOD (1876–1941), American short story writer and novelist who exercised great influence upon the novelists of Faulkner's generation. When Faulkner met him in 1925, Anderson was at the peak of his career, his best work, including *Winesburg, Ohio, The Triumph of the Egg*, and major short stories, already completed. Faulkner had previously met Anderson's wife, Elizabeth, in New York, and when the aspiring author arrived in New Orleans, he moved into the Andersons' French Quarter apartment, briefly sharing a room with their son Robert, until he moved into an apartment on Pirate's Alley. For the next two years, Faulkner spent much time with Anderson, whose work he greatly admired. Wandering the French Quarter, they collaborated on a series of tall tales about the half-alligator ''Al Jackson,'' an imaginary descendant of Andrew Jackson.

That Anderson's tutelage was instrumental in shaping the career of his disciple Faulkner later acknowledged. Anderson, he said, told him to be himself, not to be bound by conventions, and to write about his own region. Anderson also read the typescript of *Soldiers' Pay*, although Faulkner was later to claim that he had agreed to help get it published only if he did not have to read it.

In 1926 Faulkner collaborated with William Spratling on a book of caricatures of New Orleans characters entitled *Sherwood Anderson and Other Famous Creoles*. Faulkner's introduction was a parody of what he termed Anderson's "primer-like style." Anderson was not amused, and the friendship between the two cooled. The portrayal of Anderson in Faulkner's *Mosquitoes* (1927) seems to have increased the tension. After the New Orleans years the two met only once, at a New York cocktail party in 1937. Although Anderson tried to avoid him, Faulkner insisted on confronting the older writer, and something of a reconciliation occurred.

In his final evaluation of the man, the essay "A Note on Sherwood Anderson," Faulkner acknowledges Anderson's faults but also praises him as an author of purity and integrity. Elsewhere, he describes his mentor as the father of Faulkner's own literary generation (*FIU* 281).

FURTHER READING

Faulkner, William. "A Note on Sherwood Anderson." *Essays, Speeches & Public Letters by William Faulkner*, ed. Meriwether. 3–10.

W. Kenneth Holditch

APOCRYPHA. During correspondence in 1945 with Malcolm Cowley regarding the production of *The Portable Faulkner*, Faulkner agreed to making "a Golden Book of my apocryphal county" and suggested that the front jacket should read "A chronological picture of Faulkner's apocryphal Mississippi county." Cowley, however, changed Faulkner's adjective from "apocryphal" to "mythical," using as well the term "saga" to characterize Faulkner's literary project of Yoknapatawpha (*FCF* 25, 65, 69). Nonetheless, Faulkner continued throughout the 1950s to refer to his work as an apocrypha, a personal cosmos created by "sublimating the actual into the apocryphal" (*LIG* 255). The term was clearly important to Faulkner's sense of aesthetics and to the way in which he understood the relationship between the fictional Yoknapatawpha County and the actual Lafayette County. An "apocrypha" suggests an alternative to orthodoxy, especially as regards ways of perception and presentation; and as such, Faulkner may have found the term a more accurate description of his literary ambitions.

James Carothers, in *William Faulkner's Short Stories*, has found the term useful to distinguish the ways in which Faulkner understood his short story career, labeling as apocrypha those stories that were never incorporated into novels, collections, or story cycles.

FURTHER READING

Harrington and Abadie, eds. *The Maker and the Myth.*
Urgo. *Faulkner's Apocrypha.*

Joseph R. Urgo

"APPENDIX, COMPSON, 1699–1945," Faulkner's genealogical treatment of his Compson family, written in 1945. The original intent for the Appendix was as background to the "Dilsey" section from *The Sound and the Fury*, which Malcolm Cowley proposed to use in the Viking *Portable Faulkner*. Subsequently, Random House developed plans to publish a Modern Library edition of *The Sound and the Fury* and asked Faulkner to write an introduction. Faulkner declined and suggested using the Appendix instead. In its initial Modern Library appearance, therefore, the Appendix, often viewed as a fifth section of the novel, appears as an introduction; but in later printings, it is moved to the end. Recent critical concerns for authentic texts have removed it altogether, restoring the structure of *The Sound and the Fury* to its 1929 form. The location of the Appendix begs the question of its purpose. One of Faulkner's earlier introductions to *The Sound and the Fury* (they and their history are included in Minter's *Norton Critical Edition*) began, "I wrote [*The Sound and the Fury*] and learned to read." The possibility that the Appendix was intended to help readers "learn . . . to read" the difficult novel is borne out by remarks Faulkner made regarding the inconsistencies between the Appendix and the novel in some points of chronology and detail. To Cowley, Faulkner wrote, "The inconsistencies in the appendix prove that to me the book is still alive after 15 years . . . growing, changing. . . . The appendix was done at the same heat as the book. . . . [I]t's the book itself which is inconsistent, not the appendix" (*FCF* 90). And to Random House editor Robert Linscott he noted: "It is the key to the whole book . . . the 4 sections as they stand now fall into clarity and place" (1974 *FAB* 1208).

Calling its title "really an obituary," Faulkner wrote it "Compson/1699–1945" and then extended the saga back to Ikkemotubbe and the Chickasaw tribe before moving forward to include under the subtitle "These were Compsons" the Scottish migrations in the wake of the Battle of Culloden and the subsequent genealogy of the fleeing Quentin Maclachan. Thus the Appendix begins the saga with attention to the "dispossessed," the first substantive word in the work. The family of the novel's present follows the subtitle "And these," being mostly devoted to "Candace (Caddy)" and ending with her daughter Quentin's flight to escape her Uncle Jason.

The Appendix closes under the final subtitle "And that was all. These others were not Compsons. They were black." This section must be understood in the light of Faulkner's remark that the Appendix's title was "not a segregation" (Minter, *Norton Critical Edition* 225). Its last line, "They endured," appears under the name "Dilsey." Many read this as a comment on the endurance of the Negro, but grammar and context argue otherwise. Other "black" characters are referred to as "who . . ."; the choice of "they" suggests a commentary about the Compsons. In his Nobel Prize address, Faulkner asserted a belief that man would not only endure but would prevail, a promise not fulfilled for the Compsons who, far from prevailing, are said here to have merely endured.

In the Appendix readers are left with a possible sighting of Candace in Germany, Benjy in an institution, Quentin dead, Jason raging at his dispossession, and Caddy's daughter fleeing hers. Her flight parallels that of the first Quentin who opened the chronology of the Appendix, thus suggesting that paradoxes of order and flight, along with their causes and obstacles, are major themes of *The Sound and the Fury*.

FURTHER READING

Davis, Thadious M. "Reading Faulkner's Compson Appendix." *Faulkner and Ideology*, ed. Kartiganer and Abadie. 238–252.

Dickerson, Mary Jane. " 'The Magician's Wand': Faulkner's Compson Appendix." *Mississippi Quarterly* 28 (1975): 317–337.

Minter, David, ed. *The Sound and the Fury: Norton Critical Edition*. 2nd ed. New York: W. W. Norton, 1994.

Peek, Charles. "Order and Flight: Teaching *The Sound and the Fury* through the Appendix." *Approaches to Teaching Faulkner's* The Sound and the Fury. Ed. Stephen Hahn and Arthur F. Kinney. New York: MLA, 1996. 68–72.

Charles A. Peek

"L'APRES-MIDI D'UN FAUNE," Faulkner's first published literary work, which appeared in the August 6, 1919 issue of the *New Republic*, is an adaptation of the pastoral poem *L'Après-midi d'un Faune* (1876) by Stéphane Mallarmé, leading theorist and poet of the French Symbolist movement. Faulkner's poem utilizes faun/nymph imagery to describe the unfulfilled longing of the narrator for his beloved. Thus the poem introduces a theme that would become a near-constant in all of Faulkner's subsequent work: the thwarted quest for a romanticized ideal. The association between Faulkner's poem and the French poem that inspired it is explored in Gresset's *Fascination: Faulkner's Fiction, 1919–1936*.

FURTHER READING

Hamblin, Robert W., and Louis Daniel Brodsky. "Faulkner's 'L'Apres-Midi d'un Faune': The Evolution of a Poem." *Studies in Bibliography* 33 (1980): 254–263.

Arthur Wilhelm

ART. *See* **Visual Arts**.

"ARTIST AT HOME," a short story by Faulkner, was first published in *Story* in 1933 and reprinted in *Collected Stories*. It tells the story of novelist Roger Howes, a "fattish, mild, nondescript man of forty," who, having sold a book in New York, moves to Virginia and, against the wishes and better judgment of his wife Anne, opens his home to failed or would-be artists. One of the visitors, poet John Blair, falls in love with Anne, giving both himself and Roger something to write about. "Artist at Home" is told by a cynical, seemingly omniscient observer in deadpan amazement at the species of man called "artist" or "poet." Critics have seen a parallel between Howes and Sherwood Anderson, and some read the story as metafiction. The story's title suggests its central questions. Can an artist *be* an artist and have a home, or must an artist be homeless and ultimately dead? Similarly, what *is* an artist when he is home—what is left of art when stripped of its ideal or commercial value? In the end, the conflict between art and life that the story dramatizes seems diminished in the story's own self-consciousness. One believes as little in Roger's life with his wife or his children, who are conveniently away, as in the value of the story he writes about his wife and Blair's affair; and Blair's breakthrough poem, written on a menu and published posthumously, seems as much a parody of art as his standing in the rain looking up at Anne's window and his recollection of his dead mother's sherbet seem a parody of love and loss.

FURTHER READING

Bradford, M. E. "An Aesthetic Parable: Faulkner's 'Artist at Home.' " *Georgia Review* 27 (1973): 175–181.
Owens, Tony J. "Faulkner, Anderson, and 'Artist at Home.' " *Mississippi Quarterly* 32 (1979): 393–412.
Peterson, Richard F. "An Early Judgment of Anderson and Joyce in Faulkner's 'Artist at Home.' " *Kyushu American Literature* 18 (1977): 19–23.

Arthur A. Brown

AS I LAY DYING, published in 1930, is by general consensus one of Faulkner's greatest novels. It is also possibly his most audacious adventure in style, certainly unique among the Yoknapatawpha novels, and the novel in which Faulkner's mythical county receives its name. The novel was begun the day after the Wall Street panic of October 1929, which left many investors bankrupt. By December 11, a mere forty-seven days later, Faulkner had finished the novel's fifty-nine monologues. The initial printing was only 2,522 copies, and the reviews, many of which labeled the book confusing, were no more encouraging than the sales. Faulkner himself once characterized it as "a little on the esoteric side" (1974 *FAB* 818). However, he also called the novel a "tour de force" on which his reputation could stand, along with *The Sound and the Fury*, the standard he did not want *Sanctuary* to shame. The first of Faulkner's novels to appear in France, published there by Gallimard in a translation by Maurice Coindreau, its form has made it accessible for translation into other genres, notably Valerie Bettis's ballet and Lewis Lazare's drama. Faulkner recorded parts of the novel for Caedmon.

As I Lay Dying tells the story of a poor farming family from the Frenchman's Bend area. This setting connects it to the "Spotted Horses" and "Father Abraham'' materials from which Faulkner drew his Snopes stories, one section of *The Hamlet* having once been titled ''As I Lay Dying.'' *As I Lay Dying* captures the Bundren family at the time of the death of Addie, the wife and mother, and follows them through their journey to bury her in Jefferson as she made them promise they would. The journey is a series of obstacles to be overcome and dangers to be confronted, some comic, others filled with pathos, featuring the flooding of the river they must cross and the burning of the barn where her coffin rests. Beginning with the absence of two of her sons, Darl and Jewel, off to sell a load of wood at the time of her death, everything conspires to delay the transport of the body in Mississippi's August heat. Retarded by ineptness on the part of Anse, father and husband, misunderstandings of Vardaman, the youngest son, or attempts by Darl to stop it, the journey is often portrayed through the inconvenience and outrage caused the neighbors, principally the Tulls.

Even in these details it is obvious we are not witnessing a case study in Mississippi burial ritual. Several features of the novel give ample opportunity for those exploring Faulkner's mythic method, his overlay of the apocryphal on the actual. One is the title, taken from the passage in *The Odyssey* in which the shade of Agamemnon addresses Odysseus during his descent into hell; another is the parallel of the length of the journey to the nine days of the Dionysian revels. There is also the triad of Addie, daughter Dewey Dell, and neighbor Cora, representing Demeter-Persephone-Kore, and the fact that Addie's sole monologue occurs between flood and fire and after her death.

These mythic parallels emerge in Addie's death, in the conventionality that demands her family fulfill their promise to bury her with her people, and in the ulterior motives each brings to the journey. They also emerge in the psychobiology of the courtship and marriage of Addie and Anse, the pregnancy of Dewey Dell, the idea of the maternal in both Addie and Dewey Dell, the rivalries and revenges between brothers and sisters, and the insanity of Darl, taken to an asylum just before the rest of the family returns home. Embedded in the story line these materials question the meaning of death, the value of fertility and creativity, and the possibilities of community and communication. Such mythic/psychoanalytic issues have been addressed by a number of critics, including Carvel Collins, Doreen Fowler, and John T. Irwin.

Are the Bundrens exemplars of the fulfillment of moral obligation under difficult circumstances, or are they a buffoon's parade, a grotesque parody of moral dignity? Though the structure of the novel makes answers to such questions highly problematic, they occupied much of the early critical debate. More recent criticism has turned to possibly smaller but ultimately more intriguing questions. Faulkner himself has said that if there is a villain in *As I Lay Dying*, it is conventionality itself (*FIU* 112). Warwick Wadlington has explored this issue, focusing on the cause and effect of the host of family secrets the death and burial journey expose. One of these, of course, is Addie's affair with the Rev. Whitfield, from which Jewel was born, a scenario that prompted John T. Matthews's study of the relation of the novel to Hawthorne's *The Scarlet Letter* and Updike's *Month of Sundays*. But Wadlington is more concerned with the secret stories of class discontent in a world where "just about everything . . . seems to be swappable" (*Stories* 83). In a similar vein, Matthews addresses commodification and how "money silently constitutes and openly mediates the family in the agricultural South" ("Machine Age" 76). Joseph Urgo, finding in the novel a demonstration that "one's role in the drama of meaning is largely determined by one's mastery of the use of the figurative" (14), argues for the primacy of the one-line monologue ascribed to Vardaman, "My mother is a fish." Patrick O'Donnell, criticizing those who apply the "Family Romance" construct to *As I Lay Dying* and at the same time taking seriously Faulkner's own remark that Anse's troubles began with the building of the road (1974 *FAB* 635), explores how the novel deals with the role of the state, arguing for a paradoxical dependence between "the nomadic and authoritarian" (93). Wadlington also addresses how, as the last novel of the Roaring Twenties and the first of the Great Depression, it constitutes a "tightrope act" between two opposing accounts of America (*Stories* 3–8).

One of the most successful elements of the novel is the portrait of Darl as "thinker." The way Darl's reflective nature is treated by his family and neighbors draws on then-current concerns for the legacy of the frontier, its preference for action over thought, and the subsequent revolt against the village. Influenced by Faulkner's mentor Sherwood Anderson, this revolt focused on the plight of the sensitive young man, the potential artist, caught in the bifurcation of values Van Wyck Brooks had depicted in *America's Coming-of-Age* (Doubleday, 1958), forced to "lurch violently to the one extreme or the other" (13–14), discovering at one extreme that, in Joseph Wood Krutch's words, "rationality is an attribute of himself alone" (*The Modern Temper* [Harcourt, Brace, 1929] 6–7). It is not hard to see Darl and Jewel as portraits of that lurching to extremes, Darl left in a world of pure reason, Jewel in action alone, the two together highlighting a tragic legacy. Hence, the novel could be seen to constitute a critique of frontier values and the American myths (Wadlington's stories about ourselves) that drove westward expansion.

Equally engaging is the portrait of Addie as a young woman engaged in the Twenties' revolt against Puritanism. Social critics such as Harold Stearns and Elsie Clews Parsons saw Victorian moral codes and Blue Laws as one legacy of our Puritan past, a legacy partly responsible for the great gulf fixed in the American character. Faulkner embodies their rejection of hypocrisy and convention in his portrait of Addie. The times, Parsons says, "when the labels are . . . attached," her getting married and giving birth, show her how even her emotional relations are "statutory, pre-determined, [and] conventionalized" (Stearns, *Civilization of the United States* 315). Once a schoolteacher "imbued with the idea that the will of her child[ren] should be broken," Addie discovers the "duty to the alive." She breaks free of puritanical, life-denying codes and enters into her affair with Whitfield. Then, finding even sexual freedom made "love . . . less momentous" (Krutch 68–69), as did others of the "new women," she comes home to begin "cleaning up the house" and, with something like stoic resignation, getting "ready to die."

Addie's inability to escape the harsh reality of Bundren life, a reality that has already killed Anse, though "[h]e did not know he was dead," is paralleled by a similar failure for each of her older children. Cash reinjures his leg; Jewel sacrifices his horse; instead of an abortion, Dewey Dell gets seduced again; Darl is incarcerated in an asylum for burning Gillespie's barn. Worse, since the American dream held their qualities to be the keys to success, their failure to either alter or escape their world is an indictment of many of our cherished myths: work ethic and action, women's roles, reason, and sensitivity.

Yet the novel is not all indictment. Faulkner held neither a literature of indictment nor one of escape to be adequate (Minter 222). Balancing both, he does not close with Addie's readiness for death or the family's failure to escape or alter the world. However comically, it is the desire to live that reasserts itself. In Vardaman's metaphoric grasp of his mother's death, which turns it into art, in the acquisition of Anse's new teeth and a graphophone, in the return with a new "Mrs. Bundren," and in Dewey Dell's prospective child, Faulkner gives the desire to live the upper hand and last word.

FURTHER READING

Birns, Margaret Boe. "Demeter as the Letter D: Naming Women in *The Sound and the Fury* and *As I Lay Dying*." *Women's Studies* 22 (1993): 533–541.

Cox, Dianne L., ed. *William Faulkner's* As I Lay Dying: *A Critical Casebook*. New York: Garland Publishing, 1985.

Fowler, Doreen. "Matricide and the Mother's Revenge in *As I Lay Dying*." *Faulkner Journal* 4.1–2 (1988–1989): 113–125.

Luce, Dianne C. *Annotations to William Faulkner's* As I Lay Dying. New York: Garland, 1990.

Matthews, John T. "*As I Lay Dying* in the Machine Age." *Boundary 2* 19.1 (1992): 69–94.

———. "Intertextuality and Originality: Hawthorne, Faulkner, Updike." *Intertextuality in Faulkner*, ed. Gresset and Polk. 144–157.

Merrill, Robert. "Faulknerian Tragedy: The Example of *As I Lay Dying*." *Mississippi Quarterly* 47 (1994): 403–418.

O'Donnell, Patrick. "Between the Family and the State: Nomadism and Authority in *As I Lay Dying*." *Faulkner Journal* 7.1–2 (1991–1992): 83–94.

Wadlington, Warwick. As I Lay Dying: *Stories out of Stories*. New York: Twayne, 1992.

Charles A. Peek

AUTOMOBILE. During the 1966 Yoknapatawpha Conference at the University of Mississippi, a physician who had ridden to school in a carpool with Jill Faulkner reminisced about the Faulkners' automobile during the 1940s. It was a Ford phaeton so old its glass windows were missing and its floorboards admitted views of the streets passing beneath. Mr. Bill, the speaker claimed, never got it out of second gear. Such neglect of his own automobile and perhaps of driving itself seems perfectly appropriate for a writer who treated automobiles with deep suspicion and neglect.

Faulkner's neglect can be startling: In two novels, automobiles that could advance the plot simply disappear. In *Sanctuary*, Gowan Stevens's automobile, presumably still lying wrecked but identifiable at the scene of Tommy's murder, seems to vanish. Horace Benbow never seeks Stevens out; Eustace Graham never calls him to the stand. In *Light in August*, the new automobile Joe Christmas and Joe Brown have been "riding around town all day in" vanishes as well. Neither Christmas nor Brown flees in it, yet Sheriff Watt Kennedy does not spot it at the scene of Joanna Burden's murder.

Faulkner's suspicion is pervasive. Repeatedly, the automobile represents the decline of civilization in a way that other technology—the railroad, for example—does not. In particular, it seems to embody modernity's rootlessness and, more deeply, its mechanical views of human nature and of human history and society, reflecting, perhaps, behavioralism and Marxism. The old order resists automobiles, the Young Colonel huffing about "gasoline-propelled paupers" (*Sartoris*) and having automobiles banned from Jefferson. When the younger generation embraces automobiles, they often signify corruption: notably young Bayard's automobile in which he kills his grandfather (*Sartoris*), Popeye's gangster car (*Sanctuary*), Christmas and Brown's car financed by moonshine (*Light in August*), young Jason Compson's automobile bought with the money his mother believes is invested in the hardware store (*The Sound and the Fury*), the carny's automobile in which Miss Quentin flees (*The Sound and the Fury*), the general's "chromiumtrimmed sports car" her mother poses beside ("Appendix" to *The Sound and the Fury*), and Linda Snopes Kohl's Jaguar, her getaway car following the murder of Flem (*The Mansion*). Generational decline is apparent in the Kinston cab driver in *Sanctuary*—"a planter, a landholder, son of one of the first settlers," who has "lost his property through greed and gullibility" and is left with a "good, powerful car" he uses as a hack, "telling the drummers how he used to lead Kinston society; now he drove it." The faceless mob also embraces the automobile's promise of power combined with anonymity; the "Face" that had been preparing to lynch Lucas Beauchamp (*Intruder in the Dust*) flees Jefferson in a "torrent of ballbearing rubber and refinanced pressed steel." Only in Faulkner's last novel does the automobile become desirable, as the recovery of Boss Priest's Winton Flyer signals Lucius's return to family and community, as well as Boon and Everbe's departure from Miss Reba's and the establishment of their own home and family.

FURTHER READING

Carey, Glenn O. "William Faulkner on the Automobile as Socio-Sexual Symbol." *CEA Critic* 36.2 (1974): 15–17.
Milum, Richard A. "Continuity and Change: The Horse, the Automobile, and the Air-

plane in Faulkner's Fiction.'' *Faulkner: The Unappeased Imagination*, ed. Carey. 157–174.

Terrell L. Tebbetts

AVIATION. Faulkner manifested a keen interest in airplanes and aviation from the time he and his brothers, as young boys, sought to build and fly a makeshift plane in their parents' backyard. In July 1918, attracted to the romantic, adventurous image of the World War I flyer, he enlisted in the Canadian branch of the Royal Air Force; he was still enrolled in the pilot training program in Toronto when the war ended a few months later. Not having earned his wings or fought in the war, however, did not deter Faulkner from returning home to Oxford, wearing a pilot's uniform about town, and spreading stories about his participation in dogfights over Germany. In 1933 Faulkner resumed his active involvement in flying, becoming a licensed pilot under the tutelage of noted aviator Vernon C. Omlie of Memphis and encouraging his brothers John and Dean to take up the sport. A short while later, Faulkner purchased a Waco C cabin cruiser and, at first with Omlie and later with John and Dean, frequently participated in north Mississippi air shows featuring stunt flying, parachute jumps, and passenger rides. In February 1934 Faulkner and Omlie attended a huge air show that accompanied the opening of the Shushan Airport in New Orleans. Throughout the mid-1930s Faulkner remained immersed in flying, soloing several times each week, but the excitement and glamour of the sport ended for him in November 1935 when Dean, along with all three of his passengers, died in the crash of the Waco during an air show at Pontotoc, Mississippi. Just weeks before, Faulkner had transferred ownership of the plane to his brother. The following August Omlie died in the crash of a charter plane on which he was a passenger. Although Faulkner continued to fly for several more years, he did so more and more infrequently, the tragic deaths of his brother and friend having essentially ended his long love affair with the sport.

Predictably, Faulkner's involvement with airplanes, pilots, and aviation supplied him with considerable source material for his writing. Early poems such as ''The Ace'' and ''The Lilacs'' deal with World War I pilots, as do a number of early short stories, notably ''Ad Astra,'' ''Turnabout,'' and ''All the Dead Pilots''—each of which Faulkner regarded highly enough to include in *Collected Stories*. Faulkner's first novel, *Soldiers' Pay*, is a Lost Generation account of a wounded airman returning home to die; and his initial Yoknapatawpha novel, *Sartoris*, incorporates the wartime experiences of twin pilots, Bayard and John Sartoris, the latter of whom dies in air combat. *Pylon* is a treatment of barnstorming pilots like the ones Faulkner met at the New Orleans air show. In Hollywood, first in the 1930s and again in the 1940s, Faulkner successfully crafted a number of movie scripts involving pilots and airplanes—for example, *Today We Live, War Birds,* and *Battle Cry*. In his later fiction, Faulkner's treatment of aviation is diminished but still present. A principal character in *A Fable* is a young British pilot named Levine, and Chick Mallison, as he appears as an adult in *The Mansion*, has served as a bombardier in World War II.

Faulkner's early obsession and continuing fascination with flying take on significance from both biographical and literary standpoints. Personally, Faulkner seems to have been drawn to flying, as later he was to horseback riding and jumping, by the risk factor. Small in stature, effeminate in appearance and bearing, unfortunate in love, Faulkner appears to have sought to assert his manhood and courage by courting danger and death at the controls of a plane. In his fiction, airplanes serve not only to showcase the adventurous and often foolhardy actions of characters like John Sartoris and Roger Shumann but also to symbolize, with automobiles and in opposition to bears, horses, and mules, the tremendous changes that mechanization was bringing to the modern world.

FURTHER READING

Harrison, Robert L. *Aviation Lore in Faulkner*. Philadelphia: John Benjamins, 1985.

Robert W. Hamblin

B

BAIRD, HELEN. William Faulkner seems immediately to have fallen in love with Helen Baird upon first meeting her in 1925 at a party in the French Quarter. They saw each other over the next few years both in New Orleans and Pascagoula, Mississippi. Although Helen was fond of him, she rejected his proposal for marriage. In addition to dedicating *Mosquitoes* to her, Faulkner created at least two gift books for Helen, composing the texts, writing them in ornate handwriting, and illustrating one, an allegory called *Mayday* (1926), with ink drawings and watercolors. The other, *Helen: A Courtship*, was a proposal in poetry. Helen also became the prototype for a number of Faulkner characters, most notably Patricia Robyn in *Mosquitoes* and Charlotte Rittenmeyer in *The Wild Palms*.

FURTHER READING

Zender, Karl F. "Two Unpublished Letters from William Faulkner to Helen Baird." *American Literature* 63 (1991): 535–538.

W. Kenneth Holditch

BALZAC, HONORÉ DE (1799–1850), realistic French novelist whose collected works were published under the title *La Comedie humaine* (1842–1855). As early as 1830 Balzac had started grouping his novels and stories to form a comprehensive treatment of French society. By the 1840s he envisioned his "human comedy" as an interrelated series extending to twenty-six volumes presenting 4,000 to 5,000 characters. At the time of his death the work included seventeen volumes and more than 3,000 characters. Faulkner frequently acknowledged Balzac as a major influence, noting that he read "some of Balzac almost every year" and commending the Frenchman's "concept of a cosmos in miniature" (*FIU* 50, 232). "I like the fact," Faulkner further explained, "that in Balzac there is an intact world of his own. His people don't just move from page one to page 320 of one book. There is a continuity between them all like a bloodstream which flows from page one through to page 20,000 of one book" (*LIG* 217). This observation, of course, applies equally well to Faulkner's interlocking Yoknapatawpha novels and stories.

Robert W. Hamblin

"BARN BURNING," one of Faulkner's best and most widely discussed and anthologized short stories, was first published in *Harper's Magazine* in June 1939 and republished as the first story in *Collected Stories*. A truncated account of the central situation of the story is narrated by V. K. Ratliff near the beginning of *The Hamlet*. Critics have argued the priority of the one version over the other, but no clear consensus has emerged. In a 1945 letter, Faulkner described "Barn Burning" (along with "Wash") as having been written as an "induction" to *The Hamlet*, "which I discovered had no place in that book at all" (*SL* 197). This comment suggests that the story version preceded the novel version, but it leaves unclear the exact relation between the two.

"Barn Burning" is one of several works depicting the Snopes clan. Focus falls on the relationship between Ab Snopes, a sharecropper, and his son, Colonel Sartoris ("Sarty") Snopes, a boy of ten or eleven. Ab, who appears as a Civil War freebooter and horse thief in *The Unvanquished*, is here depicted (thirty years older) as a virulently angry man, given to burning barns as revenge for real or imagined slights. The story recounts Sarty's slow, reluctant emergence into rebellion against his father.

Central to the account is Ab's deliberate tracking of manure on an expensive rug owned by Major de Spain, the man with whom Ab has just contracted to farm on shares, or as he puts it, "the man that aims to begin to-morrow owning me body and soul for the next eight months." As the struggle between Ab and de Spain accelerates, Sarty finds himself torn between the demands of family loyalty and his emerging sense of ethical rightness. He finally breaks into open rebellion, opposing his father's intention to burn de Spain's barn and rushing off to warn de Spain. The story ends with the suggestion that Ab may have been shot by de Spain and with Sarty moving off toward an indeterminate future, walking "toward the dark woods within which the liquid silver voices of the birds called unceasing."

The richness of the story has invited many forms of critical interpretation. A popular reading throughout the history of Faulkner criticism presents "Barn Burning" as a "coming of age" story. Readings of this sort emphasize the psychological and mythical implications of Sarty's conflict with his father. They tend to accept Sarty's final rebellion as ethically correct and to emphasize the evil—even demonic—aspects of Ab's behavior. Recent readings, informed by cultural materialist/new historicist considerations, have challenged this view. They have sought to "decenter" the story by emphasizing the social and economic sources of Ab's anger. While not excusing Ab's behavior, these readings tend to question the ideological sophistication and ethical correctness of Sarty's rebellion.

Much critical attention has also been paid to the story's imagery and diction and to its relation to other works by Faulkner. Critics have often commented on the story's complex narrative method, in which Sarty's thoughts are rendered in a language more sophisticated than his age would seem to allow. Critics interested in decentering the story have emphasized how highly the narrator's negative rendering of Ab Snopes is colored by Sarty's anxiety and fear. A number of critics have linked Ab Snopes to Thomas Sutpen, seeing his aggressive entry into de Spain's mansion as a variation on the motif of balked entry in *Absalom, Absalom!* Some have viewed "Barn Burning" as occupying a pivotal place in Faulkner's career, both in its rendering of class and economic issues and in its depiction of father-son relations.

FURTHER READING

Saur, Pamela S. "Property, Wealth, and the 'American Dream' in 'Barn Burning.' " *Teaching Faulkner* 8 (1995): 3–5.

Watson, James G. "Faulkner's Short Stories and the Making of Yoknapatawpha." *Fifty Years of Yoknapatawpha*, ed. Fowler and Abadie. 202–225.

Yunis, Susan S. "The Narrator of Faulkner's 'Barn Burning.' " *Faulkner Journal* 6 (1991): 23–31.

Zender, Karl F. "Character and Symbol in 'Barn Burning.' " *College Literature* 16 (1989): 48–59.

Karl F. Zender

BARN BURNING (film). Six years after the appearance of "Barn Burning" in *Harper's Magazine* in 1939, Faulkner himself conceived of a film adaptation of his award-winning short story. In the summer of 1945 he and A. I. Bezzerides worked on a fifty-page sketch. Although this project was abandoned, a telefilm version was finally realized in 1954. Written by Gore Vidal and directed by Robert Mulligan, *Barn Burning* aired on CBS in its half-hour, live series *Suspense*. The most noteworthy adaptation came, however, with the 1980 production, an inclusion in the American Short Story series on PBS, which was sponsored by a grant from the National Endowment for the Humanities and the Xerox Corporation.

Produced by Robert Geller, the film was telecast in March 1980 with a running time of forty-one minutes. Peter Werner, director, worked from a screenplay by Horton Foote, who also wrote television and cinema adaptations of two other Faulkner stories, "Old Man" and "Tomorrow." The cast of *Barn Burning* included such notables as Tommy Lee Jones as Abner Snopes and Faulkner's nephew Jimmy as Major de Spain. Shawn Whittington starred as Colonel Sartoris Snopes, better known as "Sarty."

Under Werner's direction, this production offers an artful rendition, yet one that remains faithfully close to Faulkner's text. One of the most commendable aspects of the film pertains to its visual conveyance of Ab's character—his obstinacy, fierce independence, and even cruelty. Typically, he is framed in a close-up or middle shot, though by one that casts half of his face in deep shadow. This lighting provides a visual analogue to the story's central thematic thrust, namely, Sarty's need to choose between right and wrong. Additionally, Snopes's cold, flat expressions and almost unendurable periods of silence or stillness in response to accusations or even supportive, loving words from his son further testify to his defiance, rigidity, and extremism. Werner equally utilizes the setting and landscape to such ends as well.

Through a voice-over narration, we learn from the outset not only of Sarty's love for his father but equally of his despair over his recent barn burning. Sarty's thoughts are symbolically conveyed by the barren landscape, which is cold and lifeless, with the sparse, dead brush looking as if it were recently scorched by fire. Shortly thereafter, Snopes confronts Sarty about his loyalty concerning their recent appearance before the law, and he does so by luring Sarty literally and figuratively into a Spenserian wood of error. That is, as Ab talks, he draws Sarty into a swampy area and thicket of limbless trees, a scene that clearly resembles a labyrinth, hence nicely symbolizing the moral ambiguity of his talk. Ab attempts to seduce Sarty's loyalty by referring to justice and family bonding. His speech truly conveys his moral perversity, for viewers are able to weigh Abner's character not only by such actions as the sudden slap across Sarty's face but also by contrasting Abner's treatment of Sarty with that of the mother. Throughout the film, we witness Sarty's mother consistently demonstrating love and affection for the boy.

One of the film's more dramatic scenes concerns the rug that Abner has damaged. This same evening the family eats their meager meal, and as they talk, we learn more about the mean subsistence of their lifestyle. Sarty enters carrying a load of firewood, and as he passes the drying rug, he notes the hole Abner has rubbed into its surface with a rock. From a close-up of the hole, the scene cuts to the logs being thrown into the fireplace. As the sparks fly, we know, as does Sarty, that Abner will elect to burn de Spain's barn.

After Sarty has warned de Spain and watches as the barn burns, we see a shot identical to the one of the film's opening of another fire set by Snopes. This shot further reinforces the vicious cycle of the family's life, and this is again conveyed at the film's end when we see a silhouette of the family wagon moving to another destination—although this time, Sarty watches from a distance rather than follows behind.

FURTHER READING

Skaggs, Merrill Maguire. "Story and Film in 'Barn Burning': The Difference a Camera Makes." *Southern Quarterly* 21 (1983): 5–15.

Kathy G. Willingham

BARNETT, NED. "Uncle Ned" Barnett was a black family servant of four generations of Falkners and one of many individuals who participated in the ritual of telling stories about the family patriarch, William Clark Falkner, the novelist's great-grandfather. During such sessions, Barnett would wear "frock coats, broadcloth suits, and high-crowned hats, as though to evoke the Old Colonel's sartorial splendor" (Minter 4). In 1930, when William and Estelle Faulkner purchased the "Shegog Place," a rundown antebellum house they named Rowan Oak, Ned was employed as the butler. After 1938 he lived and worked at Greenfield Farm, Faulkner's farm located seventeen miles east of Oxford, though he continued to serve on special occasions as the Rowan Oak butler. In the semiautobiographical essay "Mississippi," Faulkner describes Uncle Ned as one who had been "born in a cabin in the back yard in 1865, in the time of the middleaged's great-grandfather and had outlived three generations of them" (*ESPL* 39). In his 1940 will, Faulkner, much like Zack Edmond's arrangement for Lucas Beauchamp in *Go Down, Moses*, made provision for Barnett to retain his house and acreage at Greenfield Farm, should he outlive Faulkner. Barnett seems to have served as a model for a number of Faulkner's characters, including Simon Strother of *Flags in the Dust*, Ned McCaslin of *The Reivers*, and Lucas Beauchamp.

FURTHER READING

Hamblin, Robert W. "Lucas Beauchamp, Ned Barnett, and William Faulkner's 1940 Will." *Studies in Bibliography* 32 (1979): 281–283.

Darcy Schultz

BARR, CAROLINE (c. 1855–1940), a black woman who was a lifelong Falkner family servant. "Mammy Callie," as she was lovingly called by all who knew her, could not read or write, but she contributed greatly to William Faulkner's literary background by telling him stories from memory on numerous topics. She is said to have been the model for Molly Beauchamp of *Go Down, Moses* and for Dilsey Gibson of *The Sound and the Fury*, the latter of whom, David Minter claims, "epitomizes the kind of Christian Faulkner most admired" (97). Faulkner's love and admiration of Caroline is evidenced in both his dedication of *Go Down, Moses* to her and the eulogy he delivered at her funeral service, held in the parlor of Rowan Oak, the same room in which Faulkner himself would later lie in state. In that speech, Faulkner noted that Mammy Callie had given "a half century of fidelity and devotion" to his family, that this relationship "never became that of master and servant," and that he had learned from her "to tell the truth, to refrain from waste, and to be considerate of the weak and respectful to age." He concluded the eulogy with his conviction that "if there is a heaven, she has gone there" (*ESPL* 117–118).

Darcy Schultz

BARRON, HOMER. In Faulkner's short story "A Rose for Emily," Homer Barron arrives in Jefferson with a Northern paving company hired to repair the city's streets. He begins an affair with Miss Emily Grierson who, apparently disappointed at his failure to propose marriage, poisons him. The townspeople believe he has simply walked out on Emily, but the truth is revealed after her death when they find his body in an upstairs bedroom. Evidence at the scene suggests that Emily had, on occasion, slept with the corpse. Some critics have suggested that Homer, a Northerner, may provide an occasion for an ironic triumph of the South in Miss Emily's successful commission of his murder. Others have found in Homer's strong masculine presence and whip-wielding skills an interesting resemblance to Emily's domineering father, who kept any potential suitor at a distance. They see Emily's crime as a second attempt to keep a father-figure from deserting her. In comments recorded in *Faulkner in the University*, Faulkner suggested that he was not particularly interested in Homer's symbolic value but saw him as a means of developing the tragedy inherent in Emily's inability to escape the influence of her repressive father.

FURTHER READING

Inge, M. Thomas. *William Faulkner: "A Rose for Emily."* Columbus, Ohio: Charles E. Merrill Publishing Company, 1970.
Scherting, Jack. "Emily Grierson's Oedipus Complex: Motif, Motive, and Meaning in Faulkner's 'A Rose for Emily.' " *Studies in Short Fiction* 17 (1980): 397–405.

Glenn Reed

BATTLE CRY is one of two major unproduced film projects on which Faulkner worked in the early 1940s (the other is *The De Gaulle Story*). Warner Bros. intended this to be an epic film, directed by Howard Hawks, about Allied resistance to Axis aggression on various fronts—American, British, French, Russian, Chinese, and Greek. The project would also utilize a variety of unproduced story properties and discarded scripts. With only minor exceptions, the final draft of the screenplay was entirely Faulkner's and thus provides a valuable indication of his talents as a screenwriter. The script is a comparativist extravaganza depicting a mosaic of world resistance to fascism and including, as well, a strong statement denouncing discrimination against African Americans in the United States.

FURTHER READING

Brodsky and Hamblin, eds. *Faulkner: A Comprehensive Guide to the Brodsky Collection.* Vol. IV: *Battle Cry: A Screenplay by William Faulkner.*

Joseph R. Urgo

"BEAR, THE," one of Faulkner's most highly regarded narratives, was published both as a short story in the *Saturday Evening Post* (May 9, 1942) and as a chapter of *Go Down, Moses* (1942). Portions were published separately from the version integral to *Go Down, Moses* (e.g., the story "Lion"). "The Bear" is a composite narrative of the initiation and inheritance of Isaac McCaslin (born in 1867), the last direct male descendant of Lucius Quintus Carothers McCaslin, who purchased land from the Chickasaw Indians. When he turns twenty-one, Ike chooses to repudiate his inheritance, believing that no one can own the land.

Four sections of the novel version (1, 2, 3, and 5) tell the story of Ike's initiation as a hunter and of the diminishment of the wilderness with the advent of railroading and clear-cut logging along the Tallahatchie in the later nineteenth century. In section 4, a difficult piece of narration in an otherwise accessible sequence, Faulkner depicts similar settings and relationships at different historical times and creates multiple perspectives within a frame of omniscient-objective narration by alternating narrative voices between Ike and his cousin McCaslin in dialogue—and by intercalating material from ledgers in the commissary on the "plantation" once belonging to Ike's father Theophilus ("Buck") and uncle Amodeus ("Buddy"). This section is panoramic, synoptic, and richly textured—although readers must attend closely to narrative shifts and allusions to the Bible, battles of the Civil War, and other matters as Ike and McCaslin discuss the whole estate and descent of humankind.

Sections 1–3 narrate the rising action of Ike's progressive initiation into the wilderness and the skills of hunting, reaching a climax with the deaths of the mythical bear Old Ben, Sam Fathers (one of Ike's surrogate fathers), and the dog Lion (December 1883). Taken as a whole, this sequence is mythic, heroic, male centered, and highly racialized. So strongly interwoven are elements of the story, so sacralized the ritual of the hunt, that the three totemic deaths at the conclusion of section 3 make it difficult to imagine how the narrative might return to a quotidian world. It does return, in medias res, to the colloquy of Ike and McCaslin as Ike reaches twenty-one years of age in section 4 (October 1888): Here the quotidian and the transgressive-sublime meet in their reading of ledgers that reveal miscegenation and incest stemming not from latter-day backsliding but from L.Q.C. McCaslin himself (extending, however, as the whole of *Go Down, Moses* reveals, to the last generation). The trajectory of section 4 leads to Ike's dispossession by his wife, resulting from his repudiation of his inheritance. Section 5 returns the action to 1884, where Ike enters the now-leased and invaded woods, meets and salutes a totemic snake, and finds Boon hammering his gun under a gum tree full of squirrels. Here, memories of sublime apprehension in the hunt are accommodated to an ironic realization that things are not as they were.

In the *Saturday Evening Post* version of "The Bear," Sam Fathers and other characters from the longer story appear, but the boy is unnamed and interacts with a living father who takes the place, as it were, of McCaslin in discussing the lines from Keats's ode. (Ike's father, in contrast, dies when he is three.) Unlike Ike, the boy acquiesces to his father's instruction.

During the Cold War period of modernization, urbanization, and search for a national/spiritual narrative, "The Bear" was especially attractive for undergraduate teaching. An early anthology of texts, sources, and criticism, *Bear, Man, and God*, remains a valuable reference work. Arthur Kinney's *Critical Essays on William Faulkner: The McCaslin Family* provides more recent commentary and aids, including photographs of locations, activities, and persons relevant to the story. Much current criticism treats the story in the context of *Go Down, Moses*. Faulkner's insistence on the story's dependence on the context of the novel notwithstanding, it is serious, complete, and of a magnitude sufficient to consider it a separate work. Its treatment of the themes of the wilderness and national narrative can be compared to treatment of these in works by Latin American writers (Faris). Its treatment of issues of inheritance, family, and race can be viewed both historically and from the vantage of literary tradition and influence (MacKethan). Indeed, whatever else is true about representations of race in the story, they often reveal insight, as in the passage explaining Lucas Beauchamp's name (his grandmother Tomey is both illegitimate daughter to L.Q.C. McCaslin by the slave Eunice and mother by L.Q.C. to Lucas's father Tomey's Turl): "not refusing to be called Lucius . . . not denying . . . but simply taking the name and changing, altering it, making it no longer the white man's but his own, by himself composed, himself selfprogenitive and nominate." Both "composition" (in the sense of "writing") and reading are central themes, as Ike learns to read signs of the land, reads ledgers revealing the history of generations on it, and debates the meaning of these, the Bible, and Keats's ode with McCaslin (Zender, "Reading"). Thus the story is highly self-reflexive and, like many of Faulkner's works, interrogates the paradoxical interpenetration and divergence of word and event.

FURTHER READING

Faris, Wendy B. "Marking Space, Charting Time: Text and Territory in Faulkner's 'The Bear' and Carpentier's Los pasos perdidos." *Do the Americas Have a Common Literature?* Ed. Gustavo Perez Firmat. Durham, N.C.: Duke University Press, 1990. 243–265.
Kinney, Arthur F., ed. *Critical Essays on William Faulkner: The McCaslin Family.* Boston: G. K. Hall, 1990.
MacKethan, Lucinda H. "The Grandfather Clause: Reading the Legacy from 'The Bear' to *Song of Solomon.*" *Unflinching Gaze: Morrison and Faulkner Re-Envisioned.* Ed. Carol A. Kolmerten, Stephen M. Ross, and Judith Bryant Wittenberg. Jackson: University Press of Mississippi, 1997. 99–114.
Pinsker, Sanford. "The Unlearning of Ike McCaslin: An Ironic Reading of William Faulkner's 'The Bear.' " *Topic* 23 (1972): 35–51.
Utley, Francis Lee, Lynn Z. Bloom, and Arthur F. Kinney, eds. *Bear, Man, and God: Seven Approaches to William Faulkner's "The Bear."* New York: Random House, 1964.
Zender, Karl. "Reading in 'The Bear.' " *Faulkner Studies* 1 (1980): 91–99.

Stephen Hahn

BEAR, THE (film), the 1980 screen version of Faulkner's story produced by Barr Films and directed by Bernard Wilets, offers an adaptation that highly recommends itself in a number of respects. The twenty-five-minute film isolates, from Faulkner's tale, the young Isaac McCaslin's participation in the yearly hunt at the de Spain camp. While emphasizing and foregrounding the boy's gradual initiation process into earning the right to hunt in the highly ritualized affair, the film also incorporates other thematic concerns and motifs central to the novella. In particular, the film includes Faulkner's sentiments about the encroachment of technology upon the wilderness and the potential for total dissipation of the woods. Inextricably linked with this concern is Sam Fathers' tutelage of Ike regarding the proper and respectful use of nature. One substantial deviation concerns the death of Old Ben, the bear, at the hands of Boon Hogganbeck, which the film omits altogether.

The film opens with an exposition shot of the wilderness and then cuts to a close-up of a young boy's grip upon a rifle barrel, establishing from this credit sequence the central thematic thrust. The next scene features the boy and the elder hunters gathered in Walter Ewell's sitting room, speaking of recent citings of Ben and of his terrorism. The camera cuts back and forth from the sitting room talks to shots of some of the dead animals slain by Ben. Through a voice-over narration, we learn of the boy's long-awaited desire to participate in the traditional hunt. The omniscient narrator quotes directly from Faulkner's text, and as he tells of the ritual's significance and tradition, he also speaks of "that doomed wilderness whose edges were being constantly and punily gnawed at by men with plows and axes." Simultaneously, the camera presents a visual analogue to Faulkner's pronouncements about the diminishing wilderness by rapidly cutting from the sitting room to shots of the pristine woods and then to scenes of the lumber industry's felling of trees.

As the film progresses, the setting changes to feature the woods itself. We witness significant phases of Ike's odyssey, from his first glimpse of Old Ben's footprint to his recognition that he is being observed by the bear. Simultaneously we learn more about Ike's tutelage by Sam Fathers. We hear, for instance, Sam's directive to relinquish his gun in order to earn the privilege to have an encounter with Ben. The next sequence dramatically shows Ike's deliberate yet anxious decision to leave his gun and then walking stick, compass, and knife. By way of subjective camera, we experience Ike's frightful and intimidating trek in the big woods alone, unarmed, and defenseless. Ike's sense of vulnerability is heightened by the rapid-fire cuts from one wilderness shot to another, accompanied by a musical and sound score intensifying the mood. The sequence ends with an abrupt and climactic scene featuring Ike's up-close confrontation with Ben.

Having successfully completed one of his first important tasks, he is now ready to hunt for deer and other game, and the narrator tells us that Ike has now even slain a bear, "but not the old bear." We watch as Sam Fathers places the "tribal marks [of animal blood] on his face." We next learn of the importance of having "the right dog" with which to pursue Ben. We watch as one is finally found, trained, and nurtured for the task. Shortly thereafter, Sam, Ike, and the dog spy Ben in the woods. In a slow-motion sequence, the dog chases after Ben while Ike follows. The scene climaxes with a middle shot of Ben on his hind legs and then Ike in an ideal situation to shoot.

The scene cuts to an exterior shot of Ike's home (actually the facade of Faulkner's Rowan Oak) and then an interior view of the home. Ike confronts his father (not Cass Edmonds) and attempts to wrestle with his failure to shoot Old Ben when given the ideal opportunity. His father responds by reading from Keats's "Ode on a Grecian Urn," particularly emphasizing the lines: "When old age shall this generation waste" and "Beauty is truth, truth beauty." When Ike demonstrates a bit more doubt and confusion, the father reiterates the lines about truth. After speaking further about the verity of truth, Ike says he understands the message his father is conveying, and on this note, the film closes.

Kathy G. Willingham

"BEAR HUNT, A," a short story by Faulkner, first appeared in the *Saturday Evening Post* in February 1934 and is reprinted in both *Collected Stories* and *Big Woods*. Among other, mostly minor revisions for inclusion in *Big Woods*, Faulkner changes Lucius Provine to Lucius Hogganbeck. The story presents a humorous twist to the revenge theme. To cure Hogganbeck's hiccoughs, V. K. Ratliff sends him to John Basket at the Indian village. Old Man Ash (Ash Wylie), an aged black man who works for the de Spains, arranges with Basket to frighten Hogganbeck to get even with him for having burned the celluloid collars off Ash and the other black men at a church picnic some twenty years previously. Hogganbeck is cured but so frightened he returns to the hunting camp to thrash Ratliff.

Larry Wharton

BEAUCHAMP, an African American Yoknapatawpha family whose lineage is traceable to the white patriarch and founding landowner, Lucius Quintus Carothers McCaslin, whose incestuous relationship with a half-black daughter, his slave, produces a son, Terrel ("Tomey's Turl") Beauchamp. Terrel and his wife Tennie are founders of the Beauchamp line. Important in *Go Down, Moses* and *Intruder in the Dust*, the Beauchamps also appear in *A Fable, The Town*, and *The Reivers*.

In *Intruder in the Dust*, Lucas Beauchamp, framed for the murder of a white man, coordinates from his jail cell the efforts of Chick Mallison, a white youth whom Lucas has earlier aided, to open the grave of the murder victim and thus begin Lucas's exoneration. In *Go Down, Moses*, Ike McCaslin, after learning his family's genealogy (in "The Bear"), repudiates his inheritance and makes some restitution to his Beauchamp relatives. In "Delta Autumn," however, he discovers a sexual liaison between a white relative (Carothers Edmonds, current owner of the McCaslin place) and a black one (an unnamed great-granddaughter of Tennie and Terrel) and cynically advises the woman and her child to "go back North." But in *Go Down, Moses*, Molly Beauchamp, Lucas's wife, establishes her own family's claim to the McCaslin patrimony by her insistence on a public, local burial for her grandson, who has been executed for murder in Chicago.

Faulkner's characterizations of Molly as an apparently simple old woman and Lucas as an arrogantly upright man whose resistance to white domination stems from his consciousness of McCaslin blood have not been uniformly approved. But the presence of the Beauchamps in Faulkner's work illustrates his continuing concern with the theme of the South's biracial heritage and the question of the status of black Southerners and of black inheritance in the twentieth-century South.

FURTHER READING

Kinney, Arthur F., ed. *Critical Essays on William Faulkner: The McCaslin Family.* Boston: G. K. Hall, 1990.

Meeter, Glenn. "Molly's Vision: Lost Cause Ideology and Genesis in Faulkner's *Go Down, Moses.*" *Faulkner and Ideology,* ed. Kartiganer and Abadie. 277–296.

Sowder, William. "Lucas Beauchamp as Existential Hero." *College English* 25 (1963): 115–127.

Glenn Meeter

BENBOW, a fictional family appearing in several Faulkner works. Bookish and sensitive, Horace and Narcissa Benbow are the twentieth-century generation of an old legal family in Jefferson. We hear mention of earlier Benbows: A Judge Benbow plays a part in *Absalom, Absalom!* and "An Odor of Verbena"; Cassius Q. Benbow, a black former slave, has a key role in "Skirmish at Sartoris." But Faulkner is most interested in this quiet and inward-looking brother and sister whose stories he develops at length in *Sartoris/Flags in the Dust, Sanctuary* (especially the original text), and "There Was a Queen." In their first appearance, in peacetime Jefferson after Horace's return from Europe, they are notable for their unusually close relationship and their resistance to disturbance. Yet both are drawn into complicated erotic attractions to deeply agitating opposites. Horace is eventually married to the ambitious Belle Mitchell, Narcissa to the self-destructive Bayard Sartoris. Although the Benbows' relationship survives these disastrous liaisons, the disruption and bitterness are irreversible, and their later history in *Sanctuary* deepens the rifts. The future of the imperiled Benbow family is unknown. (It converges with that of the Sartorises in the figure of Narcissa's son, Benbow Sartoris—heard of in "Knight's Gambit" on a "hush hush" mission in England in 1942.)

Sometimes seen as a descendant of Pierrot, a prototype of Quentin Compson and Gavin Stevens, Horace is an intellectual idealist whose troubled consciousness Faulkner tracks in some of his most involuted and metaphorical writing. Critics have increasingly paid him attention as an artist-figure who gives us insights into the dynamics of Faulkner's aesthetics. Meanwhile, both Benbows continue to fascinate readers as studies in sexual conflict. Horace's compulsive interest in seemingly unsuitable women—among them, his sister, his future wife's sister, and his step daughter—presents fertile ground for psychoanalytic approaches. Narcissa, too, provokes lively analysis, attracting labels ranging from "radical virgin" to "repressed hysteric," from "fantasist" to "earth-mother," from "controlled sexual opportunist" in "There Was a Queen" to "vindictive mouthpiece of convention" in *Sanctuary*. But any simple diagnoses are reductive, failing to do justice to a pair of Faulkner's most complex portraits: an intricately developed representation of genteel Southern womanhood in crisis and a powerful account of idealism discovering its own complicity with the forces that destroy it.

FURTHER READING

Cohen, Philip. "Horace Benbow and Faulkner's Other Early Failed Idealists." *South Carolina Review* 18 (1986): 78–92.

Hönnighausen, Lothar. "Personae of the Artist: Horace Benbow and Gavin Stevens." *The Artist and His Masks: William Faulkner's Metafiction*. Ed. Agostino Lombardo. Rome: Bulzoni, 1991. 127–137.

Irwin, John T. "Horace Benbow and the Myth of Narcissa." *Faulkner and Psychology*, ed. Kartiganer and Abadie. 242–271.

Young, T. Daniel. "Narcissa Benbow's Strange Loves: William Faulkner." *American Declarations of Love*. Ed. Ann Massa. Basingstoke, England: Macmillan, 1990. 88–103.

Pamela E. Knights

BERGSON, HENRI (1859–1941), French philosopher. Faulkner had two things in common with Bergson: Both desired American involvement in World War I; both received the Nobel Prize for Literature. Bergson is among the obvious influences on Faulkner's artistic experiment. Karl's biography cites Faulkner's "temporal modes" as the arena in which the influence of Bergson had its greatest play. Clearly, Bergson's idea of chronology versus duration gave modernist writers an aesthetic of time that influenced their portrait of the historicity of events, the momentum of memory, and the recurrent fluidity of past-present-future. Thus Bergson enlarged Faulkner's specific use of Keats's urn iconography, suggesting that life is a motion whose movement the artist must slow in order to focus but, in slowing, risk distorting.

Elements of Faulkner's fiction bearing the sign of Bergsonian influence would include the time zones, shifting subjectivities, varieties of frieze and fury, and the aggregation of histories in *The Sound and the Fury, Sanctuary, As I Lay Dying*, and *Absalom, Absalom!* Bergson's influence was greatest on the early novels and short fiction where decentering reality was of primary importance. It is well documented that Faulkner, as well as other writers both popular and serious, read Bergson. Joan Williams's copy of *Creative Evolution* was given to her by Memphis writer Louise Fitzhugh; seeing it in her possession prompted Faulkner to tell her, "It helped me," and to inscribe in it the injunction: "Dont work too hard at it, but read it.'' Its perspective on Darwinian evolution possibly influenced the literary paleontology of *Requiem for a Nun*.

While we cannot be certain Faulkner read other Bergson works, Bergson also addressed two other topics of importance to Faulkner, the sources of humor and morality as senses defining the human. Bergson's *Two Sources of Morality and Religion* would have helped him examine the "religion of the Confederacy" that pervaded his formative years and led him to associate his family with the fictional Sartorises, allowing him to reflect on that association in the light of the ethical dimensions of the Judeo-Christian tradition. And Bergson's ideas of comedy would have helped him shape the development of his earliest materials into, eventually, the *Snopes* trilogy and *The Reivers*, even when his experiments with time had become less central.

FURTHER READING

Ford, Daniel G. "Faulkner's Sense of Was." *Publications of the Arkansas Philological Association* 10.1 (1984): 45–56.

Gidley, Mick. "The Later Faulkner, Bergson, and God." *Mississippi Quarterly* 37 (1984): 377–383.

Ringold, Francine. "The Metaphysics of Yoknapatawpha County: 'Airy Space and Scope for Your Delirium.' " *University of Hartford Studies in Literature* 8 (1976): 223–240.

Charles A. Peek

"BEYOND," a short story by Faulkner, first appeared in *Harper's* in September 1933 and is also included in *Doctor Martino and Other Stories* and *Collected Stories*. This sad, quizzical story seems to present Faulkner's skeptical attitude toward the Christian doctrine of the immortality of the soul. The plot centers on the final moments of Judge Howard Allison, a man who has lived alone most of his life and who has long mourned his son's early and tragic death. The dying man, attended only by Dr. Lucius Peabody and his own hired help, seems to visit the "beyond," where he has conversations about immortality. He returns to his own funeral as the coffin lid is closing without confirmation of a life after death.

FURTHER READING

Gidley, Mick. "Beyond 'Beyond': Aspects of Faulkner's Representation of Death." *Faulkner's Discourse*, ed. Hönnighausen. 223–233.

Simpson, Hassell A. "Wilbur Daniel Steele's Influence on Faulkner's Revision of 'Beyond.' " *Mississippi Quarterly* 34 (1981): 335–339.

Larry Wharton

BEZZERIDES, ALBERT I. (1908–   ), author and scriptwriter best known for his film noir screenplay *They Drive by Night* (1940), which he adapted from his best-selling novel *The Long Haul* (1938). Another of Bezzerides's highly regarded film adaptations is his screenplay (1954) of Mickey Spillane's novel *Kiss*

Me Deadly. Faulkner and Bezzerides first met in 1942 at Warner Bros. Studio, where both were employed as screenwriters. More experienced as a scriptwriter but younger and awed by Faulkner's reputation as an author, Bezzerides volunteered to drive Faulkner to and from the studio, thus initiating a friendship that continued until Faulkner's departure from Hollywood in 1945. For six months during 1944 and another four-month period in 1945 Faulkner lived rent free in a room in Bezzerides's home in west Los Angeles. In July 1947 Bezzerides and his wife briefly visited Faulkner and Estelle at Rowan Oak. Bezzerides authored the script for the PBS documentary *Faulkner: A Life on Paper* (1979).

FURTHER READING

Brodsky, Louis Daniel. "Reflections on Faulkner: An Interview with Albert Bezzerides." *Southern Review* 21 (1985): 376–403.

Louis Daniel Brodsky

BIBLE. The biblical influence in Faulkner's fiction is strong and constant. Although some of this biblical influence no doubt came by virtue of his heritage and background, some he consciously sought; so we may more properly speak of Faulkner's use of the Bible than of his merely being passively "influenced" by it. When asked in a 1956 interview how he got his "background in the Bible," Faulkner responded with an illustrative anecdote about how his great-grandfather Murry required everyone at his breakfast table, child or adult, to recite an "authentic, correct verse" of Scripture before eating, even if the achievement took a special instructional session (*LIG* 250). If Faulkner had personal favorites among the biblical narratives, the stories of Abraham, David, and Christ would no doubt rank high, judging by their prominence in such works as *Sartoris, Go Down, Moses, Absalom, Absalom!, The Unvanquished, Light in August,* and *A Fable.*

As for regional influences, Faulkner as a Southern writer growing up in the first part of the century, when the term "Bible Belt" was coined during the Scopes trial, would have found the Bible an inescapable part of his material. Apart from his characters' function in any given novel, it would be natural for them to have a bedside Bible, like Mrs. Compson (*The Sound and the Fury*), or to place one in a satchel when traveling, like Ned McCaslin (*The Reivers*), or quote from it in political argument like Goodhue Coldfield (*Absalom, Absalom!*), or argue about its interpretation like Ike and Cass (*Go Down, Moses*); even displaced Southerners like Harry and Charlotte in *The Wild Palms* name their imaginary dog "Moreover," in allusion to Luke 16:21 ("moreover the dogs . . ."). The Bible for Faulkner would have been as necessary a part of the social and linguistic landscape of his fiction as the mule and the cottonfield were of the physical. In addition, on the conceptual level it was a long-standing Southern habit of mind to draw parallels between the South and biblical Israel. The Israelite prototype of course has been claimed by many American groups, including the Pilgrims, Mormons, Southern slaves singing spirituals of deliverance, and Union troops singing "The Battle Hymn of the Republic" during the Civil War. But the South's defeat in a cause it had thought of as holy, at the hands of a larger, wealthier, and more secular empire, was felt to give its use of the parallel a unique appropriateness. The meditations of Hightower on the Civil War (*Light in August*) and the arguments of Ike and Cass about Southern history (*Go Down, Moses*) owe something to this kind of thinking, as does Faulkner's own evocation, in *Absalom, Absalom!* and *The Unvanquished*, of parallels between Sutpen and Sartoris and the biblical David.

Faulkner's uses of the Bible are sometimes signaled by biblical titles like those of *Absalom, Absalom!*, *Go Down, Moses*, and *If I Forget Thee, Jerusalem* (the original title of *The Wild Palms*). In *Absalom*, Sutpen and his family have a number of features in common with the biblical house of David—and the *making* of the Sutpen story, by its later redactors Quentin and Shreve, shares features (including a setting in "exile") with the work of the biblical redactors of Israel's history. *The Wild Palms* picks up the Psalm of exile, Psalm 137, and uses it thematically (and ironically). In *Go Down, Moses* L.Q.C. McCaslin is pictured as an Abraham, with his many descendants; Mollie Beauchamp's insistence that her grandson's body be buried in Jefferson stakes her family's claim to the South as Promised Land—even as Ike, a white McCaslin descendant, like Esau, sells his birthright.

Other Faulknerian uses of the Bible are signaled by character: in *Light in August* "Joe Christmas" undergoes a scapegoat's death (and a metaphorical resurrection/ascension), whereas Lena Grove, an unwed mother whose dress and demeanor has reminded readers of the Virgin, births her baby in an out-of-the-way place. Or by plot: in *Sanctuary* "Temple's" abduction to a Memphis brothel recalls the allegories of Ezekiel 16 and 23, where Jerusalem, personified as a fallen and hypersexed woman, is carried off to Babylon by the heathen she allowed herself to be promiscuously associated with. Or by a variety of elements: In *The Sound and the Fury* apocalyptic imagery is common to Quentin and Jason, and the book of Revelation is a favorite of Dilsey and Shegog. In *As I Lay Dying* the motif of conventional wisdom, which is embodied in the characters who disparage the Bundrens' outlandish journey, also gets expressed in proverbs: Job 1:21, for example, is echoed by Peabody, Moseley, and a chorus of the Bundrens' comforters. The two female teachers of the novel, Addie and Cora, are contrasted like Lady Wisdom and Dame Folly in Proverbs; and Anse, with all his "trials," aims to see himself as Job. In *The Unvanquished*, Bayard Sartoris, the narrator, repeatedly gives his father David-like characteristics, including especially the legacy-speech delivered to Bayard just before his death, calling himself a man of bloodshed and his son a man of the law who, Solomon-like, will carry on the Sartoris agenda in a new era.

There is a suggestion, then, of an attempt by Faulkner to have his "apocrypha" (*FIU* 285) echo major portions of the English Bible. During 1940–1962 something else happens: Extending the Israelite model for Southern history into

New Testament times, Faulkner no longer makes each novel echo a segment of biblical literature but rather elaborates on his central metaphor, the mid-century South (or Yoknapatawpha) as a Roman Judaea. In *The Hamlet* he furnishes a Greco-Roman mythology for his county and in *Requiem for a Nun* gives a secularized account of its history. In *Intruder in the Dust, The Town*, and *The Mansion* he portrays Yoknapatawpha versions of Samaritans, Pharisees, Zealots, and Essenes (as well as "early Christians" like Goodyhay in *The Mansion*), in a land increasingly "Hellenized"; and in *The Reivers* he completes his array of New Testament parallels with Boss Priest's family of Sadducees.

FURTHER READING

Coffee. *Faulkner's Un-Christlike Christians*.
Meeter, Glenn. "Beyond Lexicon: Biblical 'Allusion' in Faulkner." *Mississippi Quarterly* 49 (1996): 595–602.
Ross, Stephen M. "Faulkner's *Absalom, Absalom!* and the David Story: A Speculative Contemplation." *The David Myth in Western Literature*. Ed. Jean Frontain and Jan Wojcik. West Lafayette, Ind.: Purdue University Press, 1980. 136–153.

Glenn Meeter

"BIG SHOT, THE," an early short story by Faulkner. Composed no later than January 23, 1930, "The Big Shot" remained unpublished until *Uncollected Stories*. Dal Martin, the protagonist, rises to a position of wealth and power in Memphis. He wants his daughter Wrennie to be among the debutantes of the Chickasaw Guards ball, a goal that leads to the suicide of Dr. Blount. Martin's machinations enable the bootlegger Popeye to disappear after a traffic incident in which he kills a woman. Later Martin learns that the woman is Wrennie. "Dull Tale" is a revision of "The Big Shot" without the Popeye material. Popeye reappears in *Sanctuary*, and Wrennie may prefigure Temple Drake. Like Thomas Sutpen, Dal Martin experiences a life-altering, front door rejection. Don and the unnamed narrator of this story also appear in "Mistral," "Snow," and "Evangeline."

FURTHER READING

Lang, Beatrice. "An Unpublished Faulkner Short Story: 'The Big Shot.' " *Mississippi Quarterly* 26 (1973): 313–324.

Diane Brown Jones

BIG SLEEP, THE, a 1946 film, directed by Howard Hawks, in which Humphrey Bogart plays Raymond Chandler's tough private eye Philip Marlowe. The screenplay, cowritten by Faulkner, concerns Marlowe's efforts to track down an heiress who is also a murderess, a nymphomaniac, and a drug addict. The violent action is balanced at times by a sardonic type of humorous dialogue that approximates the quality of Chandler's own taut, cynical dialogue. Chandler, accordingly, was pleased that the screenplay of the film preserved the hardboiled flavor of his novel. *The Big Sleep* was lauded by reviewers as an expert crime melodrama; it was perhaps the biggest commercial success of all the films on which Faulkner collaborated as a screenwriter.

Gene D. Phillips

BIG WOODS, a collection of hunting stories by Faulkner, published in 1955. The work includes "The Bear," "The Old People," "A Bear Hunt," "Race at Morning," and a number of interchapters that Faulkner termed "interrupted catalysts." All of the material had been previously published, although only "The Old People" is unchanged from its original form. The volume also includes drawings by Edward Shenton, who also illustrated *The Unvanquished* and a number of Faulkner's *Saturday Evening Post* stories.

Big Woods opens with an excerpt from *Requiem for a Nun* that encapsulates the evolution of the Mississippi wilderness and experience: from allusions to a fecund, lush, primordial past through the history of the appearance of man, Native American and European alike. The presentation of the rapid-fire evolution of settlement ends with a depiction of a homogeneous present, a Mississippi that, due to economic, political, cultural, and technological forces, is now indistinguishable from any other part of America. This opening vignette previews one of the novel's major thematic concerns, namely, the absolute verity of growth, change, and dynamism and humankind's subsequent reaction.

Faulkner next presents "The Bear," though without the fourth section featuring Ike McCaslin's repudiation of his inheritance. This omission serves to foreground the cluster of themes and motifs cementing the structure of *Big Woods*. Of utmost significance is, of course, the exhaustion of the wilderness and its subsequent impact on hunting, even at the most rudimentary level—that is, no wilderness, hence no game. Faulkner, however, does not entertain such a simplistic view—thus the introduction of one of the novel's key concerns, namely, the elevation of hunting from a mere sport to a profoundly significant ritual.

"The Bear" segment ends with Boon Hogganbeck maniacally and violently asserting a pathetic territorial imperative over his frantic prey, the squirrels at the gum tree, thus anticipating the theme and tone of the next vignette. Taken from "Red Leaves," this interchapter tells of the Indians' pursuit of Issetibbeha's personal slave who, according to ritual, is condemned to die with his former master. Now, man has turned his penchant for violence and cruelty onto his fellow man, signifying that with the destruction of the natural world comes equally debased interpersonal relations.

Unlike *Go Down, Moses, Big Woods* has "The Old People" following rather than preceding "The Bear," and this arrangement serves to better eulogize the wilderness as well as further demonstrate the subsequent debasement of man. "The Old People" features Sam Fathers, who embodies a code of behavior and ethics respectful of all living things. He transmits to Ike McCaslin not merely hunting expertise but moreover a transcendental set of values. To demonstrate erroneous use of nature and other men, Faulkner uses aspects of Sam Fathers's history, namely, his childhood enslavement and a portrait of his own corrupt father, Doom. The exploitation and enslavement of man, murder, and avarice characterize Doom and signify the fallen traits of man.

Largely derived from "A Justice," the next interchapter addresses the destruction of the pastoral or Edenic idyll by technology. This vignette tells of a deserted steamboat foundered upon a sand bar near the Indian Plantation and of Doom's decision to transport it some twelve miles overland, in order to attach it to the communal house. This labor lasts over five months and, significantly, is accomplished by the destruction of trees to make a path. In addition to Doom's obvious disregard for nature here, his actions also reflect an inappropriate treatment of his fellow man. Faulkner emphasizes this by writing that Doom was not content to let his people rest after this laborious task; rather, he would think "of something else arduous and unpleasant for them to do."

The motif of the deterioration of nature and humanity alike continues with the next story, "A Bear Hunt." With the procession of time, not only has old Major de Spain's hunting camp receded, but his generation has vanished as well, replaced by people who are far too alienated from the land and one another. Former settlers, farmers, hunters—persons directly linked with the land—are now representatives of a consumer society—"agents for the manufacturers of minor articles like soap and men's toilet accessories and kitchen objects." Faulkner notes the change among Native Americans as well: Dispossessed of the land, the "once powerful clan of the Chickasaw tribe" now resides on a reservation, and they have forsaken their cultural practices. Even the region's traditional hunt at old Major de Spain's camp has degenerated over time. Although the title of the story leads us to expect a bear hunt, the piece actually tells of a poker party at the camp and the group's annoyance with one hunter's severe case of the hiccups.

The fourth interchapter of *Big Woods* addresses the extensive obsolescence of the wilderness due to technological and economic forces. Railroads, sawmills, and paved highways dominate the landscape, yet Faulkner does not present an entirely futile or bleak picture of the present situation. Although man has now included the grand river in his desire for economic and technological mastery, it resists, and its occasional flooding reinvigorates the land, suggesting the great cycle of life and renewal, in spite of man's actions. The aged Ike who narrates the section laments the passing of the wilderness, but Faulkner interjects by reminding us of the seemingly "invincible and almost inattentive River—impervious" to man's destructive and foolish designs. The river, therefore, is presented as signification of hope, renewal, and regeneration.

The final short story, "Race at Morning," continues the regenerative motif begun earlier and does so structurally as well as thematically. The piece echoes the central thematic concern of the first story, "The Bear." "Race at Morning" is set in modern times, yet it features a young man's education in the manner of Ike's, and like his predecessor, the boy's instruction transcends mere hunting skills to include "the business of mankind." The nameless protagonist, a product of neglect, much like the wilderness itself, is adopted and reared by Mister Ernest, a man who teaches the boy not only the right use of nature but also the necessity for adaptation to environmental and cultural changes. The boy is instructed that he must enlarge his field of experience to include a formal education. Mister Ernest explains that by attending school the boy can possess and then, more important, pass on to others "what's right."

Faulkner closes *Big Woods* with an epilogue drawn from "Delta Autumn." Narrated by Uncle Ike, the piece reiterates the vanishing woods, loss of traditional values, and the encroachment of technology, but the vignette is not without some redemptive promise. In conversing with his companion, Ike says that God probably foresaw his fate, but He nevertheless said, "I will give him his chance, I will give him warning and foreknowledge too, along with the desire to follow and the power to slay." While the landscape no longer resembles that of Ike's youth, some wilderness has remained intact, as evidenced by the presence of the hunt on this day. And as David Paul Ragan argues, "Isaac's despair must be contrasted with Mister Ernest's insistence upon possibility: 'The best word in our language, the best of all. That's what keeps man going on: Maybe' " (317).

FURTHER READING

Burggraf, David L. *The Genesis and Unity of Faulkner's* Big Woods. Ann Arbor, Mich.: UMI Research Press, 1977.

Johnson, Glen M. "*Big Woods*: Faulkner's Elegy for Wilderness." *Southern Humanities Review* 14 (1980): 249–258.

Ragan, David Paul. " 'Belonging to the Business of Mankind': The Achievement of Faulkner's *Big Woods*." *Mississippi Quarterly* 36 (1983): 301–317.

Kathy G. Willingham

BIOGRAPHIES. Faulkner wrote to Malcolm Cowley in 1946 that he hoped "for no biography, personal matter, at all. . . . nothing at all prior to the instant I began to write, as though Faulkner and Typewriter were concomitant, coadjutant and without past on the moment they faced each other at the suitable (nameless) table" (*SL* 215, 222). This was not to be. In Faulkner's lifetime Robert Coughlan drew on two *Life* articles, written with the secret help and advice of Faulkner's sometimes friend Phil Stone, for *The Private World of William Faulkner* (1953); and a hunting companion, John B. Cullen, with Floyd Watkins, published his personal reminiscences in *Old Times in the Faulkner Country* (1961). None of this is very detailed or accurate as biography, and Faulkner considered most of it intrusive. In the years immediately following the novelist's death, his brother John Faulkner, a novelist in his own right, reminisced about their childhood in *My Brother Bill* (1963), and his brother Murry Falkner remembered general family background in *The Falkners of Mississippi* (1967). *William Faulkner of Oxford* (1965), edited by James Webb and A. Wigfall Green, is a collection of appreciative memoirs by Faulkner's townspeople. Early, critically focused biographical essays include two Carvel Collins introductions: to *William Faulkner: New Orleans Sketches* (1958), about Faulkner's life in New Orleans in 1925, and to *William Faulkner: Early Prose and Poetry* (1962), about his writing life c. 1916 to 1925. H. Edward Richardson's *William Faulkner: The Journey to Self-Discovery* (1969), though dated, treats Faulkner's early life and writing through the publication of *Sartoris*. Michael Millgate's carefully documented chapter "The Career" in *The Achievement of William Faulkner* (1966) is a substantial biographical essay that introduces one of the first and best critical studies of Faulkner.

A new era in Faulkner studies began with Joseph Blotner's monumental *Faulkner: A Biography* (2 vols., 1974; rev. 1-vol. ed., 1984). The two-volume edition traces the Falkners from their beginnings in Scotland in the late seventeenth century to William's birth in 1897 and presents his life in 2,000 detailed pages from "Childhood and Youth" (1897–1918) through the post–Nobel Prize years to his death in 1962. Reviewing the two-volume edition for *Mississippi Quarterly* in 1975, James B. Meriwether noted some problems and some errors but proclaimed, "New worlds of opportunity have been opened up by this biographer; other researchers will find their tasks made easier—or made possible for the first time" (367). The one-volume edition condenses the two-volume, aiming, as Blotner says, "to make its essence available to a wider audience and to bring the earlier account up to date by incorporating material from the enormous outpouring since [1974] of scholarship, criticism, and other writings, including posthumously published Faulkner works" (1984 *FAB* ix). The enormous outpouring since then includes considerable biographical interpretation and new matter, as well.

In reading the fiction through the life, Judith Wittenberg, in *Faulkner: The Transfiguration of Biography* (1979), and David Minter, in *William Faulkner: His Life and Work* (1980), rely exclusively on Blotner, as does Michel Gresset in his useful *A Faulkner Chronology* (1985). More recent biographies also draw on Blotner for their own interpretative schema without adding new factual information: Stephen Oates's slight and impressionistic *William Faulkner; The Man and the Artist* (1987), Frederick Karl's *William Faulkner, American Writer* (1989), and Richard Gray's theory-based *The Life of William Faulkner* (1994). Of the three, Gray is the most careful and comprehensive in his treatment of the relation between Faulkner's life and his writing. In combination with specifically historical sources, Joel Williamson's *William Faulkner and Southern History* (1993) cites and interprets materials from the Blotner Papers (now a part of the Brodsky Collection) not included in *Faulkner: A Biography*. These bear especially on Faulkner's slaveholding ancestors, on both sides of the family, and on such matters as the circumstances of Estelle's divorce.

Ben Wasson's memoir *Count No 'Count* (1983) describes his forty-year relationship with Faulkner as his friend and agent, and Meta Carpenter Wilde and Orin Borsten's *A Loving Gentleman: The Love Story of William Faulkner and*

Meta Carpenter (1976) details her memories of Faulkner in Hollywood and after and quotes from his love letters; it is usefully supplemented by Panthea Reid Broughton's "An Interview with Meta Carpenter Wilde" (*Southern Review* 18 [1982], 776–801), which contains a Faulkner-Wilde chronology. Louis Daniel Brodsky's potpourri of essays and interviews, *William Faulkner: Life Glimpses* (1990), includes an interview with Faulkner's Hollywood friend Buzz Bezzerides, whose *William Faulkner: A Life on Paper* (1980), originally produced for television, is likewise composed of interviews with family members, friends, and scholars. Susan Snell's biography *Phil Stone of Oxford: A Vicarious Life* (1991) puts into perspective Faulkner's long relationship with his mentor, friend, and lawyer. Malcolm Franklin's *Bitterweeds: Life with William Faulkner at Rowan Oak* (1977), with an introduction by his mother Estelle Franklin Faulkner, is a memoir of his childhood, important aspects of which are called into question, however, in Brodsky's long interviews in *Life Glimpses* with Estelle's daughter, Victoria Fielden Johnson. More recent memoirs and books of reminiscences include *Across the Creek: Faulkner Family Stories* (1986), by Faulkner's nephew Jim Faulkner; Sally Wolff and Floyd C. Watkins's *Talking about William Faulkner: Interviews with Jimmy Faulkner and Others* (1996); and, of peripheral interest, Herman E. Taylor's *Faulkner's Oxford: Recollections and Reflections* (1990).

Blotner himself has continued to write about Faulkner's life in essays published with the proceedings of Faulkner conferences at the University of Mississippi (1979), Rome (1989), and Vienna (1992). Carvel Collins provided new biographical information from his Faulkner collection and corrected previous errors in introductions to his editions of two Faulkner manuscript books, *Mayday* (1977, 1978) and *Helen: A Courtship* (1981). In Volume I of Louis Daniel Brodsky and Robert Hamblin's *Faulkner: A Comprehensive Guide to the Brodsky Collection* (1982), artifacts from Brodsky's large Faulkner collection are arranged into a chronological "biobibliography" of Faulkner; Volume II, *The Letters*, containing letters by Faulkner and about him, has considerable biographical interest, as do all collections of Faulkner's correspondence and editions of his interviews. Among the latter are Robert A. Jelliffe, *Faulkner at Nagano* (1956); Frederick Gwynn and Joseph Blotner, *Faulkner in the University: Class Conferences at the University of Virginia, 1957–1958* (1959); Joseph Fant and Robert P. Ashley, *Faulkner at West Point* (1964); and James B. Meriwether and Michael Millgate, *Lion in the Garden: Interviews with William Faulkner, 1926–1962* (1968). Significant photographic collections depict Faulkner's family and region, including Martin J. Dain, *Faulkner's County: Yoknapatawpha* (1964), John Lawrence and Dan Hise, *Faulkner's Rowan Oak* (1993), and especially, Jack Cofield, *William Faulkner: The Cofield Collection* (1978). In *William Faulkner: His Tippah County Heritage* (1985) and the companion volume *William Faulkner: His Lafayette County Heritage* (1992), Jane Isbell Haynes makes available facts about Faulkner's and his family's ownership of houses and lands and their precise locations. Thomas S. Hines treats the architecture of Lafayette and Yoknapatawpha Counties in *William Faulkner and the Tangible Past* (1996).

James G. Watson

"BLACK MUSIC," a short story by William Faulkner, first appeared in *Doctor Martino and Other Stories* (1934). The story presents a character who has isolated himself to atone for one misguided, if not accidental, act. The present action, set in Mexico, is seen through the eyes of an unnamed listener, who manages to coax the tale from an impoverished and exiled Wilfred Midgleston. Twenty-five years before, Midgleston, an architect's draftsman, was sent to deliver plans to the Van Dyming site where they were building a Grecian temple-like structure. After a seizure and several drinks, Midgleston imagines himself a faun in service to Pan, chases Mrs. Van Dyming about a pasture, and then disappears. Later, he sees in a newspaper article that his wife soon remarries, moving up in the world with the help of his insurance policy and a newspaper story that elevated his occupation to "architect" rather than "architect's draftsman."

Larry Wharton

BLAND, GERALD, a young Southerner of good family in *The Sound and the Fury* and probably "Ad Astra." In *The Sound and the Fury* Gerald Bland, one of Quentin Compson's Harvard classmates, is a foil for his fellow Southerner Quentin in that, unlike Quentin, he has a doting mother and success with young women. Bland's boasts about his conquests provoke Quentin to fight with him since Quentin associates Bland with the men who have sexual access to Quentin's sister Caddy, as Quentin longs to but cannot. In "Ad Astra" Bland (no first name provided) is a Rhodes scholar, Royal Air Force (RAF) pilot, and womanizer who participates in drunken discussions and fights about the meaning or meaninglessness of the war.

FURTHER READING

Collins, Carvel. " 'Ad Astra' Through New Haven: Some Biographical Sources of Faulkner's War Fiction." *Faulkner and the Short Story*, ed. Harrington and Abadie. 108–127.

Veronica Makowsky

BLOTNER, JOSEPH LEO (1923–   ), American professor, scholar, and biographer, author of *Faulkner: A Biography* (1974; rev. ed., 1984), the first—and, in the opinion of many scholars, still the definitive—biography of William Faulkner. A professor of English and member of the Balch Committee at the University of Virginia in 1957, Blotner was one of those instrumental in persuading Faulkner to accept the position as Writer-in-Residence at the university, an appointment leading to Faulkner's affiliation with the university for the remainder of his life. During this period Blotner and Faulkner established a close friendship, not only working together at the university but also attending Little League baseball and college football games, touring Civil War battlefields, and hosting dinner parties for each other's families and friends. With another English professor, Frederick Gwynn, who assisted Blotner in coordinating Faulkner's activities at the university, Blotner and Faulkner organized the Squadron Room, a departmental office furnished with model planes and other flying memorabilia, where they could meet for fellowship between classes. A bombardier and prisoner of war during World War II, Blotner shared Faulkner's interest in aviation and war stories; one story that Blotner told Faulkner about his prison camp being bombed by RAF pilots found its way, to Blotner's surprise, into the pages of *The Mansion* (1974 *FAB* 1711). On one occasion Blotner provided Faulkner with more tangible help, writing the original draft for Faulkner's acceptance speech for the National Institute's Gold Medal for Fiction. Once identified by Faulkner as "my spiritual son" (1807), Blotner served as a pallbearer for Faulkner's funeral. Following Faulkner's death, Blotner was selected by the Faulkner family to produce a biography of the author, which he worked on for the next decade and more. In addition to writing *Faulkner: A Biography*, Blotner has edited several other Faulkner volumes, including *William Faulkner's Library: A Catalogue, Selected Letters of William Faulkner, Uncollected Stories of William Faulkner*, and (with Frederick L. Gwynn) *Faulkner in the University: Class Conferences at the University of Virginia*. His other books include two studies of the political novel, a treatment of J. D. Salinger's fiction, and a biography of Robert Penn Warren.

FURTHER READING

Millichap, Joseph. "Joseph Blotner." *Dictionary of Literary Biography*. Vol. III: *American Literary Biographers, Second Series*. Detroit: Gale Research, 1991. 24–32.

Robert W. Hamblin

BRITISH INFLUENCES AND RECEPTION. What formative role did British literature play in Faulkner's development? Overall, it would be fair to say that the English influence was greater the further back in time Faulkner went. Shakespeare and the King James version of the Bible, particularly the Old Testament, were overwhelming influences; Faulkner also spoke highly of the Elizabethan poets and of Keats, whose "Ode on a Grecian Urn" came to assume iconic status in Faulkner's aesthetic, representing art's attempt to stop time with the consequent loss of fulfillment thereby entailed. Closer to his own lifetime, Faulkner acknowledged the influence of late nineteenth-century aesthetes Swinburne, Wilde, and in drawing, Audrey Beardsley. Although neither was British strictly speaking, Eliot and Joyce were, according to Faulkner, contemporaries rather than influences, though some might detect a certain anxiety of influence in this distinction. But the two British writers Faulkner always mentioned were Charles Dickens and the Polish-born Joseph Conrad, the former presumably for his creation of character and the latter both for his concern with men in extremis and for his experimentation with narrative and point of view. Otherwise, Faulkner was pretty much silent on modern British writers.

Indeed, British critics have returned the indifference, their reaction to Faulkner being largely, as Mick Gidley once observed, "peevish, blimpish and hostile" (74). The roll call of British critics who have been less than impressed by Faulkner runs from Orwell to Leavis and beyond. Still, a few—Arnold Bennett, Richard Hughes, and V. S. Pritchett—have written in praise of Faulkner, and Graham Greene at least expressed an appreciative ambivalence. But although Faulkner did affect certain English traits, particularly a fondness for "riding to hounds," and expressed his fondness for the English countryside, his literary reputation in Europe owed little to the British and much to their Gallic neighbors across the Channel.

The more interesting question is, Why? Some have suggested that Britain's London-based literary establishment had difficulty responding to the regional, frontier setting of Faulkner's work, despite Faulkner's own fascination with the code of aristocracy. This may have played some role, but it begs the question as to why the hothouse intellectuality of Paris or the postwar New York critics' urban, Jewish, left-wing background failed to foreclose interest in the Mississippi writer.

In addition, a main theme of British literary culture, at least between 1945 and the 1970s, was a general ambivalence, even hostility, toward the experimental, avant-garde dimensions of literary modernism. Such a critical bias would obviously make an appreciation of Faulkner difficult, since in its major phase Faulkner's work is as experimental and difficult as any writer's in English. To comprehend Faulkner may have required what Cleanth Brooks once referred to as "American literary professionalism" as opposed to "good old British literary amateurs" (quoted in Gidley 80), who looked on the experimental modernists, and sometimes American writers generally, as affected and artificial, willfully obscure, or incompetent in their craft.

In terms of theme and vision, Faulkner's fiction also seems foreign to the tradition of social manners and observation so central to British writing. This tradition assumes that the ground rules of the world are both shared and available for common discussion. Although Faulkner's work is filled with penetrating explorations of class, status, and racial issues, it also contains strong elements of the Gothic and the Romance, adumbrating a world no longer accessible to common sense or common evaluation. The balance is no longer there; the center has not held. Put another way, Faulkner was often fascinated by those characters and actions that were transgressive of respectability and morality. It would be hard to find British characters to match Popeye or Joe Christmas or Thomas Sutpen, even in the fiction of Dickens. Although obviously capable of the comic and the pastoral, Faulkner's deployment of those modes of writing often takes on a larger-than-life or mythic quality.

Above all, Faulkner was a novelist of the inner wound, of defeat and tragedy, whether conceived in terms of individual character or regional identity. His region's defeat in the Civil War, along with the psychological, moral, and economic legacy of slavery, made the past—and the past-in-present—problematic to him in a way foreign to British fiction. If history, as Fredric Jameson has said, "is what hurts," then Faulkner's fiction was all about a history that hurt, a far cry from the relatively unproblematic relationship between present and past in English (though not perhaps in Irish or Scottish) writing.

Several recent developments suggest Faulkner's reputation in Britain will remain precarious. One encouraging sign could be noted: The development of the study of American literature in the universities since the 1960s has generated several major works in Faulkner criticism by British academics. On the other hand, the emergence of the "postmodern" as a category of literary and cultural analysis does not bode well for Faulkner's reception. If there has ever been a modernist writer—difficult, allusive, obsessively intense, stressing the unconscious and the intensely subjective, struggling with the loss of tradition—it is Faulkner. The more coldly ironic tonalities of postmodern writing and a preoccupation with popular culture and its ease of access and relatively less serious attitude toward the past may mean that Faulkner's readership will be confined to the classroom, if it can exist even there.

Indeed, one mid-1990s example of Faulkner's persisting obscurity, even invisibility, to the British literary world is symptomatic. Early in 1997 there was a flurry of attention surrounding the revelation that Graham Swift's *Last Orders*, the 1996 winner of Britain's best-known literary award, the Booker Prize, was closely modeled on Faulkner's *As I Lay Dying*. First publicized by an Australian academic but obvious and unremarkable to anyone who knew their Faulkner, it turned out that only one British review of *Last Orders* had recognized Swift's indebtedness to Faulkner; more startlingly, it had also escaped the notice of the judges of the Booker Prize. What lessons should be drawn from the affair is uncertain, but two things are clear: British literary critics and reviewers are still largely ignorant of Faulkner's work; and British novelists, with the exception of Swift, and in striking contrast with Latin American writers of the last half century, have failed to be significantly influenced by Faulkner's technical virtuosity or his vision.

FURTHER READING

Gidley, Mick. "Faulkner and the British: Episodes in a Literary Relationship." *Faulkner: International Perspectives*, ed. Fowler and Abadie. 74–96.

Richard H. King

"BROOCH, THE," a short story by Faulkner, was first published in *Scribner's Magazine* in January 1936 and is included in *Collected Stories*. The theme of the story is a mother's suffocating love for her son, conditioned by her own fear of being abandoned by another male. Mrs. Boyd, after being abandoned by her husband, decides to be ever watchful of her son Howard. He marries late, and his estrangement from his wife is heightened when their child dies. Mrs.

Boyd orders her son's unfaithful wife out of the house. As the story ends, Boyd is so cowed and distraught that he even tries to muffle the sounds of his preparations to shoot himself.

FURTHER READING

Garrison, Joseph M., Jr. "Faulkner's 'The Brooch': A Story for Teaching." *College English* 36 (1974): 51–57.
Hult, Sharon S. "William Faulkner's 'The Brooch': The Journey to Riolama." *Mississippi Quarterly* 27 (1974): 291–305.

Larry Wharton

BROOKS, CLEANTH (1906–1994), American professor and literary critic. While the phrase "the New Criticism" derives from the title of a book by John Crowe Ransom (1941), it was Brooks who in the mid-twentieth century was the most widely influential among the so-called New Critics. Never referring to a formally organized school of criticism—and associated with a broad cast of academic critics including Ransom, I. A. Richards, Austin Warren, Rene Wellek, and most of the Fugitive/Agrarian critics—the term "New Criticism" usually implies: (1) a focus on "the work itself," excluding extrinsic biographical or historical data; (2) a concern to avoid the affective and intentional "fallacies" and the "heresy of paraphrase"; and (3) a particular emphasis on paradox, irony, or other verbal tensions in literary artifacts. Although the writing that identifies Brooks as a New Critic is more varied than the selection of one or two texts can suggest, the most influential of these are the teaching anthologies he edited with Robert Penn Warren, *Understanding Poetry* (1938) and *Understanding Fiction* (1943), and the essays collected in *The Well Wrought Urn: Studies in the Structure of Poetry* (1947).

Brooks's writing on Faulkner occurs only well after he had established his critical principles and pursued his career as a professor of English at Yale (having for some years taught at Louisiana State University and elsewhere). He met Faulkner only once, in Manhattan in November 1948, through their mutual acquaintance (and sometime editor and business advisor) Albert Erskine. Brooks's first essay on Faulkner was published in *Sewanee Review* in 1951, and a year later he contributed the essay "Primitivism in *The Sound and the Fury*" to the English Institute (published 1954). The first major work, *William Faulkner: The Yoknapatawpha Country*, appeared in 1963, along with extended commentary on Faulkner in *The Hidden God* (Yale University Press, 1963). Subsequent volumes include *William Faulkner: Toward Yoknapatawpha and Beyond* (1978), which treats much of the work set outside Faulkner's mythical county but also contains appendices on topics such as Thomas Sutpen as a presumed representative of the Southern planter class; *William Faulkner: First Encounters* (1983), which provides a useful if general introduction to individual novels; *On the Prejudices, Predilections, and Firm Beliefs of William Faulkner* (1987), which is intended to set the record straight on these matters for a general reader; and portions of the posthumous *Community, Religion, and Literature* (1995).

If "irony" and "paradox" are key terms in Brooks's writing on poetry, "community" is the key term in his writing on Faulkner. Faulkner is distinguished, Brooks argues, by his connection to an "organic community" that is exemplified in his work, principally, by yeomen farmers and their steadfast wives, figures such as Dilsey, and raconteurs such as V. K. Suratt/Ratliff. The importance of these figures in the work is that collectively they provide a standard of value against which to judge the actions of those who fall away from the community. Through their actions, these figures illustrate the self-correcting coherence of the community.

It is helpful in understanding Brooks's emphasis on community values in Faulkner to know that he was brought up (in Kentucky and Tennessee) the son of a Methodist minister and educated at Vanderbilt (a Methodist university), Tulane, and Oxford. In later life, he became a communicant of the Episcopal Church from which the Methodist Church developed as a reform movement. From this relatively liberal (as distinct from fundamentalist) religious background, Brooks evolved a concept of the autonomy and purposefulness of individuals within a totality of created being that is organized not despite but out of the diversity and difference, including moral difference, of the individuals comprising it. Not coincidentally, Brooks's liberal religious views were consonant with the emerging liberal political consensus in the United States, as reflected in Arthur Schlesinger's *The Vital Center* (1949).

Brooks's contribution to Faulkner studies has been well recognized, but his focus on the community has also been critiqued effectively in John Duvall's *Faulkner's Marginal Couple: Invisible, Outlaw, and Unspeakable Communities*, John T. Matthews's "The Sacrifice of History," Lewis P. Simpson's *The Possibilities of Order: Cleanth Brooks and His Work*, and Philip M. Weinstein's *What Else But Love? The Ordeal of Race in Faulkner and Morrison*. These critics see Brooks misreading Faulkner by eliding dissonant aspects of the texts he treats and overemphasizing portions that agree with his view of Faulkner. Ironically, in contrast to Brooks, they may see Faulkner's writing as more complexly inhabited by, and readers as more complexly interpellated by, paradox and irony—especially paradoxes involving issues of race, gender, identity, and class. But, just as ironically, they may presume that Brooks is trying to do the same sort of thing they are trying to do, and for the same audience. Although the reader of Faulkner criticism is now construed as an incredibly alert and informed fellow critic, Brooks was trying to interpret Faulkner largely for a lay audience. At the same time, Brooks's emphasis on "community" is clearly allied to a moral concern to find an image of social organization that might serve as a counterimage to current social circumstances he deplored. The formal aspects of Faulkner's fiction are seen, in Brooks's criticism, as attaining their value by recalling this antecedent image of wholeness in the community, both representing and annealing the contradictions of what Faulkner called "the human heart in conflict with itself."

FURTHER READING

Hunt, John. "Outside Yoknapatawpha County with Cleanth Brooks and William Faulkner." *Mississippi Quarterly* 31 (1978): 465–476.
Matthews, John T. "The Sacrifice of History in the New Criticism of Cleanth Brooks." *Rewriting the South: History and Fiction.* Ed. Lothar Hönnighausen and Valeria Gennaro Lerda. Tübingen, Germany: Francke, 1993. 210–221.
Simpson, Lewis P., ed. *The Possibilities of Order: Cleanth Brooks and His Work.* Baton Rouge: Louisiana State University Press, 1976.
Winchell, Mark Royden. *Cleanth Brooks and the Rise of Modern Criticism.* Charlottesville: University Press of Virginia, 1996.

Stephen Hahn

BUNCH, BYRON, as his name implies, is one of Faulkner's comic heroes, a romantic Byron who is one of the bunch. From *Light in August,* he is "the kind of fellow you wouldn't see . . . if he was alone . . . in the bottom of a empty concrete swimming pool." But he is also the one man in Jefferson with enough gumption to befriend such outcasts and strangers as Gail Hightower, Lena Grove, and the Hineses, the crazy grandparents of the pariah Joe Christmas. Early on, he had even risked offering his lunch pail to the ominous Christmas, realizing he had not eaten for days. But then, "Byron Bunch knows this." About the town's stale gossip over Hightower, he knows that "when anything gets to be a habit, it also manages to get a right good distance away from truth and fact." About Hightower, he knows a man will "cling to trouble he's used to before he'll risk a change." About Brown, he knows "that there was not even enough left of him to do a good, shrewd job of shirking." About himself, he knows, "For a fact, it looks like a fellow is bound to get into mischief soon as he quits working." Of course, the "mischief" he gets into brings him to life, for this is the moment when Byron "fell in love contrary to all the tradition of his austere and jealous country raising which demands in the object physical inviolability." And it is this love for Lena that both frees him from his time clock existence at the mill and binds him to perilous quests and dreads—of scandalizing the town, of betraying Hightower, but most of all, of losing Lena: to childbirth, to the man who betrayed her, or simply to her own indifference to his love. But having valiantly sent the villain packing, this Adonis wins the hand of his lady, both *"good stock peopling in tranquil obedience to it the good earth."*

FURTHER READING

McCamy, Edward. "Byron Bunch." *Shenandoah* 3 (1952): 8–12.
Taylor, Carole Anne. *"Light in August*: The Epistemology of Tragic Paradox." *Texas Studies in Language and Literature* 22 (1980): 48–68.

Virginia V. James Hlavsa

BUNDREN. Central to *As I Lay Dying*, there are eight Bundrens (depending on how one counts). Anse, a dirt farmer, is known for getting his family and neighbors to do his work because, he believes, "if he ever sweats, he will die," neighbor Vernon Tull saying, "I done holp him so much already I can't quit now." Most of the Bundrens are buried in the cemetery at New Hope. Anse takes to wife Addie, a former schoolteacher, whose death forms the heart of *As I Lay Dying*. Their "chapping," Anse's undignified term, produces four children. Cash, the oldest, is a carpenter, born, it would seem, soon before the turn of the century (dates and birth chronologies are not given for most of the Bundrens and are sketchy at best). Darl, next in order of birth, was in France in World War I, so he must have been born no later than 1900–1901; absorbed and abstract, wanting more than any to get Addie "into the ground," Darl tries to burn down Gillespie's barn where her body rests, leading to his committal to an asylum in Jackson, referred to again in "Uncle Willie." Addie then has Jewel from her affair with Reverend Whitfield; at fifteen Jewel acquires the last of the spotted horses. (If eighteen at the time of Addie's death, there would be over a decade between Darl's and Jewel's births.) A year younger, Dewey Dell, Anse and Addie's only daughter, becomes pregnant by Lafe and attempts, but fails, to get an abortion in Jefferson. The youngest, Vardaman, is seven to eleven at the time of *As I Lay Dying*. Finally, after Addie is buried, Anse presents the family with a new "Mrs. Bundren." Locating Anse Bundren and his people provided the occasion for Faulkner to name his fictional county, Moseley reporting, "They came from some place out in Yoknapatawpha County."

FURTHER READING

Bradford, M. E. "Addie Bundren and the Design of *As I Lay Dying*." *Southern Review* 6 (1970): 1093–1099.
Tebbetts, Terrell L. "The Bundrens in Context: Faulkner's Proprietary Family." *Publications of the Arkansas Philological Association* 16.2 (1990): 83–97.

Charles A. Peek

BURDEN, a family appearing in a number of Faulkner's novels and stories. In *Light in August*, Joanna Burden is an aging, unmarried woman who lives in a large house on the outskirts of Jefferson and has an affair with Joe Christmas, who ultimately murders her. She is the only surviving descendant of this family, whose history she relates in the novel's eleventh chapter. The Burdens are outsiders, stern Calvinist Northerners from New Hampshire who move to Jefferson around 1867 to serve the former slaves and to work for the Freedman's Bureau. Two Burden men are murdered in 1874 by John Sartoris (for trying, as *The Unvanquished* explains, to help freed slaves vote in a local election). The name *Burden* (shortened from the original *Burrington*) signifies the family's self-appointed mission to serve the black race ("[Y]ou must raise the shadow," Joanna's father tells her). In *Light in August* the Burdens exemplify obsessive subjugation to a political and moral cause, at the cost of personal suffering and sacrifice. Ironically, the Burdens view the black race as a curse (as Nathaniel Burden says, "a race doomed and cursed to be forever and ever a part of the white race's doom and curse for its sins"). Joanna Burden herself is a racist who becomes sexually excited by the knowledge that her lover Christmas may have black blood. Faulkner's portrayal of the family is ambiguous: He castigates the Burdens for their obsessive fanaticism and their intrusion into the affairs of Jefferson yet sometimes seems sympathetic to Joanna. The "Skirmish at Sartoris" chapter of *The Unvanquished* describes the murder of the Burden men.

Hugh Ruppersburg

BURDEN, JOANNA. Joanna Burden appears in *Light in August*, primarily in chapters ten through twelve. Although a native Jeffersonian, her New England roots, family history, and reclusiveness make her a town pariah. During Reconstruction, before she was born, her grandfather and brother were killed by a former Confederate colonel, John Sartoris, over their work with black voters. Fate brings Joe Christmas into Joanna's life, and for two years they carry on a strange and compelling love affair that culminates in her death at Joe's hands. After Joe's roommate, Lucas Burch, finds Joanna's body, he torches the house. This fire begins the novel's action at the end of the opening chapter when Lena Grove and her driver spot the fire. With her Puritan heritage, her toting of the "white man's burden" in working with black colleges, and her traumatic childhood memories, Joanna becomes a double of Joe Christmas. Their relationship recapitulates Joe's own tortured history, and his killing of Joanna for "praying" over him sets in motion the forces that will seal his fate. In death, Joanna is transformed from "Yankee niggerlover" to an emblem of "Southern Womanhood" whose alleged murder by an alleged black man must be avenged. The critical perception of Joanna has evolved from seeing her as one of Faulkner's "masculinized" women, whose story is subordinate to Joe's, to viewing her as one of Faulkner's "silenced" women whose story has tragic dignity in its own right.

FURTHER READING

Burgess, Miranda J. "Watching (Jefferson) Watching: *Light in August* and the Aestheticization of Gender." *Faulkner Journal* 7.1–2 (1991–1992): 95–114.
Clarke, Deborah. "Gender, Race, and Language in *Light in August*." *American Literature* 61 (1989): 398–413.
Duvall, John N. "Murder and the Communities: Ideology in and Around *Light in August*." *Novel: A Forum on Fiction* 20 (1987): 101–122.
Nielsen, Paul S. "Secrets: Ritual and Inheritance in *Light in August*." *Southern Review* 26 (1990): 801–813.

David L. Vanderwerken

BUTLER, LELIA (1849–1907), whom William Faulkner called "Damuddy," was his maternal grandmother. Not overly fond of men in general, Lelia "shared her daughter's hatred of the foul language and the drinking that went with hunting and fishing'' (Minter 11). Although forced by circumstances to relinquish a sculpture scholarship in Rome, she nevertheless became a proficient artist in several media. Lelia was especially fond of William and taught him to draw.

Darcy Schultz

BUTLER, MAUD. *See* **Falkner, Maud Butler**.

"BY THE PEOPLE," a humorous short story by Faulkner, first published in *Mademoiselle* in October 1955. A tall tale in the southwestern yarn-spinning tradition, the story was reprinted in *Prize Stories 1957: The O. Henry Awards* and *40 Best Stories from* Mademoiselle: *1935–1960*, but it is curiously omitted from *Uncollected Stories*. A considerably revised version of the text is incorporated into *The Mansion*. The plot describes the crafty and hilarious means by which V. K. Ratliff publicly humiliates ''the Honorable'' Clarence Eggleston Snopes, a despicable Mississippi legislator who aspires to be a U.S. congressman, by enticing a bunch of dogs to use him as ''a dog way-station'' or ''dog postoffice'' during a political rally. As a result of Ratliff's action, Snopes is forced to withdraw in disgrace from the campaign, his sponsor, Will Varner, angrily asserting, ''I aint going to have Beat Two and Frenchman's Bend represented nowhere by nobody that ere a son a bitching dog that happens by cant tell from a fence-post.'' As the title implies, the story pits a concern for a democratic ideal of government (''of the people, by the people, and for the people'') against the political machinations and ethical abuses of a demagogue like Senator Snopes. As political satire, the story belongs to a rich American literary tradition that reaches back to such early works as Hugh Henry Breckenridge's *Modern Chivalry* (1792–1815).

Robert W. Hamblin

C

CAMUS, ALBERT (1913–1960), Algerian-born French novelist, playwright, philosopher, journalist, and 1957 winner of the Nobel Prize for Literature. Camus is often cited, along with philosopher-playwright Jean-Paul Sartre, as a supreme example of an existentialist writer. His best-known works include the novels *The Stranger* (1942), *The Plague* (1947), and *The Fall* (1956); a collection of short stories, *Exile and the Kingdom* (1957); and the influential philosophical essay *The Myth of Sisyphus* (1942; revised and enlarged, 1945), in which he analyzes contemporary nihilism and defines the sense of the "absurd." His most important plays—*Cross Purpose* (1944) and *Caligula* (1944)—are considered landmarks in the Theater of the Absurd. In a letter published in the *Harvard Advocate* in 1951, Camus expresses his admiration for Faulkner as the greatest of contemporary writers and singles out *Sanctuary* and *Pylon* as Faulkner's masterpieces. In an interview conducted that same year by a young French graduate student at Yale, Faulkner claimed that he did not know Camus's work. In 1956, Camus's French stage adaptation of Faulkner's *Requiem for a Nun* premiered at the Théâtre des Mathurins in Paris. In his preface to Maurice-Edgar Coindreau's French translation of *Requiem for a Nun*, Camus compares the courtroom to a temple, the governor's office to a confessional, and the jail to a convent. In 1957, after hearing that Camus had been awarded the Nobel Prize for Literature, Faulkner sent Camus a congratulatory cable. In 1960, following Camus's tragic death in an automobile accident, Faulkner wrote a brief tribute to Camus that was published in a special issue of *La Nouvelle revue française*. Later collected in *Essays, Speeches & Public Letters*, the essay links Camus's premature death with Faulkner's notions on art and mortality: "When the door shut for him, he had already written on this side of it that which every artist who also carries through life with him that one same foreknowledge and hatred of death, is hoping to do: *I was here*" (114).

FURTHER READING

Wilson, Paule A. "Faulkner and Camus: *Requiem for a Nun*." *Odyssey* 3.2 (1979): 3–9.

Arthur Wilhelm

CARCASSONNE, a city in southwestern France, the site of the finest remains of medieval fortifications in all of Europe. Although Faulkner apparently never actually saw Carcassonne, its legendary and picturesque castle, walls, and towers came to symbolize for him the ideal of artistic creativity. Once asked about the source of the Southern literary renaissance, Faulkner observed: "I myself am inclined to think it was because of the bareness of the Southerner's life, that he had to resort to his own imagination, to create his own Carcassonne" (*FIU* 136). Significantly, one of the works that Faulkner created to contrast the "bareness" of life with "imagination" is a short story entitled "Carcassonne." A similar use of Carcassonne as a symbol of inventive creation is found in *Absalom, Absalom!* in the identification of Thomas Sutpen—an artist-type whose dream of creating Sutpen's Hundred may be compared to Faulkner's creation of Yoknapatawpha—with "a madman who creates within his very coffin walls his fabulous immeasurable Camelots and Carcassonnes." Time and again Faulkner identified the sources of his work as "observation, experience, and imagination" (*FIU* 123); and if it is clear that the actual world of Oxford and Lafayette County may be identified primarily with the first two of these sources, it is equally clear that Carcassonne represents for Faulkner the third component in the triad. Recognizing in Faulkner's work the polar aspects represented by Oxford and Carcassonne helps readers to understand that Faulkner's work is neither purely realistic nor wholly fanciful, but some curious mixture of the two—a superrealism that combines elements of the everyday, outer world with the inner world of the artist's creative vision.

FURTHER READING

Hamblin, Robert W. "Carcassonne in Mississippi: Faulkner's Geography of the Imagination." *Faulkner and the Craft of Fiction*, ed. Fowler and Abadie. 148–171.

Robert W. Hamblin

"CARCASSONNE," an early prose piece by Faulkner. There is widespread agreement that "Carcassonne" is one of Faulkner's most difficult, most poetic, and most intensely personal narratives. Should it be considered a story, or is it more accurately designated a prose-poem, a poetic fantasy (as Faulkner called it), a personal aesthetic credo? If for no other reason than Faulkner's own high valuation of it and its strategic placement as the final story in both *These 13* and *Collected Stories*, "Carcassonne" should be regarded as a key Faulkner composition.

The date of writing is uncertain. The earliest proposal is late 1925, based on its links with *Mosquitoes* and "Black Music" and what Cleanth Brooks calls "Faulkner's romantic prose" (*Toward Yoknapatawpha Country* 60) of the mid-1920s. The latest date argued for is 1931, a view that holds that Faulkner wrote (or rewrote) "Carcassonne" specifically as a capstone for *These 13*, where it was first published in 1931. The evidence is inconclusive, although scholarly opinion leans toward the earlier composition date.

Measured by conventional standards, it hardly seems to be a story at all: There is little or no action, no plot. However, measured by avant-garde standards in the most intensely experimental phase of Faulkner's career, it could be argued that, by virtue of its mode and force as one long sustained epiphany, "Carcassonne" is on the cutting edge of experimentation in the formal possibilities of the short story. Briefly summarized, the content of the piece is a body-soul dialogue or, more precisely, a dialogue between the skeleton and the flesh-blood-spirit of a young poet whose spirit refuses to accept his skeleton's insistence that "the end of life is lying still" and instead affirms his will *"to perform something bold and tragical and austere."* This apparent affirmation is interwoven within a reverberant fugal polyphony of historical, literary, and religious allusions.

The difficulty of reading these allusions with sufficient precision and delicacy may account for the divergent interpretations of the story, with some commentators seeing the outcome as affirmation and transcendence, others seeing despair, defeat, death. Perhaps all would agree that the story is concerned with immortality, with the possibility, or at least the hope, that the human spirit is capable of some kind of transcendence of mere fleshly decay and death.

One of the most ambitious critical treatments is Noel Polk's analysis of the protagonist as a kind of Prufrockian failed dreamer, an Eliotesque Waste-Lander whose signification is inextricably bound up with the design, imagery, and themes of *These 13* ("Carcassonne"). In another view, Robert Hamblin presents a compelling reading of "Carcassonne" as the poet's struggle "to articulate his inner vision" (355). Hamblin sees the story as a key to Faulkner's understanding of the creative process, as an affirmation of how the artist can "say No to death" (363). Both critics agree that "Carcassonne" is one of Faulkner's neglected masterpieces and deserves far more critical attention than it has received to date.

FURTHER READING

Hamblin, Robert W. " 'Carcassonne': Faulkner's Allegory of Art and the Artist." *Southern Review* 15 (1979): 355–365.

Milum, Richard A. "Faulkner's 'Carcassonne': The Dream and the Reality." *Studies in Short Fiction* 15 (1978): 133–138.

Minter, David. " 'Carcassonne,' 'Wash,' and the Voices of Faulkner's Fiction." *Faulkner and the Short Story*, ed. Harrington and Abadie. 78–107.

Polk, Noel. "William Faulkner's 'Carcassonne.' " *Studies in American Fiction* 12 (1984): 29–43.

H. R. Stoneback

CARPENTER, META DOHERTY (1908–1994), Hollywood secretary and script supervisor who had an extended love affair with William Faulkner. Faulkner had met Doherty in 1922 in Oxford and met her again in Hollywood in 1935, when he was collaborating on the script of *The Road to Glory* and she, after being briefly married to Billy Carpenter in the early 1930s, was working as secretary to Howard Hawks. Faulkner and Meta soon became lovers, a relationship that continued until her marriage to Wolfgang Rebner, a concert pianist, in 1937. Following her divorce from Rebner in 1942, and upon Faulkner's return to Hollywood that same year, Faulkner and Meta resumed their affair. The liaison ended when Meta remarried Rebner in 1945. Carpenter has left a stylized reminiscence of her relationship with Faulkner in *A Loving Gentleman: The Love Story of William Faulkner and Meta Carpenter* (Wilde and Borsten, 1976). Aside from letters in which Faulkner mentions her (see *Selected Letters*), her account may be as close as one can get to their relationship. It is fairly clear that it took place in the context of both the deterioration in his marriage to Estelle (to which, of course, it also contributed) and his grief over his brother Dean's death. Off again, on again, they were lovers—in California, New York, New Orleans. Then, typical of Faulkner after a failed love affair, they remained friends, Faulkner occasionally visiting her and Rebner and corresponding with her until his death in 1962. Meta's second marriage to Rebner also ended unhappily, partly because he was a musician whose early promise failed to produce a satisfactory career and a European whose ideas of marriage could not accommodate American habits of relationship. Although Faulkner and Carpenter became so close that he even took his daughter on outings with her, she, born in Tunica, Mississippi, could not quite handle an extramarital affair while she was in a committed relationship. Faulkner's role in the affair (which the word ''gentleman'' in her title points up) was complicated by his ties to Estelle, Jill, and their social and financial situation that would not allow him to seek a divorce, especially as Estelle threatened scandal (Karl 588). Critics who acknowledge that Charlotte Rittenmeyer in *If I Forget Thee, Jerusalem* (*The Wild Palms*) bears resemblance to Helen Baird may also note that this resemblance was triggered by his relationship with Carpenter. Faulkner inscribed the first copy of the limited edition of *Absalom, Absalom!* to her.

FURTHER READING

Broughton, Panthea Reid. ''An Interview with Meta Carpenter Wilde.'' *Southern Review* 18 (1982): 776–801.

Charles A. Peek

CARTER, HODDING (1907–1972), author, newspaper editor, and publisher, winner of a 1946 Pulitzer Prize for his editorials condemning racial injustice. A native of Louisiana, Carter moved to Greenville, Mississippi, in 1935, where, three years later, he founded the influential *Delta Democrat-Times*, which he continued to publish and edit until shortly before his death. Carter's writings—

not only his editorials but also his novel *The Winds of Fear* (1944), such autobiographical works as *First Person Rural* (1963), and articles appearing in *New Republic, Nation, New York Times Magazine*, and other periodicals—reflect his position as a leading white Southern moderate of his day. While Carter attacked racial intolerance and bigotry and chastised his native region for clinging to outmoded Jim Crow laws and attitudes, he simultaneously opposed forced intervention and warned Northerners not to underestimate the fierce loyalty of white Southerners to their long-held beliefs and practices.

Faulkner greatly respected Carter and his views, telling one interviewer, "Hodding Carter's a good man, and he's right when he says the solution of the Negro problem belongs to the South" (*LIG* 60). In February 1948, when Faulkner was working on *Intruder in the Dust*, Carter and fellow Greenvillian Ben Wasson visited Faulkner at Rowan Oak. They had traveled there to persuade Faulkner to publish something of his under the imprimatur of the Levee Press, a new publishing company that Carter, Wasson, and colleague Kenneth Haxton had recently founded; but, as Wasson records in *Count No 'Count*, they spent much of the day discussing "the burning question of the moment: 'Shall the South integrate or remain segregated?' " (162). Perhaps not coincidentally, the racial and political views expressed by Gavin Stevens in *Intruder in the Dust* are remarkably similar to those that Carter was espousing in essays of the same period.

FURTHER READING

Carter, Hodding. "The Civil Rights Issue as Seen in the South." *New York Times Magazine* 21 March 1948: 15ff.
———. "A Southern Liberal Looks at Civil Rights." *New York Times Magazine* 8 August 1948: 10ff.
Kneebone, John T. "Liberal on the Levee: Hodding Carter, 1944–1954." *Journal of Mississippi History* 49 (1987): 153–162.

Robert W. Hamblin

CATHER, WILLA. When youthful school dropout Billy Falkner determined to be a writer, he trained himself as "an omnivorous reader with no judgment, no discretion," saying, "I read everything" (*FWP* 114). Judith Sensibar indicates, "At twenty-two, Faulkner had read the major novelists of the past three centuries, as well as Shakespeare, the Romantics, the Symbolists, Swinburne, the Georgians, Yeats, and finally, Eliot, Aiken, and other Modernists" (*Origins* 8). However, he was still a self-described Victorian sexist; as he wrote Anita Loos in February of 1926, "I am still rather Victorian in my prejudices regarding the intelligence of women, despite Elinor Wylie and Willa Cather and all the balance of them" (*SL* 32). So he took notice when his reading forced him to admire current women writers of exceptional talent such as Cather.

In his doggedly determined apprentice years he not only read carefully but also obviously thoroughly absorbed Cather's major fiction, including *My An-*

tonia (1918), *One of Ours* (1922), *A Lost Lady* (1923), *The Professor's House* (1925), *My Mortal Enemy* (1926), and *Death Comes for the Archbishop* (1927). Although it is still too soon to declare finally which of these Cather works most thoroughly permeated Faulkner's creative imagination, it is clear that Cather provided Faulkner a stockpile of literary materials for use throughout his writing career.

Faulkner paid tribute to Cather on a number of occasions, frequently including her in his list of the best contemporary authors. By the time the State Department sent him to Japan, he was using Cather as a kind of literary bridge-across-the-waters: "There are some works of several people which are first rate. I can name the ones that I was impressed with that probably influenced me to an extent that I still like to read—one a woman, Willa Cather—I think she is known in Japan" (*LIG* 167–168).

Critics have just begun to measure how much Faulkner was influenced by Cather. It is clear, however, that he was one of her most astute readers. Even more evident than what he, as he would have put it, stole is the startlingly original transformations and revisions he built on her foundations. Twenty-first-century scholars, picking up on the work of Jo Ann Middleton, Merrill Skaggs, and Joseph Urgo, can determine how soon he noticed her footprints and what he did with her trail.

The novel Faulkner most ingeniously reinvented was *My Antonia*. It gave Faulkner, among other things, the names *Burden* and *Bundren*; a recognition of the brilliant effects to be achieved when linear and cyclical structural organizations are used simultaneously, as he would go on to do in *As I Lay Dying* and *Light in August*; and an idea of the thematic ironies achievable when a sensitive young man, cut loose from his roots, appropriates another's story for his own, as in *Absalom, Absalom!* While the influence of *The Professor's House* on *Mosquitoes* has been demonstrated (see Skaggs, "Thefts and Conversations"), *A Lost Lady* also provides a "myriad" of details that one can spot from *Soldiers' Pay* forward. Having already published at Ole Miss "Une Ballade des Femmes Perdus" on February 4, 1920, Faulkner would have noted Cather's similarly titled work as soon as it appeared in 1923.

Of course, Faulkner did not necessarily read Cather's work in its chronological order of publication. Because he was eager to write a war novel for his first effort, he may first have discovered Cather's *One of Ours* (*OO*), which contributed much to Faulkner's storage bin for *Soldiers' Pay* (*SP*): a war hero with a "glamorous fatality"; a brain-damaged soldier who has lost the memory of women; an emphasis on the romantic and self-destructive element of war; a portrayal of young women for whom soldiers are as remote "as the portrait of her grandfather upon the wall" (*OO* 223; *SP* 220); and the figure of a "lost American" who "remembers the books he's read better than his own life" or his own fiancée (*OO* 288; *SP* 169). Interesting, too, is Cather's figure of a pink-cheeked, hard-drinking, cynically wisecracking, insubordinate fourth berthmate on Claude's ship who is characterized by a Royal Flying Corps uniform, a cane, a "yellow hummingbird mustache," and an English accent on an Iowa tongue—all of which adds up to a caricature remarkably close to the pose Faulkner fashioned for himself as a returning war hero.

In similar manner, *My Antonia* contains dozens of details and literary possibilities that Faulkner spotted, understood, and then expanded in *The Sound and the Fury*. For example, there are the multiplied foci possible if one starts a novel more than once; or the brilliant effects to be achieved when daily, seasonal, or yearly cycles serve to organize each part of a novel; or the results observable when sensitive young men try to possess a strong, older-seeming, and unavailable but beloved young woman. There are, as well, the kaleidoscopic possibilities when particular families function, as both the Shimerdas and Compsons do, as symbolic "families of man": self-destructive fathers, self-absorbed mothers, fallen daughters, vulnerable young female children, idiots, suicides, and greedy sons; or when those family units—each with four children—stand in contrast to figures such as Jim Burden and Quentin Compson, who perceive themselves to be orphaned ("I never had a mother"), isolated, and alone. In fact, there are two families that contrast with each other in *both* novels: Cather's Burdens and Shimerdas in one and Faulkner's Compsons and Gibsons in the other. In both, the beloved woman is equated with trees: Caddy smells like trees, whereas Antonia's hand on an orchard tree suggests goodness. Moreover, both novels feature grasping brothers like Ambrosch and Jason who will cheat to amass more money, who are recognized as "too mean," who will hurt even themselves to acquire more wealth, and who are their socially inferior mothers' favorites. The idiot brothers in both novels are eventually sent to mental institutions, because both "naturals" seem to threaten violence, even though both are said to be harmless and lovable. The primary or central female figure in each does not tell her own story but is presented through the eyes of a brotherly lover (or two); yet both those beloved women are children's leaders, associated with strength and will. The act of suicide in each novel is associated with dressing cleanly and neatly and saving from damage what clothes one can. Both novels feature centrally the servants who love children better than anyone else can. Both include little girls—Yulka Shimerda and Julio's sister—who play nonspeaking, nonchalantly self-serving, enigmatic, and essentially comic roles. Both novels develop thematically the results of the disintegration of an older way of life. Crucially, both end with final sentences that are major tours de force, each encompassing both jaggedness and smooth order, immediate time and all time, all the opposites that each writer has developed throughout each novel.

FURTHER READING

Skaggs, Merrill. "Thefts and Conversations: Cather and Faulkner." *Cather Studies III*. Ed. Susan J. Rosowski. Lincoln: University of Nebraska Press, 1996. 115–136.
———. "Willa Cather's *Death Comes for the Archbishop* and William Faulkner's *The Sound and the Fury*." *Faulkner Journal* 13.1–2 (1997–1998): 91–101.

Wittenberg, Judith. "Faulkner and Women Writers." *Faulkner and Women*, ed. Fowler and Abadie. 287–293.

Merrill M. Skaggs

"CENTAUR IN BRASS," a short story by Faulkner. First published in the February 1932 issue of *American Mercury* and reprinted in *Collected Stories*, this Snopes tale belongs to the opening chapter of *The Town*, where it sets the tone for that novel. It is the first story written by Faulkner about Flem's appearance in Jefferson. In the story, Flem Snopes attempts to capitalize on a rivalry between two black men, Tom-Tom and Tomey's Turl, in order to steal brass fittings from the Jefferson power plant. But the two men overcome their division and band together to outmaneuver Flem, delivering one of very few defeats to Snopes. Alone, the story is a comic but pointed commentary on African American solidarity in the face of white efforts to divide the black community. After fighting briefly, it becomes "perfectly plain to both of them . . . that Turl's life and limbs had been endangered, not by Tom-Tom, but by Flem Snopes." In the context of *The Town*, the episode in chapter 1 has Flem Snopes ultimately failing to appreciate something foreign to his radical individualism: kinship and the human potential for common purpose. His failure to incorporate the lesson of "Centaur in Brass" foreshadows his final defeat at the hands of Mink Snopes, who kills him not for profit but for Flem's failure in kinship.

FURTHER READING

Nilon, Charles H. "Blacks in Motion." *"A Cosmos of My Own,"* ed. Fowler and Abadie. 227–251.

Joseph R. Urgo

CHILDHOOD. The bildungsroman, the story of a young person's initiation into adulthood, is one of literature's most familiar forms. Many readers have noted Faulkner's virtuosity in creating credible child characters. One thinks of the Compson children, the young Joe Christmas, Thomas Sutpen, or Isaac McCaslin. None of these grows into anything resembling a psychically healthy, well-adjusted adult. Yet more happily, late in his career Faulkner created more productive and balanced children in Chick Mallison and Lucius Priest. Faulkner's lifelong concern with human development finds expression in his presentation of the childhoods of a number of his characters. However, most of his major novels concentrate on the misdevelopment of his child characters, and they might be more accurately described as antibildungsroman.

In such works as *The Sound and the Fury, As I Lay Dying, Sanctuary, Light in August, Absalom, Absalom!*, and *Go Down, Moses*, Faulkner becomes the poet of the crippled childhood. Tracking the initiatory experiences undergone by the Compson children, the Bundren children, Popeye, Joe Christmas, Thomas Sutpen, and Isaac McCaslin, one uncovers a series of failed initiations and their mostly tragic consequences. None emerges from anything resembling a normal family. The parental figures are largely hopeless, absent, perverse, or ineffectual; as a result, the youngsters seek to adopt surrogates with varying degrees of success. Early formal education is nearly nonexistent or nugatory, while sexual education is downright disastrous. The lessons gained from traditional initiatory experiences lead to confusion instead of growth, alienation instead of security. Indeed, their initiations are so psychically and emotionally traumatizing that they seem to lock in at the age they experience them. When Thomas Sutpen, for example, is turned away from the front door of the Pettibone plantation, he undergoes the most intense, epiphanic experience of his life: the pivotal moment when he discovers his innocence of the ways of the world, becomes self-conscious, and anoints himself the Sutpen family messiah—at age thirteen or fourteen. Using his rifle analogy to think it through, Sutpen determines to dedicate his life to his design, to vindicate the insulted youth. What Wash Jones ultimately scythes down is not so much a sixty-two-year-old monster but a self-centered teenager whose thinking never developed beyond the rifle analogy and whose emotional life may never have developed at all.

Dysfunctional families pervade Yoknapatawpha County. Joe Christmas, orphaned by Milly Hines and a possibly Mexican or black father and adopted by the McEacherns, has no childhood. His formative years, from five to eighteen, consist of a series of small rewards and large punishments administered by his doctrinaire Presbyterian foster father, whom Joe finally crowns with a chair at a country dance, causing Joe to flee home at last. With an alcoholic father and a whining, hypochondriacal mother, the Compson children receive little guidance and less love. Both parents abdicate their roles, leaving the children to parent themselves. Thomas Sutpen remembers little about his mother, who died when Thomas was very young. His surviving parent Thomas remembers as a semicomatose alcoholic whose defining quality was apparently inertia. As a single parent, Pap Sutpen is on a par with Pap Finn. Isaac McCaslin also lost his parents early in life, leaving first his grandmother, then his second cousin, to oversee his childhood.

Some of Faulkner's children seek out surrogates to replace their ineffectual parents. Rebelling from the ruthless justice of McEachern, Joe Christmas adopts a model of sorts in the figure of Max, the acerbic proprietor of a diner/brothel. Joe appropriates the dress and mannerisms of this sharpy from the rural underworld. Part of Quentin Compson's problem is finding an adult who will take him seriously. The bitter wisdom of his father's absurdist philosophy hardly provides sustenance for Quentin's fragile psyche. While at Harvard, Quentin does find an adult friend in Deacon, a black man who is apparently a fixture around campus and who befriends and lives off the largesse of Southern students. The suicidal young man determines to leave one of his suits to Deacon. In lieu of his own failed father, Thomas Sutpen adopts the plantation owner, Pettibone, as an imaginary surrogate. Pettibone lying in his hammock represents all of young Thomas's fantasies of power and ease. Isaac McCaslin is perhaps the most successful in finding a mentor: Sam Fathers, the guru of the hunt, who initiates young Ike into the ethic of the wilderness. Ike undergoes a rite of passage when Sam ceremonially marks his face with blood from Ike's first deer kill. Yet the values Ike learns, while valid in a frontier Mississippi of the 1870s, prove less workable in an agrarian and industrializing twentieth-century Mississippi.

While children who suffer from abuse, neglect, and defective genetics characterize the major texts of the 1920s and 1930s, Faulkner offers more typical bildungsroman in his later work, especially through the stories of Chick Mallison in *Intruder in the Dust* and Lucius Priest in *The Reivers*. Chick and Lucius grow up in stable, loving, and nurturing extended families. Both boys also benefit from large support groups of others who have worked for or lived around the Mallisons and Priests long enough to have become, in effect, "family," too. Yet Faulkner's strategy in both novels is to separate the lads from their families and provide them with impromptu families who reinforce and confirm the values already learned at home. The two youngsters are exposed to issues and events far beyond their capacity to assimilate them, with the effect being to accelerate their rate of maturation.

Through their initiations, Chick and Lucius gain a broader sense of identification with humankind: its baseness and its nobility, their own place in the human family, and the individual's duty to try to make a difference in striving for a more humane world. Their education in the ways of the world at such tender ages has prepared them for leadership in Yoknapatawpha County. Nurtured themselves, Chick and Lucius will, in turn, be the sort of nurturer that Joe Christmas, Quentin Compson, Thomas Sutpen, and Isaac McCaslin never had and could never be.

FURTHER READING

Adamowski, T. H. "Joe Christmas: The Tyranny of Childhood." *Novel: A Forum on Fiction* 4 (1971): 240–251.

Baum, Rosalie Murphy. " 'Family Dramas': Spouse and Child Abuse in Faulkner's Fiction." *The Aching Hearth: Family Violence in Life and Literature*. Ed. Sara Munson Deats and Lagretta Tallent Lenker. New York: Plenum, 1991. 221–240.

Peavy, Charles D. " 'If I'd Just Had a Mother': Faulkner's Quentin Compson." *Literature and Psychology* 23 (1973): 114–121.

Tebbetts, Terrell L. "Finding Faulkner's Adequate Family." *Publications of the Arkansas Philological Association* 11 (1985): 67–82.

Vanderwerken. *Faulkner's Literary Children*.

David L. Vanderwerken

CHINA. At least one Faulkner short story ("A Rose for Emily") was translated into Chinese in the 1930s, and his work received some critical attention in China in that decade. Yet in spite of the fact that a few more works were translated and further critical attention was paid in the 1950s and 1960s, Faulkner's reputation in China before the late 1970s can be summed up in one word: neglect.

The situation of Faulkner studies in China is succinctly characterized by Tao Jie, one of China's leading Faulkner scholars: "It took almost half a century and the concerted efforts of scholars, editors, translators, and university professors to persuade the general public to pay serious attention to this great novelist of the American South" ("Short Stories" 174). After the years of chaos of the "Cultural Revolution" and all the political campaigns of the 1960s and 1970s, there was a great awakening of interest in Faulkner in the decades that followed. Important translations were published—*As I Lay Dying* (1980), *The Sound and the Fury* (1984), *Selected Stories of William Faulkner* (1985), and *The Unvanquished* (1994). In addition, significant critical studies appeared (e.g., *Critical Essays on William Faulkner*, 1980), and leading Chinese Faulkner scholars such as Li Wenjun, Tao Jie, and Zhou Jueliang not only published translations and critical studies but also directed student work and theses on Faulkner.

Since the nature and scope of the burgeoning Faulkner studies in China are not entirely measurable by the usual scholarly and bibliographical yardsticks, what will have to suffice is the personal testimony of one who was privileged to witness firsthand the growing interest in Faulkner as a 1984 Fulbright Professor teaching a graduate seminar in Faulkner at Peking University and presenting visiting lectures on Faulkner at numerous institutions across China. Discussions with many of the scholars, translators, and students who were at the cutting edge of Faulkner studies in China, as well as Chinese writers of fiction who had read and were, to varying degrees, influenced by Faulkner, suggested that Faulkner had a particular appeal to Chinese readers. This appeal could be explained, in part, by a shared agrarian vision; a similar sense of place, family, and community; and the common experience of small town and village life. Moreover, Faulkner's sense of the "eternal verities" resonated with a Confucian sense of benevolence, wisdom, courage, and compassion. As Chinese scholars have observed, a remarkable number of Chinese Faulkner aficionados, critics, and translators were *Southerners*.

Continuing reports of Faulkner translations-in-progress, critical studies, seminars, theses, and dissertations suggest that Faulkner is now well established as a canonical writer throughout China, both for his stylistic richness and his urgent and compelling vision of human experience. It should also be noted that the Hong Kong America Center has a substantial Faulkner collection, including some 2,000 items donated by James Meriwether. The Center has also held Faulkner Conferences and published a volume entitled *William Faulkner in China: Selected Conference Papers* (1994). The essays are in Chinese with English abstracts.

FURTHER READING

Lai, Jane, ed. *William Faulkner in China: Selected Conference Papers*. Hong Kong: Hong Kong America Center, 1994.
Stoneback, H. R. "The Hound and the Antelope." *Faulkner: International Perspectives*, ed. Fowler and Abadie. 236–256.

Tao, Jie. "Faulkner's Humor and Some Chinese Writers." *Thalia: Studies in Literary Humor* 6 (1983): 57–60.
———. "Faulkner's Short Stories and Novels in China." *Faulkner and the Short Story*, ed. Harrington and Abadie. 174–205.

H. R. Stoneback

CHRISTIANITY. "No one is without Christianity, if we agree on what we mean by the word," said Faulkner in his 1957 interview with Jean Stein. He then defined the word: "It is every individual's individual code of behavior by means of which he makes himself a better human being than his nature wants him to be, if he followed his nature only. Whatever its symbol—cross or crescent or whatever—that symbol is man's reminder of his duty inside the human race" (*LIG* 246–247). On other occasions Faulkner referred to the Christian story as among the world's best stories, as among the writer's handiest tools, and as a tale readily revised or recast. A good sign of Faulkner's complex relation to Christianity is that critics have labeled him across the theological spectrum from Calvinist to Gnostic, Episcopal, humanist, and agnostic.

There is no question that Faulkner made extensive use of Christian themes, symbols, and dramatic situations throughout his fiction. *The Sound and the Fury* is set on Easter weekend, with Reverend Shegog's Resurrection sermon providing narrative climax to the novel; *Light in August* plays upon the martyrdom of Christ, the cross of existence, and the hope of redemption, and its intersecting tales of Joe Christmas and Lena Grove reflect birth and passion narratives in the Gospels; *A Fable* boldly recasts the story of Christ, in apocryphal fashion, in the setting of World War I. In each of these cases Christian symbolism functions quite seriously as a locus of meaning. The promise of Resurrection provides a more universal, humanitarian context to the pathetic disintegration of the Compson family, transforming objects of scorn and pity into more sublime expressions of the human condition. Similarly, the crucifixion of Christ provides in *Light in August* a frame of reference that explodes racism beyond its limited expression as a Southern caste system to a more universal human quest for control over indeterminate meaning. And in *A Fable*, authorial control over Christian storytelling is exerted in a modernist gospel, where Christ returns as a mutinous soldier, sacrificed to twentieth-century militarism and authoritarianism.

The agility with which Faulkner's works interweave conservative, liberal, and apocryphal Christian stories suggests that the one label one might apply to Faulkner with confidence is that of Christian humanist. The man himself was raised in the Methodist tradition, sometimes attended an Episcopal church, and was thoroughly versed in biblical literature (including the apocrypha). The headstone on his grave in Oxford, Mississippi, reads "Beloved, Go With God." Obviously, Southern religious culture had a formative and lifelong influence on his consciousness. However, Faulkner seemed fully cognizant of the influences on his psyche, and as an author he consistently placed Christianity within a universal context of the human desire for certainty and for firm belief. Among the more critically controversial exchanges in the fiction is that between Nancy Mannigoe and Gavin Stevens in *Requiem for a Nun*. Nancy tells Gavin, "All you need, all you have to do, is just believe"; to which Gavin asks, "Believe what?" Nancy's answer "Just believe" has infuriated some and relieved others, as it retreats from an endorsement of any particular faith, suggesting either religious relativism or universalism. In either case, the exchange has humanist implications that quite undeniably contextualize Christianity within a framework larger than the South or, for that matter, Western Civilization. Another text central to any understanding of Faulkner's relationship to Christianity is *A Fable*. Centrally and thoroughly engaged with Christian theology, this bold, Gnostic retelling of the Christ story suggests immediately that its author considered the existence of Christianity as one phenomenon among a multiplicity of resources for fiction.

Christianity, for Faulkner, is thus important as a set of ideas and images to manipulate, not as a theology to explain. In other words, Faulkner's writing never simply exists within Christian theology—one would not call Faulkner a Christian writer, nor should one say that his writing was informed by faith in the peculiarities of a single Christian dogma. Nevertheless, much of Faulkner's writing engages Christianity very seriously, searching within its structures of meaning for articulations that might provide solace or explanation. In this sense Faulkner, along with writers as diverse as Kafka and Cather, Joyce and O'Connor, Malamud and Hurston, participates in one of the central traditions in modern literature: the serious exploration of religious ideas, both within and outside their Judeo-Christian context, and the importance of those ideas to human survival.

See also **Humanism; Religion, Southern**.

FURTHER READING

Brooks. *On the Prejudices, Predilections, and Firm Beliefs of William Faulkner.*
Fowler and Abadie, eds. *Faulkner and Religion.*
Hunt. *William Faulkner: Art in Theological Tension.*
Mansfield, Luther Stearns. "The Nature of Faulkner's Christianity." *Descant* 22.3 (1978): 40–48.
Urgo. *Faulkner's Apocrypha.*

Joseph R. Urgo

CHRISTMAS, JOE, perhaps the most tormented character in American fiction, dominates *Light in August*. Faulkner introduces him as a drifter who refuses any socializing with his coworkers at the planing mill. A Jeffersonian might say that Joe was a "white nigger" who murdered Joanna Burden and was eventually captured and then killed during an escape attempt. But readers learn far more. An orphan whose mother died delivering him and whose father was shot by his maternal grandfather because he "knew" the man was black, Joe spends his formative years in an orphanage being watched by the janitor, who is his grand-father. At this time, Joe absorbs the idea that he is part black from the janitor, other children, and the dietician. To avoid scandal, the orphanage director places Joe with the McEachern family, where Joe spends his teenage years battling wills with his Presbyterian foster father and rejecting offerings of love by his foster mother, while wrestling with his identity. At eighteen, Joe attacks and possibly kills McEachern when McEachern tries to "rescue" Joe from a "Jez-ebel." After a fifteen-year odyssey, Joe's life circles back to Jefferson where his final three years play out like the final act of a tragedy. Through Christmas, Faulkner explores society's racial coding, as well as the process through which his upbringing has also warped him away from women. He is one of Faulkner's most puritanical characters in his misogyny, his obsessiveness, and his search for punishment. Given this Calvinist community, Joe Christmas becomes the perfect Christ for this brand of Christianity—a haunted, driven, and alienated man who can find peace only through his own death.

FURTHER READING

Gammel, Irene. " 'Because He Is Watching Me': Spectatorship and Power in *Light in August.*" *Faulkner Journal* 5.1 (1989): 11–23.

Gibb, Robert. "Joe Christmas: Faulkner's Savage Innocent." *Journal of Evolutionary Psychology* 9 (1988): 331–340.

Greer, Scott. "Joe Christmas and the Social Self." *Mississippi Quarterly* 11 (1958): 160–166.

Haselswerdt, Marjorie B. " 'Keep Your Muck': A Horneyan Analysis of Joe Christmas and *Light in August.*" *Third Force Psychology and the Study of Literature.* Ed. Bernard J. Paris, Cranbury, N.J.: Associated University Presses, 1986. 206–224.

Kazin, Alfred. "The Stillness of *Light in August.*" *William Faulkner: Three Decades of Criticism,* ed. Hoffman and Vickery. 247–265.

David L. Vanderwerken

CIVIL RIGHTS. *See* **Race.**

CIVIL WAR. The Civil War constituted the central crisis in the history of Yoknapatawpha and the American South. Although the actual events of war and Reconstruction themselves get limited treatment in Faulkner's works, much of what happens to the people of Yoknapatawpha after 1865 is shaped by the defeat of the Confederacy, the emancipation of the slaves, the severe impact of the war on the planter class, and the enduring legacy of defeat and defiance that thus pervaded much of the South.

Faulkner's treatment of the Civil War, most notably in *The Unvanquished,* focuses on the home front, on the women, children, old men, and slaves who were left behind to cope with the hardships of war, the Union army invasion, the uprising of slaves, and the threat of bushwhackers. This approach to the Civil War anticipated trends in historical scholarship that only recently have revised our view of the war and the deterioration of Southern morale on the home front. The American Civil War is often said to be the first "total war," one that engaged much of the civilian population through not only enlistment of men in massive armies but also recruitment of women in supporting the war effort. Total war also meant that the civilian population would feel what General Sherman called the "hard hand of war" in a deliberate effort to break Confederate civilian morale. Few regions of the Confederacy were exposed to more turmoil throughout the war than northern Mississippi. It became, whether purposely or not, a testing ground for a number of radical Union strategies that included efforts to incite slave rebellion, massive confiscation of civilian food supplies, and the wholesale destruction of civilian property, most memorably the burning of Oxford in 1864.

As the war evolved and the Confederacy suffered defeats and invasion, the Confederate civilian population came under tremendous pressure. Social divisions between rich and poor, free and slave, men and women, all became aggravated. The Confederate cause, some historians now argue, was lost on the home front well before it was defeated on the battle front as each of these divisions of class, race, and gender ruptured under the pressure of war. Faulkner's fictional portrait of a society exposed to war in *The Unvanquished* provides an excellent illustration of these historical themes, which were usually repressed in traditional Southern narratives of the war at the time Faulkner was writing.

Faulkner noted the initial enthusiasm and naïveté with which most Southerners greeted secession and war before anyone realized this was not going to be a romantic adventure every young man would want to claim part in but, rather, a long, ghastly bloodbath that would bring destruction and defeat to the South. As he put it in his reprise of Yoknapatawpha's history in *Requiem for a Nun*, "[T]he first seconds of fall always seem like soar. . . ." Between the surrender of Fort Sumter in April 1861 until the Battle of Shiloh in April 1862, it may have seemed the new Confederate nation was soaring, with that "upward rush of earth . . . a soar, an apex, the South's own apotheosis of its destiny and pride." But Shiloh, just above the Mississippi state line, was the first major display of the real horrors modern warfare was to bring in the Civil War. Hundreds of young men who had left their hometowns amid celebrations of martial glory a year earlier returned now to Oxford where the university would be converted to a Confederate hospital. Maimed and infected, hundreds died and many more had limbs amputated. Women who had been sewing uniforms and flags and presenting them to military companies now served as volunteer nurses—like Faulkner's Judith Sutpen, who joined the women of Jefferson "in the improvised hospital where (the nurtured virgin, the supremely and traditionally idle) they cleaned and dressed the self-fouled bodies of strange injured and dead and made lint of the window curtains and sheets and linen of the houses in which they had been born." Before the end of the year northern Mississippi would be invaded, and by then, if not already, those who joined the cause with such enthusiasm realized they were not soaring but falling. Even then, as Faulkner put it, the impact when they hit the ground produced a "preliminary anesthetic of shock so that the agony of bone and flesh will not even be felt."

Soon after Shiloh the Confederacy introduced America's first conscription law, with a controversial provision to exempt one white man for every plantation with twenty slaves. This was bitterly referred to as "the twenty nigger law" by poor white families who were sending their own sons to what they contemptuously referred to as a "rich man's war and poor man's fight." As the war dragged on and the death tolls mounted, the loyalty of poor whites to the planter elite would be severely tested. Many joined the Confederate army grudgingly; others evaded the draft by hiding out in the woods, "moss backs" supported by family and neighbors who brought them food and warned them when to hide. One man in Faulkner's county hid out in his attic to avoid the draft, an incident that might have inspired Faulkner's story of Goodhue Coldfield in *Absalom, Absalom!*

Internal opposition to the Confederate cause became evident in other ways. As the war dragged on, as supplies grew scarce, growing numbers in northern Mississippi began engaging in "blockade running," which meant crossing enemy lines to trade cotton, often in exchange for salt and other badly needed provisions. Faulkner's own great-grandfather, the "Old Colonel," was said to have engaged in this trade during the war. Others known as "bushwhackers" were Confederate deserters or draft dodgers who preyed on their own people, taking advantage of defenseless women and elderly in a war-torn society. Because it became a "no man's land" unprotected by either army, northern Mississippi by the end of the war was crawling with bands of bushwhackers stealing horses, mules, food, and other valuables. Faulkner made a point of featuring this element in his story of the Confederate home front, *The Unvanquished*, with the Grumby gang that included Ab Snopes.

Following Shiloh, Grant's army advanced on Corinth and into northern Mississippi, establishing Oxford as its winter headquarters. But Van Dorn's raid on the Union supply depot at Holly Springs, an event featured in *Light in August*, forced Grant into a hasty retreat. Before evacuating, Grant ordered his troops to scour the countryside, foraging for food supplies and confiscating mules, horses, and wagons. Ostensibly intended to replenish the supplies lost to Van Dorn's raid, the devastating foraging was also a strategy meant to inflict punishment on the Southern civilian population for supporting the war and to demonstrate the inability of the Confederacy to protect its people. Grant recorded in his memoirs that it offered a lesson that would be applied later in the war, an assessment that was proven right with General Sherman's devastating march to the sea.

Another Union war strategy, the emancipation of slaves, was also tested during Grant's invasion. The Emancipation Proclamation had been announced in September 1862 and went into effect the following January. Union troops were able to spread the news of the emancipation throughout northern Mississippi, and the new year witnessed a massive flight to the North, which Faulkner dramatized in the slave exodus depicted in *The Unvanquished*.

Women's support for the war effort, so essential at the outset, was undermined by the demoralizing experience of losing their men at the battle front while on the home front the Confederacy left them exposed to invasion, depredation, and slave rebellion. Faulkner sometimes echoed a common Southern jest that said, Had it been up to the women, the South would never have surrendered. Recent historical studies of Confederate women suggest they were not so resolute in their support of the cause. They protested the lack of supplies and other hardships, and they protested the lack of protection. Faulkner's Granny Millard accurately illustrates the primacy women gave to their families and loved ones often at the expense of loyalty to the Confederate cause.

For the people of Lafayette County, the final act of devastation and humiliation came in August 1864 when Union forces, including a contingent of black soldiers, under the command of General A. J. "Whiskey" Smith invaded Oxford and burned the courthouse and nearly every building on the square. They ransacked and burned several homes of Confederate leaders and sympathizers as well. Faulkner repeated the error of blaming Grant for burning Oxford, but in *Requiem for a Nun* he grasped the more important truth that this kind of devastation broke the Southern will to fight on. Yoknapatawpha, he wrote, passed through its own Appomattox well before the end of the war, reconciled to defeat—and to rebuilding.

The legacy of the Civil War—defeat, destruction, slave emancipation—remained a pervasive and enduring feature of Southern life long after 1865. During the late nineteenth century Southern white women organized campaigns to raise monuments to honor the Confederate veterans and the Lost Cause for which they had fought. The typical monument, much like the one standing before the Oxford courthouse, depicted an erect Confederate soldier armed and with his back to the North, as though to deny the defeat of the cause. Erected during a time of worsening race relations and a wave of lynchings, these monuments of the Lost Cause also served to galvanize resistance to any further threat of federal interference in Southern affairs. The projection of the Civil War as a noble cause for home rule, along with romantic depictions of slavery and the Old South, served as vital bulwarks in the defense of white supremacy and segregation. Faulkner's subtle subversion of that historical mythology was in advance of most historical scholarship at the time, though it drew on his deep interest in the history of his region.

See also **Race; Reconstruction**.

FURTHER READING

Bettersworth, John. *Mississippi in the Confederacy*. New York: Kraus, 1970.

Clinton, Catherine, and Nina Silber, eds. *Divided Houses: Gender and the Civil War*. New York: Oxford University Press, 1992.

Faust, Drew Gilpin. *Mothers of Invention: Women of the Slaveholding South in the American Civil War*. Chapel Hill: University of North Carolina Press, 1996.

McPherson, James M. *Battle Cry of Freedom: The Civil War Era.* New York: Oxford
    University Press, 1988.

Don H. Doyle

CLASS. Faulkner well understood his society's system of class, caste, and race—wealthy landowners, middle-class whites, poor whites, "white trash," and then blacks (who were actually not on the bottom of the ladder but separate from it)—as he also well understood the problems inherent in such a system. Through a variety of characters and situations, he presents, questions, praises, and damns the South's view of social standing.

The Old South was built on a social and economic system that could survive only by maintaining stringently prescribed roles in every segment of society. The security of the whole depended on the separation, and yet adherence, of each of its parts: Carefully guarded divisions between classes, genders, and races kept the structure intact. After the Civil War, the circumstances and rhetoric changed, yet the New South retained much of the mythology on which it was founded. In his work, Faulkner examines the foundations of that mythology, how it changes, how it fails to change, and how the reality often differs from the appearance.

Some of the most memorable characters in Faulkner descend from "fine old families" who have fallen on hard times. The short story "A Rose for Emily" points out this circumstance and the resentment others hold toward those who live in high social standing. Miss Emily struggles to maintain her status and repeatedly demonstrates her feelings of entitlement despite the difficulties she faces from her neighbors. The townspeople feel that "the Griersons held themselves a little too high for what they really were," yet intervene when she might marry someone they consider beneath her. They even go so far, when she buys rat poison, to conclude, " 'She will kill herself'; and we said it would be the best thing." In these few pages, Faulkner shows the complicated emotional landscape of differing sides of the social ladder.

The Compsons in *The Sound and the Fury* have also fallen on hard times from previous aristocratic status. Jason Compson repeatedly bemoans the fact that his prestigious family has such problems—a sister pregnant out of wedlock, one brother mentally disabled, and another brother who committed suicide. Mrs. Compson, to "protect" her family honor, renames her mentally incompetent son so that he no longer carries the name of her brother. Through these characters, Faulkner explores the aristocratic notions of people who believe in their own aristocracy while behaving in ways that undercut any claim to being a "fine old family."

In Faulkner's narratives, rich and poor whites both depend on each other and resent and distrust each other. Ab Snopes, who sharecrops on Major de Spain's land in "Barn Burning," recognizes his place on the social ladder, yet rebels by tracking horse manure on the man's rug. His resentment leads to destruction when he sets de Spain's barn on fire. Conversely, in *The Unvanquished*, this same Ab Snopes helps the Sartoris family survive the war when the aristocratic clan turns to stealing livestock to survive. The irony here further demonstrates a point made repeatedly in Faulkner's fiction: Circumstances, primarily monetary circumstances, not behavior, decide social standing. With other criteria— honor, integrity, responsibility—the lines would fall completely differently.

While rigid on its surface, this social structure does, sometimes, allow for movement from one class to another. Flem Snopes, who begins firmly in the "white trash" category, ultimately arrives at respectability and status. However, Thomas Sutpen, in *Absalom, Absalom!*, ultimately fails in the same quest. Having once been turned away from an aristocrat's front door, he attempts to achieve that status. However, his past, including a part-black wife and son, eventually prevents his establishing the dynasty he craves.

The firmly established caste difference between blacks and whites also proves more complicated than the first glance implies. One of the clearest examples occurs in "Was" in *Go Down, Moses*. Buck and Buddy McCaslin chase their runaway slave, Tomey's Turl, who is also their half brother. This story ends happily but shows the illogic of the reverence of "family ties" and "family honor." Buck and Buddy also provide a further example of how reality often differs from appearance: They own slaves—including their half brother—yet they live in the slave quarters while allowing their slaves to live in the mansion, where the locked front door keeps no one in because the backdoor is left unlocked.

Light in August demonstrates the social constructs of race with Joe Christmas, a man who passes for white but believes he has black blood. Christmas's grandfather tries to punish him, and society condemns him the second it hears that he is part black. The same man, familiar to them all, becomes something else entirely with the utterance of one sentence. Christmas understands this, because he feels the same way about himself. In the characterization of Christmas, Faulkner presents a deeply troubled soul, a racist who turns his hatred onto himself.

In Faulkner, the interrelationship between the castes demonstrates the best and the worst of this system. Slavery and the repression that followed it show the cruelty of the whites, both upper and lower class, which belies the very superiority they attempt to prove. In "Dry September," for example, Minnie Cooper has accused a black man of violating her. McLendon, a white man, sets out to defend the white woman's honor by murdering the man who has been falsely accused. Faulkner points out the logical gymnastics of this racism when McLendon says, "Happen? What the hell difference does it make? Are you going to let the black sons get away with it until one really does it?" And after defending the honor of one white woman by murdering, he returns home and strikes his wife.

Alternately, characters can show understanding and rise above the social constructs given to them. In *The Sound and the Fury*, the qualities of honor so important to Quentin Compson are best exhibited by Dilsey, the black servant who alone in that household demonstrates true compassion, responsibility, and integrity. Chick McCaslin, in *Intruder in the Dust*, resents feeling obligated to a black man, Lucas Beauchamp, yet succeeds in clearing him of a murder for which he has been falsely accused. Lucas's refusal to behave the way whites expect from blacks also comes into play, as the town never questions his guilt or innocence, simply being satisfied that he has finally fulfilled its expectations.

Throughout the history of Yoknapatawpha County, the South's system of class and caste both changes and remains entrenched. While the surface rules never vary, and those rules cause great pain and suffering, Faulkner points out the inconsistencies, ironies, and untruths necessary to maintain the adopted social constructs. On every rung of the social ladder, characters defy expectations—both exceeding them and falling disastrously short.

Allowing the Sartorises to go from poor whites to fine old family over several generations while denying Sutpen that status for succeeding in one underscores the basic illogic behind the aristocratic class: a class who both owned slaves and fathered them, who looked down on poor whites yet descended from them, and who cherished family honor but often behaved without it. While the class structure was rigid on the surface, Faulkner shows us that underneath it was a complex, often destructive, rarely rigid system.

See also **Historical Materialism; Marxist Approaches; Race**.

FURTHER READING

Cash, W. J. *The Mind of the South*. New York: Vintage Books, 1960.
Gerster, Patrick, and Nicholas Cords, eds. *Myth and Southern History*. Urbana: University of Illinois Press, 1989.
Godden. *Fictions of Labor: William Faulkner and the South's Long Revolution*.
Jehlen. *Class and Character in Faulkner's South*.

Caroline Carvill

CLERGY. Faulkner respects only a few of his clerics. Some of them are simply ineffectual, like the Reverend Mahon of *Soldiers' Pay*, Episcopal rector, father of the dying veteran at the center of the novel, a man in whose "eyes was a despair long since grown cool and quiet," or like Doctor Worsham of *The Unvanquished*, also an Episcopal rector but even less effectual than the Reverend Mahon, having left his flock during the Civil War to refugee north to Memphis. Both men talk well, however, the former quoting the classics and fixing "dear boy" to each sad counsel, the latter remembered as one who, had he not deserted his flock, "would have thought up [something] to say, about all soldiers did not carry arms, and about they also serve and how one child saved from hunger and cold is better in heaven's sight than a thousand slain enemies."

The most prominent of these talkative failures are the Reverend Whitfield and the Reverend Gail Hightower. In *As I Lay Dying*, where a strong link between words and truth is essential, Whitfield is unredeemed. He permits himself to commit adultery with Addie Bundren and to father Jewel and then justifies false deeds with falser words: "[God] will accept the will for the deed, Who knew that when I framed the words of my confession it was to Anse I spoke them, even though he was not there.'' Faulkner, however, spoke kindly of him and he fares better in ''Shingles for the Lord.'' Gail Hightower, on the other hand, redeems himself in *Light in August*. His talk has been his failure. Perhaps like his favorite poet Tennyson, he has mounted his pulpit ''with his hands flying around him and the dogma he was supposed to preach all full of galloping cavalry and defeat and glory.'' Although the wild unreality of his talking has driven his wife to suicide and his Jefferson congregation to revolt, he comes to acknowledge that he had gone to seminary only ''to guard himself from truth,'' that he rather than his congregation ''was the one who failed,'' and that he had been the ''debaucher and murderer'' of his own wife. He even offers Faulkner's memorable description of a clergy failing truth and mercy alike: ''It seems to him that he has seen it all the while: that that which is destroying the Church is not the outward groping of those within it nor the inward groping of those without, but the professionals who control it and who have removed the bells from its steeples. . . . He seems to see the churches of the world like a rampart, like one of those barricades of the middleages planted with dead and sharpened stakes, against truth and against that peace in which to sin and be forgiven which is the life of man.'' Hightower adds deed to words, attempting to shift Joe Christmas's guilt to himself: ''Listen to me. He was here that night. He was with me the night of the murder.'' For his efforts he receives a curse: ''Has every preacher and old maid in Jefferson taken their pants down to the yellow-bellied son of a bitch?'' But he now chooses *Henry IV* over Tennyson.

Faulkner's lay preachers can fail as fully as the professionals. In *Light in August*, Doc Hines ''who very nearly depended on the bounty and charity of negroes for sustenance was going singlehanded into remote negro churches and interrupting the service to enter the pulpit and in his harsh, dead voice and at times with violent obscenity, preach to them humility before all skins lighter than theirs, preaching the superiority of the white race, himself his own exhibit A, in fanatic and unconscious paradox.'' He murders his daughter Milly at Joe Christmas's birth by denying her medical attention, removes the infant Joe from his wife's care, presides over Joe's psychological destruction at the Memphis orphanage, and calls for Joe's lynching after his capture in Mottstown.

Clergy for whom Faulkner's fiction has some sympathy, on the other hand, substitute embattled deeds for easy words. Before the Civil War, for example, Gail Hightower's father is a Presbyterian minister and a ''sanctimonious cuss,'' but he returns afterward a surgeon '' 'deodorized' . . . of sanctity somewhat,'' his ''uncompromising conviction . . . not defeated and not discouraged, but wiser.'' Doctor Worsham's replacement in *The Unvanquished*, Brother Fortin-bride, heard his call after being wounded in battle when ''Jesus came to him and told him to rise up and live.'' Unlike his predecessor, ''he never talked long,'' Bayard reports, for it ''was like he said to himself, 'Words are fine in peacetime, when everybody is comfortable and easy. But now I think that we can be excused.' '' Brother Joe Goodyhay of *The Mansion* heard a similar call in World War II, lying "safe and dead and peacefully out of it at last on the bottom of the Pacific Ocean when all of a sudden Jesus Himself was standing over him saying Fall in and he did it." A furious doer rather than a talker, Brother Goodyhay is building a church in north Mississippi, "trying to bring Jesus Christ back alive in the middle of 1946." He prays twice in the presence of Mink Snopes, whom he has hired briefly, both prayers absolutely laconic: "Save us, Christ, the poor sons of bitches."

All of these sympathetic clergy might agree with Addie Bundren's comment on "how words go straight up in a thin line, quick and harmless, and how terribly doing goes along the earth."

See also **Religion, Southern**.

Terrell L. Tebbetts

COINDREAU, MAURICE-EDGAR (1892–1990), a professor of Romance languages at Princeton University for thirty-eight years (1923–1961), described by George McMillan Reeves as "the most prestigious translator of American fiction into French," was born in La Roche-sur-Yon in the Vendée region of France. Having obtained degrees in law and Spanish literature from the University of Bordeaux, Coindreau continued his studies in Spanish and taught for three years in Madrid before coming to the United States to accept a one-year appointment at Princeton. In the mid-1920s, Coindreau met John Dos Passos, who became his lifelong friend and who encouraged him to translate *Manhattan Transfer* into French. Thus Coindreau embarked on a lengthy career (spanning more than half a century, from 1927 to roughly 1978) as literary critic and translator of American literature into French. Coindreau is appropriately given credit for introducing Faulkner to France in 1931 with the publication in *La Nouvelle revue française* of a critical appreciation entitled simply "William Faulkner," the first article on Faulkner ever to be published in French. After completing translations of Hemingway's *A Farewell to Arms* and *The Sun Also Rises* as a favor to his French publisher Gallimard, Coindreau translated *As I Lay Dying*, published in 1934 as *Tandis que j'agonise*. (René-Noël Raimbault's translation of the more notorious *Sanctuary* was published in 1932 and holds the distinction of being the first Faulkner novel to appear in French.) Coindreau's translation of *As I Lay Dying* was followed by his translations of *Light in August* (*Lumière d'août*, 1935); *The Sound and the Fury* (*Le Bruit et la fureur*, 1938); *These 13* (*Treize histoires*, 1939); *The Wild Palms* (*Les Palmiers sauvages*, 1952); *Requiem for a Nun* (*Requiem pour une nonne*, 1957); and *The Reivers* (*Les Larrons*, 1964). Coindreau also translated the Compson Appendix into French for a 1956 publication entitled *Jefferson, Mississippi*, an anthology of Yoknapatawpha materials collected and edited by Michel Mohrt. Faulkner short stories translated into French by Coindreau and the dates of French publication include "A Rose for Emily" (1932), "Dry September" (1932), "There Was a Queen" (1933), "That Evening Sun" (1935), "The Afternoon of a Cow" (1943), "Two Soldiers" (1955), "The Wishing Tree" (1969), and "Miss Zilphia Gant'' (1972). To introduce his translations of Faulkner novels to French readers, Coindreau wrote illuminating critical prefaces to *Light in August, The Sound and the Fury*, and *The Wild Palms*. These prefaces stand as important critical documents in their own right and offer insights that other critics have found extremely valuable. His preface to *Light in August* presents a psychological analysis of the doomed Joe Christmas with focus on the puritanical obsessions with sex and death. In his preface to *The Sound and the Fury*, Coindreau reveals that Faulkner confided in him that the novel had begun in his mind as a short story for which he thought it would be interesting to imagine ''the thoughts of a group of children who were sent away from the house the day of their grandmother's funeral.'' Coindreau also reveals in the preface that the novel was written ''when the author was beset with personal problems.'' Attempting to clarify some of the numerous problems confronting the reader, Coindreau analyzes the novel in musical terms, comparing its structure to a musical composition divided into four movements. In his preface to *The Wild Palms*, Coindreau argues that the alternated plots illuminate each other and that theme and plot are carefully interwoven through the use of eternal myths and primal elements. Coindreau also wrote critical reviews of *The Hamlet, Absalom, Absalom!*, and *The Unvanquished*. Most of Coindreau's reviews of American fiction were published in *La Nouvelle revue française*, but they received much wider circulation because Coindreau himself translated many of them into Spanish for publication in such Spanish periodicals as the Argentine newspaper *La Nación*. The worldwide recognition that Faulkner's work receives today can in large part be attributed to Coindreau's critical intuition and his efforts to promote twentieth-century American fiction abroad. During the 1950s, following Faulkner's acceptance of the Nobel Prize for Literature, Coindreau wrote a number of articles about Faulkner in celebration of the recognition that he felt was long overdue a gifted, dedicated writer. These articles contain many personal recollections of Faulkner as a private man as well as a writer, offer explanations of the nature of Faulkner's art, and emphasize the problems and responsibilities of the translator with particular regard to Faulkner.

FURTHER READING

Blotner, Joseph. "The Achievement of Maurice-Edgar Coindreau." *Southern Literary Journal* 4 (1971): 95–96.
Coindreau, Maurice-Edgar. *Mémoires d'un traducteur: Entretiens avec Christian Giudicelli*. Paris: Gallimard, 1974.
———. *The Time of William Faulkner*.
Wilhelm, Arthur W. "Maurice-Edgar Coindreau: America's Literary Ambassador to France." Dissertation. Georgia State University, 1992.

Arthur Wilhelm

COLLECTED STORIES OF WILLIAM FAULKNER (1950) contains forty-two Faulkner short stories, including all those in *These 13*, all but two from

Doctor Martino and Other Stories ("The Hound" and "Smoke"), and seventeen previously uncollected stories written between 1932 and 1948. Appearing relatively soon after *The Portable Faulkner* (1946) established Faulkner's reputation as a major contemporary writer and shortly before the November 1950 announcement of his Nobel Prize in Literature, *Collected Stories* marked the watershed of Faulkner's efforts in the genre and provided a timely survey of the range and variety of his short fiction. It was immediately adopted by the Book-of-the-Month Club as an alternate fiction selection for September and subsequently won the National Book Award in March 1951.

Collected Stories provided readers with a context other than the Yoknapatawpha cycle in which to read Faulkner's short fiction. From the first major reviews, the book's reception was one of "enthusiasm and often of acclaim": The New York *Herald Tribune* praised his "unmistakable lucidity" and proclaimed him "more distinctly a master of style" than any of his contemporaries, whereas the *New York Times Book Review* ranked him "above all American writers since James and perhaps since Melville" (1974 *FAB* 1329). Irving Howe argues that despite its merits *Collected Stories* "does not persuade one that Faulkner, the short story writer, is nearly as important as Faulkner, the novelist" (262) but concedes that it represents a major achievement. Although Faulkner neglected the short story from late in his life and integrated a number of later stories into novels, short fiction anthologies rarely fail to include his work and inevitably select stories from this volume.

While Malcolm Cowley made the original suggestion that Faulkner publish a cyclically arranged story collection at this juncture in his career, Faulkner had clearly demonstrated his ability to recognize and exploit the artistic possibilities of contrapuntal arrangements in previous works. *These 13*, his first published collection, contains three contrapuntally organized sections, whereas the stories in *The Unvanquished, Go Down, Moses*, and *Knight's Gambit*—which Faulkner stopped work on *Collected Stories* to assemble—comprise more unified and coherent short story cycles. Given Faulkner's experiments with contrapuntal form in *The Sound and the Fury* and *The Wild Palms*, it is not surprising that this aesthetic carries over into most of his short story collections. As Faulkner noted in a letter to Cowley, "[E]ven to a collection of short stories, form, integration is as important as to a novel" so that the volume becomes "an entity of its own, single, set for one pitch, contrapuntal in integration, toward one end, one finale" (*FCF* 15–16). Another letter expresses his desire to give *Collected Stories* "an integrated form of its own, like the Moses book [*Go Down, Moses*] if possible, or at least These 13" (*FCF* 107).

In creating *Collected Stories*, Faulkner fashioned six discrete sections: "The Country"; "The Village"; "The Wilderness"; "The Wasteland"; "The Middle Ground"; and "Beyond." He included two stories that would later become part of *The Town* ("Centaur in Brass" and "Mule in the Yard") and another that would be revised slightly for *Big Woods* ("A Bear Hunt") but omitted all the Snopes stories that went into *The Hamlet*, including one of his best—and favorites—"Spotted Horses." For various reasons, he also chose to exclude: the stories that constitute his major short story cycles *The Unvanquished, Go Down, Moses*, and *Knight's Gambit*; all the early pieces posthumously gathered as *New Orleans Sketches*; and the previously published stories "Thrift" and "Once Aboard the Lugger," which later surfaced in Blotner's posthumous edition of *Uncollected Stories*. Faulkner thus exerted deliberate selectivity when composing the volume, which displays the rich variety of subjects and techniques found in his short fiction and embodies one coherent version of his imaginative world, mapped out in short fiction.

Collected Stories' six ostensibly geographic section titles allude to metaphoric as well as literal locales and imply a thematic unity. Faulkner changed the title of the story group originally called "Indians" to "The Wilderness" so that it paralleled the others in invoking place, with "each noun in character and tone and tune with every other" (qtd. in 1974 *FAB* 1271). The volume opens with an affirmation of tragedy's role in moving a young boy forward ethically ("Barn Burning") and closes with a portrait of the artist achieving spiritual transcendence ("Carcassonne"), though no neat developmental curve is enclosed by the frame these stories create. Nonetheless, most of the Yoknapatawpha stories appear in the first three sections; the historical account of the Indians' loss of the land is juxtaposed with the spiritual desiccation of those who have left it during the war at the center; the struggles of those on the "middle ground" between life and death precede the concluding section, which provides glimpses "beyond."

The opening section, "The Country," depicts the lives of the northern Mississippi countryside's varied residents—poor whites, proud hill farmers, and Indians. These previously uncollected stories, published between 1934 and 1943, open the volume with a fresh context and with a group whose intertextuality provides a microcosm for *Collected Stories* as a whole; as Millgate notes, this section "displays a degree of unity, of mutual reverberations between stories, not exceeded by any of the other sections" (*Achievement* 272). The region's insular quality and the strength of family ties, as well as the themes of class conflict and honor, are initially established in "Barn Burning" and echoed in the section's other stories. The acts of arson that link "Barn Burning" with the next story, "Shingles for the Lord," and the reappearance of the Grier family in three stories, provide connections that complement the contrapuntal alternation between comedy and a more somber tone. The section's more serious thematic unity is perhaps best summed up in "The Tall Men," where the investigator—foreshadowing Faulkner's Nobel Prize acceptance speech—colloquially proclaims that "honor and pride and discipline . . . make a man worth preserving, make him of any value. That's what we got to learn again. Maybe it takes trouble, bad trouble, to teach it back to us." The final story, "Shall Not Perish," not only reiterates this theme of endurance but also recasts the opening conflict with the de Spains in a later era, where the sacrifice of lives in World War II bridges the gulf within Frenchman's Bend and between this rural backwater and the country at large.

The second group, "The Village," presents a variety of Faulknerian techniques, characters, tones, and themes. Moving from rural surroundings to the town of Jefferson, Faulkner establishes the mentality that breeds the town's oppressive collective outlook and anatomizes its effect on individuals, black as well as white. The section is organized more by contrapuntal mood than by similar or repeated characters. Nevertheless, a collective narrator appears in the opening story and again in the third, "Centaur in Brass," which separates the two stories featuring Hawkshaw the barber and provides a contrast to the more serious tragedy in "Dry September." The comic tone of "Centaur in Brass" is echoed in the symmetrically placed "Mule in the Yard," which appears third from last; bracketed by four stories before and after, "Death Drag" and "Elly" feature the most amoral characters. While the section begins with the analysis of Emily Grierson's sustained victory over time and death in "A Rose for Emily," it concludes with the chaos and violence of "That Evening Sun."

The third group, "The Wilderness," steps back to the time before the region's white settlement. The opening story, "Red Leaves," contrasts a slaveholding Indian tribe's decadence with the heroic resistance of a doomed slave whose death custom dictates. His tragic triumph, however, gives way to the depiction of various comic struggles for control and dominance in the other three stories, "A Justice," "A Courtship" (winner of the 1948 O. Henry Awards First Prize), and "Lo!" (previously published in 1934 but uncollected).

Evoking images from T. S. Eliot with the title of the fourth section, "The Wasteland," Faulkner placed "Ad Astra" and "All the Dead Pilots"—which he singled out as "the best one" when autographing George Oppenheimer's copy of These 13 (1974 FAB 731–732)—in the framing positions. The peace-loving subadar's pronouncements about brotherhood in "Ad Astra" echo ironically throughout the section's subsequent portraits of spiritual and moral despair. While the victors have descended to a condition of stasis, dislocation, and spiritual numbness, the marginalized subadar and the German prisoner understand that the "victorious lose what the vanquished gain." The story's repeated references to victory connect it explicitly with the heavily ironic "Victory"; the remaining stories, especially "Crevasse" and "All the Dead Pilots," carry forward the theme of the moral and spiritual deadness that emerges from war's horror and absurdity.

The eleven stories of "The Middle Ground," the largest and most miscellaneous section, are set in a variety of locales—ranging from the rural South to New York and Hollywood—and time periods—ranging from the Civil War to the depression. In "Wash," the opening story (and one of Faulkner's best), Wash Jones asserts his resistance against Sutpen's dehumanizing view of his granddaughter and rediscovers his dignity with a wild charge that will cost him his life. Similarly, the boy in the concluding story, "Mountain Victory," is killed by his pro-Union, poor white family when he cannot stand by and let them murder the one-armed Confederate officer with whom he hoped to leave his native Tennessee hollow. Millgate speculates that the idea of the "middle of the journey," with the "experience of upheaval and uprooting—geographical, social, intellectual, or emotional," might explain Faulkner's rationale for its title (*Achievement* 273); Carothers contends that "the section can be understood as a series of investigations of the twin themes of sex and death" (59). Ultimately, decline, disillusion, tragedy, and literal or symbolic death pervade most of the section's diverse stories.

Reviewers often cited the final section, "Beyond," as the volume's weakest. The title story takes place in a parklike spiritual afterlife, where the agnostic Robert Ingersol, among others, directs a deceased judge awaiting judgment in the search for his son, who died in a riding accident at ten years of age. The theme of the search is carried forward in "Black Music," which assumes a detective story tone as the narrator learns the secret of an exile whose one-day foray as a faun has made his return home impossible; his experience "beyond," like the others in this section, has been "something outside the lot and plan for mortal human man." "The Leg," featuring a haunting by an amputated limb, depicts the narrator's confrontation with another self representing his unconscious desires. The last half of "Beyond" features Americans abroad and concerns, according to Millgate, "the enlargement or extension of experience" (*Achievement* 262) in a tragic world. The paired protagonists in "Mistral" and "Divorce in Naples" confront very different types of infidelities that heighten their awareness of mutability and deceit; "Carcassonne" concludes the volume with a lyric coda focusing on transcendence through the world of imagination. While the final story's lyric form and stream-of-consciousness narrative present an aesthetic that embodies the converse of a comprehensive volume of grouped stories, perhaps *Collected Stories*—with its imaginative scope and intertextual ambition to transcend being a mere "best of"—represents one version of Faulkner's attempt to respond to the "bareness of the Southerner's life . . . to resort to his own imagination, to create his own Carcassonne" (*FIU* 136).

FURTHER READING

Kinney, Arthur F. "Faulkner's Narrative Poetics and *Collected Stories.*" *Faulkner Studies* 1 (1980): 58–79.

Robert M. Luscher

COLLECTIONS. Six major repositories of Faulkner's extant papers are identified and the collections briefly described in the 1987 "General Introduction" to *William Faulkner Manuscripts*, Volume I. The series' editors point out that "Faulkner's extant papers run to thousands of pages, comprising holograph manuscripts, ribbon and carbon typescripts, corrected and uncorrected galley and page proofs, notes, foul papers, outlines, preliminary and revised drafts, all in varying combinations, for nearly every novel and short story" (ix). The repositories they list are the University of Virginia Alderman Library, the largest and most significant of the six; the New York Public Library; the Harry Ransom Humanities Research Center, the University of Texas at Austin; the University of Mississippi, where Faulkner's Rowan Oak Papers are held; Tulane University, which houses the William B. Wisdom Collection; and Southeast Missouri State University, repository of the large private collection of Louis Daniel Brodsky. Among smaller private collections are the Holzman Collection at the University of Michigan and the Carl Petersen Collection, divided for sale in 1991. Some other letters, with some manuscripts, are at Princeton and Yale Universities and a few elsewhere. Since 1987 Joseph Blotner's papers have been added to the Brodsky Collection, and the Humanities Research Center has opened and catalogued two important collections held there since the early 1960s—the Carvel Collins Collection and the Mallard Collection of 150 letters by Faulkner to his mother and father, 1918–1925.

FURTHER READING

Blotner et al., eds. ''General Introduction.'' *William Faulkner Manuscripts*. I: ix–xii.
Bonner, comp. *William Faulkner: The William B. Wisdom Collection.*
Brodsky and Hamblin, eds. *Faulkner: A Comprehensive Guide to the Brodsky Collection.*
Howard. *William Faulkner: The Carl Petersen Collection.*
Kinney, Arthur, and Doreen Fowler. ''Faulkner's Rowan Oak Papers: A Census.'' *Journal of Modern Literature* 10 (1983): 327–334.
Massey, comp. *William Faulkner: ''Man Working,'' 1919–1962.*
Watson, James G. ''Carvel Collins' Faulkner: A Newly Opened Archive.'' *Library Chronicle of the University of Texas at Austin* 20.4 (1991): 17–35. Rpt. *Mississippi Quarterly* 44 (1991): 257–272.

James G. Watson

COLLEGE HILL PRESBYTERIAN CHURCH. The oldest Presbyterian structure in north Mississippi and the oldest church in the Oxford area, College Hill Presbyterian Church was built between 1844 and 1846 from bricks fired on the site at a cost of $2,809.75. The original congregation of early Scot-Irish settlers organized as a church in the home of Alexander Shaw on January 11, 1835, and emigrated to the present site, about eight miles west of Oxford, in 1836. The church was first named Neriah Church and later Ebenezer Church after its second pastor, Ebenezer McEwen (1836); it took its present name from North Mississippi College, which helped to found it and with which it was initially associated. The church was a main part of the small community, built on twenty-three acres for which the early congregation paid $400. The slightly slanted pulpit and dais, the pews, and the pew doors are all original; and the building is especially noteworthy for retaining the original outside doors to the slave balcony, which was taken down shortly after the conclusion of the War Between the States. This is the balcony in which Ringo might have sat in *The*

Unvanquished, able to hear but not see the service or be seen by the white congregation.

The congregation grew rapidly to include at least thirty-one families by 1860; and by church regulation, they brought their slaves to services with them, teaching them to read. In 1861 the young men of the parish formed their own militia company and with university students mustered into Confederate service as Company G of the 11th Mississippi Infantry. They saw service in every major battle fought under Lee's command, many dying in Pickett's Charge at Gettysburg on July 3, 1863, to which Faulkner refers in *Intruder in the Dust*. Meantime, Grant's forces came through College Hill, leaving Sherman's division in residence. The church became military headquarters for a time while Union soldiers raided the countryside, foraging for fresh meats and vegetables. The church itself was not damaged.

Dr. W. H. Heddleston, pastor from 1910 to 1936, married Faulkner and Estelle Oldham Franklin in 1929 but not, as was once thought, in the sanctuary, since church law did not permit church weddings of divorced persons. The couple was married either on the church porch or (as was common with Reverend Heddleston) at the parsonage a short way down the road. College Hill is located on Faulkner's map of Yoknapatawpha at the location of Sutpen's Hundred, and the church may have served as a model for the marriage of Thomas Sutpen and Ellen Coldfield—perhaps in sly reference to the Faulkners' own marriage. But according to *Absalom, Absalom!* the Coldfield family is Methodist, not Presbyterian.

A cemetery adjoins the church. In the white section are buried several families with names that appear in Faulkner: Bunch, Waddel, Buford, and Isom. A separate black graveyard is fenced off to the rear. The church was honored as one of two outstanding small Presbyterian churches in 1977 and in 1979 was placed on the National Register of Historic Places.

FURTHER READING

Lewis, Will. *The Founding and Early History of College Hill Presbyterian Church.* Oxford, Miss.: College Hill Presbyterian Church, 1985.

Arthur F. Kinney

COMMINS, SAXE (1892–1958), editor at Random House from 1933 until his death. Among the authors with whom he worked were Faulkner, Eugene O'Neill, Sinclair Lewis, Budd Schulberg, and Irwin Shaw. Beginning with *Absalom, Absalom!* in 1936, Commins guided into print twelve Faulkner titles (nine novels and three story collections), ending with *The Town* in 1957. During the 1950s, a particularly tumultuous time in the author's life, Commins and his wife Dorothy frequently opened their home in Princeton to Faulkner for days and weeks at a time. Indeed, during this period Commins served not only as Faulkner's editor but also as his principal adviser and confidant. Commins was particularly instrumental in helping Faulkner structure and complete *A Fable*, which was partly written in the Commins home. On one occasion, at Estelle Faulkner's request, Commins traveled to Oxford to assist in persuading Faulkner to seek medical treatment for a severe alcoholic collapse. On another occasion, at grave risk to his own health because of a deteriorating heart condition, Commins nursed Faulkner through another siege of alcoholism at the Algonquin Hotel in New York. Faulkner acknowledged Commins's friendship and service in the dedication of *Big Woods*, which reads in part, "We never always saw eye to eye but we were always looking at the same thing." Upon receiving notice of his friend's death in 1958, Faulkner sent a telegram to Dorothy Commins that read: "The finest epitaph everyone who ever knew Saxe will have to subscribe to whether he will or not quote He loved me unquote."

FURTHER READING

Commins, Dorothy. *What Is an Editor?: Saxe Commins at Work*. Chicago: University of Chicago Press, 1978.
Brodsky, Louis Daniel, and Thomas M. Verich. *Saxe and Bill: A Keepsake*. Oxford: University of Mississippi, 1982.

Louis Daniel Brodsky

COMPSON, one of Faulkner's major fictional families. Compsons appear prominently in *The Sound and the Fury, Absalom, Absalom!*, and the "Compson Appendix"; less centrally but still importantly in *The Unvanquished, Go Down, Moses, Requiem for a Nun, The Town,* and *The Mansion*; and singly or as a group, in several short stories, most notably "That Evening Sun." Faulkner imagines Compson history as collateral with the history of Yoknapatawpha County itself. In the Compson Appendix and *Requiem for a Nun*, the first Jason Lycurgus Compson enters the region that would become Yoknapatawpha County in 1811, obtains the "Compson Domain," and helps found Jefferson; the family history moves forward through Governor Quentin Maclachan II and Confederate General Jason Lycurgus II to its more familiar twentieth-century constituents.

In *The Sound and the Fury* this background is only partially and indirectly depicted, as emphasis falls instead on the three generations comprising Jason III and Caroline Bascomb Compson; their children, Quentin, Candace, Jason IV, and Benjamin; and Candace's daughter, Quentin. Covering the period from 1897 to 1928, *The Sound and the Fury* depicts the gradual dissolution of the family, via Mr. Compson's alcoholism and eventual death, Mrs. Compson's neurasthenia and hypochondria, Caddy's failed marriage, the male Quentin's suicide, Benjy's congenital idiocy, and the female Quentin's final flight from home.

This dissolution has been seen to bear a variety of meanings. Through the novel's Easter Week symbolism and its Southern setting, the breakup of the family is linked to the loss of religious faith in the modern world and to nostalgia for a lost Southern aristocratic social order. Implicit as well are changes occurring in economic, racial, and gender relationships in the South, and America generally, in the 1920s, as well as new understandings of family dynamics brought into prominence in the 1910s and 1920s by Sigmund Freud and his followers.

Direct depiction of the Compson family in *Absalom, Absalom!* is limited to Quentin Compson and his father, two of the four first-person narrators in the novel, who piece together and invent the story of Thomas Sutpen. Here, in contrast to *The Sound and the Fury*, the range of reference widens, shifting from emphasis on family dynamics and individual psychosexual development to concern with racial relations and Southern and American history.

FURTHER READING

Bloom, Harold, ed. *Caddy Compson*. New York: Chelsea House, 1990.
Kinney, Arthur F., ed. *Critical Essays on William Faulkner: The Compson Family*. Boston: G. K. Hall, 1982.

Karl F. Zender

COMPSON APPENDIX. *See* **"Appendix, Compson, 1699–1945."**

CONFEDERACY. *See* **Civil War**.

CONRAD, JOSEPH (1857–1924), Polish-born author who is generally acknowledged as one of the greatest prose writers in the English language. Faulkner frequently expressed his admiration for Conrad, on one occasion including him in a list of "the masters from whom we [Faulkner's generation of writers] learned our craft" (*FIU* 243). Among Conrad's works that Faulkner listed as particularly noteworthy were *The Nigger of the "Narcissus," Lord Jim, Nostromo, Heart of Darkness*, "Falk," "The End of the Tether," and "Youth." Faulkner shares with Conrad a fondness for the initiation story, as well as an essentially tragic view of life and human nature (though Faulkner's pessimism is not quite as bleak as Conrad's); but the most important Conradian influence on Faulkner would seem to lie in the area of narrative technique. One of the first writers to come under the strong influence of the impressionistic painters, Conrad constantly experimented with shifting perspectives, multiple viewpoints, disrupted chronology, unresolved textual and moral ambiguities that result from the absence of an authoritative voice that might be taken to represent absolute truth, and a consequent demand upon the reader both to shape and to interpret the text for himself or herself. All such characteristics, of course, are standard fare in Faulkner's fiction, as can be readily seen by comparing the technique of *Absalom, Absalom!* to that of *Lord Jim*.

FURTHER READING

Beach, Joseph Warren. "William Faulkner." *American Fiction 1920–1940*. New York: Macmillan Company, 1941. 123–169.
Guerard, Albert J. *Conrad the Novelist*. Cambridge, Mass.: Harvard University Press, 1958.

Guetti, James. *The Limits of Metaphor: A Study of Melville, Conrad, and Faulkner.* Ithaca, N.Y.: Cornell University Press, 1967.

Robert W. Hamblin

COOPER, MINNIE. Miss Minnie Cooper is the female protagonist in Faulkner's short story "Dry September," published in *Scribner's* in 1931. After Miss Minnie falsely accuses Will Mayes, a black man, of rape, the majority of the men in town set out to kill Mayes. One man from the town, Hawkshaw, argues for Mayes's innocence and tries to convince the townsmen that dried-up spinsters like Minnie Cooper often indulge in sexual fantasies like the one she has created about Will Mayes. Faulkner describes Miss Minnie as a "thirty-eight or thirty-nine"-year-old spinster who lives with her mother and aunt. After a brief relationship with a local widower, Faulkner says that Minnie was "relegated into adultery by public opinion." Most critics believe that Faulkner sympathetically portrays Minnie Cooper as a sexually repressed, frustrated woman, not completely responsible for her act of imagination. Irving Howe, however, describes Faulkner's characterization of Minnie Cooper as "close to stereotype."

Rebecca Rowley

CORPORAL, the Christlike leader of the failed mutiny in Faulkner's novel *A Fable.* Among the more dramatic scenes in the novel is the verbal confrontation between Stefan and his father, the Supreme Commander, in which the son's rebellion is incorporated into and used as rationale for the Generalissimo's command. The Corporal says little in the exchange except to identify authoritarianism with fear. "Don't be afraid," he tells his father. "There's nothing to be afraid of. Nothing worth it." The Corporal's rebellion inspires other characters, notably the Runner, to a renewed faith in the human capacity to effect change. Despite an attempt by his half sisters to bury his body on their farm, Stefan is interred in France's Tomb of the Unknown Soldier.

Joseph R. Urgo

CORRECTED TEXTS. *See* **Texts**.

COUNTRY LAWYER, an undeveloped film treatment that Faulkner wrote as a screenwriter at Warner Bros. Studio in 1943. Assigned to adapt Bellamy Partridge's book of reminiscences for the screen, Faulkner responded with a loose interpretation that shifted Bellamy's setting from Phelps, New York, to Faulkner's own fictional domain of Jefferson, Mississippi. Other Faulknerian aspects of the treatment include the tracing of two family lines through four generations and two world wars and the handling of white-black relationships.

FURTHER READING

Faulkner, William. *Country Lawyer and Other Stories for the Screen.* Ed. with intro. by Louis Daniel Brodsky and Robert W. Hamblin. Jackson: University Press of Mississippi, 1987.

Robert W. Hamblin

"COURTSHIP, A," a short story by Faulkner, first appeared in *Sewanee Review* in 1948, winning First Prize in the O. Henry Short Story Award for 1949. Later included in *Collected Stories*, the story is in the "tall tale" tradition and deals with the extraordinary lengths men go to in order to gain a woman's notice. The two rivals are Ikkemotubbe, before he becomes the Man, or Doom, and David Hogganbeck, who brings the steamship upriver. They attempt to win the interests of a completely disinterested, though stunningly attractive woman, Herman Basket's sister. The two, as the best specimens of manhood of each race, try to outrun, outdrink, and outeat each other. In the end, both lose out to a man who does nothing but play the harmonica. This ending suggests a concern for definitions of masculinity and the role of the artist in a masculinized society.

FURTHER READING

Cantrell, Frank. "Faulkner's 'A Courtship.' " *Mississippi Quarterly* 24 (Summer 1971): 289–295.
Hönnighausen, Lothar. "Faulkner Rewriting the Indian Removal." *Transatlantic Perspectives*. Vol. 3: *Rewriting the South: History and Fiction*. Ed. Lothar Hönnighausen et al. Tübingen, Germany: Franke, 1993. 335–343.
Howell, Elmo. "Inversion and the 'Female Principle' in William Faulkner's 'A Courtship.' " *Studies in Short Fiction* 4 (1967): 308–314.
———. "William Faulkner and the Mississippi Indians." *Georgia Review* 21 (1967): 386–396.

Larry Wharton

COWLEY, MALCOLM (1898–1989), American writer, editor, translator, and journalist. Although he was a minor if accomplished poet and a significant translator of French symbolist poetry, Cowley's principal career was as a chronicler and commentator on the literary scene and a judicious editor; from 1929 until 1940 he served as the literary editor of the *New Republic*. In 1944, Cowley published (through Viking Press) *The Portable Hemingway*, and he began his correspondence with Faulkner about the possibility of a "Portable Faulkner," which was subsequently published in 1946 (*see* **Portable Faulkner, The**).

A central theme of Cowley's critical writing is the reaction and rebellion of twentieth-century American writers—especially Cather, Dos Passos, Faulkner, Fitzgerald, and Hemingway—against the "Genteel Tradition," which had been defined in a seminal essay by George Santayana and which is the subject of Cowley's introduction to *After the Genteel Tradition: American Writers, 1910–1930* (W. W. Norton, 1937). Cowley gives considerable attention in his critical writing to the social, cultural, and intellectual context of writers he treats, but he is also attentive to forms of language and (apropos the Genteel Tradition) issues of diction. Two samples of Cowley's work as a practical critic, in addition to the introduction to *The Portable Faulkner*, are of particular interest to students of Faulkner. The first is his long critique of John T. Irwin's *Doubling and Incest/Repetition and Revenge* in "Faulkner: The Etiology of His Art" (—*And*

I Worked at the Writer's Trade [Viking, 1978] 214–230); the second is his treatment of issues of style and diction in "The Middle American Prose Style" (in *The Flower and the Leaf* [Viking, 1985]).

FURTHER READING

Bak, Hans. *Malcolm Cowley: The Formative Years.* Athens: University of Georgia Press, 1993.

Crews, Frederick. "The Strange Fate of William Faulkner." *New York Review of Books* 7 March 1991: 47–52.

Peek, Charles A. "An Interview with Malcolm Cowley." *Faulkner Journal* 5.1 (1989): 51–59.

Stephen Hahn

"CREVASSE," a short story Faulkner wrote in May 1931 for inclusion in *These 13*, also appears in "The Wasteland" section of *Collected Stories.* Possibly originally a flashback in an examination of war's aftereffects on a Scot, Alexander Gray, the published story erases identity by removing the characters' names, leaving only the Scottish dialect. A party of World War I soldiers, their water "contaminate," bandages "filthy," tumble into a cavern past the skeletons of Senegalese troops gassed in combat. A wounded soldier's repeated cry, "A'm no dead!" suggests their descent has been into hell, "where no life is." Although fourteen survive the tunneling out and "[l]ight rushes in," a wasteland is suggested by the monotonous sounds of their prayers and cries, "meaningless and unemphatic."

Charles A. Peek

D

"**DAMNED DON'T CRY, THE,**" a story treatment that Faulkner wrote in late 1941 in an attempt to secure a movie contract with Warner Bros. Studio. A reworking of another writer's previously rejected screenplay based on Harry C. Hervey's novel (1939), Faulkner's treatment features a strong female protagonist who, because of her resiliency in the face of tragedy and her association with a brothel, may be paralleled with the Temple Drake of *Requiem for a Nun*.

FURTHER READING

Faulkner, William. *Country Lawyer and Other Stories for the Screen*. Ed. with intro. by Louis Daniel Brodsky and Robert W. Hamblin. Jackson: University Press of Mississippi, 1987.

Robert W. Hamblin

"**DANGEROUS MAN, A,**" a short story by Faulkner, was submitted for publication in February 1930 but was not published until *Uncollected Stories* in 1979. It is difficult to know what is dangerous about Mr. Bowman, the protagonist; perhaps it is that beneath his benign predictability there resides potential volatility. His wife is apparently unfaithful to him, but he is faithful to his wife and especially to his snappish dogs. There is a disagreement as to whether or not manuscripts of "A Letter" and "A Letter to Grandmamma" are versions of this story. If so, then this story is one of at least three that began as ideas or drafts of Estelle Faulkner.

Diane Brown Jones

"**DANZAS VENEZUELA,**" a performance of indigenous dances that Faulkner attended at the Teatro Municipal in Caracas on April 6, 1961, during his visit to Venezuela on behalf of the U.S. State Department. Soon after attending the program, Faulkner wrote a brief, eloquent tribute to the dancers in whom he "saw the spirit and history of Venezuela caught and held in a bright and warm moment of grace and skill and happiness, by young men and women who gave one the impression that they were doing it out of love of what they were doing." The original handwritten draft of Faulkner's impressions is now in the Brodsky Collection.

FURTHER READING

Brodsky, Louis Daniel. "William Faulkner's 'Danzas Venezuela': The Original Manuscript." *Studies in Bibliography* 40 (1987): 226–229.

Louis Daniel Brodsky

DEATH seems to have been an obsession with Faulkner from an early age. Perhaps, as Jerold Howard Stock has suggested in his seminal study of death anxiety in the life and works of Faulkner, this fear of death may have derived from Faulkner's near-demise from scarlet fever at age four or from the experience, at age nine, of watching his beloved maternal grandmother, Lelia Swift Butler ("Damuddy"), being destroyed by cancer. The semiautobiographical "Sepulture South: Gaslight" (1954), while written during the later stages of Faulkner's life, nevertheless suggests the degree to which an acute awareness and fear of death significantly influenced his boyhood years.

Whatever the origin of influence, death surfaces as a major subject in Faulkner's early poetry and prose and is seldom again absent from his work. The autumnal setting and tone of *Marionettes*, the preoccupation with mutability in *The Marble Faun*, the concern with time and mortality in *Elmer* and *Mayday*, the role of the skeleton in "Carcassonne," the focus on dying soldiers in "The Lilacs" and *Soldiers' Pay*, the penning of his own epitaph ("Mississippi Hills") before he was thirty, the treatment of the passing of the generations in *Flags in the Dust*, the suicide of Quentin Compson, the death of Addie Bundren (and the frightened response to that death by her young son Vardaman)—all of these elements demonstrate the extent to which memento mori is, from the very beginning, a controlling theme in Faulkner's view of life and experience. Indeed, among American writers, only Edgar Allan Poe seems as obsessed with death, decay, corpses, and cemeteries. It seems clear that the melancholic verses of Swinburne and Housman merely confirmed feelings toward which the youthful Faulkner was already inclined; and the tragic death of his brother Dean in 1935 in the crash of a plane Faulkner had given him indelibly imprinted the ghastly vision onto his psyche.

But an existential recognition of the tragic inevitability of death is only one—and not the most important—facet of Faulkner's handling of this subject. For Faulkner the ultimate meaning is to be found not in the fact of death but in the heroic resistance to that fate, and from *Absalom, Absalom!* onward this latter emphasis becomes an overt theme in Faulkner's work. As Ernest Becker has convincingly argued in *The Denial of Death*, all individuals experience death anxiety and consequently long for immortality, whether natural or supernatural;

but Faulkner contends that this psychological tension is particularly acute and productive for artists. "Since man is mortal," Faulkner once observed, "the only immortality possible for him is to leave something behind him that is immortal since it will always move. This is the artist's way of scribbling 'Kilroy was here' on the wall of the final and irrevocable oblivion through which he must someday pass" (*LIG* 253). Perhaps Faulkner's most sublime expression of this idea is found in the foreword to *The Faulkner Reader*, in which he contends that the ultimate goal of the writer is "to uplift man's heart" by "saying No to death." "Some day," Faulkner concludes, "[the writer] will be no more, which will not matter then, because isolated and itself invulnerable in the cold print remains that which is capable of engendering still the old deathless excitement in hearts and glands whose owners and custodians are generations from the air he breathed and anguished in." Such sentiments partly explain Faulkner's immense fondness for Keats's "Ode on a Grecian Urn," undoubtedly the best known of all literary works treating the paradox of the mortal artist seeking to create immortal art.

Given his deep concern for the nature and role of artists and the art they create, it is not at all surprising that Faulkner frequently utilizes art surrogates in his work—that is, particular objects that have survived the past and continue to evoke memories or thoughts of people and incidents from earlier times. Predictably, a significant number of these art surrogates take a "literary" form, requiring the response of a "reader." There is, for example, the letter that Judith Sutpen gives to Quentin Compson's grandmother, which Quentin's father associates with Judith's compulsion "to make that scratch, that undying mark on the blank face of the oblivion to which we are all doomed." Other examples, treated by Faulkner in greater detail, are the commissary ledgers that Ike McCaslin reads in *Go Down, Moses* and the "story" evoked by Cecilia Farmer's signature scratched into a windowpane of the Jefferson jailhouse in *Requiem for a Nun*. All such surrogates express symbolically the same idea that Faulkner stated explicitly in one of his letters to Joan Williams, his lover and protégée: "That's the answer, the reason for it all, the one and only way on earth you can say No to death: the best, the strongest, the finest, the most enduring: to make something" (1974 *FAB* 1461).

FURTHER READING

Becker, Ernest. *The Denial of Death*. New York: Free Press, 1973.

Gidley, Mick. "Beyond 'Beyond': Aspects of Faulkner's Representation of Death." *Faulkner's Discourse*, ed. Hönnighausen. 223–253.

Hamblin, Robert W. " 'Saying No to Death': Toward William Faulkner's Theory of Fiction." *"A Cosmos of My Own,"* ed. Fowler and Abadie. 3–35.

Stock, Jerold Howard. "Suggestions of Death-Anxiety in the Life of William Faulkner." Dissertation. West Virginia University, 1977.

Robert W. Hamblin

"DEATH DRAG," a short story by William Faulkner, was first published in *Scribner's* in 1932 and also appears in *Doctor Martino and Other Stories* and *Collected Stories*. It tells the story of three desperate, depression-era men who earn enough money to survive by taking their unlicensed air show from small town to small town. Told by a townsperson, its point of view broadened and insights sharpened by the added perspective of Captain Warren, a former acquaintance of the air show pilot and an ex-army flier himself, the story depicts the generation doomed by World War I. It seems equally focused on the caricature of the daredevil Jew, whose preoccupation with money seems a comic symbol of man's struggle for justice, and on the portrait of the pilot, who heroically and absurdly assumes the burden of rescuing the Jew and bearing him along. Making use of anti-Semitic stereotypes, "Death Drag" presents a picture of man at odds with his metaphysical and historical circumstances: The Jew is forced by the depression out of the business world and into death-defying aerobatics the way the pilot is forced by the end of the war out of more honorable and prestigious acts of flight.

FURTHER READING

Kutzik, Alfred J. "Faulkner and the Jews." *Yivo Annual of Jewish Social Science* 13 (1965): 213–226.

Lind, Ilse Dusoir. "The Language of Stereotype in 'Death Drag.' " *Faulkner's Discourse*, ed. Hönnighausen. 127–131.

Arthur A. Brown

DECONSTRUCTION, as a form of textual analysis, grows out of the philosophical project of Jacques Derrida, which broadly questions the privilege of speech over writing in Western thought from Plato to Saussure. This privileging, which Derrida variously calls "the metaphysics of presence" and "logocentrism," means that speech is posited as a more authentic communication than the mediation of the written word, since in speech the subject is apparently fully present in the moment of the word's enunciation. Derrida sees this distinction as illusory since every claim that can be made about speech is inevitably a claim that can be made about writing, so that speech is always already a form of writing. The deconstruction is precisely that what appeared as a self-evident hierarchy (validated by a linear historical development) becomes instead a mutually constitutive pair. All metaphysical oppositions, therefore, that are hierarchically ordered so that the first term is positively marked as origin while the second term is perceived as a potentially dangerous supplement (e.g., pure/impure, cause/effect, good/evil, denotation/connotation, man/woman, master/slave) are open to deconstructive analysis. It is important to understand that deconstruction does not seek to destroy meaning but rather wishes to show that meaning is not prior to, but rather an effect of, language.

Deconstruction's implications for Faulkner studies are manifold since Faulkner represents a patriarchal Christian Southern culture that is founded on a number of oppositions of unexamined privilege and domination (white/black, planter/poor white, husband/wife, community/individual, South/North). There has, however, been little analysis of Faulkner's texts that is strictly deconstructive. Even John Matthews, whose work in the 1980s was more invested in Derridean concepts than any other Faulkner scholar, acknowledges that because he does not seek out the oppositions that ground Faulkner's discourse, he is "not performing a Derridean deconstruction of the Faulknerian text" but rather using deconstructive concepts "to explain retrospectively developments in modern literature" (23–24). Nevertheless, Matthews convincingly uses Faulkner's fiction to argue a deconstructive point: The individual's identity (or subjectivity) is not whole and complete prior to his or her use of language; rather, this identity is created through language.

Deconstruction has proved to be at least as useful as a tool for examining the a priori assumptions of previous Faulkner scholarship. Because many of the first-generation Faulkner scholars were from the South, often informed by the conservative world picture of Southern agrarianism, they tended to act as apologists for the forms of privilege and domination noted above. Deconstructive readings have mapped the contradictions of this body of earlier scholarship. Intertextual studies that see Faulkner's fiction in a larger network of texts participate in the deconstructive project to the extent that this work challenges the notion of the fully autonomous artist-as-genius. Although deconstruction has been attacked for being ahistorical, its insights live on in the way New Historicism conceives of history.

FURTHER READING

Krause, David. "Reading Bon's Letter and Faulkner's *Absalom, Absalom!*" *PMLA* 99 (1984): 225–241.
O'Donnell, Patrick. "Sub Rosa: Voice, Body, and History in *Absalom, Absalom!*" *College Literature* 16 (1989): 28–47.

John N. Duvall

DE GAULLE STORY, THE, Faulkner's first assignment with Warner Bros. Studio in 1942, was a film project suggested to Jack Warner by Franklin Roosevelt. Together with *Battle Cry, The De Gaulle Story* has numerous links to Faulkner's subsequent fiction, especially *A Fable*. Roosevelt had in mind a film that would celebrate Charles de Gaulle, but in Faulkner's hands the story would have little to do with de Gaulle himself. Instead, Faulkner concentrated on the plight of common French people who were influenced by the same ideas and forces that created de Gaulle. This populist sense of what should constitute the de Gaulle story brought Faulkner into conflict with representatives of the Free French/Fighting French who were consulted on the script. A two-page memorandum defending his approach to the story (Brodsky and Hamblin III: 395–

398) is a valuable source for Faulkner's concept of historical representation. Largely for budgetary and political reasons, the film was never produced.

FURTHER READING

Brodsky and Hamblin, eds. "Introduction." *Faulkner: A Comprehensive Guide to the Brodsky Collection*. Vol. III: *The De Gaulle Story*. ix–xxxiii.
Gresset, Michel. "The De Gaulle Story Comes Full Circle." *Faulkner Newsletter and Yoknapatawpha Review* 12:2 (1992): 1f.

Joseph R. Urgo

"DELTA AUTUMN," a prose work by Faulkner, exists in two versions: as a short story, originally published in *Story* in 1942, now most conveniently available in *Uncollected Stories*; and as the penultimate section of *Go Down, Moses*. The relation between the two versions is summarized by Joseph Blotner in an endnote to *Uncollected Stories*; The essential changes, Blotner says, are that a character named Don Boyd in the short story version "became [in the novel version] Carothers 'Roth' Edmonds, great-great-great-grandson of old Lucius Quintus Carothers McCaslin . . . ; and [that] Edmonds' mulatto mistress became the great-great-great-granddaughter of old Lucius Quintus Carothers McCaslin."

In its *Go Down, Moses* form, "Delta Autumn" concludes the account of Isaac McCaslin's life and adds greatly to the novel's exploration of the themes of racial injustice and of American and Southern history. The section's main participants are Isaac McCaslin, at this point well past seventy years old; his several-times-removed cousin, Roth Edmonds, here approximately forty; a hunter named Will Legate; and a nameless young black woman, Roth's former mistress, the mother of his infant child, and a descendant, via the Beauchamp family line, of L.Q.C. McCaslin.

Set during a November (c. 1940) hunting trip to the Mississippi Delta, "Delta Autumn" begins, seemingly inconsequentially, with veiled sexual joking, discussion of contemporary American and European politics, and elegiac reflections on the disappearance of the Mississippi wilderness. These seemingly unconnected elements come together in the final scene of the section, as Isaac McCaslin confronts the young black woman, who has journeyed to the hunting camp to learn whether Roth's rejection of her is final.

When Isaac learns, to his surprise, that the woman is both black and his and Roth's distant relative, he faces a final test in his lifelong struggle over the issue of Southern racial injustice. He fails the test abjectly, for although he recognizes in the woman's touch "the strong old blood" in "its long lost journey back to home," he cannot accept the thought of marriage between her and Roth, thinking desperately, *"Maybe in a thousand or two thousand years in America . . . But not now! Not now!"* He then links this rejection to the destruction of the wilderness, imagining that in *"Chinese and African and Aryan and Jew, all breed[ing] and spawn[ing] together . . .* the ruined woods . . . will accomplish its revenge."

The rich concatenation of themes in "Delta Autumn" has produced a wide variety of critical readings. In the early years of Faulkner criticism, when Isaac McCaslin's rejection of his inheritance tended to be positively valued, "Delta Autumn" was given less attention than the earlier sections of *Go Down, Moses*, most notably "The Bear." But as the critical consensus shifted toward negative evaluations of Isaac's decision, "Delta Autumn" gained prominence, with critics seeing Isaac's final hysterical outburst as the logical outgrowth of a political and social immaturity basically frozen into position at the age of twenty-one.

In recent years, with the rise to prominence of feminist and neo-Marxist criticism, critiques of "Delta Autumn" (and of *Go Down, Moses*) have become even more incisive—and, at times, judgmental of Faulkner himself. Philip Weinstein, for example, has argued that Faulkner's "nostalgia for immolated white innocence runs deeper than his compassion for black suffering" and that "the wilderness so dilated upon in this text [*Go Down, Moses*] seduces not least because of its imaginary innocence, its status as prehuman (presexual and preracial) uncontaminated space" ("Diving" 45–46). Expanded awareness of the range of meanings dramatized in "Delta Autumn" shows how Isaac's final crisis of choice involves not only racial but gender and class issues as well, articulated in ways specific to the time of composition of *Go Down, Moses*, at the end of the Great Depression and the beginning of World War II.

"Delta Autumn" has also been insightfully read in its structural and imagistic connections to the rest of *Go Down, Moses*, in its relation to the history of American nature writing, and in its placement in Faulkner's career. Michael Grimwood and others have advanced a reflexive reading of "Delta Autumn," seeing in Isaac's regret over the destruction of the wilderness a veiled reflection of Faulkner's midlife concern over the waning of his creativity and the disappearance of his fictional subject matter.

FURTHER READING

Godden, Richard. "Iconic Narrative: or, How Faulkner Fought the Second Civil War." *Faulkner's Discourse*, ed. Hönnighausen. 68–76.

Grimwood, Michael. " 'Delta Autumn': Stagnation and Sedimentation in Faulkner's Career." *Southern Literary Journal* 16 (1984): 93–106.

Matthews, John T. "Touching Race in *Go Down, Moses*." *New Essays on* Go Down, Moses. Ed. Linda Wagner-Martin. Cambridge: Cambridge University Press, 1996. 21–47.

Weinstein, Philip M. "Diving into the Wreck: Faulknerian Practice and the Imagination of Slavery." *Faulkner Journal* 10.2 (1995): 23–53.

Karl F. Zender

DE SPAIN, the name of a prominent family appearing in a number of Faulkner's Yoknapatawpha novels and stories. Major Cassius de Spain is omnipresent but silent in "The Old People" in *Go Down, Moses*. Owner of the hunting camp and deeply respected by the hunters, he is one of the original landowners in Yoknapatawpha County. He also appears in *Absalom, Absalom!*, "Lion," "Barn Burning," and *The Hamlet*, not always favorably. The view of Major de Spain in "The Bear" is particularly poignant. He is no longer as he appears in "The Old People"—the hunter with a profound relationship to the land and to his fellow hunters—but unwilling to go back to the hunting camp, having long before sold to the lumber company the land that would now become a planing mill, bringing log-trains into the sacrosanct wilderness. As Isaac invited him to return to the woods with him, he "did not look up again." De Spain's son, Manfred de Spain, appears in "Spotted Horses," *The Town*, and *The Mansion*—in the last two of these as the adulterous lover of Eula Varner Snopes. Manfred had gone to Cuba as a second lieutenant and came home to "modernize" Jefferson irrevocably. As the narrator of *The Town* puts it, "[H]e and Jefferson were incorrigibly and invincibly awry on one another, and . . . one of them was going to have to give. And . . . it would not be him." "Progress" was on its way.

Marion Tangum

DETECTIVE STORIES. The detective story emerged as a distinct genre or "type" of story—and the detective as both a fictional character and an actual social role—in the nineteenth century, prominently in several stories by Edgar Allan Poe and, later, in stories and novels by Wilkie Collins and Arthur Conan Doyle. Mildly parodic versions of the genre appear in Mark Twain's *Pudd'nhead Wilson* and *Tom Sawyer, Detective*. Eventually the genre became the staple of popular and juvenile literature, often through serial stories or novels involving a single detective and (frequently) one or more helpers.

Analyses of the genre sometimes consider it a restricted genre in which certain characters, sequences of plot complication, and other "rules" of representation must be deployed. More expansive analyses, which generally appear as writers themselves begin to expand the parameters of the genre, see the detective story from a quasi-religious or anthropological perspective as a variation of cultural myths. Dorothy L. Sayers, for instance, traces the detective story in Western literature to apocryphal biblical narratives (Daniel and the story of Bel and of Susanna and the Elders) as well as other classical sources. Aspects of the genre may be seen, from an expanded definition, in Sophocles's *Oedipus Tyrannus* or Shakespeare's *Hamlet*, since these works involve unexplained deaths, allegations of wrongdoing, the conduct of an investigation, and the conviction of a guilty party. At its most expansive the genre appears in works like Dostoevsky's *Crime and Punishment*.

What generally distinguishes the detective story from the background of other stories of crime or other mystery stories (those of a religious nature, for instance) is the presence of "rules of evidence" developed to determine guilt in alleged crimes. Since most criminal procedure in Western history involved investigation through torture and confession, the development of the genre, in this respect, was delayed until evidence rather than confession became the key to solving crimes. The apocryphal stories involving Daniel, cited above, interestingly fore-shadow this development (one involves a "sting" operation in which visible evidence is produced; the other, conflicting testimony that results in conviction). Historically, the method of torture and confession required a culturally approved authority figure to conduct the investigation. The emergence of a logic of de-tection through evidence enabled the investigator to work by methods that confer authority independent of the social status of the investigator. Hence, although the "detective" might eventually become professionalized, the activity of de-tection could be carried out by "outsiders," amateurs, and those who are not otherwise culturally sanctioned. In fact, one aspect of the development of the genre is the contest between the amateur detective and the culturally sanctioned police, who are either hampered by bureaucratic method or by being politically compromised, or between competing members of the police establishment. This development has relevance to at least one of Faulkner's novels that is often considered to be influenced by the detective genre, *Intruder in the Dust*, in which Chick Mallison, Miss Habersham, and Aleck Sander conduct an unofficial in-quiry on behalf of the jailed Lucas Beauchamp to prove an alternate solution to the one the sanctioned powers have asserted.

An additional formal distinguishing feature of the detective story *as story* is that it diverges from the narrative genre of romance on which the novel is based by concerning itself less with the question "What will happen?" and more with the question "What has happened?" The closer any story is to the more re-stricted model of a detective story, the more its focus will center on the solution to a past crime. But, obviously, any story in which the fate of individuals in the story is yet to be determined (e.g., Lucas Beauchamp in *Intruder*) frames the question of "What has happened?" with the question of "What will happen?" (Will he be executed?). The result is a narrative doubling that enables the de-tective formula to gain a richer dramatic texture than it might otherwise have. (The lack of that texture can be illustrated equally by Poe's "Murders in the Rue Morgue," which focuses almost entirely on past events, and by Faulkner's "A Rose for Emily," in which the solution to a mystery and the discovery of a crime occur simultaneously in the discovery of the strand of iron-gray hair.)

Much of Faulkner's writing can be considered in light of such analyses and formal criteria. He wrote some stories that come within the narrower definition of the term "detective story," collected in *Knight's Gambit*, while other works, such as *Sanctuary* (related particularly to the Dashiell Hammett/Raymond Chan-dler "hard-boiled" school of detective fiction) and *Absalom, Absalom!*, or por-tions of works (the fourth section of "The Bear") focus on crime, investigation, and the question "What has happened?" and involve investigators who attempt by their methods and logic to answer this question and determine guilt or motive. In the example already cited, *Intruder*, the novel closely mimics a detective story without perhaps exactly mirroring its structure or characterization. Mick Gidley provides a close examination of the correspondence of the stories in *Knight's Gambit* to established paradigms of the genre, but he provides as well an informed discussion of the affinities between and among Faulkner's major works and the detective genre. He also gives a brief summary of the relevant information on Faulkner's probable reading of detective fiction.

Alternatively, concerning himself with the narrative strategy of withholding information, Robert Dale Parker's *Faulkner and the Novelistic Imagination* provides a broad formal context in which to consider the relations between Faulkner's major fictions and the genre of detective fiction, or the activity of detecting. Two additional works of related interest focus on law and lawyers in Faulkner: Jay Watson's *Forensic Fictions* and J. K. Van Dover and John F. Webb's *Isn't Justice Always Unfair?: The Detective in Southern Literature* (Bowling Green University Popular Press, 1997). These works provide formal, social, psychological, and thematic analyses useful to anyone exploring the influence of the detective genre in Faulkner.

FURTHER READING

Gidley, Mick. "Elements of the Detective Story in William Faulkner's Fiction." *Journal of Popular Culture* 7 (1973): 97–123.

Irwin, John T. " 'Knight's Gambit': Poe, Faulkner, and the Tradition of the Detective Story." *Arizona Quarterly* 46 (1990): 95–116.

O'Brien, Frances Blazer. "Faulkner and Wright, Alias S. S. Van Dine." *Mississippi Quarterly* 14 (1961): 101–107.

Sayers, Dorothy L. "Introduction." *The Omnibus of Crime*. New York: Payson and Clarke, 1929. 9–47.

Skei, Hans. "Faulkner's *Knight's Gambit*: Detection and Ingenuity." *Notes on Mississippi Writers* 13.2 (1981): 79–93.

Volpe, Edmond L. "Faulkner's 'Monk': The Detective Story and the Mystery of the Human Heart." *Faulkner Studies* 1 (1980): 86–90.

Stephen Hahn

DICKENS, CHARLES (1812–1870), British novelist, author of such highly regarded works as *Oliver Twist, Dombey and Son, David Copperfield, Bleak House, Hard Times*, and *Great Expectations*. Faulkner almost always included Dickens when listing authors whom he admired and emulated. "I read some of Dickens every year," he told one group of students (*FIU* 50); and he almost certainly modeled one contemplated ending for his screenplay *The De Gaulle Story* on Sidney Carton's act of sacrificial heroism in *A Tale of Two Cities*. Faulkner praised Dickens, along with Balzac, as a writer who possessed "a concept of a cosmos in miniature" (*FIU* 232). While Dickens's separate works are not as consciously intertwined as Balzac's *La Comedie humaine* or Faulkner's Yoknapatawpha series, Dickens's works, taken as a whole, provide a portrait of nineteenth-century England as comprehensive as Balzac's France or Faulkner's Mississippi. Faulkner was particularly drawn to Dickens's realistic character portrayal, describing Sairy Gamp of *Martin Chuzzlewit* as "a cruel, ruthless woman, a drunkard, opportunist, unreliable, most of her character was bad, but at least it was character." Emphasizing the theme of endurance with which he was so concerned in his own work, Faulkner added, "Mrs. Gamp coped with life, didn't ask any favors, never whined" (*LIG* 251). Perhaps the most obvious parallel between the works of Dickens and Faulkner is a near obsession with initiation stories (bildungsroman) that trace the fate of innocent children as they engage the tragic, fallen world of adulthood. In this connection, David Copperfield might be usefully compared to Ike McCaslin and the young-sters of *Oliver Twist* to the Compson children. It might also be argued that Dickens's Mr. Dombey is a precursor of Faulkner's Thomas Sutpen.

Robert W. Hamblin

DICKINSON, EMILY (1830–1886), American poet. Dickinson published only eight poems during her lifetime; not until *Poems by Emily Dickinson* was pub-lished in 1890 did her poetry receive any critical attention. The success of this volume led to further volumes, including a second series of poems in 1891, letters in 1894, a third series of poems in 1896, and in 1924, the immensely popular *The Life and Letters of Emily Dickinson*. Furthermore, in 1924, Conrad Aiken, the writer for whom the young Faulkner arguably had the most esteem, released *The Selected Poems of Emily Dickinson*.

Although we know that Faulkner read a vast amount of American and English poetry, whether or not he read Dickinson is not documented. Faulkner did not own any of Dickinson's books, nor did he mention her in any published essays or interviews. Some critics, however, have detected Dickinson's influence on Faulkner. In his biography of Faulkner, David Minter traces Dickinson's influ-ence on Faulkner's poetry. Minter writes that "in 'Diana' we meet one who . . . 'turns to night, and weeps, and longs to die'; in other words we find a perspec-tive, like Emily Dickinson's in 'Because I Could Not Stop for Death,' that is distinctly post-mortem" (21).

Peter Hays traces a more direct link between Dickinson and Faulkner, arguing that because Conrad Aiken ranked some of Dickinson's poems "among the finest written by any American poet," Faulkner almost certainly was familiar with Dickinson's poetry (107). Pointing out such similarities as reclusiveness, having overprotective fathers, and a "shared fascination with death" (108), Hays claims that the model for Miss Emily Grierson in "A Rose for Emily" is the popularized persona of Emily Dickinson. According to Hays, "Dickinson's myth provided him with a woman who was overprotected by her father, denied marriage, became a recluse, and was intrigued with a dead lover (whether man or God), all of which he used in his story" (109). The hypothesis that Emily Grierson is indeed modeled after Emily Dickinson also, as Minter argues, pro-vides a logical explanation for why Faulkner offers a rose for Emily. Both Dickinson's prevailing themes of death and alienation, as well as her status as a neglected poet in her lifetime, reveal obvious affinities with Faulkner.

FURTHER READING

Hays, Peter L. "Who Is Faulkner's Emily?" *Studies in American Fiction* 16.1 (1988): 105–110.

Rebecca Rowley

DILSEY. *See* **Gibson, Dilsey**.

"DIVORCE IN NAPLES," a short story by Faulkner, was published in the short story volume *These 13* (1931) and republished in *Collected Stories*. The story has been included in at least one anthology of gay literature, *The Other Persuasion*. "Divorce in Naples" owes its origins to Faulkner's sojourn in Europe from July to December 1925 and to the closely related *Elmer* narrative that he wrote during this time. A first-person narrator tells the story of a group of merchant sailors out for a night of drinking and debauchery in Naples, with special attention to the homoerotic relationship or "marriage" of George and Carl, the messman and the messboy, respectively. George, a "big and black" Greek man, intends on this night that Carl, a small, blond, eighteen-year-old boy, should lose his virginity with a woman. But when George returns from the bathroom to discover that Carl has run off with an Italian woman, whom Carl later discovers to his disgust to be a prostitute, he is overcome with drunken rage and despair. When he is detained for not paying the bill, George hastily throws some money on the floor and is subsequently arrested for insulting "the king's majesty by placing foot on the king's effigy on a coin." George is eventually freed from jail and returns to the ship, waiting in despair for Carl's return. Carl returns after two or three days, but he and George ignore each other for five days more, until the ship leaves the port of Naples and heads out to sea, when they are reconciled. Dancing in their undershirts to the music of a Victrola, they join together in "decorous embrace, their canvas shoes hissing in unison."

FURTHER READING

Volpe, Edmond L. "A Tale of Ambivalences: Faulkner's 'Divorce in Naples.' " *Studies in Short Fiction* 28 (1991): 41–45.
Zeitlin, Michael. "Faulkner and Psychoanalysis: The *Elmer* Case." *Faulkner and Psychology*, ed. Kartiganer and Abadie. 219–241.

Michael Zeitlin

DIXIECRATS is the popular name given to the Southern conservative, or "states' rights," wing of the Democratic Party that opposed the civil rights policies of the Truman administration in the 1948 presidential campaign. Upset by the president's decisions to integrate the armed forces and to lobby Congress to pass legislation to enforce nondiscrimination in all areas of American life, the Dixiecrats met in a rump convention in Birmingham, Alabama, on July 17, 1948, and chose Governor Strom Thurmond of South Carolina and Governor Fielding Wright of Mississippi as their candidates, respectively, for president and vice president in the fall election. By denying the national Democratic Party the traditional support of the "Solid South" and perhaps thereby throwing the election into the House of Representatives, the Dixiecrats hoped to force Truman to abandon or modify his civil rights program. These efforts failed, however, as the Dixiecrats carried only four states (Alabama, Louisiana, Mississippi, and South Carolina) and Truman won reelection.

Faulkner's *Intruder in the Dust*, written in early 1948 as the Dixiecrats initiated their anti-Truman, anti-Northern campaign, is in part—both literally in the speeches of Gavin Stevens and symbolically in the actions of Lucas Beauchamp, Chick Mallison, and the other "intruders"—a commentary on the Dixiecratic position. While Faulkner agreed in principle with states' righters in their opposition to outside intervention in Southern affairs, he deplored the racism that inspired and fueled the movement; as he told an interviewer just days before the presidential election: "I'd be a Dixiecrat myself if they hadn't hollered 'nigger.' I'm a States' Rights man. Hodding Carter's a good man, and he's right when he says the solution to the Negro problem belongs to the South" (*LIG* 60). In effect, as contradictory and ultimately impossible as the effort proved to be, *Intruder in the Dust* may be viewed (as it was by a number of contemporary reviewers) as Faulkner's attempt to offer a states' rights platform untainted by the scourge of racism.

FURTHER READING

Berman, William C. *The Politics of Civil Rights in the Truman Administration*. Columbus: Ohio State University Press, 1970.
Garson, Robert. *The Democratic Party and the Politics of Sectionalism, 1941–1948*. Baton Rouge: Louisiana State University Press, 1974.
Hardwick, Elizabeth. "Faulkner and the South Today." *Partisan Review* 15 (October 1948): 1130–1135.

Robert W. Hamblin

DOCTOR MARTINO AND OTHER STORIES (1934), Faulkner's second volume of short fiction, contains twelve previously published stories that had appeared between 1930 and 1934 in *Harper's, Scribner's, Story*, the *Saturday Evening Post*, and *American Mercury*, along with "The Leg" and "Black Music," which Faulkner had "finally despaired of selling" (1974 *FAB* 844). With only a few exceptions, its stories (some written as early as the mid- to late 1920s) are generally inferior to those in *These 13*, although Faulkner's stories became more marketable after the 1931 publication of *Sanctuary*. Apart from "Wash" and "The Hound," Millgate comments, "none of the stories showed Faulkner at his best" (*Achievement* 264). Contemporary reviews were generally less than complimentary, judging the stories to be "slighter and more artificial" than his earlier short fiction, according to F. T. Marsh of the *Herald Tribune*. While reviews from abroad were the most favorable, *Time* labeled the stories "merely potboilers" (qtd. in 1974 *FAB* 844).

The stories in *Doctor Martino* show Faulkner experimenting with a variety of subjects, settings, and narrative techniques, as well as moving toward subsequent novels. "Wash," the volume's best story, anticipates *Absalom, Absalom!* as it enters the decaying Southern village world of Thomas Sutpen and his dehumanizing mistreatment of the poor white Wash Jones's granddaughter. Entering his protagonist's thoughts sparingly in a tightly constructed narrative,

Faulkner depicts Wash's rediscovery of the dignity that Sutpen denies him and his family, even as it costs Wash his life. "The Hound" also takes place in Jefferson and later became the Mink Snopes–Jack Houston episode in *The Hamlet.* "Mountain Victory," which shifts to post–Civil War Tennessee, depicts another fatally heroic gesture by a poor white boy who opposes his pro-Union family's plan to murder a one-armed, gentlemanly returning Confederate veteran to whom the family's daughter is attracted.

"There Was a Queen" shifts to the post–World War I South and its female survivors to portray the end of an era of gentility (and perhaps sound a note of anti-Semitism). "Death Drag" and "Honor" both concern wing-walking veterans, with the former focusing on spiritually enervated veterans for whom money has become life's prime object and the latter depicting a love triangle with potentially destructive consequences. "Fox Hunt" obliquely treats another adulterous relationship through parallels to the title action, whereas "Elly" features a manipulative tease who attempts to kill her grandmother when she threatens to report her promiscuous behavior.

Faulkner began his forays into the detective story with "Smoke," which is firmly grounded in the Poe/Doyle tradition and later became the lead story in *Knight's Gambit* (1949). A number of the *Doctor Martino* stories contain supernatural elements, although they do not rank among Faulkner's best. "Black Music" has the tone of a detective story as the narrator learns the secret of an exile whose one-day foray as a faun has made his return home impossible. The plot in "Dr. Martino" hinges on a brass rabbit that a young girl is convinced has magical powers, whereas "Beyond" takes place in a parklike spiritual afterlife, where the agnostic Robert Ingersol, among others, directs a deceased judge awaiting judgment in the search for his son, who died in a riding accident at ten years of age. "The Leg," which features a haunting by an amputated limb, is the collection's weakest story.

Several of the stories from *Doctor Martino* were included in *Collected Stories.* "Wash," "Honor," "Dr. Martino," "Fox Hunt," "There Was a Queen," and "Mountain Victory" appear in "The Middle Ground" section; "Turnabout" was added to the war stories in "The Wasteland," section IV; "Death Drag" and "Elly" were incorporated as the middle stories in "The Village" section; and "Beyond," "Black Music," and "The Leg" became the first half of the final group, which assumed the name of the opening story. "The Hound" and "Smoke" were integrated into *The Hamlet* and *Knight's Gambit*, respectively.

Robert M. Luscher

"DOCTOR MARTINO"/"DR. MARTINO," a short story by Faulkner, first appeared as "Doctor Martino" in the November 1931 issue of *Harper's* and later as the title story in *Doctor Martino and Other Stories* (1934). It is also included in *Collected Stories.* The story's main theme concerns the power of platonic love, via the mysterious affinity between a young woman and an older, infirm gentleman. Dr. Martino, suffering from an unnamed potentially fatal heart ailment, summers at the same resort as Louise King and her mother. For fifteen years, he draws his strength from her, and she learns from him that courage can be gained by facing her fears. In order to break Dr. Martino's hold on Louise, Mrs. King plots to have Hubert Jarrod fall in love and eventually marry Louise. As he spirits her away from the resort, Jarrod understands that she sees marriage as merely another fear that must be conquered. Dr. Martino is found dead back at the resort.

FURTHER READING

Knieger, Bernard. "Faulkner's 'Mountain Victory,' 'Doctor Martino,' and 'There Was a Queen.' " *Explicator* 30 (1972): item 45.
Lang, Beatrice. " 'Dr. Martino': The Conflict of Life and Death." *Delta* 3 (1976): 23–32.

Larry Wharton

DOHERTY, META. *See* **Carpenter, Meta Doherty**.

"DON GIOVANNI," an early short story by Faulkner, was written in New Orleans between January and July 1925 but was not published until it appeared in *Uncollected Stories of William Faulkner* (1979). The protagonist, Herbie, like Ernest Talliaferro of *Mosquitoes* (who is in turn partly modeled on Leopold Bloom of James Joyce's *Ulysses*), is both a thirty-two-year-old widower with thinning hair and a wholesale buyer of women's undergarments. Oppressed by celibacy and determined on this night to be "bold" and "indifferent" and so achieve the sexual "domination" of a woman (any woman), he experiences only a characteristic form of erotic humiliation: He is coolly rebuffed by the woman and displaced by a larger, more "masculine" man. Herbie belongs in that line of nervous Faulknerian protagonists running from Elmer Hodge of *Elmer* through Ernest Talliaferro of *Mosquitoes*, Horace Benbow of *Flags in the Dust* and *Sanctuary*, Quentin Compson of *The Sound and the Fury*, the reporter of *Pylon*, and Harry Wilbourne of *If I Forget Thee, Jerusalem*.

FURTHER READING

Zeitlin, Michael. "Faulkner in Nighttown: *Mosquitoes* and the *Circe* Episode." *Mississippi Quarterly* 42 (1989): 299–310.

Michael Zeitlin

DOSTOEVSKY, FYODOR. *See* **Russia**.

DOUBLE DEALER, THE, a literary magazine, originated in New Orleans in January 1921, the brain child of a group of poets and newspapermen, including John McClure and Julius Friend, and continued five and a half years. The founders, inspired to action by H. L. Mencken's description of the South as "the Sahara of the Bozart," subtitled their review "A National Magazine from the

South.'' They shared with the Nashville Agrarians a desire to see an end to the sentimental romanticism that had dominated Southern literature since the Civil War. Their success is suggested by Mencken's praise of the magazine and by the list of contributors, including Sherwood Anderson, Hart Crane, Faulkner, Ernest Hemingway, Ezra Pound, John Crowe Ransom, Allen Tate, Robert Penn Warren, and Thorton Wilder. Faulkner's first appearance in *The Double Dealer*, in the June 1922 issue, was a poem entitled ''Portrait.'' In New Orleans in 1925, he became friends with the editors, and subsequently they published several of his essays, reviews, and poems, as well as a series of sketches under the title ''New Orleans.''

W. Kenneth Holditch

DRAKE, TEMPLE, the central character in two of Faulkner's novels, *Sanctuary* and *Requiem for a Nun*. In *Sanctuary*, Temple, seventeen years old, is kidnapped and raped by a Memphis bootlegger and then succumbs to the immorality of the underworld. In *Requiem for a Nun* she is rehabilitated into a sense of sin and redemption. Critical attention to this character provides an indicator of the shifting sense of sexual responsibility in this century. Early criticism found Temple largely at fault for her rape, due to the way she dressed and conducted herself. More recently, critics have questioned that judgment and have found her a victim of the various social pressures bearing upon female adolescent development, pressures that often border on the obscene. Actions taken by Temple after her rescue from the Memphis whorehouse are equally controversial. She falsely accuses one man of murder, in *Sanctuary*, while in *Requiem* she plans to run away from her husband and child, back to the criminal world. In many respects, Faulkner's creation of Temple Drake marks the intersection of a number of major feminist issues this century, including female agency, the social construction of feminity, and pornographic representation. Postmodern theories of the self are illustrated in this characterization, too, as Temple Drake seems to possess no integral being but rather adapts herself to the demands of a series of social (and antisocial) situations.

FURTHER READING

Bassett, John E. ''*Requiem for a Nun*: Revising Temple Drake.'' *Heir and Prototype*, ed. Ford. 48–58.

Degenfelder, Pauline. ''The Four Faces of Temple Drake: Faulkner's *Sanctuary, Requiem for a Nun*, and the Two Film Adaptations.'' *American Quarterly* 28 (1977): 544–560.

Muhlenfeld, Elisabeth. ''Bewildered Witness: Temple Drake in *Sanctuary*.'' *Faulkner Journal* 1.2 (1986): 43–55.

Urgo, Joseph R. ''*Sanctuary* and the Pornographic Nexus.'' *Novel Frames: Literature as Guide to Race, Sex, and History in American Culture*. Jackson: University Press of Mississippi, 1991. 77–112.

Joseph R. Urgo

"DRY SEPTEMBER," a short story by Faulkner first published in *Scribner's Magazine* in January 1931 and subsequently revised and collected in *These 13* and *Collected Stories*. One of Faulkner's best and most frequently anthologized stories, "Dry September" treats an apparent lynching of a black man, Will Mayes, for the alleged rape of a white woman, Minnie Cooper. One must say "apparent lynching" and "alleged rape" because Faulkner's text, while it supplies strong textual clues that the rape did not occur and the lynching did, actually treats both events indirectly and implicitly, leaving the determination of the facts up to the reader.

Told in third person and masterfully plotted in five separate vignettes, the story opens on a Saturday evening in the communal setting of a Jefferson barbershop, where a group of white men are discussing the rumor, which has spread "like a fire in dry grass," of the alleged rape. Most of the men, already persuaded that the rumor is true, advocate organizing a lynch party; one, McLendon, a former soldier and a precursor of the vicious Percy Grimm in *Light in August*, enters the shop armed with "a heavy automatic pistol" and assumes leadership of the group. Hawkshaw, one of the barbers and an acquaintance of the suspect, advises caution and restraint: Will Mayes, he insists, is "a good nigger"; besides, Minnie Cooper's claim is highly suspect, since she is "about forty" and "unmarried" and "this isn't the first man scare she ever had." For such statements Hawkshaw is called a "damn niggerlover" and accused of being a Northerner. Section I ends with most of the men leaving with McLendon to look for Mayes; Hawkshaw follows, hoping somehow to prevent mob violence.

Section II temporarily suspends the action of the vigilantes to present a brief biographical portrait of Minnie Cooper. Once possessed of "a slender, nervous body and a sort of hard vivacity which had enabled her for a time to ride upon the crest of the town's social life," but later jilted by the one man who seemed to represent her only chance of marriage, she now lives out the "furious unreality" of her "idle and empty days" chiefly among women: sharing a house with her mother and aunt, shopping and going to movies with "the other ladies" who are her neighbors and former classmates. Now known to the town as "Poor Minnie," she must contend with the fact that men no longer find her physically attractive: When she puts on a new dress and walks downtown, "the sitting and lounging men [do] not even follow her with their eyes any more."

Section III returns to the actions of Hawkshaw, McLendon, and the vigilantes. Still hoping to dissuade his fellow citizens from their violent intent, Hawkshaw accompanies the group to the ice plant where Mayes works. But Hawkshaw's continuing protests are to no avail: Mayes is abducted, beaten, handcuffed, loaded into McLendon's car, and driven toward "an abandoned brick kiln—a series of reddish mounds and weed- and vine-choked vats without bottom." During the abduction, in what is one of the most puzzling and disturbing details of the story, Mayes "swept his manacled hands across their faces and slashed the barber upon the mouth, *and the barber struck him also*" (emphasis added).

A short while later, apparently convinced that he cannot alter the tragic course of events, and perhaps frightened and repulsed by his own instinctively violent act against Mayes, Hawkshaw leaps from the speeding car, refusing to accompany the kidnappers to their final destination. Not long afterward, as he is walking back to town, Hawkshaw watches as McLendon's car drives past, also returning toward town: The car now has only four occupants, whereas initially there had been six.

Section IV returns the focus to Minnie Cooper, treating her actions on the same evening that the mob abducts and, in all likelihood, kills Will Mayes. She dresses for supper and then afterward, in the company of three of her friends, walks downtown to attend a movie. This time, now that the entire town is aware of her alleged violation, she finds herself the center of attention. The drummers on the courthouse square remark, "That's the one: see? The one in pink in the middle"; and "the young men . . . tipped their hats and followed with their eyes the motion of her hips and legs when she passed." Even Minnie's friends are titillated by the prospect of hearing her story of ravishment: "When you have had time to get over the shock," they tell her, "you must tell us what happened. What he said and did; everything." Described as "feverish" and "trembling" throughout this segment, Minnie manages to control her emotions for a time, but during the movie she breaks out in uncontrollable hysterical laughter and must be led from the theater and taken home to bed. While the text of the story certainly allows for the possibility that Minnie has experienced a nervous breakdown as the result of delayed shock reaction to her assault, a key passage suggests otherwise. As she walks through the town square, all eyes upon her, the reader is told: "She walked *slower and slower, as children eat ice cream, her head up and her eyes bright* in the haggard *banner* of her face . . ." (emphases added). This comparison of Minnie's behavior to the pleasurable way that children eat ice cream seems to imply that it is not the terror of a recollected rape but a heightened pleasure that approaches orgasmic ecstasy that leads to Minnie's loss of self-control.

Section V provides a brief but powerful coda that describes—in language as sexually charged as the previous section—McLendon's return home. It is midnight, and his wife is waiting up for him. Angry at her for "sitting up like this, waiting to see when I come in," he strikes her and then moves on through the house, undressing as he goes, to the back porch, where he stands "panting," seeking relief from the oppressive heat—and probably much, much more. The final sentence of the story, "The dark world seemed to lie stricken beneath the cold moon and the lidless stars," seems a symbolic commentary not merely on the probable fate of Will Mayes but on all of the inhabitants of a "dark world" of racial hatred, violence, sexual frustration, and social irresponsibility. In such a world even the good intentions of a decent man like Hawkshaw become dangerously perverted.

"Dry September" has, deservedly, received a great deal of critical attention. Social and historical critics view Will Mayes as a scapegoat for the sexual and cultural impotence of white Southerners, both male and female. Modernists like the disjointed time pattern and the counterpointing of the Will Mayes and Minnie Cooper narratives. Psychological critics speculate about the complex motivations for the behavior of Hawkshaw, McLendon, and Minnie. Formalists commend the expert handling of imagery and symbolism, especially the recurring use of weather images as a corollary to human emotions. Reader response theorists admire the ambiguities and indeterminancies of the text that require the reader to become actively engaged in the creation of the story and its meanings.

FURTHER READING

Crane, John K. "But the Days Grow Short: A Reinterpretation of Faulkner's 'Dry September.' " *Twentieth Century Literature* 31 (1985): 410–420.

Dessner, Lawrence Jay. "William Faulkner's 'Dry September': Decadence Domesticated." *College Literature* 11 (1984): 151–162.

Ford, Arthur L. "Dust and Dreams: A Study of Faulkner's 'Dry September.' " *College English* 24 (1962): 219–220.

Kerr, Elizabeth M. "William Faulkner and the Southern Concept of Woman." *Mississippi Quarterly* 15 (1961–1962): 1–16.

Nilon, Charles. "Blacks in Motion." *"A Cosmos of My Own,"* ed. Fowler and Abadie. 227–251.

Vickery, John B. "Ritual and Theme in Faulkner's 'Dry September.' " *Arizona Quarterly* 18 (1962): 5–14.

Robert W. Hamblin

"DULL TALE," a short story by Faulkner, is a 1930s revision of "The Big Shot" with the Popeye material and the "Don and I" narrative perspective omitted. Like "The Big Shot," it was not published until *Uncollected Stories.* The plot involves Dal Martin's desire to secure his daughter's membership in the Nonconnah Guards. By offering to build an art gallery named in honor of Dr. Gavin Blount's grandfather, Martin gets the membership. Blount is more contentious in this story, and his background provides more context for his suicide. Martin's daughter, Laverne here, attends the ball and is shunned and humiliated. The story closes with her post-cotillion sobs and Martin's speculations as to what he and Blount might have accomplished together.

Diane Brown Jones

E

EDEN. Our understanding of the Edenic motif in American fiction stems largely from its articulation by three primary critics—R.W.B. Lewis, Leslie Fiedler, and D. H. Lawrence. According to Lewis, as well as numerous other literary historians, *the* most pervasive theme in American literature pertains to Edenic mythology or America as a metaphorical Garden of Eden with its central inhabitant modeled after Adam. From Brockden Brown to William Faulkner, the hero of American fiction is, according to Lewis, the history of the Adamic debate concerning the character's relationship to the Fall or to innocence, which is manifest in a tripartite reaction: "the party of Hope," "the party of Memory," and "the party of Irony" (*American Adam* 7). This triad essentially equates to either a transcendental optimism and a belief in Adamic innocence, a Calvinist pessimism and obsession with Original Sin and the fallen nature of man, and the concept known throughout Western civilization as *felix culpa*, or the belief in the advantageous aspects of the Fall upon man's nature.

In addition to a preoccupation with Adam's spiritual relationship to sin, other concerns and motifs have become evident in the myth's evolution, and the result is a fairly well delineated personality profile. Readers have generally come to expect the Adamic/Edenic metanarrative to include an extensive discourse (and one often highly overdetermined) concerning Adam's relationship to and attitudes toward nature, wilderness, or the garden itself. Additionally, the myth includes Adam's position toward community, family, women, and civilization including its political, economic, and racial issues. Generally Adam rejects all social constructs—hence, his subsequent isolation, rugged individualism, nonconformity, and bachelorhood. The American Adam also demonstrates an equally complex relationship with time, history, and the past.

Of the various American authors who have engaged the myth, Faulkner certainly stands out, demonstrating a thorough, compelling, and long-standing interest. Faulkner's contribution to the Adamic/Edenic myth was deliberate and often overtly apparent, as evidenced by the passage from *The Bear* where Isaac McCaslin tells Cass Edmonds:

[God] made the earth first and peopled it with dumb creatures, and then He created man to be His overseer on the earth and to hold suzerainty over the earth and the animals on it in His name, not to hold for himself and his descendants inviolable title forever . . . but to hold the earth mutual and intact in the communal anonymity of brotherhood, and all that He asked was pity and humility and sufferance and endurance. . . . [M]an was dispossessed of Eden. . . . He used a simple egg to discover to them a new world where a nation of people could be founded in humility.

Ike's speech nicely encapsulates many of the motifs central to the myth of America as the new Garden of Eden: isolation versus community, egotism versus humility, acquisition versus dispensation. As conveyed by this selection and numerous others, Genesis and the question of Adam's stewardship of the land particularly captured the author's imagination.

A close analysis of this thematic concern inevitably draws attention to another, namely, that an inextricable link exists between Adam's treatment of the land and his subsequent relations with other persons. For Faulkner, wrongful use of the land extends to adverse treatment of others. This interrelated characteristic enables readers to distinguish in Faulkner oppositional Adamic types, as epitomized by, say, Thomas Sutpen and Isaac McCaslin, with the former related to the party of Memory and the latter, the Irony. The settlement of the Sutpen Hundred signifies ferocity and human indifference, and Sutpen himself embodies greed, pride, obstinacy, and even cruelty—traits in total antithesis to those esteemed by Faulkner himself. The histrionics of Sutpen are so grandiose that they may blind us to the notion that he not merely represents an isolated case or individual but rather symbolizes a collective Adamic type. Acquiring land by devious or ruthless means, enslaving or mistreating fellow men and women, disregarding or transgressing moral and civic law, and having a brutish, solipsistic, and boundless egotism all characterize one group of Faulkner's Adamic figures who have debased themselves in their overzealous pursuit of some sort of Edenic ideal. From Sutpen to Ab Snopes, Faulkner exposes the various entrapments leading to Adam's fall. In this regard, Faulkner contributes to the long list of Adamic figures in our literature who are bent toward destruction: Brown's Carvin, Hawthorne's Chillingworth, Melville's Ahab, Twain's Hank Morgan, Bellow's Gene Henderson, Theroux's Allie Fox.

Lawrence and Fiedler particularly note Adam's dangerous potential. In his assessment, for instance, of one of the more quintessential Adams, Natty Bumpo, Lawrence observes that he is actually "hard, isolate, stoic, and a killer" (72). More typically, though, readers tend to perceive the American Adam (Cooper's heroes included) as the buckskinned frontiersman who is kind to animals and respectful (if not reverent) of nature. The stereotypical Adam of the Daniel Boone variety escaping from society and finding home in a vast, natural Edenic setting—what Lewis calls "spaciousness"—is definitely a stock figure, and Faulkner certainly contributes to this aspect of the myth as well.

With much frequency, critics point to "The Bear" as Faulkner's definitive Edenic tract. Ursula Brumm, for instance, convincingly likens Sam Fathers to Cooper's Leatherstocking. In addition to similar attitudes toward nature, the characters are alike in other respects as well: "Both are old, illiterate but wise, solitary, kinless, childless, without property and are held by the others in the veneration of an almost extinct species. Their deaths coincide with the death of the wilderness" (127–128). Though childless, Fathers does rear Ike McCaslin, and this fact corresponds with another important motif in the Adamic myth, namely, the bond between the white and ethnic "other." This factor plays handily into Fiedler's thesis concerning homoerotic love between Adam and his ethnic sidekick. The Fathers/McCaslin relationship clearly belongs to that tradition in our fiction featuring such couples as Deerslayer and Chingachgook, Ishmael and Queequeg, Huck and Jim.

An analysis of such unions generally triggers the debate of other closely related aspects of the Adamic/Edenic mythology that have become quite formulaic. Associated with the Edenic, garden, or nature motif is the theme of flight from society or Adam's repudiation of the mainstream community. Of Adam's relation to society, Lewis observes that "the hero" of our literature is "an individual emancipated from history, happily bereft of ancestry, untouched and undefiled by the usual inheritance of family and race; an individual standing alone" (*American Adam* 5). Lewis believes it implicit "that the valid rite of initiation for the individual in the new world is not an initiation *into* society, but, given the character of society, an initiation *away from it* . . . [a] 'deniation' " (15). (In a later piece, one devoted exclusively to Faulkner, Lewis addresses Faulkner's deviations from the more conventional renditions.)

Most emphatically, Faulkner engages the same issues and motifs of which Lewis speaks, though he does so uniquely and rather uncharacteristically. Try as they may, Faulkner's Adamic characters cannot divorce themselves from history, ancestry, family, and race. In fact, their stories usually center around their struggles with such issues or burdens. While Deerslayer, Ishmael, and Huck are orphaned (literally or figuratively) and carefreely take flight, Faulkner's characters never really manage to escape the variables that these others have managed to dodge, lack, or in some cases, readily or conveniently dismiss. True, many of Faulkner's male protagonists reject matrimonial bonds and traditional or conventional communal living, hence resembling the many bachelors in our literature preceding them; however, unlike many of these same predecessors, they simply cannot shake the past with similar efficacy or ease. In this respect their solitude, loneliness, or alienation from mainstream culture widely differs from, say, Cooper's presentation. As Frederick J. Hoffman has so aptly pointed out, history, tradition, and the past weigh heavily on all Faulkner's protagonists, often motivating "the psychology and morality of individual actions" ("Faulkner's Concepts of Time" 337).

While Faulkner's most conventional Adamic character, Ike McCaslin, may be the literary scion of Deerslayer or Leatherstocking in his love of the wilderness and his lamentation at its passing, he does not share their unrealistic Edenic existences. At his twenty-first birthday, he confronts a myriad of postlapsarian complications and ambiguities concerning inheritance—economic, familial, racial. He must wrestle with moral choices, all of which are inextricably linked to the past. His confrontation with ancestry disallows an innocence commonly associated with the party of Hope or those characters created by optimists ranging from Cooper to Thoreau. And for some of Faulkner's other Adamic characters, those in many ways antithetical to Ike, the past or inheritance in all of its many manifestations continues to beset the hero and complicate his life. This is true of such diverse characters as Sutpen or the entire Snopes clan. While Faulkner's characterization of Adam may at times vastly differ from previous renditions, he nevertheless not only demonstrates a profound interest in the mythology but, moreover, has enlarged and enhanced its significance tremendously.

FURTHER READING

Brumm, Ursula. "Wilderness and Civilization: A Note on William Faulkner." *William Faulkner: Three Decades of Criticism*, ed. Hoffman and Vickery. 125–134.

Fiedler, Leslie A. *Love and Death in the American Novel*. New York: Stein and Day, 1966.

Hoffman, Frederick J. "Faulkner's Concepts of Time." *Bear, Man, and God: Seven Approaches to William Faulkner's* The Bear. Ed. Francis Lee Utley et al. New York: Random House, 1964. 337–342.

Lawrence, D. H. *Studies in Classic American Literature*. New York: Viking, 1961.

Lewis, R.W.B. *The American Adam: Innocence, Tragedy, and Tradition in the Nineteenth Century*. Chicago: University of Chicago Press, 1955.

———. "The Hero in the New World: William Faulkner's *The Bear*." *Bear, Man, and God*, ed. Utley et al. 306–323.

Phillips, K. J. "Faulkner in the Garden of Eden." *Southern Humanities Review* 19.1 (1985): 1–19.

Spivey, Herman E. "Faulkner and the Adamic Myth: Faulkner's Moral Vision." *Modern Fiction Studies* 19 (1973–1974): 497–505.

Kathy G. Willingham

EDMONDS. Although members of the Edmonds family are mentioned in a number of Faulkner's post–World War II works, the family's only elaborated appearances are in *Go Down, Moses* and in the short stories out of which that novel was formed. One of the four families—along with the McCaslins, the Beauchamps, and the Priests—descending from Lucius Quintus Carothers McCaslin, the Edmondses appear in *Go Down, Moses* in three generations, depicted only in their male representatives: Carothers McCaslin ("McCaslin") Edmonds, great-grandson of L.Q.C. McCaslin; his son, Isaac ("Zack"); and his grandson, Carothers ("Roth"). The Edmondses function in *Go Down, Moses* to provide a philosophical and political counterweight to Isaac "Ike" McCaslin. Because Ike is born late in his father's life, only a few years before both of his parents die, he is raised by his cousin, McCaslin. In the long debate in the fourth section of "The Bear," eventuating in Ike's relinquishing his inheritance, McCaslin Edmonds opposes to Isaac's visionary idealism a conservative, "parental" attitude toward property ownership, arguing that L.Q.C. McCaslin "bought the land, took the land, got the land no matter how . . . translated it into something . . . worthy of bequeathment." Unlike Isaac, McCaslin Edmonds is willing to overlook the various forms of injustice underlying his great-grandfather's rise. The succeeding two generations extend this characterization of the Edmondses as responsible, if morally opportunistic, Southern property owners. Zack Edmonds appears briefly in "The Fire and the Hearth" in a flashback depicting a near-fatal confrontation with Lucas Beauchamp over Lucas's wife Molly, whose services as housemaid and, Lucas suspects, sexual partner Zack had commandeered after his own wife died in childbirth. In the third generation, Roth appears most prominently in "The Fire and the Hearth" and "Delta Autumn." He is characterized comically in "The Fire and the Hearth" as a modern-day farm owner harassed by governmental regulations and by Lucas Beauchamp's trickery. In "Delta Autumn" his rejection of a nameless black woman, a distant cousin descended through the Beauchamp family line with whom he has fathered a child, brings to a tragic close the novel's depiction of racial and gender injustice, historical amelioration, and property ownership, linking the novel to the immediate circumstances of its composition, at the end of the Great Depression and the beginning of World War II.

FURTHER READING

Kinney, Arthur F. *Critical Essays on William Faulkner: The McCaslin Family*. Boston: G. K. Hall, 1990.

Ragan, Donald Paul. "The Evolution of Roth Edmonds in *Go Down, Moses*." *Mississippi Quarterly* 38 (1985): 295–309.

Zender, Karl F. "Faulkner at Forty: The Artist at Home." *Southern Review* 17 (1981): 288–302.

Karl F. Zender

ELIOT, THOMAS STEARNS (1888–1965), American-British poet and critic, winner of the 1948 Nobel Prize for Literature. The influence of Eliot's poetry on Faulkner's novels is strong and constant, ranging (at least) from verbal echoes of "Prufrock" in *Mosquitoes* to thematic and verbal echoes of *Four Quartets* and "Mr. Eliot's Sunday Morning Service" in *Requiem for a Nun*. Imagery from *The Waste Land* appears in *As I Lay Dying*, and many Faulkner novels suggest the theme of civilization's decline that seems to underlie Eliot's poem. Horace Benbow (*Sanctuary*) and Quentin Compson (*The Sound and the Fury*), among others, have been called "Prufrockian"; Gail Hightower (*Light in August*) may owe something to "The Journey of the Magi," given his involvement with "birth" and "death" in the lives of Lena and Joe. Eliot's concept of the "mythical method" that he attributed to Joyce's *Ulysses*, and that he practiced in his own conflations of mythic, folkloric, and literary materials, may be seen in Faulkner's richly complex intertextuality throughout his career.

FURTHER READING

Dickerson, Mary Jane. "*As I Lay Dying* and *The Waste Land*: Some Relationships." *William Faulkner's* As I Lay Dying: *A Critical Casebook*. Ed. Dianne L. Cox. New York: Garland Publishing, 1985. 189–197.

Gwynn, Frederick L. "Faulkner's Prufrock—and Other Observations." *Journal of English and Germanic Philology* 52 (1953): 63–70.

Polk, Noel. "Afterword." *Sanctuary: The Original Text*. Ed. Noel Polk. New York: Random House, 1981. 293–306.

Glenn Meeter

"ELLY," a short story by Faulkner, first appeared in *Story IV* in February 1934. Included in *Doctor Martino and Other Stories* and in *Collected Stories*, the story presents a complex relationship between desire and guilt and the often suffocating confines of family. A young woman, Elly (Ailanthia), longs to escape her family, especially the watchful eyes of her grandmother and namesake, and the town in which she lives. She runs off with and loses her virginity to Paul de Montigny, who is rumored to have black blood. After Paul refuses to marry her, she causes a wreck that kills both him and her grandmother, although she is unscathed.

FURTHER READING

Bradford, Melvin E. "Faulkner's 'Elly': An Expose." *Mississippi Quarterly* 42 (1989): 273–280.

Petry, Alice Hall. "Double Murder: The Women in Faulkner's 'Elly.' " *Faulkner and Women*, ed. Fowler and Abadie. 220–234.

Volpe, Edmond L. " 'Elly': Like Gunpowder in a Flimsy Vault." *Mississippi Quarterly* 42 (1989): 273–280.

Larry Wharton

ELMER, written in Paris between August and October 1925, was Faulkner's second major attempt to write a novel, but he left the manuscript unfinished after about 40,000 words. *Elmer* was first published in *Mississippi Quarterly* in 1983. In Thomas McHaney's apt formulation, alluding to Joyce's *A Portrait of the Artist as a Young Man* (1916), *Elmer* may be read as Faulkner's "comic portrait of the artist," an early attempt by Faulkner to carry out a fictional self-analysis of his own deepest artistic and psychological sources. In this sense, *Elmer* may also be read as a kind of Freudian case study of the psychosexual history of the protagonist, Elmer Hodge, who aspires to be a painter. In accordance with its psychological focus, Faulkner throughout *Elmer* attempts to develop appropriate formal definitions of mental realities. Thus he experiments with various "stream-of-consciousness" textures and invents some strikingly original representations of fantasy, memory, and repression. It would be hard to overestimate the long-range effects of this narrative project upon Faulkner's subsequent work; for in *Elmer*, Faulkner establishes the principle that everyday family relations and the unconscious fantasy life to which they give rise could constitute the material and influence the structure of high modernist art. *The Sound and the Fury*, completed just three years after *Elmer*, is perhaps the century's most spectacular manifestation of this principle.

Given its attempt to render psychosexual experience, *Elmer* does not unfold in a conventional (that is, linear and progressive) manner. Rather, *Elmer* is arranged in fragments that are linked by interconnecting patterns—or "complexes"—of imagery. The central pattern involves Elmer's memory of his long-lost sister, Jo-Addie, whom Elmer loved with the most innocent, sensual, and intense of childhood passions, reminding one of Benjy Compson's love of Caddy in *The Sound and the Fury*. When Jo-Addie runs away from home, she sends her brother a box of paint tubes—transitional and "fetish" objects that enable Elmer to "sublimate" into fantasy and artistic expression the full intensity of the lost incestuous love of his childhood.

The most highly significant of these paint tubes, which Elmer obsessively fondles, is a red one, the color operating as a kind of gateway not only to Elmer's fantasy of his sister's hermaphroditic ambiguity (she used to wear a "twisted ropish length of bright red cloth" beneath her clothes) but also to the distorted memory of an early childhood trauma, the burning of the family house. As the house burns, the infant Elmer stands naked, lost, and ashamed, his back exposed to the heat of the flames as he is suddenly pressed claustrophobically against his mother and then covered by a strange, unidentified woman. In one form or another as he passes through the inevitable stages of childhood, adolescence, and adulthood, Elmer is destined to relive and "act out" the essential patterns of this highly charged emotional scene. One graphic example of the symbolic repetition of childhood experience occurs in Elmer's ludicrous military accident with a fondled grenade, when Elmer's back is again lacerated and burned, his naked back exposed to the view of the hospital nurses, "women young and old."

In sum, *Elmer* gives us a young fetishist obsessed with tubes of paint and other things such as cigar stubs; describes the infant Elmer's rich fantasy life and erotically charged relations with sister and mother; follows the growth in him of defensive moral forces, like shame and disgust, as well as his first aesthetic impulses and aspirations; and renders the history of Elmer's compulsive selection of love-objects—an older schoolboy, a schoolteacher, Velma, Myrtle, an Italian prostitute, Ethel—all of whom are determined to a greater or lesser degree on the model of childhood prototypes. The narrative breaks off after a nightmarish scene in which Elmer returns to Houston following his European sojourn and encounters his ex-lover Ethel and their five-year-old bastard son.

In exploring the entangled fantasies of incest, fetishism, narcissism, and gender ambiguity—fantasies lying at the root of Faulkner's artistic power—*Elmer* is thematically and intertextually linked with such figures as Ernest Talliaferro and Gordon of *Mosquitoes*, Horace Benbow and Narcissa of *Flags in the Dust* and *Sanctuary*, and the Compson children of *The Sound and the Fury*.

FURTHER READING

McHaney, Thomas L. "The Elmer Papers: Faulkner's Comic Portraits of the Artist." *A Faulkner Miscellany*, ed. Meriwether. 37–69.
Meriwether, James B. "Foreword" to *Elmer. Mississippi Quarterly* 36 (1983): 339–342.
Zeitlin, Michael. "Faulkner and Psychoanalysis: The *Elmer* Case." *Faulkner and Psychology*, ed. Kartiganer and Abadie. 219–241.

Michael Zeitlin

"ERROR IN CHEMISTRY, AN," a short story by Faulkner, first appeared in *Ellery Queen's Mystery Magazine* in June 1946, winning second prize in the magazine's best story contest. Later included in *Knight's Gambit*, the story treats the theme of hubris. Joel Flint, an "outsider" and an ex-carnival illusionist (Signor Canova), kills his wife of two years, is arrested, then escapes from jail. Flint kills, then masquerades as, the father-in-law, old man Pritchell. Narrated by Gavin Stevens's nephew (Charles "Chick" Mallison), the title refers to one part of Flint's undoing. While mixing a toddy, Flint/Pritchell pours whiskey into the glass with sugar. As all Southerners, and Pritchell especially, know, the sugar is mixed with water, then the whiskey is added. Stevens attributes the mistake to the Signor Canova's prideful and unnecessary flaunting of his skill before the authorities.

Larry Wharton

"EVANGELINE," an early short story by Faulkner. Although submissions of "Evangeline" are recorded as early as 1931, the story was not published until 1979, when it appeared in the November issue of *Atlantic*. It was subsequently reprinted in *Uncollected Stories*. "Evangeline" opens with a challenge from "Don" to the journalist "I" to solve the mystery of the Sutpen house. An aged and dying Henry Sutpen has lived secretly in his father's house for forty years. He kills his sister's husband Charles Bon because Charles has another wife in New Orleans. This relationship is irrevocable in Henry's view because the first wife is racially mixed. Raby Sutpen's devotion to Judith and Henry has been that of a sibling. Faulkner found important use for the subject matter, namely, Sutpen's story in *Absalom, Absalom!*

FURTHER READING

Cornell, Brenda G. "Faulkner's 'Evangeline': A Preliminary Stage." *Southern Quarterly* 22.4 (1973): 22–41.
Ryan, Steven T. " 'Mistral' and 'Evangeline': The Gothic Derivation of *Absalom, Absalom!" Kentucky Review* 5 (Autumn 1983): 56–71.

Diane Brown Jones

F

FABLE, A, a novel by Faulkner, was published in 1954. Even though it was accompanied by feature stories in *Life* and *Newsweek* and won a Pulitzer Prize and the National Book Award, some of the more astute critics, and Faulkner himself, were not convinced that it matched his earlier great fiction. One indication of its problematic status was its gestation period. The original idea—and it was an idea rather than an animating image as had been the case with *The Sound and the Fury*—came to Faulkner in Hollywood in 1943. Its focus was to fall on an Unknown Soldier who was also Jesus Christ. At the time, Faulkner spoke of it as "a fable, an indictment of war" (1974 *FAB* 1152). Faulkner spent the next decade working on his big book; at times he thought it promised great things, and at others, he suspected that it was not quite going to work. By the year of its publication, the focus had shifted. In an unpublished preface Faulkner asserted that "[t]his is not a pacifist book"; that "pacifism does not work"; and that it represented the viewpoint that "there is evil in the world and I'm going to do something about it" (1974 *FAB* 1493–1495). Such radical shifts portended no good for *A Fable*. Indeed, the novel had a lot to overcome. Overall Faulkner's ambition was that *A Fable* would, like Dostoevsky's *The Brothers Karamazov* or Thomas Mann's *The Magic Mountain*, depict human culture in urgent dialogue with itself through engagement with the seminal dilemmas of its informing traditions.

At first glance, *A Fable* could not have been more different from Faulkner's major work. Set in France in Easter week of 1918, the novel unfolds by backing and filling, cutting and fading, over ten chapters. The core of the novel concerns the efforts of a Corporal in the French army and twelve of his men to organize soldiers on both sides of the lines to lay down their arms and effect a cease-fire. Ultimately, this mutiny fails when the commanding officers on both sides of the lines agree to quash it. After meeting with the commander of the French army, the "Old General," and engaging in an extended philosophical exchange in a setting reminiscent of Jesus' temptation by Satan in the Wilderness, the Corporal is captured and put to death. But, as it turns out, the Corporal's body is chosen inadvertently to become the body buried in the tomb of France's Unknown Soldier.

Despite its distance from Yoknapatawpha, there are continuities with the rest of Faulkner's work. Faulkner gestures toward the Southern setting by embedding in his text the story of a jockey and his horse as they make a mock-epic journey around the South—nearly fifty pages of what is the strongest writing in the book. More to the point, Faulkner returns to war itself as the site where a civilization settles its most momentous conflicts, literal and symbolic. The Civil War was certainly that for the United States, while World War I marked the first installment in the decimation of European civilization. It was also a war the psychological effects of which Faulkner had written about in his early fiction.

Yet by concentrating on the mutiny, in part from the perspective of women, Faulkner also vented his skepticism about the virtues of military engagement or the wisdom of settling civilizational conflicts in this way. As mentioned, pacifism *had* been on his mind at the book's inception; and in the face of the Cold War threat of mutual annihilation, which Faulkner was also anything but complacent about, *A Fable* did still carry some deep contempt for, or at least anxiety about, war. Indeed, he had already mocked the Sartorises' derring-do in an early novel, whereas Gail Hightower's grandfather, the chicken thief, was hardly anything but mock-heroic.

As in *The Sound and the Fury*, Faulkner set *A Fable*, literally and symbolically, around the "Easter event." Both books evoke the religious resonances of their central characters but ultimately swerve away from any specific religious message. A modernist reading of both novels would emphasize that they reflect the modern world's essentially ironic relationship to the Christian message of redemption: Lives are sacrificed, but in neither case does a resurrection lend that sacrifice any sort of transcendent resonance. All that remains in *A Fable* is the rhetorically resonant but incomplete vision that Faulkner borrowed from his Nobel Prize address in Stockholm.

More to the point, the Corporal is one of several Faulkner characters—one thinks also of Lucas Beauchamp and Ike McCaslin, as well as the evocation of abolitionist John Brown—who decides to say, "Enough of this." Indeed, where the Corporal differs from Faulkner's earlier characters is that he actually organizes a collective action rather than offering an individual gesture against a morally scandalous condition. In this sense, *A Fable* can be read as a protopolitical novel and marks the culmination of Faulkner's fictional exploration of the difficulty of translating individual gestures into collective, public actions. At the same time, it also points to Faulkner's own career as a public spokesman.

Moreover, *A Fable* also reenacts one of Faulkner's classic scenes of paternal (mis)recognition, exploring once again what John Irwin expressed as the question of whether a man's father is his fate (*Doubling and Incest*). As it turns out, too neatly for a realistic novel but not for a fable, the Old General is actually the father of the Corporal. Thus the two know each other even before they know who each other is. This is a literary-philosophical territory where Hegel meets Freud and calls to mind the exchanges between Quentin and his father in *The Sound and the Fury* and the confrontation of Henry Sutpen and his father in *Absalom, Absalom!* It also recalls the missed (and mis-)recognition between Thomas Sutpen and Charles Bon and between Ike McCaslin and his grandfather, Carothers McCaslin.

There is yet another kind of fictional repetition involved here. The climactic exchange between the General and the Corporal, in which it is often difficult to tell who is saying what, echoes the earlier intellectual-moral "duets" between Gavin Stevens and Chick Mallison in *Intruder in the Dust* and between Ike McCaslin and Cass Edmonds in "The Bear," as well as the paired exchanges both in *Absalom, Absalom!* and the second part of *The Sound and the Fury*. These almost operatically staged exchanges seem to occur in Faulkner's fiction when his characters have reached a political or moral impasse. Fictionally, the resolution, such as it is, comes by parceling out the message between two characters and then making it difficult to say who says what or, in *A Fable*, why who says what:

> " . . . Because man and his folly—"
> "Will endure," the Corporal said.
> "They will do more," the Old General said proudly. "They will prevail—
> Shall we return?"

After this crucial exchange, it is no longer clear how we are supposed to read the Nobel Prize address.

But there are a couple of salient differences that mark off *A Fable*. First, in keeping with its fablelike quality, very few of the characters have specific surnames or are given locations in place, time, or even culture. For a writer who apotheosized the past and place, Faulkner was both daring and unwise to divorce his characters from their roots. The General is an orphan, and the origins of the Corporal and his men are obscure. Other figures, such as the runner, are identified only by their position or function. The effect of all this is to create a sense, not so much of timelessness in the positive sense but of abstraction in the negative sense. As Irving Howe once astutely observed, *A Fable* is too novelistic for the simple requirements of the fable, yet too symbolic and nakedly didactic to be an effective novel. Needless to say, this also affects the novel's status as an effective political novel. We never actually witness the Corporal and his men organizing the soldiers to lay down their arms. The world of the novel thus lacks not so much a mimetic as an illuminative dimension that any fable needs in order to have moral relevance. Indeed, Faulkner strains too hard for significance; as a result the irony of the Corporal's corpse being selected as the Unknown Soldier is less deep than cheap.

A Fable will, one suspects, continue to be judged harshly as fiction. Yet it is important to emphasize that Faulkner took considerable risks with the work. As

Richard Gray has observed, here Faulkner tried, as nowhere else in his fiction, to present the frightening power and independent existence of crowds. Moreover, he caught something essential about political action in concert when he wrote of the possibility of saying " 'we' and not 'I' " in striking contrast with the anonymity of the mob; and he identified the mutiny as an act not of cowardice but of "free men." Nevertheless, finally it was not enough. Too formulaic and too indeterminate at the same time, didactic yet confused, *A Fable* is a work that failed to be as good as Faulkner wanted or readers hoped it would be.

FURTHER READING

Butterworth, Nancy. *Annotations to William Faulkner's* A Fable. New York: Garland, 1989.
King, Richard H. "*A Fable*: Faulkner's Political Novel?" *Southern Literary Journal* 17 (1985): 3–17.
Urgo, Joseph R. "Conceiving the Enemy: The Rituals of War in Faulkner's 'A Fable.' " *Faulkner Studies* 1.2 (1992): 1–19.
———. *Faulkner's Apocrypha.*

Richard H. King

FAIRCHILD, DAWSON, a middle-aged novelist who is the convivial leader of the male group on board the *Nausikaa* in Faulkner's novel, *Mosquitoes*. Generally considered to be based on Sherwood Anderson, Fairchild is an indefatigable drinker, talker, and philosophizer, with a tremendous capacity for disrupting Mrs. Maurier's plans. His various pronouncements on the nature of art, words, poetry, creativity, and sex are fascinating ground for readers concerned with Faulkner's early aesthetics. His notoriously reductive remarks about women have also attracted vigorous feminist commentary. Fairchild is memorable, besides, for spinning the comic epic of the adventures of old man Jackson—some of the most preposterous tall tales in Faulkner.

FURTHER READING

Rado, Lisa. " 'A Perversion That Builds Chartres and Invents Lear Is a Pretty Good Thing': *Mosquitoes* and Faulkner's Androgynous Imagination." *Faulkner Journal* 9.1–2 (1993–1994): 13–28.

Pamela E. Knights

FALKNER, DEAN SWIFT (1907–1935), brother to William Faulkner, the youngest son of Murry and Maud Falkner. Handsome and popular, Dean was an outstanding athlete, both in high school and at the University of Mississippi. Later, William financed and encouraged Dean to take up flying and to become a member of the "Flying Faulkners." Tragically, Dean was killed at age twenty-eight in a plane crash during an air show near Pontotoc, Mississippi. The brother's death was one of the most painful experiences in William's life.

Darcy Schultz

FALKNER, JOHN WESLEY THOMPSON (1848–1922), Faulkner's grandfather. He named William after his own father, William Clark, and after Faulkner's father, Murry Cuthbert Falkner. Son of "the Old Colonel," J.W.T. was called "the Young Colonel" by relatives and servants, although he had not fought in any wars. William's bad money habits—giving it or loaning it to relatives and spending it freely—he inherited from his Grandfather Falkner. William was also favorably influenced by him as a storyteller.

Darcy Schultz

FALKNER, MAUD BUTLER (1871–1960), William Faulkner's mother. "Auntee" (Mary Holland Falkner) introduced her to Murry Falkner, whom she married on November 8, 1896. A graduate of Women's College in Columbus, Mississippi, Maud continued her mother Leila's artistic bent. If she had any ghosts, it would have been being left with her mother to shift for themselves after her father, the town marshal of Oxford, absconded with the city's funds and eloped with his mistress, reportedly a mulatto. In contrast to Murry, both Maud and her mother were Baptist teetotalers, and Maud was active in community groups, which formed the heart of Oxford society. Hers was an extended family of three generations in which, especially after the death of J.W.T. Falkner (the Young Colonel) in 1922, the women dominated. As one of the foremost influences in her son's life, she bequeathed to him her literary bent, her artistic ability, her small stature, and her high expectations. Although her devotion did not always apply to his work (she refused to read his first novel), she never deserted him. Frederick Karl records that she even sold her diamond ring to pay off one of Faulkner's debts (144). He in turn wrote to "Moms" when away (see *Thinking of Home* and *Selected Letters of William Faulkner*), visited her daily when in Oxford, took her with him on trips, and dedicated *The Marble Faun* to her. Maud was not fond of Faulkner's wife Estelle, whose manners she disdained; and this antagonism made her situation even more difficult when she became dependent on William after Murry's death in 1932, remaining so until her death at eighty-eight on October 16, 1960, only two years before Faulkner died.

FURTHER READING

Dahl, James. "A Faulkner Reminiscence: Conversations with Mrs. Maud Falkner." *Journal of Modern Literature* 3 (1974): 1026–1030.

Darcy Schultz

FALKNER, MURRY CHARLES, JR. (1899–1975), William Faulkner's brother. A veteran of both World War I and World War II, Murry, better known as "Jack," completed law school at the University of Mississippi and served for more than thirty years as a special agent of the FBI. In his memoir *The Falkners of Mississippi*, Jack provides much insight into his brother's character, noting that he "patterned his life after the Old Colonel's" (6). Of William's acceptance of a postmaster position, Jack said, "It never ceased to amaze us all. . . . Here was a man so little attracted to mail that he never read his own being solemnly appointed as, one might say, the custodian of that belonging to others" (1974 *FAB* 338).

Darcy Schultz

FALKNER, MURRY CUTHBERT (1870–1932), William Faulkner's father. Murry attended the University of Mississippi for two years, then became involved in the family railroad, working successively as fireman, conductor, engineer, supervisor, and treasurer. In 1902, after the railroad became financially troubled, he moved his family from Ripley to Oxford, where he operated a livery stable, owned a hardware store, and eventually became business manager of the University of Mississippi. Murry's demons were many, possibly stemming from the shadow cast by his own father, J.W.T. Falkner, the Young Colonel. Large and given to fights, he was once shot over a courtship; induced vomiting saved him from hemorrhage and death. Although he had attended college, he was less comfortable in academic culture than in the freedom of the railroad and livery stable—or the ranch in the West that he hoped one day to possess. Unsuccessful in his business ventures, displaced in a home of dominant women, and increasingly given to long bouts of drinking, Murry became less and less central to Oxford, his wife, and the lives of his sons, especially the literary and artistic William. Many of the elements of his character, except the drinking, suggest Jason Compson; only the drinking suggests something of William. At age sixty Murry lost his position at Ole Miss because he refused to ante up a required $500 "voluntary" contribution to Governor Bilbo. After that, Faulkner told Blotner, Murry just gave up (1974 *FAB* 782); he died suddenly on August 6, 1932, at the age of sixty-one. He was buried in the Falkner family plot in St. Peter's Cemetery in Oxford, with the "u" William had adopted added to the name on the tombstone.

Darcy Schultz

FALKNER, MURRY CUTHBERT, II ("CHOOKY") (1928–), William Faulkner's nephew, son of John Fa(u)lkner. Chooky and Faulkner's other nephews would go on airplane rides with Faulkner when the nephews were children. Chooky once had a close call in a two-seater plane William was flying when the engine died. A businessman and insurance agent in Oxford, Chooky attained the rank of brigadier general in the Mississippi National Guard, thus achieving the military rank that "the Old Colonel" dreamed of and sought but never achieved. In recent years Chooky has been a featured presenter at the annual Faulkner and Yoknapatawpha Conference at the University of Mississippi, recounting stories about his uncle and father.

Darcy Schultz

FALKNER, SALLIE MURRY (1850–1906), Faulkner's paternal grandmother, was the wife of John Wesley Thompson Falkner, "the Young Colonel," and daughter of Dr. John Young Murry of Ripley, who was said to have spoken Gaelic, worn a kilt, owned a claymore, and knitted, as a good highlander might. Sallie Murry nursed little William through a siege of scarlet fever in 1901 and was most likely the person who taught him his prayers. Indignant at a plan to erect a monument to the "Greys" on the Ole Miss campus, she resigned from the United Daughters of the Confederacy and helped start plans for another monument to honor all Confederate veterans on the square. With "Miss Rosie" Stone, Sallie Murry is said to have run the Methodist Church. Faulkner took the epitaph for Eula Varner Snopes's gravestone ("Her Children Rise and Call her Blessed") from Sallie Murry's in St. Peter's Cemetery in Oxford.

Charles A. Peek

FALKNER, WILLIAM CLARK (1825–1889), great-grandfather of William Faulkner, was, during the course of a varied and distinguished career, a jailor, lawyer, Confederate colonel, landowner, politician, railroad builder, and author. A principal influence upon the life and work of his famous great-grandson, "the Old Colonel," as Colonel Falkner came to be called, is easily recognizable as the prototype for John Sartoris in *Flags in the Dust* and *The Unvanquished*. Identifiable aspects of Falkner's experience and behavior also appear in the characterizations of Thomas Sutpen and L.Q.C. McCaslin.

Falkner was born somewhere in Tennessee as his family migrated westward, and he spent his early years in Ste. Genevieve, Missouri. About 1840 he traveled to north Mississippi to cast his lot with an uncle who resided there; settling in Ripley, he worked for a time at the local jail, completed a rudimentary education, and began his study of the law. Between 1847 and 1861 he fought briefly in the Mexican War, established a family, practiced law, became a prominent landholder and slave owner, assumed an active role in state politics, and wrote a long narrative poem and a romantic novel. During this period Falkner also became involved in a bizarre and controversial chain of violence that left two men dead at his hand. In the ensuing trials he was exonerated of any wrongdoing, but the scandal and animosity resulting from these incidents continued to hound him for many years.

Joel Williamson, in *William Faulkner and Southern History*, has convincingly argued from census records of the period that during the 1840s and 1850s Falkner may have fathered one or more children by one of his black slaves. While William Faulkner never publicly acknowledged any instances of miscegenation in his family history, his identification of Elnora, the black house servant in the short story "There Was a Queen," as the daughter of John Sartoris suggests that he had at least considered the possibility. Moreover, the introduction of miscegenation in the biographies of Thomas Sutpen and L.Q.C. McCaslin further hints that Faulkner may have been aware of the rumors of Colonel Falkner's mulatto offspring—rumors, as Williamson discovered, that are still current in Ripley among both the white and black populace.

When Mississippi seceded from the Union in 1861, Falkner helped organize a company of soldiers to fight for the Confederacy. Subsequently he was elected as colonel of a regiment of infantry, thus securing the title he would carry for the rest of his life. Proving to be a valiant, if somewhat foolhardy soldier, Falkner was commended for his courage by General Pierre G. T. Beauregard at Manassas Junction. By 1862, however, Falkner had fallen into disfavor with his troops and was voted out as commander. Disappointed but undaunted, he returned to Mississippi, organized an irregular band of cavalry, and reentered the fray. In 1863, partly because of poor health and partly because of his failure to secure the rank of general, he resigned from the Confederate army. According to family tradition, he spent the remaining war years dealing in contraband secured by running the Union blockade that encircled Memphis.

Following the war Falkner returned to the practice of law, restored his plantation, and then—in 1871—entered upon a venture that secured his reputation as an entrepreneur. The Mississippi legislature, in an attempt to speed restoration of railroads destroyed during the war, voted to pay $4,000 per mile to any company that would build a railroad at least twenty-five miles in length. Shortly after this law was passed a charter for the Ripley Railroad Company was issued to W. C. Falkner, R. J. Thurmond, and thirty-five other incorporators. The railroad, which was completed in 1872, extended north from Ripley to Middleton, Tennessee, where it intersected the Memphis and Charleston road. Colonel Falkner, as president and major subscriber, was the principal figure in the construction and early operation of the Ripley Railroad; the town that was founded at the site of the first stop on the route still carries his name: Falkner, Mississippi.

Throughout the next two decades, until his death in 1889, Colonel Falkner was actively involved in the difficult tasks of operating and expanding the railroad and of retaining control of the company. In 1873, when the company defaulted on a loan, the road passed into the hands of a New York holding company; and by 1877 R. J. Thurmond had secured majority ownership. Not until 1886 was Colonel Falkner able to reacquire a controlling interest by purchasing Thurmond's share of the company. According to local rumor, the two men, by this time bitter enemies, drew lots to see which partner would sell his stock to the other. Thurmond lost, though he would later exact a heavy revenge for his defeat. By 1888, with Colonel Falkner in charge, the railroad was merged with other lines to become the Ship Island, Ripley, and Kentucky Railroad; the line had been extended southward to New Albany and Pontotoc; and plans were under way to link the road with a network of track reaching to the Gulf Coast.

In 1880 Falkner took time out from his railroad and real estate enterprises to write a melodramatic novel entitled *The White Rose of Memphis*. Originally serialized in a local newspaper, the early chapters proved so popular that a New York publisher contracted to issue the story in book form in 1881. The novel was an instant success, selling out the first printing of 8,000 copies within a month; and the popularity of the work led to thirty-six subsequent editions, the latest appearing in 1953. Colonel Falkner later authored two additional books— *The Little Brick Church* and *Rapid Ramblings in Europe*—but his literary reputation is based almost solely on *The White Rose of Memphis*. Undoubtedly it was the success of this book that prompted young Billy Falkner to tell his third-grade teacher, "I want to be a writer like my great-granddaddy" (1974 *FAB* 105).

In 1889 Colonel Falkner stood for election to the Mississippi legislature, hoping in part to influence legislation that would benefit his railroad. Siding with one of Falkner's opponents in a virulent campaign was R. J. Thurmond. On the afternoon of November 5, when it had become apparent that Falkner had won his election bid, Thurmond, in a violent act culminating many years of frustration and bitterness, assassinated Falkner on the public square in Ripley. This tragic climax to an adventurous and controversial career would later serve as the basis for one of Faulkner's finest narratives, "An Odor of Verbena," the concluding chapter of *The Unvanquished.*

FURTHER READING

Duclos, Donald Philip. *Son of Sorrow: The Life, Works, and Influence of Colonel William C. Falkner, 1825–1889.* Bethesda, Md.: International Scholars Publishing, 1997.

Robert W. Hamblin

FATHER ABRAHAM, an unfinished prose narrative by Faulkner, was written c. 1926–1927. This manuscript, published as *Father Abraham* (limited edition by the Red Ozier Press, 1983; trade edition by Random House, 1984), develops a narrative parallel to the opening of *The Hamlet,* including the arrival of the Snopeses in Frenchman's Bend and thence Jefferson, as well as material related to the "Spotted Horses" episodes. The text thus provides evidence that Faulkner conceived the broad outlines of the story of the Snopeses before writing *Flags in the Dust* and well before beginning *The Hamlet.* It is also significant that the scene setting in *Father Abraham* is conducted in a mock-heroic style more pointed even than that in *The Hamlet*—for example, introducing an unnamed "he" as symbolic of the "astonishing by-blows of man's utopian dreams actually functioning; in this case the dream is Democracy," suggesting less authorial hostility toward the class of characters treated than is sometimes alleged. Comparing this text with *The Hamlet* reveals Faulkner's deliberate manipulations of language as the story matured for him.

FURTHER READING

Mitgang, Herbert. "Key Faulkner Tale Is Published at Last." *New York Times* 1 June 1983: C14.

Stephen Hahn

FATHERS, SAM, is a major character in *Go Down, Moses*; he also appears in "Red Leaves" and "A Justice." Son of the last of the Chickasaw chiefs, Ikkemotubbe, and a "quadroon" woman whom Ikkemotubbe forced to marry a slave (thus Sam's name denoting dual fathers), Sam was sold to the McCaslin plantation by Ikkemotubbe himself. Sam is notable, however, for independence.

When Isaac implores his cousin Cass, then owner of the plantation, to "let him go!" Cass replies with the obvious: "Did you ever know anybody yet . . . that ever told him to do or not do anything that he ever paid attention to?" Sam is chief of the deep woods, where his word is authority: "Did he do all right, Sam?" Cass asked when Isaac shot his first deer. "He done all right," Sam says. Sam talks to Isaac, as he does to no one else. "And as he talked about those old times and those dead . . . vanished men of another race . . . gradually to [Isaac] those old times would cease to be old . . . and would become a part of [his] present." The effect on Isaac is both profoundly enriching and stunting: Spiritually and emotionally, he stayed in the woods with Sam the rest of his life.

FURTHER READING

Matthews, John T. "Touching Race in *Go Down, Moses.*" *New Essays on* Go Down, Moses. Ed. Linda Wagner-Martin. Cambridge: Cambridge University Press, 1996.
Millgate, Michael. "William Faulkner: Tales of a Grandfather." *Essays by Divers Hands: Being the Transactions of the Royal Society of Literature.* Ed. Richard Faber. Wolfeboro, N.H.: Boydell, 1988. 41–58.
Schliefer, Ronald. "Faulkner's Storied Novel: *Go Down, Moses* and the Translation of Time." *Modern Fiction Studies* 28 (1982): 109–127.

Marion Tangum

FAULKNER, JAMES MURRY ("JIMMY") (1923–), William Faulkner's nephew. In his lectures and stories, Jimmy has provided Faulkner admirers with many insights into the uncle he knew familiarly as "Brother Will." The son of John Wesley Thompson III, William Faulkner's second youngest brother, and Lucille Ramey Faulkner, Jimmy was born in Oxford in 1923. He attended high school in several Mississippi communities, as well as in Whitehaven, Tennessee, graduating from Oxford's University High in 1941. After a brief enrollment at the University of Mississippi, Jim served in World War II as a U.S. Marine Air Corps fighter pilot. Later, he would also see action in the Korean War, earning a Distinguished Flying Cross. In 1950 Jim married Nancy Jane Watson; he operated a construction firm until retiring in 1983. Now a widower, Jim lives on College Hill Road near Oxford at Cedar Hill Farm, an antebellum structure designed in 1850 by the same architect who designed Faulkner's Rowan Oak. His daughter, a champion equestrian, and her husband share the residence. His two sons and his four grandchildren also live in Oxford. With an uncle who won the Nobel Prize for Literature and a father who was a novelist in his own right, Jim has in turn produced a number of magazine pieces and a volume of stories about his illustrious family. A gifted raconteur, Jim has delighted academic audiences all over America with his stories about "Brother Will." Since 1974, Jim has been a staple attraction at the University of Mississippi's Faulkner and Yoknapatawpha Conference. Jim and his uncle shared similar passions and avocations—hunting, aviation, athletics, horses, dogs. Some of Jimmy's attributes might be discerned in Faulkner's characterization of Chick Mallison in *Intruder in the Dust, The Town*, and *The Mansion*. The last family member to see Faulkner alive, Jim drove his uncle to the sanitorium in Byhalia on July 4, 1962. Two days later, Faulkner died of a heart attack. Fittingly, Jim supervised many of the arrangements for Brother Will's last rites.

FURTHER READING

Faulkner, Jim. *Across the Creek: Faulkner Family Stories.*
———. "Brother Will's Passing." *Southern Living* March 1992: 108–109.
Wolff and Watkins, eds. *Talking about William Faulkner.*
Wooly, Bryan. "Remembering Brother Will." *Dallas Morning News* 25 Sept. 1997: C1–3.

David L. Vanderwerken

FAULKNER, JILL (1933–), the daughter of William and Estelle Faulkner. As a young girl, Jill often went with her father to the beach, where he enjoyed telling her stories and watching her play. Jill did not see a great deal of her father while growing up except during certain periods such as her eleventh summer and at age eighteen, when he took her to Europe for his Nobel Prize acceptance. Faulkner spoke at both her high school and junior college graduation exercises and dedicated *A Fable* to her. Jill married Paul D. Summers, Jr., a West Point graduate and lawyer, in 1954. Residents of Charlottesville, Virginia, Jill and her family were influential in Faulkner's acceptance of a writer-in-residence appointment at the University of Virginia in 1957.

FURTHER READING

Inge, Thomas. Introduction. "The Homesick Letters of William Faulkner." *Oxford American* 18 (1997): 44–55.

Darcy Schultz

FAULKNER, JOHN WESLEY THOMPSON, III (1901–1963), William's brother, called "Johncy," often played with William in the woods near Oxford and joined the male members of the family on hunting and fishing trips. One account of William's adult relationship with this particular brother involves William's purchase of Greenfield Farm in 1938. Faulkner insisted on raising mules instead of cattle on the farm despite the protests of John, who managed the farm and who realized the day of the mule was gone. A talented writer and artist, John authored several popular books, including *Men Working* (1941), *Dollar Cotton* (1942), *Chooky* (1948), *Cabin Road* (1951), *Uncle Good's Girls* (1952), and *My Brother Bill* (1963), and executed a number of impressive oil paintings, including several that depict scenes in William's books.

Darcy Schultz

FAULKNER, LIDA ESTELLE OLDHAM (1896–1972), wife of William Faulkner. Estelle came from a Republican and musical family, with connections to generals, bishops, congressional representatives, and Sam Houston. The Oldhams moved to Oxford in 1903, and sometime in youth Estelle reportedly pointed at William as a little boy on his pony and declared she would marry him when they grew up. She attended Mary Baldwin College before entering Ole Miss in 1914. Though in love with Faulkner, she succumbed to pressure from her parents and married Cornell Franklin in April 1918, although she expressed surprise that he had taken their engagement seriously and, at the wedding, voiced doubts as to whether she loved him. Most of her years with Franklin were spent in the Far East, where he held various official positions; but she often returned to Oxford with their two children, Victoria and Malcolm. Faulkner inscribed volumes of his verse to her and saw so much of her during her Oxford visits that he was dubbed Major Oldham's yard boy. Estelle began divorce proceedings against Franklin in 1926, during which she made her first attempt at suicide. In June 1929 she and Faulkner were married near Oxford at College Hill Presbyterian Church or its manse—a marriage Faulkner attributed to both desire and necessity. Estelle again attempted suicide on their honeymoon on the Mississippi Gulf Coast, and she is said to have cried when she first saw the condition of Rowan Oak after Faulkner purchased it in 1930. Patterns of infidelity in her previous marriage, both her and Faulkner's alcoholism, and his extramarital affairs made their marriage difficult. Estelle eventually sought treatment for her drinking and apparently became resigned to her husband's infidelity. She and Faulkner had two daughters, Jill (Mrs. Paul Summers) and Alabama, who died shortly after birth and to whom, along with Estelle, *These 13* is dedicated. Estelle was a partial source for Faulkner's female characters, beginning with Cecily Saunders in his first novel, and she would later provide Faulkner with some story ideas (e.g., "Idyll in the Desert") as well as the title for *Light in August*. Estelle produced a novel in manuscript, "White Beeches," but destroyed it when Boni and Liveright rejected it. She did not attend the Nobel Prize ceremony.

FURTHER READING

Sensibar, Judith L. " 'Drowsing Maidenhead Symbol's Self': Faulkner and the Fiction of Love." *Faulkner and the Craft of Fiction*, ed. Fowler and Abadie. 124–147.

Charles A. Peek

FAULKNER, WILLIAM (1897–1962). The well-documented disasters incumbent on receiving the Nobel Prize did not spare William Faulkner. His award fatally tipped the delicate balance between his two intense desires: one for undisturbed privacy, another for belated recognition. The new desperation with which he gripped both his personal integrity and his public responsibilities contributed to the increasingly destructive behavior that shortened his life. He was buried beneath the cooling shade of trees in St. Peter's Cemetery in the same

Oxford, Mississippi, he had been in the process of leaving. But Oxford (and Ripley and New Albany) and Lafayette County and the Yocona River were unquestionably that life of which he had been exceptionally aware.

Seemingly equally aware of his impending death, he closed off his remarkable chronicle with *The Reivers*, a comic adventure with Freudian implications. He had claimed to know nothing about Freud. But he had never denied being that special kind of thief of time called a writer. And the core of his writing is unquestionably structured by an epic account of the migration of those Scots from whom he was descended, replete with ironies of conflict between Clan— the clandestine, the clannish, the desire to belong—and Celt—the roverman, famous for wanderlust, desiring to be only and purely oneself. That he saw, assuredly at first through a glass darkly but increasingly with more and more clarity, the parallels of these same ironies in the African American culture in proximity to which he grew up gives his work what is quite possibly its most remarkable and controversial feature.

Who was this man, praised by his earliest admirers, especially the French, for his psychological insight and linguistic innovations; condemned by his critics for an obscurely rendered dark vision of an unreconstructed Southern apologist; and eventually seen as the keenest critic of his own social order and the spiritual and material issues composing and facing it? Not surely one author but several, not William Faulkner but several other fellows of the same name.

Born William Cuthbert Falkner in New Albany, Mississippi, on September 25, 1897, he later added the ''u'' to his name just as Hawthorne (a novelist whose influence he disavowed) had added the ''w'' to his. The greatest influences of his youth seem to have been his mother and her artistic interests, the cavalier conception of the Confederacy as a model of adventure and daring, the ''big woods'' as a threatened source of spiritual renewal, and his small physical stature, a goad to his identity-seeking masquerades.

Gifted at drawing, he became a poet in imitation of Keats and Swinburne, then in imitation of Eliot and Joyce, and finally in his own right, creator of ''a keystone in the universe [that], if it were ever taken away, the universe itself would collapse'' (*LIG* 255). He made the novel form a new site for poetry, creating works less parallel to *Tom Jones* and *Oliver Twist* than to the works of Homer and Chaucer. Shelby Foote claims that the frequent distinction of Hemingway as realist and Faulkner as romantic was just the opposite of the truth (Harrington and Abadie, *The South* 155). Indeed, Faulkner's lasting contribution was a paradigm shift in how the real and the poetic might touch, not in angels on the head of pin as the Medievals thought, nor in the pituitary as Descartes postulated, but in the compelling conception of Yoknapatawpha and its analogs on the envelope surrounding his postage stamp of native soil.

Even within the native environs of Bilbo's Mississippi, he was less the rural oaf than his early mentor Phil Stone sometimes seemed to make him out to be. After all, the world came sometimes to Oxford; by 1915 he and Estelle Oldham, his first love and later wife, were going to dances played by W. C.

Handy's Memphis band. For modern Americans, increasingly distanced from the village, it is hard to grasp how important to lives that began there were those outside winds that stirred the native dust. And a quite different world was not so far away, no farther than the juke joints of the Delta. Surprisingly, the Faulkner biographies do not index *bootlegger, brothel, gangster, mobster*, or *underworld* (though Blotner does list *prostitute*). But Faulkner had been where he later followed his creation, Temple Drake, and he would not be the first to have found in the demimonde an escape from the mannered world of his origins, an alternative to Estelle's high-toned social strata, whose adults were not amused with his aspirations. Later, Faulkner would suggest that the job he had been offered as landlord in a brothel would have been perfect (*LIG* 239). But then he also said he would have liked to have been a Lay Reader in the Episcopal Church. Apparently some of Faulkner went out to the Delta, some stayed home.

It may have been through his rougher friends that he discovered New Orleans. In any event, by January 1925 he was there, having left in Oxford his employment at the post office and his volunteer leadership of a Boy Scout troop—both of which he had been forced to resign. He departed just after Estelle arrived there with her husband. Of course, he had been away before: to New Haven and New York and Canada, where he sought to qualify as an RAF (Royal Air Force) pilot. But New Orleans was his first chance to be among a literary community, those around Sherwood Anderson in the Vieux Carré and the larger impetus toward a Southern Renaissance given expression in *The Double Dealer* and *Times-Picayune*, outlets for expanding his own writing interests beyond the apprenticeship poems of *The Marble Faun*.

It was through his association with the *Times-Picayune* that he met, fell in love with, and wrote poetry for Helen Baird, a devil-may-care girl whose mother cared enough to take her to Europe to get her away from this particular devil. Now a Bohemian, the high-toned were still not amused. It was New Orleans where he first told someone he was a genius, and there he developed the idea of Al Jackson, half alligator, half horse, Faulkner's own two halves, the self that would not take a rider and the mannered gentleman who often took to saddle. In New Orleans he wrote his first novel, *Soldiers' Pay*; and he would later use the locale as the setting for other works: *Mosquitoes, Pylon, The Wild Palms*.

In Anderson, Faulkner found encouragement and recognition, but their relationship ended, self-confessedly, in a pattern that was to become typical of Faulkner's relationships: "unhappily." By that time, Anderson was not going anywhere, and Faulkner was on his way—to Europe, immediately France and the shortest expatriation ever (from June when he sailed out of Savannah until September when he arrived in New York) and eventually Sweden (1950 but the Nobel Prize for 1949, his life seemingly filled with such anomalies).

His first trip to Europe, as his letters home to his mother Maud attest, afforded him the chance to experience the newest artistic movements, which helped him to the first transformation of his art and his own craft of revision. And it cata-lyzed his transformation from a son of the South, ever imagining "it's still not yet two oclock on that July afternoon in 1863" (*Intruder in the Dust* 190), to a man of letters destined for the world. His experience, especially of France and of the beautiful innocence of the children in the Luxembourg Gardens, would haunt his feelings and fiction (*Sanctuary*). Yet even while there, he was working on the "Elmer" material that would appear in so much of his later fiction and lead him to the creation of Yoknapatawpha.

Back in the South, but already being transformed by the world outside it, he quickly discovered the apocryphal uses of his own family, black and white (*Flags in the Dust*), and other families (*The Sound and the Fury*); the signifi-cance of the dislocations of his age (*As I Lay Dying*, the *Snopes* trilogy); and the inescapability of the questions that vex American history: race, sex, and nature (*Light in August, Absalom, Absalom!, Go Down, Moses*).

His career now fully under way, Faulkner rejected his own Hightower's ad-vice and married the recently divorced Estelle, apparently both dreading and dearly desiring life with her. It is widely felt they often were not very good for each other, did not treat each other well, and used alcohol to silence the haunting sounds of their sorrow. Less obvious but equally real were the love that drew them to one another and possibly her own talent. In rapid order he became a stepparent and propertied citizen, the purchase of Rowan Oak further establish-ing his personal myth.

Family, of course, but principally their high-maintenance property and rec-reations (his flying, her clothes) created needs for cash and goodly amounts of it, much more than he was earning from his fiction. So he turned to Hollywood and screenwriting. It was there he met and fell in love with Meta Doherty (a.k.a. Carpenter, Rebner), whom he would pick up in the morning, driving over bare-footed—Mississippi in Hollywood. But while there he would long to escape back home to write his novels, and those he did write in later years showed the influence of his movie work—Hollywood in Mississippi.

Hollywood was important for more than paying his bills. There, among the people he met both in the studios and in the scripts, he once again found a world of larger possibilities, some realized in characters in his later fiction; and his immersion in Hollywood's world of images, on-screen and off-, once again transformed his craft as writer, adding to his repertoire the style of subsequent works, especially *Intruder in the Dust* and *The Reivers*.

Still not much in vogue, Faulkner was about to be transformed again, this time by Malcolm Cowley's *Portable Faulkner*. Whatever the controversies over whether Cowley "made" Faulkner's reputation or confined him in categories that delayed full recognition of the richness of his work, the *Portable* most certainly assisted him to new recognition, especially to the Nobel Prize. From the late 1940s on, he emerged as a public presence whose life was moving hectically toward its end.

In Oxford, he met and fell in love with Joan Williams about the time he was starting *Requiem for a Nun* and, in St. Moritz, with Jean Stein as he worked on *Land of the Pharaohs*, another movie for Howard Hawks. Armed with a protective bottle, he was all the while traveling for the State Department as a goodwill ambassador in Latin America and Japan. These appearances gave him a forum in which to address his sense of the century's besetting sin, the diminution of freedom and individuality and the drive toward collectivization. His use of such forums, however, led to his being asked to pronounce judgments on the increasingly heated subject of race, a subject on which his stands had already distanced him from friends and family, from Phil Stone and John Faulkner in particular. Unfortunately, Faulkner often made remarks disappointingly less sensitive and insightful than the portraits in his fiction.

Faulkner soon found himself again on the run from Oxford: Riding to the hounds in fox-hunt pinks seemed more becoming the escutcheon of the Virginia gentleman he had begun to think himself. But he had lived long enough to see a child die shortly after birth, see his and Estelle's daughter Jill, through school and into adulthood and marriage, and see Estelle escape, if not her demons at least the need to drown them. Faulkner escaped only in death, on July 6, 1962, in an asylum at Byhalia, Mississippi, where, as the common answer to his drinking, his nephew Jimmy had taken him. He had taken along Jeremy Taylor's *The Art of Holy Living* and *The Art of Holy Dying*.

An obituary pictorial by Willie Morris and William Styron in *National Geographic* takes us to the place where his often bare feet came to rest deep beneath the shade of trees, his "green woods . . . dreaming here to wake." His whole life had not been writing—he had sailed, golfed, flown, and ridden. But writing had been his life. More and more, we know about his writing; it cannot be said we know even yet much about the man.

Charles A. Peek

FAULKNER READER, THE, a representative collection of Faulkner's work. Part of the celebratory marketing of Faulkner in the wake of the Nobel Prize, this substantial anthology of entire works and of extracts from novels, assembled under the guidance of Saxe Commins, was published on April 1, 1954, by Random House and adopted as a Book-of-the-Month Club selection. This anthology has received less critical attention than *The Portable Faulkner*, but even though it consists of already published material, it is not without interest in itself. Compiled as Faulkner came to the end of his long struggle with *A Fable*, at a time when he was exhausted, depressed, and beset with problems in his personal life, the volume opens, nevertheless, with a specially written foreword, dated November 1953. These pages sound some of the most powerfully upbeat notes in Faulkner's entire career. Their theme, which colors the subsequent selection, is the endurance of the writer in his art. Early memories of books in his grandfather's library lead Faulkner to recall the preface to a historical story by the heroic Polish nationalist writer, Henryk Sienkiewicz—the first foreword, he claims, that, as a boy, he ever took time to read. Sienkiewicz's suggestion that he wrote "to uplift men's hearts" gives Faulkner the clue to his own, and all writers', driving and anguished compulsion to get books written. Whatever else the motivation, the excitement of writing, communicated to others, is "completely selfish, completely personal" because in that way the writer guarantees his immortality: "he can say No to death." By the end of this short essay, even Faulkner's gently amused reminiscences at the start, about the faded romantic fictions bought by Southern women like his grandmother, fall into place as part of the artist's credo. The writer will endure in the "old deathless excitement" engendered from "the isolation of cold impersonal print." This is invulnerable and will remain "capable and potent" long after all that is left of him is "only a dead and fading name."

The foreword is close in spirit to the first item in the selection, the Nobel Prize acceptance speech, with its own affirmations of endurance and immortality, and the truths of the human heart in the face of fear of death. This leads on to the complete text of *The Sound and the Fury*, including the "Compson Appendix" ("They endured"), then to what the dust jacket describes as three "novellas"—in fact, novel excerpts, separated from their larger contexts—to maintain the focus on the themes of man, struggle, and resilience: "The Bear" (*Go Down, Moses*), "Old Man" (*The Wild Palms*), and "Spotted Horses" (*The Hamlet*). Eight short stories follow, all of which continue to be the staple of anthologizers today: "A Rose for Emily," "Barn Burning," "Dry September," "That Evening Sun," "Turnabout," "Shingles for the Lord," "A Justice," and "Wash" (all from *Collected Stories*). Three additional extracts from novels complete the volume: "An Odor of Verbena" (*The Unvanquished*), "Percy Grimm" (*Light in August*), and "The Courthouse" (*Requiem for a Nun*). The final page catches up the echoes of the foreword and of the Nobel Prize address in the striking of the courthouse clock, and the long vistas of hours since Genesis, returning the reader with a flourish to time and eternity, to the "loud dingdong of time and doom."

Pamela E. Knights

FEMINIST APPROACHES examine, among other things, the societal roles, perceptions, and biases that influence an author's views and the literary portrayal of women. In Faulkner's work, which includes numerous perspectives of the role of women in the South, this approach finds fertile ground, as he explores the mythologies, the expectations, and the consequences of his society's views of women, creating portrayals as complex as the fiction itself.

Characters in Faulkner respond to women on multiple levels, beginning with the purely biological. Quentin Compson remembers his father's description: "Delicate equilibrium of periodical filth between two moons balanced." Joe Christmas struggles to deal with the same knowledge: "[T]he smooth and superior shape in which volition dwelled doomed to be at stated and inescapable intervals victims of periodical filth." Both characters share a loathing, even a fear, of women equated with their bodies and bodily functions.

Another level of responses deals with women's sexuality. Faulkner explores, for both male and female characters, the territory beneath society's surface touting of "chasteness" of its women. Whether Quentin Compson's obsession with his sister's loss of virginity (even though his father says, "Purity is a negative state and therefore contrary to nature"), Darl's eerie "knowledge" of his sister Dewey Dell's pregnancy, the rape of Temple Drake, or Rosa Coldfield's "rank smell of female old flesh long embattled in virginity," the issue of women's sexuality recurs.

Along with biology and sexuality, Faulkner shows the conflicts within a society that simultaneously viewed women as inferior human beings and the standard bearers for all that is moral and good. This contradictory outlook creates similarly contradictory characters. A good example is Miss Emily Grierson in "A Rose for Emily." The town spent years glorying in their "pity" for her, only to be shocked after her death by the real events in that house. Caroline Compson claims weakness, sick headaches, and the full burden of the family "dishonor" yet controls everyone in her reach.

The paradoxical paradigm of women results in a range of perceptions and misperceptions about women's power, or lack thereof. Mr. Compson says, in *Absalom, Absalom!*, "Years ago we in the South made our women into ladies. Then the War came and made the ladies into ghosts." This confusion between the ghosts of ladies and actual women can be seen in McLendon in "Dry September," who, after apparently murdering an innocent black man to preserve the "honor" of a white woman, goes home and strikes his wife. In other works, those "ghosts" shock other characters by refusing to act as such. Hightower's wife in *Light in August* is a case in point.

Many of these perspectives come together in *The Sound and the Fury*, which revolves around the Compson brothers' views of their sister Caddy. In this one novel, we see a variety of responses to and associations with the cultural perspective of "Southern womanhood." To Benjy, Caddy appears as his beloved, caring sister who "smelled like trees." To Quentin, she is "some concept of Compson honor precariously and (he knew well) only temporarily supported by the minute fragile membrane of her maidenhead as a miniature replica of all the vast globy earth may be poised on the nose of a trained seal." To Jason, she is simply, like all women, "[o]nce a bitch, always a bitch."

Caddy Compson never speaks directly in the novel (she inhabits it only as a ghost would), but the idea of her—her brothers' expectations of and reactions to her—drives the course of events and consequences. All views of her come from others: from Benjy, who still waits by the fence; from Quentin, who claimed paternity of her child; from Jason, who blames her for his own failed life; from her mother, who does not allow her name to be spoken in the house; and from Dilsey, who did what she could for her, just as she is doing for Caddy's daughter. We see the range of fear, love, distrust, and responsibility her family forced on her.

The reaction to women in this novel and other works includes the interrelatedness of gender and race in the ideology of the South. The relationship between the bitter, manipulative Caroline Compson and her servant Dilsey shows the different expectations, strengths, and weaknesses of Faulkner's white and black women. The relationship of Dilsey and Jason IV underscores the paradoxical centrality and marginality of blacks in the life of this fine old family that had run its course.

Joe Christmas's views of women and his own black blood intersect often in *Light in August*, nowhere more starkly than the scene in which he tells a white woman with whom he has just had sex that he is part black. Finding a woman who does not care enrages Joe, so much that ''[I]t took two policemen to subdue him.'' ''He was sick after that. He did not know until then that there were white women who would take a man with a black skin. He stayed sick for two years.'' One word represents what both attracts and disgusts him: ''womanshenegro.''

Faulkner captures the complexity of women's roles, the stereotypes placed on them, the expectations others have, and the very real consequences of the interplay of myth and reality, of ''ghosts'' and the living. In his fiction, there exists no ''truth'' about women, no simply ''good'' or ''fallen,'' no stereotypes, but many. From Addie Bundren, who sees herself ''tricked'' by words, to Joanna Burden, who carves out an independent life, to Dilsey, who ''seed de first en de last'' of the Compson line, and many others, Faulkner's women provide a rich and varied spectrum of human hopes, fears, failures, and triumphs. Feminist critics often critique a writer's or a society's paradigm of women, their expected roles, and the reality. In his fiction, Faulkner does that for us.

See also **Women**.

FURTHER READING

Fowler and Abadie, eds. *Faulkner and Women*.
Gwin. *The Feminine in Faulkner*.
Minnick, Cheryl. ''Faulkner and Gender: An Annotated Select Bibliography, 1982–1994.'' *Mississippi Quarterly* 48 (1995): 523–555.

Caroline Carvill

"FIRE AND THE HEARTH, THE," the second section of Faulkner's *Go Down, Moses*. At the heart of ''The Fire and the Hearth'' are the earlier stories, ''A Point of Law,'' in which the old black sharecropper Lucas Beauchamp is caught operating a still on the property of Roth Edmonds; ''Gold Is Not Always,'' in which Beauchamp uses a ''divining machine'' to hunt for gold on the same property (both published in 1940); and a third story (never published) called ''The Fire and the Hearth.'' Of this last story at least three typescripts exist, one of which bears the title ''An Absolution.'' Thinking about this title, one expects the plot to revolve around the remission of guilt. For this association to work, however, stronger ties between the characters were necessary than had existed in ''A Point of Law'' and ''Gold Is Not Always.'' Indeed, Faulkner adds here a psychological closeness between the black sharecropper and the white landowner, who now remembers the old man as important to his coming of age, having been present when he first learned to ride a horse and carry a gun. Yet, obviously, Faulkner saw the need to push the attachment still further back in time, making it psychologically even more essential. In the second typescript, Beauchamp's wife Molly not only delivers young Roth, but when his mother dies, she moves into the big house with her "milktwins"—"a dark baby at one breast and a white one at the other," to use the words of Lillian Smith. Thus the typescript first establishes the reference to what James Early calls "the 'tragic complexity' of the white man's motherless childhood" (8) and the deep attachments between black and white in the South.

For many critics the story, as it appears in *Go Down, Moses*, is not completely successful, due in part to the emphasis on the complicated genealogy and the intrusion of the original comic material but also to the disturbing voicelessness of the female protagonist. When Faulkner sent the dedication to *Go Down, Moses* to his publisher on January 21, 1942—"To Mammy CAROLINE BARR Mississippi (1840–1940)"—it was clear just how personal the question of the relationship between black and white in the South was to him.

FURTHER READING

Duvall, John N. "Silencing Women in 'The Fire and the Hearth' and 'Tomorrow.' " *College Literature* 16.1 (1989): 75–82.
Early, James. *The Making of* Go Down, Moses. Dallas, Tex.: Southern Methodist University Press, 1972.

Ineke Bockting

FLAGS IN THE DUST. See *Sartoris*.

FLAUBERT, GUSTAVE (1821–1880), French novelist born in Rouen, Normandy, and foremost figure of the Realist movement, is best known for *Madame Bovary* (1856), a work noted for its mastery of style and narrative technique. Flaubert's dedication to the perfection of his art is embodied in his quest for what he termed "le mot juste." In numerous interviews Faulkner cites Flaubert—along with Balzac, Dostoevsky, Conrad, Dickens, Tolstoy, and Shakespeare—as one of the great writers who profoundly influenced his own work. In separate interviews with Cynthia Grenier (1955) and Jean Stein (1956), both published in *Lion in the Garden*, he mentions having read Flaubert in his youth and refers to Flaubert's *The Temptation of Saint Anthony* (1874) as the standard by which he measured the success of his own work. In a 1955 colloquy (IV) at Nagano, Japan, he claims to have taught himself French by reading Flaubert.

FURTHER READING

Kinney, Arthur F. "Faulkner and Flaubert." *Journal of Modern Literature* 6 (1977): 222–247.

Yonce, Margaret. "His True Penelope Was Flaubert: *Madame Bovary* and *Sanctuary*." *Mississippi Quarterly* 29 (1976): 439–442.

Arthur Wilhelm

"FOOL ABOUT A HORSE," a short story by Faulkner. First published in *Scribner's* in August 1936 and reprinted in *Uncollected Stories*, the story belongs (wholly reworked) to the second chapter of Book I ("Flem") of *The Hamlet*. In the original tall tale, a boy's father, Pap, is outtraded by Pat Stamper's chicanery and is thus humiliated. In *The Hamlet*, the foolish father is revealed to be Ab Snopes, and his son, Flem Snopes. As a result of his humiliation, Ab abandons any sense of the "honor and pride of Yoknapatawpha" that he may have had before, moving away from any sense of community toward a simple belief in personal survival, even if criminal. The original tale thus evolves from a comic *Scribner's* tale to an explanation of the process by which "Snopes" is created by local community trading practices. In *The Hamlet*, Ratliff narrates the tale on the veranda of Littlejohn's hotel. Ratliff was Ab's associate during the horse trading ("I was a fool about a horse too, same as he was"), and he explains simply that the experience "soured" Ab and accounts for his barn-burning tendencies. The episode also estranges Ab from his wife because in the trading he loses her milk cow. The loss of property and the decline in his status at home lead Ab to criminal activity and teaches his son, Flem, that the most important aspect of life is the accumulation and control of property.

Joseph R. Urgo

"FOX HUNT," a short story William Faulkner first published in *Harper's* in 1931, is included in *Doctor Martino and Other Stories* (1934) and *Collected Stories*. It tells the story of the unhappy marriage of the wealthy Harrison Blair and Mrs. Blair. In an expression of hatred, seemingly for his wife—who is linked to the fox by her sex and comments made by others about her hair and eyes—Blair kills the fox that he had been pursuing for three years, while at the same time Mrs. Blair consummates an adulterous affair with a man whom she seems to care for as little as she cares for her husband. The story suggests that the use of others, or of the land, as objects of pursuit or possession destroys beauty, or life itself, and that given man's nature, particularly the white man's, this destruction is inevitable. Told in third person, the story switches back and forth between the perspective of a citified and sardonic valet or secretary and that of an old "clay-eater" and his young companion.

Arthur A. Brown

FRANCE. The association of William Faulkner with France suggests a symbiotic relationship that proved mutually beneficial. His affinity for France and French people has been well documented by Joseph Blotner and others. Faulkner's interest in the literature, history, and culture of France is evidenced in literary works ranging from his first published poem, "L'Apres-Midi d'un Faune," to one of his last published novels, *A Fable*. That interest is also reflected in the several versions of the unfinished "Elmer," which he wrote while in Paris in 1925; in the short story "Carcassonne"; in the novels *Sanctuary* and *Absalom, Absalom!*; and in the screenplays *Battle Cry* and *The De Gaulle Story*. Faulkner's early interest in French literature was partly due to the influence of Phil Stone, who introduced him to the poetry of the French symbolists. While he was enrolled as a student at the University of Mississippi, French, which he studied under Professor Calvin Brown, another important figure in Faulkner's early development, was the one subject in which he did well. During the early 1920s, his period of literary exploration and experimentation, Faulkner made frequent visits to New Orleans, a city with culture and history steeped in French associations. In July 1925, after long and careful planning and several disappointing postponements, Faulkner departed New Orleans for what was originally intended to be a two- or three-year European sojourn. For several months he lived in Paris on the Left Bank, near the Luxembourg Gardens and the Luxembourg Galleries, where he may have seen paintings of Cézanne and other post-Impressionists whose techniques influenced his later writings (Millgate, *Achievement* 20). After returning from Europe in late 1925, he lived temporarily in New Orleans before settling more permanently in Oxford and entering the period of his most intense creative activity.

Faulkner's affinity for France has been repaid by the critical acclaim that his works received in France. The first French critical appreciation of his work was written by Maurice-Edgar Coindreau and published in *La Nouvelle revue française* in 1931. Faulkner's rise to literary fame was assured in 1932 with the appearance of René-Noël Raimbault's French translation of *Sanctuary*, for which André Malraux wrote the preface. Every year from 1933 until the outbreak of war in 1939, a new translation of one of Faulkner's novels appeared, each greeted with favorable criticism. During the German occupation of France, when no new novels were published and French critics were forbidden to write about American literature, reading American novelists such as Hemingway and Faulkner became a French symbol of resistance. After the war ended in 1946, French translations of Faulkner's novels and short stories resumed, and numerous critical studies appeared. Coindreau, Jean-Paul Sartre, and Albert Camus were among those who promoted Faulkner's work and reputation. Interestingly, in his own country at this time Faulkner's works were nearly out of print and largely ignored by American critics and scholars. When Faulkner won the Nobel Prize for Literature in 1950, therefore, French intellectuals and writers justifiably claimed a great deal of the credit.

French and American criticism and scholarship of the 1960s and 1970s recognized Faulkner as one of the strongest influences on French writing and suggested that his themes and techniques played important roles in the development of two major French literary schools—Existentialism and the New Novel. Undeniably the most influential French critic and translator of Faulkner's works has been Coindreau, whose reviews, prefaces, and translations span more than fifty years of Faulkner scholarship. Three French scholars widely recognized for their contributions to Faulkner criticism during the last thirty years are André Bleikasten, Michel Gresset, and François Pitavy. Three younger French scholars currently making significant contributions are Nicole Moulinoux, Jacques Pothier, and Marie Liénard.

See also **Paris**.

FURTHER READING

Biron, Beth Dyer. "Faulkner in French: A Study of the Translation of His Major Works and Their Influence in French Literature." Dissertation. University of Georgia, 1986.

Makuck, Peter L. "Faulkner Studies in France: 1953–1969." Dissertation. Kent State University, 1977.

Wilhelm, Arthur W. "An Assessment of Current Faulkner Scholarship in France: The Bibliographies of André Bleikasten, Michel Gresset, and François Pitavy." *Mississippi Quarterly* 43 (1990): 417–430.

———. "Maurice-Edgar Coindreau: America's Literary Ambassador to France." Dissertation. Georgia State University, 1992.

Woodworth, Standley D. *William Faulkner en France (1931–1952).* Paris: Lettres Modernes, 1959.

Arthur Wilhelm

"FRANKIE AND JOHNNY," an early short story by Faulkner, first published in *Mississippi Quarterly* in 1978 and reprinted in *Uncollected Stories*. The story has connections with "New Orleans" and "The Kid Learns" in *New Orleans Sketches*. Frankie, young, uneducated, and pregnant, declares her personal freedom: "I dont need Johnny nor any other man to keep me, and I never will." Frankie grows up without a father and with a mother who earns a living through prostitution. Johnny, Frankie's lover, withdraws his support for her when she becomes pregnant. Her shows of confidence are always linked with images of ignorance, conditional phrasing, or other subtle undercutting. The story suggests that Frankie's confidence will be undone by life.

Diane Brown Jones

FREUD, SIGMUND (1856–1939), a Viennese medical doctor and neuropathologist, the inventor of psychoanalysis, the twentieth century's most influential theory of human subjectivity and culture. His major works, collected in twenty-four volumes, include *The Interpretation of Dreams* (1900; English translation 1913), *Three Essays on the Theory of Sexuality* (1905; English translation 1910), and *Beyond the Pleasure Principle* (1920; English translation 1922). In *The Ego and the Id* (1923; English translation 1927), Freud gives a one-sentence summary of his theory: "The division of the psychical into what is conscious and what is unconscious is the fundamental premise of psychoanalysis." Nicolaus Copernicus (1473–1543) had struck the cosmological blow to humanity's natural assumption that the sun revolved around the earth, until that moment known and felt to be at the very center of the universal order. And Charles Darwin (1809–1882) had devastated humanity's narcissistic conception of its place in the economy of nature by speaking of the animal descent of human beings, of the struggle of all organisms to seize a place in the economy of nature, and of the radically contingent and unforgiving character of biological causality unfolding according to entirely immanent, that is, nontranscendent, laws and forces. Just so, Freud decentered the human subject with respect to itself by dividing its domain into two separate, conflicting, yet also in some sense overlapping and mutually interpenetrative regions, one part conscious, the *greater* part unconscious, "the very centre of the human being . . . no longer to be found at the place assigned to it by a whole humanist tradition," to quote the French psychoanalyst Jacques Lacan.

Indeed, that region of what had commonly been known and felt to be "the self" or "the ego" was reconceived in Freud's theory as a relatively small and besieged entity, surrounded by powerful and unruly unconscious forces. In this sense, the theme of "the human heart in conflict with itself," to cite Faulkner's famous formulation from his Nobel Prize acceptance speech, suggests the gist of Freud's revolutionary emphasis on the dynamic contestation of inner (and "internalized") forces that were seen to dominate human subjectivity. These forces included, on the one hand, emphatic sexual and aggressive drives and fantasies and, on the other, the excessive and irrational demands and prohibitions of conscience, or what Freud would call the "superego." Neurosis, defined as the continuous and unresolved struggle of innermost desire against the more or less internalized demands of a repressive reality, was humanity's common condition. In this view, the distinction between what was "normal" and what was "abnormal" or "pathological" in human thought and behavior was predicated upon culturally contingent mores, subtly shifting degrees of emphasis, and notoriously inconstant and permeable borders between the ego and the external world. As Freud put it in his essay "Delusions and Dreams in Jensen's *Gradiva*" (1907), "[T]he frontier between states of mind described as normal and pathological is in part a conventional one and in part so fluctuating that each of us probably crosses it many times in the course of a day." One thinks of the tragedy of Darl Bundren of *As I Lay Dying* and Cash's poignant struggle at the end of that novel to distinguish between "sane" and "crazy."

For Freud, the ability to love and to work was the ultimate goal and measure of successful adaptation to the harsh conditions imposed by civilization upon the pleasure-seeking subject. For this reason, Freud placed into focus all that tended to invade, displace, or decenter that ego or self that aspired toward satisfaction, social stability, and self-mastery: involuntary and excessive emotions, cravings, fears, obsessions, self-reproaches; daydreams, nightdreams, and nightmares; slips of the tongue and bungled actions; and most important, the never-ending flow of unconscious fantasy into the everyday mental and social experience of the subject. Insofar as, for Freud, the unconscious was always "present and operative,'' the goal of psychoanalysis was to illuminate its determinative force so as to enable the subject to ''get in accord'' with it.

Freud's major technique for analyzing this flow of unconscious psychosomatic force was called ''free association,'' in which the analysand (or patient) was asked to give verbal form to all that was passing at that moment through the mind, without exception, deliberate selection, or prejudice. Like its modernist formal equivalent, the ''stream-of-consciousness'' narration, the flow of association through the mind was never absolutely ''free'' but always more or less inhibited by the internalized forces of repression and censorship. Quentin's narrative in *The Sound and the Fury* is perhaps the purest instance of this phenomenon in Faulkner's work.

The wellspring of unconscious drives, emotions, phantasies, and proscriptions was childhood experience, scene of that Oedipal ''complex'' of forces that, surviving into the present, continued to structure the subject's eccentric orientation to his or her own self-definition and gender identity. In this sense, the Freudian subject was seen as always entangled—at the level of fantasy life and so in symbolic repetition through changing social contexts—in the struggles and the conflicts of the original family drama (cf. Gavin Stevens's observation in *Requiem for a Nun* [1951] that ''The past is never dead. It's not even past''). There is virtually no major Faulknerian protagonist, from Elmer Hodge to Horace Benbow, from Quentin and Benjy Compson to Darl Bundren and Joe Christmas, from Rosa Coldfield to Harry Wilbourne, who is not implicated in this ''acting out'' and ''transference''—this actualization and displacement—of the past into the present. In one form or another, the tensions and traumas of family life are invariably at the center of Faulkner's work.

As a self-conscious and sophisticated modernist artist and, finally, a genius, Faulkner during the 1920s was fluent in the artistic and intellectual currents of his time, including those associated with Freudian psychoanalysis. (See, for example, his early review entitled ''Books and Things: American Drama: Inhibitions,'' published in *The Mississippian* on March 17, 1922.) It may be worth recalling, however, that much of the ambiguity surrounding the question of his knowledge of Freud is traceable to his own frequent denials that he was ever significantly touched by any contemporary influence. When asked about Freud at the University of Virginia in 1958, Faulkner replied with characteristically misleading humor and ingenuity: ''What little of psychology I know the characters I have invented and playing poker have taught me. Freud I'm not familiar with'' (*FIU* 268). In 1956 he told Jean Stein, ''Everybody talked about Freud when I lived in New Orleans, but I have never read him. Neither did Shakespeare. I doubt if Melville did either, and I'm sure Moby Dick didn't'' (*LIG* 251). Naturally, in the 1920s, the sources of Freudian knowledge were myriad and inescapable, and no writer in America would come to have a more profound grasp of that knowledge than the author of *The Sound and the Fury* and *Light in August*. Faulkner very likely read Freud in translation; certainly he was exposed to Freudian ideas by virtue of his contact with Conrad Aiken, Sherwood

Anderson, Phil Stone, and the famous "pollen of ideas" that floated in the air of the 1920s and contaminated the offices of the literary journal *The Double Dealer* in New Orleans where Faulkner lived from January to July 1925. Most important, Faulkner assimilated into his fiction of the 1920s and 1930s the psychoanalytic insights that he encountered in the work of other writers, from William Shakespeare and Fyodor Dostoevsky to his most influential contemporary, James Joyce.

Psychoanalysis during the time of Faulkner's development and maturation as a novelist was at once a therapeutic method, a theoretical vocabulary, and a complex of assumptions about narrative and human subjects. An historically rooted system of ideas, psychoanalysis was thoroughly embedded in that rich "modernist" scene in which Faulkner took an active (indeed, a creative and momentous) part, and in one demonstrable form or another, it helped define and enable his fiction's fundamental subject matter and unique forms of expressive power. *Soldiers' Pay, Elmer, Mosquitoes, Flags in the Dust, The Sound and the Fury, Sanctuary, As I Lay Dying, Light in August, If I Forget Thee, Jerusalem*: These are the most fundamentally Freudian of Faulkner's novels. Each builds into its fictional definitions of psychological reality the logic of dreams and the fantasy work of the unconscious, the psychopathology of everyday life, and the determining power of childhood experience in shaping the pathways of adult being. Each explores in often radically new formal ways the many-layered symbolic texture of subjective experience, along with the ways in which human subjectivity is overdetermined and constrained within powerful symbolic fields of law, language, and social force. Each explores what psychoanalysis would call its universal themes: the loss of the loved object; the fear of bodily violence and castration—hardly a disguised theme in *The Sound and the Fury* and *Light in August*; the fatefulness of the instincts and the manner in which they force the subject into patterns of compulsive repetition and symbolic substitution. Incest, fetishism, and the power of involuntary sexual fantasy dominate the lives of Elmer, Talliaferro, Horace Benbow, Byron Snopes, Benjy Compson, Quentin Compson, Darl Bundren, Popeye, Joe Christmas, and Harry Wilbourne. Also present are the ambiguities of gender identity and the pressure of a culture's definitions of masculinity and femininity, with respect to which the Faulknerian protagonist is invariably *misaligned*, the dialectically involved and sexually ambiguous figures of Horace Benbow and Temple Drake being representative of this theme. In sum, as one reads Faulkner, the encounter with Freud is, at some point, inevitable.

See also **Jung, Carl G.; Psychoanalytic Approaches**.

FURTHER READING

Irwin. *Doubling and Incest/Repetition and Revenge.*
Kartiganer and Abadie, eds. *Faulkner and Psychology.*
Matthews, John T. "The Elliptical Nature of *Sanctuary.*" *Novel* 17 (1984): 246–265.
McHaney, Thomas L. "At Play in the Fields of Freud: Faulkner and Misquotation." *Faulkner, His Contemporaries, and His Posterity*, ed. Zacharasiewicz. 64–76.

Michael Zeitlin

G

GERMANY. On his frequent transatlantic tours in the 1950s, Faulkner seems to have avoided Germany as much as possible; his one visit to Germany was a stopover in Munich (September 17, 1955) that lasted just long enough for him to give a short interview on the occasion of the German publication of *A Fable*. However, despite his "violent antipathy to things German" (1974 *FAB* 470), he publicly admired Thomas Mann, whom in 1932 he rated among "the best living writers" (1974 *FAB* 787) and whose *Buddenbrooks* (1901) he eulogized as "the greatest novel of this century" (*LIG* 49). Several critics have commented on the numerous structural and thematic parallels between *Buddenbrooks* and Faulkner's family novels, especially *Sartoris* and *The Sound and the Fury*; and further connections have been detected between Mann's short story "Mario and the Magician" and Faulkner's "An Error in Chemistry," and between Mann's *Death in Venice* (1913) and *Flags in the Dust, Mosquitoes*, and *Elmer*.

Slight as the traces of German literature in Faulkner's works are, the reverse influence of Faulkner on German writers is more obvious. For the postwar generation of German authors, Faulkner (beside Hemingway and Thomas Wolfe) was *the* literary model; the German writer Elizabeth Langgässer even stated in 1947 that a German author would not be accepted by the German readers unless she or he wrote like Hemingway or Faulkner. Wolfgang Koeppen's novel *Tauben im Gras* (1951, *Pigeons on the Grass*) presents the events of a single day in 110 narrative units and as seen through the perspectives of thirty people. Even more obvious are the Faulknerian echoes in works by Alfred Andersch, who had been a prisoner of war in the United States (1944–1945): His novel *Sansibar oder der letzte Grund* (1957, *Flight to Afar*) is fragmented into five narrative perspectives, the titles of the chapters give the names of the character whose perspective is adopted in that chapter, and italics are used to indicate the perspective of one of the five characters. Andersch's novel *Die Rote* (1960, *The Redhead*) also shows Faulkner's influence in three ways: at a structural level, under the headings of four successive days, simultaneously telling two stories that develop quite independently of each other; at a formal level, using italics for stream-of-consciousness passages; and at a thematic level, the nonconformist protagonist reading Faulkner's "very wild" novel *The Wild Palms*, which she rates as "unbelievably good." More recently, Uwe Johnson's fictional county of Jericho shows strong ties with Faulkner's Yoknapatawpha. Similarities between *The Sound and the Fury, Absalom, Absalom!*, and *Light in August* and Johnson's *Mutmassungen über Jakob* (1959, *Speculations about Jacob*) and *Jahrestage* (1970–1983, *Anniversaries*) have been seen not only at the story level but also as concerns sentence construction, point of view, narrative technique, the use of italics and appendices, and the treatment of time and racism. Johnson openly acknowledged his debt to Faulkner and admitted that after reading *The Sound and the Fury* he revised *Mutmassungen* into a polyphonic narrative. For Johnson's intellectual circle in socialist Leipzig, Faulkner personified contemporary "Western" literature.

The history of German translations of Faulkner's works was strongly influenced by the political situation of the 1930s to the 1950s. From 1933 to 1938 three novels (*Light in August, Pylon*, and *Absalom, Absalom!*) and four stories ("That Evening Sun," "There Was a Queen," "Honor," and "That Will Be Fine") were published in German and extensively reviewed. Faulkner's popularity in Germany during this period is also indicated by the publication of *Pylon*, "Smoke," and *The Unvanquished* in English by German publishers. The fact that in the early Third Reich Faulkner texts (in contrast to those of other American writers, such as Hemingway) were allowed to appear in Germany was probably due to a misunderstanding: Nazi officials misinterpreted Faulkner's regionalism as akin to the Nazi "blood-and-soil" ideology; thus they took Faulkner for a conservative agrarian whose *Absalom, Absalom!* argued in favor of racial purity and against miscegenation. Soon, however, Faulkner's novels, too, met with official Nazi disapproval. After World War II the reading public had to wait until 1951 for another translation of a Faulkner novel—*Intruder in the Dust*. This delay was due to several facts. First, because of what was considered Faulkner's negative depiction of the United States, Faulkner's works were not included in the official translation program of the U.S. military government for Germany. Second, the situation of the German publishing houses was very difficult—Rowohlt, who had published the first German translations of three of Faulkner's novels, had been closed by the Nazis; and during World War II the copyright had been given to a Swiss publisher, Fretz & Wasmuth of Zurich. When Faulkner received the Nobel Prize, only the three novels translated in the 1930s were available in German. The order in which his novels were then translated in the 1950s and 1960s seems totally random: His early novels had to wait over thirty years to be published in German (*Soldiers' Pay*, 1958; *Mosquitoes*, 1960; *Sartoris*, 1961), and his most highly esteemed works did not fare any better (*The Sound and the Fury*, 1956; *As I Lay Dying*, 1961). Faulkner's later novels were translated almost immediately and published only one year after the original (*A Fable*, 1955; *The Town*, 1958; *The Mansion*, 1960; *The*

Reivers, 1963). Today, an almost complete paperback edition of Faulkner's works is available in German (Diogenes, Zurich). German-language productions of *Requiem for a Nun* preceded the New York premiere (January 1959) by years: the play saw its world premiere in Zurich on October 9, 1955, and its German premiere in Berlin on November 11, 1955.

Because of the official Nazi disapproval, the highly promising Faulkner criticism of the early 1930s was silenced during World War II. When Rowohlt published second editions of *Absalom, Absalom!* (1948) and *Light in August* (1949), a new wave of critical reception started. At first Faulkner's works were read in the light of the atrocities experienced during the preceding decade, and consequently the entanglement of the past and the present was emphasized, Faulkner being seen as a pessimistic determinist. But gradually a more existentialist reading of his works emerged, regarding him as an optimistic, humanistic, and religious author and his South as the focal point of the universal problems of humankind. Over the decades German critics have increasingly participated in the Faulkner "industry," and in 1987 the International Faulkner Symposium convened in Bonn, organized by Lothar Hönnighausen, the most prominent German Faulknerian, who also edited the papers presented (*Faulkner's Discourse*; Tübingen, 1989). Hönnighausen was also guest editor of the 1997 Faulkner issue of *Amerikastudien*, a collection of German responses to the Faulkner centenary.

FURTHER READING

Lennox, Sara. "Yoknapatawpha to Jerichow: Uwe Johnson's Appropriation of William Faulkner." *Arcadia* 14 (1979): 160–176.
Zacharasiewicz, ed. *Faulkner, His Contemporaries, and His Posterity.*
Zindel, Edith. *William Faulkner in den deutschsprachigen Ländern Europas: Untersuchungen zur Aufnahmeseiner Werke nach 1945.* Hamburg: Luedke, 1972.

Juergen C. Wolter

GIBSON, DILSEY. Of the several African American domestic servants in Faulkner's novels whose characterizations are drawn from the real-life Caroline Barr (1840–1940), the "Mammy" in the house of Faulkner's youth to whom he dedicated *Go Down, Moses*, Dilsey is by far the most famous. She is a major character in *The Sound and the Fury* and appears also in the "Compson Appendix" and "That Evening Sun." In the novel Dilsey is the major source of stability in the once proud, now fallen, Compson family. In the first section we see her, in place of the increasingly dipsomaniac father and hypochondriac mother, disciplining the Compson children, comforting especially the retarded Benjy, and, in the novel's "present" in 1928, protecting Miss Quentin against her Uncle Jason's petty tyrannies. The second and third sections, told, respectively, from Quentin's and Jason's viewpoints, confirm her in these roles. The last section, where she becomes the chief third-person point-of-view character, follows her to church on Easter along with her daughter, her grandson, and

Benjy; and we see her afterward, with Benjy on her lap, in a kind of "Pietà" tableau. Dilsey has been praised for her Christlike selflessness of character and her simple, benevolent faith, although her portrayal is sometimes criticized as owing too much to the stereotyped plantation mammy. But Dilsey also reveals a good deal of anger, especially in her verbal and physical abuse of her grandson (she threatens, for example, to tear his ears off his head, cut his hand off with a butcher knife, and have him beaten with a stick); and her faith, like the Easter sermon she attends, contains an apocalypticism that echoes, though it finally transcends, the imagery and themes of death, punishment, judgment, and vengeance that preoccupy the other characters.

FURTHER READING

Mellard, James M. "Faulkner's *Commedia*: Synecdoche and Anagogic Symbolism in *The Sound and the Fury.*" *Journal of English and Germanic Philology* 83 (1984): 534–546.

Glenn Meeter

"GO DOWN, MOSES," a Faulkner short story, from *Collier's* of January 25, 1941, which became, with slight revision, the concluding and title chapter of *Go Down, Moses*. The story, which has been reprinted in *Uncollected Stories*, is told mainly through the third-person view of Gavin Stevens, county attorney for Yoknapatawpha; but the heroine is Mollie Beauchamp, a "little old Negro woman." Mollie is a visionary who intuits that her grandson, whom she raised, is in trouble. Having been ordered off the McCaslin place by its current owner, Carothers Edmonds, the grandson has been absent for five years. "Pharaoh got him," Mollie says. She seeks Gavin's aid, and when he informs her that the grandson has been executed for murder in Chicago, she insists that the body be brought back for public burial on McCaslin land. Stevens, with some misgivings, makes the arrangements and collects community contributions for the funeral. The story has been unfairly neglected and is sometimes denigrated as nostalgic for Southern paternalism. But Mollie's radical use of biblical imagery should be recognized: If Old Carothers McCaslin was a founding Abraham, Mollie here makes good her claim as a matriarchal Rachel, claiming the McCaslin property as the land of promise for its black as well as its white inhabitants.

FURTHER READING

Meeter, Glenn. "Molly's Vision: Lost Cause Idealogy and Genesis in Faulkner's *Go Down, Moses.*" *Faulkner and Ideology*, ed. Kartiganer and Abadie. 277–296.
Selzer, John. " 'Go Down Moses' and *Go Down, Moses.*" *Studies in American Fiction* 13.1 (1985): 89–95.

Glenn Meeter

GO DOWN, MOSES. When Faulkner received his copies of *Go Down, Moses, and Other Stories* in 1942, he promptly thanked Random House for the shipment. Yet in 1949, when Random was planning to reissue the volume, Faulkner wrote to Robert K. Haas, urging him to drop *and Other Stories* from the title, insisting that *Go Down, Moses* was "indeed a novel" (*SL* 284). All subsequent editions have honored Faulkner's request. Random House might be forgiven its original confusion since almost all parts of the text had previously been published in magazines, and Faulkner had written Haas in May 1941 that last year "I mentioned a volume, collected short stories, general theme being relationship between white and negro races here" (*SL* 139).

Whether *Go Down, Moses* is a novel or a collection of stories has been a major critical issue since its appearance. Over seven months, Faulkner revised the published stories, reassembling their order and inventing new material to arrive at a coherent sequence of narratives. He sent sections to his editor, Saxe Commins, trusting Commins to keep it all straight. In December 1941, Faulkner begged his publisher's indulgence since he was adding a fourth section to the piece called "The Bear," "a section now that I am going to be proud of and which requires careful writing and rewriting to get it exactly right" (*SL* 146). Also, he was expanding "Delta Autumn," tripling its original size. Faulkner delivered these additional parts in mid-December. In January, Faulkner sent Haas a dedication, "To Mammy, Caroline Barr," and the project was complete.

The capstone of Faulkner's "major phase," 1929–1942, *Go Down, Moses* continues Faulkner's exploration of family, incest, race, miscegenation, and the relationship between humankind and the natural world. The framework is the tangled genealogy of the McCaslin family, the most intricate family tree in Yoknapatawpha County. Genealogical charts provided by critics prove helpful since Faulkner distributes the complex family relationships in jigsaw puzzle fashion throughout the text. The historical sweep of the narratives covers 1859 to 1940, but documents and conversations cut back through earlier centuries to Roman antiquity and even biblical Eden. *Go Down, Moses* may then be viewed as one of Faulkner's "Old Testament" narratives, its historical record interrupted at times with symbolic tales, "Pantaloon in Black" its book of Job. The leading characters are the white Isaac McCaslin and black Lucas Beauchamp, two cousins descended from the "old Abraham," Lucius Quintus Carothers McCaslin—dead since 1833 yet dominating the work.

"Was," placed first, begins with a prelude of appositives that introduces Isaac "Uncle Ike" McCaslin, a childless widower of seventy-four. Yet the story is about to be told from the viewpoint of Ike's second cousin, McCaslin Edmonds, sixteen years Ike's senior and the current owner of the plantation that Ike *should* own, being L.Q.C. McCaslin's grandson, while McCaslin Edmonds is only L.Q.C.'s great-grandson. The tale takes place in 1859 when McCaslin is a nine-year-old orphan living with his twin bachelor uncles, Theophilus "Buck" McCaslin and Amodeus "Buddy" McCaslin. Since Ike is not born until 1867, the tale to follow is "not something he had participated in or even remembered except from the hearing, the listening." As the book unfolds, readers learn there is much "Uncle Ike" McCaslin never participates in.

"Was" may be the funniest unfunny story ever written when it is reread in light of later information. "Was" begins the novel's hunt motif as Buck and Buddy pursue Tomey's Turl, apparently an escaped slave, while Miss Sophonsiba Beauchamp pursues becoming Mrs. Theophilus McCaslin. But Turl, simply off courting Tennie Beauchamp at the neighboring plantation, is the master of the situation, while only Uncle Buddy's poker prowess and Turl's ability to stack the deck earn his brother a temporary reprieve from marriage. Turl and Tennie do achieve their goal of being together, while Sophonsiba will eventually get her man. Subsequent narratives reveal that Turl is Buck and Buddy's quadroon half brother and that he is the incestuous issue of their father and his mulatto daughter. While these grimmer realities emerge later and modify the initial comic enjoyment of the story, in "Was" the reader learns that Turl, as well as all other blacks owned by their father, has been freed by the twins and that the rough-hewn Mississippi abolitionists live in a cabin they built themselves, moving the blacks into the half-completed McCaslin mansion. Faulkner will reprise the poker hand, in which Tennie Beauchamp is one of the major stakes, five times, each repetition deepening an understanding of its meaning.

The second section, the novella-length story of Lucas Beauchamp, "The Fire and the Hearth," serves as the comic first movement in which Lucas protects his moonshine business from being disrupted and becomes obsessed with finding buried gold, nearly succumbing to greed and having his wife of forty-five years, Molly, divorce him. Both issues are happily resolved in court. Yet again, amid the domestic comedy, Faulkner interpolates two major flashbacks: Lucas as a young man confronting his cousin, Zack Edmonds, over Molly in an affair of honor that nearly ends in catastrophe; and the two kinsmen growing up like brothers, as will their sons Roth Edmonds and Henry Beauchamp, but growing apart because of the culture's racial coding, its "wrong and shame." White McCaslins denying the humanity of their black kin, often trying to assuage their guilt with money, becomes one of Faulkner's major patterns in *Go Down, Moses*.

The function of "Pantaloon in Black," the third story, has puzzled many. As moving as the story is, its only links with the McCaslin-Edmonds-Beauchamp narratives are that Rider and Mannie rent a cabin on the plantation and that they imitate Lucas and Molly in lighting a fire on the hearth that will burn throughout their marriage. (Faulkner would later explain that Rider is another of the black McCaslins, but that point is not made in the text.) Rider's sawmill work, his unassuageable grief over the death of his bride, his killing of the white sawmill watchman, his subsequent lynching, and the white community's misunderstanding as represented by the deputy sheriff prepare readers for upcoming events where the violation of black people will be foregrounded and environmental issues will move into the spotlight. Moreover, "Pantaloon in Black" signals the text's shift in focus from a farming/industrial society to a primitive hunting realm.

"The Old People" introduces the new movement by focusing on Isaac

McCaslin's initiation into the community of hunters when he kills his first deer at age twelve in 1879. The orphan boy's wilderness mentor and "spirit's father" is Sam Fathers, possessor of Faulkner's most interesting gene pool since Sam is part red, black, and white. Faulkner's style takes on a nearly incantatory quality in presenting the hunt ritual of "The Old People," "The Bear," and "Delta Autumn."

"The Bear" reprises Ike's initiation at age twelve and covers the years leading up to it and the killing of the legendary two-toed bear, Old Ben, the embodiment of the vanishing wilderness. When Ben dies, so does the bravehearted dog Lion, so does Sam Fathers, and so does an era. In its fourth section Ike McCaslin, having reached twenty-one, relinquishes all title to the McCaslin estate. To try to explain his forfeiture, Ike draws upon his mythical interpretation of world history in which God established America as a second chance for humankind, which slaveholders like his grandfather betrayed. Yet God, according to Ike, also established the McCaslin family as partial redeemers of the tainted paradise. Since Ike's father and uncle did what they could to atone for the evil of their father, Ike believes that the logical extension would be for him to simply give up the plantation. His decision completes five years of brooding since he read his family's history in the plantation ledgers and discovered the inhumanity of his grandfather, who refused to acknowledge his son begotten on his own daughter and then cavalierly left that child a money legacy; "*cheaper than saying My son to a nigger,*" Ike bitterly reflects. The fourth section closes with a powerful flash-forward scene in which his unnamed wife uses her body in an attempt to force Ike to renounce his renunciation. Ike's refusal to do so ensures that he will be "uncle to half a county and father to no one." "The Bear" concludes with a fifth section, set when Ike is eighteen, in which Ike laments the passing of the wilderness now that the hunting grounds have been sold to a Memphis timber company.

A fifty-year gap separates "The Bear" from "Delta Autumn." Ike has lived to see the wilderness shrink to a tiny remnant. Ike spends his first night of an annual deer hunt in camp reviewing his life; and into this vestigial male paradise walks a young woman carrying a male child in her arms, a child fathered by Ike's younger cousin, Roth Edmonds. The young woman is a Beauchamp, a partially black descendant of L.Q.C. McCaslin. The text comes full circle when Ike rejects the prospect before him. Once again, a white McCaslin abuses a black McCaslin. And true to family history, Roth Edmonds provides some guilt money. It comes home to Ike that his relinquishment has not changed the history of injustice in his family.

The title and concluding story offer some hope for Southern society as an aged Molly Beauchamp and an equally aged white woman, Miss Worsham, join forces to bring home from Chicago the body of Molly's grandson, an executed cop killer. Unlike the black and white male pairings, these two women remain lifelong friends. County Attorney Gavin Stevens affirms the bonds of family and community. The story takes place in Jefferson, not in the woods or on the plantation. When Miss Worsham tells Stevens, "It's our grief," her words speak for the South and for America as well. Only in this final story does family identity outweigh racial identity.

Most of the critical attention on *Go Down, Moses* focuses on the nature of Ike's attempt to redeem his family's history of choosing race over kinship. Is he a saint of renunciation, an emulator of Christ, or the very embodiment of avoidance, a Pontius Pilate who washes his hands of his tainted heritage? Certainly most recent criticism echoes Faulkner's own assessment that withdrawing from life never alleviates social ills. Ike's choice leads to the sterility suggested by the half-century gap in his narrative: There was nothing to report. The values Ike learned in the woods at the feet of Sam Fathers are of the woods alone, hardly applicable to the social world in a transforming Mississippi. Faulkner endorses only Ike's sacramental attitude toward what is left of the natural world. *Go Down, Moses* is in some respects a visionary eco-text as well as a major examination of racial anguish in America. In Faulkner's mind, the two issues are inextricable—violation of human beings is a violation of nature itself.

FURTHER READING

Early, James. *The Making of* Go Down, Moses. Dallas, Tex.: Southern Methodist University Press, 1972.

Kinney, Arthur F. Go Down, Moses: *The Miscegenation of Time*. New York: Twayne, 1996.

Kuyk, Dirk, Jr. *Threads Cable-Strong: William Faulkner's* Go Down, Moses. Lewisburg, Pa.: Bucknell University Press, 1983.

Litz, Walton. "Genealogy as Symbol in *Go Down, Moses.*" *Faulkner Studies* 1.4 (1952): 49–53.

Sundquist. "Half Slave, Half Free: *Go Down, Moses.*" *Faulkner: The House Divided.* 131–159.

Taylor, Nancy Dew. *Annotations to William Faulkner's* Go Down, Moses. New York: Garland, 1994.

Thornton, Weldon. "Structure and Theme in Faulkner's *Go Down, Moses.*" *Costerus* 3 (1975): 73–112.

Tick, Stanley. "The Unity of *Go Down, Moses.*" *William Faulkner: Four Decades of Criticism*, ed. Wagner. 327–334.

Wagner-Martin, Linda, ed. *New Essays on* Go Down, Moses. New York: Cambridge University Press, 1996.

David L. Vanderwerken

GOLDEN BOUGH, THE. With the explorations and settlements among ever-more exotic peoples, nineteenth-century Europeans became increasingly aware that patterns of human behavior and belief could also be discovered and indeed related to their own. The greatest compiler of comparative religions and folk practices, Sir James Frazer, published his first volume of *The Golden Bough* in 1890 and his twelfth in 1915, with the one-volume version appearing in 1922.

Frazer began his encyclopedic study with a single image of the priest who must prowl Diana's sacred grove near Lake Nemi, protecting the Golden Bough, a mistletoe, god-empowered because it was apparently "planted" by lightning onto Diana's sacred oak. Since this bough stayed alive in winter, suspended (like Christ) between heaven and earth, it must hold the soul of the "dead" oak, and it alone could kill the apparently "deathless" god. Now, even though, as Diana's consort, the priest is "King of the Wood," he must prowl, sword in hand, awaiting his successor, a runaway slave, who will kill him for his job, who will in turn prowl, sword in hand, waiting for his successor to kill him (1.11). With this incident as his central focus, Frazer set out to explore why the savage slaughter of the sacred—human or animal—is so disturbingly universal. As he proceeded he distinguished the "civilized" from the "primitive" either by using an arch humor (quoting an African king—"God made me after his own image; I am the same as God"—he footnotes: "A slight mental confusion may perhaps be detected in this utterance of the dark-skinned deity" [1.396n]) or by applying Darwin's principle of evolution: Bloody sacrifice could evolve into ritual wafer; myth and magic, into religion and science; superstition and even orthodoxy would continue to evolve into full enlightenment.

Although the modernists used other sources (such as Bulfinch and Weston), *The Golden Bough* became their primary source of myth. Eager to overthrow European traditions, writers such as Joyce, Mann, and Lawrence turned to archetype by reason not of Darwin but of Freud (who published contemporaneously with Frazer). Like Picasso's using African masks to suggest the unconscious, the modernists had their characters enact early belief and practice to suggest the dreams, fantasies, and even behavior of the people around them. Himself a modernist, Faulkner evidently found Frazer fascinating. Rowan Oak, the name he gave his Oxford home, is actually one type of the sacred golden bough (11.281). When Faulkner stayed with Sherwood Anderson in New Orleans in 1925, much of their talk was of Freud, Eliot, and Frazer, with an abridged *Golden Bough* on Anderson's coffee table. Later, Faulkner would be observed reading Frazer at the time he was writing *Light in August*.

Myth and folk practices from Frazer have been noted in many of Faulkner's works. The battle for the priesthood at Nemi has been found in *Sanctuary*; Dionysus in *As I Lay Dying*; Attis in *The Hamlet*; the Persephone/Demeter myth in *The Sound and the Fury, As I Lay Dying*, and *Sanctuary*; the association of the palm tree with fertility in *The Wild Palms*. In *As I Lay Dying*, when Vardaman bores a hole in Addie's coffin (and her head) after twice opening the window, the act mirrors a practice described in Frazer of releasing the soul from the body (4.189).

Faulkner's most systematic infusion of material from Frazer is found in *Light in August*. Having patterned his main characters on Christian figures, Faulkner also assigned them pagan counterparts from Frazer: Lena/Mary as Isis, Byron/Joseph as Adonis, Joe Christmas/Christ as Dionysus. Moreover, Joanna Burden, called "manlike," her name the feminine form of John, brings her message of brotherhood before JC (Joe Christmas), whom she immerses in a "black pool,'' and her head is cut off. She is, in other words, a John the Baptist, JB. But Joanna is also the moon-goddess, Diana of the Woods, ''patroness of wild beasts'' and pregnancy, who ''heard the prayers of women in travail'' (2.128). Having a ''clump of oaks'' in the ''exact center'' of her property, described as one body of ''two moongleamed shapes,'' Joanna advises the local Negro women in their travails and decides that she herself is pregnant.

The twenty-one chapters of *Light in August* parallel the twenty-one chapters of the St. John gospel, but Faulkner further expanded each Johannine story with material from Frazer. For example, the description of the first stage of Joe's affair with Joanna occurs in chapter 11—in John, the raising of the dead Lazarus. So Joanna is often spoken of in relation to death; indeed, beneath Joe's hands, her ''body might have been the body of a dead woman not yet stiffened.'' But called ''priest'' and ''tree,'' she and Joe also enact the battle of the priesthood at Nemi. Reflecting Christ's ability to raise the dead, this battle is over the secret of life over death. But since that secret resides in the symbolic golden bough, like the ''runaway slave,'' Joe fights with Joanna ''as if he struggled physically with another man for an object of no actual value to either, and for which they struggled on principle alone.''

Faulkner probably used the abridged *Golden Bough* for most of his myth-making, but *Light in August* echoes material found only in the complete version. For example, John's chapter 5 presents the halt man waiting to be immersed at the ''troubling'' of the waters at Bethesda. Believed to be a healing spa or hot springs, the periodic ''troubling'' of Bethesda's pool would be the boiling up of noxious vapors. Since odors were used medicinally in primitive societies, chapter 5 of *Light in August*, featuring the ''halted'' Joe, frequently mentions smells, breathing, and even the nose and reflects Frazer's discussions of ancient volcanic regions, known for their curative powers, especially to heal ''diseases of the skin'' (5.209). This material is not in the abridged Frazer. Nor is the description of the shepherds' festivals of St. George, which Faulkner features in chapter 10 to develop John 10's discourse on the Good Shepherd.

Although, like Frazer, Faulkner often reached for humorous effect (for example, paralleling Lazarus with Joanna's ''body of a dead woman not yet stiffened''), such levity must be placed in the context of Faulkner's abiding compassion. By using what Eliot called ''the mythical method,'' he sought to give a deeper, older significance to our most savage impulses and profound yearnings.

FURTHER READING

Cross, Barbara M. ''*The Sound and the Fury*: The Pattern of Sacrifice.'' *Arizona Quarterly* 16 (1960): 5–16.

Dickerson, Mary Jane. ''Some Sources of Faulkner's Myth in *As I Lay Dying*.'' *Mississippi Quarterly* 19 (1966): 132–142.

McHaney, Thomas L. ''*Sanctuary* and Frazer's Slain Kings.'' *Mississippi Quarterly* 24 (1971): 223–245.

Virginia V. James Hlavsa

"GOLDEN LAND," a Faulkner short story. Faulkner mentioned "Golden Land" in correspondence as early as the summer of 1934, and it was completed by the end of the year. He had hopes its "flavor of perversion" would sell it to *Cosmopolitan* for a high price (*SL* 88). However, it was first published in *American Mercury* in May 1935 and later reprinted in *Collected Stories*. Deserving of more attention than it has received to date, the story contains vintage Faulknerian place writing, and it is surely his definitive landscape study of California as anti-Edenic cacotope—the epitome of displacement, rootlessness, and corruption. Thus "Golden Land" suggests Faulkner's contribution to a major motif in American literature: the Myth of the West.

With little action and plot, "Golden Land" is primarily an evocation of place and mood, a set of thematic variations on California as a place of corruption. The central character, Ira Ewing, Jr., having fled from the hard frontier farming life of his native Nebraska, is now a prosperous real estate broker in Beverly Hills. His marriage is empty, his son is an embittered transvestite (tellingly named Voyd), and his daughter—rechristened April Lalear for her film career— is involved in a scandalous sex orgy trial. Yet Ewing, who seeks business profit from his daughter's scandal, is shown as the center of corruption. The only positive character is his mother, who longs to return to Nebraska. Ewing visits her every day and takes care of her physical needs, but he refuses to give her the money she needs to return to Nebraska. After years of sitting in her rocking chair, her one cherished item from her Nebraska life of "hardship and endurance" that had taught her the honor, courage, dignity, and pride lacking in her family, she dreams of escaping the golden emptiness of California, where everything is "too easy." But she seems to give up her dream in the story's final sentence: "I will stay here and live forever." Whether this is an expression of despair, defeat, seasoned resignation, or triumphant irony is the crux of the tale.

The sparse critical commentary on "Golden Land" has generally judged it to be a failed story, with excessive sociological commentary in its so-called puritanical reaction against the golden wasteland of California. Read as psychobiography, the story may be seen as Faulkner's shadowy revelation of self-hatred based on his own experiences and conduct in Hollywood. But such judgments may be a bit harsh, especially when arrived at without any real explication of this tale that at least one critic, Dorothy Tuck, values as "a subtle story of success and disillusionment" (167). For any reader concerned with agrarianism (Southern or otherwise), or with Faulkner's place writing, or with the illumination of values through place and placelessness, rootedness and deracination, "Golden Land," with its evocation of the agrarian frontier of Nebraska juxtaposed against California's "curious air of being rootless," is an important minor text.

FURTHER READING

Bradford, M. E. "Escaping Westward: Faulkner's 'Golden Land.' " *Georgia Review* 19 (1965): 72–76.

H. R. Stoneback

"GOLD IS NOT ALWAYS," a short story by Faulkner. A string of rejections preceded the November 1940 publication of the story in *American Mercury*. It was revised for "The Fire and the Hearth" in *Go Down, Moses* and later included in *Uncollected Stories*. Lucas Beauchamp and George Wilkins seem the dupes in a hunt for buried gold. Beauchamp's savvy soon turns a salesman's gold detector into a certain moneymaker for Beauchamp. The salesman becomes frenzied hunter, and Carothers Edmonds is furious.

FURTHER READING

Millgate, Jane. "Short Story into Novel: Faulkner's Re-writing of 'Gold Is Not Always.' " *English Studies* 45 (1964): 310–317.
Weinstein, Philip M. " 'He Come and Spoke for Me': Scripting Lucas Beauchamp's Three Lives." *Faulkner and the Short Story*, ed. Harrington and Abadie. 229–252.

Diane Brown Jones

GORDON, a major character in Faulkner's second novel, *Mosquitoes*. Gordon is a brooding, muscular sculptor, the most asocial and intense of the artists in *Mosquitoes*, so self-contained he remains impervious to the insects that plague the rest of them. But he becomes fascinated by Patricia Robyn as the living image of the girl he has "locked up" in the marble torso that dominates his studio. This sculpture, his relations with Patricia, and his reflections upon his feminine ideal have long interested readers. So too has his final artwork. For many critics, the clay face of Mrs. Maurier that Gordon produces after the yachting party represents a significant development within the course of *Mosquitoes*, a hint of transformation, rare in this static narrative.

FURTHER READING

Carothers, James B. " 'The Dead Tranquil Queens': Sculptors and Sculpture in Faulkner's Fiction." *The Artist and His Masks: William Faulkner's Metafiction*. Ed. Agostino Lombardo. Rome: Bulzoni, 1991. 65–78.
Daüfenbach, Claus. "The Aesthetics of Form: Sculpture and Sculptor in *Mosquitoes*." *The Artist and His Masks*, ed. Lombardo. 79–88.

Pamela E. Knights

GOTHIC. Putting aside questionable claims made on behalf of the Gothic in order to establish its presence in early American writings such as sermons or captivity tales, by the end of the eighteenth century Charles Brockden Brown had undeniably developed the Gothic's narrative pattern in an American setting. His *Wieland* and *Edgar Huntley* are premier examples. Subsequent writers, such as Poe, whose Virginia upbringing and years in Maryland arguably link him to the South, were to develop the tradition further. If Poe's ties to the South are tenuous, no one could deny the credentials of William Gilmore Simms, who, while best known for his novels of frontier adventure in the manner of Scott, wrote several Gothic novels as well. These novels, including *Martin Faber, Castle Dismal*, and *Confession*, provide a literary foundation beneath the settings, plots, and themes often discussed under the rubric of Southern Gothic.

The terms *Gothic* and *Southern Gothic* have often been used disparagingly, and many Southern writers have resisted having their work so categorized. Despite such resistance, the labels have stuck for Faulkner as well as such distinguished others as Truman Capote, Tennessee Williams, Carson McCullers, Eudora Welty, and Flannery O'Connor.

Certainly several characteristic American settings for the Gothic are to be found in Faulkner's work: the collapsing mansion (and often an associated family), the wilderness, the small town populated by eccentric and obsessed figures. *Absalom, Absalom!* features a climax in which the great house of Colonel Sutpen, haunted by a man long presumed dead, goes up in flames, consumed, as was the House of Usher, by one of the elemental powers. Even Rosa Coldfield's house in the same novel, a much more modest affair, is closed and shuttered, haunted by the chimerical presences of Sutpen and her father. The novel also features a nightmarish hunt through the wilderness for a wily French architect by townsmen, the single-minded Sutpen, and his animalistic slaves. Finally, the small community of Jefferson provides a cornucopia of obsessed and frustrated personalities, among them Rosa Coldfield, who is fascinated by and ultimately betrayed by the larger-than-life Gothic machinations of Sutpen.

Gothic plot elements are similarly readily identified. These include the quest for knowledge, the intrusion of the past into the present, the cyclical pattern of capture-escape-pursuit-recapture, the manipulation of others for selfish ends, and the unintelligibility of life. Quentin Compson in both *The Sound and the Fury* and *Absalom, Absalom!* exemplifies the quest for knowledge and the dangers of that quest. Many of Faulkner's families are unsettled by events that occurred in the past: for example, the Compsons, the Sartorises, and the Sutpens. Individual characters, such as Quentin Compson and Rosa Coldfield, are obsessed imaginatively with whole congeries of events rising from the past. And who better to exemplify the manipulation of others for selfish ends than Anse of *As I Lay Dying*, Colonel Sutpen of *Absalom, Absalom!*, or Jason Compson of *The Sound and the Fury*.

Also prominent in Faulkner are Gothic themes centering on the capacity of the oppressed to endure and triumph, on the power of emotion, on the darkness lying directly beneath the thin veneer of civilization, and on the relation between perception and reality. Dilsey, in *The Sound and the Fury*, stands preeminently forth as an example of the human spirit's capacity to triumph in the midst of oppression. Countless characters in Faulkner's fiction are driven by emotions they only dimly understand; most of the Snopeses in their various manifestations are so driven. *Sanctuary*'s Popeye darkly exemplifies the theme that bestiality and cruelty lurk just below the surface of civilization. Finally, one of the most prevalent Gothic themes in Faulkner is that of the role of perception in the creation of reality. One has only to read *The Sound and the Fury* or *As I Lay*

Dying, the narrative structures of which provide a variety of perceptions, to observe a masterful exemplification of this theme. The best example, however, occurs in *Absalom, Absalom!* when Quentin and Shreve bring the past to life through the force of their own passionate desire to understand. Of course, characteristically Gothic, this novel, like many of Faulkner's other works, avoids closure. This is done in part as a means of involving the reader in a construction of the narrative's meaning and in part as a means of suggesting thematically that all such reductive attempts are necessarily tentative.

Faulkner's most decidedly Gothic short work is "A Rose for Emily." This much-praised story features an old dark house and a protagonist, Emily Grierson, whose distorted sexuality and resistance to change become the driving force behind murder and necrophilia. Among the novels, *As I Lay Dying* has clearly Gothic elements, particularly in what has been called the inverted quest to attain a resting place for Addie's corpse; but *Absalom, Absalom!* is the novel closest to the conventions of the Gothic, including those mentioned above as well as secret confinements, hints of incest, a desperate protagonist, and victimized women.

To confirm the presence of Gothic elements in Faulkner's works is not to diminish the power or richness of those works. Unquestionably Faulkner's works are much more than conventional Gothic constructions. However, the Gothic narrative tradition contributes to their power and richness, and that tradition reflects the heritage of a man who loved to tell wonderfully frightening ghost stories to the children of Oxford.

FURTHER READING

Kerr. *William Faulkner's Gothic Domain.*
Wells. *The Ghosts of Rowan Oak.*

Glenn Reed

GREAT MIGRATION. In 1910, when Faulkner was thirteen years old, 90 percent of the African American population—almost 8 million—lived in the Deep South. When he died in 1962, 50 percent of the African American people lived outside the South; and Ole Miss, which was still a bastion of white privilege, would soon be forced to admit its first black student. In the intervening years, over 6 million Afro-Southerners had migrated, changing history and life throughout the United States.

Apart from the comparatively small Exoduster movement to Kansas in 1879, African American migration from the South did not occur in great numbers until 1915, when the sudden halt in Eastern and Southern European immigration and a shortage of labor in the war industries of the North created a demand for Afro-Southern labor outside the South. Although African Americans had powerful reasons for wishing to leave the South, their mobility was vigilantly restricted and their opportunities for resettlement were slim. The lure of jobs outside the South—with labor recruiters to spread the word, arrange transportation, and offer the (frequently false) promise of help with the process of relocation and resettlement—resulted during the years of World War I in a net out-migration from the South of nearly 500,000 African Americans. Another 800,000 followed during the 1920s and, in spite of the depression, nearly 400,000 in the 1930s. World War II inaugurated a period in which these numbers would triple; 1.5 million African Americans migrated in the 1940s and another 1.5 million migrated in the 1950s. Only in the 1960s did this dramatically rapid pace of migration begin to slow. By this time, however, the wider dispersion of African Americans to cities throughout the United States had already made deep and lasting impressions on American culture.

As one might imagine, the Southern white response to African American migration was far from uniform, particularly across class and over time. At the outset, however, the sudden opportunity for Southern blacks to escape the South was powerfully opposed by middle- and upper-class Southern whites, who had relied for generations on the unpaid or barely paid labor of Afro-Southerners. More than simply economic, however, black migration posed a threat to the very foundation of white identity, whose socially constructed position of superiority and privilege depended on a vigilant maintenance of black disadvantage and the position of black dependency and inferiority that flowed from it. Striking at the heart of racialized identities in the South, black migration demonstrated not only that Southern blacks could take charge of their own lives but also that Southern whites were in a variety of ways "lost" without them. As black migration eroded the material and ideological infrastructure that supported the myth of black inferiority and dependency, it also opened and exposed profound fissures in the infrastructure on which the myth of white strength and independence resided—an infrastructure born in slavery and reconstructed in the post-Confederate era via new institutions and practices, from sharecropping and debt peonage to the black codes.

From his first novel, *Soldiers' Pay*, to his last, *The Reivers*, Faulkner analyzed the dislocation of identities with remarkable depth and precision; and his own experiences of geographical and cultural displacement enabled him to better understand and investigate the impact of migration on identity formation and reformation. Eighteen years old in 1915, when the Great Migration first began, Faulkner joined the stream of migration in 1917 at the age of twenty. Like the journeys of thousands upon thousands of African Americans leaving at this same time, Faulkner's trip by train from Oxford, Mississippi, to New Haven, Connecticut, represented his first departure from the South. As with these Afro-Southerners, Faulkner's travels to the North led him to observe that black people seemed much more free, as they were not in the Jim Crow South, to move about in public space, specifically, on trains and streetcars, and to address white people without the strictly regulated etiquette of deference imposed in the South. Faulkner's observations may be found, for example, not only in the letters he wrote home from New Haven but also in the treatment this journey received more than a decade later in *The Sound and the Fury* (1929). The spatial and temporal bifurcation of this novel's mise-en-scène structures it as a kind of comparative analysis of North and South before and after the commencement of the Great Migration. Notably, the novel offers this comparative analysis from the point of view of the Southern white male, a personage whose dissolving subject position is depicted variously in terms of idiocy, suicide, and moral decay. Through its structure and plot, then, the novel suggests what it never explicitly declares: namely, that a certain way of life, corresponding to the construction and maintenance of a certain type of Southern white man, reached a conclusion with the commencement and development of the Great Migration.

To understand the marginalization of a phenomenon as massive and significant in historical, social, and cultural importance as the Great Migration, which is only today entering collective historical consciousness, one must look beyond Faulkner. Black migration was kept quiet in the South because of the meanings it conveyed about black people. The agency, independence, and self-determination that were evident in each act of migration interfered with the series of racialized polarities whose circulation privileged Manhood, Whiteness, and Southernness. Learning once and for all that these polarities were ungrounded was not simply unpleasant for Southern white men; rather, it was a lesson that unsettled the very ground of their being, leaving them to survive, if they survived at all, in the tragic, decadent, or buffoonish manners figured in the male characters that appear throughout Faulkner's writings. In fact, Faulkner seems to have required that nearly all his major characters grapple with the experience of annihilation, perhaps so that he could examine whether and how— for better or for worse—they endure it. With marginalized phenomena like the Great Migration only just beginning to elbow their way into mainstream narratives of American history, we have much to learn from Faulkner and the South about such exclusions and the possessive investment in Whiteness that has perpetuated them.

The process through which Faulkner recognized that the racialized polarities that constructed identity in the South were groundless was, in spite of all the cultural mechanisms intended to inhibit such recognition, triggered by black migration. When the opportunity presented itself, people to whom Faulkner was attached, people he believed were similarly attached to him, chose to leave him and the South in favor of making a life on their own. Evidence of such leave-takings appears throughout the footnotes of Joseph Blotner's two-volume biography of Faulkner. Moreover, Faulkner's writing consistently explored the depth of white Southerners' attachments to black Southerners, denial and repudiation of this attachment, and resistance to black agency. Only in later writings, such as *Intruder in the Dust*, did Faulkner more directly explore the asymmetry or one-sidedness of this attachment, to which black migration was already clear testimony. Not until the publication of the 1946 Compson Appendix, for example, was Faulkner willing to suggest that Dilsey left the Compson family to live with her daughter in the "Negro residence section" of Memphis. Never was Faulkner willing or able to imagine the reconstruction of Southern identity outside the South—for white or black Southerners—in anything but negative terms. Examples of his depiction of the deleterious effects of geographical and cultural dislocation can be readily found in *Soldiers' Pay, Flags in the Dust, The Sound and the Fury, Sanctuary, Light in August, Absalom, Absalom!, Pylon,* and *Go Down, Moses.* These narratives are informed and enriched when examined in the context of other versions of the migration experience, which are readily available in the burgeoning canon of African American migration narratives.

FURTHER READING

Griffin, Farah. *"Who Set You Flowin'?" The African-American Migration Narrative.* Oxford: Oxford University Press, 1995.

Grossman, James R. *Land of Hope: Chicago, Black Southerners, and the Great Migration.* Chicago: University of Chicago Press, 1989.

Lester, Cheryl. *"If I Forget Thee, Jerusalem* and the Great Migration: History in Black and White." *Faulkner in Cultural Context,* ed. Kartiganer and Abadie. 191–217.

———. "Racial Awareness and Arrested Development: *The Sound and the Fury* and the First Great Migration (1915–28)." *The Cambridge Companion to William Faulkner,* ed. Weinstein. 123–145.

Rodgers, Lawrence R. *Canaan Bound: The African-American Great Migration Novel.* Champaign-Urbana: University of Illinois Press, 1997.

Cheryl Lester

GREEN BOUGH, A, a volume of poems by Faulkner, published in 1933. Shortly after the publication of his second novel, *Mosquitoes,* in 1927, Faulkner approached his publisher about the possibility of publishing a second volume of verse (*SL* 37). Portions of poems subsequently included in *A Green Bough* appear in variant forms ascribed to the hand of the lesbian poet Eva Wiseman in *Mosquitoes,* and other related passages appear in *Soldiers' Pay,* Faulkner's hand-lettered volumes, and magazines such as *Contempo.* Thus Faulkner was actively, if sporadically and ambivalently, engaged in writing and revising poems throughout the 1920s. While he judged the results "2nd class poetry" in a letter to Harrison Smith (*SL* 54), he also told Smith that for *A Green Bough* he "chose the best ms. and built a volume just like a novel" (*SL* 67). Yet *A Green Bough* is less clearly an exercise in developing a poetic sequence than is *The Marble Faun* or the hand-lettered volumes he produced—and Faulkner's diffident participation in assembling the collection suggests his avowed resignation to "failure" as a poet.

It is difficult to place *A Green Bough* as a unified volume in a trajectory of authorial or representational development, but intertextual relations among the poems are intriguing and significant. Study of these relations must be guided, however, by information about manuscripts and prior publication; hence, Judith Sensibar's *Faulkner's Poetry: A Bibliographic Guide to Texts and Criticism* is essential to critical inquiry. The most extensive and persuasive critical treatment of the poems of *A Green Bough* in the context of Faulkner's development is by

Michel Gresset in *Fascination*. Gresset reads *A Green Bough* as signifying Faulkner's escape from early narcissistic immobility (evident, for him, in *The Marble Faun*) and engagement with the world as an ethical subject (borrowing from Kierkegaard the paradigm of development from the "aesthetic" approach to life to the "ethical"). Gresset describes the genesis of the Faulknerian text—focusing on "Poem X" of *A Green Bough*, the early sketch "The Hill," and the unpublished (in Faulkner's lifetime) short story "Nympholepsy"—skillfully interweaving textual and biographical approaches to argue that one can read "Poem X"/"The Hill" as Ur-texts for representation of the Faulknerian landscape. The landscape analogized to an urn and the laborer as a figure on it become a recurrent ground (scene) and figure (action) that is revised, reworked, and recontextualized throughout the major fiction.

As the work of a writer who had reached maturity in his prose writing by 1933, the poems in *A Green Bough* are remarkable for the degree to which they reveal the influence of other poets without ostensibly being imitations: Eliot (Poems I, II, XXV), Pound (IV), Housman (VI, XI, XII, XIII, XV, XXIII), Poe (XIX), Shelley (XX), Shakespeare (XXVII, XXXIX, XL), and others among his near-contemporaries. "Poem VII" even borrows four lines from the tenth section of *The Marble Faun*. Yet many images and turns of phrase clearly belong to the Faulknerian repertoire. Much as Gresset can see a central intertextual relevance in "Poem X," one can note other parallels and intertextual relations. "Poem XL," for instance, is echoed in the description of Narcissa Benbow and her relationship with Bayard Sartoris in *Sartoris/Flags in the Dust*. These verbal relations indicate not only Faulkner's frequent reuse of material but also the importance of particular tropes to his imaginative life and the necessity for readers of attending to the idiosyncratic significance of particular words and to dispersed and submerged verbal patterns in Faulkner's poetry and prose.

Stephen Hahn

GREENFIELD FARM. Early in 1938 Faulkner bought a 320-acre farm, which he named Greenfield Farm, just north of Highway 30, seventeen miles northeast of Oxford and almost exactly midway to his birthplace in New Albany. The farm, now owned by the University of Mississippi, is in Beat Two, then the toughest part of Lafayette County, near Woodson Ridge. Perhaps not coincidentally, it had been the family home of Joe Parks, a banker and putative model for Flem Snopes, who had just purchased Murry Falkner's home on North Street. The land consisted of hills with blue-green pines and bottom land for raising corn and hay for livestock; Faulkner planned from the first to raise mules there. His brother John and his family initially lived on and managed the farm; Faulkner kept the studbook and made frequent trips from Rowan Oak to oversee the work. Faulkner had admired mules since his tribute to them in *Flags in the Dust*, and the terrain may have reminded him of Sartoris farmland and the farm the tall convict plows; in time, Faulkner would arrange for the construction of a cabin, called "The Lodge," to which he would occassionally retreat to meditate and write. Greenfield Farm, with its own commissary, became the model for the McCaslin plantation. The hills there are reminiscent of the landscapes of many of Faulkner's early poems, including his self-epitaph concerning "these green woods. . . . Within my heart" and the "earth that holds me fast." Although Faulkner never worked the farm itself, he visits it and poses there on a tractor in the closing scenes of the Ford Foundation *Omnibus* film made for television in 1952. Stories are told in Oxford of Faulkner's creating farm jobs to provide employment for hard-pressed locals.

Arthur F. Kinney

GRIERSON, EMILY, the protagonist of Faulkner's well-known short story "A Rose for Emily." She lives in the shadow of her domineering father, who, while her contemporaries court and marry, keeps any potential suitors for Emily's hand at bay. After his death she is left with only an old house and her pride. The summer following her father's death, Emily has a brief affair with Homer Barron, the foreman of a Northern paving company, which scandalizes the town. A Baptist minister and two relatives are unable to change her behavior. Then Homer disappears concurrently with Emily's purchase of arsenic. The town takes his absence as evidence of his jilting of Emily, whose life thereafter is increasingly circumscribed by the four walls of her father's house. For a time she gives china-painting lessons to young women but eventually becomes a recluse. The community approaches her, first, over an unpleasant odor coming from the house. The town's aldermen feel they cannot ask a lady to deal with such a matter, so instead they try to dissipate it by coming at night to sprinkle lime about the foundations of her house. Second, the alderman asks her to pay taxes. She responds by calling upon the promise of a dead patron, Colonel Sartoris, to justify her nonpayment. After her death, the townspeople discover Homer Barron's corpse in an upstairs bedroom and find evidence that Emily has slept with the corpse of the man she murdered.

Certain critical concerns have dominated the discussion of Emily's characterization: the oppressive patriarchy of her father and her presumed Electra complex, the extent to which her life and misfortune symbolize the South and its conditions, and the nature and significance of her relationship to the community of Jefferson.

See also **Gothic**.

FURTHER READING

Inge, M. Thomas. *William Faulkner: "A Rose for Emily."* Columbus, Ohio: Charles E. Merrill Publishing Company, 1970.

Glenn M. Reed

GROVE, LENA, a major character in Faulkner's novel *Light in August*. As with most of his characters, Faulkner never described Lena's physical features, but we still picture her in that joyous opening chapter, wandering afoot, saving her dusty men's shoes for town. With her nine-month belly, this "lady" arrives in August (the time of Caesar Augustus), wearing Mary's blue and carrying a palm leaf fan, a happy blend of madonna and the fertility goddess, Isis (whose images were early confused with Mary's), who also took to the road.

Lena comes from Doane's Mill, Alabama, where she helped her brother's family after he had taken her in, an orphan at twelve. When Lucas Burch got her pregnant, she quietly climbed out her window, following the "word" of the father, who had promised to send for her, "serene" in her faith that the Lord would provide. And she is right. The folks she meets question her sharply about that father, but in the end they help her along.

A confusion of names sends Lena to Byron Bunch. Oddly, she is suspicious of him, and he does unwittingly reveal that Lucas is that worthless fellow calling himself "Joe Brown." In love with her, Byron brings Lena to Mrs. Beard's boardinghouse and then to a cabin on Joanna Burden's property; later he gets Hightower to help deliver her baby and determines that he will "whip" Brown.

Often cited in theories on Faulkner's misogyny, Lena is called "bovine" and "mindless" based on that tranquil opening chapter when she moves along the "peaceful corridors" with "calm unreason." But Lena is no placid earth mother when she looks at her birthing body "with wailing and hopeless terror." Nor is she mindless about Lucas; as Byron says, part of her "knows that he is a scoundrel." And although Isis was a cow-goddess, Lena is not bovine in her initial suspicion of Byron or her final teasing acceptance, the two of them traveling on beyond Jefferson.

FURTHER READING

Douglas, Ellen. "Faulkner's Women." *"A Cosmos of My Own,"* ed. Fowler and Abadie. 156–157.

Hlavsa, Virginia V. "The Woman in Faulkner." *Women's Studies* 22 (1993): 543–551.

Kazin, Alfred. "The Stillness of *Light in August*." *Partisan Review* 24 (1957): 519–538.

Lind, Ilse Desoir. "Faulkner's Women." *The Maker and the Myth*, ed. Harrington and Abadie. 89–104.

Mortimer, Gail L. "The Smooth, Suave Shape of Desire: Paradox in Faulknerian Imagery of Women." *Women's Studies* 13 (1986): 149–161.

Virginia V. James Hlavsa

"GUEST'S IMPRESSION OF NEW ENGLAND, A," a personal essay Faulkner wrote describing a trip he took through rural Connecticut and Massachusetts with Malcolm Cowley in October 1948, first published in *New England Journeys Number 2: Ford Times Special Edition* in 1954 and reprinted in James B. Meriwether's *Essays, Speeches & Public Letters by William Faulkner* (1965). In this somewhat fanciful narrative Faulkner respectfully contrasts the taciturn, stoical, self-reliant New Englander with the more garrulous and sociable inhabitants of the West, the Midwest, and the South.

Louis Daniel Brodsky

H

"HAIR," a short story by Faulkner, was first published in *American Mercury* in May 1931; it also appears in *These 13* (1931) and *Collected Stories*. A traveling salesman tells the story of a barber called "Hawkshaw" in Jefferson, who twice remains faithful in love despite unfortunate circumstances. His first fiancée dies young, and Hawkshaw dedicates himself to fulfilling his promise to pay the mortgage on her dead father's property. His second love, linked to the first by her hair—not yellow and not brown—is an orphan who grows up to be sexually promiscuous by the time she is in her early teens. Hawkshaw ignores the townspeople's way of seeing things and, once he has fulfilled his promise to his first love, marries his second love and disappears. Though at times sardonic, the narrator seems largely sympathetic toward Hawkshaw, respectful of his silent ways; and the narrative distance created in the story by the salesman's limited point of view serves to isolate the honorable, if curious, Hawkshaw out of the talking and disparaging world. As critics have pointed out, storytelling itself seems a primary focus of "Hair." Hawkshaw also appears as a principal character in another Faulkner story, "Dry September."

FURTHER READING

Flynn, Peggy. "The Sister Figure and 'Little Sister Death' in the Fiction of William Faulkner." *University of Mississippi Studies in English* 14 (1976): 99–117.

Watson, Judson D., III. " 'Hair,' 'Smoke,' and the Development of the Faulknerian Lawyer Character." *Mississippi Quarterly* 43 (1990): 349–366.

Arthur A. Brown

HAMLET, THE (1940), one of the longest of Faulkner's novels, is the first volume of a trilogy focusing on the Snopes clan, the latter two volumes of which—*The Town* and *The Mansion*—were not published until the 1950s. The setting is the rural community of Frenchman's Bend southeast of the fictional

Jefferson, sometime after 1890. All the major characters are white, and the action revolves around their economic and amorous interactions. Faulkner began writing the novel in the mid-1920s (*see* **Father Abraham**), and substantial portions derive from revisions of short stories written and mostly published during the 1930s: "Lizards in Jamshyd's Courtyard," "The Hound," "Spotted Horses," and "Afternoon of a Cow." "Barn Burning," which provides a kind of back story to the action at the opening of the novel, was originally the first chapter, but it was removed in the later stages of composition and published separately. For a number of early critics, Faulkner's stitching together of previously existing material, however much it may have been revised, supports claims that the novel lacks unity or appears to have only thematic unity.

The novel is divided into four "books" ("Flem," "Eula," "The Long Summer," and "The Peasants"), and the narrative is, on the surface, loosely structured, episodic, and digressive. Despite this apparent looseness, however, the various constituent narratives, each with its own structure, coalesce around the story of the incursion of the Snopes clan into Frenchman's Bend and the central event of the murder of Jack Houston by Mink Snopes. It is Flem Snopes (son of "Ab" or "Abraham") with his persistent insinuation of himself into the fabric of the community, displacing the rustically seignorial Will Varner, who lends continuity to the action in the novel—being involved in nearly all actions either by his presence or, in the case of his cousin Mink's trial and conviction and of his own civil trial, by his telling absence. Flem's influence is felt throughout, despite the fact that he is taciturn and spends a good portion of the novel in Texas. Likewise, while the story is told by an omniscient narrator, the peddler and raconteur V. K. Ratliff is a central narrative presence: Privy to both domestic and public spheres, his imputed consciousness provides the reader (and his interlocutors) with information and insight about relationships and actions throughout the countryside. Thus, it is not the least of the novel's many ironies that it ends with a tale of Ratliff being outwitted by Flem Snopes in a scheme to sell the "Old Frenchman's Place."

Stylistically, the novel is as variegated as any of Faulkner's narratives that appear to be told by a single omniscient narrator—modulating from classical Balzacian realism to periodic, mock-epic historical narration, to lyrical mock-pastoral in the narrative of Labove's enthrallment to Eula and Ike Snopes's to a cow, to something more like psychological and social realism in the story of the conflict between Houston and Mink, and finally to the tall-tale humor in the stories of the spotted horses and the misguided treasure hunt on the Old Frenchman's Place. Thematically, the novel treats a series of transgressions against approved norms of the community. These include, for instance: Eula Varner's unconscious transgressions of feminine propriety and the corresponding actual or putative transgressions of male characters against the rule of virginity (and, in the case of Labove, both sanity and pedagogic propriety); Ike's transgression of the rule against bestiality; Mink's transgression of the rule against murder; and Flem's consistent transgressions of the rule against false witness and false representation. It can be said, then, that transgression—and the response of the community to it—is a central, unifying thematic element about which the concerns with economy, self-control, sexuality, and husbandry cohere. The effect is to dramatize the tension and play between notions of what is natural and what is ordered by precept.

Michael Millgate (*Achievement*) provides a comprehensive summary of the textual history of the novel, as well as insightful critical analysis of the novel's stylistic virtuosity, sociological richness, and complex handling of themes of greed and self-interest. More specialized subsequent studies include Philip Cohen's examination of the oft-noted influence of Balzac on Faulkner; Barbara Monroe's treatment of honor and humor as they are involved in the comic tone of the book (and as they involve gendered reading); Daniel Hoffman's study of the novel in relation to American folk- and joke-lore; and James Snead's post-structuralist analysis of the ideology of "equalization" at play in the economic interactions among characters and in modes of narration, both authorial and embedded.

As Snead argues, for those who would read *The Hamlet* primarily as a story of the displacement of one order, identified with the reign of Will Varner, and the emergence of another, identified as Snopesism, an important element is Faulkner's structuring of the story as a myth of origin. If the arrival of "Snopes" into the land is the beginning of the end for some, is it because the Snopes principle is fundamentally different from the Varner principle? Or does Snopes simply supply an organizing principle similar to Varner's, which entails strategies for the expropriation of value in a system of exchange? Put another way, is the pre-Snopes milieu of Frenchman's Bend more "natural" (and therefore, presumably, good) than the post-Snopes milieu—or is each generation caught up in getting and spending, having and holding, by then current means? How does the attitude ascribed to those who owe fealty to Varner—"*What do you* [Varner] *think you would like for me to do if you was able to make me do it*"— differ from the attitude with which people approach a Snopes? The interactions among the characters, particularly in the auction of the spotted horses, suggest that one person's gain depends on the acquiescence of others to that person's right to gain under a social fiction of the equality of exchange. In this regard, it is not so much the presumptive "taking" on the part of either Snopes or Varner that matters as it is the blind willingness of others to cede control of their will—as the auction of the worthless animals cannot proceed until someone makes a bid on one of them. The ideology of economic self-interest as a universal is therefore illusory and already premised on a contradiction: The self-interest of one is inimical to the self-interest of all or any. The reductio ad absurdum of self-interest, murder (whether physical or psychic), is simply the extension of the principle to the point that it destroys itself. As Mink thinks to himself (without irony, though we are meant to read the passage with irony), "It's like just about everything was in cahoots against one man killing another."

Despite the absence of African American characters as significant actors in the narrative, Faulkner inserts into the novel a critique of racist attitudes parallel to the implied critique of self-interest taken to its [il]logical extreme. In jail awaiting trial for having murdered Jack Houston in cold blood, and thus for having violated one of the most fundamental precepts of any society, Mink watches his "negro" fellow prisoners ascend the stairs for supper: "Are they going to feed them niggers before they do a white man? he thought, smelling the coffee and the ham." The degree to which, for Mink, his sense of superiority appears to him as a fact of nature rather than a historical outcome of oppression is a measure of the degree to which critical consciousness—the ability to discern the difference between what is given and what is made—fails to function for him. To a large extent, it is precisely the discernment of the discrepancy between what is given and what is made that funds the irony and both the grim and genial humor of the novel. Despite its being focused almost entirely on the milieu of rural Southern whites, *The Hamlet* has broad cultural implications.

FURTHER READING

Beck, Warren. *Man in Motion: Faulkner's Trilogy*. Madison: University of Wisconsin Press, 1961.
Cohen, Philip. "French Peasants and Southern Snopeses: Balzac's *Les Paysans* and Faulkner's *The Hamlet*." *Mississippi Quarterly* 40 (1987): 383–392.
Hoffman, Daniel. *Faulkner's Country Matters*. 71–106.
Holmes, Catherine D. *Annotations to William Faulkner's* The Hamlet. New York: Garland, 1996.
Monroe, Barbara. "Reading Faulknerian Comedy: Humor and Honor in *The Hamlet*." *Southern Quarterly* 26.4 (1988): 33–56.
Urgo. *Faulkner's Apocrypha*.
Watson, James G. *The Snopes Dilemma: Faulkner's Trilogy*. Coral Gables, Fla.: University of Miami Press, 1968.

Stephen Hahn

HAWTHORNE, NATHANIEL. *See* **American Renaissance**.

HEAT. Of all the regionalist aspects of Faulkner's fiction, none is more noticeable than Mississippi's climate. Heat is the element evoking Faulkner's relation to the native place, both the "real" and the "apocryphal." "Element" should be understood in Gaston Bachelard's sense, when he describes the four elements as vectors of the creativity of our minds rather than as mere perceptions of the world. In Faulkner's work, heat provides a rich source of poetic and symbolic associations. Faulkner's handling of heat oscillates between the syntagmatic axis (the metonymic, literal level) where heat is experienced as a climatic factor, desiccating and oppressive, and the paradigmatic axis, where heat becomes a narrative device functioning as token of the unsaid.

Heat is channeled into a climatic expression: summer. The Faulknerian summer dominates the cycle of the seasons and orchestrates the temporal space around its imagination. The insistence on summer manifests what Charles Mauron calls a "personal myth" defined as "correspondence between the dramatic structure of the work and the writer's deep, fundamental phantasm." Heat is thus a synecdoche of Faulkner's imaginary world and of the Southern imagination fixated in the contemplation and commemoration of its August season. Yet the glorious sun of the August season of the South entailed murder and destruction—a past that can neither be represented nor forgotten but returns through the motif of the aggressiveness of heat.

Heat emerges as an agent of erosion—erosion of the soil and of people. The fierceness of the climatic factor is translated to the land and the characters' psychological tensions. Heat is exacerbated and exacerbates and functions as a Derridean "trace" of the violence underlying the foundation of the South. Faulkner's handling of heat thus orchestrates a principle of substitution and analogy. Suggestive heat motifs evoke the violence of animated discussions. In *Absalom, Absalom!* public opinion is outraged at Sutpen's enterprise, and things smolder until "civic virtue came to a boil" because something "transpired" in Sutpen's deeds. By locating the violence in terms of the weather, Faulkner translates (shifts) social tensions, in particular racial tensions, as in "Dry September" where the lynching is never described but suggested through the description of the ambient stifling heat.

The handling of heat underlines the traces of the founding history of the South, a history shaped by violence and destruction. Yet the use of heat as the vector of the unsaid testifies to an impossibility or a refusal to describe such violence and an attempt to poeticize it. The poetics of heat results in the creation of an oppressive and obsessive climate in keeping with the Southern motifs of doom and obsession. The multiple aspects of heat represent the ambivalence informing the imaginary world of the South: shame (guilt) and pride, expiation and glorification, amnesia and nostalgia.

FURTHER READING

Bachelard, Gaston. *Fragments of a Poetics of Fire*. Trans. Kenneth Haltmann. Dallas, Tex.: Dallas Institute of Humanities and Culture, 1990.
———. *The Psychoanalysis of Fire*. Boston: Beacon, 1964.
Liénard, Marie. "Poetics of Heat in Mauriac's Landes and Faulkner's Yoknapatawpha County." Dissertation. Cornell University, 1996.

Marie Liénard

HELEN: A COURTSHIP, a poetry sequence that Faulkner created in 1925 for Helen Baird, whom he had met earlier that year in New Orleans. The "single manuscript impression," as he termed it, dated "Oxford-Mississippi-June-1926," contains sixteen poems, all handwritten in his ornate script. "To Helen, Swimming" describes its subject as having the breasts and flanks of a boy, reflecting Faulkner's concept of the epicene ideal of women. "Bill" is a portrait of the poet himself, a man cursed with "the gift of tongues" who falls in love with silence as exemplified by Helen. Another sonnet, "Proposal," indicates that the book was, as its subtitle states, "a courtship." *Helen: A Courtship* was first published in 1981, in both a limited facsimile edition by Tulane University and as part of a joint trade edition with *Mississippi Poems*.

FURTHER READING

Collins, Carvel. "Biographical Background for Faulkner's *Helen*." *Helen: A Courtship and Mississippi Poems*. Oxford, Miss.: Tulane University and Yoknapatawpha Press, 1981. 9–10.

W. Kenneth Holditch

HEMINGWAY, ERNEST (1899–1961), American writer, winner of the 1954 Nobel Prize for Literature. Now that the twentieth century is almost over, it seems quite clear to most students and aficionados of American literature that Faulkner and Hemingway are our two greatest artists in fiction in this century—indeed, many would argue, in all centuries. Yet this critical anomaly persists: In spite of many shared aspects of characterization, subject matter, technique, and theme, and in spite of resonant intertextualities in their works and in the shape and conduct of their lives, very little serious scholarly attention has been devoted to reading and to studying Faulkner and Hemingway *together*. For the most part, both Faulkner and Hemingway studies have been content to make the usual brief passing nods to the other writer, to repeat the usual platitudes, and to avoid engaged comparative analysis of the two writers.

One exception to this rule may be found in Thomas L. McHaney's critical volume, *William Faulkner's* The Wild Palms: *A Study*. McHaney, particularly in his first chapter, "Anderson, Hemingway, and the Origins of *The Wild Palms*," considers Faulkner's novel and its many Hemingway allusions and echoes "in the significant context of a broad relation to Hemingway's work" (8). Taking his discussion well beyond the perplexing "hemingwaves" pun in *The Wild Palms*, McHaney usefully surveys and analyzes the "parallels" and "important links" between Faulkner's novel and Hemingway's work (especially *A Farewell to Arms*) that "have been overlooked" (12–13). However, McHaney falls far short of a complete discussion of crucial Faulkner-Hemingway intertextualities; moreover, his view of Hemingway (e.g., as "solipsist") needs rethinking in the light of recent Hemingway scholarship. Clearly, there is a kind of Faulkner-Hemingway dialogue present in their works, early to late, and that allusive dialogic intensity has barely begun to receive the necessary critical and scholarly attention. Thus, for example, McHaney's argument concerning Hemingway's presence in *The Wild Palms* needs to be extended to Hemingway's *The Garden of Eden*, which is, in one sense, a response to *The Wild Palms*.

Among others, Cleanth Brooks also notes, rather perfunctorily, the Hemingway allusions in *The Wild Palms*, placing them in the context of an appendix discussion of the sustainability of "the intensity of romantic love" (*Toward Yoknapatawpha* 408). In his classic study *William Faulkner: The Yoknapatawpha Country*, Brooks makes only four brief passing references to Hemingway.

Interesting and revealing references they are, to be sure; for example, Brooks devotes one sentence to his observation that *Sartoris* "most resembles . . . a novel by Ernest Hemingway" (114); and he notes in passing, more than once, that Faulkner had "a traditional society behind him as Hemingway did not" (207). The former perspicacious aside could well be developed in articles, books, dissertations; the latter observation needs to be carefully reexamined with adequate recognition that Hemingway's key characters are generally engaged in questing a truly traditional society, that indeed Hemingway's life and work are invested and conducted in a *more* traditional (i.e., Catholic and European) society than Faulkner's.

In general, what is needed in those Faulkner-Hemingway studies that may yet appear is a deeper recognition and exact understanding that Hemingway's "code" of multiple forms of "grace under pressure" and the "secret" of "the values" that Count Mippipopolus talks about in *The Sun Also Rises*, the Priest discusses in *A Farewell to Arms*, and Santiago embodies in *The Old Man and the Sea* are in precise accord with Faulkner's "eternal verities," with the vision incarnate in Ratliff, Sam Fathers, Ike, and Cass McCaslin. We need to study the connections, the direct lines of relationship between young Bayard Sartoris and Jake Barnes, between Caddy Compson and Brett Ashley, Harry Wilbourne and David Bourne, Lena Grove and Maria (and Pilar), Sam Fathers and Santiago. We need to meditate on the resonances of the allusions that both writers make to such matters as Carcassonne, Roland, and Roncevaux and grasp the significance of these allusions. We need close comparative readings of their World War I and Waste Land themes and images. And we need to see with exactitude that Faulkner's Bear and Hemingway's Marlin, and all who pursue them, are brothers—blood brothers and code brothers—in the eyes of God, Nature, and the creators who make them.

Faulkner studies and Hemingway studies are perhaps the two most widely practiced pursuits of American literary scholarship, yet they remain separate, isolate, lacking any real critical or creative communication or communion. The evidence of this curious lack of communion is pervasive. For example, some of us—very few—have taught, for decades, courses and seminars that extensively and intensively combine Faulkner and Hemingway. Yet when this writer conducted an informal nationwide and worldwide survey in the 1970s and 1980s, only *four* regularly taught Faulkner-Hemingway courses could be identified at the hundreds of institutions queried. Indeed, some of us—the number may be counted on one hand—have attended both Faulkner conferences and Hemingway conferences around the world for decades, and we have noted what strikes us as one of the great oddities of our literary and academic milieus: Faulkner enthusiasts generally know or care little about Hemingway, and Hemingway aficionados generally know or care little about Faulkner. Perhaps it is the business of the twenty-first century to study these two great creators of fictional worlds in a proper fructifying mutuality.

On the biographical front, there are also platitudes to be swept away. It seems that everyone is prepared to parrot what is still referred to as Faulkner's low "ranking" of Hemingway as artist. Yet, as Faulkner said, he had to explain for two decades that it was not a serious "ranking." As Faulkner also said, Hemingway did "consistently probably the most solid work of all of us" (*FIU* 143–144). And Hemingway consistently expressed his admiration for Faulkner's work. One sometimes hears the regret expressed, among the few true aficionados of *both* writers, that they never met, even though, for example, they lived near each other in Paris, walked the same streets, went to Mass at the same Cathedral (St. Sulpice), probably passed each other in the Luxembourg Gardens, which they both loved, which they both frequented in 1926. Yet they almost did meet, years later, when Hemingway went to Oxford specifically to see Faulkner, a biographical fact that has recently been revealed. After the contretemps over Faulkner's reported "ranking" of Hemingway, they exchanged letters; Faulkner apologized. Hemingway wrote back, a warm and revealing letter, offering a lament for how his native country had been ruined by gas stations and subdivisions, how the trees had all been cut down, and thus he had been a "chickenshit dis-placed person" for as long as he could remember. And he told Faulkner that he was his "brother" (*Ernest Hemingway: Selected Letters* [Scribner, 1981] 623–625). Thus, in 1947, Hemingway acknowledges Faulkner as a man and writer with a rooted sense of place, and he laments his own lack of place, his displacedness. A few weeks later Hemingway makes his pilgrimage to Oxford, to the Capitol of Place in American Literature, to see Faulkner. But Hemingway does not tell Faulkner he is coming, and Faulkner is not at home because, according to Hemingway's driver, Faulkner is being honored in some kind of community observance. So Hemingway leaves Oxford, goes up the northbound highway to the only location where he ever felt profoundly *placed*, to northern Michigan. There is no more important moment in American literary history.

H. R. Stoneback

HIGHTOWER, GAIL, the aptly named defrocked clergyman, is the most reclusive of Jefferson's considerable population of hermits in *Light in August*. Twenty-five years earlier, Reverend Hightower came to Jefferson with his bride, ostensibly to assume the pastorate of the Presbyterian Church. In reality, Hightower arrives in Jefferson to serve his private obsession with his namesake grandfather, a Confederate cavalry officer killed in a raid on Jefferson long before his grandson was even born. After Mrs. Hightower dies scandalously, his church forces Hightower to resign. Of the novel's prisoners of the past, Hightower may be the most fettered—and perhaps the most pathetic since grandfather Gail did not die a glorious death in the service of the "lost cause" but suffered a ludicrous demise in being blown out of his saddle while stealing chickens. Yet of the characters crippled by the past, Hightower is the only one who achieves some illumination in this August. Prodded by his only friend, Byron Bunch, Hightower reinvolves himself in life by delivering Lena Grove's child and attempting, albeit futilely, to provide an alibi for Joe Christmas. In chapter 20, after Joe's death in his kitchen, the aging minister reviews his life as he sits in his study window facing the street his grandfather charged down. He realizes that he betrayed his calling, that he was accountable for his wife's misery, and that the private deal he thought he had with the universe was fallacious and self-serving. His agonizing meditation, a sort of Gethsemane, leads him to see that life is interconnected, that we are responsible to and for others, and that seeking "immunity" from life is actually death.

FURTHER READING

Benson, Carl. "Thematic Design in *Light in August.*" *South Atlantic Quarterly* 53 (1954): 540–555.

Berland, Alwyn. Light in August: *A Study in Black and White*. New York: Twayne, 1992.

Collins, R. G. "*Light in August*: Faulkner's Stained Glass Triptych." *Mosaic* 7 (1973): 97–157.

Hungerford, Harold. "Past and Present in *Light in August.*" *American Literature* 55 (1983): 183–198.

Lind, Ilse Dusoir. "The Calvinistic Burden of *Light in August.*" *New England Quarterly Review* 30 (1957): 307–329.

David L. Vanderwerken

"HILL, THE," an early narrative by Faulkner, was published in *The Mississippian* (March 10, 1922) and reprinted in *Early Prose and Poetry* (1962). A man climbs a hill at sunset; he looks out over a calm valley; he briefly forgets his daily trouble to find work and food; he slowly descends. This very short story, a prose poem in five paragraphs, is viewed, like "Nympholepsy," as a pivotal piece by many critics. Here, Faulkner brings the visionary, nymph-haunted landscape of his poems into the realistic world of toil and labor that would become the little patch of ground of his major fictions. He would continue to use the evening setting, the strangely lit hill and valley, with the air of a hovering revelation, at heightened moments in his later narratives. In the person of the "tieless casual," Faulkner gives us a glimpse, too, of a new kind of hero, very different from the dandy figures of his poems: a poor man, laborer, and wanderer, like many of his future protagonists.

FURTHER READING

Gresset, Michel. "Faulkner's 'The Hill.' " *Southern Literary Journal* 6:2 (1974): 3–18.

Momberger, Philip. "A Reading of Faulkner's 'The Hill.' " *Southern Literary Journal* 9.2 (1977): 16–29.

Pamela E. Knights

HISTORICAL MATERIALISM. For the historical materialist, reality is more made than found, being made primarily by human work. In the process of making their material and social conditions, men and women also make their natures, which—since they are constructed—are mutable and historically particular. Language, too, is a made thing, made meaningful by what is done with it; so that the meaning of a word depends upon how it is used by socially located speakers. Consequently, readers of fiction read what is in several senses "work," and materialist critics are particularly concerned to trace how specific systems of labor condition linguistic work and to discern how, in turn, that work of grounded words finds its way into the stylistic habits and narrative options of the literary work.

Faced with Benjy Compson's claim, "Caddy smelled like trees," a historical materialist might ask, "What are the conditions of his utterance?" Early among them would be that it is unuttered; Benjy is incapable of speech. Thirty-three, with a mental age of perhaps three, analogy, too, should elude him. Given that he has been read as largely devoid of consciousness, the conditions attendant upon his untypical mental act should be revealing. In 1898, Caddy climbed a tree to see into a room containing her grandmother's corpse. Looking up from the base of the tree, Benjy saw a muddy stain on her underpants. Faulkner claimed that *The Sound and the Fury* stems from that "mental picture" (*LIG* 244), as does Benjy's consciousness since none of his perceptions predates the tree climbing episode. It follows that until 1898, and Damuddy's death, Benjy (born 1895) is a blank. Indeed, of the 100-plus pieces that make up the day of his monologue (April 7, 1928), the majority occur before 1910 (the date of Caddy's wedding), suggesting that Benjy has temporal preferences—that he would rather be earlier, and nearer the unclimbed tree with his sister, than later and at a loss for the smell of trees and for Caddy, married and gone away.

Benjy's tree comes biblically dressed: As Caddy climbs, a paternal prohibition is voiced; a snake crawls from under the house, and Dilsey cries, "You, Satan." The point is not to rehearse Genesis but to locate conditions that may be said to give rise to Benjy's analogy. For a materialist, those conditions are necessarily external and determining, which is to say they are social before they are conscious, and they are historical prior to their linguistic realization. If Benjy "falls" into consciousness and language in 1898, his own sense of that lapse stems from the sexual practices and fears of those among whom he lives. Benjy's analogy implies two plots: Smelling his chosen smell, he can either jump back into a silent and prelapsarian space iconicized as clean undergarments and a sister's hymen, or he can fall forward into noisy, stained, and deathly times associated with a sister's sexual knowledge.

What conditions Benjy's analogy is therefore his sister's sexuality. But why should a hymen matter quite so much? The question begs a further question of those who would read from context to text: If conditions always have conditions, where does a reader stop? Or, if she cannot stop, will it not be necessary, in order to say one thing (about an analogy), first to say everything else? A materialist's emphasis on labor ends this otherwise potentially infinite critical regression. The condition of Caddy's sexuality (itself the conditioner of Benjy's language, consciousness, and temporal sense) is conditioned by a racial pathology, which in turn arises from a labor circumstance. At this point, the holistic impulse of the materialist finds its causal source, grounded in work.

To put flesh on these summary bones: Like Benjy, the other Compson brothers struggle to preserve the hypothetical hymen of their sister but do so in ways that evoke the fear that her sexual activity will "blacken" her and her family in more than name. For Quentin, Caddy's suitors are repeatedly "blackguards," encouraging her to *"do like nigger women do in the pasture the ditches the dark woods."* But he, too, is a suitor, of incestuous inclination, and so may be a "black[. . .]guard." Jason, too young to police Caddy's promiscuities, practices on the surrogate form of her daughter, Miss Quentin, protesting, voyeuristically, that he is a "slave" unequal to the task of preventing her "going on like a nigger wench," when "it's in her blood." By implication the hymen functions as a color line: Intact, it expels the ethnic foreigner; broken, it admits him—though elements in the brother's rhetoric imply their sense that he has long since entered.

Reasons for Quentin and Jason's secret and fascinated fear that their sister's body may harbor a black transcend pathologies about miscegenation, since in the South, as the historian Joel Williamson argues, whites are the persons black people make by the sheer manner and number of their regional presence. Consequently, to do as the Compson brothers would do, to expel the notional black from the notionally pure body of Caddy (and so from the family "blood"), would be to expel what makes them what they are. Williamson asks: "How [does one] take the racism, the unreality of seeing black as either child or beast, out of the Southern mind without killing the Southerner? How does one excise a functioning part of the body and yet preserve the life of the patient?" (*The Crucible of Race* [Oxford University Press, 1984] 499). These questions are particularly acute for a Southern writer in the 1930s, since, historically speaking, the white owning class are experiencing a radical shift in the manner and presence of black people among them.

The above comments demonstrate how a historical materialist might read in order to exemplify the critical procedures of that methodological habit. Such a reading carries one a long way from Benjy's sense of smell and toward issues of labor history, though for a materialist the two (odor and work) are necessarily related. Benjy's whiff of trees is deeply double (prelapsarian and lapsed; hymenal and penetrated; white and black). The smell's duplicity repeats, at some remove, a ramifying structural duplicity within the experience of work in the South.

From the Civil War to the late 1930s, the region's labor system was characterized by "dependency." In effect, from Lincoln's Emancipation Proclamation (1863) to the New Deal's Agricultural Adjustment Program (1933–1938), the Southern owning class conducted a long counterrevolution, resisting all attempts to translate the bound laborer into the free employee. They struggled on behalf of dependency in the face of autonomy, seeking to preserve their status as masters rather than employers. Put reductively, from 1791 to 1933, the planter demands some version of what Mark Tushnet calls the "total relations" of slavery (*The American Law of Slavery* [Princeton University Press, 1981] 8). The names change; the tethers that bind are modified; but the goal remains—a system of production turning on relations of personal dependency and involving the whole life of the slave (tenant) and the whole life of the master (employer). As an Arkansas sharecropper put it in 1939, "De landlord is landlord, de policeman is landlord, de shurf is landlord, ever'body is landlord, en we ain't got nothing" (Kirby, *Rural Worlds Lost* [LSU Press, 1987] 239). The experience of having next to nothing may not have changed for many Southerners in the 1930s, but the manner in which they received nothing was radically altered by the Agricultural Adjustment Act of 1933. Responding to an ever-falling price for cotton and a glutted market, the act sought to restrict overproduction by offering landowners cash incentives to plough their crop under. Fifty-three percent of the South's cotton acreage went out of production. Since a sharecropper, cropping on a half the crop agreement, would by rights receive half the federal payment for the sacrifice of any of his acres, it paid the landowners not to sign sharecropping contracts for the following year. Instead, they might hire the same cropper on a wage, pay him to plough the crop under, and reap the entire subsidy themselves. Between 1933 and 1940 the Southern tenantry declined by more than 25 percent, whereas the number of hired laborers increased, though not proportionately, since landowners might simply evict any unnecessary "dependents." A "New South" was born. Eviction, enclosure, and drastically increased tenant mobility are the visible marks of a structural change, as sharecroppers are made over into cash workers, "free" to be underemployed or unemployed in a region where dependency is finally ousted by autonomy as a cultural dominant.

However, Faulkner was raised within an economy and culture defined by codependency between owner and owned, and so, for a materialist, his writing necessarily reflects the coerced affinities of dependency. To say as much is not simply to note that there are a lot of white planters and black tenants in his books. Rather, it is to explore how the difficulties of his fiction may be said to be generated by a central contradiction within Southern culture.

For the owner, committed to the "total relations" of bound labor, what he owns—his properties and his body—results from black work. From such a recognition it is a small step to the conclusion that whites are blacks in white-face. The step is both likely and, for the owning class, untenable. Ab Snopes, a sharecropper on de Spain's land, can call de Spain's plantation house "Nigger sweat." Sutpen, in *Absalom, Absalom!*, knows as much but can say so only indirectly; he calls his black son Charles Bon. Bon: Good: goods—the pun is cruelly obvious and allows him to declare that his son, being black goods, is no son of his. However, the pun contains, residually, the psychic cost of Sutpen's dismissive act of naming. Bon: Good—i.e., all that is of value and springs from Sutpen is black. The word "Bon" is as split as Benjy's fondness for the smell of trees; both divide along a social impulse to expel the body of the black as that which is structurally integral to the body of the white. Expulsion, however, must remain incomplete, since without the effects of black work (without, that is, the extended body of the black), secreted about his person and his properties, the white owner, be he a planter or the idiot son of a house built on plantation profits, will not be Southern. He will instead be modern, lacking the generative and archaic contradiction from which his doubt-filled Southern integrity takes its form. A historical materialist might wish to hazard the suggestion that it is from within just such a constellation of difficulty that the dis-integrity of Faulkner's major fiction is generated.

FURTHER READING

Godden. *Fictions of Labor.*

Lester, Cheryl. "Racial Awareness and Arrested Development: *The Sound and the Fury* and the Great Migration." *The Cambridge Companion to William Faulkner*, ed. Weinstein. 123–145.

Mandle, Jay. *Not Slave, Not Free: The African American Experience Since the Civil War.* Durham, N.C.: Duke University Press, 1992.

Matthews, John T. The Sound and the Fury: *Faulkner and the Lost Cause.* Boston: Twayne Publishers, 1991.

Williams, Raymond. *Problems in Materialism and Culture.* London: Verso, 1980.

Richard Godden

HISTORY. Intrinsic uncertainty in the interpretation of history is an important focus in various works of William Faulkner. In recent years, history has been seen as little more than myths that are agreed upon by particular groups of people. These myths determine the group's past in cultural and traditional ways that are distorted. As Bleikasten ("A Furious Beating of Hollow Drums") points out, when Faulkner fictionalized the history of the South, thereby foregrounding that history is a literary creation, he questioned the very premises upon which classical historiography rests.

The impossibility of finding the truth of history, or the many visions of that truth, at times arrived at through complicity or evasion, informs Faulkner's *Absalom, Absalom!, Light in August, The Sound and the Fury, As I Lay Dying*, and *Requiem for a Nun*. In *Absalom*, as Faulkner holds back information, readers as well as Quentin, Shreve, and Rosa are forced to puzzle out the past, since what they know seems inexplicable. In their search for truth, they grasp certain evidence that appears to be fact; but, as they proceed, that truth is shattered, so they must loop back to find new pathways to follow: They become detectives of history.

Faulkner develops *Light in August* in zigzags of loose, unstructured memory/history and time shifts: Joe's ethnic background, his childhood, Joanna's family history, Hightower's evocations of the Civil War, different perspectives of the same materials by first-person narrators interspersed with third-person omniscient narrators who at times are speaking for the first-person protagonist.

The social, historical, and political affairs of the South formed the background against which Faulkner presents his works. He breaks the basic traditional plot continuity, syntax and coherence of language, and ways of presenting characters in his novels, so that they reflect the condition of human beings in traditional societies. These traditions, which have no meaning in the twentieth century, psychologically destroy the person living in a meaningless society in which, rather than hope for change, there is only ennui, stasis, destruction. Faulkner obfuscates history since it cannot be verified, only read or heard, not experienced.

FURTHER READING

Bleikasten, André. "A Furious Beating of Hollow Drums Toward Nowhere: Faulkner, Time, and History." *Faulkner and History*, ed. Coy and Gresset. 77–96.
Hamblin, Robert W. *"No Such Thing as Was": William Faulkner and Southern History.* Cape Girardeau: Southeast Missouri State University, Center for Faulkner Studies, 1994.
Williamson. *William Faulkner and Southern History.*

June Townsend

"HOG PAWN," a short story by Faulkner, was likely composed in 1954 but not published until its inclusion in *Uncollected Stories.* Narrated by Charles Mallison, the tale revolves around a feud between Otis Meadowfill and Orestes Snopes, backgrounded by the long-suffering Mrs. Meadowfill and a daughter, Essie, who quietly but firmly raises herself out of the situation. A foraging hog provides the narrative turn, but the real source of conflict is land. James Carothers observes of the combatants: "There is little, if anything, to choose between them, except that Snopes is willing to risk murder for the sake of victory in the feud" (135). Faulkner later used the narrative in *The Mansion.*

Diane Brown Jones

HOLLYWOOD. Faulkner's work in Hollywood was crucial to the development of his craft. Misunderstood initially as something he did only out of a desperate need for money, it has since been established not only that Faulkner's career as a scriptwriter afforded opportunities to recast and create new fictional forms but also that California itself provided a suitable physical environment for writing portions of a number of novels, including *Absalom, Absalom!* and *The Wild Palms.* In addition, Faulkner did fine work for the movies, contributing to over fifty film projects and proving to be a highly adaptable, cooperative, and productive film writer. The fact that some of Faulkner's scripts (for example, *The De Gaulle Story* and *Battle Cry*) were never filmed may have a great deal to do with the disparaging remarks Faulkner often made about Hollywood. For a writer who finished almost everything he started, even things some critics believe he perhaps ought not have completed, to work for months on a project only to have it scrapped by "higher ups" far removed from the actual work was surely exasperating. In Japan in 1955, when asked about moviemaking, Faulkner's primary reservation was that "there's no chance for the individual to make something as he himself thinks it should be made" (*LIG* 153). Faulkner worked well with other writers and was a productive collaborator; nonetheless, in direct contradistinction to his career as a fiction writer, much of what he worked on in Hollywood went unproduced.

Faulkner spent four months in 1932 working for MGM Studios, three weeks in July 1934 at Universal Studios, five weeks in December–January 1934–1935 at 20th Century–Fox, where he worked again for two separate periods in 1936 and 1937, one for three months and another for a full year. These were productive and successful years, characterized by a steadily rising salary, starting at $500 a week and peaking at $1,000 a week in 1937. In the 1930s, according to Bruce Kawin's filmography, Faulkner worked on twenty projects, including such productions as *Today We Live* (MGM, 1933) (adapted from Faulkner's short story, "Turn About"), *Sutter's Gold* (Universal, 1936), *The Road to Glory* (20th Century–Fox, 1936), and *Drums Along the Mohawk* (20th Century–Fox, 1939). In 1942 Faulkner returned to Hollywood to work for Warner Bros. (WB) Studio under a distinctively unfavorable contract. Desperate for money to pay accumulating debts, he signed a seven-year contract, at $300 per week, in which Warner Bros. would own the rights to everything he wrote—including print fiction. The lasting effect of this experience produced the misconception that Faulkner's work in Hollywood was damaging to his career as a whole. There is no question that the Warner Bros. contract was detrimental to Faulkner's productivity in the 1940s, directly contributing to the slowed pace of fiction writing in the years during which Warner Bros. "owned Faulkner." Ironically, these were critical years in the establishment of Faulkner's literary reputation, aided by the work of critics such as Malcolm Cowley, whose *Portable Faulkner* was first published in 1946. Random House was instrumental in getting Faulkner released from the Warner Bros. contract that same year.

Despite the humiliating conditions under which he worked in the 1940s, Faulkner continued to produce material of high quality in Hollywood. The period of 1944–1945 was particularly fruitful, as Faulkner devoted nearly all of his energies to film instead of fiction. Although certain major projects would continue to go unproduced, including his screen adaptation of Stephen Longstreet's novel *Stallion Road*, Faulkner contributed to three important productions in this period: *To Have and Have Not* (WB, 1944), *The Southerner* (United Artists, 1945), and *The Big Sleep* (WB, 1946). After his release from the Warner Bros. contract, Faulkner continued to do paid work on movie scripts, including collaboration on *The Land of the Pharaohs* (WB, 1955) as a special favor to Howard Hawks.

The relationship between Hollywood and Faulkner's writing career is intricate. In the 1930s, Faulkner's work on movies was crucial in the advancement of his own fictional style, as is seen especially in the debt owed to moviemaking in *Absalom, Absalom!* and in the multiple ties to film in *The Wild Palms*. However, critics have also recognized the film aesthetic in novels such as *The Sound and the Fury* and *Sanctuary*, written prior to Faulkner's arrival in California; hence, Faulkner's early novels may have influenced filmmaking as much as his later novels were influenced by his work on movies. Faulkner's emotional life was also nurtured by his sojourns to Hollywood. In addition to a close friendship with Howard Hawks, Faulkner was involved in an extended love affair with Meta Carpenter during much of his time in California. Hollywood thus provided Faulkner with an invaluable outlet for experiences unavailable to him in Mississippi and a level of collaborative exchange unprecedented in Faulkner's biography. Working with other writers provided the opportunity to discuss writing and storytelling as a professional calling. People in Hollywood were serious about stories, and the entire film industry underscored the importance of storytelling to human survival. Sam Marx at MGM, for example, would review some 400 stories every week, looking for potential film plots. Faulkner thrived in this professional atmosphere and enjoyed as well the ways in which writers in this lucrative business would spend their leisure hours.

The collaborative nature of film production makes it often as difficult to attribute credit for specific contributions as it is to attribute sources to an author's final work. The question of who did what, who wrote this or that line, or who is responsible for this or that scene must go unanswered in most cases. This condition of indeterminacy alone was a challenge to Faulkner's sense of individuality, but at the same time it reinforced his sense of being an articulation— on more than one occasion he commented that if he had not written his books, someone else would have had to do so. At the same time, this indeterminacy is echoed throughout Faulkner's writing: for example, in the futile efforts to ascribe causal connection in *Go Down, Moses*. The fact is that Faulkner had two careers that he found mutually reinforcing: the writing of fiction, which he did largely alone and did not like to talk about, and film writing, which he did collaboratively, as a product of "some happy marriage of speaking and hearing" (*Absalom*).

FURTHER READING

Dardis, Tom. *Some Time in the Sun: The Hollywood Years of F. Scott Fitzgerald, William Faulkner, Nathanael West, Aldous Huxley, and James Agee*. New York: Penguin, 1981.
Harrington and Abadie, eds. *Faulkner, Modernism, and Film.*
Urgo, Joseph R. "*Absalom, Absalom!*: The Movie." *American Literature* 62 (1990): 56–73.
Wilde and Borsten. *A Loving Gentleman.*

Joseph R. Urgo

HOMOSEXUALITY. Although Cleanth Brooks in 1963 identified Joe Christmas as a latent homosexual, relatively little work was done on the issue of same-sex desire in Faulkner's work until the 1990s when the scholarship of gay and lesbian critics, increasingly known as queer studies, began to complicate the feminist sex/gender distinction. If feminist gender theory emphasized that sex is biological (female, male) and gender is culturally determined (femininity, masculinity), queer gender theory has noted the residual heterosexist bias in that formulation and allowed for a more fluid understanding of the individual's enactment of gender.

The term *homosexuality* can be understood in relation to two other related terms—*homosociality* and *homoeroticism*. Homosociality refers to same-sex activities. Male bonding rituals in Faulkner's hunting stories, for example, could be described as homosocial activity. With homosocial communities such as those in Faulkner's World War I stories, what happens between men is frequently figured through homoerotic imagery (wherein fighting another man, for example, becomes a displaced expression of unacceptable homosexual urges). The homoerotic, the figurative and often unconscious expression of same-sex desire, in effect is a mediating concept in a culture such as Faulkner's South that celebrates homosociality yet villainizes homosexuality.

There is little overt representation of homosexuals in Faulkner's fiction; Carl and George in "Divorce in Naples" and Voyd Ewing in "Golden Land" may be the most overt and stereotyped examples. But the presence of overt homosexuality is not necessary to see that Faulkner's texts engage the issue of same-sex sexuality. As recent criticism has demonstrated, the more open figuration of homoerotic desire in *Mosquitoes* (especially in the manuscript version) helps us better understand the more veiled homoerotic implications in the delineation of Quentin Compson in *The Sound and the Fury* and *Absalom, Absalom!* and Popeye and Horace Benbow in *Sanctuary*.

Background material for the study of homosexuality in Faulkner's works is provided in the psychobiography of Faulkner by Fredrick Karl, who emphasizes Faulkner's various youthful friendships with other men who are identified as homosexuals.

FURTHER READING

Butler, Judith. *Gender Trouble: Feminism and the Subversion of Gender*. New York: Routledge, 1990.

Gwin, Minrose. "Did Ernest Like Gordon?: Faulkner's *Mosquitoes* and the Bite of 'Gender Trouble.' " *Faulkner and Gender*, ed. Kartiganer and Abadie. 120–144.

Michael, Frann. "William Faulkner as a Lesbian Author." *Faulkner Journal* 4.1–2 (1989–1990): 5–20.

Sedgwick, Eve Kosofsky. *Epistemology of the Closet*. Berkeley: University of California Press, 1990.

Watson, Jay. "Overdoing Masculinity in *Light in August*; or, Joe Christmas and the Gender Guard." *Faulkner Journal* 9.1–2 (1993–1994): 149–177.

John N. Duvall

"HONOR," a short story by Faulkner, was first published in July 1930 in *American Mercury* and included in *Doctor Martino and Other Stories* and *Col-*

lected Stories. Linked by theme and subject to stories such as "Death Drag" and "Ad Astra," "Honor" presents a World War I pilot who cannot adjust to civilian life years after the war is over. The story is told by the pilot himself, whose name we learn only at the end of the story when his boss says to his secretary, "We are letting Mr. Monaghan go. Send him to the cashier." Monaghan's postwar death-in-life is dramatized in his inability to hold a job and to have an enduring relationship with a woman. His story about quitting the job he held for three weeks frames the story of his love affair with the wife of his friend Rogers, a fellow ex-flier. Monaghan and Rogers achieve a kind of honor not only as wing-walker and air-show pilot but also in Monaghan's willingness to commit suicide and Rogers's act of saving him. For Monaghan, honor is perpetually incompatible with domestic life; the best he can do is leave Rogers and his wife alone and quit his job with a corrupt automobile dealer.

Arthur A. Brown

HORSE. Some of the horses in Faulkner's fiction bear names—the Compsons' Queenie, John Sartoris's Jupiter, Drusilla Hawk's Bobolink, and *The Reivers'* Acheron/Lightning. But many go nameless, even significant ones—Jewel Bundren's spotted horse, for example, as well as Rafe McCallum's murderous stallion in "Knight's Gambit" and the stolen thoroughbred in *A Fable*. Such anonymity is fitting for creatures that function less as individuals than as extensions, even embodiments, of particularly masculine power.

Joe Christmas connects the horse to masculinity: "Even a mare horse is a kind of man." The fiction bears out Joe's claim: Consistently the strongest of Faulkner's men of action ride horses—Jewel Bundren, John Sartoris, Thomas Sutpen, Roth Edmonds, Jack Houston—while the garrulous, the ineffectual, and the lost must walk or drive—Quentin Compson on his last day, Jason on his two quests for Miss Quentin, Horace Benbow throughout *Sanctuary*, Gail Hightower (who lets his grandfather ride for him), Joe Christmas in his last week, Mink Snopes on the road from Parchman to Jefferson. And women certainly walk—Dilsey on the trip to and from the Easter service, Lena Grove to and from Jefferson, Molly Beauchamp seeking her "voce," Eula Varner through Frenchman's Bend—or they travel in trucks or cars—Miss Habersham in *Intruder in the Dust*, Linda Snopes in *The Mansion*, riding in Flem's sedan and tooling away in her own Jaguar. The only female exception is the masculinized Drusilla Hawk, "riding astride like a man."

A man's ability to control a horse seems to represent his ability to control the "maelstrom of unbearable reality" (*Absalom*) that Faulkner's characters thrash about in. Often that fearsome maelstrom seems distinctly female. Thomas Sutpen gallops about Sutpen's Hundred on a fine black stallion, the would-be captain both of the land and of women and their breed (Eulalia, Ellen, Rosa, Milly). Jewel Bundren rides a "durn spotted critter wilder than a cattymount," a horse no one else can handle, apparently to satisfy his drive to possess the woman that gave him birth—''It would just be me and her on a high hill and me rolling the rocks down the hill at their faces.'' One of Jewel's brothers, at least, makes the connection: ''Jewel's mother is a horse,'' Darl says. If Jack Houston exercises unbearable control over the somewhat feminized Mink Snopes (always afoot, confined for forty years, tricked into a Mother Hubbard), Mink deprives him of that power by ambushing him off the back of the horse that embodies his mastery, a stallion with an ''arrogant vicious head.'' By contrast, Joe Christmas, who fears women and hates them because he needs them so much, fails to complete his one ride, from the McEachern farm to Bobbie's house, just before he fails to win Bobbie in marriage: ''the horse . . . slowed into the curb and stopped. . . . He went to the horse's head and began to tug it. . . . The horse did not move. . . . Then Joe raised the stick and fell to beating the horse about its motionless head. . . . [H]e threw the stick away and turned, whirled, already in full stride. . . . [H]e ran as completely out of the life of the horse as if it had never existed.'' What if Christmas had been able to control that horse? Would he have needed to acknowledge fifteen years later that he had ''never got outside that circle'' in which he had been running (not riding) for thirty years, a circle distinctly feminine? Would he repeatedly attack women of both races as he ''gropes for the masculine in all things''? (Davis 140)

If the horse suggests masculine power, those who are still young and weak yet are destined for power demonstrate their growing prowess in horsemanship. In ''An Odor of Verbena,'' Ringo, one of Faulkner's strong young black characters, has ''talked Hilliard at the livery stable out of a good horse'' and rides beside Bayard. In *The Reivers* not only does a strong Ned McCaslin manage a racehorse, but the young Lucius Priest completes his passage into manhood by riding the horse to victory. The novel makes him the ''father'' of Everbe Hogganbeck's child at the tender age of twelve. Gavin Stevens, repeatedly defeated by rivals in love, finally wins a wife in ''Knight's Gambit'' after thwarting both Max Harriss and Captain Gauldres, a cavalry officer with ''a hard ruthless unimaginative maleness to him,'' in the matter of a horse. Imagination has become a chief weapon in masculine agonistics.

The use of imagination in the ability to trade horses signifies masculine control as well. In *The Hamlet* Pat Stamper's defeat of Ab Snopes in trading presages Ab's defeat by his wife when she ends up with her separator and he with neither horse nor mule. In ''Spotted Horses,'' on the other hand, Flem Snopes demonstrates the power that he will use to acquire Eula Varner and Manfred de Spain's bank and mansion by unloading a corral of horses on lesser men who cannot manage them. In *The Reivers* Ned McCaslin proves himself a master trader; true to pattern, by the time he dies at seventy-four he has ''run through four wives.'' Swap horses, swap wives: no commitments. The male who controls horses demonstrates the will and the ability to acquire sufficient power to control the female, from the specific woman to the archetypically female earth, which always in Faulkner is threatening to reenvelop him: ''[T]he ground itself never let a man forget it was there waiting, pulling gently and without no hurry at him between every step, saying, Come on, lay down; I aint going to hurt you. Jest lay down'' (*Mansion*).

Yet this masculine agenda has to fail. The ground will win, does win every time. In the final analysis, therefore, the horse suggests a masculine desire not only to master a threatening feminine world but to transcend it, as if in riding a man might escape the earth and its yawning graves, become a god, and ascend into the heavens. Thus the poet of "Carcassonne," kept in a garret by a patroness, dreams of himself *"on a buckskin pony with eyes like blue electricity and a mane like tangled fire, galloping up the hill and right off into the high heaven of the world."*

Wash Jones, an equally powerless piece of transiently articulated clay, has a similar vision, with Thomas Sutpen as its model: "[I]t would seem to him that . . . the actual world was the one where his own lonely apotheosis . . . galloped on the black thoroughbred, thinking . . . 'If God Himself was to come down and ride the natural earth, that's what He would aim to look like.' " In *A Fable*, the groom is a man so befouled by the earth that he is the "emissary" of the underworld entered through the grave if not "its actual prince and master," yet he finds in his stolen thoroughbred, the winner of every race he enters, an "apotheosis" of the everlasting love story, a way up and out of the underworld befouling him. Man escapes the feminine world on his horse because the relation of man and horse supersedes that of man and woman: Between the groom and his horse there is "no mere rapport but an affinity . . . from heart to heart and glands to glands," an affinity based on "truth, love, sacrifice, and something else even more important than they: some bond between or from man to his brother man." With their horses some men in Faulkner try to create homosocial relationships enabling them to evade the feminine, in microcosm and macrocosm alike. For them, especially, even a mare horse is a kind of man, a god-man in a heaven entirely masculine.

Terell L. Tebbetts

"HOUND, THE," a short story by Faulkner. First published in *Harper's* in August 1931 and reprinted in *Doctor Martino and Other Stories* and again in *Uncollected Stories*, "The Hound" belongs to the second chapter of Book III ("The Long Summer") in *The Hamlet*. In the original story, an indigent farmer named Ernest Cotton kills his cavalier neighbor, Houston, and tries to conceal the body in a tree. A dog's howl accentuates Cotton's mental trauma. In the revision for *The Hamlet*, Cotton is Mink Snopes, and what in the story is an almost purely psychological drama becomes a tale of class antagonism as well, another futile attempt by a Snopes to transcend property distinctions.

Joseph R. Urgo

HOUSMAN, A. E. (1859–1936), British poet and classicist. Housman's finely crafted lyrical ballads in three small collections—*A Shropshire Lad* (1896), *Last*

Poems (1922), and posthumously, *More Poems*—treat elemental themes of life, love, guilt, cuckoldry, suicide, and death by hanging or drowning in an ambiance of stoicism and despair ("'Dust's your wages . . . But men may come to worse than dust" [*Shropshire Lad*, XLIV]). Housman's characteristic speakers are men from the agrarian Welsh border country of Shropshire, west of his birthplace, who affirm ambivalence and irony as their response to life. A number of Faulkner's poems in *A Green Bough* show the influence of Housman, and numerous parallels to these poems appear in *The Sound and the Fury*, where Mr. Compson quotes from poem XLVIII ("Let us endure an hour and see injustice done") and where themes of love-suicide (XLIV and LIII, "The True Lover"), narcissism, and death by water (XX) are developed in the characterization of Quentin. In addition, as late as the time of his Nobel Prize speech, Faulkner alluded to Housman, using the phrase "When will I be blown up?" (cf. *Shropshire Lad*, XXVIII, "The Welsh Marches," "When shall we be slain?"), and more obliquely to poem IX, *Last Poems* (see Meriwether, "A. E. Housman"). The speaker of Housman's most famous poem, "To an Athlete Dying Young," is a representative of the community or town comparable to some narrator-elegists in Faulkner's fiction (e.g., the narrator of "A Rose for Emily").

FURTHER READING

Brogunier, Joseph. "A Housman Source in *The Sound and the Fury*." *Modern Fiction Studies* 18 (1972): 220–225.
Meriwether, James B. "A. E. Housman and Faulkner's Nobel Prize Speech: A Note." *Journal of American Studies* 4 (1971): 247–248.

Stephen Hahn

HUMANISM. Despite its amorphous history, the outlines of the humanistic tradition are clear enough to suggest seeing Faulkner as not only included in the tradition but as one who defines its future. Whether associated with the Renaissance's rediscovery of classical culture and reassertion of the significance of human affairs, or seen as an anthropology whose origins were in Augustine's *City of God* and that flowered in the ideals of *Gerusalem Liberata*, humanism asserts a dignity to the place human beings occupy, believes in a common nature and universal values, and shapes liberal institutions to harness human powers for the improvement of human society. In sum, humanism sees humanity as having a spiritual nature as well as various material cultures.

Many critics, most notably Cleanth Brooks, found in Faulkner's address on receiving the Nobel Prize explicit expression of the humanistic themes they had already identified in his work. Particularly congenial to humanism was his focus on "the old verities and truths of the heart" and his evocation of "the human heart in conflict with itself." The remarks map his fiction's conception of mankind defined by conflicting emotions created by the need for identity, on the one hand, and for belonging, on the other, between freedom to make one's own meaning and the meaning imposed by the social order into which one is born.

Characters from many walks of life can be seen in his fiction moving between their own caprice and their best reason, just as families and societies are seen ranging between restricting conformity and life-giving community. This does not mean, of course, that Faulkner could as easily portray a character across cultural differences as he could one more closely associated with his own background—only that he thought it worthwhile to try to do so. This rich complexity of characterization, chosen with little regard to caste or class, suggests seeing Faulkner as humanist.

So, too, does the source of his materials. The authors who most influenced Faulkner—Joyce, Dostoevsky, Conrad, for instance—were themselves apt critics of the humanistic tradition; but their reliance on ancient myths, Greek epics, scriptural stories, and literary traditions marks them also as participants in the tradition they critiqued. So, too, with Faulkner. Still, literary history is itself artificial, a way of making connections. And the Nobel address, however beautiful its sentiments, was a ritual performance for a public ceremony. Neither, therefore, provides the best evidence for placing Faulkner in the humanistic tradition. That evidence must come from the fiction itself.

Faulkner's own humanism can be seen most directly in three features of his fictional work. The first of these is the place occupied by the human capacity to struggle with oppositions, the striving of individuals and communities with the complexity of their history and present moment. Perhaps this can be seen best in his "heart's darling," Caddy Compson. In his 1933 introduction to *The Sound and the Fury*, Faulkner wrote significantly: "[H]ers was the courage which was to face later with honor the shame which she was to engender, which Quentin and Jason could not face." Here, Faulkner conceives of Caddy's humanity as found equally in her having engendered shame as in her having faced it, that is, in her own sense of responsibility to, for, and with her family. Second, Faulkner prizes her because she assumes this responsibility regardless of whether her brothers love or hate, accept or reject, honor or abuse her. Her humanity is seen in exemplifying that "Love is not love/Which alters when it alteration finds" (Shakespeare, Sonnet CXVI). And finally, her courage, honor, and love are not seen as something Jason and Quentin *would* not but *could* not show (emphasis added). That is, these virtues are seen as moral emblems of the human condition, not causes for praise or blame of individual actions.

Once again, a similar feature is present in the Snopes trilogy as Faulkner characterizes Eula's suicide as being intended to allow Linda to live with the sympathy given a bereaved daughter rather than the disapprobation displaced on a daughter from her mother's notoriety. Eula's suicide and the awareness of community that prompts it suggest Faulkner's concern for community as the second evidence of his humanism. Community, meant to support the human enterprise, easily degenerates into pernicious societies. Indicting such societies for their inhumanity upholds the ideals from which they have fallen. One instance is Faulkner's concern in *A Fable* for the replacement of community with the collective. And in the Yoknapatawpha chronicle, sometimes community degenerates into a mob, or into a mere aggregate of separate individuals, or into a life-denying demand for conformity. These may be seen, for example, in Percy Grimm's lynch mob in *Light in August*, in the "secret and selfish selves" of *As I Lay Dying*, and in Flem's sacrifices to "respectability" in *The Town*.

Faulkner's concerns for community inform his conception of the Snopes invasion. Although not much stands in their way, Faulkner poses against them in the trilogy Gavin Stevens who, though he may show that human beings can stand only so much reality, also shows the ultimate power and appeal of those humanizing forces for which he most stands. It is, in fact, in his all-too-imperfect but sincere devotion to ideals that he represents the humanistic tradition, glimpsed also in the actions of a variety of other characters, such as Ike McCaslin, Lucius Priest, V. K. Ratliff, and even Eck Snopes.

Best exemplifying humanism, however, is that the Snopeses' ultimate collapse comes from within, caused by both the comic and tragic excesses of their egos, the internal rivalry and betrayal among them, and the suffocating weight of their own pretensions. If Kant's Categorical Imperative can be seen as the ethical statement of humanism, then the Snopeses are its living antithesis; and their internal contradiction spells their own doom as well as their danger to society. Their story began in the small hamlet where Will Varner's avarice had already stamped out what might be called community. Their Frenchman's Bend follies become enlarged as they move from little hamlet to town, finally to be dealt a mortal blow in the death of the last patriarch, Flem, in the isolation of his mansion, when Mink takes his revenge and makes his escape with Linda's assistance. Begun with the "Abraham" of the tribe, Ab Snopes, they end in the wild dispersion promised in the first story material, the episode of the spotted horses, the last of which to survive is Jewel's horse in *As I Lay Dying*.

The Snopeses' collapse suggests the third humanistic feature of Faulkner's fiction: his conception of the human being as capable of moral self-destruction, of becoming something less than human. As humanism values that within us that makes us human, so it can conceive of our doom where such inner qualities are absent or destroyed. Here the portrait of Sutpen in *Absalom, Absalom!* comes most readily to mind. Faulkner conceives of Thomas Sutpen as one capable of a grand design, of wresting out of wilderness something of order, grandeur, and purpose. In Jason Compson's account, Sutpen remains to the end unable to understand how the design could have failed; thus, in this one sense, he remains innocent unto the end. Yet Sutpen's innocence, like that of the American Adam he embodies, is doomed by his own misconceptions, cursed by his own fall.

Sutpen's conception of man against the wilderness obscures for him the more spiritual fight against principalities and powers lurking within his own soul. Seeking order, he lives in wild abandon; driven by purpose, he destroys the purposes of everyone around him; building a grandeur of his own designing, he remains, spiritually, unable to move beyond the lacerating shame of being turned away from the front door of the "big house," a shame he associates with issues of race, gender, and origin at the heart of history. Thus, though the final blow is administered by Wash Jones, Sutpen's death is actually an event of self-destruction, the result of his own abdication of the human long before the rusty scythe harvests his soul. At the root of what is perhaps Faulkner's most complex work lies the simple conception of the seasons of man's life, of reaping what is sown, a conception that, borrowed from biblical sources, informs humanism's ideas of value and dignity. Robert Hamblin best represents this humanism when he draws out the dynamic in *Absalom, Absalom!* between history and art, between empirical reality and transcending vision.

Postmodernism, particularly that of Derrida and Foucault, has taught us the negative side of the humanistic tradition, principally its naïveté regarding the pervasiveness of ideological factors and its consequent privileging of various social arrangements and groups. More generally, the rise of the social sciences has had humanism on the run since Darwin's tangled bank displaced the Great Chain of Being as the primary conception of human affairs. Nevertheless, with a protean capacity for reshaping itself—Christian humanism, secular humanism, humanistic existentialism—the essence of humanism is the belief that human beings can forge "the link between comprehension and the production of meaning" (Urgo, "Drama of Meaning" 21). Various voices in the twentieth century have kept alive, not so much in the public addresses as in the structures of their fiction, a belief in this ability. Not the least of these voices has been Faulkner's. Not in spite of but because of this unflinching focus on our fallen state, because of the "horror, the horror" he so artfully depicts, Faulkner arouses in us a hope for transcendence and makes credible the timelessness of that enterprise that asks, "What a piece of work is man?" Or, as Faulkner himself put it in an interview with Henry Nash Smith, "Everyone is capable of almost anything" (1974 *FAB* 760).

See also **Christianity**.

FURTHER READING

Gold. *William Faulkner: A Study in Humanism.*
Hamblin, Robert W. " 'Longer Than Anything': Faulkner's 'Grand Design' in *Absalom, Absalom!*" *Faulkner and the Artist*, ed. Kartiganer and Abadie. 269–293.
Urgo, Joseph R. "William Faulkner and the Drama of Meaning: The Discovery of the Figurative in *As I Lay Dying*." *South Atlantic Review* 53 (May 1988): 11–23.

Charles A. Peek

HUMOR. Because William Faulkner dealt so frequently with the tragic side of life and human experience, with the alienated and the dysfunctional, with violence and Gothicism, it is easy to overlook the important part humor and comedy play in his fiction. In a 1949 review of *Intruder in the Dust* for the *Hudson Review*, Eudora Welty noted, "The complicated and intricate thing is that his stories aren't decked out in humor, but the humor is born in them, as much their blood and bones as the passion and poetry." Katherine Anne Porter, in a 1956 television interview, said, "He is one of the funniest men in the world. . . . I love Mark Twain and I never forget him really; but when you speak of humor, [Faulkner is] my standard.''

The entire body of Faulkner's major published work is imbued with a comic spirit and attitude, from the smug, sophisticated, ironic style of *Mosquitoes* in 1927 through the lively, exaggerated, and bawdy narrative of *The Reivers* in 1962. Even his first published and best known short story, "A Rose for Emily," of 1930, can be seen from one perspective as a sustained joke about a genteel Southern lady who feeds rat poison to her unfaithful Yankee lover, with a startling punch line at the end. If incongruity is at the heart of what makes things funny, the disparity between our expectations and what actually happens, then hardly anything Faulkner ever wrote, *The Sound and the Fury, As I Lay Dying*, and *Absalom, Absalom!* included, escapes the category of grand drama in the comic mode. Quentin Compson, Anse Bundren, and Thomas Sutpen are outrageous caricatures of human beings who pursue their goals to extreme lengths far beyond levels of normalcy and serious behavior. When we consider the simple things that motivate their epic contortions—a sister's maidenhead, a pair of false teeth, and an absurd belief in racial purity—then their labors become less tragic than comic.

As in the work of all great writers—Cervantes, Shakespeare, Dostoevsky, and Joyce among them—comedy and tragedy are deeply intertwined in Faulkner and not easily extricated for the sake of discussion. In the case of Faulkner, he is so thoroughly in the American grain as a comic writer and draws so frequently on the entire body of distinctively American forms and techniques of comic writing and performance that an understanding of the history of American humor is almost necessary to an appreciation of his accomplishment.

For example, the way a story is told, who narrates it, and from what point of view were major preoccupations of Faulkner's. He learned these techniques from the early experiments of the humorists of the Old Southwest, who permitted skillful raconteurs to tell of their fantastic frontier exploits in their own metaphorically rich vernacular, such as George Washington Harris, whose yarns about Sut Lovingood he read with amused appreciation. Also there is Mark Twain's masterpiece in the first-person comic narrative tradition *Adventures of Huckleberry Finn*, which Faulkner considered one of the two greatest books in American literature, the other being that grand tall tale *Moby Dick*.

Keeping in mind, too, Joseph Conrad's brilliant use of the narrator Marlow as tragic witness, Faulkner proceeded to build upon this tradition. In *The Sound and the Fury*, he charted the decline of a Southern family by telling their story through the consciousnesses of three of its members, one of whom is an idiot, before speaking in his own voice. In *Absalom, Absalom!* to recount the history of Thomas Sutpen, a nineteenth-century Faustus, Faulkner used at least four tale tellers. None of them has all the facts, however, and the reader must piece together the story without conclusive help from the author, the point being that history as truth is beyond knowing anyway. The most elaborate experiment of this type may be *As I Lay Dying*, in which no less than fifteen narrators are used to chronicle the journey of a poor white family to bury the wife and mother in her home soil. The seriousness of the difficult trip, fraught with natural and physical disasters, is undercut when we learn at the end that husband Anse Bundren mainly wanted a set of false teeth and a new wife.

Faulkner sometimes turned to burlesque to treat serious subjects frivolously. One of his finest comic episodes, and one of the few examples of pure fantasy in his fiction, is the story in *The Hamlet* of what would happen if Flem Snopes went to hell and confronted Satan himself. The journey through hell is an honored event in Western literature, most effectively treated by Milton and Dante, but Faulkner travesties the tradition by putting it in the language of an itinerant sewing-machine salesman and finally turning it upside down by allowing Flem to win. Another form of burlesque, in which a frivolous subject is treated seriously, is the love story of Ike Snopes and his cow, basically a comic interlude in which animal sodomy is described in the rich language of Elizabethan love poetry. Like Mark Twain and other American humorists before him, Faulkner in effect ridicules European literary and cultural attitudes in such passages.

The fiction abounds in numerous examples of typically American comic materials. The Pat Stamper horse swap in *The Hamlet* borrows from Augustus Baldwin Longstreet's *Georgia Scenes*, the wild pony episode in the same novel from *Sut Lovingood's Yarns* by Harris, and "The Bear" from Thomas Bangs Thorpe's classic tale "The Big Bear of Arkansas."

Familiarity with a lengthy history of oral narrative, folklore, masculine humor, and backwoods dirty jokes is discernible in the stories of the Snopes boys who sleep at a Memphis bordello in *Sanctuary* under the impression it is a rooming house, the teacher who stays after class to smell the desk seat where Eula Varner sat, Lump Snopes who sells tickets so others can watch Ike bugger a cow in *The Hamlet*, and the drugstore clerk in *As I Lay Dying* who persuades the pregnant Dewey Dell (the name itself, like many in Faulkner, an erotic joke) that more sex will undo her condition. This is salacious high comedy. A darker strain of American humor can be found in many parts of *Sanctuary*, such as how Temple Drake is raped or how the macabre funeral of the gangster Red is held in a nightclub. The master of acerbic irony and sarcasm may be Jason Compson who delivers a steady series of sardonic one-liners and wisecracks in *The Sound and the Fury*, as would later stand-up comedians like Lenny Bruce and Don Rickles.

Finally, however, the basis for Faulkner's humor resides in his attitude toward life and the universe, best expressed in his Nobel Prize address where he affirmed the possibility of salvation and charged the writer with the duty "to help man endure by lifting his heart." To believe in redemption and salvation is to posit a comic vision, and surely the hearts of his readers have been lifted by the resulting humor in Faulkner's fiction.

FURTHER READING

Fowler and Abadie, eds. *Faulkner and Humor.*

M. Thomas Inge

HUNTING. Faulkner enjoyed hunting as a pastime throughout his life. As a child, he first encountered the hunt with his father in bottom lands along the Tallahatchie River in northern Lafayette County, where hunters could bag bear and wolves as late as the 1920s. (The location roughly correlates to the site of Major de Spain's hunting camp on Faulkner's map of Yoknapatawpha County published in *Absalom, Absalom!*) Later, as a young adult, Faulkner went on annual hunting parties at a camp near Batesville, Mississippi, on the edge of the Delta, owned by "General" James Stone, father of Faulkner's friend and mentor Phil Stone. When this property was sold to lumber interests in the 1930s, the hunts moved progressively southward into the Delta in a search for virgin wilderness. As he grew older, Faulkner developed a distaste for killing animals, but he continued to relish the companionship and experience of the hunt. Late in life, after he became writer-in-residence at the University of Virginia, he took an active interest in fox hunting on horseback, finding himself strongly attracted not only to the formalized rituals of the sport but also to its thrills and dangers.

Hunting is referred to obliquely in a number of novels (*Sartoris*, for example) and short stories, but it finds its most significant treatment in *Go Down, Moses*. In a series of episodes relating to the McCaslin family, Faulkner uses hunting as a recurrent metaphor of initiation and maturation, particularly in the case of Isaac McCaslin, arguably the novel's protagonist; of companionship and communion, both among men and with the natural world; and of wanton and deliberate destruction of the wilderness, symbolized most potently by the killing of Old Ben in "The Bear." Faulkner's depiction of hunting also suggests a comparison to the struggles and pursuits of life itself and, especially in his treatment of the rituals and mythologies of hunting, an act by which humans determine their position in life between the wilderness and civilization. Specific hunting practices depicted throughout the novel reveal how patrimonial attitudes of ownership, whether of land, animals, or humans, can devastate both present and future generations.

One additional book by Faulkner also relates closely to hunting. *Big Woods: The Hunting Stories* (1955) is a collection of four previously published stories connected by extracts from other Faulkner works.

FURTHER READING

Creighton, Joanne V. "Revision and Craftmanship in the Hunting Trilogy of *Go Down, Moses*." *Texas Studies in Literature and Language* 15 (1973): 577–592.

Duvall, John N. "Doe Hunting and Masculinity: *Song of Solomon* and *Go Down, Moses*." *Arizona Quarterly* 47.1 (1991): 95–115.

Howell, John M. "McCaslin and Macomber: From *Green Hills* to *Big Woods*." *Faulkner Journal* 2.1 (1986): 29–36.

John B. Padgett

I

"IDYLL IN THE DESERT," a short story by Faulkner, was first published in 1931 by Random House as a signed limited edition; it also appears in *Uncollected Stories*. The narrator of the story, Lucas Crump, a mail rider in Arizona, tells a companion about Darrel House, a tuberculosis patient seeking recuperation in the western air. His lover, a married woman and wife of his former employer, joins him. Darrel recovers and leaves. His lover, now ill, waits eight years for his return, supported by money sent secretly by her husband. When she dies, Lucas arranges to transport her body by train just as Darrel and his new bride arrive. The auditor surmises that Lucas has profited from his devotion.

Diane Brown Jones

IF I FORGET THEE, JERUSALEM. *See* **Wild Palms, The**.

"IF I WERE A NEGRO," an essay by Faulkner, appeared in *Ebony* in September 1956 and is reprinted in *Essays, Speeches & Public Letters by William Faulkner*. The essay contains Faulkner's denial that he had ever advocated "shooting down Negroes in the street." He also clarifies an earlier appeal to black reformers to "go slow" by insisting that what he meant was "be flexible." According to Faulkner, Negroes should adopt "an inflexible and unviolent flexibility." The goals should be fixed—if he were black, Faulkner claimed, he would joint the NAACP (National Association for the Advancement of Colored People)—but tactics should be variable. Faulkner ended by insisting that Negroes should "earn" their rights and accept "responsibility." This was, he concluded speaking as a Negro, necessary since the white man "has not taught us that." Faulkner's mixture of (sometimes) shrewd advice, awkward paternalism, and misjudged ventriloquism in this and other articles in the mid-1950s found

little positive response among African Americans and prompted a strong rebuttal from James Baldwin in *Partisan Review* (reprinted in *Nobody Knows My Name*).
    See also **African American; Race**.

FURTHER READING

Baldwin, James. "Faulkner and Desegregation." *Nobody Knows My Name*. New York: Delta Books, 1962. 117–126.

Richard H. King

IKKEMOTUBBE, an Indian character who appears in a number of Faulkner works. Ikkemotubbe assumes a number of names and titles ranging from "l'Homme," "The Man," "Doom," "a Mingo subchief," to the alias "David Callicoat." Although noted primarily for trading off or selling land to Jason Lycurgus Compson, Carothers McCaslin, and Thomas Sutpen, hence forfeiting that which becomes the fertile heart of Jefferson and the rich plantation lands in Yoknapatawpha County, Ikkemotubbe is a striking character in his own right. As a young Chickasaw, he demonstrates a passionate intensity for athletics, dancing, and revelry and is admired by his male peers and many women of the tribe. At twenty-two, he valiantly competes with David Hogganbeck for the affections of Herman Basket's sister but, once rejected, departs by steamboat for New Orleans and begins his descent into moral disintegration. While old Issetibbeha, his maternal uncle and tribal chief, has long suspected a baser side to Ikkemotubbe, accusing him of possessing a "bad" eye and capacity for evil, he does not demonstrate blatant character flaws until Basket's sister jilts him. (Ikkemotubbe's genealogy differs in *Go Down, Moses* with Ikkemotubbe featured as son to old Issetibbeha and not nephew.)

After a seven-year absence from the plantation, and with the moral transformation now very obvious, he returns home, accompanied by the Chevalier Soeur Blonde de Vitry, a Parisian rogue who nicknames Ikkemotubbe "Du Homme" or "The Man." Ikkemotubbe, whom Faulkner calls "a man of wit and imagination as well as a shrewd judge of character," now has designs on usurping Issetibbeha's rule. As a result of Ikkemotubbe's devious rituals involving poison and the death of several puppies, not only do the chieftain and his son die mysteriously, but the next heir apparent, Sometimes Wakeup, is likewise affected by such antics and abdicates his rule.

Immediately after the burials, Ikkemotubbe, now chief, turns his attention to retrieving a floundering steamboat, cultivating some of the land, and acquiring Negro slaves. He eventually marries and impregnates a West Indian woman who gives birth to a son, Issetibbeha. Importantly, Ikkemotubbe is also associated with the noted character Sam Fathers. In "The Old People" Faulkner casts Ikkemotubbe as Sam's father, but in "A Justice" he is said to have owned Sam's mother and given Sam the name "Had-Two-Fathers." Ikkemotubbe appears in "Red Leaves," "A Justice," *Absalom, Absalom!*, "The Old People,"

The Bear, the Appendix of the Modern Library edition of *The Sound and the Fury*, "A Courtship," *Requiem for a Nun, The Town*, and *The Reivers*.

FURTHER READING

Doyle, Don H. "The Mississippi Frontier in Faulkner's Fiction and Fact." *Southern Quarterly* 29.4 (1991): 145–160.

Gidley, Mick. "Sam Fathers's Fathers: Indians and the Idea of Inheritance." *Critical Essays on William Faulkner: The McCaslin Family*. Ed. Arthur F. Kinney. Boston: G. K. Hall, 1990. 121–131.

Taylor, Walter. "Yoknapatawpha's Indians: A Novel Faulkner Never Wrote." *The Modernist Studies in Literary Phenomenon*. Ed. Lawrence B. Gamache. Rutherford, N.J.: Fairleigh Dickinson University Press, 1987.

Kathy G. Willingham

IMPRESSIONISM, an influential movement in painting and music during the late nineteenth century. Dated roughly from 1867 to 1886, the movement in painting, including such French artists as Claude Monet, Edouard Manet, Pierre Auguste Renoir, and Edgar Degas, held its first independent exhibition in 1874 after having been rejected by the official French Academy's Salon. Its name derives from a painting entitled *Impression: Soleil Levant* by Claude Monet. As a reaction against conventional academic notions of painting, Impressionist artists focus on the impressions made by the artistic subject on the artist's consciousness. The method stresses freedom in technique, as well as the use of lighting, color, and perspective to create an emotional impact and atmosphere rather than objective reality, conventional subject matter, and idealized images of nature.

Literary artists such as Joseph Conrad, James Joyce, Virginia Woolf, Djuna Barnes, and Henry James became influenced by the emphasis on subjective impressions. They use an impressionistic style to convey an individual character's responses to the outside world and his or her inner thoughts—the latter of which is characteristic of the "stream-of-consciousness" technique for which modernist novelists are noted. Literary Impressionism, as critic Maria Elisabeth Kronegger has noted, focuses on "an interplay of the individual's consciousness and the surrounding world" and is characterized by the use of multiple perspectives and shifts in time and chronology where the reader must "seize the impressionist works spatially in a moment of time, rather than as a time sequence" (13).

Faulkner's interest in painting and the Impressionists in particular was carried over into his fictional style and technique through the use of pastiche, image, color, lighting, and nonlinear time. His greatest narratives focus on the individual's consciousness in relationship to the outside world. Noted for his complex exploration of various subjectivities, Faulkner emphasizes the individual impressions of his characters through his use of interior monologue. *As I Lay Dying*, for example, focuses on the perspectives of fifteen different characters, including the dead Addie Bundren. With *Absalom, Absalom!*, also an exploration of narratives within narratives, Faulkner interweaves present time with past history to tell the stories of Colonel Thomas Sutpen and Quentin Compson—again with multiple narrators. Shifts in time and perspective play significant roles in *The Sound and the Fury* (told by four distinct narrators, including Benjy, the idiot child, whose responses to the outside world and inner reality are not much more than impressions and images, and Quentin, on the day of his suicide), as well as in *Light in August*, particularly with the flashback to Joe Christmas's boyhood and adolescence.

FURTHER READING

Hönnighausen. *William Faulkner: The Art of Stylization in His Early Graphic and Literary Work.*
Kronegger, Maria Elisabeth. *Literary Impressionism.* New Haven, Conn.: College and University Press, 1973.
Tate, Allen. "William Faulkner, 1897–1964." *Sewanee Review* 71 (1963): 160–164.
Wynne, Carolyn. "Aspects of Space: John Marin and William Faulkner." *Arizona Quarterly* 16 (1964): 59–71.

Dean Shackelford

INDIANS. William Faulkner's work is most often associated with descendants of the Old South suffering in the shadow of slavery and the Civil War. The significant portion of his work that interacts with Native American legend and literature has attracted less critical attention. Although most of the Indians had been removed by this time, the interracial and cultural mixes in his self-stamped Yoknapatawpha County, Mississippi, rise partly from the mists of the region's Indian past.

Aspects of his symbolism—the ritual and significance of hunting, animal totemism, and the central motif of the bear in his acclaimed story of that name— are influenced by the practices and beliefs of the Mound Builders and the Southern Ceremonial Cult. Furthermore, as a worker with the oral tradition, drawing upon a love of narrative inherited through gossip sessions at his father's livery stable and the country stores of his youth, Faulkner can align himself, through the Sam Fathers of "A Justice" and "The Bear," with a culture that survives through mythmaking. Indians appear in several places in Faulkner's work, albeit sometimes in stereotypical portraits. Often, he uses characters who become larger than life in order to carry the weight of a symbolism incorporated into their construction. At other times, the Indians are brutally realistic. Stories such as "A Courtship," "A Justice," and "Red Leaves" feature the Chickasaws and Choctaws before the forced relocation via the Trail of Tears. "Lo!" yields a comic view of politically savvy resisters, whereas "The Old People" and "The Bear" reach further back to a fictionalized but immutable and noble past. Faulkner's writing about Indians in the South is informed by stories of extensive slavery within the Five Civilized Tribes, and for violence and fatalism he needed look no further than the heritage of the Natchez, feared and abhorred by the whites for their deification of the Sun Nobles and human-sacrifice funeral rites.

Faulkner believed in the inherent integrity and capability of all people, regardless of race—even if the trait lay dormant until exigency demanded emergence—and subscribed firmly to the unity of mankind. Underlying many of his heroes victimized by circumstance is a sense of the natural cycle and laws, a code of honor that is at stake, though it may also prove their undoing. Within the cosmogony of some of his protagonists, the world does not stretch beyond the familiar—they are bounded and often limited by their heritage, as in *As I Lay Dying*. Behind the conflicts lies a backdrop of cultural clash, oppression, bigotry, and ingrained intolerance. Faulkner does not avoid the unwelcome truths envisioned in his convoluted plots but turns his attention less caustically on certain segments of human society—the agrarians, simple folk of the soil, keepers of a mythical, idealized existence.

Faulkner acknowledges the plight of the dispossessed, juxtaposes poverty and power. Social stratification figures into the formula; he crafts story lines in which rigid class structure, enforced by an ideology of exclusion, sets the stage for a demonstrable wrong. Quick to point out flaws in established society, especially transplanted faux nobility from eastern tidal planters, he notes the harms that follow his characters' inabilities to cross caste or racial boundaries. The answers to human contention are often found among the old, established mores of an indistinct but vital history. That is not to say that he monolithically champions or sanctifies "the primitive" but that his yarn spinning incorporates a respect for earthiness, the intrinsic truth of the natural. Of course, this naturality can result in impulsive and dangerous reaction; yet it can also foster rationality and wisdom derived from former generations in tune with their terrestrial surroundings.

Faulkner urges unity by exploring disunity, especially through persons caught in the no-man's-land between cultures, whether by accident of birth, social affiliation, or circumstance. His work has been noted for its integration of ethnicities, not always with reassuring conclusions for either the character or the reader, and seldom without tension, yet in this way addressing community. Mixed-blood characters appear: Joe Christmas in *Light in August*, of black and white lineage; Boon Hogganbeck, part Indian, part white; Sam Fathers, Indian and black. Many of the earliest workers in published Native American literature were themselves of merged descent, as are their characters. Faulkner's themes are universalized beyond the immediate and his characters made more complex through his reluctance to sentimentalize and see Indians like Ikkemotubbe as pure victims. Instead, they are partly complicit in their own culture's demise, in this case via a regionalized version of original sin, the selling of the land. Personal weakness and mistakes are reckoned on the same scales as other evils.

Native Americans are also creating literature built upon the paradoxes of the human condition. Leslie Marmon Silko's Tayo must perform his "ceremony" because the "destroyers" would reduce all conflict to one of solely red versus white, and the holy man forces Tayo to realize that the causes are too disparate to lay at the feet of a single enemy. Here, too, individual perversities compound problems created by hatred or oppression between groups, and the individual is responsible to resist factions that promote division.

Faulkner's influence on Native American literature is difficult to separate from his influence on twentieth-century American literature as a whole, by virtue of the intensity of his prose and psychological probing. Correlatives to his pioneering stream of consciousness and integration of authentic non-European perspectives can be located in later literature by Indian writers as diverse as Laguna, Kiowa, Blackfoot, Ojibwa. Native chroniclers such as Silko and N. Scott Momaday, now brought into the broadened mainstream of American literary tradition, gained recognition by documenting the psychic trauma of disenfranchisement. Both *House Made of Dawn* and *Ceremony* treat the struggle with tradition in the face of a search for cultural and personal identity, as does James Welch. Simon Ortiz demonstrates how an oppressed minority is forced into violence by systematic bullying and recounts the terrible, and to the reader poignantly unwarranted, consequences of misunderstanding the dictates of the dominant culture. Authors such as Louise Erdrich, with *Love Medicine* and her related novels, Linda Hogan, and Paula Gunn Allen bring Native American consciousness more into focus, as have spokesmen like Vine DeLoria, Jr.

There are instances of more specific influences. Lewis Dabney connects the tracking of the bear in Momaday's *House Made of Dawn* to the regularized, ritualized stalking of Old Ben in "The Bear," vibrations he, in turn, thinks first emanated from Keats's "Ode on a Grecian Urn." He notes in both hunting sequences the solidarity achieved for a hunter initiated into the community of hunters, the import of the similarities lying not only in the borrowing but in tapping the universally human reservoir of attitude, behavior, and emotion.

Faulkner and Indian authors often toil in the same fields, to protest what has become of the Anglo "errand into the wilderness." An appreciation of tragedy that Faulkner inherited through the conquered South is manifest in his attempts to document the Vanishing American and is expanded to the disappearing frontier. Correspondingly, his work at times yields to hopelessness and inevitability. Many of his characters resist change, which, when it does come, is often unjust and irresistible, and his narrative then takes on an element of the apocryphal; figures like Sam Fathers who evoke power from what-once-was in moments of epiphany are also the last of the line. In similar fashion, Native American writers work from a historical record in which the threat of cultural demise is already proven. Justice is not always rendered for them either, and resolution, if it comes, also only comes about on the level of the individual. On the other hand, protagonists in contemporary Indian literature are not as apt to view themselves as subject to inexorable history, with something of value in the background always being lost. The new warriors, of any gender, struggle to construct not a replica of former circumstance but a new, altered existence, and they are hindered by other characters, frozen in time, who refuse to bring the best from their tradition to bear upon an emerging world.

The technique of stream of consciousness may not be the direct literary antecedent of the shifting awareness evident in many Native American characters, but it prepared the ground with the American reading public for the drama of perceived reality. So, too, Faulkner's disrupted and sometimes seemingly unreliable narration parallels *magical realism*, an imaginative realm ambiguously hovering between fact, psychosis, and alternative reality, which, though not itself native, appears in a great deal of Latino and Native American fiction such as Louise Erdrich's *Trader* or Louis Owens's *Bone Games*. The reading audience must grant the efficacy of visions and extraworldly intervention, the aid resulting not from supplication to a regimented Christian God but from the sphere of nature. One is brought into the confusion between objective reality and possibility, and as in many of Faulkner's extended, discursive passages, one is expected to embrace rather than resent the blur. It is perhaps one step past the turbulence and urgency of Faulkner's human-based psychology, but the effect is the same—a reader accepts the premonition or prophecy, comprehends the distortion of actuality, because one is viewing the universe through the mind's eye of a character rendered believable precisely because of imprecisions or human foibles. Through the "willing suspension of disbelief" the reader is brought into belief, because the alternative view is plausible when placed in the immediate.

Thus Faulkner cannot necessarily be seen as an impetus for the entrance upon the literary scene of realistic Native American portrayal in fiction, but his blending of fabled ancient values, of actual history, truth, pain, and self-possession into his own rainbow coalition of characters has contributed to a spirit in which other voices can be heard. If he brings European echoes to bear upon the wilderness experience, that combination is carried forward by even more knowledgeable witnesses. To writers of truth, the world is not always a place in which a new order equates with fairy-tale endings, but what cannot be redressed in life can be captured in art, a lasting record. In the universe of ideas and prose, through the freedom of style and play of language, Faulkner is joined to the Native Americans. And it is here, too, that his voice whispers into the future.

FURTHER READING

Dabney. *The Indians of Yoknapatawpha.*

Henry, Jeannette, ed. *The American Indian Reader.* San Francisco: Indian Historical Press, 1973.

Jeltz, Wyatt F. "The Relations of Negroes and Choctaw and Chickasaw Indians." *Journal of Negro History* 33 (1946): 26.

Kreft, James Harvey. *The Yoknapatawpha Indians: Fact and Fiction.* New Orleans, La.: Tulane University Press, 1976.

Porter, Kenneth W. "Relations Between Negroes and Indians Within the Present Limits
of the United States." *Journal of Negro History* 16 (1932): 321.

Garry R. Alkire

INFLUENCES. *See* particular country, region, group, or individual.

"INNOCENT AT RINKSIDE, AN," one of two descriptive essays (the other
was "Kentucky: May: Saturday") Faulkner wrote on assignment for *Sports
Illustrated* in 1955. A treatment of a hockey match played in New York's Madison Square Garden between the New York Rangers and the Montreal Cana-
diens, "Innocent at Rinkside" was first published in the January 24, 1955 issue
of *Sports Illustrated* and later reprinted (with the inclusion of a final paragraph
omitted from the magazine version) in James Meriwether's collection, *Essays,
Speeches & Public Letters by William Faulkner.* Not surprisingly to anyone
familiar with Faulkner's distinctions between "facts" and "truth," the essay is
not at all a factual account of a hockey match (the first and perhaps only one
that Faulkner, the "innocent" of the title, ever witnessed) but rather the poignant
reflections of an aging artist who saw symbolized in the sporting event before
him the ongoing if absurd human quest for perfection in a world delimited by
space and time. A number of familiar Faulkner themes surface in the vivid
description of the hockey players and their competitive zeal: motion versus
stasis, experience versus art, dream versus fact, individuality versus anonymity,
life versus death.

FURTHER READING

Hamblin, Robert W. "*Homo Agonistes,* or, William Faulkner as Sportswriter." *Aethlon:
The Journal of Sport Literature* 13:2 (1996): 13–22.

Robert W. Hamblin

INTRUDER IN THE DUST, a novel by Faulkner, published in 1948. Faulkner
conceived of the story that became *Intruder in the Dust* as early as 1940, when
he described the idea in a letter as "a mystery story, original in that [the] solver
is a negro, himself in jail for murder and about to be lynched" (*SL* 128). By
1948, however, when Faulkner actually got around to writing the book, his
concept of the story had altered significantly: It would now be "a mystery story
plus a little sociology and psychology" (*SL* 267). The "mystery story" involves
the wrongful arrest, near-lynching, and eventual exoneration of Lucas Beauchamp, the black man (actually a mulatto), for the murder of a white man,
Vinson Gowrie. To prove his innocence, Lucas must rely upon an unusual set
of detectives—a white teenager, Chick Mallison; his black companion, Aleck
Sander; and an elderly white woman, Miss Eunice Habersham (a biracial pair
of Hardy boys assisted by a Miss Marple)—and a macabre plot that culminates
in the act of digging up a grave in a rural Mississippi cemetery. The "little
sociology and psychology," presented largely through the speeches of lawyer

Gavin Stevens to his nephew Chick Mallison, presents Faulkner's social thesis that "the new white people in the [S]outh, before the North or the government or anyone else, owe and must pay a responsibility to the Negro" (*SL* 262). This thesis, as most early reviewers recognized, represented Faulkner's contribution to the national debate on race that, at the very time Faulkner was drafting and revising the text of his novel, was surfacing as a major issue in the Southern states' rights revolt against the Truman administration in the 1948 presidential campaign (*see* **Dixiecrats**).

Intruder, correctly grouped with Faulkner's lesser works, is a very uneven novel, partly because the Hollywood-style "whodunit" action (Faulkner had spent much of the early 1940s writing screenplays in Hollywood) seems incompatible with the stream-of-consciousness, high modernist style that is Faulkner's hallmark and partly because the story is frequently set aside (as in chapters 7, 9, and 10) for the effusive propagandizing of Gavin Stevens on the issues of race and sectionalism.

Despite its weaknesses, however, *Intruder* shows occasional signs of brilliance. The opening two chapters, for example, represent one of the most discerning treatments of race in all of Faulkner. There Faulkner dramatizes the indebtedness that Chick Mallison unwillingly incurs when Lucas Beauchamp rescues the boy from an icy creek, takes the boy home with him, dries his clothes, and feeds him dinner. What is crucial in this section is how Faulkner inverts the traditional racial hierarchy (this inversion being effectively symbolized by Chick's fall, followed by Lucas's towering over Chick on the creek bank and then issuing commands to the boy) and why this inversion creates such profound embarrassment and shame in the young boy. All of the further action of the novel evolves from this scene—first in Chick's instinctive desire to reestablish the lost racial order (hence his wish to see the community "make a nigger out of [Lucas] once in his life anyway") but eventually in Chick's growth and maturation, which enables the youngster to see Lucas not as a stereotypical black but as an individualized fellow human being.

This last point introduces what is clearly the most impressive feature of *Intruder in the Dust*: the characterization of Lucas Beauchamp. One of the slave-line descendants of old Carothers McCaslin from *Go Down, Moses*, in which Lucas plays an important but secondary role, Lucas is here moved center stage and presented as a proud, defiant individualist who refuses to allow others to define him, either as a person or as a member of his society. Interestingly, while early readers of the novel, in the heightened race-conscious atmosphere in which it appeared, understandably viewed Lucas as a militant "black" seeking to throw off white oppression, the fact is that Lucas views himself as being as much white as black and ultimately refuses to allow either color to control his own definition of self. This, it would appear, is the point of the final scene when Lucas insists on paying his legal fee and getting a receipt for the payment.

The heart of *Intruder in the Dust*—and what keeps it from devolving into a standard murder mystery—is the relationship between Chick and Lucas. That relationship, much like the one between Huckleberry Finn and Jim, which almost certainly influenced Faulkner's novel, begins in opposition (white/black, youth/age) and ambivalence but ends in mutual acceptance, respect, and a degree of friendship. For that development to occur, however, both Lucas and Chick must become "intruders"—Lucas by militantly refusing to accept the ethnic definitions that the community thrusts upon him and Chick by daring, through actions that make a mockery of his uncle's mere rhetoric, to challenge the long-held belief in white supremacy. What Lucas and Chick both unsettle (with help, of course, from Aleck and Miss Habersham) is the "dust" of Southern tradition. A final irony is revealed in the denouement of the novel when a society so blind to the evils of racism and mob lynching recoils in horror at an act of fratricide.

FURTHER READING

Bassett, John E. "Gradual Progress and *Intruder in the Dust.*" *College Literature* 13 (1986): 207–216.

Clark, Keith. "Man on the Margin: Lucas Beauchamp and the Limitations of Space." *Faulkner Journal* 6.1 (1990): 67–79.

Monaghan, David M. "Faulkner's Relationship to Gavin Stevens in *Intruder in the Dust.*" *Dalhousie Review* 52 (1972): 449–457.

Rigsby, Carol R. "Chick Mallison's Expectations and *Intruder in the Dust.*" *Mississippi Quarterly* 29 (1976): 386–399.

Samway, Patrick H. *Faulkner's* Intruder in the Dust: *A Critical Study of the Typescripts.* New York: Whitson, 1980.

Robert W. Hamblin

INTRUDER IN THE DUST (film), directed by Clarence Brown, is the 1949 screen adaptation of the Faulkner novel. The story centers on an elderly black man, Lucas Beauchamp, falsely accused of shooting a white man in the back. Chick Mallison, a white youngster, convinces his uncle, Gavin Stevens, a high-minded lawyer who figures in several Faulkner stories, to defend Lucas. Meanwhile Chick, aided by Miss Habersham, sets out to protect Lucas and investigate the crime with which he is charged.

Brown shot the bulk of the movie on location in Faulkner's own hometown of Oxford, Mississippi, where he met the novelist. Faulkner accepted Brown's invitation to touch up the final shooting script of the film, although he wanted no screen credit for doing so. Screenwriter Ben Maddow wrote the script for the film. He not only interpolated several episodes from the novel directly into the screenplay but worked into the script portions of Faulkner's own dialogue as well. Small wonder, then, that the film continues to win critical plaudits as the most faithful movie version of a Faulkner novel ever filmed.

FURTHER READING

Fadiman, Regina. Intruder in the Dust: *Novel into Film.* Knoxville: University of Tennessee Press, 1978.

Thomas, Tony. *The Films of the Forties.* New York: Carol, 1993.

Gene D. Phillips

J

JAMES, HENRY (1843–1916), American author, often considered the first of the "modern psychological novelists." The only works of James that brought him much acclaim were "Daisy Miller" (1878) and *The Portrait of a Lady* (1881). Most of James's other novels were considered by both readers and critics to be obscure and convoluted. The primary subject matter of James's work involves Americans abroad or the vulgarity of American manners.

Like William Faulkner, James considered the novel a unique art form and experimented with it as such. Joseph Blotner cites Conrad Aiken's comment on Faulkner's similarity to James: "[W]hat sets him above . . . all his American contemporaries, is his continuous preoccupation with the novel as *form* . . . and a degree of success with it which would clearly have commanded the interest and respect of Henry James himself" (1984 *FAB* 412). Aiken's observation succinctly characterizes James's influence on Faulkner.

Although the style of Faulkner's novels demonstrates strong affinities with Henry James's style, Faulkner's comments on James are ambiguous. When asked by students at the University of Virginia if he had read Henry James, Faulkner replied, "Yes, without much pleasure. Henry James to me was a prig, except *The Turn of the Screw*, which was very fine *tour de force*" (*FIU* 16). In another lecture at the University of Virginia, however, Faulkner ranks James as among the best novelists, English and American (243). According to Blotner's catalogue of Faulkner's library, Faulkner owned copies of *The Portrait of a Lady, The Turn of the Screw*, and Robert Marks's edition of *James's Later Novels*.

Faulkner stated that he actually considered James a European rather than an American novelist: "Hawthorne or Henry James are not truly American writers. Their tradition was from Europe. They wrote in the tradition of European writers. They were not true Americans in the sense that I mean—indigenous American writers who were produced and nurtured by a culture which was completely

American'' (*LIG* 168). Faulkner appears to consider James's emphasis on manners, as well as his subtlety in describing psychological matters, rather than the powerful and often graphic nature of Faulkner's own psychological delineations, as distinctly European rather than American. Moreover, Faulkner sees James's penchant for subtlety as a shortcoming and recognizes that James himself would have considered the graphic aspects of Faulkner's work as ''vulgarity.'' In his biography of Faulkner, Blotner quotes Faulkner's observation in ''describing Myrtle Monson's [of *Elmer*] 'humanness' . . . that 'Henry James would have called it vulgarity' '' (1984 *FAB* 169). James's influence, then, resides in his emphasis and experimentation with the novel as form, rather than in particular subject matter or themes.

FURTHER READING

Reesman, Jeanne Campbell. *American Designs: The Late Novels of James and Faulkner.* Philadelphia: University of Pennsylvania Press, 1991.

Rebecca Rowley

JAPAN. During his three-week stay in Japan in 1955, Faulkner mentioned that he had been introduced to Japanese poems through Ezra Pound, had read Tanizaki's *Some Prefer Nettles*, and had admired Kurosawa's film *Rashomon.* Faulkner compared Japanese culture with the Southern tradition, using the term ''Samurai'' spirit. When Cleanth Brooks explains Quentin Compson's suicide, he, too, refers to this central figure in Faulkner's canon as ''the true samurai,'' calling Quentin's suicide Faulkner's ''version of a bloodless hara-kiri'' (*Toward Yoknapatawpha* 310). Beyond these few traces, it is difficult to find a significant influence of Japanese culture in Faulkner's works even after his successful visit to Japan.

By contrast, Faulkner had caught the attention of writers and scholars in Japan before he was awarded the Nobel Prize. Interestingly, Faulkner was first introduced to Japan through French translations and French literary magazines. Yukio Haruyama (1902–1994), a famous modernist poet reading Faulkner in French, published an essay entitled ''William Faulkner'' in 1932. In the same year, a Japanese translation of ''A Rose for Emily'' appeared in a literary magazine Haruyama edited. He again introduced four of Faulkner's poems in 1933. In 1934, Matsuo Takagaki, a professor of American literature, explained in an essay that Faulkner's ''*Soldiers' Pay* is filled with an extraordinary power that he had never felt with Sherwood Anderson,'' and ''*The Sound and the Fury* is a wonder and a fascination.'' However, it was not until the 1950s that Faulkner's novels started to be read and studied among scholars and students. Certainly the prestigious Nobel award triggered a tremendous interest in this writer from the American South, and the enthusiasm was confirmed with Faulkner's visit to Japan—as the record of that visit, Robert A. Jelliffe's *Faulkner at Nagano*, confirms.

The publication history of Faulkner's works translated into Japanese is as follows: *Sanctuary* and *The Wild Palms* (1950), *Intruder in the Dust* and *Knight's Gambit* (1951), *Soldiers' Pay* (1952), *The Sound and the Fury* and *Pylon* (1954), *Absalom, Absalom!* and "The Bear" (1958), *As I Lay Dying* (1959), *A Fable* (1960), *Light in August* (1961), and numerous short stories, including "Dry September," "That Evening Sun," and "Delta Autumn" (1952). Today several versions of the popular novels are available from different translators. Fuzambo Publishing House in Tokyo began a project entitled "The Complete Works of Faulkner" in 1967 with a translation of *Requiem for a Nun*. Now all twenty-seven volumes have been published, and the whole project was completed in 1997.

The first book-length critical study on Faulkner's novels in Japan appeared in 1958. With the development of the critical commentaries on Faulkner in the United States in the 1960s, Faulkner's novels and short stories were widely taught at college and graduate levels in Japan, using these materials. In the 1970s and 1980s, Faulkner studies in Japan vigorously flourished. Now Faulkner has become one of the most popular topics for students as well as for conference discussions. In fact, there are now thirty-five books on Faulkner written by Japanese scholars, including the monumental three-volume study of Faulkner by Kenzaburo Ohashi, an internationally acclaimed figure in Faulkner studies. Just recently a Japanese Faulkner Society has been organized with an initial membership exceeding 200.

In 1978 Ohashi, with Kyoichi Harakawa and Kiyoyuki Ono, started a journal entitled *William Faulkner: Materials, Studies, and Criticism*, twelve issues of which were published by 1985; and three issues of another journal, *Faulkner Studies*, edited by Michel Gresset, Kenzaburo Ohashi, Noel Polk, and Kiyoyuki Ono, were published from 1991 to 1994. In 1985 *Faulkner Studies in Japan*, edited by Thomas McHaney, was published in the United States (University of Georgia Press). Also in 1985, the International Faulkner Colloquium was held at Izu, seventy-five miles south of Tokyo, to commemorate the thirtieth anniversary of Faulkner's visit to Japan in 1955, with Cleanth Brooks as a special guest. The Colloquium papers were compiled as *Faulkner: After the Nobel Prize*, edited by Michel Gresset and Kenzaburo Ohashi.

During the talk with six prominent Japanese authors at the PEN club in Tokyo, Faulkner impressed them with his ideas about land, continuity, and history. After the end of the war, Japan shared many serious problems with the American South in its process of modernization. Once Faulkner was introduced to Japanese readers, he made a dramatic impact on the postwar generation writers and the leading contemporary Japanese writers. Faulkner's modernistic style of innovations was a fresh stimulus to young Japanese poets and novelists such as Takehiko Fukunaga (1918–1979), who discovered Faulkner via France as early as the 1930s. Soon most of the writers were fascinated by Faulkner's powerful imagination and insight into the human condition in the modern world, as well as Faulkner's techniques of nonchronological narrative, stream of consciousness, and multiple points of view. Mitsuharu Inoue (1926–1992) was attracted by a strong sense of community in Faulkner's world, which he could not find in the postwar confusion in Japan. Kenji Nakagami (1946–1992), a guest speaker at the Izu Colloquium, created his own Yoknapatawpha out of his homeland and adopted the Faulknerian technique of storytelling. Yuko Tsushima (b. 1947), one of Japan's most important women writers, has shown strong interest in Faulkner's female characters such as Caddy Compson. Above all, Faulkner has always been among 1994 Nobel Prize winner Kenzaburo Oe's (b. 1935) most influential predecessors. Oe finds in Faulkner's novels a sense of "salvation," which he believes should be a major function of literature. Oe has been specifically impressed by Faulkner's penetrating observations of human beings; he frequently quotes the idea of "grief" from Faulkner in his essays and novels. Moreover, Oe admires Faulkner's creation of a cosmological model of human life from the individual issues in a small Southern county. In *The Silent Cry* (1967, English edition, 1974), Oe invents his own mythological cosmos based on his small village, just as Yoknapatawpha, Mississippi, became a "postage stamp of native soil" for Faulkner.

FURTHER READING

Nakagami, Kenji. "Faulkner: The Luxuriating South." Trans. Michiyo Ishii. *Faulkner: After the Nobel Prize*. Ed. Michel Gresset and Kenzaburo Ohashi. Kyoto: Yamaguchi, 1987. 326–336.
Ohashi, Kenzaburo. " 'Native Soil' and the World Beyond: William Faulkner and Japanese Novelists." *Faulkner: International Perspectives*, ed. Fowler and Abadie. 257–275.
Yoshida, Michiko. "Kenji Nakagami as Faulkner's Rebellious Heir." *Faulkner, His Contemporaries, and His Posterity*, ed. Zacharasiewicz. 350–360.

Ikuko Fujihira

JESUS, an African American character in Faulkner's "That Evening Sun." Jesus is more notable for his absence, than his presence, in the story. In the bluesy world of the tale, Jesus is the estranged common-law husband of Nancy, laundress and sometimes cook for the Compson family, who Nancy fears intends to return and kill her for moonlighting as a prostitute for white men. On one level, Jesus represents the latently violent "bad nigger" of Southern culture who threatens white supremacy. On another, Jesus is a prophecy of the future in his refusal to be treated as less than a man. And on a more symbolic plane, Jesus is an ambiguous redeemer, one who offers retribution rather than forgiveness.

FURTHER READING

Hamblin, Robert W. "Before the Fall: The Theme of Innocence in Faulkner's 'That Evening Sun.' " *Notes on Mississippi Writers* 11 (1979): 86–94.
Johnston, Kenneth G. "The Year of Jubilee: Faulkner's 'That Evening Sun.' " *American Literature* 46 (1974): 93–100.

Kuyk, Dirk, Jr., Betty M. Kuyk, and James A. Miller. "Black Culture in William Faulkner's 'That Evening Sun.' " *Journal of American Studies* 20 (1986): 33–50.

Perrine, Laurence. " 'That Evening Sun': A Skein of Uncertainties." *Studies in Short Fiction* 22 (1985): 295–307.

David L. Vanderwerken

JONES, WASH, a character created by Faulkner, first appears in a story called "Wash," published in *Harper's Magazine* in 1933. As Faulkner often did, he revised the story and incorporated it into a novel, *Absalom, Absalom!* A representative of the class of poor whites, or "white trash" or "rednecks," Wash establishes squatter's rights in a cabin on the land of Thomas Sutpen, owner of Yoknapatawpha County's largest and richest cotton plantation. The two men establish a master and retainer relationship, even drinking together for long afternoons in Sutpen's scuppernong arbor. During the Civil War, Jones claims to be "looking after" Sutpen's property while Colonel Sutpen is leading his regiment. After the war, Sutpen returns to his ruined land, his wife dead, his son vanished. Sutpen and Jones open a country store together. Jones has a granddaughter, Milly, who serves as a convenient female for Sutpen in his next attempt to sire a male heir. When Milly produces an infant girl, however, Sutpen insults and repudiates her. Jones, having heard his beloved Sutpen callously scorn his and Sutpen's own blood, confronts and kills Sutpen with a scythe. A posse of Sutpen's peers kills Jones shortly after he cuts the throats of Milly and his great-granddaughter. Although Jones learns this man whom he idolizes as brave, noble, and caring suffers from elephantiasis of the ego, he never knows that Sutpen is really an Appalachian hillbilly, a double of Jones himself, whose hubristic quest to triumph over time by establishing a kind of biblical dynasty in north Mississippi is brought to an end by Jones, an emblem of father time with his scythe.

FURTHER READING

Callen, Shirley. "Planter and Poor White in *Absalom, Absalom!*, 'Wash,' and *The Mind of the South*." *South Central Bulletin* 23.4 (1963): 24–36.

Howell, Elmo. "Faulkner's Wash Jones and the Southern Poor White." *Ball State University Forum* 8.1 (1967): 8–12.

MacLelland, Jackie. "Honor and Milly Jones in *Absalom, Absalom!*" *Mount Olive Review* 6 (1992): 52–55.

David L. Vanderwerken

JOYCE, JAMES (1882–1941), Irish novelist and poet. Joyce was a tidal force in the cultural and artistic transformations that have come to be designated by the term "modernism." Born in Rathgar, a suburb of Dublin, Ireland, he was one of the first of the great "expatriates," leaving Dublin with his common-law wife, Nora Barnacle, in 1904, and spending the rest of his life in Trieste, Zurich, and Paris, which Joyce helped make into the world capital of the avant-garde movements. His major works include the short story collection *Dubliners* (published in 1914, some seven years after it was completed), *A Portrait of the Artist as a Young Man* (serialized in *The Egoist*, 1914–1915, and published as a book in 1916), *Ulysses* (serialized in *Little Review*, 1918–1920, and published as a book in 1922), and *Finnegans Wake* (begun in 1923 and published in fragments from 1924 until its completion and publication as a book in 1939). Reviewing *Ulysses* in 1923, T. S. Eliot observed, "I hold this book to be the most important expression which the present age has found; it is a book to which we are all indebted, and from which none of us can escape."

It is demonstrably clear that Faulkner was a close and careful reader of *Ulysses*, that his relationship with Joyce's novel was sustained throughout his formative years as a novelist, and that it was deepened and renewed, very likely by means of fresh readings, as he composed his first novels between 1925 and 1931: *Soldiers' Pay, Elmer, Mosquitoes, Flags in the Dust*, the two versions of *Sanctuary*, and *The Sound and the Fury*. Faulkner is linked to Joyce by complex patterns of influence and emulation; borrowing and "theft"; imitation and resistance; rereading and rewriting; sometimes playful and sometimes polemical forms of "dialogue, parody, and contestation" (Roland Barthes's phrase).

It is possible to mark four interrelated aspects of *Ulysses* that were of primary importance for Faulkner. First, *Ulysses* offered a series of radically experimental narrative techniques for representing psychological reality, including the "interior-monologue" and "stream-of-consciousness" forms of narration. With these techniques Joyce was able to explore and render the moment-to-moment being and consciousness of its central protagonists during the course of one full day, June 16, 1904. Moreover, Joyce established the principle that each character's unique processes of thought and experience should be matched with an appropriately unique and distinctive stylistic texture. For example, comprising the final chapter of *Ulysses*, the stream-of-consciousness monologue of Molly Bloom runs for some forty-five pages without a single punctuation mark and is dominated both by the memory of her own erotic history and by the word "yes," which is woven into the flow of her narration countless times. In the third chapter of *Ulysses*, in contrast, the flow of the thinking of Stephen Dedalus (whose childhood, early maturity, and artistic awakening are the subjects of *A Portrait of the Artist as a Young Man*) is governed by the "seamorse" evoked by the memory of his dead mother and by the recondite philosophical speculation and complex aesthetic theorizing of the young genius-in-the-making. Joyce was equally committed to representing the unconscious fantasy life of his protagonists, especially that of Leopold Bloom, as in the harrowing "Walpurgisnacht" or "Nighttown" chapter, "Circe." These fictional definitions of psychological reality were revolutionary and suggested to Faulkner, as he conceived such figures as Elmer Hodge, Horace Benbow, Benjy Compson, Quentin Compson, or Addie Bundren, a rich array of possible ways to organize the narrative of the inner life and represent its dynamic processes of consciousness and memory, fantasy and repression.

Second, *Ulysses*, as its very title suggests, was famous for its mythic intertextuality, the sometimes disguised, sometimes explicit manner in which it structured the events of the present day, June 16, 1904, upon an epic series of adventures recounted in Homer's *Odyssey*. Each chapter of *Ulysses* is entitled according to, and thus modeled upon, a different Homeric episode: *Telemachus, Nestor, Proteus, Calypso, Lotus-eaters, Hades, Aeolus, Lestrygonians, Scylla and Charybdis, Wandering Rocks, Sirens, Cyclops, Nausicaa, Oxen of the Sun, Circe, Eumaeus, Ithaca, Penelope*. As Eliot again noted: "In using the myth, in manipulating a continuous parallel between contemporaneity and antiquity, Mr. Joyce is pursuing a method which others must pursue after him." One thinks, for example, of Faulkner's use of fertility myths in *Soldiers' Pay*, of James Frazer's *The Golden Bough* in *Sanctuary* and *Go Down, Moses*, or of the Easter story in *The Sound and the Fury*. In addition to what Eliot called Joyce's "mythical method," *Ulysses* is additionally overdetermined by an elaborate, multistaved schema, according to which each chapter is interwoven with its own unique images, symbols, colors, bodily references, and so on. In an analogous way, Faulkner always gives us a many-layered and richly elaborated symbolic discourse.

Third, the power of *Ulysses* was inseparable from its compelling display of linguistic *jouissance* and musicality, its radically unconventional forms of expressive freedom. With each unfolding sentence of *Ulysses*, Faulkner encountered the kind of seamless fusion of prose and poetry that would come to characterize his own writing. No better imitation of Joycean expression can be found than Faulkner's description of Ike Snopes and the cow in *The Hamlet*.

Fourth, and most generally, *Ulysses* dramatized a lesson of the utmost importance for Faulkner: that everyday family relations, along with the most intimate personal experiences, conflicts, and fantasies involved therein, could constitute the material and influence the structure of great modernist art. Moreover, based as *Ulysses* was on Joyce's memory of Dublin's inexhaustible array of social types, the largest context of this art could be based on the conflicts, tensions, and tragedies inherent in the mutually entangled social and economic lives of an entire region. As Faulkner, as if by analogy, would put it in a famous interview, "Beginning with *Sartoris*, I discovered that my own little postage stamp of native soil was worth writing about and that I would never live long enough to exhaust it, and that by sublimating the actual into the apocryphal I would have complete liberty to use whatever talent I might have to its absolute top. It opened up a gold mine of other people, so I created a cosmos of my own" (*LIG* 255).

When asked about the influence of Joyce on his own writing during the early years of his fame, following the publication of *The Sound and the Fury* and *As I Lay Dying*, Faulkner tended to be understandably evasive. In a 1932 interview with Henry Nash Smith, for example, Faulkner claimed, in fact, that he had never read *Ulysses*, invoking instead a vague aural source for his knowledge of Joycean methods: " 'You know,' he smiled, 'sometimes I think there must be a sort of pollen of ideas floating in the air, which fertilizes similarly minds here and there which have not had direct contact. I had heard of Joyce, of course,' he went on. 'Some one told me about what he was doing, and it is possible that I was influenced by what I heard' " (*LIG* 30). In a moment of irony that may not have been lost on the interviewer, Faulkner reached over to his table and handed Smith a 1924 edition of the book; Smith politely accounted for it in his description of the interview by supposing that Faulkner had borrowed the copy at some point during his recent trip to New York. Faulkner, it is worth pointing out, did in fact own a copy of *Ulysses* (Paris: Shakespeare & Co, fourth printing, January 1924) that bears his signature.

By 1947, Faulkner hardly needed to be so coy, telling an English class at the University of Mississippi that Joyce was "the father of modern literature" (1974 *FAB* 1230). By 1957, Faulkner's pronouncements on Joyce had become fully classical: "James Joyce was one of the great men of my time. He was electrocuted by the divine fire" (*LIG* 280).

FURTHER READING

Adams, Robert Martin. *After Joyce*. New York: Oxford University Press, 1977.
Eliot, T. S. "*Ulysses*, Order, and Myth." *Selected Prose of T. S. Eliot*. Ed. Frank Cermet. London: Faber, 1975. 175–178.
Grodin, Michael. "Criticism in New Composition: *Ulysses* and *The Sound and the Fury*." *Twentieth Century Literature* 21 (1975): 265–277.
Zeitlin, Michael. "Faulkner, Joyce, and the Problem of Influence in *The Sound and the Fury*." *Faulkner Studies* 2 (April 1994): 1–25.
———. "Versions of the 'Primal Scene': Faulkner and *Ulysses*." *Mosaic* 22 (1989): 63–77.

Michael Zeitlin

JUNG, CARL G. (1875–1961), Swiss psychiatrist and author. The process of psychic growth described by C. G. Jung as "individuation" provides an avenue for investigating how historical social arrangements relate to individual identity and freedom, thus deepening readers' understanding of individual characters and of three social groups in Faulkner's fiction—white males, black people, and women.

Jung's analytical psychology understands each individual's *Self* to consist of a gender-specific *ego*, a gender-opposite *anima* (in males) or *animus* (in females), and a *shadow* containing characteristics the ego considers unacceptable. According to Jung, individuals are first conscious only of the ego and take it to be the entire Self. Immature individuals unconscious of the anima/animus and shadow deny the existence of these counterparts of the ego and project them upon other individuals and groups, thus essentially claiming to have nothing to do with the qualities characteristic of the counterparts and seeing them entirely as the qualities of outsiders radically different from themselves. Individuals grow psychically and achieve "individuation" as the ego becomes aware of and eventually accepts its gender-opposite and shadow counterparts, allowing the full Self to emerge.

Both the alienated white males and the rigid patriarchal societies of Faulkner's fiction suggest the individual and social damage that occurs when an immature white male ego denies anima and shadow and projects them in demeaning social roles for women and black people. Alienated white males abound in the fiction. Some express their alienation in disaffection—young Bayard of *Flags in the Dust*, the Compson sons, Darl and Jewel Bundren, Popeye, Joe Christmas, and the tall convict of *The Wild Palms*. Married males, who, notably, are often widowers, more often express their alienation in a will to subdue—especially the patriarchs. John Sartoris, for example, has "intolerant eyes" and a "violent and ruthless dictatorialness and will to dominate." Thomas Sutpen can "swagger even on a horse," and Carothers McCaslin expresses "contempt for all his get." The last of the alienated widowers is not a patriarch but a modern man, Flem Snopes, whose will to dominate has led him to his mansion and whose alienation leaves him sitting alone each night, known even to his admiring cousin Montgomery Ward as *"THE son of a bitch's son of a bitch."*

Faulkner's alienated white males repeatedly damage themselves and others as they alternately fear and try to dominate the women and black people they interact with, actions typical of the ego damaging itself by denying anima and shadow and projecting them upon others. Doc Hines in *Light in August*, for instance, rants against "womanfilth" and "bitchery," and he preaches white supremacy in black churches; yet readers see his true need of women and blacks in the revelation that he eats through the "bounty and charity of negroes," specifically of the "negro women carrying . . . dishes of food [into] the rear [of] the house . . . and emerging emptyhanded." The younger Jason Compson in *The Sound and the Fury* similarly denigrates women—"Once a bitch always a bitch, what I say"—as well as black people—"Let these dam trifling niggers starve for a couple of years, then they'd see what a soft thing they have"; yet his need is as clear as Doc Hines's, for he lives on income derived from his mother, sister, and niece, and he eats the food prepared and served by a black woman, Dilsey. These white males' needs mirror Jung's view that immature individuals very much need the counterparts that their egos deny, denigrate, and project.

In *Light in August*, Joe Christmas begins like Doc Hines and Jason Compson but finally matures in a distinctly Jungian manner. Initially, he flees from the essence of "womanshenegro," which he senses first at the scene of his attempted sexual initiation and later in his walk through Freedman Town: "It was as though he and all other manshaped life about him had been returned to the lightless hot wet primogenitive Female." He fears, apparently, his own shadow connected to his "black blood," as well as his own repeatedly unfulfilled orphan's need for mothering, mothers being responsible for developing anima in males. However, during the days of his flight following Joanna Burden's death, he comes to new acceptance of women and black people. Although first sensing himself sinking "at last into the black abyss which had been waiting, trying, for thirty years to drown him," he subsequently becomes able to wonder that the black people who have fed him were "Of their brother afraid." Brotherhood with women and black people suggests the ego's acceptance of the legitimacy of its counterparts, as well as this white male's social acceptance of other persons viewed not as flat projections but as fully human brothers.

When two of Faulkner's major patriarchs—Thomas Sutpen and old Carothers McCaslin—fail to reach this point of brotherhood suggestive of Jungian psychic maturity and wholeness, their narrow social designs collapse. According to Quentin Compson's telling in *Absalom, Absalom!*, Thomas Sutpen's design for a patriarchal line fails because Sutpen will not accept his son Charles Bon, whom he sees as black and whom he sends his white son Henry to kill. Henry and Bon articulate the question of whether the white male can accept the black male as a brother: "You are my brother," says Henry. "No I'm not," replies Bon. "I'm the nigger that's going to sleep with your sister." A shot from Henry's pistol completes the conversation. In *Go Down, Moses* the McCaslin white male line fails similarly: Ike, the sole white McCaslin grandson, repudiates his inheritance after uncovering Carothers's violation of his own slave daughter Tomey. Carothers has begotten a son upon her, Turl, and then has left Turl a bequest Ike sees as a contemptuous sop, *"cheaper than saying My son to a nigger."*

Both white patriarchs—Sutpen and McCaslin—disregard black and female children so thoroughly as to destroy not only their designs but even the white masculinity they hold separate and aloof: Their last white male descendants— Henry Sutpen and Ike McCaslin—are both childless and either dead or enfeebled by the ends of the novels. Jung suggests this precise fate for the unindividuated masculine ego, which has no chance of renewal apart from its gender opposite and its shadow. Meanwhile, the patriarchs' denied black descendants have become wild men, Jim Bond howling in the wilderness that was once Sutpen's Hundred and Butch Beauchamp executed for murder. Such is the fate of Jung's denied shadow, which presents itself in the forms of beasts and criminals.

In contrast to these patriarchs who cannot say "My son to a nigger," young white males in Faulkner's later novels form productive partnerships with women and black people that grow perhaps from psychic maturity strong enough to produce mature human beings freed from projection and committed to societies where brotherhood can thrive. Three novels turn on the partnerships of young white males, black males, and white females—compelling comparison with Jung's white male ego, shadow, and anima. They include *The Unvanquished* with Bayard Sartoris, Ringo, and Granny/Aunt Jenny; *Intruder in the Dust* with Chick Mallison, Aleck Sander, and Miss Habersham; and *The Reivers* with Lucius Priest, Ned, and Everbe.

Though all three novels are bildungsromans ultimately interested in the maturation of their young white male characters, those characters are oddly subordinate through much of the novels. In *The Unvanquished*, Granny Millard directs all the major actions until her death, and Ringo rather than Bayard is her second in command: "Father was right," thinks Bayard; "[Ringo] was smarter than me." Even in the fatal confrontation with Grumby after Granny's death, Ringo must save Bayard, who is overpowered in Grumby's assault. In *The Reivers*, though Lucius Priest rides the race horse, his black cousin Ned McCaslin has created the crisis and finds the key to Lucius's victory in the race, saving the white boy as Ringo has saved Bayard. In *Intruder in the Dust*, though the white boy Chick Mallison must save the black man Lucas Beauchamp, he does so compelled by a sense of this black man's superiority to him: "[H]e could never give up now who had debased not merely his manhood but his whole race too." By its end the novel has made Lucas Beauchamp as much the savior of Chick Mallison as Chick is of Lucas. This pattern of subordination follows the Jungian principle that individuation requires the ego's subordination to the larger Self and acceptance of its need of anima/animus and shadow.

If these novels end with the white boys' maturation, they tie that maturation to visions of human equality in societies that stop seeing black people and women in the flat, stereotypical terms of Jungian projection. In *The Unvanquished* Bayard turns aside from his father's will to dominate, accepting passivity as he stands before Redmond's pistol, a passivity his society demands not of white men but of women and black people. It is as if he triumphs by becoming black and female, just as Jung insists that the ego triumphs only as it finds its role alongside anima/animus and shadow in the mature Self. The Bayard who has thus matured is the narrator of *The Unvanquished*, the narrator who begins his tale by claiming Ringo as a brother: "Ringo called Granny 'Granny' just like I did, until maybe he wasn't a nigger anymore or maybe I wasn't a white boy anymore, the two of us neither." In *The Reivers*, after Boss has lectured Lucius on the impossibility of avoiding one's own shadow—"Live with it, Grandfather said"—the mature Lucius now narrating the story declares that "now I knew what Grandfather meant: that your outside is just what you live in, sleep in, and has little connection with who you are and even less with what you do." Having learned to accept his own shadow, he refuses to see black people as dark and threatening aliens. The more explicit *Intruder in the Dust* brings Chick Mallison full circle. At its end the white boy who once insisted that Lucas Beauchamp had *"to admit he's a nigger"* now tacitly accepts his uncle's lecture that human rights must prevail "no matter what pigment" and that they must be defended until "Lucas will no longer run the risk of needing without warning to be saved."

The maturation of Faulkner's white protagonist in each of these bildungsromans follows the Jungian pattern, each boy establishing a harmony among ego and its counterparts and extending that harmony into a social vision of harmony among white males, females, and black people. Certainly Faulkner understood how forcefully the past impinges on the present, but Jung helps readers see how fully Faulkner also understood that the present lies in the hands of those inhabiting it and that the future will depend not just on the past but on the degree to which living individuals mature enough to alter social arrangements.

See also **Freud, Sigmund; Psychoanalytic Approaches**.

Terrell L. Tebbetts

"JUSTICE, A," a short story by Faulkner, first appeared in *These 13*. It was also included in *Collected Stories*, and a small portion is used as the prelude to "A Bear Hunt" in *Big Woods*. The story's theme presents a Machiavellian examination of power. A young Compson (Quentin) begins telling the story that Sam Fathers heard from Herman Basket about how Sam Fathers was first named Had-Two-Fathers. Imbedded are two tales. The first relates the manner by which Ikkemotubbe becomes chief or The Man (*du homme*: Doom) by poisoning the chief and his relations. The second concerns The Man's Solomonic attempts at keeping Crawfishford's attentions away from a slave's wife, who is Sam Fathers's mother.

FURTHER READING

Bradford, Melvin E. "That Other Patriarchy: Observations on Faulkner's 'A Justice.' " *Modern Age* 18 (1974): 266–271.

Hönnighausen, Lothar. "Faulkner Rewriting the Indian Removal." *Transatlantic Perspectives*. Vol. 3: *Rewriting the South: History and Fiction*. Ed. Lothar Hönnighausen et al. Tübingen, Germany: Franke, 1993. 335–343.

Howell, Elmo. "William Faulkner and the Mississippi Indians." *Tennessee Studies in Literature* 12 (1967): 149–153.

Kinney, Arthur F. "Teaching Narrative as Meaning in 'A Justice' and *The Sound and the Fury*." *Approaches to Teaching Faulkner's* The Sound and the Fury. Ed. Stephen Hahn and Arthur F. Kinney. New York: Modern Language Association, 1996. 140–143.

Larry Wharton

K

KEATS, JOHN (1795–1821), British romantic poet. Keats was born the son of a livery stable owner, orphaned at an early age, apprenticed as an apothecary, and studied to become a surgeon. He broke off his medical studies and, with the assistance of Percy Shelley, published his first volume of poems in 1817. By 1819 he had written his most accomplished work in the odes, especially "To a Nightingale" and "On a Grecian Urn." He died of tuberculosis in Rome two years later.

Keats's relatively small body of poetry and highly speculative letters established his place in the canon of British poetry; and they had a wide influence among American writers of the early twentieth century, including Faulkner. His two most significant odes and the narrative poem "La Belle Dame Sans Merci" were widely disseminated through the agency of such collections as Palgrave's *Golden Treasury* in a period when lyrical poetry was widely regarded as the epitome of literary expression—an evaluation that Faulkner himself made on numerous occasions. There was sustained critical interest in Keats throughout Faulkner's formative and early years as a writer, including biographies by Sir Sidney Colvin (1917) and Amy Lowell (1925).

The primary aspects of Keats's influence on Faulkner can be seen in Faulkner's adoption of the "urn" as a metaphor for representation and his related exploration of the theme of the quest as a consequence of a nympholeptic encounter. (See, for example, the 1925 story "Nympholepsy.") In "Verse Old and Nascent," Faulkner asked, in a well-practiced tradition, "Is there nowhere among us a Keats in embryo, someone who will tune his lute to the beauty of the world?" (*EPP* 118). In one significant poem written during this period, published later as Poem X in *A Green Bough*, Faulkner depicts a laborer wending homeward at twilight as "a terrific figure on an urn." The use of the urn as a metaphor of representation enables Faulkner to write of the landscape of northern Mississippi in terms that suggest equivalencies and contrasts between the Arcadian milieu represented on a putative classical urn and his own environment, even as it evokes the cinematic or stereoptic quality of narrative and imagery (the figures depicted on a circular urn telling a sequential narrative that can itself be imagined as circular). The most striking example is the introduction of Lena Grove approaching Jefferson from Alabama, "moving forever and without progress like a figure on an urn."

Keats's ode is quite literally recalled in the colloquy between McCaslin and Ike in the commissary in Part 4 of "The Bear," where they differ on the interpretation of lines from the poem, which McCaslin apparently reads from a volume stored among the ledgers of the commissary. While McCaslin claims that the speaker of the poem is referring to "truth," "all things which touch the heart—honor and pride and pity and justice and courage and love," Ike insists that "he's talking about a girl." The difference in interpretation is indicative of the characters, McCaslin representing an insight into life as an allegory and Ike representing a stubborn literal-mindedness. But the scene is not without irony regarding the blindness of both interlocutors.

A number of studies have pondered the significance of Keats's ubiquitous influence on Faulkner, but the rich suggestiveness of Faulkner's allusions and the depth of Keats's influence remain topics to be explored more fully.

FURTHER READING

Hahn, Stephen. " 'Life Is Motion': Keats and Faulkner in the Classroom." *Teaching Faulkner* 10 (Fall 1996): 5–9.

———. " 'What Leaf-Fring'd Legend Haunts about Thy Shape?': *Light in August* and Southern Pastoral." *Faulkner Journal* 1.1 (1985): 30–40.

Kobler, J. F. "Lena Grove: Faulkner's 'Still Unravish'd Bride of Quietness.' " *Arizona Quarterly* 28 (1972): 339–354.

Korenman, Joan S. "Faulkner's Grecian Urn." *Southern Literary Journal* 7 (Fall 1974): 3–23.

Stephen Hahn

"KENTUCKY: MAY: SATURDAY," the second of two impressionistic essays (the other was "Innocent at Rinkside") that Faulkner was commissioned to write for *Sports Illustrated* in 1955. An on-the-scene description of the eighty-first annual running of the Kentucky Derby, the essay was first published in the May 16, 1955 issue of *Sports Illustrated* and later collected in James Meriwether's edition of *Essays, Speeches & Public Letters by William Faulkner* (1965). Unconcerned with the factual details of the race, disdaining even to name the winning horse and jockey, Faulkner instead seeks to capture the spirit or essence of the horse race, finding in the event symbolic expression of paradoxes he found inherent in the human condition: life and death, past and present, reality and dream, victory and defeat.

FURTHER READING

Hamblin, Robert W. "*Homo Agonistes*, or, William Faulkner as Sportswriter." *Aethlon: The Journal of Sport Literature* 13 (Spring 1996): 13–22.

Tower, Whitney. "Prose for the Roses." *Sports Illustrated* 28 April 1986: 38ff.

Robert W. Hamblin

KNIGHT'S GAMBIT, a collection of six mystery stories by Faulkner, published in 1949. Only the title story, actually a novella, had not been previously published; the other five—"Smoke" (*Harper's*, April 1932), "Monk" (*Scribner's*, May 1937), "Hand upon the Waters" (*Saturday Evening Post*, November 4, 1939), "Tomorrow" (*Saturday Evening Post*, November 23, 1940), and "Error in Chemistry" (*Ellery Queen's Mystery Magazine*, June 1946)—had appeared from three to seventeen years earlier; and one of these, "Smoke," had been included in *Doctor Martino and Other Stories*. In seeking to group and unify a number of previous stories, Faulkner was repeating the pattern of *The Unvanquished* and *Go Down, Moses* but in this case with far less successful results.

All of the stories in *Knight's Gambit* feature Gavin Stevens as a detective/lawyer who shares the ratiocinative powers of Poe's Inspector Dupin and Arthur Conan Doyle's Sherlock Holmes and the courtroom strategems of Erle Stanley Gardner's Perry Mason. In "Smoke," almost universally viewed as the weakest of the stories because of its extreme incredulity, Stevens introduces into a trial a piece of fabricated evidence to trick Granby Dodge into revealing that he hired a Memphis gangster to perform a murder. In the cruelly ironic "Monk," Stevens secures the pardon of the mentally retarded Monk Odlethrop, who has been wrongfully imprisoned for one murder, only to later discover that Monk has been set up by a fellow prisoner to commit another murder, for which he is hanged. In "Hand upon the Waters" Stevens solves the murder of Lonnie Grinnup, another feebleminded individual who is the last descendant of the original founders of Yoknapatawpha County. In "Tomorrow" Stevens uncovers, years later, the motives of a juror who had hung the jury in a murder case Stevens had tried as a young lawyer. In "An Error in Chemistry" Stevens assists in exposing a murderer's disguise when the individual reveals his ignorance of the proper way to mix a cold toddy. In the title story that concludes the volume Stevens foils a murder plot involving the use of a wild stallion as the intended weapon.

As Michael Millgate has pointed out, Faulkner seems concerned to elevate the book above the level of mere potboiler, casting Stevens as "a knight of many gambits, as embodiment of justice, a fearless, skillful and yet compassionate campaigner for the right" (*Achievement* 268). A close reading of the text reveals that Stevens's role goes far beyond that of solving a number of particular crimes. Moreover, the framing of Stevens's actions by an opening story narrated by a communal "we" and a coda focusing on a representative member of the next generation, Chick Mallison, suggests that a concern for the creation and preservation of community is a principal subtext of the work. Part of this concern is that Yoknapatawpha County, already being threatened from within by the Snopesism that Faulkner had treated in *The Hamlet*, is now being subjected to sinister outside forces as well. The murderer of Anselm Holland is "that gorilla, that thug, down here from Memphis"; and the murderer of Lonnie Grinnup is hiding out in rural Yoknapatawpha County, "it was said, not from the police but from some of his Memphis friends or later business associates." Joel Flint, the murderer who is unfamiliar with a Southern toddy, is "the foreigner, the outlander, the Yankee"; and Harriss, the first husband of Melisandre Backus, who rebuilds the old Backus house into one that looks "like the Southern mansion in the moving picture, only about five times as big and ten times as Southern," is reported to have made his fortune as a big-time New Orleans bootlegger, "successful not even despite the Law but over the Law as though the Law itself and not failure were his vanquished adversary." That the threat to Yoknapatawpha is not merely local or even national is revealed in the final story, the climax of which occurs on the day before the bombing of Pearl Harbor, beginning the war that will pull Chick Mallison and other local youths into ever widening circles of evil and danger. To counter such growing threats to his home region, Stevens, who significantly spends his spare time translating the Old Testament into Greek, promotes the traditional values of justice, honor, decency, and community. One character tells him, "Mr. Stevens, you are what my grandpap would have called a gentleman. . . . And you are trying to bring the notions of 1860 into the politics of the nineteen hundreds. And politics in the twentieth century is a sorry thing. In fact, I sometimes think that the whole twentieth century is a sorry thing, smelling to high heaven in somebody's nose."

It is Gavin's role as a traditionalist in a corrupt modern world that is captured in the effective image of Faulkner's title, *Knight's Gambit*. The phrase, as Stevens explains to his nephew Chick, describes a move in chess whereby a knight simultaneously checks the opposing queen and rook. The only viable defensive response, as Chick understands, is "to save the queen and let the castle go." While Gavin applies the metaphor to Captain Gauldres's situation in the concluding story, Faulkner, by choosing the term as the collective title for the entire volume, seems to be directing the chief import of the phrase toward Stevens. Caught as he is in the paradoxical human world of law and crime, right and wrong, love and hate, past and present, individual and community, Stevens must make difficult and sometimes painful decisions, often between the lesser of two evils, saving the queen but losing the rook. Considerably altered from his roles in *Light and August* and *Intruder in the Dust*, this characterization of Stevens will be reprised and expanded in *The Town* and *The Mansion*.

FURTHER READING

Samway, Patrick. "Gavin Stevens as Uncle-Creator in *Knight's Gambit*." *Faulkner and Idealism*, ed. Gresset and Samway. 144–163.

Schlepper, Wolfgang E. "Truth and Justice in *Knight's Gambit*." *Mississippi Quarterly* 37 (1984): 365–375.

Skei, Hans H. "Faulkner's 'Knight's Gambit': Detection and Ingenuity." *Notes on Mississippi Writers* 13.2 (1981): 79–83.

Robert W. Hamblin

"KNIGHT'S GAMBIT," a short story by Faulkner, the title story of *Knight's Gambit* (1949). This is a long, convoluted story, almost a novella, using the knight's ability to move in two directions at once as the central metaphor to express a thematic distinction between truth and justice. Narrated by Charles Mallison, Gavin Stevens's nephew, the story's present action occurs on the three days prior to Japan's attack on Pearl Harbor. Stevens is able to prevent a crime, the death of Captain Gauldres in a trap set by his future brother-in-law. In addition, Stevens manages to right an old wrong by marrying the woman he had jilted some twenty years before.

FURTHER READING

Irwin, John T. " 'Knight's Gambit': Poe, Faulkner, and the Tradition of the Detective Story." *Arizona Quarterly* 46.4 (1990): 95–116.
Kalfatovic, Martin R. "Faulkner's 'Knight's Gambit.' " *Explicator* 45.3 (1987): 47–48.
Volpe, Edmond L. "Faulkner's 'Knight's Gambit': Sentimentality and the Creative Imagination." *Modern Fiction Studies* 24 (1978): 232–239.

Larry Wharton

L

LAND OF THE PHARAOHS (1955) is the least significant of the five films that Faulkner coscripted for director Howard Hawks. The movie deals with the building of the great pyramids. Faulkner conceded that he had no idea how a pharaoh talked and accordingly wrote the pharaoh's dialogue as if the Egyptian were a Kentucky colonel. Withal, the critical consensus is that the picture, starring Jack Hawkins, emerged as one of the better sword-and-sandal sagas to come out of Hollywood.

FURTHER READING

Halliwell, Leslie. *Film Guide*. Rev. ed. New York: HarperCollins, 1998.
McBride, Joseph. *Hawks on Hawks*. Berkeley: University of California Press, 1982.

Gene D. Phillips

LATIN AMERICA. William Faulkner's writings have greatly influenced Latin American literature of the last sixty years, and Latin American writers have widely acknowledged his literary presence. Because of the varied and diverse nature of Faulkner's literary works, and because literary influence is relational and specific to each writer, they have expressed a bond with Faulkner through a variety of different literary devices and forms. Faulkner's concepts of community, time, history, and tragedy; his sense of solitude; his expressions of the relationship between people, nature, land, and industrialization; and his methods for representing an ambiguous, plural, and changing sense of reality all strike a common chord with these New World authors also seeking to define themselves as writers, express the vision and values of their relatively new countries and cultures, and capture their rich and diverse lives.

Latin American writers became familiar with Faulkner in the 1930s through both English and French versions of his texts and through the texts of writers whom Faulkner influenced. "All the Dead Pilots" was the first literary work translated from English to Spanish. It was translated in 1933 in *Revista de Occidente*. Cuban writer Lino Novás Calvo, who readily acknowledged Faulkner's influence on his own work, translated *Sanctuary* in 1934. Because of his English ancestry, the Argentinean Jorge Luis Borges learned to read English before he could read Spanish. He discovered Faulkner in the original and between 1936 and 1939 wrote reviews of Faulkner's *Absalom, Absalom!*, *The Unvanquished*, and *The Wild Palms* to help introduce Hispanic readers and writers to Faulkner. In the review of *The Unvanquished* Borges states: "Rivers of brown water, rundown mansions, black slaves, equestrian wars—lazy and cruel: the peculiar world of *The Unvanquished* is consanguineous with this America and its history, and it is also *criollo*" (93). Borges did the first Spanish translation of *The Wild Palms* in 1940.

A number of Latin American novelists writing in the 1930s and 1940s are either consciously indebted to Faulkner or developed a similar artistic vision. The Argentine novelist Eduardo Mallea knew of Faulkner's works and expressed a somewhat similar sense of solitude, tragedy, and community in novels such as *La bahía de silencio* (*The Bay of Silence*), *Todo verdor perecerá* (*All Green Will Perish*), *Las Águilas* (*The Eagles*), and *La torre* (*The Tower*). However, *Fiesta en noviembre* (*Fiesta in November*), which weaves together two unrelated narratives much as Faulkner does in *The Wild Palms*, was published a year before Faulkner's novel. Agustín Yáñez, the Mexican writer, captures a sense of community, land, and nature similar to Faulkner's in *La tierra pródiga* (*The Prodigious Land*), *Las tierras flacas* (*The Barren Lands*), and especially *Al filo del agua* (*The Edge of the Storm*), although Yáñez points to Dos Passos rather than Faulkner as an influence. *Al filo del agua*, in particular, proved important to other Mexican writers such as Juan Rulfo and Carlos Fuentes.

The Uruguayan writer Juan Carlos Onetti also attracted attention to Faulkner through his own writing. Onetti, who came to Faulkner first through French translations of "All the Dead Pilots" and *Sanctuary*, was attracted to Faulkner's sense of ambiguity, concept of place, sense of time, and manipulation of narrative devices. Onetti, whose works have been associated with the beginning of the Boom, frequently refers to Faulkner's influence on his work.

The "Boom" in Latin American literature was a period marked by explosive growth and the use of innovative techniques. It attracted international attention and helped define Latin America's distinctive literary qualities. Taking root in the 1950s and reaching its apex in the 1960s, its writers and their works achieved international acclaim. Real/marvelous or magical realism is often associated with the Boom, although it is certainly not limited to that one feature. The Boom brought international recognition to writers such as Juan Rulfo, Gabriel García Márquez, Mario Vargas Llosa, José Donoso, Carlos Fuentes, Alejo Carpentier, Julio Cortázar, and others. A number of these writers have readily admitted their indebtedness to Faulkner.

Juan Rulfo's novel *Pedro Páramo* and his collection of short stories *El llano en llamas* (*Burning Plains*) were an important early expression of the Boom. In

Pedro Páramo, Rulfo uses the multiple narrative voices of ghosts to relate the history of the small rural Mexican village of Comala and its "*cacique*," Pedro Páramo, who is similar to Faulkner's Thomas Sutpen in certain respects.

Mario Vargas Llosa, the Peruvian novelist, states that he learned the importance of structure from Faulkner: that it can be a character and perhaps the most important one in a novel. He admits that Faulkner's influence was particularly visible in his first novel, *The Time of the Hero*. While acknowledging Faulkner's immense talent, Vargas Llosa believes that talent alone does not explain totally his widespread appeal in Latin America:

But there are more specific reasons for which Faulkner has such appeal in Latin America. The world out of which he created his own world is quite similar to a Latin American world. In the Deep South, as in Latin America, two different cultures coexist, two different historical traditions, two different races—all forming a difficult coexistence full of prejudice and violence. There also exists the extraordinary importance of the past, which is always present in contemporary life. In Latin America, we have the same thing. The world of Faulkner is preindustrial, or at least resisting industrialization, modernization, urbanization—exactly like many Latin American societies. Out of all this, Faulkner created a personal world, with a richness of technique and form. It is understandable that to a Latin American who works with such similar sources, the techniques and formal inventions of Faulkner hold strong appeal. (75–76)

Mexican novelist Carlos Fuentes has written and commented on the Faulkner relation to Latin America as well. He argues that the South, in coming to terms with its Civil War defeat, lives a reality that is common to Latin America, one marked by "defeat, separation, and doubt: the image of tragedy" (Vegh 23). Fuentes asserts that the baroque quality of Faulkner's language is appropriate for capturing an uncertainty and indeterminacy that challenges clarity, rationalism, and positivism. Novels such as *La muerte de Artemio Cruz* (*The Death of Artemio Cruz*), *Gringo viejo* (*Old Gringo*), *Una familia lejana* (*A Distant Family*), and *Terra nostra* show a relationship to Faulkner.

Perhaps the most celebrated Latin American writer whom Faulkner influenced is the Colombian Gabriel García Márquez. García Márquez's *Cien años de soledad* (*One Hundred Years of Solitude*), the saga of the Buendía family and of the village of Macondo from its founding days to its destruction, with its focus on land and family, achieved international acclaim and drew immediate comparisons to Faulkner. García Márquez once remarked that when he read Faulkner, he thought he had to be a writer. After critics focused on that comment, he retracted it, saying that Kafka, not Faulkner, made him think he needed to be a writer. In another interview, he states that Faulkner's *The Hamlet* was "the best South American novel ever written" (Kennedy 57). *La hojarasca* (*Leaf Storm*) is García Márquez's most Faulknerian novel, although Faulkner's influence is present in a number of other works as well, including *La mala hora* (*The Wicked Hour*) and *El otoño del patriarca* (*The Autumn of the Patriarch*). His comments in a dialogue with Vargas Llosa sum up the Faulkner relation in Latin America:

I think that the major debt that we, the new Latin American novelists have is with Faulkner. Faulkner is present in all the novels of Latin America. I believe . . . probably exaggerating, . . . that the great difference between us and our grandparents . . . is Faulkner. He was the only thing that happened between those two generations.

The Faulknerian method is very effective for relating Latin American reality. Unconsciously, it was that which we discovered in Faulkner. That's to say, we were looking at this reality and wanted to tell it, and we knew that the European method would not work, nor the traditional Spanish method; and suddenly we found the Faulknerian method was very adequate to represent this reality. Actually, that's not strange, because Yoknapatawpha County has banks on the Caribbean Sea. So, in some ways he is a Latin American writer. (García Márquez and Vargas Llosa 52–53)

See also **Spain**.

FURTHER READING

Borges, Jorge Luis. *Borges: A Reader: A Selection from the Writings of Jorge Luis Borges.* Ed. Emir Rodriguez Monegal and Alastair Reid. New York: E. P. Dutton, 1981.

Frisch, Mark. *William Faulkner y su influencia en la literature hispanoamericana: Mallea, Rojas, Yáñez, García Márquez.* Buenos Aires: Corregidor, 1993.

García Márquez, Gabriel, and Mario Vargas Llosa. *La novela en América Latina: Diálogo.* Lima, Peru: Carlos Milla Batres, 1968.

Kennedy, William. "The Yellow Trolley Car in Barcelona and Other Visions." *Atlantic* 231 (1973): 50–59.

Oberhelman, Harley D. *The Presence of Faulkner in the Writings of García Márquez.* Lubbock: Texas Tech University Press, 1980.

Vargas Llosa, Mario. *A Writer's Reality.* Ed. Myron I. Lichtblau. Syracuse: Syracuse University Press, 1991.

Vegh, Beatriz, ed. Special Issue: "A Latin American Faulkner." *Faulkner Journal* 11. 1–2 (1996).

Mark Frisch

LAW. Faulkner's writing is remarkable for its various attempts to explore the complex nature, developments, and sources of law. Lawyers (and law students) abound in his work, and law as a deeply felt personal vocation, implicit political activity, system of rules, social construct, and often thwarted hope for justice pervades his representations of communal crisis and communal self-definition. Not only the stylized contentions and heavy formalities of public courtroom argument but private, searching discussions between lawyers and clients and lawyers and family members account for a vital but, until recently, critically neglected aspect of Faulkner's imaginative project.

Even a brief survey of the fiction indicates the preponderance of represented legal activity and speculative thought on the definitions and practice of law. *Sanctuary* collapses the boundaries between respectable Jefferson society and the Memphis underworld to the extent that the novel's interrupted trial becomes only an exercise in political and social containment. At the novel's center, underneath the bureaucratic violence of the highly unusual courtroom scenes, are Temple Drake, Horace Benbow, and Narcissa Benbow, the adult children of judges and lawyers. Each of these three characters is instrumental to the novel's legal narrative but positioned differently to the culminating trial and its compressed issues of widespread corruption, bootlegging, prostitution, and legitimate power's hidden connections to law's supposedly criminal opposite. After many unexpected legal, political, and social collisions, Faulkner presents law in *Sanctuary* as finally the instrument of the class and gender attitudes of the powerful, rather than any genuine search through evidence and procedure for redress of wrongs.

The generally underestimated *Knight's Gambit* is composed of five stories that also interrogate the conditions of justice in Yoknapatawpha while subtly complicating the characterization of the usually valorized recurring legal figure Gavin Stevens, who appears throughout most of Faulkner's novels and many stories. In "Smoke," for example, one of the stories in the collection, Stevens's dubious creation of a legal space (an inquest) for investigating a judge's murder depends entirely on his own manufactured evidence, thereby casting a cloud over the public trust of his position and the legal system itself. The County Attorney's willingness to stretch the conditions of justice by any means to ensure a conviction troubles the story's narrator, a member of the inquest jury, enough that this layman's anxiety over the treatment of evidence provides the engine for the story. "Monk," another *Knight's Gambit* story, chronicles the unjust murder conviction of a severely mentally challenged individual. A very young Charles "Chick" Mallison narrates this story based on his uncle's account. The community's indifference to Monk's circumstances is counterpoised by Chick's abiding concern, as indicated by his desire to narrate and to provide the only comprehensive written account of Monk's life beyond the inaccuracies of the trial's version of events. Since "Monk" signals Chick's first awareness of the potential of law as a manipulative (and performative) linguistic and political activity and not merely an arena of mimetic representations, the story chronicles the awakening of this character's particularly idealistic legal consciousness.

Not surprisingly, Chick is later poised at the end of *The Mansion*, the final volume of the Snopes trilogy, to be graduated from law school. In fact, the whole of the Snopes trilogy is substantially characterized by legal concerns and conflicts. The "Spotted Horses" section of *The Hamlet* parodies the often arid (often absurd) rationality of legal judgments when a judge allows a fraudulent contract to stand that supposedly transfers ownership of a group of runaway wild horses to some local men in exchange for their meagre family savings. When Mrs. Tull brings suit against the alleged owner, Flem Snopes, to recover money for goods entirely unobtainable, the court's ruling that the exchange is valid enables Flem to profit and succeed in his first of a series of exploitative moves through which he will eventually attain considerable authority in Jefferson. *The Town* and *The Mansion* deal with a number of off-the-record legal deals that increasingly implicate County Attorney Gavin Stevens in dubious extralegal maneuvers to dictate Yoknapatawpha affairs and conserve his own power against the perceived Snopes threat. "Law" again emerges here, particularly with the manufacture of a bootlegging charge against Montgomery Ward Snopes in *The Town*, as a set of unaccountable stratagems deployed by the representatives of the law; law in Faulkner becomes a screen through which the preferences and desires of particular personalities are played out in what is only apparently a communal ground. With Stevens's implication in Mink Snopes's murder of Flem in *The Mansion*, the crisis of what "law" is and where it may be located apart from the actions and decisions of its representatives reaches its culmination in Yoknapatawpha. "A Rose for Emily," *Light in August*, "Barn Burning," "Old Man," *Go Down, Moses, Intruder in the Dust*, and *Requiem for a Nun* also engage specific legal issues as painful flashpoints in Faulkner's imaginative community and expose the ambiguous underpinnings of what is, or passes for, law.

Faulkner arrived at his insistent legal concerns both by way of family history, which included a large number of notable lawyers for five generations, and through the cultural milieu of Mississippi, which was complexly characterized by traditional respect for lawyers (often gentlemen planters in the antebellum period) and by infamous contempt for and mass resistance to the rule of law itself. Faulkner's many returns to matters of law and lawyers also appear to be the inevitable move of a gifted and struggling writer who likely felt resentful of the lawyer's cultural capital and social authority in the Southern oral economy.

The history and status of law in the Southern United States offered its own bottomless paradoxes for Faulkner to engage. While many famous Southern writers, such as Mark Twain, Charles Chestnutt, Harper Lee, and Robert Penn Warren, have turned their attention to both the promises and failures of law, no Southern or even literary American writer interrogates the principles and presuppositions behind law as insistently in as many stories and novels as Faulkner. For the most part, his concern with legal narrative seems to revolve around the quixotic project of attempting to distinguish the domain of law from social influences such as racism, classism, sexism, influential private opinion, and the vagaries of public politics. The recurring issue of how law operates to construct and regulate society while embedded itself in a social narrative marks his work with a philosophical seriousness approaching its own form of literary jurisprudence. In fact, Faulkner's working definition of law appears to anticipate that of one of the most influential writers on the sources and definition of law in contemporary jurisprudential debates, Judge Ronald Dworkin. Both Faulkner (implicitly) and Dworkin (explicitly) define law as that which legal officials decide to do about legal disputes. In Faulkner, however, this only apparently simple definition is usually enacted with cynical, even nihilistic, implications. Faulkner's only sustained but qualified hope for a recognizable justice—communal and procedural—emerges as Chick Mallison, who has been intellectually nurtured as a type of "legal child," prepares near the end of Faulkner's canon to enter the adult world of Southern power imbalances as a young lawyer.

The relative critical neglect of such a complex and layered topic in Faulkner's writing is hard to explain, particularly since an interdisciplinary study of law and Southern literature holds such promise for any number of literary, theoretical, cultural, and historical projects. While some early articles exist on law and lawyers in Faulkner, the only book-length study to date is Jay Watson's *Forensic Fictions: The Lawyer Figure in Faulkner*, which concentrates on Stevens's role as powerful official and unofficial storyteller whose performative language relentlessly shapes his community. Watson's study commands an array of literary, narratological, historical, and legal critical sources and, apart from the 1984 *Mississippi College Law Review* special edition on law and Southern literature (featuring a number of informative Faulkner articles), represents the most sustained analysis of law in Faulkner.

FURTHER READING

Bodenhamer, David J., and James W. Ely, Jr. *Ambivalent Legacy: A Legal History of the South*. Jackson: University Press of Mississippi, 1984.
Lahey, Michael E. "The Complex Art of Justice: Lawyers and Law-Makers as Faulkner's Dubious Artist Figures." *Faulkner and the Artist*, ed. Kartiganer and Abadie. 250–268.

Michael E. Lahey

"LEG, THE," an early Faulkner short story, written in England or France in 1925, was published first in *Doctor Martino and Other Stories* (1934) and later in the "Beyond" section of *Collected Stories*. Probably the story characterized by Faulkner as "a queer short story, about a case of reincarnation" (*SL* 31), "The Leg" describes the experiences of two young World War I soldiers— George, an Englishman, and his friend Davy, an American, before the war a student at Oxford University. During the battle of Givenchy, George is killed and Davy is critically wounded, losing a leg. In the hospital, Davy engages in conversations with his dead friend, asking him to find the lost leg and make sure it is dead. Later, however, Davy discovers that the leg has been reincarnated in another person, a physical likeness of himself, who has caused a series of tragic events, including the death of a young English woman he and George had known before the war. As in "Beyond" and other stories in this grouping, Faulkner's text leaves ambiguous the question of whether key incidents represent supernatural occurrences or merely the imaginary products of an unsettled mind. Read symbolically, "The Leg" presents a Lost Generation contrast between the idyllic life the two friends shared before the war and the terrible grief and tragedy wrought by the war.

Robert W. Hamblin

LETTERS. William Faulkner's letters fall roughly into three categories: private letters, constituting the great majority, which were generated primarily by absences from his home and family; business letters, to publishers and editors, involving his writing; and public letters, most written in the last decade of his life and generated primarily by social issues, especially civil rights. Major repositories of Faulkner's letters are the Alderman Library at the University of Virginia, the Harry Ransom Humanities Research Center at the University of Texas at Austin, the Louis Daniel Brodsky Collection at Southeast Missouri State University, and the New York Public Library. A great number of letters are in the Jill Faulkner Summers Archive, and other collections are in private hands, including the thirty-one letters listed in the Carl Petersen Collection, which has been divided and sold. There are three book-length collections: Joseph Blotner's *Selected Letters of William Faulkner* (Random House, 1977) publishes full letters and excerpts from 1918 to 1962 and is representative rather than inclusive; Malcolm Cowley's *The Faulkner-Cowley File: Letters and Memories, 1944–1962* (Viking, 1966) publishes Faulkner's side of the 1944–1945 correspondence along with Cowley's narrative of the creation of *The Portable Faulkner*; James G. Watson's *Thinking of Home: William Faulkner's Letters to His Mother and Father, 1918–1925* (Norton, 1992) transcribes one 1912 letter and the 145 letters and telegrams Faulkner wrote from New Haven, New York, Toronto, New Orleans, and Europe in a period of which less has been known about his life than any other. Louis Daniel Brodsky and Robert W. Hamblin's *Faulkner: A Comprehensive Guide to the Brodsky Collection.* Vol. II: *The Letters* (University Press of Mississippi, 1984) publishes 145 letters by Faulkner and some 350 about him by family members, friends, agents, editors, and scholars, starting in 1924. The strength of the collection is from the 1940s forward. Public letters are transcribed in James B. Meriwether's *Essays, Speeches & Public Letters by William Faulkner* (Random House, 1965). Magazine correspondence is available in Meriwether's "Faulkner's Correspondence with *Scribner's Magazine*" (*Proof* 3 [1973]) and "Faulkner's Correspondence with the *Saturday Evening Post*" (*Mississippi Quarterly* 37 [Summer 1977]). Letters are quoted broadly, in whole or in part, in Joseph Blotner's *Faulkner: A Biography* (Random House, 1974, 1984) and in personal memoirs such as Meta Carpenter Wilde's (with Orin Borsten) *A Loving Gentleman: The Love Story of William Faulkner and Meta Carpenter* (Simon and Schuster, 1976).

The letters are of biographical and critical interest in that they record Faulkner's ideas, attitudes, and states of mind and feeling at the times and places from which he wrote them. They document personal relationships with family members, friends, professional associates, and intimates; and they trace his travels away from Oxford, especially in the years before he had regular business correspondence and signed contracts that located his whereabouts. Like all letters, Faulkner's portray him in the multiple roles in which he subjectively presented himself as letter writer. Together, his letters to his correspondents constitute a set of personal narratives, variously detailed and interesting in different ways and contexts. Letters to Random House editor Saxe Commins and others that bear upon *A Fable* help to trace stages in the long compositional history of that novel. The sixty-three letters and telegrams to his mother and father from Toronto in 1918 tell the story of his adventure in the North, recounting his successes as a Royal Air Force cadet and expressing his hopes and ambitions for the immediate future. Written an average of one every two and a half days of his service, the Toronto letters testify to his devotion to Maud Falkner (whom he frequently addresses as "Mother darling" and whose surname he spells with a "u," like his own) and to the importance of his epistolary relation to his father, Murry, to whom he wrote both singly and in conjunction with Maud. Often, as with the 1918 New Haven and Toronto letters, Faulkner's correspondence seems to have served him as a kind of journal or day-book from which actual and imagined experience later passed into fiction. Fiction passed into letters, as well. When Faulkner wrote Joan Williams at the end of their brief love affair, in August 1952, that "between grief and nothing, I will take grief" (1974 *FAB* 1431), he was quoting Harry Willbourne in *If I Forget Thee, Jerusalem.*

As a rule, Faulkner seldom commented on his fiction in his letters or on himself as artist, but there are as many exceptions as there are contradictions in what he did say there. From New Orleans in late March 1925, he wrote his mother what he had learned from Sherwood Anderson: "What really happens . . . never makes a good yarn. You have to get an impulse from somewhere and then embroider it" (Watson, *Thinking of Home* 194). Love letters to Meta Carpenter held at the Ransom Center and the New York Public Library, and to Joan Williams at the Alderman and in the Brodsky Collection, portray a passionate and devoted lover whose imaginative expression of his feelings occasionally included feelings about himself as writer. "And now, at last, I have some perspective on all I have done," he wrote Williams in April 1957. "I realise for the first time what an amazing gift I had: uneducated in every formal sense, without even very literate, let alone literary, companions, yet to have made the things I made. I don't know where it came from. I dont know why God or gods or whatever it was, selected me to be the vessel . . . I wonder if you have ever had that thought about the work and the country man whom you know as Bill Faulkner—what little connection there seems to be between them" (*SL* 348). In a postscript to a letter about *The Hamlet* in 1939, he told Robert Haas, "I am the best in America, by God" (*SL* 113).

FURTHER READING

Krause, David. "Reading Bon's Letter and Faulkner's *Absalom, Absalom!*" *PMLA* 99 (1984): 225–241.

———. "Reading Shreve's Letters and *Absalom, Absalom!*" *Studies in American Fiction* 2 (1983): 153–169.

Watson, James G. *William Faulkner, Letters and Fictions.*

James G. Watson

"LETTER TO THE NORTH, A," one of several articles Faulkner wrote in the mid-1950s to explain himself as massive resistance to desegregation began in the South. In the article, published in *Life* (March 5, 1956) and collected in *Essays, Speeches & Public Letters by William Faulkner*, Faulkner declared that just as "I was against compulsory segregation, I am just as strongly against compulsory integration." He went on to assert two things: first, "being in the middle" between the "Citizens Councils and the NAACP [National Association for the Advancement of Colored People]," he warned of the tenuous nature of the moderate position; and second, he urged the NAACP to "Go slow now" and that the North not try to change the Southern racial situation by "mere force of law or economic threat." Above all, he contended, racial polarization had to be avoided.

Richard H. King

"LIFE AND DEATH OF A BOMBER, THE," a propagandistic film treatment that Faulkner wrote for Warner Bros. Studio in 1943. Never developed into a full-length script, the story pleads for civilian support of American military forces in World War II by dramatizing how selfish interests jeopardize the construction and delivery of a bomber needed in the war effort.

FURTHER READING

Faulkner, William. *Country Lawyer and Other Stories for the Screen.* Ed. with intro. by Louis Daniel Brodsky and Robert W. Hamblin. Jackson: University Press of Mississippi, 1987.

Robert W. Hamblin

LIGHT IN AUGUST, one of Faulkner's greatest novels, was published in 1932. Among its many themes is an emphasis on taking responsibility for others. This is what Faulkner had been doing when he began this seventh novel in the depths of the depression (and the South's Jim Crow laws). Having married to stop "running away from my own devilment," Faulkner had moved Estelle and her two children into the newly purchased Rowan Oak, and soon after, he was burying their firstborn, Alabama. Waiting for royalties from *Sanctuary* (which would never come), Faulkner was "whoring," selling stories to popular magazines to meet expenses.

On August 17, 1931, he began a work he called "Dark House" with Gail Hightower, Jefferson's ex-minister, sitting by his darkened window. He later said the book was conceived with an image of the full-term pregnant Lena Grove, walking from Alabama to find the father of her child, Lucas Burch. At least some of his conception involved modernist techniques, for not only would his characters suggest figures from the Christ story (and their pagan counterparts), but the twenty-one chapters of *Light in August* would also parallel the twenty-one chapters of the St. John gospel, with John's stories enriched by mythic and folk material from Frazer's complete *Golden Bough*. For example,

John 19, the crucifixion chapter, is paralleled in *Light in August* by Percy Grimm's "crucifixion" of Joe Christmas. Grimm represents not only the Roman soldier/executioner from John but also, from Frazer, a "mock king," one of the castrating Priests of Attis, to whom civil authority was briefly relinquished before normal order was restored.

But Lena's story encircles the book, as she sets out with her "calm unreason," wandering the "peaceful corridor," serene in her madonna-like faith in the "word" of the father. Because someone mistakes "Burch" for "Bunch," Lena comes to Jefferson (where Lucas has become "Joe Brown") and meets Byron Bunch, who lives by the whistle of the planing mill. By novel's end, Joseph-like, he will take on the more difficult responsibility for the placid Lena, traveling beyond Jefferson with her newborn son.

Meantime, we witness the earlier arrivals at the mill of the Christ-as-scapegoat figure, Joe Christmas and, later, Joe Brown, who becomes his "disciple" in bootlegging. Byron and the other men immediately size up both Joes, sensing the one's grim fatality and the other's swaggering worthlessness. While Byron lives by his watch, by night he visits Hightower, who, like Nicodemus (or Pilate) lives "by the book." Brought in to serve his parishioners, Hightower instead serves the South's ghosts, revisiting in his reveries and his mad sermons the brave "phantom horsemen" at his grandfather's death; the intellectual, he loves the delicious irony that the fatal cavalry charge was merely a raid on a chicken coop. Most notoriously, because "he couldn't or wouldn't satisfy her himself," his wife had fallen into promiscuity, madness, and suicide. Now all but forgotten by the town, nightly engaging in his masturbatory "charge" (even after, at book's end, his elegiac vision reveals he has failed others, failed life), he embodies the danger that reviving the dead—even if potently—can deny the living, a crucial message for the South and for Faulkner himself.

But another town outcast, Joanna Burden, whose New England forebears hated slavery, will take on too much. Charged by her father to "raise the shadow," she has burdened her life for Negro charities. A John the Baptist figure (she carries a message, her head is cut off), it is to her house that Joe Christmas comes some three years before the "passion week" in the current time of the novel. To tell their story, Faulkner returns to the "sootbleakened" orphanage of Joe's childhood where he was left on Christmas Eve by his grandfather, Euphues Hines. Like Yahweh in his vengeful fanaticism for the chosen (white) race, Hines had let Joe's mother die after he had killed Joe's father, whom he believed to be part black. The ambiguity is crucial. First named "Christmas," Joe is nailed as "nigger bastard" when he inadvertently catches the dietitian having illicit sex. Because of her and the janitor, who is Hines come to work "His vengeance," Joe forever connects sex to what Faulkner felt was his tragedy, "that he didn't know what he was."

With the hint that Joe might be a "nigger," he is placed "at once" with Simon McEachern, a rigid Pharisee, who, unaware of Joe's problematic "blood," raises him "to fear God and abhor idleness and vanity despite his origin.'' When his father beats him to teach him his catechism, what Joe learns is the man's cold ruthlessness. When his mother sneaks him favors to soften the brutality, Joe learns not her warmth but her deviousness.

Falling for the waitress, Bobbie (the woman taken in sin), the adolescent Joe learns to accept her ''periodical filth'' and her prostitution, but with despair. At first she treats him kindly, even when he admits he may have ''some nigger blood,'' but when he strikes down McEachern, who has caught them at a dance, Bobbie lashes out: ''Son of a bitch! Getting me into a jam, that always treated you like you were a white man. A white man!''

Joe takes to ''a thousand savage and lonely streets,'' becoming white or black to provoke rejections from the women he beds. Arriving at Joanna's, he moves into a cabin on her property, and they begin a three-stage affair, all involving her perception of him as black. In the first, nightly he must ''despoil'' her manlike resistance as, daily, she sets out dishes—as he says—'' *''for the nigger.''* When she finally yields, it is ''in words''; as with Bobbie, the couple's tenderness is depicted in their quiet talk rather than in sex. Indeed, the second stage involves their descent into a ''black pool,'' with Joanna in ''the wild throes of nymphomania,'' pounding ''Negro, Negro, Negro!'' In the third stage, she refuses all sex and insists he go to a Negro college, advocate the Negro cause. Faced with her ultimatum—and her loaded pistol—he kills her. But when he realizes that she had also intended to die, saying, ''For her and for me,'' he takes to the woods, circles the town, seizes the pulpit of a black church, dons a black man's shoes, eats food tendered by black hands, at last assuming the role of the community's scapegoat, the black man. Finally, asking the day—it is Friday—at peace, because he ''dont have to bother about having to eat anymore,'' Joe delivers himself up to be captured.

The word ''nigger'' from Brown, betraying Christmas for the reward money, inflames the community against ''nigger-murderer'' of the woman they had once called ''nigger-lover.'' When Christmas is captured, the Hineses arrive, asking Hightower to give their grandson an alibi, but he shouts, ''I wont!'' He does help to deliver Lena's baby, which brings him briefly to life. Brown, on the other hand, faced with having to take responsibility for Lena (and Byron's sudden heroism), lights out again—minus the reward.

Christmas's final hour is determined by the newly introduced Percy Grimm, about whom Faulkner said he had created a Nazi before Hitler did. A jingoist and a racist, he marshals his own ''force'' until the community gives over its responsibility, awed by the dedication of this ''young priest,'' and when Christmas escapes—as if ''to passively commit suicide''—Grimm and his men run him down in Hightower's house. At the minister's belated attempt to save Joe, Grimm cries, ''Jesus Christ! . . . Has every preacher and old maid in Jefferson taken their pants down to the yellowbellied son of a bitch?'' Then he fires five shots into Christmas and—to the horror of his men—castrates him, storming, ''Now you'll let white women alone, even in hell.'' Still, Joe achieves his peaceful apotheosis, "soaring into their memories" as a suffering "man," forever "serene" and even "triumphant."

Light in August has provided critics with many images—the wheel, the urn, the shadow—and many themes—racism, puritanism (Calvinism), Protestantism, community versus outcast, circular versus linear movement, movement versus stasis, darkness versus light, or Faulkner's view of women. The three stories of Joe/Joanna, Lena/Byron, and Hightower have prompted discussions of *Light in August*'s unity or its anomalies or how the stories are interwoven or who the main protagonist is or whether the book is tragic or comic or if the introduction of major characters late in the book makes the ending a failure. Now seen as expanding our notion of how a novel works, these issues have come to be of less concern.

The Christian parallels have troubled many. Although Lena is no virgin, she could be a Mary; but to equate Christmas with Christ must be our wrong interpretation or, worse, Faulkner's bad technique. But if the characters are judged not as icons but as figures in what Faulkner called "the Christian legend," they function like the many pagan parallels such as Isis, mistakenly worshiped as Mary, who, like Lena, took to the road, looking for her man (Osiris); or Dionysus, like Joe, known for his orgiastic rites and his final mutilation, in some stories, as a black-skinned goat. Many such stranger-gods arrive in Jefferson—how are "the least of these" treated? In this poignant, savage portrayal of an ancestor-haunted South, Faulkner offers no easy answers, discovering abiding strengths in those who, short of becoming fanatics, will take responsibility for life.

FURTHER READING

Berland, Alwyn. Light in August: *A Study in Black and White*. New York: Twayne, 1992.

Bloom, Harold, ed. *Modern Critical Interpretations of William Faulkner's* Light in August. New York: Chelsea, 1988.

Hlavsa, Virginia V. James. *Faulkner and the Thoroughly Modern Novel*. Charlottesville: University Press of Virginia, 1991.

Millgate, Michael, ed. *New Essays on* Light in August. Cambridge: Cambridge University Press, 1987.

Pitavy, François L. *Faulkner's* Light in August. Rev. ed. Bloomington: Indiana University Press, 1973.

———, ed. *William Faulkner's* Light in August: *A Critical Casebook*. New York: Garland Publishing, 1982.

Porter, Carolyn. "The Problem of Time in *Light in August.*" *Rice University Studies* 61 (1975): 107–125.

Ruppersburg, Hugh M. *Reading Faulkner*: Light in August. Jackson: University Press of Mississippi, 1994.

Vickery, John B., and Olga W. Vickery, eds. Light in August *and the Critical Spectrum*. Belmont, Calif.: Wadsworth Publishing, 1971.

Virginia V. James Hlavsa

LILACS, THE, an illustrated booklet of poems that Faulkner hand-produced in 1920. The only known copy, the one Faulkner dedicated and presented to his friend Phil Stone, is now preserved in the Brodsky Collection. Although the booklet was severely damaged in the fire that destroyed Stone's house in 1942, enough remains to identify the red velvet cover, the dedication dated "Jan. 1, 1920," and a number of the poems. The contents include "The Lilacs," "Cathay," "To a Co-ed," "O Atthis" (first line), "L'Apres-Midi d'un Faune," "Une Ballade des Femmes Perdues," "After Fifty Years," "Sapphics," "A Dead Dancer," and four unidentified poems. Several of the poems had appeared the previous year in *The Mississippian*, the campus newspaper of the University of Mississippi. Faulkner also included in the thirty-six-page booklet a full-page water color drawing of a female figure and a small pen-and-ink drawing of a nude woman.

FURTHER READING

Brodsky and Hamblin, eds. *Faulkner: A Comprehensive Guide to the Brodsky Collection.* Vol. V: 43–57.

Robert W. Hamblin

"LION," a short story by Faulkner, was written in early 1935 and published later that year in *Harper's*. In the story Quentin Compson recalls a trip to Major de Spain's hunting camp when Boon and the dog Lion, at the cost of Lion's life, kill the enigmatic bear Old Ben. In the final scene Quentin witnesses Boon's hammering furiously on a broken gun while squirrels scamper above them in the tree. The narrative is substantially revised in the version that appears in "The Bear" in *Go Down, Moses*.

Diane Brown Jones

"LIZARDS IN JAMSHYD'S COURTYARD," a short story by Faulkner, was first published in the *Saturday Evening Post* on February 27, 1932, and reprinted in *Uncollected Stories*. The story belongs to *The Hamlet*, where it forms part of Book One, chapter 3; and Book Four, chapter 2. The title comes from Edward Fitzgerald's translation of *The Rubáiyát of Omar Khayyám*. The story is based upon the folkloric "salted-mine" trick, in which money is planted on relatively worthless property to trick treasure hunters into buying it. In this case, Flem Snopes tricks Ratliff (Suratt in the original story) and his cohorts into buying the worthless Varner property Flem had acquired as part of Eula's dowry. It is the second time Flem has gotten the better of Suratt/Ratliff; the first involved a deal in goats.

Joseph R. Urgo

"LO!," a satiric short story by Faulkner, first published in *Story* in November 1934 and later included in *Collected Stories*. A fanciful blend of tall tale, trickster myth, American history, and the quest for justice, "Lo!" draws upon the July 1932 Bonus Expeditionary Force debacle when protesting World War I veterans were routed by troops led by Patton, MacArthur, and Eisenhower, as well as upon actual presidential visits by Mississippi Choctaw chiefs: Pushmataha's to President James Monroe in 1824 and Greenwood Leflore's to President Andrew Jackson in 1831. Faulkner's title may derive from a passage in Alexander Pope's "Essay on Man": "Lo, the poor Indian! Whose untutored mind / Sees God in clouds, or hears him in the wind / His soul proud Science never taught to stray."

The native Americans of this story are not Ikkemotubbe's people; they are merely vaguely identified as title holders to all of Mississippi west of an unspecified river. The mythical Indians march on Washington, ostensibly to hand over the Chief's nephew for judgment by the "white father" for murdering an eccentric white man, a coureur de bois who had secured title to the only ford across the river for 300 miles and then promptly constructed a toll booth. The man thereafter died of a strange white man's disease, a "split skull." When the Chickasaw agent commences an investigation, the Indians organize a pilgrimage to the "White Chief's capital" in order to coerce him into settling the case himself. The President, ironically defined as "the conqueror of men, the winner of battles diplomatic, legal and martial," is reduced to the "baffled helplessness of a child" when confronted by thousands of Indians descending on Washington to camp out in a gigantic "sit-in" demonstration. The shrewd Chief deftly threatens to wait until all his other people arrive (a matter of months) unless the ritual trial of the nephew takes place in the White House, which it eventually does, with the nephew being cleared of all charges. The next fall, another white man, with like designs on the ford, is drowned in the river during a swimming contest with the feckless nephew. Chief Weddel writes to his Great White Father that he must again bring the nephew to the national bar, after which the President immediately dispatches a cavalry officer to deliver an official proclamation that the ford is ceded to Weddel and his heirs in perpetuity.

"Lo!" lampoons national policy and public officials by caricature and through ridicule of the sacred institutions desecrated by the arrival of Indians who wear "pantaloons," but amidst frivolity runs a vein of iron scorn. Faulkner critiques stereotypes of ethnicity when he renders the national leader incapable of identifying individual Indians, recognizing only "the Face," one that appears "dark, a little flat, a little Mongol; secret, decorous, impenetrable, and grave." Washington politicians are reactionary, petulant, and self-serving; the Indians devious and inscrutable. In the end, as often happens in Faulkner, the simple folk of the soil win out over the sophisticates: The meek shall inherit the earth. As in Boccaccio and Chaucer, the meek may have to create that destiny by deviousness or falsehood, and the sweetest victory arises from the elaborate cultural framework being turned in upon itself through manipulation by the disenfranchised, yet the end justifies the means and justice is finally served.

Within its context of composition, during the social chaos of the Great Depression, the motif of powerless, faceless masses gaining ascendency over a political aristocracy would surely have struck a vibrant chord.

FURTHER READING

Bradford, M. E. "Faulkner and the Great White Father." *Louisiana Studies* 3 (1964): 323–329.
Howell, Elmo. "President Jackson and William Faulkner's Choctaws." *Chronicles of Oklahoma* 45 (1967): 252–258.
————. "William Faulkner and Tennessee." *Tennessee Historical Quarterly* 21 (1962): 251–262.

Garry R. Alkire

LONG HOT SUMMER, THE, a feature film of 1958 derived from Faulkner's novel *The Hamlet*. Several episodes in the novel constitute self-contained units. Hence the screenwriters, Irving Ravetch and Harriet Frank, Jr., simply picked the incidents they judged screenworthy and discarded the rest. They also added some characters and incidents of their own devising. The film's central character is an impecunious fellow named Ben Quick (Paul Newman). Ben falls in love with Clara Varner, a character who is not in the book; she is the daughter of Will Varner, a wealthy landowner (Orson Welles). Quick is a decent chap who aspires to prove himself worthy of Clara. Hence he is a much better human being than Flem Snopes, his counterpart who, in the novel, is a crafty con man, bent on marrying for money, not for love. The movie was a huge success, given Martin Ritt's spirited direction and the appealing screenplay by Ravetch and Frank.

The television version of *The Long Hot Summer* (October 5 and 6, 1985) is a remake of the 1958 feature film. The two-part miniseries once again portrays how Ben Quick (Don Johnson) wins the daughter of rich landowner Will Varner (Jason Robards, Jr.). The new material added to the miniseries departs from *The Hamlet* to a much greater degree than the previous movie did. The miniseries drew a large audience, but several reviewers judged the television version of *The Long Hot Summer* to be roughly twice as long and about half as good as the theatrical feature.

FURTHER READING

Kael, Pauline. *I Lost It at the Movies.* New York: Boyars, 1994.
McGilligan, Pat. "Ritt Large: An Interview with Martin Ritt." *Film Comment* 22.1 (1986): 38–46.

Gene D. Phillips

LOST GENERATION is a phrase that was used extensively in Britain and France in the first years after World War I to refer to a generation of young soldiers "lost" in the fighting during the war. The American usage of the phrase is attributed to Ernest Hemingway, who actually heard it in Paris from Gertrude Stein. Hemingway introduced American readers to the Lost Generation in the epigraph to his book *The Sun Also Rises*, which was originally titled "The Lost Generation—A Novel." The phrase became a kind of craze in the mid-1920s and was later popularized by Malcolm Cowley in his book *Exile's Return* (1934). The Lost Generation, then, typically refers to a generation uprooted by World War I and subjected, as a result, to intense philosophic despair and disillusionment with traditional ideals and beliefs, especially the values of prewar middle-class America.

It was Cowley, in *A Second Flowering*, who attempted to codify a group of eight American writers as representative of the Lost Generation. Cowley considered William Faulkner a prominent member of this group. The other seven writers Cowley discussed as representative figures are F. Scott Fitzgerald, Ernest Hemingway, John Dos Passos, E. E. Cummings, Thornton Wilder, Thomas Wolfe, and Hart Crane, all of whom were born between the years 1894 and 1900 and had important works published in the 1920s. Cowley also described the works of these writers as "a second flowering of American literature," the "first flowering" having come in the mid-nineteenth century and represented by such writers as Thoreau, Emerson, Whitman, Melville, and Hawthorne. The limitations of Cowley's construction of an all-male, all-white group of authors to represent this second flowering of American literature have been pointed out by a number of recent critics, who have noted that the 1920s was also the decade of the Harlem Renaissance and the decade in which a number of American women writers also produced important works.

More recent critical discussions of Faulkner and the Lost Generation tend to focus on whether or not he should be considered a member of such a generation. Marc Dolan argues that F. Scott Fitzgerald "campaigned for the job of generational spokesperson with his first published novel, *This Side of Paradise*" (14). According to Dolan, Fitzgerald seemed to capture in this novel three of the traits commonly associated with the Lost Generation: disillusionment, iconoclasm, and greed. In a famous essay entitled "My Generation," Fitzgerald defined what he meant by a *generation*: "By a generation I mean that reaction against the fathers which seems to occur about three times in a century. It is distinguished by a set of ideas, inherited in moderated form from the madmen and outlaws of the generation before; if it is a real generation it has its own leaders and spokesmen, and it draws into its orbit those born just before it and just after, whose ideas are less clear-cut and defiant."

Can William Faulkner, then, be claimed as a member of the Lost Generation? Does his work embody the traits most commonly associated with this generation? Does his own biography conform with that of other so-called Lost Generation American writers, who went off to war and later became exiles living in Paris?

Although he never fought in World War I, Faulkner attempted to do so. Like other young men of his generation, he wanted to experience firsthand the events that shook Europe and the world in 1917. Given his childhood interest in flying, it is not surprising to learn that Faulkner attempted to be a pilot in the war. He was rejected, however, at the recruiting station in Oxford, Mississippi, for being too ''short'' and too ''frail.'' Not to be deterred from his goal, Faulkner traveled to New Haven, Connecticut, where he visited his friend Phil Stone and befriended members of an ROTC unit at Yale University, some of whom were members of the Royal Air Force. Subsequently, Faulkner made his way to a Royal Air Force Recruiting Office in New York, where he arranged to enlist for pilot training in Toronto. When the war ended in November 1918, Faulkner was in the third and final phase of his training. As a result, he never did go off to war. Thus, he did not have the firsthand experience of a fighter pilot, or ambulance driver, or foot soldier, as did some of the other Lost Generation writers identified by Cowley.

Nevertheless, the war profoundly affected Faulkner, and his early work as a fiction writer was influenced by it. Faulkner's first novel, *Soldiers' Pay* (1926), suggests his imaginative engagement with the war. Two of the major characters in the novel, a cadet and a scarred Royal Air Force pilot, owed their creation, respectively, to Faulkner's own stymied war experience and his imaginative rendering of what he heard about the war from those who personally fought in it. The creation of the character Lieutenant Donald Mahon, who returns from the war wounded and loses his sight, represents a figure of estrangement representative of the ''lost generation.'' At the time of writing *Soldiers' Pay*, Faulkner also wrote a nonfiction piece entitled ''Literature and War,'' in which he reviewed how other writers used the war in their work.

After finishing *Soldiers' Pay*, Faulkner set sail for Europe. He took with him letters of introduction, written by his friend Phil Stone, to Ezra Pound, T. S. Eliot, and James Joyce. But Faulkner did not live the romanticized life of an artist in exile. Rather, he embarked on a number of walking tours in France and England and spent very little time with any of the writers Stone had hoped he would develop friendships with. In Paris Faulkner began the writing of *Mosquitoes*, which became his second novel. In all, he spent five months abroad and then returned to Oxford, Mississippi. Like other members of Cowley's group of Lost Generation writers, Faulkner did spend time abroad as a ''writer-in-exile,'' but unlike several of his contemporaries, his stay in Europe was comparatively short and not nearly as adventurous or bohemian. In other words, his experiment with ''exile'' was not nearly as significant as it was for writers like Hemingway and Pound. Faulkner knew early on that his best material would be found on native ground, that his work would have to probe the depths of his experience in Oxford, Mississippi, to become truly great.

Faulkner's third novel, *Sartoris* (1929), the first of the Yoknapatawpha novels, has at its center the protagonist Bayard Sartoris. Bayard suffers from the sense of despair associated with those who survived the war. His grief and guilt over the death of his brother John, killed in an aerial dogfight, has been suggested by critics to represent the general sense of gloom that permeated the consciousness of fictional characters created by writers of the Lost Generation. Hyatt Waggoner notes that "the content of Bayard's awareness is like that which shapes the sensibility of the old waiter in Hemingway's 'A Clean, Well-Lighted Place' " (23). Waggoner also sees a parallel between Bayard and Nick in Hemingway's "Big Two-Hearted River," as both characters struggle to find physical activities to divert or shield themselves from the acuteness of their own consciousness.

Faulkner's early novels, then, present the sensitive young man of the lost generation but with varying degrees of success. It would not be until *The Sound and the Fury*, published at the end of the 1920s, the decade most closely identified with the Lost Generation, that Faulkner, in creating Quentin Compson, realized his imaginative capabilities in a character whom some critics have seen as embodying the psychological and philosophical perspectives of the Lost Generation.

FURTHER READING

Broer, L., and J. Walther. *Dancing Fools and Weary Blues: The Great Escape of the Twenties.* Bowling Green, Ohio: Bowling Green State University Press, 1990.
Cowley, Malcolm. *A Second Flowering: Works and Days of the Lost Generation.* New York: Viking, 1973.
Dolan, Marc. *Modern Lives: A Cultural Re-reading of the Lost Generation.* West Lafayette, Ind.: Purdue University Press, 1996.

Steven P. Schneider

LUSTER, a black male character who figures prominently in *The Sound and the Fury* and less significantly in *Absalom, Absalom!*, the "Compson Appendix," and *The Reivers*. Discrepancies in chronology and affiliation make it difficult to view all of the individuals who bear the name as the same character. Luster is seventeen or eighteen in 1928 in *The Sound and the Fury* and the "Compson Appendix," whereas in *Absalom* and *The Reivers* he is that age or older circa 1905–1909. He is a servant of the Compson family in the earlier works, but in *The Reivers* he is an employee of Maury Priest. Possibly Faulkner associated the name more with a type—"youthful black male servant or employee"—than with an individual.

In *The Sound and the Fury* Luster appears most prominently in the first and fourth sections. His primary function is as Benjy Compson's caretaker, a duty he discharges competently, casually, and with occasional adolescent cruelty. Throughout the first section, he is absorbed in trying to find a quarter he has lost, which he needs if he is to attend a carnival that evening. This search forms an analogue to various other "quests" in the novel, most notably to Jason Compson's pursuit of the female Quentin and of the money she has taken. Luster's relative inattention to Benjy contributes to the novel's theme of failed communication, as he persistently misconstrues the causes of Benjy's moaning and bellowing. Some recent critics see in Luster's relationship with Benjy—a youthful black acting as "master" to an adult white male—a commentary on racial and economic changes occurring in the South in the 1920s. The tenuousness of the Compsons' economic and social status is suggested by their having to rely on an adolescent who, like his uncles, Versh and T. P., may leave the Compson employ upon reaching adulthood.

Luster's appearance in the fourth section serves primarily to add depth and color to the novel's depiction of black family and religious life. His desire to emulate the man from the carnival who could play a tune on a saw foreshadows the Reverend Shegog's sermon, with its emphasis on the transforming power of voice and sound.

In *Absalom, Absalom!* Luster is the subject of Mr. Compson's casual teasing. When Mr. Compson and Quentin seek shelter in a cedar copse containing the Sutpen family graves, Luster remains outside in the rain, despite Mr. Compson's repeated invitations. The scene relies on a stereotypical view of black superstition and fear, but its primary purpose is to illustrate Quentin's awareness of similar feelings in himself.

Karl F. Zender

LYNCHING refers to the extralegal killing of someone usually accused of a crime, such as rape or murder, by a group of people who see themselves carrying out vigilante justice on behalf of a majority of the community or the family of the crime victim. Lynching often interrupted the legal process, which would likely have led to legal execution, in order to deny the accused the honor of a legal trial and execution. Furthermore, a lynching often included prolonged and cruel torture, burning, branding, mutilation, and humiliation before and after the killing. Many lynchings were also carried out in retribution for some noncriminal behavior, such as a black male whistling at a white woman.

Whatever the alleged provocation, the killing typically took place by hanging by the neck with a rope. Before World War I, after which public pressure heightened the threat of federal intervention, Southern lynchings were very public events, attended by large crowds, often including women and children. The corpse was often put on display afterward. In many cases the corpse would be mutilated and body parts taken home by people as souvenirs or put on display at local stores. Lynching was a public event, a shared ritual of violence and social domination, which in the South meant white supremacy.

In the South, though there were also white victims (as Faulkner demonstrates in the lynching of Lee Goodwin in *Sanctuary*), lynching was primarily a form of violence inflicted by whites on black males. Lynching of slaves had been virtually unknown before the Civil War; slave owners would never have allowed valuable slave property to be wantonly destroyed. After Emancipation there was a widespread belief among whites that blacks, no longer subject to the discipline of slavery, would degenerate to primitive instincts, with black male sexual lust for white women regarded foremost as a danger. During Reconstruction the Ku Klux Klan and other night riders used violence and terror to intimidate and kill blacks and other Republican adversaries. This violence was politically motivated and was typically done in the dark of night by secret societies with men in hoods.

It was not until the late nineteenth century, after the withdrawal of federal troops in 1877 and coinciding with the disfranchisement of blacks, that a new form of violence began to be seen across the South. Lynching was now a community ritual, something done openly during the day, and often with the leadership of prominent citizens in the community. Between 1889 and 1932 there were over 3,700 reported lynchings, almost all in the South and mostly (nearly 3,000) blacks lynched by whites. Mississippi alone accounted for approximately 600 lynchings. In Mississippi lynchings of blacks were most prevalent in counties outside the Delta, in the "white counties" where blacks were a minority; and they were often blamed, sometimes unfairly, on the lower-class whites, or "rednecks."

During Faulkner's lifetime his home county, Lafayette County, witnessed several lynchings of blacks. The most dramatic was the lynching of Nelse Patton in September 1908. Patton was a prisoner at the county jail on leave to deliver a message to the wife of another prisoner. Reportedly intoxicated, Patton apparently threatened to molest the woman or her daughter, and when the woman went to get a pistol, Patton slashed her throat with a razor, nearly decapitating her. Patton fled, and a posse went in pursuit. Patton was wounded, apprehended, and jailed. That night a large mob of men and boys gathered outside the jail and began an assault that went on through the night, using sledge hammers and other tools to break through the thick walls of the jail. Patton was killed by gunfire in the jail before he was hanged on a telephone pole in front of the courthouse, a few blocks from where Faulkner lived. It would not be until September 1935 that Oxford witnessed another lynching. A black male named Ellwood Higginbotham stood trial, accused of killing a white man whom he claimed had entered his house at night with a drawn pistol. Higginbotham had fled for his life and, following a long manhunt, was apprehended, jailed, and given a trial. While the all-white jury deliberated his fate, a mob, apparently provoked by the idea that the jury was deliberating at all, broke into the jail, dragged Higginbotham out, and hanged him from a tree outside of town. By this time, the threat of federal intervention and the organized protest of the NAACP (National Association for the Advancement of Colored People) and other antilynching groups had made the practice both more rare and far less public. The Higginbotham lynching was the last in Lafayette County.

Faulkner was only eleven at the time of the Nelse Patton lynching and did not witness this or any other lynching; however, he treated the subject of lynching in several of his writings. Many consider the killing of Joe Christmas in *Light in August* to be a lynching, but it is not. Percy Grimm and his posse are legally deputized agents of the law and *technically* chased and killed a fugitive who had escaped and resisted arrest. Grimm's mutilation of Christmas, cutting off his genitals so that he could not attack any other white women, was, however, just the kind of ghoulish act that accompanied many genuine lynchings. *Intruder in the Dust* is the story of a planned lynching that was averted by the efforts of a young white boy, his young black friend, and an elderly woman who challenge the prejudice that has led other whites to assume Lucas Beauchamp is guilty of killing a white man. Although it was published long after lynching had diminished as a threat to blacks, *Intruder* was a powerful indictment of racial injustice and of the complacency of whites who allowed it. Faulkner still follows a familiar tendency of blaming the lower-class poor whites for the violence against blacks. The Gowry clan represents a kind of rural redneck bigotry against which the Mallisons stand for a refined racial paternalism. Actual lynchings often involved prominent community leaders at the head of the mob. Earlier, in his 1931 short story "Dry September," Faulkner told the story of another black man, Will Mayes, who had been accused of violating a white woman. In this story neither inconsistencies in the charge nor the objections of the barber Hawkshaw stop the lynching. The story and others reflect Faulkner's distaste for lynching and his uncertain faith in white racial paternalism as a counterforce to redneck racism.

FURTHER READING

McMillan, Neil. *Dark Journey: Black Mississippians in the Age of Jim Crow*. Urbana: University of Illinois Press, 1989.

Raper, Arthur F. *The Tragedy of Lynching*. New York: Dover, 1970.

Williamson, Joel. *The Crucible of Race: Black/White Relations in the American South Since Emancipation*. New York: Oxford University Press, 1984.

Don H. Doyle

M

MAHON, DONALD, is the aviator in Faulkner's *Soldiers' Pay* who is returned home from Flanders, hideously scarred and terminally wounded, and who lies dying as the entire narrative unfolds. He can be read through a psychoanalytic lens, as a perceptive case study of acute shell shock, and in poetic and mythic terms as a descendant of Faulkner's Marble Faun, a Pan-like, even Christlike figure, a denizen of the Waste Land. He is one of Faulkner's present-yet-absent figures, around whom the design of the novel and the desires of other characters all revolve. Although virtually silent and almost completely passive, Donald nevertheless represents a powerful force at the center of *Soldiers' Pay.*

FURTHER READING

Scoblionko, Andrew. "Subjectivity and Homelessness in *Soldiers' Pay.*" *Faulkner Journal* 8.1 (1992): 61–71.

Yonce, Margaret. " 'Shot Down Last Spring': The Wounded Aviators of Faulkner's Wasteland." *Mississippi Quarterly* 31 (1978): 359–368.

Zeitlin, Michael. "The Passion of Margaret Powers: A Psychoanalytic Reading of *Soldiers' Pay.*" *Mississippi Quarterly* 46 (1993): 351–372.

Pamela E. Knights

MALRAUX, ANDRÉ (1901–1976), French novelist, critic, and statesman, shared with Albert Camus the view that Faulkner was a modern tragic thinker. Malraux's preface to the French translation of *Sanctuary* (1933) focuses on Faulkner's portrayal of Fate and demonstrates the "intrusion of Greek tragedy into the detective story." Malraux's understanding of the human condition is analogous to Faulkner's tragic vision, but he saw action and art as the redeeming forces that enable man to "prevail." Malraux was the European writer "Faulkner most admired" (1974 *FAB* 1504). Faulkner was familiar with Malraux's works, in particular *The Psychology of Art* and *Man's Fate*. He gave copies of

Malraux's Goncourt Prize–winning *Man's Fate* to Joan Williams and Phil Stone, saying: "He's the best of us all." However, he declined Hal Smith's invitation to write a preface for *Man's Fate* with the following statement: "I don't read French easily enough to do justice to Malraux's book" (1974 *FAB* 827). In May 1952 he participated in the Writers' Congress on the same panel of speakers as Malraux. Both Malraux and Faulkner shared an acute awareness of history and were keenly interested in the destiny of man in the world.

FURTHER READING

Horvath, Violet M., trans. "Preface to William Faulkner's *Sanctuary*, by André Malraux." *Southern Review* 10 (1974): 889–891.

Marie Liénard

MANNIGOE, NANCY, in *Requiem for a Nun*, is a reformed "dopefiend whore" hired by Temple Drake as personal companion and nursemaid to her children. A closely similar character, also named "Nancy" but with no last name specified, appears centrally in "That Evening Sun," a story published two decades earlier. Most Faulkner scholars view the Nancy Mannigoe of *Requiem* as a reuse of the Nancy of "That Evening Sun," even though in that story she believes she is soon to be murdered.

The motivating action of *Requiem for a Nun*, occurring prior to the time of the novel, is Nancy's murder of Temple Drake's infant son, an act she performs to prevent Temple from running away from her husband and her other child with a gangster named Pete. During the novel proper, Nancy waits passively for her execution, as Temple struggles to overcome the guilt occasioned by her sense that she herself has been the proximate cause of the murder. Visited by Temple and Gavin Stevens the night before the execution, Nancy urges Temple toward a renewal of hope and faith, saying repeatedly, "Just believe."

Critical controversy centers on what moral valuation is to be placed on Nancy's actions and attitudes. Many early critics, seeing Nancy as a type of the biblical "suffering servant," read her moral views as Faulkner's own. But a number of later critics—most notably Noel Polk—have argued that the bizarre nature of Nancy's attempt to hold together Temple's family undercuts her ability to serve as the novel's moral norm. Other critics have interpreted the Nancy Mannigoe of *Requiem* in racial and gender contexts, seeing her as a late variation on Dilsey Gibson of *The Sound and the Fury*. Some of this commentary is critical of Faulkner's tendency to assign blacks subsidiary roles in works focusing on the moral struggles and development of white characters.

The Nancy of "That Evening Sun" is a richly imagined tragic character. A part-time servant of the Compson family, she fears that her husband, Jesus, intends to murder her, apparently because she has become pregnant by a white man, one of her clients as a prostitute. Some critics have read "That Evening Sun" as a study in hysteria and paranoia; more usually, that Nancy's fears are well founded but dismissed by the Compson family. Read this way, the story is a tragedy of failed communication across generational, gender, and racial lines.

FURTHER READING

Broughton, Panthea. "*Requiem for a Nun*: No Part in Rationality." *Southern Review* 8 (1972): 749–762.

Slabey, Robert M. "Faulkner's Nancy as 'Tragic Mulatto.'" *Studies in Short Fiction* 27 (1990): 409–413.

Karl F. Zender

MANSION, THE, published in 1959, is the final volume of Faulkner's *Snopes* trilogy. After completing work on *The Town* in August 1956, Faulkner began working on *The Mansion* in December. Unlike work on the second volume, which Faulkner reported to be quite taxing, work on the final volume seems to have been characterized by the pleasure of completion. He interrupted work on the book early in 1957 to become writer-in-residence at the University of Virginia and to travel to Greece in March. Returning to *The Mansion* in 1958, Faulkner reportedly was writing with the kind of energy he associated with his earlier compositions, saying little about his work in progress and writing steadily.

When the manuscript was submitted, editors began noticing discrepancies in the retelling of stories from one volume to the next in the trilogy. Faulkner engaged in a lengthy correspondence with Random House editors concerning inconsistencies in the three volumes of *Snopes*, giving rise to a number of revealing authorial statements regarding the narrative project as a whole. In May 1959, Faulkner decided to write a brief but pointed preface to the novel in which he explained the significance of these "discrepancies and contradictions in the thirty-four-year progress" of the Snopes chronicle—counting back to 1925, to the writing of "Father Abraham" and the genesis of *Snopes* in his imagination. The difference of opinion between Faulkner and his editors concerning inconsistencies in the *Snopes* texts is indicative of the gulf between them regarding the significance of the trilogy as a whole. The prefatory statement to the novel defends the centrality of narrative revision to the *Snopes* project, implying that to correct discrepancies in the early volumes would be to misrepresent the "progress of this particular chronicle." The fact that certain incidents and characterizations should alter over the course of the chronicle was one fact Faulkner sought to defend.

The preface refers to the novel as both "final chapter" and "summation" of the trilogy. Structurally, the novel combines methods from Volumes I and II: It is divided into separate books, as is *The Hamlet*; but it is narrated not only by an omniscient narrator but also, in several chapters, by individual narrators, thus echoing the structure of *The Town*. In addition, *The Mansion* retells many of the events and stories that originate in the first two volumes, often redefining significance of these events in the process. Such redefinition is particularly true in the case of Mink Snopes. In *The Hamlet*, Mink appears as a rebellious, ornery, dispossessed farmer who turns criminal out of economic frustration. He is virtually absent from *The Town* except to be maligned by Ratliff as "mean without no profit consideration or hope at all." In *The Mansion*, however, Mink returns as a major figure, an immensely sympathetic character, almost heroic, the criminal foil to Flem Snopes's quasi-legal career as a capitalist. The evolution of Mink, and the way in which his story assumes prominence in the chronicle of Snopes after being dismissed by the narrators of *The Town*, is a good indication of the complex narrative strategy employed by Faulkner in the trilogy.

In *The Mansion* the bourgeois imperatives of *The Town* reappear only to clash with the peasant, or folk, values of *The Hamlet*. Stevens and Ratliff continue to represent the town's reaction to the assault on propriety, decorum, and orthodox social structure by the Snopeses. Both men continue to use extralegal maneuvers and dirty tricks to enforce their vision of civil behavior—such as Stevens's withholding information from Meadowfill in order to get rid of him or Ratliff's spoiling Clarence Snopes's election bid in the "By the People" episode. The men refer to such efforts as having "carried on the good work of getting things into the shape they're in now." Incidents such as these contribute to the theme of pragmatism in the novel, suggesting that there exist no purely good nor purely evil actions but rather a gauge of usefulness on which actions may be measured. The difference between what a Snopes will do and what anyone else would do becomes increasingly blurred in the novel as individual Snopeses begin to establish integral places in the community.

Stevens, in fact, participates in the ultimate Snopes act in his scheme to have Mink released from prison. When Mink outwits him and carries out his original plan to assassinate Flem, Stevens is driven to an alliance with Flem, thus admitting the worth of Snopes's life and garnering an unprecedented expression of gratitude from Flem. After Flem's death, Stevens is compelled to reexamine the moral standards by which he judges others and to confess that what he defined as moral is in fact political. "There aren't any morals," he concludes. "People just do the best they can." At this conclusion, Stevens and Ratliff each apply to Snopes the novel's signal statement of empathy: "The poor sons of bitches." At this point each man realizes that Flem, like any other son of a bitch in the community, has always simply done the best he could, given his place and time and ambition. Their "Snopes alarm" is thus canceled upon the recognition of a basic affinity between self and other.

The rehabilitation of Mink Snopes in *The Mansion* contributes as well to the novel's summation theme of empathy. Mink and Flem share identical origins as dispossessed Snopeses; but whereas Flem's antagonism for his environment manifests itself in single-minded ambition, Mink's manifests itself in murder. Out of a shared disdain for the community, produced by each man's consciousness of dispossession, emerge two kinds of actions: criminal and entrepreneurial. The story of Mink told in *The Mansion* makes clear Mink's class antagonisms and recasts Will Varner, the rather jovial patriarch in *The Hamlet*, into an oppressive figure compelled to protect the class structure even at the cost of betraying justice. Mink kills Flem by the same logic with which he convinced himself that Houston had to be killed, Houston having symbolized the general oppression Mink experienced from above, Flem the general betrayal he experienced from his equals.

The local and isolated drama of *The Mansion* is played out within a national context, represented by Linda Snopes Kohl's return to Jefferson and the revelation that she is a member of the Communist Party. Made deaf by artillery fire in the Spanish Civil War, where her husband, a Jew, was killed, her subsequent employment in a wartime shipyard and her work with local Negroes make her an iconic connection to the world beyond Yoknapatawpha. The fact that she is subject to harassment, both by the FBI and by local townspeople, makes the connection between Snopes and the "other" unmistakable, reverberating back across the entire trilogy. Linda supports a plan that allows Mink to kill Flem, whom she believes is her father, and then arrives on the scene of the murder to help Mink escape. When she enlists the support of Gavin Stevens, County Prosecutor, in helping Mink, she displays the collapsing of Snopes, Stevens, and human nature into a single continuum.

Critics have generally seen *The Mansion* as a better book than *The Hamlet*, but it suffers from the same critical neglect associated with much of Faulkner's later fiction. Attention has more recently been given to Linda Snopes Kohl as one of Faulkner's more compelling female characters.

FURTHER READING

Beck, Warren. *Man in Motion: Faulkner's Trilogy*. Madison: University of Wisconsin Press, 1961.

Crabtree, Claire. "Plots of Punishment and Faulkner's Injured Women: Charlotte Rittenmeyer and Linda Snopes." *Michigan Academician* 24 (1992): 527–539.

Creighton, Joanne V. "The Dilemma of the Human Heart in *The Mansion*." *Renascence: Essays on Value in Literature* 25 (1972): 35–45.

Fulton, Keith Louise. "Linda Snopes Kohl: Faulkner's Radical Woman." *Modern Fiction Studies* 34 (1988): 425–436.

Kang, Hee. "A New Configuration of Faulkner's Feminine: Linda Snopes Kohl in *The Mansion*." *Faulkner Journal* 8.1 (1992): 21–41.

Polk, Noel. "Idealism in *The Mansion*." *Faulkner and Idealism*, ed. Gresset and Samway. 112–126.

Urgo. *Faulkner's Apocrypha*.

Watson, James G. *The Snopes Dilemma: Faulkner's Trilogy*. Coral Gables, Fla.: University of Miami Press, 1968.

Joseph R. Urgo

MARBLE FAUN, THE, published in 1924, was Faulkner's first commercially produced volume of poetry. It included a preface by his erstwhile mentor Phil Stone, who may have paid charges to the Four Seas Company of Boston for printing either 500 or 1,000 copies. The status of the volume as Faulkner's first book-length commercial publication in any genre (there were earlier hand-printed "books"), rarity of extant copies, and uncertainty about how many copies were printed have made it subject to as much bibliographic discussion as critical analysis. Bibliographic questions are addressed by Joan St. C. Crane and by William Boozer, who provides a census and description of known copies.

The volume comprises nineteen pastoral eclogues, organized around seasonal and diurnal motifs and spoken by a marble statue in a formal garden. As Judith Sensibar (*Origins*) indicates, at least one prior unpublished collection by Faulkner bore the same title, comprising fourteen poems, divided into titled sections, of which several are dated later than the "April, May, June 1919" date in the published volume. This dating significantly implies that the poems were completed in their published form years prior to publication (thus by a much younger author) and marks the centennial of Keats's composition of his great odes.

It was for many years commonplace simply to deprecate *The Marble Faun* as mannered and derivative. George Garrett, Jr., is one of the few earlier critics to treat *The Marble Faun* seriously. Beginning in the late 1970s, however, several reassessments appear, including those by Robert Hamblin, who sees *The Marble Faun* articulating Faulkner's interest in the dialectic of life and art, and Martin Kreiswirth, who sees Faulkner attempting to modify pastoral forms and conventions in early drafts of the poem. The most sustained reassessment is by Judith Sensibar (*The Origins of Faulkner's Art*), who places Faulkner's achievement in the context of a theory of his development from the psychologically challenged role of an "impostor" (compensating for real and imagined defects of character and station) to that of a conscious and reflective artist manipulating fictional "masks." Michel Gresset (*Fascination*) reads *The Marble Faun* as a "detour of inauthentic aestheticism" overcome in passing from the "cold pastoral" of this poem to the more engaged and humanized writings that follow. Also extremely useful for understanding the context of Faulkner's early poetry (as well as his artwork) is Hönnighausen's *William Faulkner: The Art of Stylization in His Early Graphic and Literary Work.*

The trope of the "speaking statue" and the figure of the faun become important to Faulkner's later work, whether in the characterization of Benjy (narrating though speechless and enclosed in his body), Horace Benbow, Ike Snopes, or others. The trope also connects Faulkner to literary antecedents, such as Hawthorne in the American tradition, Keats and Wilde in the British, Mallarmé and the seventeenth-century philosopher Condillac in the French, and to now lesser-known writers such as George Moore and Robert Nichols. At its best, *The Marble Faun* affectingly evokes the spirit of adolescent ennui, arrested desire, and the dilemmas of bounded consciousness.

FURTHER READING

Boozer, William. *William Faulkner's First Book*: The Marble Faun *Fifty Years Later.* Memphis, Tenn.: Pigeon Roost Press, 1974.

Crane, Joan St. C. "Faulkner's *The Marble Faun* Redivivus." *American Book Collector* September–October 1983: 11–22.

Garrett, George, Jr. "An Examination of the Poetry of William Faulkner." *William Faulkner: Four Decades of Criticism*, ed. Wagner. 44–54.

Hamblin, Robert W. "*The Marble Faun*: Chapter One of Faulkner's Continuing Dialectic on Life and Art." *Publications of the Missouri Philological Association* 3 (1978): 80–90.

Stephen Hahn

MARIONETTES, THE, a handcrafted book that Faulkner wrote, illustrated, and bound in six copies in 1920 for presentation to close friends. The work, which treats the love story of Pierrot and Marietta, was not commercially printed until 1977. Marionettes were a significant motif in European Symbolist aesthetics around the turn of the century. In works by Gordon Craig, Arthur Symons, Aubrey Beardsley, and others, the marionette, like the Greek mask, served to stylize and distance reality and to express generalized, impersonal emotions. Whether in the actual theater or as a figure in poetry, sculpture, or painting, the puppet exemplified a purity beyond the powers of the human actor—its gestures were both timeless and universal. The motif remained important to many avant-garde American artists in the early 1920s. Faulkner was aware of such contemporaries as the Provincetown playwrights (Edna St. Vincent Millay, Eugene O'Neill, and Alfred Kreymborg, among others), who were influenced by Symbolist modes. In 1920 he joined an Oxford drama group called "The Marionettes," and he took the motif as the title and framing metaphor for his own attempt at a Symbolist playlet, *The Marionettes*, which captures the fin de siècle tone.

References to marionettes recur throughout Faulkner's prose and poetry. In his early review of Joseph Hergesheimer's *Linda Condon* for *The Mississippian* (December 15, 1922), Faulkner criticizes the characters as puppets. Yet he is clearly fascinated by them as "unforgettable figures in silent arrested motion, forever beyond the reach of time and troubling the heart like music" (*EPP* 101). This transmutation of reality into a stylized puppet theater becomes part of his repertoire for creating similar effects in his own writing. The appearance of the motif at moments of intensity signals a dreamlike state of frozen motion, which connects narratives as seemingly diverse as "The Hill" and *A Fable*. The marionette image also emerges in some of Faulkner's most powerful visions of human beings in extremis. In *The Wild Palms* he marks Charlotte Rittenmeyer's desperation by transforming this special motif into something grotesque and menacing. Charlotte makes puppets (based on some of Faulkner's favorite literary characters) to turn into commercial art; and one, the "Bad Smell," symbolizes everything that threatens her relationship with Harry. In *As I Lay Dying*, Darl sums up our lives as the "dead gestures of dolls," and Faulkner seems to confirm this vision elsewhere: in *Light in August* in the image of Doc and Mrs.

Hines, led puppetlike to be interviewed by Hightower; or in the representation, in *The Unvanquished*, of Granny's dead body as a collapsed heap of sticks and cords; or perhaps most memorably, in Judith Sutpen's fervent description in *Absalom, Absalom!* of "trying to, having to, move your arms and legs with strings only the same strings are hitched to all the other arms and legs and the others all trying and they don't know why either."

FURTHER READING

Hönnighausen, Lothar. "Faulkner's Graphic Work in Historical Context." *Faulkner: International Perspectives*, ed. Fowler and Abadie. 139–173.
Polk, Noel. Introduction. *The Marionettes*. By William Faulkner. Charlottesville: University Press of Virginia, 1977.

Pamela E. Knights

MARXIST APPROACHES. In his sociological study *The Great Tradition* (1933; rev. ed. 1935), Granville Hicks typifies the disdain of American Marxist critics in the 1930s for Faulkner's fiction. Focusing on economic and political matters relating to class struggle, Hicks finds Faulkner inferior to John Dos Passos. For Hicks, Faulkner's focus on individual pathology undercuts his ability to represent social issues: "Faulkner's unwillingness to try to understand the world about him not only robs his novels of true importance but brings them dangerously close to triviality" (267).

During the 1940s and 1950s, Marxist critical concerns continue in the more covert form of the New York Intellectuals' preference for realism over the perceived elitism of modernism. In *On Native Ground* (1942), Alfred Kazin, although distancing himself from a purely sociological approach, nevertheless expands on Hicks's brief assertion that Faulkner's writing is motivated by hatred. For Kazin, Faulkner is a misanthrope whose bitterness results from being "a Sartoris (the Southern aristocrat *manquè*) in a Snopes world" (455). Despite exploiting "the devices of naturalism," Faulkner "actually represent[s] a rejection of naturalism"; this for Kazin is unfortunate because it means that "the violence of Faulkner's novels is, at bottom, not the violent expression of a criticism of society, but the struggles of a sensibility at war with itself" (466).

At the height of the Cold War, Richard Chase's *The American Novel and Its Tradition* (1957) so encoded the discussion of Faulkner in a distinction between novel and romance that Chase's Marxian impulses are rendered nearly invisible. Nevertheless, Chase's insistence that American romance is a form of realism allows him to argue that Faulkner's art is not merely an aesthetic exercise but also represents social contradictions.

Not until Myra Jehlen's *Class and Character in Faulkner's South* (1976) is there a book-length treatment of Faulkner from a Marxian perspective. Jehlen sees Faulkner as closer to nineteenth-century European realism than to modernism because the interiority of his characters grows out of class differences. On this view, Faulkner's concern with historicizing his society becomes his very claim to our attention: "Where other American writers failed ultimately to grasp the tangibility of social context because, believing in the American myth of classlessness they could visualize society only as a universal and neutral setting, Faulkner treats society itself as his central character" (11). Jehlen's insistence on the interrelation between the literary and the social prepares the ground for the ideological and New Historical work that has been done on Faulkner since the 1980s.

FURTHER READING

Chase, Richard. *The American Novel and Its Tradition*. New York: Anchor, 1957.

Hicks, Granville. *The Great Tradition: An Interpretation of American Literature Since the Civil War*. Rev. ed. New York: Macmillan, 1935.

Kazin, Alfred. *On Native Grounds: An Interpretation of Modern American Prose Literature*. New York: Reynal and Hitchcock, 1942.

John N. Duvall

McCALLUM, a fictional family appearing in a number of Faulkner works. The McCallums are "The Tall Men" in the story of that name. The family is introduced (as the "MacCallums") in *Sartoris/Flags in the Dust*, and individual members make briefer appearances in *Intruder in the Dust*, "Knight's Gambit," *The Town*, and elsewhere. Even with inconsistencies of detail between novels, the McCallums remain a distinctive and important presence in Yoknapatawpha. Spanning the Civil War to World War II, they are a close-knit, exclusively male, family group of father, six sons, and later, twin grandsons. In spite of considerable differences in temperament, abilities, and experience, all the brothers, from Rafe the horse breeder to Buddy the war hero, bear an unmistakable patrilineal likeness. Sturdily independent, living in a log house in the hills beyond Jefferson, the McCallums represent solid yeoman stock, at the point of encounter with the changing world after 1919. Their isolated household, seen as a refuge by young Bayard Sartoris and as a hideout by the draft investigator, gives readers a glimpse of a vanishing rural South. For most critics, they have offered an alternative vision (some would say a nostalgic one) to the Snopeses, as a firm center of traditional values founded on admirable principles. The McCallums walk tall, maintaining their moral integrity in the face of larger cultural disturbances. But, for some, the persistent images of intrusion and change suggest that their fierce male self-sufficiency cannot outlast the assaults of twentieth-century society: Like the Sartorises, the McCallums are a doomed and declining clan.

FURTHER READING

Nordanberg. *Cataclysm as Catalyst: The Theme of War in William Faulkner's Fiction*.

Pamela E. Knights

McCANNON, SHREVLIN, Quentin Compson's Canadian roommate at Harvard, undergoes a name change from MacKenzie in *The Sound and the Fury* to McCannon in *Absalom, Absalom!* In the earlier novel, Quentin describes Shreve as a rosy-cheeked, chunky young man who wears glasses and is notable for a heavy-handed sense of humor that he liberally applies to his Southern roommate. Some critics have discerned a homoerotic attraction between them. Shreve also acts solicitously toward Quentin, although he, like everyone else, fails to read Quentin's suicidal intentions on June 2, 1910. In *Absalom, Absalom!* Faulkner tells us that Shreve looks exactly nineteen and that he eventually becomes a surgeon in Edmonton, Alberta, after World War I. While his role in *The Sound and the Fury* is negligible, Shreve is an inventive narrative voice in *Absalom, Absalom!* Together the two freshmen recreate the story of Thomas Sutpen and his family, with Shreve offering many conjectures and hypotheses as they try to make a comprehensible narrative out of the facts at their disposal. Shreve assumes a playful attitude toward the material he has learned from Quentin, seeing Sutpen as an outrageous tall-tale hero whose exploits could have happened only in that peculiar region, the American South. Although he has been drawn in by the compelling story, Shreve finally returns to jocularity at the end. For him, the storytelling has been an academic exercise, a way to pass the time on a cold January night. Yet Shreve's outsider's voice creates perspective and balance for a story that those closer to the principals deem "incredible."

FURTHER READING

Doody, Terrence. "Shreve McCannon and the Confessions of *Absalom, Absalom!*" *Studies in the Novel* 16 (1974): 454–469.

Gray, James D. "Shreve's Lesson of Love: The Power of the Unsaid in *Absalom, Absalom!*" *New Orleans Review* 14.4 (1987): 24–35.

Michel, Pierre. "Shreve McCannon: The Outside Voice in *Absalom, Absalom!*" *American Literature in Belgium.* Ed. Gilbert Debusscher and Marc Maufort. Amsterdam: Rodopi, 1988. 117–126.

Pitavy, François. "The Narrative Voice and Function of Shreve: Remarks on the Production of Meaning in *Absalom, Absalom!*" *William Faulkner's* Absalom, Absalom!: *A Critical Casebook.* Ed. Elisabeth Muhlenfeld. New York: Garland, 1984. 189–205.

Redekop, Magdalene. "*Absalom, Absalom!* Through the Spectacles of Shreve McCannon." *William Faulkner: Materials, Studies, and Criticism* 5.2 (1983): 17–45.

David L. Vanderwerken

McCASLIN, an important fictional family appearing in several Faulkner works. Of Faulkner's major fictional families, the McCaslins have by far the most complex and thematically suggestive genealogy. Although mentioned in a number of novels and short stories, ranging from *Absalom, Absalom!* through *The Unvanquished, Go Down, Moses, Big Woods, Intruder in the Dust, The Town, The Mansion,* and *The Reivers,* the story of the family is fully elaborated only in *Go Down, Moses*, whose central action is the coming of age of Isaac Mc-Caslin, the grandson of the family's founding patriarch, Lucius Quintus Carothers McCaslin.

Begun as tutelage in the values of the wilderness and into a hunter's code, Isaac's coming of age shifts at the age of sixteen into an exploration of his family's history, through his reading of aging ledgers housed in the commissary of the family plantation. His grandfather had fathered a son, Terrel ("Turl"), by a slave named Tomasina; Isaac discovers that Tomasina is herself his grandfather's daughter by another slave, Eunice. Horrified at the discovery of inter-mingled incest and miscegenation, Ike relinquishes his inheritance to his cousin, McCaslin Edmonds, remaining thereafter "uncle to half a county and father to no one."

In addition to Isaac and L.Q.C. McCaslin, the McCaslin surname is borne by Isaac's father, Theophilus ("Uncle Buck") and his twin brother, Amodeus ("Uncle Buddy"). Both appear as Confederate partisans in *The Unvanquished*; in *Go Down, Moses*, the brothers seek to redress their father's inequity by man-umitting as many of their slaves as possible. In *Go Down, Moses*, the McCaslin genealogy interlinks with those of the Edmondses, descendants of the McCaslin Edmonds to whom Isaac relinquishes his inheritance, and the Beauchamps, a black family descended from L.Q.C. McCaslin via Terrel. Lucas Beauchamp is an approximate coeval of Isaac, born seven years later. His attitude toward property ownership, as depicted in the section of *Go Down, Moses* entitled "The Fire and the Hearth," provides ironic commentary on Isaac's decision to relin-quish his inheritance.

In *The Reivers*, Faulkner links the McCaslin family to the Priest family, through L.Q.C. Priest's marriage to one of Isaac's cousins. The central black character of the novel is Ned McCaslin, a rogue and trickster who accompanies Boon Hogganbeck and the youthful Lucius Priest (L.Q.C. Priest's grandson) on their journey to Memphis. Ned claims, on no authority other than his own, that his mother was "the natural daughter of old Lucius Quintus Carothers himself and a Negro slave."

FURTHER READING

Benert, Annette. "The Four Fathers of Isaac McCaslin." *Southern Humanities Review* 9 (1975): 423–433.

Donaldson, Susan V. "Isaac McCaslin and the Possibilities of Vision." *Southern Review* 22 (1986): 37–50.

Kinney, Arthur F. *Critical Essays on William Faulkner: The McCaslin Family*. Boston: G. K. Hall, 1990.

Karl F. Zender

MELVILLE, HERMAN. *See* **American Renaissance**.

MIGRATION (African American). *See* **Great Migration**.

"MISSISSIPPI," Faulkner's long essay on his native state, commissioned by *Holiday* magazine where it first appeared in 1954 and reprinted in *Essays, Speeches & Public Letters by William Faulkner*, is an elegiac and often powerful mixture of fiction and autobiographical reminiscence. Its message is one of nostalgia and regret but without bitterness. Overall, the essay expresses the ambivalence about Mississippi and the South Faulkner manifested throughout his work and life. Echoing Quentin at the end of *Absalom, Absalom!* but in calmer tones, Faulkner writes near the end: "Home again, his native land: he was born of it and his bones will sleep in it; loving it while hating some of it."

FURTHER READING

Meriwether, James B. "Faulkner's 'Mississippi.' " *Mississippi Quarterly* 25 (1972): 15–23.

Richard H. King

MISSISSIPPI POEMS, a group of twelve poems in carbon typescript that Faulkner presented, along with an inscribed copy of *The Marble Faun*, to his friend and former schoolmate Myrtle Ramey on December 30, 1924. A typed cover sheet, which Faulkner signed and dated, accompanied the poems, listing the title of the collection as "Mississippi Poems" and identifying the place and time of composition or compilation as "Oxford, Mississippi/October, 1924." That date, however, is misleading, since four of the individual poems carry November or December 1924 dates. This discrepancy of dates suggests that Faulkner had expanded the contents of the manuscript beyond his original intention. Eight of the "Mississippi Poems" were subsequently revised for inclusion in *A Green Bough* (1933), and the entire group of poems was published under Faulkner's original title in a limited facsimile edition by Yoknapatawpha Press in 1979. That edition includes an introduction by Joseph Blotner and an afterword by Louis Daniel Brodsky that explain the provenance and textual history of the manuscript, which is now housed in the Brodsky Collection. In 1981 Yoknapatawpha Press and Tulane University issued a joint trade edition of *Mississippi Poems* and *Helen: A Courtship*.

FURTHER READING

Brodsky and Hamblin, eds. *Faulkner: A Comprehensive Guide to the Brodsky Collection*. Vol. V: 75–84.
Faulkner, William. *Mississippi Poems*. Oxford, Miss.: Yoknapatawpha Press, 1979.

Louis Daniel Brodsky

"MISS ZILPHIA GANT," a short story by Faulkner, was published in 1932 by the Book Club of Texas in a limited edition of 300 copies. Reprinted in *Uncollected Stories*, the story is particularly intriguing to readers who are interested in Faulkner's characterizations of women. The title character's mother confines her to keep her from males, but when Zilphia is in her twenties, she elopes. Mrs. Gant orders Zilphia into the house and the husband off the property. After Mrs. Gant dies, Zilphia learns of her husband's subsequent marriage and keeps up with his new life, new wife, and infant daughter, who becomes orphaned. After a three-year absence from Jefferson, Zilphia returns with a daughter. Zilphia's parenting suggests the pattern of her mother. Zilphia's dreams reveal unfulfilled sexual desire.

FURTHER READING

Morell, Giliane. "Prisoners of the Inner World: Mother and Daughter in *Miss Zilphia Gant.*" *Mississippi Quarterly* 28 (1975): 299–305.

Pitavy, François. "A Forgotten Faulkner Story: 'Miss Zilphia Gant.' " *Studies in Short Fiction* 9 (1972): 131–142.

Diane Brown Jones

"MISTRAL," a short story by Faulkner, was first published in *These 13* (1931) and is included in *Collected Stories*. It tells the story of two young American men, who, in part due to their cynical curiosity and in larger part due to their own "objectless and unappeasable desire," become virtual participants in the romantic and murderous events that take place in a small Italian village. Traveling by foot and without a place to stay for the night, they learn of a priest's passion for his young ward, the murder of the rich man she was to marry, and her love for a soldier—a love that in the end seems triumphant, as though its illegal consummation had been God's will. The story is told by one of the two travelers years later, for whom the mistral they had faced that night—"that black chill wind full of dust like sparks of ice"—seems to have become symbolic of the terrible and secret frustration experienced by the priest and by man universally. Critics have observed that this early story demonstrates Faulkner's developing storytelling techniques and more recently have focused on the story's connection to other works by Faulkner in its presentation of an idealized woman who rebels against her social confinement.

FURTHER READING

Carothers, James B. "Faulkner's Short Story Writing and the Oldest Profession." *Faulkner and the Short Story*, ed. Harrington and Abadie. 38–61.

Paddock, Lisa. " 'Trifles with a Tragic Profundity': The Importance of 'Mistral.' " *Mississippi Quarterly* 32 (1979): 461–465.

Arthur A. Brown

MITCHELL, a fictional family created by Faulkner. Harry, a cotton speculator, his wife Belle, and their small daughter, Little Belle, are seen as a family in *Flags in the Dust* (more briefly in *Sartoris*) until Belle breaks with Harry to embark on a new marriage with Horace Benbow. Cut entirely in Faulkner's reworking of *Flags in the Dust* into *Sartoris* was another family member, Belle's sister, the striking Joan Heppleton. In a meteoric appearance late in *Flags* *in the Dust*, she has an affair with Horace while Belle awaits her divorce. Belle, Little Belle, and the stale Benbow marriage ten years later also figure significantly in *Sanctuary*, particularly in the original version. As newcomers to town, living in one of its ugliest and most ostentatious houses, the Mitchells are Jefferson's nouveau riches. In their conspicuous hospitality, Belle's tea-and-tennis parties, and Harry's vulgarly expensive consumer goods, Faulkner satirizes fashionable pretensions and establishes the postwar ambience. He uses Belle and Joan, further, to create an atmosphere of fin de siècle decadence, representing them, in their different ways, as man-eating predators who engulf their male victims. Belle, especially, is repeatedly associated with rank sexuality: filth, unpleasant smells, heat, flesh, and rottenness. In *Sanctuary* Faulkner extends this treatment to Little Belle, with strong suggestions that she too has now become perversely fascinating to Horace, her stepfather. Critics interested in Faulkner's constructions of female sexuality have found rich material in the treatment of all three women, although, with new feminist approaches, inquiry has turned away from the characters' offenses to the assumptions underlying their representation.

FURTHER READING

Cohen, Philip. "Ahenobarbus' Vestal: Belle Mitchell and Nero." *Notes on Contemporary Literature* 14 (1984): 8–9.

Pamela E. Knights

MODERNISM, a movement in literature and art that arose in the early part of the twentieth century, developed largely from a new view of human beings provided by Charles Darwin, James Frazer, and Sigmund Freud. Evolution suggested that we have the same physical ancestry. Comparative religion suggested that we have similar beliefs and behavior. Psychology suggested that the unconscious governs us all. But how might one call on that unity—physical, social and psychic—in a world where the individual felt isolated, where, in Yeats's famous phrase, "the center cannot hold," bound as it was merely by pietistic traditionalism?

Given this dilemma, artists sought to reach the reader on the unconscious, or perhaps primal, level of understanding, a possibility suggested by Freud's revelations about the word's ability to handle richly potent ideas. Studying dreams and slips of the tongue, Freud had discovered four types of word play that protect us from our repressed thoughts: displacement (shifting emphases), condensation (compressing meanings), representation (making symbols), and misrepresentation (garbling and gainsaying with puns and adversatives). Moreover, as if responding to Nietzsche's complaint over the lack of myth in the modern consciousness, Freud suggested that these old stories may still be operative within.

Modernism was created when, to the influences of William James's concept of a "stream" of consciousness and Henri Bergson's concept of the presentness of the past, the widely discussed Gertrude Stein added Freud's insights into the economy of the word, using repetitions, which drew attention to the words, along with minute variations, which drew attention to the syntax. Her use of the concrete could suggest abstractions; her time shifts, a "continuous present."

To catch what Joyce called that "great part of every human existence . . . which cannot be rendered sensible by the use of wide-awake language, cutand-dry grammar and goahead plot," modernists deliberately transgressed the traditional methods of creating fiction. Characters could be drawn according to archetypal figures; narratives could be structured, not chronologically but according to the outlines of other stories or the principles of other disciplines; and literary devices such as shifting point of view, incremental repetition, and stream of consciousness could be used to suggest a complexity of perception. Thus, surface plots often had subplots, unknown to the characters themselves, which nevertheless metered their actions. Such substructures could be "planted" by word clusters, calling on readers' unconscious ability to recognize the whole from the fragments.

Just as *Oedipus Rex* defines Greek tragedy, so Joyce's *Ulysses* defines the modernist novel. Patterning his three main characters on Telemachus, Odysseus, and Penelope in their primary modes of quest, return, and stasis, Joyce structured his work on eighteen episodes in the *Odyssey*, with each chapter further representing parts of the body, disciplines of the mind, times of the day, or techniques of discourse. Moreover, he established his parallels with what he called "mosaics"—lexicons of synonyms, homonyms, and images. As Eliot wrote in his now-famous review of *Ulysses* (*Dial*, November 1923), "In using the myth, in manipulating a continuous parallel between contemporaneity and antiquity, Mr Joyce is pursuing a method . . . of giving a shape and a significance to the immense panorama of futility and anarchy which is contemporary history. . . . Instead of narrative method, we may now use the mythical method."

A professed admirer of Bergson and Joyce, Faulkner showed he had been influenced by the modernists as early as his poem "Love Song," which practically paraphrases Eliot's "Prufrock." Modernist techniques are found throughout his novels. In his early book *Mosquitoes*, Faulkner parodies the fact that *Ulysses* never actually mentions the *Odyssey*: by calling the mosquitoes only "it" or "they," with much fighting of epic battles. *The Sound and the Fury* not only uses incremental repetitions, shifting point of view, and stream of consciousness but also links characters and actions to archetypal figures and external structures found in (among others) the New Testament, *The Golden Bough*, Eliot, Dante, Virgil, Hawthorne, Poe, Jeffers, Shakespeare, Wordsworth, Housman, and Freud.

To take another example, the substructure of Faulkner's *Absalom, Absalom!* is a two-stage trial in equity, a branch of civil law concerned with providing remedies for wrongs that cannot be compensated for in money. The main characters enact roles in the trial: Rosa, as plaintiff, has "a summons" sent to Quentin, the defendant, or defender of the defeated South (since his "very body'' held that ''commonwealth'') with Shreve as judge. Moreover, repetitions of word and phrase in each of the nine chapters gather thematically to represent nine types of evidence given in testimony. For example, chapter 2 represents hearsay by phrases such as ''Miss Coldfield told Quentin,'' ''Sutpen told Quentin's grandfather,'' or elaborate constructions such as ''There were probably others besides Quentin's grandfather who remarked,'' or even ''General Compson was the first man in the county to tell himself.'' But the structure is ironic. In the pretrial hearing, the first four chapters, the testimony of the eyewitnesses violates the four exclusionary rules regarding opinion, hearsay, immateriality, and best evidence withheld. In the trial itself, the last four chapters (following the sworn statement of Rosa in 5), the testimony of those most removed from the events is more believable because it includes viewing the scene (a practice widespread before photography), admissions and confessions, presumptions, and real evidence.

Modernism is often identified for its ''objectivity,'' and no doubt many modernist writers intended an ironic detachment. But since we are all subjects of our own times, such detachment means only that authors could be more objective than their predecessors in areas that had lost their significance (such as religion). Moreover, while all the modernists could speak more frankly of sex, some (such as Joyce) could be more objective about women's sexuality than others (such as Eliot and Faulkner). Where any writer feels testy, a God-like remove is hard to summon. Ending with ''The Dead,'' Joyce's *Dubliners* is a series of fierce indictments of Ireland. Just so, in the apocalyptic ending of *Absalom, Absalom!*, responding to the judge's closing question, ''Why do you hate the South?'' Quentin can only repeat his final, desperate indictment by denial, ''*I dont hate it. I dont hate it.*''

See also **Joyce, James**.

FURTHER READING

Baldanza, Frank. ''Faulkner and Stein: A Study in Stylistic Intransigence.'' *Georgia Review* 13 (1959): 274–286.

Ellmann, Richard, and Charles Feidelson, Jr., eds. *The Modern Tradition: Backgrounds of Modern Literature*. New York: Oxford University Press, 1965.

Werner, Craig. ''Beyond Realism and Romanticism: Joyce, Faulkner, and the Tradition of the American Novel.'' *Centennial Review* 23 (1979): 242–262.

Virginia V. James Hlavsa

"MOONLIGHT," one of Faulkner's earliest stories, possibly written in 1920. Although Faulkner tried to sell it, ''Moonlight'' was not published until *Uncollected Stories*. The adolescent protagonist plans a rendezvous with his girlfriend Susan. He steals whiskey, has his friend Skeet pick up Susan (in exchange for two sips of whiskey), and carries Susan to an uncle's empty home. She balks when she understands his intentions. The story closes with his soothing the shaken Susan. His thoughts now turn from seduction to a simpler desire for sharing the whiskey with Skeet. Susan Reed also appears in "Hair."

Diane Brown Jones

MOSQUITOES, Faulkner's second novel, was published in 1927. Faulkner began drafts of a narrative he called "Mosquito" in 1925, while touring Europe following his sojourn among writers and artists in New Orleans. On completion, he dated the typescript of *Mosquitoes* "1 September 1926." The published novel is heavily and significantly edited, however, and several sexually explicit passages are deleted.

Characters in the novel can be keyed in part to Faulkner's acquaintances in New Orleans, including Sherwood Anderson. The tone is clearly satirical, and the novel is an excellent example of what is called "Mennippean satire": There is much talk about art in the novel—talk that is weighed against an emphasis on bodily functions and the insistence on physicality (signaled among other things by the bites of mosquitoes, omnipresent but never named) and a disorder between desire and its fulfillment. Prominent artistic symbols of desire—Gordon's sculpture, for instance—depend for their significance on their immobility in antithesis to the mobility of flesh, while desire in the flesh (as it were) is constantly complicated—both incited and deferred—without being satisfied.

Until recently, critics have generally given only passing attention to *Mosquitoes* except to say that it represents an advanced stage of Faulkner's pre-Yoknapatawpha apprenticeship and to note its similarity to other satirical works of the 1920s—especially Aldous Huxley's *Chrome Yellow*. In addition, much has been made of the setting of the novel in cosmopolitan New Orleans in contrast to Oxford, Mississippi, or the fictional Jefferson (perhaps underestimating the cultural milieu of middle-class Oxford). Yet the pastoral ideal of rusticity is satirized in the characterization of Fairchild as the cosmopolitan ideal of urbanity is through that of Mark Frost.

Numerous passages in the novel reflect Faulkner's stylistic and thematic experimentation, not precluding indebtedness to authors such as Joyce and Wilde; and comparison of this novel with the popular fiction of the time reveals its inventiveness. Both Lillian Hellman and Conrad Aiken reviewed it favorably. Still, it lacks the evident formal integrity that might recommend it to New Critical approaches and the obvious focus on historically significant settings and issues that might distinguish it for social critics during the post-Nobel reception of Faulkner, who himself described it as "not an important book on my list" (*FIU* 257). A notable exception to the absence of early critical discussion of the novel is the prescient and lyrical preface by Raymond Queneau, himself a satirist, to a French translation in 1948. More recently, the novel has been subject to a reevaluation on the grounds that it explicitly represents and interrogates gender as a social construct. For example, Lisa Rado writes that while it "displays little of the poised and mature brilliance of his later works" (28), "it is crucial and necessitates careful study because of its foregrounding of Faulkner's sexual and artistic anxieties'' (18).

The dominant tropes of the novel are verbal and situational irony, paradox, simile, and metonymy. One sustained performance in which all these tropes are deployed is the narration of Fairchild's telling of the story of the two-seat outhouse. What at first may seem meretricious verbal excess appears on close examination to serve the corrective purpose of revealing fetishism and over-intellectualization as characteristics of a social world in which a presumably natural order is reversed: ''The Thing is merely the symbol for the Word.'' It is not merely coincidental that this is also a critique, however breezily developed, of Puritan and Emersonian ideals. As is typical of satire in this mode, observations and verbal formulations presenting an incipient critique of identifiable beliefs and attitudes are dispersed among many characters, so that it is difficult to construe an authorial ''philosophy'' or ''point of view''—a difficulty that proved to be a harbinger of things to come in Faulkner and a real strength of the novel. Indeed, for the genetic-textual critic, the steward David's fondling of a slipper belonging to the nymph he cannot kiss and the description of their trek through the swamp (especially ''The Third Day: Four O'Clock'') conjure verbal echoes and parallels to Benjy in *The Sound and the Fury* and Byron Bunch and Lena Grove in *Light in August*. Further, what at first may seem an arbitrary narrative scaffolding—citing day and hour in linear sequence to mark the chief narrative divisions—bears some relation to the narrative sequence of *The Marble Faun* and looks forward to the depiction of Lena's journey in *Light in August*: ''from day to dark and dark to day again,'' as this petty pace moves from dawn to dusk and dusk to dawn again. The discovery by Talliaferro of a ''small round metal box'' on which he reads ''Agnes Mabel Becky'' intriguingly highlights intertextual connections to a similar discovery in *The Sound and the Fury* and suggests the circulation of physical objects in a South real and imagined (the object is a condom tin) while it inescapably marks the circulation of words and images in the Faulknerian text. Only serious failures to read this text closely can account for the fact that it has been so generally considered not worth reading or studying—failures that recent critics are doing well to correct.

FURTHER READING

Arnold, Edwin T. *Annotations to William Faulkner's* Mosquitoes. New York: Garland, 1989.

Gwin, Minrose C. ''*Mosquitoes*' Missing Bite: The Four Deletions.'' *Faulkner Journal* 9.1–2 (1993–1994): 31–41.

LaLonde, Christopher A. ''*Mosquitoes* and the Rites of Passage: Making Space and Time.'' *William Faulkner and the Rites of Passage*. 37–64.

Rado, Lisa. '' 'A Perversion That Builds Chartres and Invents Lear Is a Pretty Good Thing': *Mosquitoes* and Faulkner's Androgynous Imagination.'' *Faulkner Journal* 9.1–2 (1993–1994): 13–30.

Stephen Hahn

"MOUNTAIN VICTORY," a short story by Faulkner, was first published in the *Saturday Evening Post* on December 3, 1932. Later collected in *Doctor Martino and Other Stories* and again in *Collected Stories*, the story opens with a Tennessee mountain family watching two mounted figures approach their cabin. Saucier (Soshay) Weddel, just recently a Confederate major under Longstreet and now on his way back to Mississippi after the close of the Civil War, and his "boy," the Negro Jubal, come seeking shelter from the rain. One of the family has to be stopped from shooting them as they approach. There is little development of plot outside of Jubal's getting drunk and delaying their departure until daybreak, thus making them easier targets. Prompted by their mean circumstances and the brutality of the oldest brother, Vatch, the two youngest members of the mountaineer family are desperate to leave: the barefoot girl to go as Saucier's future wife if the fancy Mississippi ladies Jubal has told her about would accept a girl without shoes; the youngest boy, Hule, to go as companion if his brother's mistaken idea that Saucier is a "nigra" proves untrue.

Jubal is a racial stereotype, a comic caricature of mispronounced words and rolling eyes, often compared to a monkey. His reports of the old plantation, Countymaison (Contalmaison), show him attached to his old condition of slavery and loyal to his old "Mistis" whom he refuses to acknowledge no longer exists. Meanwhile, Jubal complains about "deyser ign'unt mountain trash." Faulkner is still testing the post-Confederate apology, Saucier believing Jubal "is only a Negro, member of an oppressed race burdened with freedom." To Weddel, it is he the war freed, except from the noblesse oblige instanced in wrapping Jubal's feet with fur from the lining of his cape.

Faulkner allows Saucier to echo a version of Darl Bundren's reflection, "to lie under a broken roof, thinking of home." Likewise, no distruster of words, Saucier reflects, "Our lives are summed up in sounds and made significant. . . . That's why we must do so much to invent meanings." "Afraid that I shall find that I have forgot how to be afraid," Saucier repeats the ironic view that it is better to be defeated than victorious. Presumably the title reinforces this irony when, at the close, Vatch gets his way in killing Saucier but mistakenly also kills his brother Hule and in turn is killed by his father. The reader is left watching Jubal, at the end again simply the Negro, "[c]rouching . . . like a cornered animal."

"Mountain Victory" represents Faulkner's foray into subjects he would later develop more fully: miscegenation, racial misidentification, the relation between Southern black and white, and family lineage. Weddel's father was "a Choctaw chief named Francis Weddel," his Choctaw grandmother having married "a French emigre of New Orleans, a general of Napoleon's and a knight of the Legion of Honor . . . Francois Vidal."

FURTHER READING

Meriwether, James B., ed. "An Unpublished Episode from 'A Mountain Victory.' " *Mississippi Quarterly* 32 (Summer 1979): 481–483.

Charles A. Peek

"MR. ACARIUS," a short story by Faulkner, initially entitled "Weekend Revisited," is based partly on Faulkner's personal experiences with sanitariums. First submitted for publication in February 1953, it was published in the October 9, 1965 issue of the *Saturday Evening Post* and is included in *Uncollected Stories*. The protagonist, aged fifty, devises a plan "to experience man, the human race." Otherwise, he feels he will leave the earth having made no mark. He enters an upscale detoxification center, but he lasts less than a day. The desperate strategies of the patients to smuggle alcohol and the death of one patient are more than he can bear, so Acarius escapes. After a chase, his doctor takes him home. The failure of his experiment is the success of his lesson.

FURTHER READING

Gresset, Michel. "Weekend, Lost and Revisited." *Mississippi Quarterly* 21 (1968): 173–178.

Diane Brown Jones

"MULE IN THE YARD," a Faulkner short story, was first published in *Scribner's* in August 1934 and later included in *Collected Stories* and, in revised form, as chapter 16 in *The Town*. The story opens on a hilarious chase scene, Mannie Hait and her longtime friend, Old Het, chasing a mule belonging to I. O. Snopes that is loose in Mannie's yard. Mannie's first words, "Them sons of bitches," set the tone of the story. What first appears as hapless comedy, however, becomes in the narrator's words "an invulnerable compact of female with female against the world of mule and man." The complicated and outlandish plot hinges on the revenge and financial compensation gained by Mannie not only for the earlier death of her husband, a partner in Snopes's scheme to defraud the railroad, but also in the present tense of the story for the destruction of her house in the fire caused by the runaway mule. Thus Mannie becomes one of the few Faulkner characters to get the better of a Snopes and the world that elsewhere grants the Snopeses their rising status. Old Het sums up the experience in the story's closing line: "Ain't we had a day!"

Charles A. Peek

MUSIC. To believe Faulkner indifferent to music, as some have claimed, would be similar to thinking Emily Dickinson was indifferent to society just because she neither went out in it nor engaged in its sociological study. Faulkner was often indifferent to attending performances, showed no more theoretical interest in music than in any other arts, including his own, and was openly hostile to mediums for music's popular consumption: radio and the juke box. Nevertheless, Faulkner loved music. While listening to Beethoven, he once remarked to Ben Wasson: "Even light can be too much distraction when music is being played. . . . Listen to those horns of triumph and joy crying their golden sounds in a great twilight of sorrow" (Peters 27). Coinciding with later interview responses indicating Beethoven, Mozart, and Prokofiev were his favorite composers (1974 *FAB* 1506), this comment suggests the association music may have had with his beloved twilight.

One story, not quite apocryphal, suggests that music was not only an aesthetic pleasure but also a tool in his writing: He told a visitor that he had gone through three recordings of Gershwin's "Rhapsody in Blue" in his attempts to "set the rhythm and jazzy tone" of *Sanctuary*. He was possibly exaggerating—Estelle thought so. However, we know he liked Gershwin and that "Rhapsody in Blue" was on the table in his room when another guest visited him in mid-July 1940 (1974 *FAB* 754, 1054, 107n). This and his contribution of a drawing, entitled "A Jazz Band with Dancers," to the 1920–1921 issue of *Ole Miss* would lend credence to the truth if not accuracy of his account (Peters 29).

As to not attending performances, George Oppenheimer probably wished that had been so when he was forced to leave a performance of *Bolero* that Faulkner, drunk and disorderly, kept loudly proclaiming to be "too soft" (1974 *FAB* 740). Earlier in his life, he had written in letters home of hearing "bands play Massanet [*sic*] and Chopin and Berlioz and Wagner," commenting, "It is lovely, the way music sounds. And these people really love good music." In another letter, among humorous comments about the state of undress of the dancers at the Moulin Rouge, he still notes they were dancing "to real music," mentioning Rimsky-Korsakoff and Sibelius by name and concluding, "It was beautiful" (1974 *FAB* 466, 465).

Many elements in his literature reflect his interest in music; and several titles, some of them of early submissions to *The Mississippian*, suggest not only a knowledge of musical genre but also his awareness of other authors' experiments in using music for their own ends. These would include: "Nocturne" (signed Prof. Fiddle D. D.), "L'Apres-Midi d'un Faune" (a debt in part to Debussy), "Aria Con Amore" (a former title for "Spotted Horses"), "Une ballade des Femmes Perdues," "Une balade d'une Vache Perdue," "Frankie and Johnny," "Don Giovanni," "Naiads' Song," "Hymn," "Aubade" (an imitation of Swinburne imitating dialect ballads), "A Song," and "A Symphony," not to mention *Requiem for a Nun*, as easily associated with the musical genre as the religious ritual.

Significantly, Faulkner sets his story "Black Music" in Rincon where, in "Carcassonne," he enacted his fable of the artistic spirit, suggesting he understood the creative powers of spirituals, blues, and jazz, which in turn strongly inform the style, structure, and substance of "That Evening Sun." Here the influence is so strong, the materials used with such accuracy, that it is evident not only that Faulkner loved the music he had heard wafting over Oxford as a boy but also that he had divined its significance to African American culture and its embodiment of the spiritual resources that had allowed African Americans to survive and would eventually lead them to prevail.

FURTHER READING

Bennet, Ken. "The Language of the Blues in Faulkner's "That Evening Sun.'" *Mississippi Quarterly* 38 (1985): 339–342.

Davis, Thadious. "From Jazz Syncopation to Blues Elegy: Faulkner's Development of Black Characterization." *Faulkner and Race*, ed. Fowler and Abadie. 70–92.

Charles A. Peek

"MY GRANDMOTHER MILLARD AND GENERAL BEDFORD FORREST AND THE BATTLE OF HARRYKIN CREEK,"

a Faulkner short story, was first published in the March–April 1943 issue of *Story* and reprinted in *Collected Stories*. In the midst of battles, the swooning, romance-reading Cousin Melisandre is united in marriage to the dashing Confederate lieutenant Cousin Philip Backhouse through the machinations of Granny Rosa Millard and her old acquaintance and unwilling accomplice General Forrest. The narrator is Rosa Millard's grandson Bayard Sartoris, as in *The Unvanquished*, and the story is a comic treatment of topics Faulkner handles more darkly in that novel, namely, the vicissitudes of the Sartoris family during the Civil War and Granny's ingenuity, humor, and fortitude in meeting them. The story has been rendered as a performance script by Evans Harrington.

FURTHER READING

Bradford, M. E. "A Coda to *Sartoris*: Faulkner's 'My Grandmother Millard and General Bedford Forrest and the Battle of Harrykin Creek.'" *Critical Essays on William Faulkner: The Sartoris Family*. Ed. Arthur Kinney. Boston: Hall, 1985. 318–323.

Ditsky, John. "Faulkner's Harrykin Creek: A Note." *University of Windsor Review* 12.1 (1970): 88–89.

Veronica Makowsky

MYTH. Myths are anonymous, their origins religious, probably ritualistic but certainly communal. Like dreams, they may function as societal discharges for individual fantasies such as incest or parricide. Their evolution takes millennia, the transmission involving historical accretions and distortions such as projection, elaboration, and displacement. Recognizing that their distillation produces potent brews (and complaining of his 1870s culture), Nietzsche proclaimed, "Mythless man stands eternally hungry."

Following T. S. Eliot and the other modernists, Faulkner repeatedly turned to myth and archetypal figures to create his own mythic tales, using, among others, Nietzsche's *The Birth of Tragedy*, Frazer's *The Golden Bough*, Bulfinch's *The Age of Fable*, Murray's *Manual of Mythology*, and since he referred to "the Christian myth," the King James version of the *Holy Bible*. Often using his source's specific words, Faulkner's allusions are deliberate; but because he chose universal themes like the quest or the castrated god, it is hardly surprising that source hunters find echoes of different myths behind the same characters and stories.

See also **Bible; Modernism**.

FURTHER READING

Dickerson, Mary Jane. "Some Sources of Faulkner's Myth in *As I Lay Dying*." *Mississippi Quarterly* 19 (1966): 132–142.

Vickery, John B. *Myth and Literature: Contemporary Theory and Practice*. Lincoln: University of Nebraska Press, 1966.

Yonce, Margaret. "Faulkner's 'Atthis' and 'Attis': Some Sources of Myth." *Mississippi Quarterly* 23 (1970): 289–298.

Virginia V. James Hlavsa

N

NAGANO. Faulkner visited Japan for three weeks in August 1955 as part of a round-the-world trip designed under the auspices of the U.S. Department of State, principally to participate in the Nagano Seminar Colloquies. From his arrival on August 1 to his departure for Manila on August 23, Faulkner was interviewed by the press, a group of writers, and editors of the literary journals. In Nagano, 140 miles northwest of Tokyo, he stayed at a Japanese-style inn for twelve days and talked with fifty Japanese professors of American literature in seven afternoon sessions. *Faulkner at Nagano* includes most of the interviews Faulkner undertook during his stay in Japan, his essays written on his visit to Japan, the Nobel Prize acceptance speech, and all the verbatim reproductions of the Nagano Colloquies. The texts of all the interviews and colloquies were later compiled into *Lion in the Garden* (84–198). The essays "Impressions of Japan" and "To the Youth of Japan" were, with the Nobel speech, reproduced in *Essays, Speeches & Public Letters by William Faulkner* (76–85).

The subjects raised by the Japanese scholars and writers ranged from Faulkner's philosophy of art, the nature of truth, racial issues, his literary influences and preferences, the content of his novels, and the meaning of the titles of his books to the problems of mothers-in-law, caused by the conservative family system in Japan. In discussing these topics Faulkner paid his listeners the ultimate compliment of treating their inquiries and comments as arising from a genuine concern for truth. His answers were filled with seriousness, sincerity, and a good sense of humor. Faulkner made penetrating and illuminating comments on a number of his own works, specifically *The Sound and the Fury*, "The Bear," and *A Fable*.

In the early interviews Faulkner stated his interest in Japanese culture and his desire to perceive the Japanese spirit and what makes all men human beings. Asked about what phases of Japanese culture he was interested in, Faulkner replied that it is a "culture of intellect," by which he meant the "rules which men should observe to get along best, of courtesy, of politeness, of courage at the right time.'' Faulkner further associated this ''culture of intellect'' with the ''samurai'' tradition in Japan. Later at the Nagano seminar, Faulkner attempted to find an analogy of patriarchal loyalty between Southern planter aristocracy and the Japanese samurai tradition.

At the sixth meeting at Nagano, Faulkner read from a book he was writing to be called *The American Dream*. He spoke of segregation, of how it was based on the fear that the Southern economy depended on cheap black labor. Faulkner affirmed the American spirit and asserted that democracy is the only salvation for the world. The Japanese participants were deeply moved by Faulkner's fervor. The chapter Faulkner read was later published as ''On Fear: The South in Labor.'' This essay was a follow-up of ''On Privacy (The American Dream: What Happened to It?),'' just published in *Harper's* that July. What makes the Nagano seminars valuable is how Faulkner managed to convey to the foreign audience the terrible dilemmas of the South and his effort to grapple with them.

Faulkner was liked and respected by all the Japanese people he met during his stays in Tokyo and Nagano, and his four-day visit to Kyoto. The Japanese admired the courtesy, politeness, and paternal qualities of the almost sixty-year-old Faulkner. His silences, modesty, and good manners were contrary to the Japanese preconception of the loud, aggressive American. Once he was liked, whatever words Faulkner uttered were taken as scripture. Thus despite some early difficulties, the Nagano seminars proved to be a success; Faulkner's mission as cultural ambassador to better Japanese-American cultural relations was superbly performed.

FURTHER READING

Blotner, Joseph, ed. ''Faulkner's Speech at Nagano, August 5, 1955.'' *Mississippi Quarterly* 35 (1982): 309–311.

Ikuko Fujihira

NATURE. Faulkner showed no more interest in theoretical physics than in anything else theoretical, yet his attention to ''nature'' goes beyond the usual sensations evoked by flora and fauna to register the pull of physical forces, the material substance of which things were composed. Few readers miss his evocation of the natural landscape: for instance, in *The Mansion*, how ''in the hills, all the land would be gold and crimson with hickory and gum and oak and maple, and the old fields warm with sage and splattered with scarlet sumac.'' But under the colorful land, there is the stuff of which it is made, the dirt itself—''the ground, dirt, the earth,'' the ''power and drag of the earth,'' and its relation to the solar system where ''[t]he sun had crossed the equator, in Libra now.''

Such elements were present from the origins of Yoknapatawpha, as in *Flags in the Dust*, whose evocations of the time when ''[m]an became amphibious and lived in mud'' introduce a cycle of nature that in turn becomes the emotional metaphor that tells how ''coming dazed out of sleep, out of the warm summer valleys where people lived . . . the cold peak of [Bayard's] stubborn despair stood bleakly among black and savage stars and the valleys were obscured with shadow.'' In *The Hamlet* he depicts the discovery ''that dawn, light, is not decanted onto earth from the sky, but instead is from the earth itself suspired.'' This discovery is extended into the chemistry of it, depicting the ''grass-roots and the roots of trees, dark in the blind dark of time's silt and rich refuse—the constant and unslumbering anonymous worm-glut and the inextricable known bones,'' producing eventually ''first root, then frond . . . from whose escaping tips like gas it rises.'' Similarly, Faulkner was attracted not only to sounds but to what made sound possible, in *The Hamlet* writing of how a voice lacked ''even the weight of breath to give it volume'' or capturing ''the very capacity of space and echo for reproducing noise.''

Very often these forays allow Faulkner to extend the life of otherwise trite comparisons. Thus, in *Absalom, Absalom!*, the metaphor of Ellen as a forgotten butterfly gains new depth as Faulkner follows the metaphor into ''the substanceless shell . . . impervious to . . . dissolution because of its very weightlessness'' until it becomes a ''powder-light paradox beneath the thousand pounds of marble monument.'' Or a common occurrence, such as the ''dustcloud in which the buggy moved,'' is compared to ''some old dead volcanic water refined to the oxygenless first principle of liquid,'' thus allowing displacement values drawn from physics: ''cubic foot for cubic foot of dust for cubic foot for cubic foot of horse and buggy.''

Such forays into chemical and physical description assist Faulkner in the development of the ironies that abound in his works. In *Absalom, Absalom!*, for example, he makes us well aware that the man ''plowing and planting and harvesting'' is himself destined one day to be ''translated quick into so much rich and rotting dirt,'' or how ''the dynamite which destroys the house and the family and maybe even the whole community'' was once ''old quiet chemicals that had rather be still and dark in the quiet earth.'' And often the irony is precisely that characters perceive metaphorically at precisely that point when physical reality is too much for them, as when Darl in *As I Lay Dying* sees ''the log [that] surged up out of the water . . . like Christ'' because he cannot face the reality represented by the river, ''skummed with flotsam and with thick soiled gouts of foam.''

What one might term the ''meta-biology'' of the fiction receives its fullest expression in *Requiem for a Nun*, where we are given a guided tour of earth as it proceeds through its evolutionary process, a tour quite accurate in the details poetically evoked. Here, for example, beneath the ''cotton taller than the head of a man on a horse'' and the ''density of brier and cane and vine'' is the ''rich deep black alluvial soil,'' and behind it ''the steamy chiaroscuro, untimed unseasoned winterless miasma not any one of water or earth or life yet all of each . . . that . . . vast incumbent ejaculation already fissionating in one boiling moil of litter from the celestial experimental Work Bench.''

FURTHER READING

Lind, Ilse Dusoir. "Faulkner and Nature." *Faulkner Studies* 1 (1980): 112–121.
Sherry, Charles. "Being Otherwise: Nature, History, and Tragedy in *Absalom, Absalom!*" *Arizona Quarterly* 45.3 (1989): 47–76.
Volpe, Edmond L. "Faulkner's 'Red Leaves': The Deciduation of Nature." *Studies in American Fiction* 3 (1975): 121–131.

Charles A. Peek

NEW HISTORICISM, a recent critical method, first developed during the late 1970s in Renaissance studies; its genealogy may be traced broadly in poststructuralism and Marxism and particularly in the work of Michel Foucault, who argues that subjectivity emerges from historically specific institutional practices. It draws on a deconstructive understanding of textuality and intertextuality and the structuralist Marxist position of Louis Althusser, who sees ideology as those unconscious systems of representation that mediate one's relation to everyday life. New Historical work is founded on two intertwined principles: The text is always historical, and history is always textual. This formulation articulates New Historicism's difference both from older forms of historical scholarship that tended to speak of the past in terms of unified world pictures and from New Criticism, which agreed with the modernist view of the work of art as autonomous and transcendent.

New Historicism takes the position that the institutions of a culture (church, school, family, law, medicine, etc.) produce an individual's subjectivity. But this production of subjectivity does not mean a reduction to historical determinism; what it means is that an individual's, including the artist's, agency is implicated in and constrained by concrete social practices.

New Historical studies of Faulkner began to appear in the latter half of the 1980s. Despite the French theoretical underpinnings of the method, New Historical work on Faulkner has been the exclusive province of American and British scholars. Their work generally is linked to that of the current generation of scholars who emphasize ideological issues surrounding Faulkner's treatment of racial, sexual, and class identities. Not all ideological analysis, however, is New Historical. Only those studies that see Faulkner's representation of race, gender, and class as embedded in other contemporary cultural and discursive practices of Faulkner's South participate in the New Historical project.

FURTHER READING

Greenblatt, Stephen. "Towards a Poetics of Culture." *The New Historicism*. Ed. H. Aram Veeser. New York: Routledge, 1989.
Kartiganer and Abadie, eds. *Faulkner and Ideology.*
Morris and Morris. *Reading Faulkner.*

John N. Duvall

NEW ORLEANS. William Faulkner's residence in New Orleans, in 1925 and 1926, was relatively brief, but its effect on his work was immense. In November 1924, he presented himself at the apartment of Sherwood Anderson and his wife in the Upper Pantalba building. Faulkner had worked briefly in 1921 in a New York bookstore Elizabeth Prall managed before her marriage to Anderson. If Anderson is to be believed, Faulkner arrived wearing a greatcoat into which numerous pockets had been sewn to transport bottles of whiskey. He told the Andersons and others in New Orleans that he drank to ease the severe pain in his head, resulting from a silver plate implanted there following a plane crash during the war. That 1924 stay in New Orleans was a short one, but on January 4, 1925, he was back, ready to learn what he could from Anderson. The older author was out of town, but Elizabeth offered Faulkner a spare room in the Pantalba apartment, where he would remain until Anderson returned at the end of February.

The French Quarter had become by that time more or less a slum, the white Creoles having left the area to Italians and Sicilians who had immigrated to the city at the end of the nineteenth century and to the blacks and Creoles of color. A number of factors contributed to making the Vieux Carré a gathering place for artists, writers, and assorted bohemian types. In the old Creole townhouses and cottages, rents were cheap; the food was tasty and exotic, a marked contrast to that in the rest of the United States; and despite Prohibition, liquor was readily available. Faulkner, a confirmed Francophile, was attracted to the romance of the Vieux Carré, a fact clearly demonstrated in the ''Mirrors of Chartres Street'' columns he wrote for the *Times-Picayune* newspaper and for *The Double Dealer*, an exciting new literary journal based in New Orleans. In addition, the presence of Sherwood Anderson, termed by Faulkner the ''father'' of his generation of writers, was an added incentive to remain. The Andersons would provide support, both moral and physical, for the aspiring young author.

At the end of February, when Anderson returned to the city, Faulkner moved into 624 Orleans Alley (now Pirate's Alley), where he and a newspaper reporter rented three rooms from the artist-architect William Spratling. There Faulkner could look out upon the garden of St. Louis Cathedral and observe the priests, nuns, altar boys, and communicants, a new experience for a north Mississippi native. He wrote regularly to his mother, describing his delight in the Quarter, its sights and its people. He was working on a novel, receiving help from the Andersons, and completed *Soldiers' Pay* in five months, on May 11, 1925. He also continued to write sketches, to enjoy a busy social life with his Quarter friends, ''my New Orleans gang,'' including authors Roark Bradford, Lyle Saxon, Hamilton Basso, Oliver Lafarge, and Anita Loos, and to visit the Gulf Coast, where he sometimes saw Helen Baird, a young woman to whom he was strongly attracted.

On July 7, 1925, Faulkner sailed with William Spratling for Europe, where he remained for almost six months, returning to the United States in late December 1925. By February 1926, he was back in New Orleans, sharing an apartment with Spratling around the corner from Pirate's Alley. For the rest of that year, he shuttled between New Orleans, Pascagoula, and Oxford, working on a number of manuscripts, including his second novel, *Mosquitoes*, a parody of the bohemian life of the Quarter, and fiction that would ultimately become *Flags in the Dust* and *The Hamlet*. In addition, he wrote the introduction and labels for Spratling's caricatures of their friends and others in *Sherwood Anderson and Other Famous Creoles*.

Faulkner's trip to Oxford for Christmas 1926 ended the New Orleans period, though he returned periodically, most notably in 1934 for the opening of Shushan airport and in 1951 to receive the French Legion of Honor. Although he lost touch with most of the "Famous Creoles" circle, he remained friends with Helen Baird, who continued to fascinate him, even after she married another man. The influence of New Orleans on his work was powerful: From Anderson he learned much about his art, and the Quarter and the people he met and observed inspired him. In addition to the "New Orleans Sketches" and *Mosquitoes*, several works use the city as setting, including *Pylon*, about the Shushan airport opening, and *The Wild Palms*, in which Faulkner's passion for Helen Baird is reflected. In the French Quarter, Faulkner surely found the kind of freedom another Mississippian, Tennessee Williams, termed "integral" to his career, a freedom that, in contrast with the Calvinist upbringing of both writers, supplied them with important materials for their works.

W. Kenneth Holditch

NEW ORLEANS SKETCHES, published originally as a collection in 1957, revised and expanded in 1958, and edited by Carvel Collins, is a collection of sixteen early stories and sketches from Faulkner's apprentice years as a fiction writer, reflecting his decision to give up his desire to be a poet. Suggestive of his later abilities to explore multiple narrative perspectives and some of his central themes and character types, the stories are of interest primarily in terms of what they anticipate in the later fiction. All but one of the sketches were originally published in 1925 in the New Orleans *Times-Picayune*; an early text of the selection entitled "New Orleans" had appeared in *The Double Dealer*, a New Orleans literary magazine.

"New Orleans," dated January–February 1925, is a series of vignettes and prose poems employing various narrative techniques, including interior monologue, about various people one might meet on the streets of the city. These include a number of outsider characters and thus anticipate such aliens in the later fiction as Quentin Compson and Joe Christmas. The "Wealthy Jew," while playing upon conventional anti-Semitic stereotypes, praises the Jew for his longevity and history; "The Priest," which focuses on the conflict between flesh and spirit, contains descriptive passages reminiscent of Faulkner's poetry and anticipates later representations of Christianity and Catholicism. Other sketches of interest include "Frankie and Johnny," based on the folk legend about awe-struck lovers; "The Longshoreman," whose African American speaker anticipates later representations of race; "The Cop," whose treatment of childhood innocence versus adult disappointment represents a frequent Faulkner theme; and "Magdalen," which uses the "fallen woman" motif Faulkner later developed with Caddy Compson and Temple Drake.

The remainder of the sketches were originally published in the *Times-Picayune*. Most interesting and significant for a reading of Faulkner's later fictional techniques, themes, and characters are "Damon and Pythias Unlimited," which deals with a trip to the races and employs the confidence man motif associated with Flem Snopes and the influence of southwestern humor on Faulkner's fiction; "Jealousy," which deals with a husband's inability to trust his wife and the waiter who works for him and calls to mind the pistol murder in *Absalom, Absalom!*; "Out of Nazareth," a frame story about ideal beauty and the making of the artist with heavily Christian symbolism and impressionistic descriptions resembling *Light in August* and other works; "The Kingdom of God," which relays the experience of an idiot figure, anticipating Benjy in *The Sound and the Fury*, who admires his narcissus during one of his bootlegger brother's deliveries; "The Cobbler," which uses interior monologue to show the loss of romantic idealism, the failure of the American dream, and the inability to recapture the past—frequent Faulkner themes; "Sunset," an almost tragic story reflecting and rendering exotic an African American's experience of trying to find his way back to Africa; "The Liar," which deals with Ek, a teller of tall tales in the tradition of southwestern humor (and anticipates later works such as *The Hamlet*), and his frustration over accidentally telling the truth in front of a murderer; and "Country Mice," an anecdote including aviation references about the failure to make a successful transfer of liquor due to cops who turn out to be tricksters rather than "hicks" as city bootleggers suspected.

FURTHER READING

Watson, James G. "New Orleans, *The Double Dealer*, and 'New Orleans.' " *American Literature* 56 (1984): 214–226.

Dean Shackelford

NEW YORK CRITICS. Despite their radical political and urban ethnic backgrounds, the New York intellectuals wrote often and sympathetically about Faulkner. Poet Delmore Schwartz contributed an early essay on Faulkner to the *Southern Review* in 1941, and *Partisan Review* printed some of Faulkner's fiction and regularly reviewed his post–World War II work. The first major study of Faulkner was written by New Yorker Irving Howe. His *William Faulkner: A Critical Study* (1951; rev. ed. 1962) recognized, for instance, that Faulkner displayed a "wider range and deeper sounding of the Negro character than any other American writer" (131). The New York critic with the most long-standing interest in Faulkner was Alfred Kazin. In *On Native Grounds* (Harcourt, Brace, 1942) Kazin wrote ambivalently of Faulkner, noting his "lack of a center" and "greatness moving in a void" (457, 459). Yet Kazin's essay "The Stillness of

Light in August'' (1958) offered a much more sympathetic view of Faulkner. The novel depicted ''the search of the 'stranger,' *l'etranger*, to become a man'' (265). Overall, the New York critics contributed to an understanding of Faulkner as a modern, as much as a Southern, writer.

FURTHER READING

Kazin, Alfred. ''The Stillness of *Light in August*.'' *Faulkner: Three Decades of Criticism*, ed. Hoffman and Vickery. 247–265.

Richard H. King

NOBEL PRIZE ACCEPTANCE SPEECH. Faulkner's brief but powerful speech upon accepting the 1949 Nobel Prize for Literature was delivered on December 10, 1950, and reprinted in world newspapers the next day. A slightly revised version was printed in the *New York Herald Tribune Book Review* on January 14, 1951, and has been anthologized often (e.g., *ESPL* 119–121). The speech attests to the power of the human voice. Even though Faulkner's own voice in Stockholm was largely inaudible due to his rapid articulation and his standing too far from the microphone, once in print the address had an immediate impact for its concise statement of affirmation. Those who wish to hear the speech reread by Faulkner should consult the Caedmon recording, *Faulkner Reads from His Works* (CDL 51035), recorded in New York in 1954.

Faulkner's address transcends its Cold War context as powerfully as it reflects it. The speech encourages its audience to look beyond immediate concerns (''When will I be blown up?'') to confront ''the problems of the human spirit in conflict with itself.'' These and other phrases have tantalized Faulkner's readers for generations, as has the paradoxical relationship between the speech's insistence that humanity will ''endure and prevail'' and the darker vision of that promise in much of Faulkner's previous fiction.

The speech's negation of terror and apocalypse (''I refuse to accept this'') is part of the fabric of resistance that appears in novels such as *Go Down, Moses*, *A Fable, Requiem for a Nun*, the *Snopes* trilogy, and *The Reivers*. On receiving the Nobel Prize, Faulkner declared that it is the writer's duty to construct alternatives to inherited predicaments and to provide the bases on which human beings may ''refuse to accept'' them. The writer's task is thus to remind humanity of its potentiality. Although not always accepted at face value, this speech has influenced the way readers understand Faulkner more than any other critical statement he uttered in his lifetime.

FURTHER READING

Grimwood, Michael. ''The Self-Parodic Context of Faulkner's Nobel Prize Speech.'' *Southern Review* 15 (1979): 366–375.

Joseph R. Urgo

"NOTE ON SHERWOOD ANDERSON, A," published in the June 1953 *Atlantic* and collected in *Essays, Speeches & Public Letters by William Faulkner*, is Faulkner's evaluation of his literary mentor, his memoir of their association, and a sort of apology for having offended Anderson. Faulkner identifies Anderson's literary virtues as simplicity, purity, fidelity, and integrity; and he comments on the older author's anger at Ernest Hemingway and Faulkner, two disciples who, Anderson felt, had turned against him—in Faulkner's case, by the preface to *Sherwood Anderson and Other Famous Creoles* in which Faulkner imitates what he termed Anderson's "primer-like style." In the later essay Faulkner credits Anderson with having taught him to be what one is and to write about his own region, concluding that, despite faults, Anderson was "a giant" in a world of "pygmies."

W. Kenneth Holditch

"NYMPHOLEPSY." When Faulkner wrote the story "Nympholepsy" early in 1925, it was the third time he created the image of a young man climbing a hill. In 1922, *The Mississippian*, the student newspaper of the University of Mississippi at Oxford, had published a very short sketch called "The Hill," in which, as Michel Gresset puts it, "nothing happens; only, the character had failed to reach an awareness of 'something' that was offered him for revelation" ("Faulkner's 'The Hill' " 6). Three years later, in the story "Out of Nazareth," published in the New Orleans *Times-Picayune*, Faulkner again presents a man climbing a hill, this time not a simple laborer as in "The Hill," however, but a beautiful young man with "poetic sensibility and inspiring faith" (1974 *FAB* 413). "Nympholepsy," written not long afterward in New Orleans, though it would remain unpublished until *Uncollected Stories* (1979), combines the two earlier stories in that it takes up again the young laborer of "The Hill" but endows him with some insight and poetic awareness. Having reached the summit, and seeing a woman walking in the descending sun, there is for a moment "an old sharp beauty behind his eyes." Following her through the fields and the woods, he falls into a stream, where he has the sensation of briefly touching her body, but she escapes him. "In a fine agony of disappointment," he flings himself on the ground, and "feeling twigs beneath his face and arm," he cries out: "I wouldn't have hurt you . . . I wouldn't have hurt you at all." At this voicing of his anguish, the young man feels his muscles relax, and the moon can soothe him now, making him briefly forget the morrow.

The theme of the young man climbing a hill, and finally "finding his voice," however briefly, can be linked to Faulkner's own experience of his writership at the time. The period of the early 1920s marks the time in which Faulkner tried to effect a transition "between the poetry behind and the fiction ahead" (1974 *FAB* 332), away from poetry that "was no longer working as it had" toward prose that "was not yet working as it would" (Minter 41–42) and toward his first experiments with using "his own little postage stamp of native soil."

FURTHER READING

Gresset, Michel. "Faulkner's 'The Hill.' " *Southern Literary Journal* 6.2 (1974): 3–18.
Meriwether, James B. "Nympholepsy." *Mississippi Quarterly* 26 (1973): 403–409.

Ineke Bockting

O

"ODOR OF VERBENA, AN," the last of the seven chapters that make up Faulkner's novel *The Unvanquished* (1938). "An Odor of Verbena" is the only section of the novel not previously published as a short story. (After finishing the story in 1937 Faulkner sent it to the *Saturday Evening Post*, where it was rejected.) Although best seen in the context of the whole novel, to which it furnishes the conclusion by showing us Bayard as an adult, "An Odor of Verbena" can also be read as a short story on its own.

The action of the story occurs in October 1873, eight years after the conclusion of "Skirmish at Sartoris." Bayard, now a twenty-four-year-old law student at the University of Mississippi, learns that his father has been shot by Redmond, a former partner now turned enemy, and that he, Bayard, is now "The Sartoris." Knowing that according to the Southern gentleman's code of honor he is expected to face and kill his father's murderer, or be killed by him, he nevertheless decides, without telling anyone, that he will repudiate this duty as a matter of principle.

When he rides home we learn in flashback that the men John Sartoris has killed include a former soldier who helped vote him out of command of his infantry regiment; Sartoris was replaced by Colonel Sutpen, of *Absalom, Absalom!* Bayard in fact prefers Sutpen's less bloody "dream" to his father's and has told Drusilla so. Drusilla (his cousin and his father's wife) disagrees. She does an odd thing: She asks Bayard to kiss her (which he does, twice) and then says he must "tell" his father. Presumably she wishes to compromise the pacifist message about which she and Bayard have been arguing (Hinkle and McCoy 195), but most readers have felt that she means for Bayard to tell about the exchange of kisses. Whatever it is that Bayard "tells," Sartoris pays no attention but instead gives his son the kind of legacy speech that the dying King David gives to Solomon: He is tired of killing men, he says; he has acted as the times demanded, but now in a new, more legalistic era, he expects Bayard, trained in the law, to carry on the Sartoris agenda without violence.

Bayard arrives home; his demeanor as Drusilla presents him formally with the dueling pistols shocks her with the recognition that he does not intend to face Redmond. In the morning, however, Bayard does confront Redmond in his office in town. Redmond is ready for the classic guns-drawn confrontation; but Bayard simply walks toward his desk, unarmed. Redmond fires two shots, aiming wide, and then leaves town. Having acquitted himself idiosyncratically but courageously, Bayard wins puzzled approval on the grounds that perhaps there has indeed been too much killing in his family. When Bayard reaches home, he finds that Drusilla has gone, leaving on his pillow a sprig of verbena, her personal symbol of courage.

The story is easily read as that of a young man redefining "courage." Against the background of war and violence, "An Odor of Verbena" presents a new kind of courage, the principled self-risk meant to appeal to the conscience of an enemy. Thus his father's principles of vengeance have become Bayard's principles of conscience and law—a triumph of sorts for Bayard, and perhaps for civilization, though the storytellers of Yoknapatawpha will persist in making John and his heroic age, not his son Bayard, their chief subject.

Controversial in the story are the motives of Sartoris and Drusilla—and Faulkner. How close are the author's values to those of Bayard, his nineteenth-century narrator? Some readers regret Bayard's seeming recantation of the vengeance code he held to earlier. Others regret Drusilla's lapse into an overwrought upholding of the code. In particular, contemporary readers are uneasy at Bayard's relapse into racialist attitudes in demoting Ringo from the friend and companion of earlier stories to the mere "boy" of this one. We have to learn, however, to separate the Bayard who narrates within a nineteenth-century plantation context from the Faulkner who narrates such works as *Light in August*, "There Was a Queen," *Absalom, Absalom!*, and *Go Down, Moses*. Hearing Bayard's tale from the immediate post–Civil War period, we have to think about it in much the same way that Quentin and Shreve, in *Absalom, Absalom!*, think about the stories of the Sutpens that they have inherited from that period.

FURTHER READING

Donaldson, Susan V. "Dismantling the *Saturday Evening Post* Reader: *The Unvanquished* and 'Changing Horizons of Expectations.' " *Faulkner and Popular Culture*, ed. Fowler and Abadie. 179–195.

Frazer, Winifred L. "Faulkner and Womankind—'No Bloody Moon.' " *Faulkner and Women*, ed. Fowler and Abadie. 162–179.

Hinkle, James C., and Robert McCoy. *Reading Faulkner*: The Unvanquished. Jackson: University Press of Mississippi, 1995.

Taylor, Nancy Dew. " 'Moral Housekeeping' and Colonel Sartoris's Dream." *Mississippi Quarterly* 37 (1985): 353–364.

Witt, Robert W. "On Faulkner and Verbena." *Southern Literary Journal* 27 (1994): 73–
    84.

Glenn Meeter

OLD BEN. "An anachronism indomitable and invincible out of an old dead
time, a phantom, epitome and apotheosis of the old wild life which the little
puny humans swarmed and hacked at in a fury of abhorrence and fear like
pygmies about the ankles of a drowsing elephant." Such is Faulkner's Old Ben,
the actual bear with mythic attributes, "too big for the very country which was
its constricting scope," according to the old man Isaac as he narrates "The
Bear," the centerpiece of *Go Down, Moses*. During the boy Isaac's and his adult
guardians' annual December pilgrimage into the wilderness, the last day was
reserved for a battle with the bear. Or, rather, the battle was a self-testing with
no real expectations of defeating him, since he was "no living creature but only
the wilderness," as Isaac puts it. Symbol, then, to all, Old Ben is "the man"
to Sam; "alma mater" to Isaac; and finally, at his death by the jaws of the great
dog Lion and the unrelenting knife of the character Boon Hogganbeck, the end
of an era: "Well," murmurs Major de Spain, looking down at Ben as he dies,
in tribute and with the tenor of remorse.

FURTHER READING

Brunauer, Dalma H. "Worshipping the Bear-God." *Christianity and Literature* 23.3
    (1974): 7–35.
Schliefer, Ronald. "Faulkner's Storied Novel: *Go Down, Moses* and the Translation of
    Time." *Modern Fiction Studies* 28 (1982): 109–127.
Zender, Karl F. "Reading in 'The Bear.' " *Faulkner Studies* 1 (1980): 91–99.

Marion Tangum

OLDHAM, LIDA ESTELLE. *See* **Faulkner, Lida Estelle Oldham**.

"OLD MAN," one of the two narratives that comprise Faulkner's novel *The
Wild Palms*, published in 1939. When Malcolm Cowley sought in 1946 to publish "Old Man" in *The Portable Faulkner* separately from its original inclusion
in *The Wild Palms*, Faulkner gave him his blessing. But in August he nevertheless indicated to Saxe Commins that "Old Man" would lose something by
the separation: "Dismembering 'THE WILD PALMS' will in my opinion destroy the over-all impact which I intended" (*SL* 352). Despite Faulkner's protest,
a focus on "Old Man" illuminates the force of the Mississippi River in the
throes of a ten-year flood—its character or, rather, its force *as* a character—and
simultaneously exemplifies its inability to defeat a human being armed with
single-minded intent. No matter the overpowering brutality of the river's attack
on him, there is nothing that the convict, the story's central human character,
cannot withstand. No doubt that is the reason Faulkner, in a letter to Malcolm
Cowley, August 16, 1945, compared "Old Man" to *As I Lay Dying*, down-

playing his success in the latter and pointing instead to the power of "Old Man." In Cowley's opinion, "It is the only other story of the Mississippi that can be set beside *Huckleberry Finn* without shriveling under the comparison" (*PF* 540).

In "Old Man," the Mississippi is indeed Old Man: as alive, as apparently premeditative in its viciousness, as commanding as any creature in American literature. Note, for example, what the convict (handed a skiff and a paddle and charged with the mission of rescuing a woman in a tree and a man on the roof of a cotton house) is confronted with as he begins to carry out his charge: Ten feet above where it had been just a moment before, the river "reared, stooping; the crest of it swirled like the mane of a galloping horse and, phosphorescent too, fretted and flickered like the fire." But the convict, unable to swim, watching "entire trees leaping and diving like porpoises, . . . in an expression of aghast and incredulous amazement, continued to paddle directly into it." He went through the motions of paddling, anyway, as he waited for a chance to scream but never had the time to do so. Instead, the river "regurgitated him onto the wild bosom of the Father of Waters."

The story continues as it begins: a humanizing of the unrelenting force that the convict unrelentingly, and rather stupidly, refuses to bow to. We see him "trying with his fragment of splintered plank merely to keep the skiff intact and float among the houses and trees and dead animals (the entire towns, stores, residences, parks and farmyards, which leaped and played about him like fish)." Meanwhile, he finds the woman in the tree who is his charge, who greets him with "It's taken you awhile." He remains philosophical about what the narrator describes as "the outrageous idea of a volume of moving water toppling forward, its crest frothed and shredded like fangs" and pauses to draw an analogy: "[T]he River was now doing what it liked to do, had waited patiently the ten years in order to do, as a mule will work for you ten years for the privilege of kicking you once." His ability to view fear in perspective is evident, too: "[I]f you just held on long enough a time would come in fear after which it would no longer be agony at all but merely a kind of horrible outrageous itching."

There is a certain humor in both that philosophic perspective and in his paradoxical total indifference to the woman—dislike even—and his undaunted commitment to complete his charge and deliver her to safety, as well as his unrelenting search for the man on the cotton house, undaunted by the fact that he is miles away from where the man would have been and clearly days too late. He wanted to do his job "right," when no one, especially the prison warden who had proclaimed him dead, would have expected or believed he could have done so. As a most frequently quoted line in the story reveals, spoken by the convict when he finally finds Mississippi soil and a prison officer, to the convict a job to do is a job to do: "Yonder's your boat, and here's the woman. But I never did find that bastard on the cotton house." Very much to his liking, he is rewarded for his efforts with an extra ten years tacked on to his sentence.

FURTHER READING

Zender, Karl F. "Faulkner and the Power of Sound." *PMLA* 99 (1984): 89–108.
———. "Money and Matter in *Pylon* and *The Wild Palms*." *Faulkner Journal* 1.2 (1986): 17–29.

Marion Tangum

OLD MAN (film). Screenwriter Horton Foote adapted the material entitled "Old Man" from Faulkner's 1939 novel *The Wild Palms* for a Hallmark Hall of Fame television movie, which was telecast by CBS on February 9, 1997. The telefilm is a remake of the 1958 television version of the same story, also scripted by Foote. When the Mississippi River—personified as "Old Man"—causes a disastrous flood, J. J. Taylor, a convict, is ordered to rescue Addie, a pregnant woman, who is stranded by the flood (both characters are nameless in Faulkner's story). Taylor eventually gets her back home and fulfills his promise to return to prison. The telefilm effectively fleshes out the two principal characters; but its ending, with the prospect of future happiness for the pair, is at odds not only with Faulkner's novel but also with Foote's original script. For this reason Foote sought, unsuccessfully, to disassociate himself from the Hallmark project.

FURTHER READING

Mills, Bart. "Faulkner Story Is Rich with Heroism, Humanity." *Chicago Tribune* 15 February 1997, sec. 11:5.
"William Faulkner's *Old Man*." *TV Guide* 14 February 1997: 108.

Gene D. Phillips

"OLD PEOPLE, THE," a short story by Faulkner, first published in the September 1940 issue of *Harper's* and then reworked for use in *Go Down, Moses*. "Oleh Chief, . . . Grandfather": This salute to the phantom buck, "taller than any man, . . . Its head high and the eye not proud and not haughty but just full and wild and unafraid," is offered by Sam Fathers, one of the literal Old People to whom the title refers. The statement implies broadly inclusive possibilities for the title, revealed as the chapter unfolds. Those possibilities include not only individuals—Sam and Jobaker (and Boon Hogganbeck, too), the last of the Chickasaws in Yoknapatawpha County; Issetibbeha and Ikkemotubbe, the royal lineage from which Sam's blood has sprung, whose stories are told here; but especially their oneness with the life of the wilderness—their peer relationship to that life within it, which Isaac sees as the special purview of those Old People.

"The Old People" is told by the boy Isaac as he remembers it when he is in his eighties. The story captures the nostalgia of Isaac as boy and old man and his idolizing of Sam as the person whom he thought could literally take him back to the old times:

As [Sam] talked about those old times and those dead and vanished men of another race, gradually to the boy those old times would cease to be old times and would become a part of the boy's present, not only as if they happened yesterday but as if they were still happening, the men who walked through them actually walking in breath and air and casting an actual shadow on the earth they had not quitted. And more: as if some of them had not happened yet but would occur tomorrow, until at last it would seem to the boy that he himself had not come into existence yet.

This last sentence becomes prophetic, for Isaac's adult life never does quite come into existence, for reasons more complicated than his idyllic view of those past times but enabled by them. This chapter is thus particularly important to the whole of Isaac's story in *Go Down, Moses*. For example, in "Delta Autumn," "he seemed to see the two of them—himself and the wilderness—as coevals, his own span, . . . transmitted to him . . . from . . . old Sam Fathers who taught him to hunt . . . the two spans running together, not toward oblivion, nothingness, but into a dimension free of both time and space."

Obviously, Sam Fathers does much more than teach the boy Isaac to hunt. As Isaac puts it, looking back on it at the age of more than eighty, "[I]t was he . . . who was the guest here and Sam Fathers' voice the mouthpiece of the host," telling him of the old days and the Old People and taking him into that time as well, so that his entry into the wilderness each winter was entry into that old time itself: "Sam Fathers marked him indeed, not as a mere hunter, but with something Sam had had in his turn of his vanished and forgotten people." For Isaac, then, those people and those old times would be brought to life again—but, ultimately, as the novel reveals, with a price that Isaac pays. He does not ever really live beyond them.

As a hunter, too, Sam marked him, dipping "his hands in the hot smoking blood and wiping them across the boy's face" when he shot his first deer. The experience of the hunt itself is unforgettably told here. But its power is as symbol for Isaac, who "would never hear that shot nor remember even the shock of the gun-butt." What he did remember was "the old dark man sired on both sides by savage kings, who had marked him, . . . the hands, the touch, the first worthy blood which he had been found . . . worthy to draw, joining him and the man forever."

Sam is important to Isaac as symbol of a past people and time that the boy (and man) Isaac embraced as eternal: a time—or timelessness—in which all life in the wilderness was embraced, in which, as Isaac's cousin Cass explained, "all the blood hot and strong for living, pleasuring, that has soaked back into it" may find room to roam in "places still unchanged from what they were." Sam is representative of that time, perceiver of that phantom life and imparter of that perception to Isaac, who will, forever, salute it: "Oleh, Grandfather."

FURTHER READING

Harrison, James. "Faulkner's 'The Old People.'" *Explicator* 44 (Winter 1986): 41.
Millgate, Michael. "William Faulkner: Tales of a Grandfather." *Essays by Divers Hands: Being the Transactions of the Royal Society of Literature*. Ed. Richard Faber. Wolfeboro, N.H.: Boydell, 1988. 41–58.

Sundquist, Eric J. "Faulkner, Race, and the Forms of American Fiction." *Faulkner and*
       Race, ed. Fowler and Abadie. 1–34.

Marion Tangum

"ONCE ABOARD THE LUGGER," a short story by Faulkner, exists in two
distinct versions. Perhaps written in 1926, the first version was submitted to
Scribner's in November 1928 but was rejected. It was published in *Contempo*
in 1932, reprinted in *Lillabulero* in 1967, and collected in *Uncollected Stories*.
The story is told by a member of a four-man crew of alcohol smugglers. His
companions are the captain, Pete (horribly seasick), and a black man. From New
Orleans, the men sail to an uninhabited island to retrieve the alcohol. Darkness,
wild cattle, mosquitoes, and shifting sand make for a miserable and slow recovery effort. By 3:00 A.M., the task is completed, and the men sleep.

In December 1928, *Scribner's* received another copy of "Once Aboard the
Lugger," most likely the second version. It, too, was rejected and remained
unpublished until its appearance in *Uncollected Stories*. Whereas the first version
is dark with the cover of night, "Lugger" (II) is dark with violence and morbidity. It begins at daylight with the narrator's efforts to repair the pump. Another boat comes broadside, the crew boards, and in the ensuing action, the
pirates kill the cook and Pete and take the liquor. The captain and narrator are
left to return home.

FURTHER READING

Bonner, Thomas, Jr. " 'Once Aboard the Lugger': An Uncollected Faulkner Story."
       Notes on Modern American Literature 3 (1978): item 8.

Diane Brown Jones

"ON FEAR: THE SOUTH IN LABOR," an essay by Faulkner. The central
question in "On Fear," which first appeared in the June 1956 issue of *Harper's*
and was reprinted in *Essays, Speeches & Public Letters by William Faulkner*,
was what the South had to fear in the emerging racial crisis. States' rights,
Faulkner insisted, could no longer provide a refuge from desegregation; nor
could a preference for inequality: "[T]o be against equality because of race or
color is like living in Alaska and being against snow." He also noted the importance of America's commitment to equality in global terms and praised the
great progress Africans had made rising from alleged primitive conditions in
Africa with hardly any help from whites. As always, he warned against racial
polarization, here in global terms.

Richard H. King

"ON PRIVACY" (*Harper's*, July 1955), one of the very few discursive essays
Faulkner wrote and published in his later career, is best understood against the
background of Faulkner's long resistance to having his life or those of family
members examined in the press. Faulkner had begun to achieve national noto-

riety in the late 1930s, when a cover story by Robert Cantwell (who would later write several essays on the Fa[u]lkner family) appeared in *Time* (January 23, 1939) in conjunction with the publication of *The Wild Palms*. Within a few years, Malcolm Cowley proposed to do a profile of Faulkner in *Life*, similar to one he had done on Hemingway, but Faulkner refused to cooperate. Moreover, in collaborating on Cowley's introduction to *The Portable Faulkner*, Faulkner asked that biographical material be kept to an absolute minimum. Eventually, Robert Coughlan was assigned by *Life* to do a two-part story on Faulkner for the magazine (September 28 and October 5, 1953), which soon became the substance of *The Private World of William Faulkner*. By 1954, Bennett Cerf—a media personality himself and chief of the editors at Random House—was asking Faulkner to accede to a cover story in *Time* "to synchronize with the publication of [*A Fable*]." Faulkner continued to refuse, and his editors acquiesced.

Like many of Faulkner's writings, "On Privacy" evolved through several drafts. The germ of the essay appears in a letter to Donald Klopfer, an editor at Random House, during the exchanges of 1954. In it, Faulkner is prophetic about the intrusions into privacy that can occur in the guise of "Freedom of the Press": "One individual can protect himself from another individual's freedom, but when monied organizations such as the press . . . begin to federate under moral catchwords . . . in the structure of which all individual members or practitioners are absolved of all moral restraint, God help us all" (*SL* 366). His ideas were expanded in a draft essay Faulkner sent to Saxe Commins, titled "Freedom: American Style" (*FCF* 132–137), which narrates the genesis of Faulkner's concerns. In its final form, "On Privacy" does not advance a novel legal argument about the so-called right to privacy, but it is an effective personal plea for his readers to consider the moral consequences that ensue in what we now recognize as a culture of celebrity.

FURTHER READING

Hahn, Stephen. "William Faulkner on Privacy." *Columbia Library Columns* 38.3 (1989): 27–35.

Stephen Hahn

ORDER OF ANDRÉS BELLO, THE, Venezuela's most prestigious civilian honor, was presented to Faulkner on April 6, 1961, during his U.S. State Department visit to Caracas. Upon receipt of the award, named after the famous Venezuelan poet, Faulkner delivered a Spanish translation of his one-page speech, the original manuscript of which is now in the Brodsky Collection. In words, phrases, and ideas that echo the Nobel Prize speech, Faulkner celebrates the artist's attempt "to put into some more durable form than his own fragile and ephemeral life—in paint or music or marble or the covers of a book—that which he has learned in his brief spell of breathing—the passion and hope, the beauty and horror and humor—of frail and fragile and indomitable man struggling and suffering and triumphing amid the conflicts of his own heart, in the human condition.''

FURTHER READING

Brodsky, Louis Daniel. ''The 1961 Andrés Bello Award: William Faulkner's Original Acceptance Speech.'' *Studies in Bibliography* 39 (1986): 277–281.

Louis Daniel Brodsky

P

"PANTALOON IN BLACK," the third story in *Go Down, Moses*, is both a powerful installment in Faulkner's brooding 1942 rumination about race relations in the South and a tale that stands independently as a portrait in extended mourning and almost inconsolable grief. The story opens as Rider, a black sawmill worker of near legendary physical prowess, furiously shovels dirt onto the grave of his wife Mannie; it ends with Rider being lynched for murdering a white man. Between these melodramatic events lies the story itself—an account of Rider's existential arc toward a violent, even tragic destiny. That Faulkner can render a black man's consciousness with sympathy and understanding tends to be overlooked by those who claim that Faulkner could write *about* blacks but was not able to plumb their psychological depths. Indeed, "Pantaloon in Black" often has the look and feel of the stories that Richard Wright, African American writer and fellow Mississippian, wrote during the 1940s, published posthumously as *Eight Men* (1961).

Faulkner's narrative perspective allows us to see as Rider sees, with a growing awareness of what his life with Mannie was and what it could no longer be: "his eye touching the objects—post and tree and field and house and hill—her eyes had lost." As Hoke Perkins points out, the title "Pantaloon in Black" suggests the comic butt of cruel jokes from Italian comedy; but Rider is the buffoon only to such whites as the deputy sheriff who has the story's last ironic words. Nor is he a black version of Shakespeare's Hamlet. Rather, Rider is a man at odds with Life itself and especially with the God, who "come messin wid me." Although his extended family and fellow mill hands offer their support, Rider cannot adjust to a life stripped of the "fire in the hearth" that symbolizes the stability of his domestic life with Mannie: the daily regimen of hard work, clean clothes, a warm meal. Unlike Lucas Beauchamp (whose story "The Fire and the Hearth" precedes Rider's in *Go Down, Moses*), Rider is reduced to raw emotion. Neither bootleg liquor nor extraordinary feats of strength can quiet his unquiet mind. As he puts it, "Hit looks like Ah just cant quit thinking. Look lack Ah just cant quit." His overpowering grief causes him to act strangely and eventually to cut the throat of the white boss whose crooked dice games had been cheating his black workers for years. If it is true that many of the story's details—from the jug of whiskey with its cob stopper to the straight razor Rider wears inside his shirt suspended by a loop of cotton string— suggest a stereotype, it is even truer that Rider's pain, his *humanity*, is what we watch as he moves inexorably toward death.

Faulkner forces readers not only to see Rider as a person but, more important, to accord him large measures of our empathy. All of this makes the concluding section a bitterly ironic study in contrapuntal rhythms. Here, a deputy sheriff offers his assessment of blacks in general and Rider in particular: "[T]hey [blacks] ain't human. They look like a man and they walk on their hind legs like a man . . . but when it comes to the normal human feelings, they might just as well be a damn herd of wild buffaloes." It may be that the deputy falls back on the traditions of Southern race prejudice because he, too, cannot bear to "think" about what has unfolded before his very eyes and that his efforts to share what happened with his wife are really efforts to convince himself about assumptions now cast into doubt. This line of speculation may give the deputy far too much credit; even more clearly, his wife has no interest whatsover in thinking about Rider at all. As she puts it in the story's unflinching, crushingly ironic lines: "I think if you eat any supper in this house you'll do it in the next five minutes. . . . I'm going to clear this table then and I'm going to the picture show."

"Pantaloon in Black" is not among the charmed circle of Faulkner stories widely anthologized or written about; but it suggests a truth about our best fiction writers: that literature is a way of experiencing another person's experience. This includes the possibility of a white male Southerner writing sensitively about blacks.

FURTHER READING

Perkins, Hoke. " 'Ah Just Can't Quit Thinking': Faulkner's Black Razor Murderers." *Faulkner and Race*, ed. Fowler and Abadie. 222–235.
Stephens, Rosemary. "Mythical Elements of 'Pantaloon in Black.' " *University of Mississippi Studies in English* 11 (1971): 45–51.
Taylor, Walter. "Faulkner's Pantaloon: The Negro Anomaly at the Heart of *Go Down, Moses*." *American Literature* 44 (1972): 430–444.

Sanford Pinsker

PARIS. "As all roads lead to Paris, all of us are now there." So Gertrude Stein put it in her *Autobiography of Alice B. Toklas*, and indeed, at one point or another during the era of High Modernism, they all came to Paris: Ernest Hemingway, E. E. Cummings, Robert Frost, Ezra Pound, T. S. Eliot, F. Scott Fitzgerald, Nathanael West, John Dos Passos, Edith Wharton, Robert McAlmon,

Henry Miller, Djuna Barnes, Anaïs Nin, Sherwood Anderson, Katherine Anne Porter, and William Faulkner, among others. For aspiring American writers who sought to modernize themselves, a sojourn of some length in Paris—the world capital of the avant-garde movements—was inevitable and obligatory. Paris exerted its own gravitational pull, but there were also many forces that drove the "expatriate" migration from America, of which the legal restriction on the consumption of alcohol was representative and symptomatic (the Prohibition lasted from 1920 to 1933). Paris, in contrast, in Stein's words, was where "the twentieth century was." It was a place that encouraged the artistic and the experimental and the bohemian life; it was a place where one could, without disapprobation, spend long hours in the cafes of Montparnasse, drinking legally and, as Faulkner notes in his letters home, cheaply. One could go to the galleries and museums and bookstores or simply stroll as a flaneur along the Left Bank of the Seine or through the Luxembourg Gardens, meditating, observing, storing up impressions for later artistic transfiguration. Faulkner wrote to his mother on August 30, 1925, "Think of a country where an old man, if he wants to, can spend his whole time with toy ships, and no one to call him crazy or make fun of him!" (*SL* 15). One could grow a beard; one could write.

Faulkner's trip to Paris had a long preparation, but it was only after he had resigned his position of Postmaster at Ole Miss on October 31, 1924, that he began to plan his trip in earnest. Already a published if an unmistakably minor poet, and urged on by his friend and mentor Phil Stone, who possibly had the example of Robert Frost's European discovery and triumph in mind, Faulkner came to New Orleans at the end of 1924 in order to find a boat to take him to Europe. For a young Mississippi writer eager to meet in his own work the "international standard" of literature, the gesture toward Paris was compulsory. However, instead of departing immediately for Europe, Faulkner ended up staying in New Orleans for six months, a period of momentous creative activity during which he transformed himself from a poet first into a writer of prose sketches, many of which he sold to the *Times-Picayune*, and finally into a full-fledged modernist novelist of world-class standing. With his first novel, *Soldiers' Pay*, completed and soon to be published by Horace Liveright, Faulkner was eager for his long-suspended journey, and on July 7, 1925, with the artist William Spratling, his Pirate's Alley roommate, he set out for Italy aboard the freighter *West Ivis*, arriving at Genoa on August 2. After detours through Italy and Switzerland, Faulkner and Spratling arrived in Paris on August 13, finding a hotel, as he wrote to his mother, "in Montparnasse. On the left bank of the Seine, where the painters live . . . not far away from the Luxembourg gardens and the Louvre, and from the bridge across the Seine you can see both Notre Dame and the Eiffel tower" (*SL* 11). After a brief stay in Montparnasse, on August 18 they moved to 26 rue Servandoni, closer to the Luxembourg Gardens.

The principal sources of information about Faulkner's Paris period are the letters he wrote home, mainly to his mother, and the reminiscences of his traveling companion, William Spratling. From these sources and others we learn that Faulkner visited Sylvia Beach's famous bookstore, Shakespeare and Co., saw James Joyce sitting with friends at a cafe, and attended the Moulin Rouge, where he was repelled by its extravagant display of human flesh. Walking the streets of Paris he observed the grim effects of the Great War on France's "lost generation": "so many young men on the streets, bitter and gray-faced, on crutches or with empty sleeves and scarred faces" (18). He saw the tombs of Napoleon and Oscar Wilde, the palaces at Versailles and Vincennes, the paintings of Matisse and Picasso, the sculptures of Rodin. In the Louvre, he saw "the Winged Victory and the Venus de Milo, the real ones, and the Mona Lisa etc. It was fine, especially the paintings of the more-or-less moderns, like Degas and Manet and Chavannes" (13). Of one painter he wrote: "And Cezanne! That man dipped his brush in light like Tobe Caruthers would dip his in red lead to paint a lamp-post" (24). He also "went to a very very modern exhibition the other day—futurist and vorticist. I was talking to a painter, a real one. He wont go to the exhibitions at all. He says its all right to paint the damn things, but as far as looking at them, he'd rather go to the Luxembourg gardens and watch the children sail their boats. And I agree with him" (13).

Indeed, the Luxembourg Gardens was a place of cherished and special value for Faulkner, a place of peace and beauty and fascination where he could gratify his intense pleasure in the activity of looking: "I have come to think of the Luxembourg as my garden now. I sit and write there, and walk around to watch the children, and the croquet games. I always carry a piece of bread to feed to the sparrows" (17). As the conclusion of *Sanctuary* demonstrates, the Luxembourg Gardens aroused in Faulkner the deepest kind of creative and aesthetic response. He wrote to his mother on September 6, 1925: "I have just written such a beautiful thing that I am about to bust—2000 words about the Luxembourg gardens and death. It has a thin thread of plot, about a young woman, and it is poetry though written in prose form. I have worked on it for two whole days and every word is perfect" (17). Equally, to his Aunt 'Bama four days later: "I have just finished the most beautiful short story in the world. So beautiful that when I finished it I went to look at myself in a mirror. And I thought, Did that ugly ratty-looking face, that mixture of childishness and unreliability and sublime vanity, imagine that? But I did. And the hand doesn't hold blood to improve on it" (20).

Along with sketches, poems, and short stories, Faulkner wrote during his time in Paris a chapter of a novel he called "Mosquito." Putting it aside, he started a new novel, "a grand one," about a young painter named Elmer Hodge: "I think right now its awfully good—so clear in my mind that I can hardly write fast enough" (13–14). This novel, left unfinished and eventually published posthumously as *Elmer* (1983), took the form of an intensive, quasi-autobiographical self-analysis whose lasting importance it would be almost impossible to overestimate. Certainly the effects of this Paris period of work on *Elmer* resonate throughout the major novels he would begin to write in succession, from *Mosquitoes* (1927) through *If I Forget Thee, Jerusalem* (1939) to *A Fable* (1954).

After writing thousands of words on the Elmer novel, Faulkner put it aside to begin another one, "a sort of fairy tale that has been buzzing in my head. This one is going to be the book of my youth, I am going to take 2 years on it, finish it by my 30th birthday" (22). This work is likely the allegorical novelette *Mayday*, which Carvel Collins has linked with the original conception of *The Sound and the Fury*.

In sum, Faulkner's time in Paris in 1925 was of immense importance in his creative development. Although Phil Stone provided Faulkner with letters of introduction to Joyce, Pound, and Eliot, Faulkner made no use of them and made no conspicuous effort to become known or recognized. Instead, Faulkner went to Paris to explore the city and himself, to gather "material," and to write. For a writer as self-conscious, ambitious, and confident as Faulkner, the person to emulate and surpass was not Sherwood Anderson but James Joyce, and Paris was Joyce's city. Indeed, with the publication of *The Sound and the Fury* in 1929, it had become clear that Paris had done its duty. Faulkner left Paris for New York and then home, arriving in Oxford on December 9, 1925. He would not return to Paris until December 1950, just after he had won the Nobel Prize.

FURTHER READING

Collins, Carvel. Introduction. *Mayday*. By William Faulkner. London: University Press of Notre Dame, 1976. 3–41.

Polk, Noel. "Faulkner in the Luxembourg Gardens." *Études Faulknériennes*. Vol. 1: *Sanctuary*. Ed. Michel Gresset. Rennes, France: Presses Universitaires Rennes, 1996. 27–34.

Michael Zeitlin

"PENNSYLVANIA STATION," a short story by Faulkner, was first published in the *American Mercury* in February 1934 and appears in *Collected Stories*. An omniscient narrator introduces the dialogue of two homeless men, one young and one old, who attempt to wait out a snowy night in Pennsylvania Station, anticipating the man in uniform who will force them to move on. The old man's account of his sister and her son Danny turns out to be the story of his own confusion and financial undoing. The old man believes in his nephew's goodness despite accumulated evidence of his criminality and of his having stolen the money his mother had been paying in advance to a disreputable undertaker. The old man's blindness to evil seems to coincide with his ability to survive one winter after another. When the railway man arrives, the two men are forced to walk in the cold to Grand Central, the old man pleasantly surprised by the night's advance toward day. In places predictably stylized and in places quietly powerful, the story reflects Faulkner's admiration of man's ability to endure the absurdity of moving only toward death.

Arthur A. Brown

PEOPLE-TO-PEOPLE PARTNERSHIP, a program of the Eisenhower administration designed, according to the official announcement, "to encourage

American citizens to develop their contacts with the peoples of other lands as a means of promoting understanding, peace and progress." In June 1956 Faulkner was invited by President Dwight Eisenhower to serve as chairman of a Writers' Committee, which was asked to make recommendations to the People-to-People officials concerning the ways that American ideas and values might be communicated to the citizens of other nations. Faulkner enlisted literary critic Harvey Breit as cochairman, and the committee met in Breit's home in New York City on November 29, 1956. Among the writers who attended the meeting were Saul Bellow, Donald Hall, Edna Ferber, Robert Hillyer, Elmer Rice, John Steinbeck, and William Carlos Williams. Faulkner opened the meeting by observing that "artists, writers, painters, and musicians . . . have spent all our lives already doing this very job which President Eisenhower discovered last year is a critical necessity." After considerable discussion, the group approved a summary report, issued in January 1957, recommending that visa requirements for Hungarian refugees be liberalized, that foreign citizens be brought to the United States for two-year visits, and that the U.S. government distribute American books, plays, and movies to foreign countries. Appended to these recommendations was a suggestion that Ezra Pound be freed from his incarceration in a mental institution. The transcript of the Writers' Committee meeting, along with other documents related to Faulkner's involvement in the program, has been published in Volume V of Brodsky and Hamblin's *Faulkner: A Comprehensive Guide to the Brodsky Collection* (340–355).

Robert W. Hamblin

"PETER," an early unpolished prose sketch by Faulkner. Although associated with the New Orleans sketches from the mid-1920s, "Peter" was not published until *Uncollected Stories*. The focal character, a young son of a prostitute, keeps watch for his working mother. He talks with Spratling, who is sketching, and Spratling's unidentified friend. The frank dialogue that drifts from the rooms contrasts with Peter's more innocent observations. The narrator remarks that Peter is an amalgam of the "severed yet similar despairs of two races."

FURTHER READING

Carothers, James B. "Faulkner's Short Story Writing and the Oldest Profession." *Faulkner and the Short Story*, ed. Harrington and Abadie. 38–61.

Diane Brown Jones

PINE MANOR COMMENCEMENT ADDRESS, a speech Faulkner delivered to his daughter Jill's graduating class on June 8, 1953. Published in the *Atlantic Monthly* in August 1953 under the title "Faith or Fear" and reprinted in *Essays, Speeches & Public Letters by William Faulkner*, the address was initially sketched on deleted manuscript pages of *A Fable*. Central to the speech is the idea of an unfinished universe awaiting human action, the duty of the artist to "remind us that man can revolt and change," and the conviction that political action must be rooted in local issues, within home communities.

Joseph R. Urgo

POE, EDGAR ALLAN (1809–1849), American writer. Poe's metier was the short story, and he made unique contributions to the development of the genres of the "detective" or "mystery" story, as well as the grotesque and arabesque. His identity as a Southerner is neither happy nor untroubled, as essays by Allen Tate and David Leverenz reflect. Criticism of Faulkner during the 1930s, and especially after the publication of *Absalom, Absalom!*, tended to compare Faulkner to Poe to the credit of neither, nor to the South. Distinctive characteristics noted were obscurity, verbosity, and morbidity. Besides some superficial similarities of style, a deeper affinity between the two writers may point back to Pascal's assertion that "the slightest movement affects the whole of nature; a stone cast into the sea changes the whole face of it" (qtd. in Tate 73). While not unique to them, a vision of the possibility of such an interconnectedness of events, material or spiritual, or some combination of both, animates the fiction of each writer.

FURTHER READING

Hubbell, Jay B. "Edgar Allan Poe and the South." *The South in American Literature.* Durham, N.C.: Duke University Press, 1965. 100–122.

Leverenz, David. "Poe and Gentry Virginia." *The American Face of Edgar Allan Poe.* Ed. Shawn Rosenheim and Stephen Rachman. Baltimore, Md.: Johns Hopkins University Press, 1995. 210–236.

Tate, Allen. *The Forlorn Demon: Didactic and Critical Essays.* Chicago: Regnery, 1953.

Stephen Hahn

"POINT OF LAW, A," a Faulkner short story, written in 1939 and published by *Collier's* in June 1940 and in *Uncollected Stories.* The text was revised for "The Fire and the Hearth" in *Go Down, Moses.* The central characters are Lucas Beauchamp and George Wilkins, who raise charges of moonshining against each other. Lucas learns that a marriage between his daughter and Wilkins will limit damaging testimony in court. The two men enter a new moonshining partnership, and Nat, Lucas's daughter, frets over home repairs that were supposed to be part of the marriage bargain.

FURTHER READING

Weinstein, Philip M. " 'He Come and Spoke for Me': Scripting Lucas Beauchamp's Three Lives." *Faulkner and the Short Story*, ed. Harrington and Abadie. 229–252.

Diane Brown Jones

POINT OF VIEW, in literary technique, relates to the perspective from which an author chooses to narrate a story. Point of view in Faulkner's fiction grows out of his conception of the nature of truth and of knowledge and his belief that bonds of family and community are the most basic of human connections. Beginning with *The Sound and the Fury* (1929) and continuing through the rest of his career, Faulkner used point of view to control how information is passed among characters, to secure reader involvement in his narratives, and to illustrate family and community relationships both in the present moment and as they evolve over time. The characteristic narrative relationship in Faulkner's novels is that of speaker, listener, and reader. Often the listener and reader seem to be nearly identical. The speaker may be a character or a so-called third-person narrator uninvolved in the story, and often the speaker and the author himself seem nearly indistinguishable, since the narrator's and the author's voices seem to merge.

Faulkner's use of point of view typically falls into one of three modes: stream-of-consciousness narration; "told" or "directed" narration, spoken by one character to another; and external narration, where an uninvolved (or third-person) narrator focuses on the thoughts and perceptions of a single character. Faulkner often used these modes in combination. His use of point of view was influenced by James Joyce, who in *Ulysses* made stream-of-consciousness narrative a primary modernist technique, and Joseph Conrad, whose *Heart of Darkness, Lord Jim*, and "Youth!" employ the convention of a narrating character (Marlow) speaking to a group of listeners. Faulkner also adopted Conrad's practice of using an external narrator (sometimes a character) to "frame" the story by introducing and describing Marlow as he begins to tell his story. Faulkner was not the only modern American writer to be influenced by these two novelists (the narrative structure of *The Great Gatsby*, for instance, is distinctly Conradian, and Dos Passos's *USA* trilogy is directly modeled on *Ulysses*), but he exploited these influences in diverse and highly effective ways. No modern American writer experimented more widely with point of view.

In his first three novels, Faulkner employs a relatively traditional point of view, but in *The Sound and the Fury* and *As I Lay Dying* he creates a series of stream-of-consciousness narratives to convey the thoughts and impressions of characters. No actual listener is present to hear the narratives, which are presented as if the speaker is seeking to explain and justify himself to a hypothetical listener. A listener is implied, then, and one might also argue that behind the first-person voice of the stream-of-consciousness narrator is an unseen authorial narrator who manipulates and controls the narrative. Although Joyce used stream of consciousness to create the illusion of presenting the unmediated contents of a character's mind, Faulkner's use of this device is highly stylized—he aggressively seeks to penetrate the minds of his characters, uncovering what they feel, explaining and analyzing their thoughts, dredging up thoughts of which they are unaware. This becomes increasingly evident in such novels as *Light in August* and *Pylon*, where at certain moments the author seems to substitute a narrating authorial voice for the voice or the conscious mind of a character at the center of a stream-of-consciousness narrative.

In the novels following *As I Lay Dying* and in the short stories, Faulkner frequently employed a number of narrative techniques in combination. Even in *The Sound and the Fury* he combined stream of consciousness in the first three sections with the more traditional third-person narrative of the fourth section, which focused on Dilsey. *Light in August*, for example, employed a variety of techniques. The predominant narrative mode is that of an external narrator describing the action through the perceptions of a central character. However, the personality and perhaps even the character of the narrator appear to change from one chapter to the next. In the opening chapter, which focuses on Lena Grove, the narrator seems simply to be an uninvolved external observer. In the next chapter, and in a number of the chapters focused on the community of Jefferson, the narrator almost seems to present himself as a resident of the town (similar to the narrator in ''A Rose for Emily,'' where the narrator is an unnamed townsperson). In the fifth chapter, which is focused on Joe Christmas as he wanders through Jefferson the night before he kills Joanna Burden, the narrator seems to be omniscient, penetrating deeply into the character's mind. On some occasions the narrator functions as an omniscient or semiomniscient spokesperson for a single character (chapters 2 and 3, for instance, which concern Hightower), whereas on other occasions he seems to represent the entire community (chapter 19). Moreover, the character on whom the narrator focuses also changes from one chapter to the next. The result is a sequence of constantly shifting views of people and events.

The overall effect of these narrative methods is multidimensional and multivocal. The reader sees the town and its characters from numerous perspectives, through differing voices, many of which clash and contrast markedly, most of which are not presented as more credible than any of the others. Faulkner in effect divests his external narrator of narrative authority, choosing instead to invest that authority in the reader, who must enter into the text, receive its contents, and assess its significance.

Faulkner uses to great effect in this novel the device of having narrators narrate narrators: The external narrator describes and introduces a character and then presents a story told by that character, or the narrator summarizes something that the character has learned, often from yet another character. The result is a story that seems to have been passed down from one speaker to another. We are compelled to question the story itself, at the same time as we are compelled to recognize the involvement of the town in telling it. Narrators narrating narrators is the central narrative strategy in *Absalom, Absalom!*, where Faulkner's use of point of view reaches a sublime culmination, encompassing not merely the source of narration and the sequence of characters who pass the information along but also the place and time of narration. An external narrator presents the first four chapters, which are set in Jefferson, Mississippi, in September 1909. The fifth chapter is a stream-of-consciousness narrative of an old woman, Rosa Coldfield, who in her earlier years had known Thomas Sutpen, the novel's main subject. The last four chapters are external narratives, told in a Harvard University dormitory room in January 1910, about the same series of events described in the opening chapters. Quentin Compson is the narrative focal point throughout the novel in the sense that he gathers from various sources the information that makes up the novel's story. He listens to his father and to townspeople talk. His father passes down to him accounts that he heard from his own father, who in turn had heard Sutpen talk about himself. He listens to Rosa Coldfield reminisce about Sutpen. Later Quentin hears and incorporates into his own understanding of the events versions of the story suggested by his Harvard roommate, Shreve, who knows the story only from what Quentin himself has revealed and from what he and Quentin together have imagined. The result is an astonishingly complex narrative of elusive credibility. Virtually no aspect of the narrative is certifiable fact, though much of it seems likely to have occurred. Faulkner's manipulation of point of view helped him to make this novel a deeply compelling narrative that is one of the greatest achievements in American literature.

None of Faulkner's later novels offers the same narrative virtuosity evident in *Absalom, Absalom!*, although he continued to employ point of view in diverse ways to tell his stories and to involve his readers. Later novels grow increasingly episodic, and point of view may vary from one episode or chapter to the next, as in *The Wild Palms/If I Forget Thee, Jerusalem, The Hamlet*, and *Requiem for a Nun*, the last of which intersperses chapters of narrative with chapters of drama. In *Go Down, Moses*, for instance, Faulkner builds a novel out of stories that appear to be only loosely connected but that in reality are tightly unified in theme and tone. The point of view is third person, but once again Faulkner subverts the predominant mode of narration by mixing in other methods, including dialogue, tales passed down by ancestors, and in "The Bear," plantation journal entries. *The Hamlet* is similarly episodic, although it is constructed of chronologically ordered and related chapters focused on the exploits of the Snopes family as they put down roots in Yoknapatawpha County. Here the primary narrative structure is that of a narrative framed by an external narrator. Even in his final novel, *The Reivers*, Faulkner uses point of view to great effect: The novel begins with the words "Grandfather said," thereby establishing the story that follows as a tale told by an elderly man to his grandson, about his experiences as a young man and his relationship with his own grandfather. Such a framework enforces the narrative situation of a coming-of-age novel, of lessons passed down through the generations from one family member to the next, and illustrates once again that for Faulkner narrative storytelling was at heart an oral event.

See also **Stream of Consciousness**.

FURTHER READING

Beck, Warren. "Faulkner's Point of View." *College English* 2 (1941): 736–749.

Hugh Ruppersburg

POLITICS. The initial wave of Faulkner critics found Faulkner's writing to be apolitical; he was assessed this way by contemporaries across the political spectrum, including *New Masses'* literary critic Granville Hicks, novelist Robert Penn Warren, and biographer Joseph Blotner. The next generation of critics would overturn the consensus. The first to rebel at length was Myra Jehlen, who described her book as existing outside the critical tradition (viii); indeed, it inaugurated another. André Bleikasten (''For/Against'') later faulted critics for failing to discern the political content of Faulkner's fiction and for censuring any ideological inquiry into his writing.

In his public statements, Faulkner was far more inclined to polemic than to advocating political engagement. His most vigorous political positions had to do with the right of privacy more than political action. On the matter of civil rights, his public record is contradictory and often irrelevant. However, his most political novel, *A Fable*, concerns the capacity of human beings to engage in deadly rebellion against entrenched systems of authority, and the *Snopes* trilogy contains discussion of a variety of political strategies. Since the 1980s, Faulkner's writing has itself been read across the political spectrum, and Faulkner has been labeled a Marxist, a feminist, a reactionary, and a prophet of rebellion.

Recently, Lawrence Schwartz has amassed evidence assessing the political interests behind the elevation of Faulkner to the status of major writer. Schwartz suggests that the stylistic challenges posed by Faulkner's prose served the interests of Departments of English in the 1950s, especially in the creation of graduate programs in American literature and in the formation of a literary canon of U.S. authors. To this day, the encompassing nature of Faulkner's writing rewards the politically minded literary critic. Faulkner critics may be divided between those, on the one hand, who see his writing as chronicling something essential about the South and about America, a crossing of the ways, the passing of a way of life, and those, on the other hand, who see Faulkner making assaults on the South and on American culture, bringing the marginal into the center, proffering apocryphal ways of seeing and hastening the passage of an old order. Heated, critical debates involving political perspectives are common in Faulkner studies.

In his overriding concern with form and juxtaposition, Faulkner reinforces critical interest in the structural dimension of political and social power. This relation is particularly apparent as his characters so often find themselves trapped by structures that they had no part in making but for which they must either apologize, if they profit by them, or bend, if they do not. Furthermore, Faulkner's insistence that the final authority, the last word, or the ultimate meaning be eternally deferred, and that the world—social, political, racial, sexual, economic, aesthetic—is an unfinished one and will be unfinished until the last dingdong of time and doom sounds forth from the last tideless rock, and so forth, indicates that any authority, word, or structure can be replaced, redefined, or reconstructed, making Faulkner's world a highly politicized place, whatever its politics.

FURTHER READING

Bleikasten, André. "For/Against an Ideological Reading of Faulkner's Novels." *Faulkner and Idealism*, ed. Gresset and Samway. 27–50.
Jehlen. *Class and Character in Faulkner's South.*
Schwartz. *Creating Faulkner's Reputation.*
Urgo. *Faulkner's Apocrypha.*

Joseph R. Urgo

POPEYE. *See* **Vitelli, Popeye**.

POPULAR CULTURE. Following the example of Walt Whitman in the nineteenth century, many twentieth-century American writers have attempted to establish a presence in the popular culture of their time. Ernest Hemingway and F. Scott Fitzgerald most prominently succeeded, to the point that the grinning, bushy face of the great white hunter and the sophisticated, handsome image of the jazz-age philosopher seem permanently embedded in the American imagination. Thomas Wolfe, Norman Mailer, and Truman Capote are others who seemed to thrive in the public eye, such efforts no doubt calculated to encourage book sales, as well as feed the ego. Notable exceptions include J. D. Salinger, Thomas Pynchon, and William Faulkner, the first two extreme examples of writers avoiding public scrutiny altogether.

For the most part, Faulkner saw the media as a mixed blessing, wanting to promote and sell his books so as to support his family and his patrician way of life in Oxford but also resisting the intrusiveness of interviewers and promoters into his private life. Basically a shy man, he developed rude strategies for dealing with intruders, turning them away at his doorstep, no matter how far they may have come to meet him, resisting offers of prominent magazines to feature his life story in their pages, or pretending to be a farmer or country rustic who knew nothing about literature or the world at large.

Yet the occasional student, reporter, young writer, or professor was allowed in, courteously received, and generously treated, for reasons only Faulkner knew. Provoked by some controversy, especially civil rights, he would write letters to newspapers and magazines to let his views be known. Because he saw it as a patriotic duty, he allowed the State Department to send him off on diplomatic cultural missions to Europe, Japan, and South America and involve him in the People-to-People program. In his later years, he settled into Charlottesville as writer-in-residence at the University of Virginia, where he answered the most pedantic questions about his fiction and personal beliefs, even though he thought that a trip to Washington at the invitation of President John Kennedy to have dinner with Nobel Laureates was too far to travel "to eat with strangers."

Faulkner expressed himself most explicitly on the subject in his 1955 essay for *Harper's* magazine, "On Privacy," where he explained "that only a writer's works were in the public domain, to be discussed and investigated and written about, the writer himself having placed them there by submitting them for publication and accepting money for them. . . . But that, until the writer committed a crime or ran for public office, his private life was his own.'' But a more revealing statement may be something he said in response to a student's question at the University of Virginia in 1958 about success: ''Success is peculiar. If you beg and plead she scorns you. If you show her the back of your hand, she will cling to your knees.''

Ironically enough, Faulkner's contradictory attitudes and actions served only to generate even more interest. If a reporter is denied access, he or she will try even harder to get the story, usually turning to secondary information or less reliable sources, which is why the Faulkner public print record is filled with errors and misinformation. Refusing a presidential invitation to dinner will create more publicity than accepting it would. Sometimes one has the suspicion that Faulkner knew exactly what he was doing and was using the media to his own calculated ends.

Given these attitudes, along with the complexity of his fiction, which created difficulties for all of his readers, as well as his reputation for drinking to an excess, Faulkner has emerged in the popular perception as a rude, drunk, backwoods genius with pretensions to social status that he didn't deserve but a reputation for literary greatness that he did. Thus one advertisement for a product features a photograph of Faulkner in full hunting regalia looking the aristocrat with the caption ''Literature's glib escort into modern Southern Lifestyles,'' but the text goes on to note that, like the product, his work is ''bound to last.'' In the satiric literary history *American Lit Relit* (McGraw-Hill, 1964), Richard Armour notes that when *The Marble Faun* failed, Faulkner ''began to write stories and novels peopled with idiots, drunkards, thieves, murderers, prostitutes, and perverts, and won a devoted following among readers who wished to learn how things were going in the South.'' When David Levine caricatured him for the *New York Review of Books*, Faulkner was dressed like Huckleberry Finn. In a 1996 comic strip sequence of *Zippy*, artist Bill Griffith satirizes the Nobel Prize speech, particularly the phrase ''last ding-dong of doom,'' Hostess Ding Dongs being Zippy's favorite junk food.

Aside from his image or presence in popular culture, Faulkner made contributions to at least two of its genres—detective fiction and motion pictures. Of the detective stories collected in *Knight's Gambit*, at least one won second prize in a contest sponsored by *Ellery Queen's Mystery Magazine*, and Ellery Queen himself cited the book as a ''major cornerstone'' of detective fiction. *Intruder in the Dust* is also basically a detective novel and can be paired with *Knight's Gambit* as another chapter in the adventures of Gavin Stevens and his ''boy-Watson'' Chick Mallison.

His contribution to motion pictures is problematic. Clearly Faulkner knew how to construct a film script, as his work on *Today We Live, The Big Sleep, To Have and Have Not*, and *The Land of the Pharaohs* demonstrates, and the middle two of these are counted classics. These, as well as his uncredited work on Jean Renoir's *The Southerner*, all reflect familiar themes and phrases found in Faulkner's fiction. *Land of the Pharaohs* may even be reviewed as a rewrite of *Absalom, Absalom!* But Faulkner always discussed his Hollywood work with disdain and reflected the typical high-brow attitude of the elites toward the movies. Critics have been too quick to adopt Faulkner's statements literally and given too little serious attention to the actual films. It was not a practice of Hollywood producers to hire writers at good salaries who did not produce creditable material.

As for the adaptations of Faulkner's novels, these range in quality from the badly altered *The Sound and the Fury* by producer Jerry Wald and director Douglas Sirk's conventional Rock Hudson melodrama *The Tarnished Angels* based on *Pylon* to such excellent versions as director Mark Rydell's entertaining *The Reivers* and the compelling *Tomorrow* as scripted by Horton Foote, Jr., and performed by Robert Duvall. In between are the once praised but now seemingly didactic *Intruder in the Dust*, directed by Clarence Brown, and the still engaging *The Long Hot Summer* based on *The Hamlet* and directed by Martin Ritt with powerful performances by Orson Welles, Paul Newman, and Joanne Woodward (the 1986 remake for television with Don Johnson and a script coauthored by novelist Rita Mae Brown was a disaster, although it moved closer to the text by reintroducing the Ab Snopes figure and other elements from "Barn Burning"). A respectable rendition of "Barn Burning" was scripted by Horton Foote, Jr., and acted by Tommy Lee Jones in 1980, but a version of "A Rose for Emily" with miscast Anjelica Huston as Emily Grierson in 1982 turned the characters into cardboard figures.

FURTHER READING

Fowler and Abadie, eds. *Faulkner and Popular Culture*.

M. Thomas Inge

PORTABLE FAULKNER, THE, a representative collection of Faulkner's work, edited by Malcolm Cowley in cooperation with Faulkner and published by Viking Press in 1946. The contents include the Compson Appendix, which Faulkner wrote specifically for this volume; the previously published stories "A Justice," "Red Leaves," "Was," "Wash," "A Rose for Emily," "Death Drag," and "Delta Autumn"; and excerpts from the novels *The Wild Palms, Absalom, Absalom!, The Unvanquished, The Hamlet, The Sound and the Fury, Sanctuary*, and *Light in August*. The endpapers of the book show a reproduction of Faulkner's revision of the map of Yoknapatawpha County that had appeared in *Absalom, Absalom!*

By virtue of the development of *The Portable Faulkner*, Cowley is sometimes credited with the heroic rescue of Faulkner from critical and publishing oblivion, although there is sense to O. B. Emerson's claim that the real turning point of Faulkner's general reputation (if not publishing fortunes) began around 1938–1939. Whatever the truth in that matter, it is clear that Cowley conceived and brought forth for both the informed reading public and academia the idea that Faulkner's work centers on the territory of Yoknapatawpha and that in the works he had produced and was yet to produce there is an overarching design, an "organic unity" (*PF* [First Edition] 24). Faulkner endorsed the idea and assisted in persuading readers of that unity by providing a map of Yoknapatawpha specifically keyed to the material in the volume (he had previously drawn one for the first edition of *Absalom, Absalom!*) and by writing the account of the Compson family that was first published in *The Portable* (and that would raise later questions about its relation to the Compson novel, *The Sound and the Fury*). A revised edition of *The Portable Faulkner* was published in 1966, with additional introductory material by Cowley and passages from *Requiem for a Nun* and Faulkner's Nobel Prize address incorporated to bolster the Yoknapatawpha thesis.

Cowley himself tells the story of the development of *The Portable Faulkner* and his later association with Faulkner by interweaving letters, other documents, and reminiscences in *The Faulkner-Cowley File: Letters and Memories, 1944–1962.* A substantially different view of Cowley's role in Faulkner's postwar career is presented in Lawrence H. Schwartz's *Creating Faulkner's Reputation: The Politics of Modern Literary Criticism.* Examining what he calls "the sudden inflation of Faulkner's literary reputation after World War II" (1), Schwartz sees Cowley as serving both the economics of the publishing industry and the ideology of Cold War consensus politics. Schwartz's account is extremely useful as a narrative of events and the persons involved in them, but its analysis of Faulkner as a cultural commodity and ideological resource is less persuasive. In any case, both Cowley and Schwartz depend on the premise that publication of *The Portable Faulkner* was the central event in Faulkner's gaining a broad American audience.

FURTHER READING

Crews, Frederick. "The Strange Fate of William Faulkner." *New York Review of Books* 7 March 1991: 47–52.
Emerson, O. B. "William Faulkner's Literary Reputation in America." Dissertation. Vanderbilt University, 1962.
Schwartz. *Creating Faulkner's Reputation.*

Stephen Hahn

"PORTRAIT OF ELMER, A," a short story that Faulkner completed and attempted to sell to Bennett Cerf of Random House in October 1935, offers a revised and condensed version of Faulkner's unfinished novel *Elmer*, which he wrote in Paris between August and October 1925. The story, which is also linked to "Divorce in Naples," was first published in *Uncollected Stories of William Faulkner* (1979). The aspiring painter Elmer Hodge and his friend Angelo are drinking at the Dome cafe in Paris. In a series of flashbacks the narrative recapitulates the main events of Elmer's life, including the loss of his sister, Jo-

Addie, and his attempts to find a suitable replacement for her in the world of art and personal relations. Returning to the present, the narrative recounts Elmer's frantic need to find a lavatory in order to relieve himself. He hurries to his lodgings only to find that his fiancée Myrtle and her mother are there waiting for him. Emptying his bowels but finding no paper, he is compelled to use the only work of art he has produced so far: a painting that he had planned to use as his entry into the world of art. Like a number of other early Faulkner works, "A Portrait of Elmer" explores the paradoxical relationship between life and art.

FURTHER READING

McHaney, Thomas L. "The Elmer Papers: Faulkner's Comic Portraits of the Artist." *A Faulkner Miscellany*, ed. Meriwether. 37–69.
Zeitlin, Michael. "Faulkner and Psychoanalysis: The *Elmer* Case." *Faulkner and Psychology*, ed. Kartiganer and Abadie. 219–241.

Michael Zeitlin

POSTMASTER. Faulkner was living with his parents on the University of Mississippi campus, where his father Murry was Secretary of the University, when the University Postmaster position became vacant in late 1921. Although Murry had recommended that the position be given to Murry C. Falkner, Jr., it was William who landed the job, beginning on an acting basis on December 5, 1921. He was probably appointed because of the influence of his friend Phil Stone and District Attorney Lemuel E. Oldham, his future father-in-law.

According to Stone, Faulkner accepted the position so he could "have some money and leisure to go ahead with his writing, for which he shows a rather unusual talent" (May 1, 1922, letter from Phil Stone to Senator John Sharp Williams). Accusations were that he wrote on the job, often failed to distribute the mail, sometimes discarded mail he thought unimportant, kept irregular hours, ignored patrons, permitted unauthorized persons entrance to the office, and kept poor records; some of his letters, however, demonstrate that on occasion he responded to mail and took care of necessary details.

The job lasted only until the end of October 1924. Faulkner biographers have assumed that Faulkner resigned and chose not to respond to a September 2, 1924, letter from Postal Inspector Mark Webster. Joan St. C. Crane makes a convincing case, however, that the letter was written, as a hoax, by Phil Stone. Although the versions differ slightly, Faulkner probably did comment to friends something to the effect, that "Now I won't be at the beck and call of every son of a bitch who happens to have two cents" (Coughlan 57). He was replaced on November 1, 1924, and made his way to New Orleans shortly thereafter.

FURTHER READING

Crane, Joan St. C. " 'Case No. 133733-C': The Inspector's Letter to Postmaster William Falkner." *Mississippi Quarterly* 42 (1989): 229–245.

"The Postmaster." *New Yorker* 46 (21 November 1970): 50.

Walton, Gerald W. "The Falkners and the University, Mississippi, Post Office." *Faulkner Journal* 5 (Fall 1989): 49–50.

———. "William C. Falkner, Postmaster: Some Correspondence." *Journal of Mississippi History* 51 (February 1989): 1–15.

Gerald W. Walton

POUND, EZRA (1885–1972), arguably the most influential modernist poet, introduced innovations in poetry that impacted most important early twentieth-century writers, including Joyce, Frost, and Yeats. Pound initiated imagism and exhorted his followers to "Make it new!" His influence on William Faulkner is somewhat unclear. Faulkner was first introduced to Pound's writing through Phil Stone, his early mentor. Although Faulkner was familiar with Pound's poetry, he does not seem to have cared very much for it: He consistently omits Pound from the list of poets he enjoys reading. When Faulkner went to Europe as a young man, Phil Stone sent letters of introduction to Pound, Eliot, and Joyce, but Faulkner apparently did not attempt to meet any of these writers.

Even though Faulkner seems rather indifferent to Pound's poetry, several critics have pointed out Pound's influences on Faulkner. According to Lothar Hönnighausen, one of the most significant similarities between Pound and Faulkner is their ostensible connection through Swinburne and the pre-Raphaelites. Pound's cantos demonstrate the influence of Swinburne, and Faulkner acknowledged Swinburne as a vital early influence on his own poetry. Hönnighausen cites Faulkner's poem "The Lilacs" as a clear example of "his combination of Modernist elements and Swinburne material" and links Faulkner to Pound and Eliot through "the poetic intelligence displayed by Faulkner in handling and controlling the sensuality of the material from Swinburne" (*Stylization* 102). Direct influences from Pound in specific lines of Faulkner's verse have also been discerned. Cleanth Brooks believes the line "above the narrow precipice of thy breast" in Faulkner's Poem XVII from *A Green Bough* is a clear indication of Pound's influence (*Toward Yoknapatawpha* 373). In addition, Hönnighausen notes (174) that Faulkner's use of nymphs in "Nympholepsy" and "The Lilacs" appears strongly influenced by Pound's poem "A Girl," and Joseph Blotner argues that *The Marionettes* "echo[es] . . . some of the imagery in Ezra Pound's translations of Chinese poems" (1984 *FAB* 94).

Ironically, the same William Faulkner who was too shy to attempt to meet Ezra Pound in Italy (1984 *FAB* 156) was connected to the effort to free Pound from St. Elizabeth's Hospital, where Pound was incarcerated after being charged with treason during World War II. Faulkner attended a meeting of the People-to-People program (which focused on bringing people from Communist countries to the United States) with other important literary figures. At the meeting, William Carlos Williams argued for Pound's release from the institution. Blotner cites poet Donald Hall's reaction to Faulkner's response: "It seemed to Hall that Faulkner had assented mildly to . . . the freeing of Ezra Pound'' (1984 *FAB* 629).

Rebecca Rowley

POWERS, MARGARET, is the young war widow in *Soldiers' Pay* who helps Donald Mahon home, marries him, and leaves town again after his death. Worshiped by all the returning soldiers, she is described explicitly in terms of an 1890s beauty, but she is also one of the most contemporary characters in the novel. Framed by critics as an archetypal femme fatale, a black widow who destroys men, a nurturing mother, a victim of sexual trauma, a hard-boiled heroine, and a complex portrayal of a 1920s New Woman, Margaret Powers remains among the most enigmatic figures in *Soldiers' Pay*.

FURTHER READING

Zeitlin, Michael. "The Passion of Margaret Powers: A Psychoanalytic Reading of *Soldiers' Pay*." *Mississippi Quarterly* 46 (1993): 351–372.

Pamela E. Knights

"PRIEST, THE," an early story by Faulkner. Although numbered fifth among sketches planned for Faulkner's series in the New Orleans *Times-Picayune* in 1925, this story was not published as such. A segment was published in *The Double Dealer*, and the complete story was published in 1976 in the *Mississippi Quarterly* and in 1979 in *Uncollected Stories*. On the eve of his becoming an ordained priest, the unnamed protagonist walks the streets and wonders if his choice is correct or a casting off of life "through abnegation." His thoughts are drawn to and repelled by the young women he sees and imagines. He longs for the morning and the ordination that, he hopes, will ease the conflicting urges of body and spirit.

FURTHER READING

Morrison, Gail M. "Faulkner's Priests and Fitzgerald's 'Absolution.' " *Mississippi Quarterly* 32 (1979): 461–465.

Diane Brown Jones

PRIMITIVISM, an idea dated at least as early as Michel de Montaigne's essay "Of Cannibals" from the French Renaissance, celebrates the natural state of humanity and elevates those in primitive societies who are close to nature and thus more noble and like human nature as it was before the corruption of social forces. As an intellectual idea, primitivism became popularized during the Romantic Age. This was due in part to the work of French Romanticist Jean-Jacques Rousseau, who posited the concept of the "noble savage." After Freudian notions about human sexuality became influential on Western ideology, primitivism became associated not only with "natural" goodness but also with the libido and primordial forces. Elements of primitivism appear in James

Joyce's *Ulysses*, D. H. Lawrence's writings, John Steinbeck's fiction, and other twentieth-century works—as well as in American art of the Harlem Renaissance, which celebrates the "exotic" nature of African Americans.

Faulkner's fictional representations of primitivism vary greatly. For example, the idiot in his works is often elevated to a noble status superior to more complex and evil characters such as Jason Compson in *The Sound and the Fury* and the Snopeses in *The Hamlet* and other novels. Benjy, the idiot child in *The Sound and the Fury*, and Ike Snopes, his counterpart in *The Hamlet*, both have a childlike appreciation of nature and respond to the world innocently without regard to socialized behavior. This latter point is particularly evident in Ike's love affair with the cow. In *The Sound and the Fury*, Caddy represents a female nymph lacking inhibitions with regard to sexual instincts, as can be demonstrated in Faulkner's frequent explanation of the novel's origin: "It began with the picture of the little girl's muddy drawers, climbing that tree to look in the parlor window with her brothers that didn't have the courage to climb the tree waiting to see what she saw" (*FIU* 1). Like Caddy, Lena Grove, an earth mother figure in *Light in August*, is celebrated for her primitivistic nature.

In "The Bear," Faulkner's greatest celebration of primitive nature, Ike McCaslin is led by nature priest Sam Fathers beyond civilization, as represented by the town of Jefferson, to experience spiritual communion with nature, as symbolized by the sacred bear, Old Ben. By contrast, Colonel Sutpen in *Absalom, Absalom!*, who has frontier and mountain origins in West Virginia, illustrates the corruption of primitivistic man, the fall of American frontier idealism, and the loss of the American Adam's innocence.

Critics have emphasized particularly the connections between primitivism and the portrayal of African American characters in Faulkner's works. For example, Dilsey in *The Sound and the Fury*, Rider, the central character in "Pantaloon in Black," and Joe Christmas in *Light in August* have been traditionally viewed as illustrating Faulkner's idealization of African American characters and their connection to the land and instinct.

FURTHER READING

Brooks, Cleanth. "Primitivism in *The Sound and the Fury*." *English Institute Essays, 1952*. Ed. Alexa P. Parker. New York: Columbia University Press, 1954.

Carey, Glenn O. "William Faulkner as a Critic of Society." *Arizona Quarterly* 21 (1965): 101–108.

Gladstein, Mimi Reisel. *The Indestructible Woman in Faulkner, Hemingway, and Steinbeck*. Ann Arbor, Mich.: UMI Research Press, 1986.

Dean Shackelford

PSYCHOANALYTIC APPROACHES. Faulkner himself always denied any acquaintance with psychological or psychoanalytic theory. As he put it jokingly on different occasions: "What little of psychology I know the characters I have invented and playing poker have taught me. Freud I'm not familiar with" (*FIU*

268); "I have never read him [Freud]. Neither did Shakespeare. I doubt if Melville did either, and I'm sure Moby Dick didn't" (*LIG* 251). Faulkner's biographer Joseph Blotner, on the other hand, reports one of Faulkner's early childhood memories, in which he "ran away to a doctor in the family and . . . browsed through his books." As Faulkner put it: "I learned plenty from them. I was interested in the brain. I learned that it had parts—a section for speech, for touch, and so on" (1984 *FAB* 34). What is more, Faulkner seems to have had access to Freud's early theories in some of the books that his friend and mentor Phil Stone ordered for him, including Havelock Ellis's *Little Essays of Love and Virtue* and *Studies in the Psychology of Sex*. When he lived in New Orleans, he associated with people who certainly were greatly interested in Freudian theory. One must expect such encounters to have left traces on the writer.

Indeed, critics have found Freudian imagery in Faulkner's early story "Elmer," and the novel *Mosquitoes* even features two characters who, while discussing the personality of a third, mention Ellis as well as Freud—a fact that led John Irwin to observe that "if the author of the novel was not familiar with Freud, his characters certainly were" (5). Other critics have pointed to more general aspects of Faulkner's work. Lee Jenkins, for instance, emphasizes Faulkner's "intuitive perception of the depth and character of mental aberration and the various modes of mental functioning—as they appear in his characters" (148). It is certain, in any case, that his characters were of the utmost importance to Faulkner. In talks and interviews, he reminded his audience again and again of their reality as "flesh-and-blood people that will stand up and cast a shadow" (*FIU* 47) and their independence from him as their creator. "There is always a point in the book," Faulkner once said, "where the characters themselves rise up and take charge and finish the job" (*LIG* 244). To him this might even extend beyond the work in question: "When the book is finished, that character is not done, he still is going on at some new devilment that sooner or later I will find out about and write about" (*FIU* 78). In his early works, especially, the complexity, the layeredness and fluidity, and the paradoxical qualities of personality—"the human heart in conflict with itself"—form the most important focus of interest. Not surprisingly, then, Faulkner's work has invited various psychoanalytic approaches.

Classical Freudian theory, with its emphasis on the layeredness of consciousness, comprising the constructs of the conflicting *id, superego* and *ego ideal*, as well as the mediating functions of the *ego*, has proven to be extremely useful in analyzing the complex personalities of some of Faulkner's most remarkable characters. John Irwin's classical Freudian approach in *Doubling and Incest/Repetition and Revenge* has been most influential, centering around the Oedipus complex and its relation to the problem of incest, which figures so prominently in Faulkner's work. Thus Irwin is able to throw considerable light on the rivalry between Henry Sutpen and Charles Bon in *Absalom, Absalom!*, on the involvement of Quentin Compson with these two characters in the same novel, and on the agony and eventual suicide of Quentin in *The Sound and the Fury*. Additional psychoanalytic approaches, Lacanian as well as Freudian, were presented at the 1991 Faulkner and Yoknapatawpha Conference at the University of Mississippi. Collected in Kartiganer and Abadie's *Faulkner and Psychology* (1994), these essays treat characters such as Joe Christmas, Elmer, Horace Benbow, Narcissa Benbow, Temple Drake, and Caddy Compson.

With their emphasis on pre-Oedipal phases of development, post-Freudian approaches such as those of Melanie Klein bring to light the earliest stages of personality development, which Freud recognized but was unable to analyze satisfactorily. Freud's "instinct theory," with its emphasis on rivalry with the father, which finds its resolution through introjection, is replaced here by "object theory," focusing on the earliest love object, the mother's breast. Julia Kristeva has brought this pre-Oedipal personality development into the realm of discourse. Her "semiotic" refers to a preverbal discourse of mother and child that is based on childbirth and breast-feeding and presents itself as fragmentary and impulsive. Such post-Freudian approaches have been used to illuminate the pathological fixation on mothers and surrogate mothers by the Compson brothers in *The Sound and the Fury*, Darl Bundren in *As I Lay Dying*, and Joe Christmas in *Light in August*.

Neo-Freudian approaches, with their interpersonal rather than intrapersonal orientation, stress more specifically the importance of the family and the society at large for psychological development. Karen Horney, for instance, identifies a drive toward self-fulfillment that all individuals naturally possess, as well as specific defensive strategies that are developed in the course of life under adverse circumstances and that obstruct this drive. Thus she is able to explain the divergence between drive and capacity, on the one hand, and performance, on the other. Based on the different defense strategies, Horney has distinguished three types of neurotic personality configurations: the compliant, the aggressive or arrogant-vindictive, and the detached, which show themselves as habitual reactions to social stress of any kind. The neo-Freudian approaches of Horney and others, where they take into account all the experiences of an individual rather than only those of infancy, have been used by Karen Ann Butery and Marjorie Haselwerdt to throw light on the origin and development of, and paradoxes in, the various forms of antisocial behavior shown by characters such as Joe Christmas and Jason Compson.

More recently, psychoanalysts such as Roy Schafer and Donald Spence have stressed especially the narrative nature of psychoanalysis and indeed of psychic life itself. Different authors have, for instance, explored the connections between certain personality classifications in psychiatry and the narrative structure of stories. Ernest Keen discusses "how the paranoid person narratizes his life," taking as a starting point the three polarities that form the structure of experience: temporality, morality, and sociality. Approaches such as these hold important promises for the psychoanalytic analysis of Faulkner's texts, in which the narrative often develops on many different levels of consciousness. One has only to think of the passage in *Light in August* in which Joe Christmas thanks his stepfather for a calf he was given: "Joe thanked him. Then he could look at the calf and say, aloud: 'That belongs to me.' Then he looked at it, and it was again too fast and too complete to be thinking: *That is not a gift. It is not even a promise: it is a threat* thinking, 'I didn't ask for it. He gave it to me. I didn't ask for it' believing *God knows I have earned it.*"

Finally, some critical works take Faulkner himself rather than, or in addition to, his characters as the object of psychoanalytic investigation. In *Faulkner and Psychology* (Kartiganer and Abadie), for instance, Donald Kartiganer discusses the trio Faulkner, Freud, and Joe Christmas, whereas Jay Watson, Jay Martin, Anne Goodwyn Jones, and David Wyatt speak of various aspects of masculinity and the construction of gender.

It would seem that the different psychoanalytic theories have been, and will continue to be, fruitful approaches to the work of Faulkner. Freud himself might well have agreed to the opposite also, as he strongly believed in the links between psychoanalysis and literature. His essay "Delusions and Dreams in Jensen's *Gradiva*," in any case, concludes with the words: the "creative writer cannot evade the psychiatrist nor the psychiatrist the creative writer, and the poetic treatment of a psychiatric theme can turn out to be correct without any sacrifice of its beauty."

See also **Freud, Sigmund; Jung, Carl G**.

FURTHER READING

Butery, Karen Ann. "From Conflict to Suicide: The Inner Turmoil of Quentin Compson." *American Journal of Psychoanalysis* 49 (1989): 211–224.

Collins, Carvel. "The Interior Monologues of *The Sound and the Fury*." *English Institute Essays 1952*. New York: Columbia University Press, 1954.

Gidley, Mick. "Another Psychologist, a Physiologist and William Faulkner." *Ariel* 24 (1971): 78–86.

Haselwerdt, Marjorie B. " 'Keep Your Muck': A Horneyan Analysis of Joe Christmas and *Light in August*." *Third Force Psychology and the Study of Literature*. Ed. Bernard Paris. Rutherford, N.J.: Fairleigh Dickinson University Press, 1986.

Woodbery, Bonnie. "The Abject in Faulkner's *As I Lay Dying*." *Literature and Psychology* 40.3 (1994): 26–42.

Ineke Bockting

PYLON, a non-Yoknapatawpha novel published in 1935, is singular in Faulkner's canon in being set within the margins of an American city—New Valois, Franciana, Faulkner's apocryphal version of a mid-depression New Orleans during Mardi Gras week. Many of the major events of the novel are based on those Faulkner himself witnessed at the opening of the Shushan Airport in New Orleans in February 1934.

The brand-new Feinman Airport has just opened, and a tall, "cadaverous" reporter for the city newspaper is sent to cover the dedication ceremonies, which are organized around a three-day air show. A crowd gazes at the spectacle of the high-powered machines and the daredevils who compete for cash prizes in such events as aerial acrobatics, airplane racing, and parachute jumping. All the while the amplified voice of an announcer describes the scene. Inevitably there is death in spectacular crashes, as if promised and foretold by the newspaper that publishes the air meet's program: "Special Mardi Gras Evening Event. Rocket Plane. Lieut. Frank Burnham."

Moving into the human heart of the spectacle behind the scenes, the reporter encounters an itinerant set of barnstormers joined together in a radically unconventional arrangement: one woman living openly with two men and a child. The reporter, becoming obsessed and fascinated with this scene of mingled erotic cooperation and competition, tries to insinuate himself into its very center. When the barnstormers' plane finishes second in the first race and they must wait for two days in order to collect the prize money, the reporter surrenders his apartment to the assembled "family": Laverne Shumann, a strikingly sexual, androgynous woman who is married to Roger Shumann, a brilliant pilot and more or less head of the household; Jack Holmes, the sardonic and mustachioed parachute jumper, who is probably the biological father of Jackie Shumann, Laverne's six-year-old son; and Jiggs, the hard-drinking mechanic, who spends much of his time obsessing over a new pair of boots.

When Roger Shumann wrecks his airplane in the next race because Jiggs, drunk and hungover, had failed to do the necessary repairs on the engine, the reporter helps Shumann acquire another plane so that he may compete for the big prize money of $2,000 in the final race of the air show. This plane belongs to the famous pilot Matt Ord, who had refused to sell it because it was too dangerously overpowered for its snub-nosed body. After a series of tricky maneuvers, Shumann, with a note signed by the reporter, manages to acquire the plane anyway and get it qualified by the race officials, who are none too particular about the lives of the pilots. During the race, in a stunning and courageous performance, Shumann is about to overtake Ord's superior machine when the plane Shumann is flying, the one Ord himself tried to prevent him from buying, begins to come apart. Steering out over the lake in order to avoid the grandstand full of spectators, he crashes and is killed. His body is never found, and so a wreath is dropped from an airplane over the spot at which he disappeared.

In the last section of the novel, Laverne and Jack take little Jackie to Roger Shumann's parents in Ohio. Here Dr. Carl Shumann, Roger's father, tries unsuccessfully to get Laverne to say that Roger is the actual father of the little boy. Laverne is unable to do so and, pregnant probably with Jack's baby, leaves with Jack. Dr. Shumann, desperate and enraged that he cannot be certain of the boy's paternity, discovers Jackie's little toy plane and stomps it to bits when he discovers $175 that had been hidden inside the fuselage where the reporter, knowing that Laverne would not accept money from him, had hidden it. Dr.

Shumann assumes that Laverne had obtained the money by prostitution and burns it in the fireplace. On the last page of the novel, the reporter writes the obituary of Roger Shumann and heads out to get drunk on Amboise Street.

There has been much critical discussion about the proper way to view the place of *Pylon* in Faulkner's career. Faulkner himself claimed in 1957 that he had written *Pylon* because he had "got in trouble" with *A Dark House*, the novel to which Faulkner would return after *Pylon* and bring to completion under the new title *Absalom, Absalom!* However, it would be a mistake to view *Pylon* as a minor or secondary work. At the minimum it brings into crystalline focus Faulkner's own lifelong fascination with airplanes from the time of his Royal Air Force training in Canada in 1918; and it ironically foreshadows the death of his brother Dean in November 1935 (after *Pylon* had been published), in an airplane belonging to Faulkner, himself a licensed pilot. More important, *Pylon* is a novel focused upon modernity's hostile and alienating though no less fascinating forces, which, in Faulkner's fictional analysis, dominate and define a set of interlocking structures and agencies, among them the city room of a mass circulation newspaper, as the invasive power of the mass media boldface newspaper headlines "abrupt" throughout the text of the novel. Around the pylons, phallic icons of modernity, the airplanes revolve in dizzying, pointless, and ultimately fatal elliptical orbits as the diminutive human figures of the crowd gaze upward in idiot fascination; it is clear that the mob has come to see the high flyers come crashing to the ground, to see the immolation of man and machine, presided over by the metallic voice of the amplifier and the menacing electric gaze of the searchlights.

This is Faulkner's stunning and remarkable figure for modernity. His fictional analysis of this figure drives the novel's turbulent and multilayered textuality, which involves and transfigures such classical modernist texts as James Joyce's *Ulysses* (especially its "Aeolus" chapter), T. S. Eliot's *The Waste Land*, and "The Love Song of J. Alfred Prufrock." Faulkner turns to this intertextual material in search of an appropriately "alienated" narrative idiom with which to represent the new modern realities, a narrative idiom now determined by the imperatives of a mechanized culture. In *Pylon* the characteristic form of that idiom is the composite, the portmanteau word, the neologism: "corpseglare," "wirehum," "gasolinespanned," "pavementthrong," "trafficdammed," "machinevoice," "gearwhine," "slantshimmered," "typesplattered"—weird, defamiliarizing "machinelanguage" appearing with Joycean strangeness upon the page. With *Pylon* Faulkner emerged from the nightmare of the contemporary scene—his estrangement having generated a powerful renewal of language—and brought *Absalom, Absalom!* (the nightmare of history) to a decisive completion.

FURTHER READING

Johnson, Susie Paul. *Annotations to William Faulkner's* Pylon. New York: Garland, 1989.

Matthews, John T. "The Autograph of Violence in Faulkner's *Pylon.*" *Southern Literature and Literary Theory.* Ed. Jefferson Humphries. Athens: University of Georgia Press, 1990. 247–269.

Torchiana, Donald. "*Pylon* and the Structure of Modernity." *Modern Fiction Studies* 3 (1957–1958): 291–308.

Zeitlin, Michael. "Faulkner's *Pylon*: The City in the Age of Mechanical Reproduction." *Canadian Review of American Studies* 22 (1991): 229–240.

———. "*Pylon*, Joyce, and Faulkner's Imagination." *Faulkner and the Artist,* ed. Kartiganer and Abadie. 181–207.

Michael Zeitlin

R

RACE. Faulkner's public interventions on the subjects of race relations and civil rights were largely confined to the 1950s when he wrote letters to and articles in local, regional, and national publications and spoke before various groups. In what were the initial years of massive resistance in the South—1955 to 1958—Faulkner demonstrated considerable courage but also a good deal of confusion. His injunctions and advice were often seen as betrayals by fellow Southerners, including members of his family and residents of Oxford, Mississippi, while Northern liberals, regardless of their race, tended to take a dim view of his public pronouncements.

Attentive readers of his fiction between the early 1940s and the mid-1950s might have seen what was coming. Faulkner had been powerfully impressed by the historical changes that World War II would bring in race relations in the South. Although it appeared only just after the war started, *Go Down, Moses* (1942), with its complex exploration of a Southern heritage tainted by slavery and exploitation of the land and in need of absolution from the guilt of racism, revealed something of what was on Faulkner's mind. There and in *Intruder in the Dust* (1948), Faulkner introduced his most fully explored and autonomous black character, Lucas Beauchamp, a man who possessed no hint of the stereotypical buffoonery of some of Faulkner's early black characters; little of the detached, Olympian moral sensibility of Dilsey in *The Sound and the Fury*; and none of the self-laceration of Faulkner's mixed-blood characters, such as Joe Christmas in *Light in August*. Lucas is his own man and nobody else's, almost to a fault.

Intruder in the Dust also foreshadowed Faulkner's own later pronouncements on race in the person of lawyer Gavin Stevens, who expounds at some length upon his vision of how the South's racial dilemma might be solved. Stevens's basic position is what might be called a liberal paternalist version of the states' rights argument: The South, which is to say, the white South, must solve its racial problem without outside interference from the North or the federal government. According to Stevens, "I only say injustice is ours, the South's. We must expiate and abolish it ourselves." Where Faulkner had once written to Robert Haas that white people had a "responsibility to the Negro" (*SL* 262), now Gavin Stevens speaks bizarrely of the "privilege" of setting blacks free. Yet Faulkner has Chick Mallison, a twelve-year-old boy, challenge Stevens's pronouncements; and it is Chick, not Gavin, who takes action to save Lucas from a false murder charge. In fact, Faulkner was even quoted as saying that if the South's racial agonies were to be solved, it would be the children who would do it.

Needless to say, many critics jumped on Stevens's views as wrongheaded and hopelessly confused. They were confused, but clearly also the product of a complex and conflicted mind. This became clear when Faulkner began speaking out in his own voice as the South faced its most serious crisis since 1861. Faulkner objected strongly to the lynchings of Willie McGee and Emmett Till; less dramatically but just as important, he carried on a spirited exchange in the Memphis *Commercial Appeal* about the public schools in the South and hammered at the absurdity of maintaining dual school systems when neither system, white or black, provided an adequate education for its children. His longer articles in *Life, Harper's*, and *Ebony* in the mid-1950s were a mixture of shrewd insights (the dangers of racial polarization and the need for Negroes to find new strategies to attack segregation), a prescient awareness of the global implications of the racial struggle (Faulkner visited several countries for the State Department in the decade), and bad history. He could combine an insulting characterization of Africa as barbaric with fulsome praise for American blacks for having come so far, despite the handicap of having come from backward Africa and also in spite of the abject failure of whites to meet their paternalistic responsibilities to blacks in slavery and afterward.

Sensitive as Faulkner was to the psychological stresses blacks lived with, and aware as he was of the role whites had played in "creating" the Negro, he never completely shook off the deeply ingrained assumption of black inferiority and the need for whites to take blacks firmly in hand. In what was his last lengthy pronouncement on the racial crisis in 1958, he suggested that the more white blood a black person had, the more capable he or she would be; he went on to advocate school integration in order to teach blacks how to match up to whites. He saw that the issue was the enforcement of legal equality, not integration as such. At the time, such distinctions sounded like the special pleading of a man who had backed himself into a corner.

Overall, several general points need making. First, Faulkner had grown up at the nadir of Southern race relations and the peak period of white Southern racism, including lynching. Little wonder that he could never fight completely free of these formative experiences and views. Second, Faulkner's views on race and civil rights revealed just how deeply unpolitical he was. If there was any cornerstone to his world, it was the importance of privacy and the right of the individual to his/her own views and way of life. From this position, his opposition to federal intervention in the affairs of the Southern states draws its own logic. Still, against all the prejudices with which Faulkner was raised, he clearly—though through clenched teeth at first—called for compliance with the 1954 Supreme Court's *Brown v. Board of Education* decision. Something about the Court's decision and the emergence of race into the public realm touched a moral and psychological chord in him and fitted with the way his own thoughts on racial matters had been tending over a couple of decades.

Neither Faulkner's fictional nor his personal world generally made much room for politics or the public realm. Somehow the truths of the human heart, as he saw them, could scarcely find a hearing in the public world. But whether it was Faulkner's self-styled aristocratic sense of responsibility or whether he simply assumed his citizenly duty to speak out, Faulkner took a public stand when very few other white writers in the South or in Mississippi did. That the results were not always happy or helpful, were at times even embarrassing, is undeniable. But that they issued from some deep affection for his region and displayed considerable civic courage is also undeniable.

See also **African American; Civil War; Slavery**.

FURTHER READING

Brodsky, Louis Daniel. "Faulkner and the Racial Crisis, 1956." *Southern Review* 24 (1988): 791–807.
Fowler and Abadie, eds. *Faulkner and Race*.

Richard H. King

"RACE AT MORNING," a short story by Faulkner, first appeared in the *Saturday Evening Post* on March 5, 1955. Revised for *Big Woods*, it also appears in *Uncollected Stories*. This is another ritual hunting story, the theme of which is that the chase can be more important than the kill. The narrator is an unnamed twelve-year-old boy who, after having been abandoned by his mother and then his father, has been adopted by Mister Ernest. The chase begins early in the morning, and Mister Ernest and the boy pursue the twelve-point buck until dark, when Ernest decides to abandon the chase so that the deer can be hunted the following year.

FURTHER READING

Bradford, Melvin E. "The Winding Horn: Hunting and the Making of Men in Faulkner's 'Race at Morning.' " *Papers on Language and Literature* 1 (1965): 272–278.

Larry Wharton

"RAID," a Faulkner short story, was published in the *Saturday Evening Post* on November 3, 1934, and revised as the third chapter of *The Unvanquished*. In a Yankee raid, the Sartoris family has lost silver, mules, and slaves. Granny Rosa Millard, with the help of her grandson Bayard Sartoris and his African

American playmate Ringo, successfully counterraids when her losses are recompensed many times over through a Yankee bureaucratic mishap. Bayard's cousin, Drusilla Hawk, has lost her fiancé, as well as her place as a Southern woman, through her fiancé's death in battle; she now wears men's clothing and wants to become a Confederate raider. Drusilla takes Granny, Bayard, and Ringo to watch a "flood" of freed slaves, as lost as Southern women, attempting to cross a river, their Jordan.

FURTHER READING

Gibb, Robert. " 'Moving Fast Sideways': A Look at Form and Image in *The Unvanquished.*" *Faulkner Journal* 3.2 (1988): 40–47.

Van Devender, George W. "William Faulkner's Black Exodus: Multiple Narratives in *The Unvanquished.*" *South Central Bulletin* 42.4 (1982): 144–148.

Veronica Makowsky

RATLIFF, VLADIMIR KYRLYTCH, a Faulkner character who appears most notably in the *Snopes* trilogy but also in *Sartoris, As I Lay Dying, Requiem for a Nun*, and several short stories. "Pleasant, affable, courteous, anecdotal and impenetrable," the narrator of *The Hamlet* says of Ratliff, a traveling sewing machine salesman. "Perceptive" and "forthright" should be added, as well. Ratliff, occasionally spelled "Ratliffe" and also known as "V. K. Suratt," lives in Jefferson but travels and trades throughout four counties, carrying not only sewing machines but "personal messages from mouth to mouth about weddings and funerals and the preserving of vegetables and fruit with the reliability of a postal service." Intervening, advising, well intentioned, he is the antidote to Faulkner's Snopes family. "A fellow can dodge a Snopes if he . . . starts lively enough," he says as he tries to reason with the crowd of fellows who are hoodwinked into considering the purchase of Flem's worthless horses. "You folks ain't going to buy them things sho enough, are you?" When Ratliff realizes how he has been "Snoped" himself, he provides a memorable description: "I went as far as one Snopes will set fire to another Snopes' barn . . . but I never went on to where that first Snopes will turn around and stomp the fire out so he can sue that second Snopes for the reward."

FURTHER READING

Kane, Patricia. "Adaptable and Free: Faulkner's Ratliff." *Notes on Contemporary Literature* 1 (1971): 9–11.

Moses, Edwin. "Faulkner's *The Hamlet*: The Passionate Humanity of V. K. Ratliff." *Notre Dame English Journal* 8 (1973): 98–109.

Trimmer, Joseph F. "V. K. Ratliff: A Portrait of the Artist in Motion." *Modern Fiction Studies* 20 (1974–1975): 451–467.

Marion Tangum

RECONSTRUCTION was the political process of bringing formerly rebellious states back into the Union during and following the Civil War in the period from 1863 to 1877. In a broader sense, the term refers to the effort to repatriate the South by elevating former slaves to full citizenship, diminishing the power of the planter elite, and generally reforming the South's economic and social life in the transition from slave to free labor.

Under President Lincoln and then Johnson, Reconstruction followed a moderate and limited course. Johnson allowed the quick reentry of former Confederate states and a liberal policy of amnesty toward former Confederate leaders. The state of Mississippi demonstrated just how thoroughly unreconstructed much of the South remained. Despite the verdict of the battlefield and the abolition of slavery, many former rebels demonstrated their intent to resist any further effort toward reform, particularly involving former slaves. The Mississippi constitutional convention refused in 1865 to ratify the Thirteenth Amendment that formally abolished slavery (a refusal that stood until 1995). Lafayette County delegate Hugh Barr (the former owner of Faulkner's beloved Caroline "Mammie Callie" Barr) proposed substitute language stating it was the United States that abolished slavery in Mississippi. Mississippi's legislature then went on to promulgate the infamous "Black Codes," a set of laws that denied former slaves vital civil rights and coerced them to labor for whites, in effect reintroducing a form of slavery that in some respects was worse than the original system.

Mississippi's defiance brought swift reaction from the Radical wing of the Republican Party, led by Thaddeus Stevens, Charles Summer, and others in Congress. The Radicals were convinced that all the blood shed during the war would be for nothing unless the federal government saw to it that the source of rebellion was attacked at its foundations. They depicted the South as a society at odds with fundamental American beliefs in equality and progress, a society ruled by a selfish aristocracy whose power and affluence came at the expense of a subjugated race of blacks and an impoverished, illiterate mass of poor whites. The Radical agenda included, first, the elimination of the planter elite, whom they held responsible for the rebellion, from political power and, in the most extreme proposals, confiscation of their land. Second, Radicals wanted to bring former slaves into full citizenship and protect their civil rights through federal power whenever state governments proved unwilling or unable to do so.

Beginning in 1867, Radicals introduced the Fourteenth Amendment, which at once restricted the political power of former Confederate leaders and guaranteed the rights of citizenship to former slaves, rights that could not be denied without due process. The Fifteenth Amendment extended voting rights to former slaves by disallowing any restrictions based on race, religion, or previous condition of servitude. Despite the profound hopes of former slaves, more radical programs to redistribute land, the famous "forty acres and a mule," remained nothing more than a disappointed dream.

With the voting power of newly enfranchised freedmen, Republicans could win victories in Deep South states like Mississippi where blacks constituted a majority. Even in more racially balanced counties, like Lafayette County where black voters were in the minority, there were sufficient numbers of "scalawags"

(Southern white Republicans) to win elections. The threat of Republican political power provoked a violent backlash from the Conservative-Democratic opposition across the Deep South. Much of this came in the form of election fraud, the intimidation of voters, and violent attacks on Republican leaders black and white. The Ku Klux Klan, first organized in 1867 in response to Radical Reconstruction measures, along with similar secret societies of night riders, constituted the terrorist wing of the Conservative-Democratic opposition. The Klan implemented an organized campaign of terror and violence aimed primarily at countering the political power of the Republicans but more broadly at any effort to empower, educate, and uplift black citizens. Across the South schools for freedmen were destroyed, and schoolteachers, typically Northern women and former antislavery missionaries, were terrorized into leaving.

Because it was racially and politically balanced, Lafayette County, Mississippi, became violently contested ground. Nathan Bedford Forrest is credited with organizing the Klan at a meeting held in the small brick office building later occupied by Faulkner's friend Phil Stone. Violence had erupted earlier with the attack by former slaves on the home of overseer Sam Ragland, which resulted in the brutal murder of his wife Elizabeth. Retaliation by whites resulted in the killing of large numbers of blacks by lynching or drowning in the Yoknapatawpha River. The part of the county in the proximity of what Faulkner called Frenchman's Bend became notorious for racial violence and became forbidding territory for most blacks after the bloody times of 1866.

In Mississippi, as throughout the South, the Freedman's Bureau attempted to protect the former slaves by supervising labor contracts and dispensing food and health care when necessary. Although it did much to shield former slaves from the worst forms of exploitation and retribution, the Bureau never had sufficient power to serve as much more than a watchdog. In many places, including Lafayette County, the Bureau fell into the hands of the opposition.

Radical Reconstruction had anticipated the need for more powerful agencies of enforcement and used the power of the federal government through the military and the courts to guarantee the rights of black and white citizens. Much of the former Confederacy was divided into military districts, and garrisons of the U.S. Army were installed to guarantee proper elections and otherwise intervene wherever the state could not protect the rights and safety of its citizens. In northern Mississippi there was a garrison at Holly Springs, and during times of political and racial violence, troops were dispatched to Oxford. Some of the soldiers serving in the South were former slaves, many of them recruited during the war. The continued presence of federal troops in the South provoked white resentment twice over.

Additionally, federal authorities used the power of the federal courts under the terms of the Klan Enforcement Act of 1871 to prosecute Klansmen and others accused of violating the civil rights of former slaves. Oxford witnessed the first Klan trial, during which there occurred a violent confrontation between Klan defender L.Q.C. Lamar and federal authorities. The intransigent refusal of

Southern whites to recognize the legitimacy of Republican rule and the black citizenship it rested upon left the Republicans at the state and federal level with the choice of ongoing rule at the point of a bayonet or giving up. Mississippi's "redemption" by the Conservative Democrats came in 1875 following what nearly became a racial war between black state militia forces and armed white militia. Following the tragic conflict of the Civil War and more than ten additional years of violence and turmoil in the South, the American public and Republican leaders seemed morally exhausted. By 1877 all federal troops were withdrawn from the South, leaving state government firmly in the hands of white Democrats. Later, Mississippi led the way in devising laws that disenfranchised black citizens, thereby ending, for the next half century, any further threat of black political power in the South. The supposed atrocities of "Black Republicans" became ensconced in popular thinking and historical scholarship as the Black Legend of Reconstruction.

As demonstrated by the above summary, Faulkner had rich historical material to draw upon for his fictional treatment of Reconstruction; but although he revisited the period frequently, he rarely did so with the kind of probing, even subversive talent, one finds in his treatments of other epochs in Mississippi history. Among the featured characters in the story of Yoknapatawpha's Reconstruction era are the Burdens, religious fanatics intent upon repenting for white sins by lifting up the former slave. They are treated at some length in *Light in August*, in which Joanna Burden, the surviving daughter, recounts the story of how John Sartoris ruthlessly shot her father and uncle to death at the election polls in Jefferson.

The same story is told in *The Unvanquished*, but from a point of view far more sympathetic to John Sartoris. The story begins, however, with a comical but remarkably savvy analysis of the meaning of Reconstruction by the former slave Ringo. "This war ain't over. Hit just started good," Ringo tells Bayard Sartoris, the son of his former master. As usual, Ringo has sized up the situation well ahead of his white friend and is filling him in. "You know what I ain't?" he tells Bayard. "I ain't a nigger any more. I done been abolished." When he goes on to tell Bayard that Cassius Q. Benbow, another former slave, is preparing for permanent election as marshal, Bayard responds incredulously, "A nigger?" " 'No,' Ringo said. 'They aint no more niggers, in Jefferson nor nowhere else.' " The carpetbaggers, led by the Burdens, were here to "organise the niggers into Republicans," just what John Sartoris and other whites were determined to stop from happening.

Another principal character in Faulkner's rendition of Reconstruction is Ben Redmond, the carpetbagger who joins forces with John Sartoris to organize a railroad through northern Mississippi. Redmond represents the carpetbagger as economic opportunist, as opposed to religious reformer or political ally of former slaves. Redmond's partnership with John Sartoris is modeled after that of John Thurmond with the author's great-grandfather and namesake, "Old Colonel" William C. Falkner. In 1889, following a political and personal feud, Thurmond shot Falkner dead on the streets of Ripley, just as Redmond kills Sartoris in *The Unvanquished*. As shown by John Sartoris's conversation with his son just before he is killed, Faulkner uses this episode to mark the passage of the entire era of violence that hitherto marked Yoknapatawpha's history. The new age, John Sartoris predicts, will belong to lawyers and other men whose shrewdness, rather than physical courage and violence, will secure their ascendance. Bayard, in turn, applies this logic in challenging the older Southern code in "An Odor of Verbena."

It was not until the time of the modern civil rights movement in the 1950s that revisionist scholarship began to undermine the stock interpretations that shaped American views of Reconstruction in the North as well as the South. Although he questioned many facets of black/white relationships, Faulkner seemed never to venture into any serious questioning of the Black Legend of Reconstruction he and his generation of white Southerners had imbibed.

FURTHER READING

Foner, Eric. *Reconstruction: The Unfinished Revolution*. New York: Harper and Row, 1988.

Garner, James Wilford. *Reconstruction in Mississippi*. 1901. Gloucester, Mass.: Peter Smith, 1964.

Harris, William C. *Presidential Reconstruction in Mississippi*. Baton Rouge: Louisiana State University Press, 1967.

Kendel, Julia. "Reconstruction in Lafayette County." *Publications of the Mississippi Historical Society* 13 (1913): 223–271.

Rable, George C. *But There Was No Peace: The Role of Violence in the Politics of Reconstruction*. Athens: University of Georgia Press, 1984.

Trelease, Allen W. *White Terror: The Ku Klux Klan Conspiracy and Southern Reconstruction*. Westport, Conn.: Greenwood, 1979.

Don H. Doyle

"RED LEAVES," a short story by Faulkner, first published in the October 25, 1930 issue of the *Saturday Evening Post*. Although often considered an inferior story, it appears in *These 13, The Portable Faulkner*, and *Collected Stories*. Set at the site of Indian quarters, the latter half of the story recounts the flight and return of Issetibbeha's Negro slave, brought on by the ritual demand that he be buried with his just dead master. The first half is the anticipation of this flight as a fulfillment of a pattern. Three Baskets and Louis Berry's conversation recalls the lives of Doom, Issetibbeha, and Moketubbe and comments on the institution of slavery.

While apparently accurate in its portrait of Chickasaw customs, including their ownership of slaves (see Dabney), the story is not meant as a historical portrait of the Chickasaw. By transferring the institution of slavery to another culture, Faulkner gains a hearing for his exposure of slavery's effect on the slaveholder; by making that culture one in which ritual is given its due, he can explore universals regarding the passages of life. The story's effect is to draw the reader from the particulars of the scene to a reflection on emotions and motive forces that transcend cultural boundaries. "Man must die," Three Baskets asserts. "Let him; there is still the Man," Louis Berry replies. *"Le Roi est mort; viva le Roi"* in Yoknapatawpha.

Despite historical elements, it is Faulkner's inventions—Doom's time in New Orleans, his relationship with the Chevalier Soeur Blonde de Vitry, his acquisition of a Negro wife—that draw our attention to how long these Chickasaws have been borrowing from other cultures, diluting their own ethos, until all that is left of their earlier strength and nobility is the hollow ritual being played out in the story. Here, somewhat in the fashion of Conrad, the Indians seem like "carved heads on a ruined wall in Siam or Sumatra," Moketubbe ("Mongolian") appears "like an effigy, like a Malay god," and another wears a "long linen frock coat and a beaver hat." Never quite leaving the Indian camp, never quite arriving at the wasteland, each seems a likely locus for the other as the story ranges in between.

Faulkner manages to draw the past into the present through the enormous oddities of two central images. One is the "deck house of the steamboat" that serves as "the Man's" house, brought originally "on cypress rollers twelve miles home overland," but now the site of the death of Issetibbeha and Moketubbe's succession to his role. Here, Faulkner's adjectives—"rotting," "fading," "gutted," "rusted"—play out the ruin of the present. The second image is a pair of red slippers, brought from Paris by Doom on the trip paid for by his sale of "forty head" of slaves. They become inverse signs of rule. Now, as Moketubbe first tries them on before Issetibbeha is yet dead, then faints away from their constriction of the blood flow from his feet, they become a token of greed, a testimony to indolence, and a "monstrous repudiation of fact."

Notably, historicity is reserved for the Negro slaves and the attitudes toward them. During the chase, we learn how, in coming to America, the fleeing slave had "lived ninety days in a threefoot-high 'tween-deck in tropic latitudes"; in bitter irony he recalls hearing the drunk captain reading aloud from what he later learns is the Bible while he wears "the white garment which the trader, a deacon in the Unitarian church, had given him." True to what we know of how slaves communicated across language barriers, his flight is triggered by the "talk" of the drums that the Negroes kept, "hidden in the creek bottom." (Like Sutpen's slaves, several of these blacks are pictured coating themselves with mud to ward off mosquitoes.)

As the middle passage and early survival are recapitulated in brief, the apology of slave owners echoes through these Indian masters who, in selling slaves back to the whites, have come full circle from first having become slave owners through whites' example and trade. To these owners, the Negro slaves are "without honor and without decorum," while the owners, far from profiting from the ownership, must work harder than the slaves at finding work for "them who prefer sweating to do." They are a great bother, but, an anonymous voice notes pointedly, "We must do as the white men do." Black, white, red are here not so much colors as cultures, less lives than histories: In a microcosm of America, as black and white encroach, red leaves.

As the chasers pursue the slave on his circuitous route first away from and then back to the encampment referred to as a "plantation," a ritual enactment of death in life and life in death, we come to see the story's essential mystery: Why would the ruined and indolent welcome death while such as slaves "would even rather work in the sun than to enter the earth with a chief"? And more: Whatever their differences, they wait together at burial, "patient, grave, decorous, implacable; clansman and guest and kin."

FURTHER READING

Beidler, Peter G. "A Darwinian Source for Faulkner's Indians in 'Red Leaves.' " *Studies in Short Fiction* 10 (1973): 421–423.

Hönnighausen, Lothar. "Faulkner Rewriting the Indian Removal." *Rewriting the South: History and Fiction*. Ed. Lothar Hönnighausen and Valeria Gennaro Lerda. Tübingen, Germany: Francke, 1993. 335–343.

Muller, Gilbert H. "The Descent of the Gods: Faulkner's 'Red Leaves' and the Garden of the South." *Studies in Short Fiction* 11 (1974): 243–249.

Watkins, Floyd C. "Sacrificial Rituals and Anguish in the Victim's Heart in 'Red Leaves.' " *Studies in Short Fiction* 30 (1993): 71–78.

Charles A. Peek

REIVERS, THE: A REMINISCENCE. Published in June 1962, one month prior to Faulkner's death, the novel won a Pulitzer Prize in 1963. As indicated by the title, a Scottish term meaning "robbers," this book is about stealing: stealing guns, stealing cars, stealing horses, and most significantly, stealing experience and meaning from those in control of such phenomena. Narrated by a persona identified as "Grandfather" and dedicated by Faulkner to his own grandchildren, *The Reivers* makes clear the necessity that the young "reive" from the old authority over their inherited world. What Grandfather says in the novel is to beware of making him into the kind of icon that prohibits, or even inhibits, future creation. To make his point, he explains how and why he stole and how important the act was in forming his character.

The novel opens with an immediate disavowal of the narrator's credibility: "I'm sure you have often noticed how ignorant people beyond thirty or forty are." The narrative continues to present a balanced presentation of wisdom and knowledge as equally dependent upon the experience and guidance of elders and upon the resources and imaginative powers inherent only in the young. Yet the young are not given their chance until the elders die away. In fact, until their authority is negated in death, the old stand in the way of young people's creative life experiences. The symbol through which much of this theme is communicated is the automobile, the icon of the future in 1905, the year the novel takes place. Lucius Priest's grandfather bought an automobile not to use but to keep up with a rival who also bought one. To young Lucius, however, the automobile embodies and holds promise to the future, to his maturity, and to his inheritance of freedom, authority, and power. His grandfather, significantly called "Boss," wishes to keep the car locked up. Lucius steals the car not because he wishes to keep it but because he desires the kinds of experience available only to those with mobility.

The idea of experiential reiving is masked in the novel beneath a narrative that verges on the trivial and harmless. Critics have often read the novel superficially, owing to an assumption that this last novel lacks the power and vitality of earlier works. Oddly for Faulkner critics, the narrator's words (despite his admitted ignorance by virtue of age) are taken at face value, so that many have read the book as being about the "gentlemanly code" so important to Grandfather. However, any deceptively comfortable reading of *The Reivers* that stresses male generational bonding and adolescent initiation ought to be tempered by readings of most other Faulkner novels where narrators cannot be trusted entirely. As interest in Faulkner's later career develops, critical perspectives on the novel may become more complete.

Faulkner's last novel pairs the willingness to reive with the need to say no to authority when its demands run counter to desires or ambitions within one's conscience. Lucius thus says no to Boss's locked garage; Everbe says no to her life as a prostitute; and Boon is transformed by the realization of his capacity to refuse. The novel, therefore, endorses the will to take what is needed to accomplish a movement, peacefully or by force, away from the ignorance of age and establishment. The stakes involved are life and death, money and power; and the transition of authority is far from ritualistic or even orderly. Instead, it is compelled and reived. The details of the transition are indeed trivial; in this case, they involve a stolen car, a prostitute, and a racehorse. Lucius, Boon Hogganbeck, and Ned McCaslin travel to Memphis because Boon wants to visit Corrie, a prostitute at Miss Reba's bordello. While there, Ned trades the stolen car for a racehorse. To get the car back, a race is arranged for the racehorse to win, which it does. Corrie reforms and marries Boon, and Lucius learns quite a bit about character. Then they all go home to confront Grandfather.

Critics have noted parallels between this novel and Mark Twain's *The Adventures of Huckleberry Finn*, another novel of travel and revelation. Regarding mistakes made by Lucius, his grandfather can only say, "Live with it," and deliver various homilies about being a gentleman. Grandfather has an interest, of course, in providing a more conservative reading of what Lucius has been through. Nonetheless, it is the reivers, not the elders, who triumph in the book. Boon makes his visit to Memphis and marries Corrie, Ned makes a bundle on the racehorse, and he and Lucius withhold information from Boss regarding just how much they won. It is youthful stealth and the subterfuge of the underclass (and race), not a gentlemanly code or an acceptance of the human condition, that wins the race in *The Reivers*.

Faulkner died, dramatically, one month after the publication of *The Reivers*. He left no novel-in-progress and had no stated plan to follow this book with another. Given these circumstances, the importance of the book as a self-conscious last statement poses a particular challenge to Faulkner readers, especially biographical critics. The comic vision of the novel is unmistakable, particularly the revisiting of Miss Reba's whorehouse (from *Sanctuary*) as comic center. Faulkner's dark vision is equally in focus, as much of what Lucius learns and the way in which he encounters it are far from genteel. As well, the backward glance of the novel is undeniable. It is set in the world of Faulkner's childhood and draws upon personal as well as textual reminiscence. The tone of the novel implies nostalgia, but its narrative events contradict sentimentality. For a man in the last years of his life, *The Reivers* displays a remarkable faith in the future and in the rising, reiving generations.

FURTHER READING

Carothers, James B. "The Road to *The Reivers*." *A Cosmos of My Own*, ed. Fowler and Abadie. 95–124.

Moses, Edwin. "Faulkner's *The Reivers*: The Art of Acceptance." *Mississippi Quarterly* 27 (1974): 307–318.

Taylor, Walter. "Faulkner's Reivers: How to Change the Joke without Slipping the Yoke." *Faulkner and Race*, ed. Fowler and Abadie. 111–129.

Urgo. *Faulkner's Apocrypha.*

Wittenberg, Judith Bryant. "*The Reivers*: A Conservative Fable?" *Faulkner: After the Nobel Prize*, ed. Michel Gresset and Kenzaburo Ohashi. Kyoto, Japan: Yamaguchi, 1987. 201–228.

Yoshida, Michiko. "Faulkner's Comedy of Motion: *The Reivers*." *Faulkner: After the Nobel Prize*, ed. Gresset and Ohashi. 197–210.

Joseph R. Urgo

REIVERS, THE (film), is filmmaker Mark Rydell's 1969 movie version of Faulkner's novel, the story of young Lucius Priest's first trip to Memphis in the company of his older friend Boon Hogganbeck (Steve McQueen), where Lucius learns a great deal about the dark side of adult life. When he returns home, his grandfather seeks to help him to profit from the experiences he had during his journey. Since the novel is narrated by Lucius as an old man, the screenplay by Irving Ravetch and Harriet Frank, Jr., attempts to approximate the book's narrative point of view by having the elderly Lucius (voice by Burgess Meredith) give a running commentary on the action, voice-over on the sound track, as the plot unfolds on the screen. Most of the aging narrator's remarks are taken verbatim from the novel. The film reflects Faulkner's humor and earthy characterizations in a most satisfying fashion. All in all, *The Reivers* remains one of the better films derived from Faulkner's work.

FURTHER READING

Crist, Judith. *Take 22: Moviemakers on Moviemaking*. New York: Viking, 1981.

Kael, Pauline. *5001 Nights at the Movies*. New York: Holt, 1991.

Gene D. Phillips

RELIGION. Following this country's break with Europe, voluntary choice of religious denomination increased, many leaving their childhood affiliation. As de Tocqueville said, in a democracy "each generation is a new people," and with *self-improvement* an American by-word, individual choice could be determined by a desire to move up the "establishment" ladder or, by a transforming religious experience, being "born again." On the frontier and particularly in the postbellum South, infused with evangelicalism, church membership swelled.

Amid this piety, Faulkner's "Southern country boy" background included having to memorize a Bible verse before breakfast when he visited his great-grandfather and attending Sunday School in his father's Methodist Church and revival meetings with his mother. Married in the Presbyterian Church, Faulkner became an Episcopalian (even though he could not marry the divorced Estelle in that church), attended if only occasionally, and was buried with the rites of the church. And although he doubted personal immortality, he abjured doubts about God, saying, "You question God, and then you begin to doubt . . . and God fades away by the very act of your doubting Him" (*LIG* 70).

But if Faulkner himself for the most part rode the religious mainstream, his novels reveal a more rebellious mind. There the religious heroes are few; the villains many. If not doctrinaire like Cora (in *As I Lay Dying*), the faith of humble folk like Lena (in *Light in August*) or Dilsey (in *The Sound and the Fury*) could justify his belief that humankind would "prevail." Otherwise, we find "a young Baptist minister, a fiery-eyed dervish, who had served in the Y.M.C.A." (in *Soldiers' Pay*); an Association that could make you "rich" (in *Sartoris*); the Methodist steward, Goodhue Coldfield, whose home had "a grim mausoleum air of puritan righteousness" (in *Absalom, Absalom!*); or Flem Snopes gracing the Baptist Church as deacon in *The Town*, whose settlers had "quitted home and security . . . to find freedom in which to be incorrigible and unreconstructible Baptists and Methodists."

Light in August teems with religious fanatics. The ruthless Calvinist, Simon McEachern, teaches by beating; catching his son at lying, he gives a "luxurious" sigh of "satisfaction and victory." Old Doc Hines preaches the supremacy of the chosen (white) race to blacks, and Percy Grimm, resembling a "young priest," kills and castrates Joe for the same reason that Hines had killed Joe's father and wants Joe, his grandson, killed—because of his "black blood." The Presbyterian ex-minister, Gail Hightower, D.D. (or "Done Damned"), refusing to engage himself with the living, not only fails his parishioners but also sends his wife into madness and suicide. Yet Hightower sees the Church controlled by "professionals" who have "removed the bells from its steeples." He sees the buildings "empty, symbolical, bleak, skypointed . . . in adjuration, threat, and doom." Listening to the "stern and implacable" music of the choir, he realizes that, unable to bear "pleasure or ecstasy," the congregants "escape . . . in violence. . . . *And so why should not their religion drive them to crucifixion of themselves and one another?*"

Like others in the avant-garde, Faulkner was reading his H. L. Mencken. In

a 1915 article, "Puritanism as a Literary Force," excoriating the American Phil-
istine, Mencken describes Calvinism as "a luxuriant demonology" that "still
survives in the barbaric doctrines of the Methodists and Baptists, particularly in
the South." This more virulent brand of New England Puritanism "is not ascetic, but militant. Its aim is not to lift up saints but to knock down sinners."
Its "professional sinhound" is not the ecclesiastic but the layman. Power-driven,
the Puritan has "an ineradicable liking for cruelty . . . and very often his blood-
lust leads him into lamentable excesses." But he can also seduce converts by
moneymaking "schemes" such as the Y.M.C.A.

As if heeding Mencken's call for aesthetic guts, Faulkner willingly broke the
taboos of his day, no more so than in the realm of what John Crowe Ransom
called the "terrible incubus of piety." Faulkner's use of what he termed "Christian lore and imagery" can make conventional readers squirm: All three Compson brothers in *The Sound and the Fury* have been linked to Christ, including
the thirty-three-year-old slobbering idiot Benjy, "de Lawd's chile," riding
around the town monument on Easter Sunday, holding a narcissus, symbol of
the Resurrection, but broken, oblivious of entreaties that fuse with those given
the horse: "Git up! Git up dar! Benjy, fer God's sake!"

Repeatedly, Faulkner brings "the Christian legend" unnervingly to life by
knocking it about, smudging it with the pagan and the primitive. As Barbara
Cross has noted, Benjy is also Attis; Quentin, Adonis. While Benjy "treats
Caddy's slipper as if it held her soul," Quentin sees her "through his horror of
the feminine cycle"—both beliefs described in James Frazer's *Golden Bough*.

While many modernists could use archetypal materials with detachment, ironically, as he admitted, Faulkner was a puritan, so his works often have a double
irony that creates moral purpose. In *A Fable*, recounting the Passion amid World
War I horrors, Christ is crucified as the French Corporal, the English Boggan,
the American Brzewski, and the Negro, Rev. Sutterfield, alias Tooleyman (Tout
le Monde). Less allegorical is the parallel of the twenty-one chapters of *Light
in August* with the twenty-one chapters of the St. John gospel, with each story
expanded by material from Frazer. For example, Joe Christmas, a bootlegger
from the underworld, is introduced in chapter 2, which in John recounts the
changing of water to wine. Moreover, this JC not only represents Christ; he is
also that early scapegoat, Dionysus, the underworld god whose mysteries involved the changing of water to wine, described in Frazer. Not that Joe is Christ
changing water to wine; rather he, like others in 2, enacts the theme of "change"
central to that chapter in John. Thus, this figure's ties to Christ add an element
of sympathy for "the least of these"; his ties to Dionysus and folk behavior
add an element of universality (and often, humor); yet he remains Joe Christmas,
the boy who refuses the name McEachern, the young man who falls for the
fallen woman, and the thirty-three-year-old lover and murderer of Joanna Burden
who, forcing himself to rejoin the rejecting human community, becomes Christ-
as-scapegoat.

Faulkner believed that "human beings are terrible," not from a Calvinistic sense of Original Sin—his sympathy for children is Dickensian—but rather from believing that human beings could choose to be decent and courageous. By setting his Christian and pagan figures in contemporary moral dilemmas, he reveals humanity's age-old, desperate yearning for relief from life's terribleness, for belief in a savior.

See also **Christianity; Clergy; Religion, Southern**.

FURTHER READING

Brumm, Ursula. *American Thought and Religious Typology*. New Brunswick, N.J.: Rutgers University Press, 1970.
Cross, Barbara. "*The Sound and the Fury*: The Pattern of Sacrifice." *Arizona Quarterly* 16 (1960): 5–16.
Culley, Margaret M. "Judgment in Yoknapatawpha Fiction." *Renascence* 28 (1976): 59–70.
Fowler and Abadie, eds. *Faulkner and Religion*.

                                                              Virginia V. James Hlavsa

RELIGION, SOUTHERN. Religion can be seen as a social indicator and political force, a part of the cultural fabric of a region. As such, despite strong traditions of Roman Catholicism and Judaism, the "religion of the South" has historically been Protestant. This is largely true of African American religion in the South, as well. Protestantism gave such churches their focus on biblical patterns that explained and ameliorated hardship while offering hope for the future. These patterns—the exodus from slavery, the vulnerable birth of the baby in the manger, and the apocalyptic promises of John the Divine—shaped Southern black religion into its own phenomenon. Further, the black church's Protestantism was from the beginning annealed to West African cultural traditions, not the least those that emerged as call/response singing and preaching. These traditions were directly tied to black liberation, whether being taught or being denied the master's Bible, and gave black Southern religion an even more distinct practice. Faulkner's awareness of it and respect for it are unmistakable. His most memorable evocation is perhaps Reverend Shegog's sermon in *The Sound and the Fury*.

Until the post–World War II era, however, it cannot be said that the religious practices of African Americans affected the social and political practices of the South. In social impact historically measured, Southern religion is not only Protestant but white. Despite the social prominence of such denominations as the Episcopalians and Presbyterians, its religious practice has on the whole been evangelical: conservative in outlook, Puritan in morals, and orthodox in doctrine. As such, there was for the generations that encompassed the Civil War through World War I something of a unified religious expression that cast its lot with the rise of the Lost Cause, the revival of chivalry, and advancement of agrarian social values. In many cases, Southern denominations severed ties with their Northern counterparts altogether.

Although Anglicans had once been the state religion in Virginia, their off-spring, the Episcopalians, had to join others in making their own way in the "new voluntary system of religious affiliation" that followed the Revolutionary War (Wilson 2). Yet because of their old prominence, they continued to enjoy a place in the social order that allowed them to contribute a ritualism to Southern social observances somewhat at odds with the less ritualistic manner of those denominations who came to dominate following the Great Revival of 1787–1805, namely, the Southern Baptists and Methodists.

Up to World War I, the "old time" religion generally found in Israel's travails and Christ's passion apt figures for both the South's sense of loss and its sense of itself as a region with a separate identity and even cultural mission. As the Old South became the object of nostalgic longing and endurance of travail an icon, the figure of the faithful Negro retainer (Mammy, Old Uncle Ned) emerged in the Southern folk pantheon. For the white South, however, the war effort began the reidentification with American ideology and the restoration of the celebration of national holidays. Soon, two civil religions existed side by side in the South; both focused on how the New South, capitalized and industrialized, could resist the forces of modernity and materialism seen now as the legacy of the North. For blacks, however, World War I was the beginning of a new determination to resist both the American and the Southern civil religion.

These were the religious forces that, transporting to the South the Calvinist traditions once associated with New England and uniting them to Southern po-litical and racial issues, influenced Faulkner's upbringing. His forebears, espe-cially the Butlers, were steeped in Southern religion, and Faulkner imbibed it early. He did not imbibe it uncritically, however. Although himself a spiritual man, his portraits of clergy (*Light in August*'s Hightower, for instance) and his satires on Protestantism (*Requiem*'s "roaring with Protestant scripture and boiled whiskey," for instance) make clear his disdain for the white South's unified Protestant voice.

See also **Christianity; Clergy; Religion**.

FURTHER READING

Bercovitch, Sacvan. *The Puritan Origins of the American Self*. New Haven, Conn.: Yale University Press, 1975.

Wilson, Charles Reagan. *Baptized in Blood: The Religion of the Lost Cause, 1865–1920*. Athens: University of Georgia Press, 1980.

Woodward, C. Vann. *Origins of the New South, 1877–1913*. Baton Rouge: Louisiana State University Press, 1951.

Charles A. Peek

REQUIEM FOR A NUN, title of a play and of a novel published on September 27, 1951. Although begun as early as October 1933, Faulkner set it aside until 1950 when, prompted by Ruth Ford's hope he would write her a play, he began to shape elements of *Requiem* for the stage. As a play it would see production

in Paris, London, and New York. Ford, Lemuel Ayers, and Albert Marre collaborated by assisting Faulkner, not a playwright, to transform his art into that
of the theater. Portions of it would conjoin in the movie *Sanctuary*.

The dramatic elements of the novel version of *Requiem* are framed by a
narrative superstructure that sets the stage for "seven play-scenes inside a
novel" in which the prose is "an integrated part of the act itself" (1974 *FAB*
1322, 1387). These narratives—"The Courthouse," "The Golden Dome," and
"The Jail"—offer an amalgam of Faulkner's representation of Mississippi history and the evolutionary development not only of its legal institutions but of
the very geologic and biologic foundations on which everything else depends.

Faulkner represents much of this history in "The Courthouse" as of a people
"obsolete: anachronism out of an old dead time and a dead age." His lament
is for how supposed progress drives "each year further back the wilderness and
its denizens." The lament turns more bitter in "The Golden Dome," where he
decries the pioneer, "roaring with Protestant scripture and boiled whiskey . . .
felling a tree which took two hundred years to grow, in order to extract from it
a bear or a capful of wild honey." This crescendo grows into "The Jail," where
Gavin Stevens "was wont to say, if you would peruse in unbroken . . . continuity
the history of a community, look not in the church registers and the courthouse
records, but beneath . . . the walls of the jail."

Even in these narratives, Faulkner makes use of the metaphor of drama, fig-
uring the displacement of the original people of the land as being "hurled, flung
. . . like a float or a piece of stage property dragged rapidly into the wings across
the very backdrop and amid the very bustle of the property-men setting up the
next scene and act before the curtain had even had time to fall." In all three,
Faulkner seems to evoke the need for a sense of place by narrating its void, the
need to connect with others by depicting the bizarre lengths to which people
will go to do so. In one of *Requiem*'s most memorable moments Cecilia Farmer
catches through the window of her father's jail just the momentary glance of a
soldier who, a year later, rides back on a mule from Pennsylvania, walks up to
the door of the jail, "patient and urgent," and takes her off on the mule to
Alabama. Here Faulkner seems to be exploring that human capacity to lift itself
by saying, "Listen, stranger, this was myself: this was I."

Still, these narratives are meant only as frames for the dramatic action that
conveys the novel's story of Temple Drake from *Sanctuary*, Nancy Mannigoe
from "That Evening Sun," and Gavin Stevens from *Knight's Gambit* (and elsewhere). Temple was last seen in denial of the experience she took part in at a
Memphis brothel. Here, a changed Temple broods over this past. Faulkner noted
that, in creating *Requiem*, he asked himself what might have become of the sad
girl he left in the Luxembourg Gardens at *Sanctuary*'s end and of her vain
boyfriend, Gowan Stevens (1974 *FAB* 1309). By *Requiem* she has married him,
had two children—Bucky, eight, whose paternity is in question, and an infant
six months old. Temple is preparing to leave Stevens and run off with the thug
brother of a gangster she had loved before. She is propelled by the need for

"[s]omebody to talk to, as we all seem to need, want, have to have." She and we may be in doubt as to what attracts her to the demimonde; there's never any doubt about the emptiness of her life in the upper world of Jefferson's social set. As she laments: "The Gowan Stevenses, young, popular: a new bungalow on the right street to start the Saturday-night hangovers in."

Nancy is the "nun" of the title. Faulkner had described the work to his publisher in 1933 as "about a nigger woman," not meaning the racial epithet himself but using it as an indication of the way Nancy Mannigoe was regarded in Jefferson (1974 *FAB* 818). She enters this action because Temple "had chosen the ex-dope-fiend nigger whore for the reason that an ex-dope-fiend nigger was the only animal in Jefferson that spoke Temple Drake's language." Nancy first acts as Temple's confidante when she thinks Temple is being blackmailed over love letters she had written. She discovers, however, that she is being used to spy on Gowan, that the thug does not need blackmail to get Temple. These realizations propel Nancy's concern, as she watches Temple preparing to run off: What of the infant, damned if taken, damned if left behind? In desperation, Nancy kills the child, is arrested, tried, and convicted for the crime. The play opens on her sentencing to be hanged and the shock given the spectators when she responds, "Yes, Lord," to the addendum, "May God have mercy on your soul." "Violation of procedure," mutters one of the "invisible spectators."

At the heart of the drama stands Temple Drake's visit to the Governor in the middle of the night, ostensibly to plead for Nancy's life. There, before a mythical State and symbolic Governor, prodded by her attorney and our philosophical guide, Gavin Stevens, she tries to come to grips with her motivation and the degree of her culpability, not only for her past actions but primarily for the death of her child. How did this Smart Set couple come to the point where the like of Nancy had become "nurse: guide: mentor, catalyst, glue, whatever you want to call it, holding the whole lot of them together"? For Temple the poignancy here is enhanced by her recognition that hers is "a household, a family, that anybody should have known all the time couldn't possibly hold together." Finally confessing in the third person, "Temple Drake likes evil," she becomes ready to seek absolution yet with the plea, "What about me? . . . [N]obody there, nobody waiting to forgive me." Nancy alters the dimensions the novel explores with her last word, the single word reply: "Believe."

The surrounding narratives both exacerbate and mitigate Nancy's seemingly simple faith and Temple's seemingly complex guilt. The interaction of narratives and drama draws together the intense personal issues of the characters and Faulkner's scathing reconstruction of history. Karl Zender has described Faulkner's relation to his work: "[U]niversal, public meanings always have at their core a meditation on some aspect of his psychic life or of his relation to the world" ("Uses" 273). *Requiem* also drives that street in the other direction: Aspects of Temple's, Gavin's, and Nancy's psychic lives and relations to the world have at their core a meditation on universal, public meanings. As in *Sanctuary*, we are left to explain the attractiveness of evil, the depths of human culpability, and their place in the condition both of the individual and of the state.

Requiem contains memorable scenes and lines, not least Gavin Stevens's "The past is never dead; it's not even past." Still, perhaps through the impossibility of interior monologues of whose uses Faulkner was such a master, the novel fails to rise into the ranks of Faulkner's greatest work. The murder does outrage us, as Millgate claims (*Achievement* 223). However, true to Zender's reading, the book goes beyond that atrocity to become a meditation "on the contrast . . . between an unfallen and a fallen language" (287). Cleanth Brooks judged elements of this novel "the most daring but perhaps the least successful" (*Yoknapatawpha Country* 140) of Faulkner's work. It has great significance for Yoknapatawpha, which is no doubt why Blotner uses excerpts for chapter epigrams in his biography and a subsequent edition of *The Portable Faulkner* includes two of the narratives.

FURTHER READING

Fowler, Doreen. "Time and Punishment in Faulkner's *Requiem for a Nun*." *Renascence* 38.4 (1986): 245–255.
Parsons, Marnie. "Imagination and the Rending of Time: The Reader and the Recreated Pasts of *Requiem for a Nun*." *Mississippi Quarterly* 41 (1988): 433–446.
Polk, Noel. *Faulkner's* Requiem for a Nun: *A Critical Study*. Bloomington: Indiana University Press, 1981.
Zender, Karl F. "*Requiem for a Nun* and the Uses of the Imagination." *Faulkner and Race*, ed. Fowler and Abadie. 272–296.

Marion Tangum

"RETREAT," a short story by Faulkner, first published in the *Saturday Evening Post* on October, 13, 1934, and revised as the second chapter of *The Unvanquished*. Granny Rosa Millard, with her grandson Bayard Sartoris and his African American playmate Ringo, attempts to retreat to Memphis from the battle zones around their Mississippi plantation. The boys are separated from Granny and advance in a farcical raid on Union troops with Bayard's father Colonel John Sartoris. Granny and the boys ultimately retreat to the Sartoris plantation but learn that their slave Loosh is advancing, not retreating, as he questions their ownership and betrays the location of the family silver to the Yankees.

FURTHER READING

McHaney, Thomas L. "An Episode of War in *The Unvanquished*." *Faulkner Journal* 2.2 (1987): 35–44.

Veronica Makowsky

"RETURN, A," a short story by Faulkner, is a revision of the 1930 story "Rose of Lebanon." "A Return" was not published until *Uncollected Stories*. "Rose of Lebanon" was published in 1995. "A Return" follows Lewis Randolph from her trip to Memphis in 1861 to her return in 1930. In 1861 Lewis married Charles Gordon, who left for war four hours later. Lewis and her son, Randolph Gordon, are both strong-willed survivors. Randolph achieves professional and personal success in Memphis. Randolph's acquaintance, Dr. Gavin Blount, obsesses over the Civil War, and his meeting Lewis offers a tangible connection. Blount apparently commits suicide shortly thereafter:

   See also **"Big Shot, The"; "Dull Tale."**

Diane Brown Jones

RIDER, the main character in Faulkner's short story "Pantaloon in Black," the third narrative in *Go Down, Moses*. On one level the story concerns Rider's anguished attempt to live on after the death of his wife Mannie; on another level the narrative points to the gulf of consciousness separating whites and blacks in Yoknapatawpha County, seen when Rider's grief is summarily dismissed by the white sheriff as an inhuman response to death.

FURTHER READING

Akin, Warren, IV. " 'The Normal Human Feelings': An Interpretation of Faulkner's 'Pantaloon in Black.' " *Studies in Short Fiction* 15 (1978): 397–404.

Limon, John. "The Integration of Faulkner's *Go Down, Moses*." *Critical Inquiry* 12.2 (1986): 422–438.

Joseph R. Urgo

RIMBAUD, ARTHUR (1854–1891), an adolescent prodigy and French poet associated with the Symbolist movement and often considered a forerunner of the surrealist school, is closely linked with Paul Verlaine (1844–1896), French lyric poet with whom he had a brief, tempestuous love affair. Verlaine's influential essay "Les Poètes maudits" (1884; "The Accursed Poets") brought attention to his own poetry as well as to the poetry of Rimbaud, Mallarmé, and Baudelaire, all three of whom influenced Faulkner. In his best-known poems "The Drunken Boat" (1871), "A Season in Hell" (1873), and "Illuminations" (1886)—all written before he was age twenty—Rimbaud uses visionary grouping of images and hallucinatory writing characterized by distortion of meaning and syntax to convey his concept of the poet as seer, or *voyant*. In 1873, during a violent quarrel, Verlaine shot and wounded Rimbaud. Two years after his release from prison, Verlaine's attempt to reconcile with Rimbaud resulted in another violent quarrel. Rimbaud subsequently abandoned poetry and left France to spend the last eighteen years of his life as a trader in Africa. In several interviews Faulkner acknowledged the influence of Verlaine and Rimbaud on his work. This influence is clearly evident in Faulkner's early poems; in 1920, for example, he published in *The Mississippian* adaptations of four poems by Verlaine. In a 1955 interview with Cynthia Grenier, he mentions Verlaine as one of his "old friends which I still read over" and expresses the view that "every novelist is a failed poet" (*LIG* 217). In a 1952 interview in which he elaborates on the difficulties and responsibilities confronting the artist, Faulkner remarks that he sometimes thinks of doing what Rimbaud did—that is, abandon his writing—yet knows that he will keep on writing as long as he lives (*LIG* 71).

FURTHER READING

Kreiswirth, Martin. "Faulkner as Translator: His Versions of Verlaine." *Mississippi Quarterly* 30 (1977): 429–432.

Arthur Wilhelm

"RIPOSTE IN TERTIO," the fourth chapter in Faulkner's *The Unvanquished*, was originally titled "The Unvanquished" when published in the *Saturday Evening Post* on November 14, 1936, as the fourth in a series of Civil War stories about the Sartoris family. Except for its new title, the story remained virtually unchanged in the novel. Set during late 1864, the story relates an ongoing scheme by which Granny Rosa Millard, with the help of Bayard and Ringo, uses forged documents to requisition mules from the Union army, which in turn are sold back to the army. After an officer discovers her scheme and confiscates the remaining mules, she is murdered while trying to obtain four thoroughbred horses from Grumby, the leader of a ruthless band of Confederate raiders.

FURTHER READING

Donaldson, Susan V. "Dismantling the *Saturday Evening Post* Reader: *The Unvanquished* and Changing 'Horizons of Expectations.' " *Faulkner and Popular Culture*, ed. Fowler and Abadie. 179–195.
Wilson, G. Jennifer. "Faulkner's 'Riposte in Tertio.' " *American Notes and Queries* 16 (1978): 88.

John B. Padgett

RITTENMEYER, CHARLOTTE, is the central female character in the "Wild Palms" narrative of Faulkner's novel *The Wild Palms* (*If I Forget Thee, Jerusalem*). A sculptress, the wife of Francis "Rat" Rittenmeyer, and the mother of two young daughters, Charlotte falls in love with Harry Wilbourne, a medical internist nearing the end of his residency at a New Orleans hospital. The two run away together, determined, in Charlotte's words, to live their lives as "all honeymoon, always." This effort, impeded first by financial anxieties, is defeated entirely by a botched abortion, performed on Charlotte by Harry at her insistence. The failed abortion results in Charlotte's slow and agonizing death and, at the end of the novel, in Harry's long-term imprisonment.

Charlotte Rittenmeyer is perhaps the most vividly realized of Faulkner's gallery of unconventional women characters, a type he seemed particularly drawn to depict in the middle and late 1930s, in such figures as Joanna Burden, Laverne Shumann, and Drusilla Hawk. Although Charlotte was the recipient of a number of sympathetic and insightful readings in the 1960s and 1970s, much of the early commentary was strongly negative in judgment, emphasizing her "nymphomania," "mannishness," and "lack of maternal values." At times, Charlotte's characterization was taken as evidence of Faulkner's misogyny.

Recently, under the influence of feminist criticism, Charlotte Rittenmeyer has been more sympathetically interpreted, as an advocate of romantic love and as an image of the female artist. Biographical revelations of the last twenty years have found models in Faulkner's early infatuation with Helen Baird and in his mid-1930s affair with Meta Carpenter. In her final status as an absent female whose loss a male character mourns, Charlotte Rittenmeyer has been interpreted as a fictional descendant of Caddy Compson.

Charlotte's unusual last name has been plausibly interpreted by Thomas McHaney as a pun on "written Maya," where "Maya" is the Hindu term—appropriated by Faulkner from Schopenhauer—for "the web of phenomenon which masks primal reality" (*A Study* 29). This pun pairs with the more obvious "will borne" in Harry's last name. Taken together, the names reflect the novel's pervasive concern with the opposition between freedom and constraint.

FURTHER READING

Bernhardt, Laurie A. " 'Being Worthy Enough'; The Tragedy of Charlotte Rittenmeyer." *Mississippi Quarterly* 39 (1986): 351–364.

Eldred, Joyce Carey. "Faulkner's Still Life: Art and Abortion in *The Wild Palms*." *Faulkner Journal* 4.1–2 (1988–1989): 139–158.

McHaney, Thomas L. *William Faulkner's* The Wild Palms: *A Study*. Jackson: University Press of Mississippi, 1975.

Karl F. Zender

ROAD TO GLORY, THE (1936), is a film set during World War I that Faulkner coscripted with Joel Sayre for director Howard Hawks. The film recalls Faulkner's screenplay for *Today We Live*, for it likewise treats the inescapable cycle of death by which war alters the lives of comrades and loved ones. Captain Laroche is obsessed by his sense of responsibility for sending men to their deaths in battle. His position is made even more intolerable when his own father becomes a soldier in his company. The screenplay was lauded by reviewers when the film was released. In fact, screenwriter George Garrett observes that the script for this film proves that Faulkner could tackle a job that he was hired to do—and do it well.

FURTHER READING

Garrett, George. Afterword. *The Road to Glory: A Screenplay*. By William Faulkner and Joel Sayre. Ed. Matthew Bruccoli. Carbondale: Southern Illinois University Press, 1981.

Halliwell, Leslie. *Film Guide*. Rev. ed. Ed. John Walker. New York: HarperCollins, 1998.

Gene D. Phillips

ROMANTICISM. Literary term; period of English literary history, circa 1785–1825. As a critical or historical term, "romanticism" has proved as pliable as it is vague in its application. In modern critical discourse the term has frequently taken its meaning by being placed in opposition to other terms, such as "classicism" or "realism," often to the disparagement of the object to which it is applied. Some of the principal meanings and connotations of the term include a renewed interest on the part of writers of the late eighteenth and early nineteenth centuries in the themes of medieval romance, the matter of ancient Britain, a return to nature, or a focus on common people and their traditional idioms; or they may include the rise of the novel and a concomitant rise in the importance of domesticity in literary representation, resistance to the reductiveness of scientific or positivistic modes of analysis and explanation, or sympathy with revolutionary democratic sentiments. Whatever the critical and scholarly perspectives on the term, they are never free from the popular use of the word "romantic" to connote illusory desire, escapism, and sentimentality.

For criticism of Faulkner, the term can be understood primarily in its use for the generation of critics gaining prominence after World War II, loosely identified with the so-called New Criticism, who were strongly influenced themselves by the high modernism of T. S. Eliot and others. A key concept for these critics is "irony" or, as Cleanth Brooks put it, "irony as a principle of poetic structure." For critics during the period in which Faulkner emerged as a major writer, there was both a suspicion of "romanticism" as a tendency in literature and a marked suspicion of the propensity of Southern writers toward romantic escapism. Thus a good deal of criticism views Faulkner as captivated by romantic influences in his early writing and struggling to jettison the verbal props borrowed from romantic poetry in order to discover his own idiom and subject. Moreover, in many formulations of the issue, there is a concern as well with the question of the identity of an American writer, and an American idiom, as distinct from an inherited British tradition.

Perhaps the most succinct example of a critic of this persuasion treating Faulkner's involvement with "romanticism" is Lawrance Thompson's brief "Afterword" to the Signet edition of *Sartoris*. While Thompson reads this work as pivotal in Faulkner's career, his thesis is indicative: "All the romantic characters in this novel are treated in an ambivalent manner by Faulkner, whose attitude toward them is at once sympathetic, critical, ironic; but, more than that Faulkner's various uses of irony here provide him with his most important artistic controls of underlying meanings" (304). The invocation of Keats's image of a Grecian urn, of medieval French romance, of the romantic novels of Sir Walter Scott, of Byron and Shelley—all these are conditioned, according to Thompson, by the principle of irony, which enables the author to assert control over his "material."

Cleanth Brooks also charts Faulkner's relations to romantic precursors, but with a somewhat contrasting view. His discussion of "Faulkner as Nature Poet" (*William Faulkner: The Yoknapatawpha Country*) points out numerous parallels between Faulkner's writings and Wordsworth's pastoral and georgic poems. But the differing approaches of Thompson and Brooks perhaps show only that "romanticism" includes many diverse characteristics.

While later critics have observed in Faulkner's texts phenomena similar to those Thompson and Brooks note, and have likewise commented on Faulkner's relation to a romantic inheritance, the concern with "irony" as an antidote to romantic excess and with authorial "control" has abated. Instead, recent critics are concerned with discourses of gender and race, and with the inheritance of romanticism as it is involved in these discourses as they supersede authorial control and enact a complex dialectic between reader and text. Thus, no general study or common set of terms focused on romanticism per se has supplanted this former mode in criticism of Faulkner. Beginning with Judith L. Sensibar's *The Origins of Faulkner's Art*, the close study of Faulkner's allusive early texts has tended to see a continuity in his appropriation of romantic and fin de siècle or decadent poetry and a greater complexity in the attitudes evoked by intertextual play than earlier critics would have found satisfactory.

Stephen Hahn

"ROSE FOR EMILY, A," perhaps Faulkner's most famous short story. *Forum* magazine published "A Rose for Emily" in April 1930; it was the first of Faulkner's short stories to find publication in a national magazine. The story, said to be Faulkner's most widely read, has appeared frequently and is included in *These 13* (1931) and *Collected Stories*. It has been translated into a variety of languages. The story reflects Faulkner's interest in the literary possibilities of the particular type of woman represented by Emily Grierson, especially in her repressed sexuality, her relationship with her father, her resistance to change, and her place in the community. In these regards critics have noted comparisons with Zilphia Gant, Rosa Coldfield of *Absalom, Absalom!*, and Minnie Cooper of "Dry September." Various suggestions have been made regarding the story's origins, one, interestingly, that it may have begun with Faulkner's knowledge of a courtship in his own community. However, that courtship, unlike the courtship of Emily and Homer, triumphed over disparities between partners and produced a happy marriage.

"A Rose for Emily" chronicles the life of Emily Grierson as perceived by an anonymous narrator whose "we" often speaks for the community. Emily, while young, is dominated by a father who expects her to look after his needs and who discourages any romantic attachments. After his death and the ensuing struggle with representatives of the community who want her to release his body for burial, Emily succumbs to a lengthy illness. Then, having recovered, to the surprise and increasing consternation of the community, Emily unexpectedly encourages the attentions of Homer Barron, a Yankee foreman with a paving company recently arrived to work on Jefferson's streets. Attempts to interfere with Emily's romantic involvement with Homer, of much interest to the town, are unsuccessful. The gossip ends when Homer apparently departs from Jefferson, an event slightly preceded by Emily's purchase first of what appear to be wedding presents for Homer and then of arsenic. With Homer gone, or as the reader later discovers, dead, Emily returns to her life of genteel withdrawal, broken for a time when she teaches the art of painting china to young girls. It is also broken by the townspeople, once when several of the town fathers sprinkle lime about the foundations of her house to combat a curious smell that has troubled the neighbors and again when the town's aldermen skirmish with her about taxes she owes. After her death, mention of which both opens and closes the largely retrospective narrative, representatives of the community enter a sealed upstairs room in her house and find the decomposed body of Homer Barron in a bed. The bed's pillow bears evidence that Emily had continued to sleep with Homer's remains long after she had murdered him.

Such a summary does scant justice to the richness of Faulkner's techniques of presentation. Considerable critical attention has been paid to the deliberately complex narrative structure, a structure that Faulkner was to employ throughout his career and that, by its achronological account of events and ambiguous point of view, involves the reader creatively in the re-creation and comprehension of Emily Grierson's life. Similarly, scholars have also called attention to the story's examination of abnormal psychology and the dynamics of social class, particularly as they provide a context for the interaction between the individual and the community.

In many ways, Emily's relationship with her father resembles the behavior of captives as described in accounts of the "Stockholm syndrome," a desire to please so strong as to forge a lasting identification with the captor. After her father's death, Emily at first will not permit the townspeople to take him from her. Then, following her failure to secure Homer as a substitute for her father, she takes on several of her father's characteristics as if to keep him alive as a significant element of her own persona. Some critics, aware of Faulkner's interest in Freud, have suggested that Emily suffers from an Electra complex and that later, when she refuses to allow the second male in her life, Homer Barron, to leave her, she is motivated by that complex.

Similarly, her large Southern Victorian house mirrors her resistance to change as it gradually comes to stand alone among the utilitarian structures of industry and commerce that mark the neighborhood's changing character. This refusal to let go of the past, a recurrent theme in Faulkner, is made manifest not only in Homer's murder but in Emily's reluctance to part with her father's body and her refusal to pay taxes on the basis of an agreement long since abrogated by the death of her patron, Colonel Sartoris.

The town's interest in Emily is in part due to the oddity of her behavior derived from her isolation and resistance to change, but it is also a curiosity energized by her class. As a member of one of the oldest families in Jefferson, Emily embodies, for the community, the vision of the "lady" as incorporated in the mythology and the reality of the antebellum South. The community respects her position, while it simultaneously evinces a certain degree of *Scha-*

denfreude as it delights in her eccentricities and fall from grace. In this context her isolation, her assumptions about the power of class, and her increasingly bizarre behavior culminating in necrophilia suggest—to a reader if not to the narrator—the dangers of clinging too closely to the past and refusing to accept change. The community, caught up in change, functions through the narrator to provide a chorus to what Faulkner considered Emily's tragedy. Emily is metaphorically described twice in the story as appearing like an idol: once as the townsmen scurry beneath her distant gaze using lime to cover up the odor that they refuse to associate with a "lady"; again as she sits unchanging while all changes about her. In both instances she is an idol without worshipers.

Many critics are convinced that Emily's actions—her assertion of the prerogatives of class, her withdrawal, and her refusal to participate in change—provide a critical commentary on tendencies in Southern society. Other critics, among them most notably Cleanth Brooks, have denounced such observations as pointless exercises in symbol hunting.

FURTHER READING

Allen, Dennis W. "Horror and Perverse Delight: Faulkner's 'A Rose for Emily.' " *Modern Fiction Studies* 30 (1984): 685–696.

Heller, Terry. "The Telltale Hair: A Critical Study of Faulkner's 'A Rose for Emily.' " *Arizona Quarterly* 28 (1972): 301–318.

Inge, M. Thomas, ed. *William Faulkner: "A Rose for Emily."* Columbus, Ohio: Charles E. Merrill Publishing Company, 1970.

Powell, Janice A. "Changing Portraits in 'A Rose for Emily.' " *Teaching Faulkner* 11 (1997): 1–4.

Glenn Reed

ROSE FOR EMILY, A (film). In 1982 Chubbuck Cinema Company released *A Rose for Emily* based on the famous and highly anthologized short story of the same name. Originally published in *Forum* magazine in April 1930, Faulkner's piece tells of Emily Grierson's profound isolation and subsequent descent into madness. Emily, an eccentric, aristocratic, Southern spinster, falls in love with a Yankee laborer, Homer Barron. His social standing, transient vocation, and confirmed preference for bachelorhood all make for a highly unlikely prospect for marriage. Once Emily realizes this, she poisons him, and in a scene strikingly similar to Dickens's *Great Expectations*, she entombs the body in an upstairs bedroom (which clearly signifies a wedding suite), where it lies for the remainder of Emily's life.

The Chubbuck production offers a very compact (only twenty-seven minutes) yet faithful adaptation of Faulkner's tale. From the very outset, it is clear that the filmmakers, Lydon Chubbuck and H. Kaye Dyal, attempt to convey cinematic equivalents to the story's major thematic preoccupations and motifs: the interplay between modernity and traditions of the Old South; class tensions between the aristocratic Griersons and the bourgeoisie; the community's paradoxical, perhaps even obsessive, love/hate relation to Emily and her family's standing, as signified by the rose motif and their constant gossip.

The film opens to jazz music and snippets of a President Roosevelt speech on the radio and then cuts to the funerary preparations of Emily's dead body, hence establishing the upcoming and constant thematic interplay between the present and the past. Simultaneously we learn, via one of its members, of the town's preoccupation with Emily and her legendary status through the voice-over narration delivered by the esteemed John Houseman. As the narrator begins to unfold the story of Emily's life—her overbearing father (John Randolph), crazed great-aunt Wyatt (Frances Bay), and familial links to the ruling class of the Confederate past—the film cuts once again, and these key aspects of her early history are dramatized by Anjelica Huston.

In addition to conveying the absence of any normal courtships or romances, viewers also begin to increasingly detect emotional or mental abnormalities, and this is particularly evident when Emily refuses to acknowledge her father's death and resists removing the body from the house. (This latter action presages, of course, her treatment of Homer's corpse.) We witness further psychic deterioration when, soon after her father's demise, she contemplates suicide with a straight razor. It is the sudden and unexpected appearance of Homer Barron (Jared Martin) that saves Emily from such action and sets into motion her attraction to him.

Rather than celebrate Emily's withdrawal from seclusion, the townspeople criticize her public carriage rides and the courtship in general. And, ironically, their derision or disapproval seems largely motivated by class division and antagonisms. That is, while they, themselves, resent her family's aristocratic and upper socioeconomic history, they find Homer an unfit suitor for a woman of such standing and would prefer that she, too, would deem him unsuitable and unacceptable. As the action unfolds, we witness Emily engaging in two seemingly unrelated actions: buying both arsenic and very refined men's clothing and a toiletry set. Shortly thereafter we also witness Homer's public declaration against marriage in general, and only later do viewers see that Emily not only intuited the town's attitudes and expectations but Homer's as well. At the completion of his job, Homer leaves, and the town, believing that she had "seriously compromised herself," half expects her to kill herself and not Homer. Even his decaying body with its horrific smell does not alert the town to the nature of his true disappearance.

In a very erotic sequence we witness the actual murder. Emily and Homer first have a romantic dinner, and then Emily enacts a ceremony that she alone clearly perceives as a wedding night ritual—yet with a perverse twist. Gradually disrobing from her white dress and standing before white candles not unlike those found upon an altar, Emily hands Homer the fatal drink. To reinforce both the sexual seduction and the imminent tragedy, the scene cuts to Emily's man-servant in the kitchen who peels an apple with an unnecessarily large butcher knife. After the narration and dramatization of such subsequent events as the town's efforts to obliterate the smell around her house and the futile attempt to collect taxes, the direction of the film returns again to the present, namely, to Emily's funeral. At the film's end, two distant relatives who are present to claim potentially valuable heirlooms insist on entering the locked room where, unbeknownst to them, Homer lies (as does evidence that Emily had lain with Homer long after his death and decay).

Throughout this cinematic production, effort was made to incorporate and reinforce the importance of the rose motif central to Faulkner's title and story toward conveying the town's ambivalent and contradictory attitude toward Emily, that is, their reverence as well as their resentment. Very early in the film the motif is introduced by way of a close-up of the long-stemmed rose etched into the glass pane of the Griersons' front door, and the filmmakers once again reinforce its significance at the story's end. In addition to a townsperson's graceful and thoughtful placement of a rose in Emily's coffin, the motif is foregrounded again when the camera slowly pans the barren and lifeless rooms of Emily's home and then focuses on a bold stained-glass window featuring a large red flower in its center. Most notable, though, is the rose-tinted wallpaper that graces one wall of the otherwise colorless, dusty, cobweb-filled wedding chamber.

Kathy G. Willingham

ROWAN OAK, Faulkner's home in Oxford, Mississippi. Faulkner named Rowan Oak after the legend of the mythic Rowan trees believed by Celts to harbor magical powers of safety and protection. The house was originally built in 1844 by Robert Shegog, an Irish planter from Loughbrickland, County Down, who came to Lafayette County by way of Tennessee. One of the wealthiest early settlers, he continued to expand his holdings and at his death owned more than 6,000 acres in four counties and nearly ninety slaves. The original house was designed in the Greek Revival style, popular between 1830 and 1850; it had two stories, wooden clapboard siding, a hipped roof, interior end chimneys, a front facade five bays in width, a front door surrounded by narrow side lights, and a central pedimented portico supported by a pair of Doric capitals. The builder was a local carpenter, William Turner, although in time he became fabled as an English architect, much as the large plantation house Thomas Sutpen built was said to be designed by a French architect. Across the road in another antebellum house lived the town's leading citizen, Jacob Thompson, a lawyer, congressman, and later Secretary of the Interior for President James Buchanan; during the War Between the States, Thompson's property was used by the Union's Major General A. J. Smith to bivouac soldiers during the Northern army's brief occupation of Oxford in 1864.

After Shegog's death, his widow, who called the place "The Mansions," resided there until her own death in 1871. The house was then sold to Mrs. Ellen Bailey, for whom the neighboring woods are still named, and, known locally as "the Bailey Place," passed to her unmarried daughter Ellen, who died in 1923. The house next passed to Ellen's married sister Sallie, who with her husband, W. C. Bryant, residents of Coffeeville, rented it out. When Faulkner purchased the property on August 12, 1930, it was being used by the Claude Anderson family as a dairy.

Faulkner paid $6,000 for the property, with no money down and monthly payments of $75. The house was in nearly total disrepair: There was no electricity, plumbing, or heat; the foundation was rotting; the roof leaked; there were no screens on the windows or doors; and the house had not been painted in years. Over the next decade and more, Faulkner repaired much of the house himself, as his finances permitted, calling on no more than one helper at a time. Shegog had constructed three outbuildings: a detached brick kitchen; a wooden servants' quarters where Faulkner would place Caroline Barr and later Ned Barnett; and a hewn-timber barn; in time, Faulkner added a stable. The original address was 719 Garfield Avenue, since Oxford officials had expected to extend that street. It never did, and the house has therefore always been on Old Taylor Road south of the town square.

Faulkner kept the line of cedars along the drive and planted narcissus, Benjy Compson's favorite flower, along the walkway; he restored the magnolia garden; and he added a rose garden and scuppernong arbor. He also added to the house the balustraded brick terraces on either side of the front portico, a porch off the dining room, and a porte cochere on the west side. In the early years he and his wife sat on the front porch; later he sat on the east side of the house, often writing on an Adirondack chair in the garden. As he became better known, he posted "No Trespassing" signs at the entrance to his drive and eventually published a notice in the Oxford *Eagle*:

The posted woods on my property inside the city limits of Oxford contain several tame squirrels. Any hunter who feels himself too lacking in woodcraft and marksmanship to approach a dangerous wild squirrel, might feel safe with these. These woods are a part of the pasture used by my horses and milk cow; also, the late arrival will find them already full of other hunters. He is kindly requested not to shoot either of these.

Like his first predecessor, Faulkner also expanded his holdings, buying three adjoining lots to the east and (in 1938 with earnings from the sale of movie rights to *The Unvanquished*) a sizable portion of Bailey's Woods, where he and his daughter Jill frequently rode horses. With this addition the original four acres became more than thirty-one.

The interior of Rowan Oak is essentially an enlarged dog-trot design with a central hallway on both floors. The house is presently restored as Faulkner knew it. The library, to the left of the front hall, still has his books on his handmade bookshelves and his mother's portraits of him and other Falkners; behind the library, the porch he enclosed as his "study" or "office" has marked on the walls the outline of each day's events for *A Fable*. His typewriter, on his desk, still faces the stable he built. When Faulkner moved into Rowan Oak the year after his wedding, he brought with him Estelle and both her children by her former marriage, Malcolm and Victoria. Their own daughter Jill was born there in June 1933. Other members of his extended household lived there off and on. It was at Rowan Oak that Jill's wedding reception was held in 1954. In 1940 Faulkner held funeral services for Caroline Barr, ''Mammy Callie,'' in the front parlor, to the right side of the entry. His own funeral was held in the same room on July 7, 1962.

Estelle Faulkner continued to live at Rowan Oak, off and on, until her death in 1973. Then Jill sold the property to the University of Mississippi, where it has become a part of the campus open to visitors during limited hours. Rowan Oak was placed on the National Register of Historic Places in 1977.

FURTHER READING

Hise, Dan, and John Lawrence. *Faulkner's Rowan Oak.* Jackson: University Press of Mississippi, 1993.

Arthur F. Kinney

RUSSIA. Faulkner's heritage, if looked upon from the point of view of literary tradition, is obviously related to Russian classic literature of the nineteenth century, especially to Leo Tolstoy's and Fyodor Dostoevsky's creative work. Faulkner's library, composed of his favorite books, contains Tolstoy, Turgenev, Dostoevsky, and Chekhov. Faulkner's romantic treatment of the Southern gentry, ousted by Northern parvenu and doomed to death as a class, can be traced to Turgenev's swan song to Russian gentry of the middle of the nineteenth century, also doomed by history, which constitutes the essence of his novels. Soviet critics consider that Faulkner inherited from Tolstoy the belief that morally healthy people are, first of all, common people who are close to nature and have to toil from morning till night. The next important feature of this inheritance is Faulkner's ability to embody an idea into an artistic image, into a full-blooded literary character.

Faulkner himself confessed more than once the influence produced upon his work by Dostoevsky's books, mentioning *The Brothers Karamazov* among the books he reread every year. Faulkner appreciated most of all Dostoevsky's ability to portray subconscious contradictory human feelings. The striving to analyze the depth of the human psyche, to explain its complexity and its paradoxes, leads critics to see in Faulkner Dostoevsky's student. Like Dostoevsky, he was interested in studying the crisis of a personality who found himself amidst crisis in society.

Faulkner is always interested in a family as the foundation of society, as the main cell of which society consists. Like Dostoevsky, he shows a family in the process of disintegration and decay and, again like Dostoevsky, saw his task not only in the portrayal of this decay but also in the discovery of its causes. In spite of the fact that the families described by Faulkner and Dostoevsky were quite different in sociohistoric and national aspects, a very important trait unites them—the breach of family traditions and relations. Both writers also put to the test families belonging to various social strata.

The psyche of Faulkner's heroes is endowed with the same extreme tension, the same intensity of interior life, that marks the inner life of Dostoevsky's characters. Professor Vladimir Kostyakov considers that Faulkner inherited from Dostoevsky the principle of the characters' relative independence—that is, when the author's consciousness does not dominate the consciousness of the characters he has created but treats them as independent, equal consciousnesses, as complicated and integral as his own. Linda Snopes is an example of such an independent consciousness, of an idea embodied into a full-blooded artistic image. Faulkner does not share her ideological concept but lets her exist and develop on the pages of his novel, demonstrating all the tendencies of her personality. Thus, he is true to his principle of considering variant ways in his search for truth and, like Dostoevsky, letting every variant exist on equal rights in his books.

Of all the great literary masters of the nineteenth century, Dostoevsky was the first who recreated the inner world of his heroes with the help of a very minute record of all shades of their feelings and thoughts changing each other in close succession. He was one of the first to introduce interior monologue, or the stream of consciousness, and amply used and developed it in his art. In the use of these techniques, it may be argued, Faulkner is Dostoevsky's follower rather than Joyce's. Faulkner's treatment of these devices is, like Dostoevsky's, directed at the cognition of the world and, especially, the inner world of man.

Scenes in Faulkner's books show Dostoevsky's influence upon Faulkner. Flem's meeting Satan in hell in *The Hamlet* may be traced to a corresponding scene in *The Brothers Karamazov* when Ivan speaks to the Devil. Similarly, the exchange between the Old General and the corporal in *A Fable* echoes the Grand Inquisitor scene in *The Brothers Karamazov*.

It is noteworthy that neither writer preferred any ideology, any rigid system of political views; both were alien to orthodox thinking and given to a dialectical approach to life. Both understood life as complexity, and this understanding is reflected in their depiction of the contradictions of life and the absence of a complete or inflexible system of belief. Both admitted many variants of truth but came to the realization of the coexistence of these variants in different artistic ways. Dostoevsky in his search for truth makes the personages of his novels clash; Faulkner changes the interpretation of the same scenes, characters, and the plot, showing them through the perception of various personages of the novel. The role of the storyteller is exclusively important in Faulkner's novels; the change of one means a new approach, a new perspective upon reality.

Some Russian critics consider that Faulkner, at least partially, accepted that part of the Southern myth that believed there was one integral community existing in the prewar South in which both black and white lived as members of one family. In their opinion, Faulkner in this respect is close to Dostoevsky, who maintained the idea of a spiritual proximity between Russian aristocracy and the common people, the belief that held him back from choosing revolution as the solution of social and moral problems.

Looking into Faulkner's work in search of parallels with writers contemporary to him in Russian literature, some critics compare his Southern saga to Sholohov's *Quiet Flows the Don*. Pyotr Palievsky bases his assumption upon Faulkner's definition of the Indian word *Yoknapatawpha* as "quiet flows water along the flat plain." The epic idea of the slow passage of life is common to both writers, and the word "quiet" acquires in both cases an opposite meaning. Both the American South and Sholohov's Don are treated as parts of a whole, patriarchal and at the same time reactionary in character, yet being subjected to basic changes. The idea of a "motherland" is also present in the books of both writers. Faulkner's unvanquished heroes who are always ready to fight a losing battle are close as types to Sholohov's Melehov and Acksinya, and both writers treat their heroes with both sympathy and soberness.

Studying Faulkner's novels, Russian scholars concentrate their attention on two main aspects of Faulkner's work: first, his position as the most important representative of the Southern school that came into existence in the 1920s and reacted to the changes caused in the South by the Civil War; and second, his creative method. These critics study Faulkner's treatment of such elements as the former grandeur of the South, refined and noble Southern gentlemen, the proud Southern belle, and idyllic patriarchal relations existing between black slaves and their white owners. They emphasize Faulkner's critical examination of the Southern myth, especially his treatment of slavery. Russian scholars maintain that Faulkner sees the source of Southern misery in the institution of slavery, which distorted the fates of slaves, corrupted the souls of slave owners, and created the burden of historical fault that even nowadays mars the lives of people in the South. Faulkner sees blacks and whites bound together by the irony of history, involved in an inextricable web of shame, guilt, and evil, corrupting both. However, Russian scholars are of the opinion that Faulkner's approach to the racial problem is not primarily social but aesthetic, moral, and philosophical.

Dwelling upon Faulkner's creative method, Russian scholars stress Faulkner's realism, or, rather, his painful way to it, overcoming his modernistic tendencies. This concern about the artist's creative method was born of the ideological situation in the Soviet Union, when modernism was looked upon as a manifestation of bourgeois culture and, hence, prohibited. The desire to secure publication for the best foreign men of letters made Soviet scholars pronounce them realists or emphasize realistic tendencies in their books. Thus, Faulkner's work was looked upon as a slow progress toward realism, evident not only in his creative work taken as a whole but in separate books as well. Analyzing Faulkner's books, Russian scholars studied the evolution of Faulkner's method from the modernism of such novels as *The Sound and the Fury, As I Lay Dying*, and *Sanctuary* to the realism of what were considered his best works: *Light in August, Intruder in the Dust*, and *The Mansion*; and they stressed realistic tendencies, obvious in the change of his method from *The Hamlet* to *The Mansion*, or even in the progression in *The Sound and the Fury* from the stream of consciousness of an idiot to the author's realistic narration. Soviet scholars view the *Snopes* trilogy as Faulkner's attempt at a social analysis of his contemporary society. Faulkner treats the character of Snopes as a new social phenomenon. The heroes of these books are presented on the concrete social and historical background, and the delineation of characters becomes more socially determined, as in the case of the development of Mink Snopes from the first to the third book of the trilogy. Female characters in the trilogy also undergo vivid transformation. Thus, the interpretation of Eula's character changes from the embodiment of sexual attraction in *The Hamlet* to more human and elevated presentation of her personality in *The Town*; Linda's character is presented as the only force capable of putting an end to Snopes and the bourgeois avarice that he personifies. Faulkner's style in *The Mansion* becomes more lucid, his manner of writing more traditional.

Russian scholars explain Faulkner's tragic vision by his pessimistic view on the development of the South: his rejection of the new vulgarized and industrialized bourgeois society. The violence, irrationality, and aberration found in his fiction are interpreted as a symbol of Southern decline. Tatyana Komarovskaya presents *Absalom, Absalom!* as a predecessor of the philosophical historical novel that flourished after World War II and secured fame for this literary genre.

Russian scholars emphasize Faulkner's humanism and optimism, vivid in his wild heroes who do not take defeat, who refuse to be conquered—in the fact that humanism and those who practice it, like Dilsey in *The Sound and the Fury*, survive in every one of his novels, giving hope of survival to others. They maintain that Faulkner's place in modern literature is determined by the philosophical depth, psychological subtlety, and great aesthetic merits of his fiction.

FURTHER READING

Blotner, Joseph. "Faulkner in the Soviet Union." *Michigan Quarterly Review* 24 (1985): 461–476.

Chakovsky, Sergei, and M. Thomas Inge, eds. *Russian Eyes on American Literature.* Jackson: University Press of Mississippi and A. M. Gorky Institute of World Literature, 1992.

Morozova, Tatiana. "Faulkner Reads Dostoevsky." *Soviet Literature* 12 (1981): 176–179.

Vashchenko, Alexandre. "The Perception of William Faulkner in the USSR." *Faulkner: International Perspectives*, ed. Fowler and Abadie. 194–211.

Tatyana E. Komarovskaya

S

SANCTUARY. If *The Sound and the Fury* was Faulkner's "heart's darling" among his novels, then *Sanctuary*, issued in 1931, was his wayward stepchild. The myth of the former claims that he wrote it for himself, that it created in him the most exhilaration as well as the most anguish. The myth of the latter novel contends that it was base and cheap, contemptuously written for an indiscriminate, thrill-seeking public. Faulkner propounded this myth in his notorious introduction to *Sanctuary* for the Modern Library edition published in 1932, a year after the novel's original appearance from Cape & Smith. Such pejorative remarks were taken at face value by early critics. But in the same introduction Faulkner also notes that he extensively revised the novel at his own expense after it had been typeset, concluding that he had finally achieved a performance that would not embarrass *The Sound and the Fury* or *As I Lay Dying*. As Michael Millgate, Noel Polk, and others have wisely argued, Faulkner's ultimate assessment of his wayward child says more about his lofty aesthetic standards than it does about the quality of his efforts in *Sanctuary*.

The seed for *Sanctuary* was planted in Faulkner's imagination in the mid-1920s when he heard a young woman in a Memphis night club talking about a gangster named "Popeye" Pumphrey, who, although rumored to be impotent, had raped a woman in some grotesque fashion and then kept her isolated in a brothel. In January 1929 Faulkner started a narrative about this grisly incident. *Sartoris*, the severely truncated version of *Flags in the Dust*, came out that same month, while *The Sound and the Fury*, very fresh on Faulkner's mind, would appear in October. He dated the completion of the new novel manuscript as 25 May 1929. Then Faulkner apparently forgot about this text, caught up in getting married and reading galley proofs of *The Sound and the Fury* even on his honeymoon.

When Faulkner received the *Sanctuary* galleys in November 1930, he began a month of furious revision: reassembling chapters, rewriting others, adding new sections and even new chapters. The salient features of the revision included deemphasizing Horace Benbow, bringing the story of Temple Drake to the forefront, and inserting a biography of the psychopathic Popeye. Also, Faulkner made a number of stylistic changes to emulate the Hemingwayesque, hardboiled, laconic style of detective fiction made popular by Dashiell Hammett and Raymond Chandler. The result was the most noir novel in Faulkner's canon.

The novel opens with a three-chapter unit on Horace Benbow, an attorney who does not practice and a husband who has left his wife, encountering a gang of Memphis bootleggers at a ruined antebellum mansion called the Old Frenchman place. The urban gang is under the leadership of a small, peculiar-looking fellow named Popeye, whose trademarks are his black suits and lethal .45 automatic, a figure Benbow sees as a personification of cosmic evil. The operators of the whiskey still are Lee Goodwin, his common-law wife Ruby Lamar, and a simpleton named Tommy. The other permanent residents of this house of horrors are the Goodwins' sickly baby and an old man, just Pap, whose kinship to the characters is left uncertain. After a night of drinking, Benbow hitches a ride to Jefferson on the liquor truck and goes to visit his widowed sister, Narcissa Benbow Sartoris, in his native Jefferson.

The next ten chapters track the extracurricular doings of a first-year student at the University of Mississippi, Temple Drake, the daughter of the prominent Judge Drake of Jackson. While Temple sneaks out with townies during the week, formal weekend dances require more respectable escorts, such as Gowan Stevens, a dipsomaniacal Jefferson aristocrat newly graduated from Virginia. This weekend, after the Friday dance, Temple plans to jump off the train en route to Starkville for a baseball game so she can go to the game by automobile with Stevens. In making a liquor run to the Old Frenchman place, the drunken Stevens rolls the car, and the young couple find themselves in the clutches of the criminals. Stevens eventually abandons Temple, who spends a terrifying night in a houseful of men who do not respect her status as the virgin belle, the Judge's daughter. Ruby Lamar and the feebleminded Tommy protect Temple through the harrowing night. On that beautiful Sunday morning in May, however, Popeye murders Tommy and violates Temple with a corncob. Faulkner handles the scene so obliquely that the reader does not realize what actually takes place until much later.

When Goodwin is arrested for Tommy's killing, Benbow takes on his pro bono defense. From this point Faulkner alternates between the stories of Benbow's attempt to play detective and Temple's captivity by Popeye, who has transported her to Memphis and imprisoned her in Miss Reba Rivers's house of pleasure. When Benbow locates Temple, she tells the story of her terror-induced fantasies on that night, a narrative that nauseates Benbow, who has associated Temple with his own stepdaughter.

Interpolated into the main plot lines are two comic chapters: one concerning the adventures of Virgil Snopes and his friend Fonzo, who end up as guests of Miss Reba's while attending barber college; the other, the chaotic funeral of a gangster named Red, whom the impotent Popeye has employed as a surrogate lover for Temple before murdering him.

At the trial, Benbow suffers a humiliating defeat as his own sister has betrayed his case to the district attorney and Temple shows up at the trial, sealing Goodwin's doom with her perjured testimony. After she testifies, her father and brothers escort her from court and out of the country. In a fit of righteousness, a mob burns Lee Goodwin. Horace returns to his wife, Temple goes to France with her father, and Popeye, en route to visiting his mother in Pensacola, ends up being wrongly arrested, tried, and executed for killing an Alabama police officer.

By common consent, *Sanctuary* is Faulkner's darkest vision, his most schematic analysis of evil, corruption, and hypocrisy. His strategy is to create an upper world of respectable middle-class citizens apparently separate from an underworld of lowlifes, then blur the surface distinction. Madame Reba is as respectable as any middle-class widow, and Narcissa Benbow Sartoris turns out to be as corrupt as Senator Clarence Snopes. The rule of law collapses into the law of the jungle. The middle class cares only about preserving its facade of respectability, not at all about equal justice before the law. *Sanctuary* deftly parodies the Roaring Twenties gangster novel and portrays the moral bankruptcy at all levels of modern American society.

Sanctuary is also a novel of disturbing images and strange ellipses in its presentation. Old Pap, Ruby's sickly baby, Miss Reba's toy poodles, the enigmatic one-handed clock in Temple's room at the brothel, the beer-drinking little boy, Uncle Bud—all suggest a warped, unstable, and grotesque reality. Faulkner's multiperspective technique calls cognition itself into question as readers try to sort out the baffling, overlapping action at the Old Frenchman place, which turns into a nightmarish funhouse whose mirrors everywhere distort what happens when, to whom, and from whose viewpoint. The novel makes voyeurs of us all as we watch everyone watching everyone watching everyone else. Confusion and chaos reign supreme. Readers are as bewildered as Horace Benbow at Lee Goodwin's trial as we realize much more is going on than meets the eye—and such is the pattern of the entire novel.

The complexity of the novel's vision has been reflected in the critical response to the characters, especially Temple Drake. The early appraisals of Temple as a young vamp who invites and deserves what she gets, or as an ingenue who discovers her dark side, have shifted to more sympathetic considerations of Temple as a study in psychological terror, as a victim of brainwashing and hostage syndromes, and as a rebel with a cause—to subvert the patriarchy. Likewise, Horace Benbow is now seen more as a walking textbook of psychological dysfunctions than as a quixotic hero defeated by overwhelming forces of evil intent. Even Popeye has become less a symbol of malignancy in the nature of things than a dysfunctional child, a product of venereal disease and an irrational gene pool.

The "theorizing" of *Sanctuary* has helped us to see the novel as less an anomaly in Faulkner's canon than was originally thought. Recent criticism has illuminated the interesting experiments in gender construction Faulkner conducts in the novel in his characterizations of Temple, Horace, Narcissa, Popeye, Red, Ruby, and Reba. Faulkner's equally interesting portrayal of social classes and subcultures has been the subject of much recent critical scrutiny. Further, recent psychologically based work has helped us better understand the apparently deviant and aberrant behaviors that formed so much of *Sanctuary*'s alleged notoriety.

It may well be that critics are just now catching up with *Sanctuary*. The macabre, grotesque, absurd, and blackly comic text appeared only a year after the Southern Agrarians had published *I'll Take My Stand*. If *Sanctuary* were to be viewed as a reply to that document, its message would be that the South is hardly immune to the predations of the modern wasteland. The seventy miles between Jefferson and Memphis contain an abyss that makes David Lynch's *Twin Peaks* look like a Norman Rockwell painting.

FURTHER READING

Arnold, Edwin T. *Reading Faulkner*: Sanctuary. Jackson: University Press of Mississippi, 1996.

Bloom, Harold, ed. *Modern Critical Interpretations of William Faulkner's* Sanctuary. New York: Chelsea, 1988.

Boon, Kevin A. "Temple Defiled: The Brainwashing of Temple Drake in Faulkner's *Sanctuary.*" *Faulkner Journal* 6.2 (1991): 33–50.

Canfield, J. Douglas, ed. *Twentieth Century Interpretations of* Sanctuary. Englewood Cliffs, N.J.: Prentice-Spectrum, 1982.

Irwin, John T. "Horace Benbow and the Myth of Narcissa." *American Literature* 64 (1992): 543–566.

Matthews, John T. "The Elliptical Nature of *Sanctuary.*" *Novel: A Forum on Fiction* 17 (1984): 246–265.

Rousselle, Melinda McLeod. *Annotations to William Faulkner's* Sanctuary. New York: Garland, 1989.

Wilson, Andrew J. "The Corruption in Looking: William Faulkner's *Sanctuary* as Detective Novel." *Mississippi Quarterly* 47 (1994): 441–460.

David L. Vanderwerken

SANCTUARY (film) (1961), scripted by James Poe and directed by Tony Richardson, ingeniously merges the original plots of Faulkner's *Sanctuary* and its sequel *Requiem for a Nun*, into a continuous narrative that smoothly blends incidents from the two books into a single movie. Following Faulkner's *Sanctuary*, the film depicts how Temple Drake is kidnapped by a gangster (whose name is changed from Popeye to Candy Man in the movie) and taken to a Memphis brothel to be at his disposal there. Temple stays on with Candy because of her morbid fascination with his sordid world, but she eventually returns to her family. Popeye, Candy's counterpart in the novel, is executed as a murderer; but in the film Candy Man lives on to figure in the last half of the picture, drawn from Faulkner's *Requiem for a Nun*, where Temple plans to leave her husband and run away with Candy—instead of with another racketeer, as in the book. Otherwise, the rest of the film follows Faulkner's work fairly closely. Temple's maid Nancy smothers Temple's baby girl to death in order to keep Temple from taking her baby with her and exposing the innocent and helpless child to the debased and perilous underworld existence that Temple would surely lead with Candy Man. Convinced she did the right thing, Nancy serenely goes to the gallows for having taken the child's life. Although both critical and popular response to the film was lukewarm, this picture retains some of the flavor of the Faulkner works on which it was based.

FURTHER READING

Richardson, Tony. *The Long Distance Runner: An Autobiography*. New York: Morrow, 1993.

Gene D. Phillips

SARTORIS, Faulkner's first Yoknapatawpha novel, was published in 1929. In the second half of 1926 Faulkner interrupted the writing of a manuscript entitled ''Father Abraham'' to work on a novel that he later decided to call *Flags in the Dust*. He finished it on September 29, 1927 (according to the date he wrote on the manuscript's last page), and submitted it to Liveright, publisher of his first two novels. This third novel, he felt, would make his reputation. ''I have written THE book . . . ,'' he wrote to Liveright, ''it is the damdest best book you'll look at this year'' (*SL* 38). Two months later in a letter that both surprised and shocked him, Liveright turned down the novel and recommended he not try to place it elsewhere: ''We're frankly very much disappointed by it. It is diffuse and non-integral with neither very much plot development nor character development'' (1984 *FAB* 205). Liveright advised Faulkner not to attempt revision; the flaws were too deep. Downcast, Faulkner waited several months before submitting the manuscript to another publisher. He finally asked his friend Ben Wasson, who was working as a literary agent in New York, to try to place the book. After eleven houses declined it, Harcourt, Brace and Company accepted it, on the condition that it be cut substantially. Wasson agreed to do the cutting, feeling that Faulkner could not or would not do the work himself.

Wasson reduced the novel's length by a fourth. Removing episodes concerning Byron Snopes, Horace Benbow, and less important characters, he turned the narrative focus more sharply on the Sartoris family, especially the twin brothers John and Bayard. He especially paid attention to passages suggesting perverse sexual inclinations in Horace Benbow, who in the *Flags in the Dust* version is clearly attracted to his own sister and has a torrid affair with the sister of the woman he finally marries. Wasson either deleted these scenes entirely or reduced them in length. The abridged novel was published as *Sartoris* in January 1929. Reviews were mixed, and Faulkner was disappointed with the reception. The full-length version of the novel under its original title was not published until 1973. Most readers find *Flags in the Dust* more satisfactory than the shortened

Sartoris, and it does represent the book that Faulkner wrote and wanted to see published.

Sartoris tells the story of the Sartoris clan, the representative aristocratic Old Southern family of Yoknapatawpha County. The center of the novel is Bayard Sartoris, who feels responsible for the death of his twin brother John in a World War I air battle. At the novel's beginning, Bayard returns to Jefferson after the end of the war and attempts to reestablish his life. His grandfather Bayard and his maiden aunt Jenny worry over his recklessness and his apparent disinterest in a conventional existence. Jenny in particular sees his self-destructiveness as the primary trait of the males in the family. Jenny's brother was killed in a Civil War raid on a chicken coop. Bayard's great-grandfather was shot to death twenty years after the Civil War by a jealous business rival. John Sartoris jumped to his death from a burning plane over France. After a time, however, Bayard seems to settle down. He marries Narcissa Benbow, and they enjoy a brief idyll before he becomes restive once again. After wrecking his automobile and causing his grandfather to suffer a fatal heart attack, he disappears from town. On the day Narcissa gives birth to their child, he is killed test-flying an aircraft of questionable design.

Bayard and his brother John may be paralleled to Hemingway's Krebs in "Soldier's Home" and to the narrator in "Big Two-Hearted River." Their self-destructive recklessness, combined with the effects of their war experiences, cut them off from their former lives in Jefferson. Both brothers in effect commit suicide because they cannot adjust to the postwar world, and Faulkner suggests in a larger sense that the post–Civil War Sartoris family is doomed to extinction or at the least to irrelevance by their inability to adjust to changes occurring in the Modern South. Both Hemingway and Faulkner were attracted to the romantic figure of the war veteran whose physical and emotional wounds leave him unable to function in a conventional world. But Faulkner complicates the situation by portraying a family heritage of self-destructiveness and decay and of obsession with the past. Even the humorous and vividly portrayed Aunt Jenny is obsessed with her tale of her brother's death in a chicken-house raid.

Sartoris/Flags in the Dust occupies a crucial place in Faulkner's development as a novelist. In it he displayed for the first time his true power as a literary artist. Tracing the affairs of the Sartorises over four generations, he uncovered the metaphoric potential of the family chronicle, to which he returns repeatedly in such novels as *Light in August, Absalom, Absalom!, Go Down, Moses*, and *The Hamlet*. The perverse sexual inclinations of Horace Benbow (which were mostly cut from *Sartoris*) are echoed in the Quentin/Caddy relationship in *The Sound and the Fury* (which he was writing while he sought publication for *Flags*), in the obsession with grotesque sexuality in *Sanctuary* (which he began writing about the time *Sartoris* was published), and later still in *Light in August*. One might argue that Faulkner's despair over the failure of *Flags in the Dust* to find a publisher, and the lukewarm reviews of *Sartoris*, exorcised his ambitions for public success, freeing him to write the long succession of great novels for which he is known. Most significant, *Flags* is the novel in which he dis-covered the essential roots of his regional sensibility: "my own little postage stamp of native soil. . . . I would never live long enough to exhaust it" (*LIG* 255).

FURTHER READING

Cohen, Philip. "*Flags in the Dust, Sartoris*, and the Unforeseen Consequences of Edi-torial Surgery." *Faulkner Journal* 5.1 (1989): 25–43.

Day, Douglas. Introduction. *Flags in the Dust*. By William Faulkner. New York: Random House, 1973.

Kinney, Arthur F., ed. *Critical Essays on William Faulkner: The Sartoris Family*. Boston: G. K. Hall, 1985.

McDaniel, Linda Elkins. *Annotations to William Faulkner's* Flags in the Dust. New York: Garland, 1991.

Millgate, Michael. "Faulkner's First Trilogy: *Sartoris, Sanctuary*, and *Requiem for a Nun*." *Fifty Years of Yoknapatawpha*, ed. Fowler and Abadie. 90–109.

Hugh Ruppersburg

SARTORIS FAMILY. The world of Faulkner's characters is often composed of clans; of these, the Sartoris family looms large not only as the subjects of his first major work about Yoknapatawpha County (*Sartoris*, 1929) but also as the focus for Faulkner's complicated understanding of Southern history. The legends surrounding Colonel John Sartoris (1823–1876), filled as they are with chivalry and swashbuckling heroism, bravery, and recklessness, create both a lost Eden and a living hell for early twentieth-century figures such as Bayard Sartoris (1893–1920). What seemed once the very stuff of Southern manhood degenerates into death wish as codes of behavior become instances of tragic doom.

Colonel Sartoris is the prototype of larger-than-life figures such as Thomas Sutpen (*Absalom, Absalom!*, 1936) who formulate grand designs and then devote their lives to bending reality until it fits their dream. Word and deed thus become one. By contrast, the Old Colonel's descendants seem less capable and most certainly less voracious. Thus, word, too, often becomes dangerously divorced from action, and the resulting psychological split leads to psychic disintegration. Bayard Sartoris is a case in point. The legacy of his great-grandfather lives on as an increasingly shaky inheritance. His own grandfather is known as the Young Colonel; and while certain aristocratic forms persist, the reality is reduced to a telling image: the carriage in which he is ceremonially driven through a landscape that bears scant relationship to the antebellum South over which Colo-nel Sartoris and his kind presided. Not only do the white trash drive their au-tomobiles over the same roads that "quality folks" like the Young Colonel travel, but the plantation system itself, with its grand mansions, cultivated man-ners, and slaves, has been replaced by sharecroppers and tawdry modernity.

The Sartorises, then, emerge as a palpable index of decline and fall, albeit with the complicating factor of Faulkner's ambivalence about the past. Young Bayard Sartoris, who watched as his twin brother John fell to his death as an aviator in World War I, can neither connect with his Sartoris past nor accommodate to his Sartoris present. Guilt is his identifying character trait, and alienation its major expression.

What distinguishes the Sartorises from other clans—the Compsons or McCaslins—is their direct involvement in the Civil War. This presumably secures their place in contemporarary society, as well as their pride. In this connection critics call attention to the biographical roots that link Colonel Sartoris with the old Colonel Falkner who passed his own exploits onto increasingly unsuitable, or unwilling, shoulders.

FURTHER READING

Kinney, Arthur F. *Critical Essays on William Faulkner: The Sartoris Family*. Boston: G. K. Hall, 1985.

Sanford Pinsker

SARTRE, JEAN-PAUL (1905–1980), French novelist, playwright, and existentialist philosopher who declined the 1964 Nobel Prize for Literature, played a significant role in establishing Faulkner's literary reputation. The favorable critical reception given Faulkner's work by Sartre and other French intellectuals before, during, and after World War II was an essential factor in Faulkner's winning the Nobel Prize for Literature in 1950. Writing to Faulkner in 1945 to elicit his cooperation in *The Portable Faulkner*, Malcolm Cowley quoted Sartre as having said that for the young people of France Faulkner was a god. In the first of his three influential Faulkner criticisms, an essay on *Sartoris* published in *La Nouvelle revue française* in 1938, Sartre argues that Faulkner's novels draw their greatest power from their silences and that the chief characteristic of Faulkner's technique is his "disloyalty"—his art of withholding and deceiving. The following year, Sartre's "Time in Faulkner: *The Sound and the Fury*," widely recognized as a seminal essay in Faulknerian criticism, appeared in *La Nouvelle revue française*. Sartre describes *The Sound and the Fury* as a novel in which nothing happens—a novel in which everything takes place offstage. Sartre compares Faulkner to Proust and describes Faulkner's vision of time as the vision "of a man seated in an open car, looking at the receding landscape." According to Sartre, for Faulkner's characters there is no escape from the past and there is no future. Sartre's 1946 essay "American Novelists in French Eyes," published in *Atlantic Monthly*, offers an assessment of Faulkner's impact in France and cites Faulkner along with Dos Passos, Hemingway, and Steinbeck as major influences on Sartre's generation of writers and intellectuals.

FURTHER READING

Sartre, Jean-Paul. "American Novelists in French Eyes." *Atlantic Monthly* 178 (August 1946): 114–118.

———. "*Sartoris,* par William Faulkner." *Literary and Philosophical Essays.* New York: Criterion, 1955. 73–78.

———. "Time in Faulkner: *The Sound and the Fury.*" *William Faulkner: Three Decades of Criticism,* ed. Hoffman and Vickery. 225–232.

Arthur Wilhelm

"SEPULTURE SOUTH: GASLIGHT," a semiautobiographical Faulkner short story first published in *Harper's Bazaar* in December 1954 and reprinted in *Uncollected Stories.* Inspired by a Walker Evans photograph of a cemetery, the story describes a young boy's impressions of his grandfather's death and funeral. The tone of the story is somber and elegiac, and the theme reprises a familiar Faulkner emphasis that reaches all the way back to the poems of *The Marble Faun*: the ironic contrast between the peaceful dead, "in marble now, durable, impervious, heroic in size, towering above their dust," and the living "anguish and grief and inhumanity of mankind."

Robert W. Hamblin

SHAKESPEARE, WILLIAM (1564–1616), British dramatist and poet who is generally considered to be the greatest writer in the English language. Although Faulkner's claim in 1921 that "I could write a play like *Hamlet* if I wanted to" (1974 *FAB* 330) may be dismissed as an act of youthful posturing, the statement serves to indicate that Shakespeare was the standard by which Faulkner would judge his own creativity. In later years Faulkner consistently acknowledged Shakespeare as a major inspiration and influence, noting, "I have a one-volume Shakespeare that I have just about worn out carrying around with me" (*FIU* 67). Faulkner's recorded interviews and conversations contain references to a number of Shakespeare's works and characters, including *Hamlet, Macbeth, Henry IV, Henry V, A Midsummer Night's Dream, Romeo and Juliet,* the sonnets, Falstaff, Prince Hal, Lady Macbeth, Bottom, Ophelia, and Mercutio. Faulkner acknowledged that his title *The Sound and the Fury* derived from the famous speech Macbeth delivers upon hearing of the death of his wife (*LIG* 169–170), and the recurring uses of shadow and bell imagery extend the echoes of Shakespeare's play in Faulkner's text. The title of the short story "Tomorrow" also seems to derive from the same Macbeth speech. Quentin Compson, as presented in both *The Sound and the Fury* and *Absalom, Absalom!,* shares several character traits with Hamlet, most notably a brooding introspection, a romantic longing for purity and truth, and an obsession with death. A major change in Gail Hightower's attitude and behavior in *Light in August* is symbolized by the minister's act of laying aside his copy of Tennyson's poems to begin reading *Henry IV,* which the narrator describes as "food for a man."

While Faulkner occasionally employed specific borrowings from and allusions to Shakespeare such as those listed above, the greater influence of the British bard upon the Mississippi novelist seems to have been in more general terms. A number of dominant themes and emphases are common to both writers, including the imaginative use of historical materials, the incorporation of both tragic and comic views of life, and the paradoxical tension between fate (in Faulkner's case, determinism) and free will. Moreover, the recurring emphasis in a number of Shakespeare's sonnets (for example, XV, XVIII, and LV) upon the brevity of life and the immortality of art may well have influenced Faulkner's notions on the interrelationship of life, death, and art. Finally, both writers exhibit a fascination for experimental form and language, flouting conventional rules to create new narrative structures and delighting in neologisms, puns, and other forms of word play.

FURTHER READING

D'Avanzo, Mario L. "Love's Labours: Byron Bunch and Shakespeare." *Notes on Mississippi Writers* 10 (1977): 80–86.

Robert W. Hamblin

"SHALL NOT PERISH," a short story by Faulkner, was first published in *Story* in 1943 and is included in *Collected Stories*. Told through the eyes of a nine-year-old boy who loses his brother in World War II, the story attempts to make sense of the sacrifice of human life for one's country. Upon news of the death of another boy from Yoknapatawpha County, the only son of the wealthy Major de Spain, the narrator and his mother, members of a poor farming family, travel twenty miles by bus to Jefferson to pay their respects. While the bitter and apparently suicidal de Spain repudiates his country, the boy's mother speaks of something in her own son that "must have been strong to have lasted through all of us" and that "must have been all right for him to be willing to die for it after that long time and coming that far." The story goes on to tell of the boy's great-grandfather, a Civil War veteran who relives a cavalry charge during a cowboy movie and whose outburst comes to stand for the spirit of all those who have crossed deserts and wildernesses and who have died in battle for "the places that men and women have lived in and loved"—in other words, for "America." Written and published during World War II, "Shall Not Perish" moves from a quiet and personal point of view to a statement that seems simplistically nationalistic.

FURTHER READING

Bradford, M. E. "Faulkner and the Jeffersonian Dream: Nationalism in 'Two Soldiers' and 'Shall Not Perish.' " *Mississippi Quarterly* 18 (1965): 94–100.
Carothers, James B. " 'I Ain't a Soldier Now': Faulkner's World War II Veterans." *Faulkner Journal* 2 (1987): 67–74.
Howell, Elmo. "William Faulkner and *Pro Patria Mori*." *Louisiana Studies* 5 (1966): 89–96.

Arthur A. Brown

SHEGOG, REVEREND. Limited in his appearance in Faulkner's work to one scene in *The Sound and the Fury*, in which as a visiting preacher from St. Louis he delivers the Easter sermon at Dilsey's church, the Reverend Shegog nevertheless makes a powerful impression. This church service dramatizes for the reader the kind of faith—communal, emotional, mystical—that underlies the daily, unpretentious heroism of Dilsey's life. Its effect on Dilsey may be judged by her tears and by her words from Revelation claiming a vision that transcends earthly time: She has seen, she says, the "first and the last," the "beginning and the ending." Others in the congregation are equally moved by Shegog's sermon; even Benjy's constant whimpering is quieted, although it begins again after the service when the party reach the Compson gate. The sermon scene has been praised as a richly realistic evocation of African American preaching, notably in Shegog's modulations through several levels of discourse, and of the black Southern church service. The description of Shegog's "monkey face" has sometimes been called racist; but the sermon absorbs this in its theme of how earthly insignificance (the minister is shabby and small, much as Faulkner sometimes portrayed himself) is transcended through the power to "see" and "believe." More controversial is the question of the sermon's place in the novel. Is it the key to an affirmative understanding of life, or is it merely a private and ironic vision that is immediately negated by Jason's viciousness, Mrs. Compson's callousness, and Benjy's continuing moans? Faulkner has it both ways. Like his creator, Shegog is an artist, and his vision imparted to Dilsey provides her the same comfort and unburdening, joyous though transient, that Faulkner's vision in the novel provides his readers.

FURTHER READING

Fleming, Robert E. "James Weldon Johnson's *God's Trombones* as a Source for Faulkner's Rev'un Shegog." *College Language Association Journal* 36.1 (1992): 24–30.

Ross, Stephen M. "Rev. Shegog's Powerful Voice." *Faulkner Journal* 1.1 (1985): 8–16.

Urgo, Joseph R. "A Note on Reverend Shegog's Sermon in Faulkner's *The Sound and the Fury.*" *Notes on Modern American Literature* 8.1 (1984): 4.

Glenn Meeter

SHERWOOD ANDERSON AND OTHER FAMOUS CREOLES. *See* **Anderson, Sherwood**.

"SHINGLES FOR THE LORD," a short story by Faulkner. Published in the *Saturday Evening Post* on February 13, 1943, and reprinted in *Collected Stories*, the comic tale concerns the changing understanding of work and its relation to personal profit and community service, as well as the relationship of grace and works. While repairing a church, Res Grier and Solon Quick negotiate dog ownership in terms of WPA (Works Progress Administration) "work units";

they end up setting the church on fire because they are less occupied by their work than they are by profiting. One of the men working on the church is called Snopes, and its pastor is Nevard Whitfield; the story bears resemblance in tone to the Reverend Goodyhay church-raising episode of *The Mansion*, and a Res (for Orestes) Snopes appears in *The Mansion*.

FURTHER READING

Folks, Jeffrey J. "Honor in Faulkner's Short Fiction." *Southern Review* 18 (1982): 506–516.

Hahn, Stephen. "Comedy and Social Construction: Teaching Faulkner's 'Shingles for the Lord.'" *Teaching Faulkner* 13 (1998): 5–7.

Howell, Elmo. "Faulkner's Country Church: A Note on 'Shingles for the Lord.'" *Mississippi Quarterly* 21 (1968): 205–210.

Joseph R. Urgo

SILVER, JAMES WESLEY (1900–1988), professor of American history at the University of Mississippi from 1936 until 1964, controversial civil rights activist, author of *Mississippi: The Closed Society* (1964) and *Running Scared: Silver in Mississippi* (1984). A close personal friend of the Faulkner family, Silver frequently discussed the politics of race with Faulkner. As program chairman, Silver arranged for Faulkner to speak at the annual meeting of the Southern Historical Association in Memphis on November 10, 1955. Faulkner's speech, entitled "American Segregation and World Crisis," represents one of his most forceful statements on racial justice and equality. Although he was much more centrist in his views than the liberal Silver, Faulkner cooperated with Silver and Mississippi newspaperman P. D. East on the composition of *The Southern Reposure* (1956), an underground newspaper that satirized segregationists and that was surreptitiously distributed on university campuses throughout Mississippi. Also a close friend of photographer Martin Dain, Silver assisted in arranging for some of the photographs that appear in Dain's *Faulkner's County: Yoknapatawpha* (1964).

FURTHER READING

Silver, James W. "Faulkner and the Teaching of History." *Running Scared: Silver in Mississippi*. Jackson: University Press of Mississippi, 1984. 206–215.

Louis Daniel Brodsky

"SKIRMISH AT SARTORIS," a Faulkner short story published in *Scribner's Magazine* in April 1935 and reprinted in *Uncollected Stories*. Faulkner revised the text as the sixth chapter of *The Unvanquished* (1938). During Reconstruction, John Sartoris kills the Burdens, who are attempting to have the freed slaves vote. He holds the election for white men at his plantation, Sartoris, winning that skirmish; but he loses his skirmish with the ladies of Jefferson, who force him to marry his cousin Drusilla Hawk in the name of Southern honor because she shared a bivouac with him during the war. Sartoris may have lost that skirmish, but Drusilla and the former slaves have lost their war for autonomous new roles.

FURTHER READING

Taylor, Nancy Dew. " 'Moral Housecleaning' and Colonel Sartoris's Dream.'' *Mississippi Quarterly* 37 (1984): 353–364.

Veronica Makowsky

SLAVERY. A system of labor and social institution before Emancipation and a legacy that continued to bear on the South long afterward, slavery pervades much of Faulkner's fictional world. As a Deep South cotton state Mississippi had been heavily committed to slavery as its chief source of plantation labor, and more than half of the population was made up of African American slaves by the time of the Civil War. Although northern Mississippi had a large non-slaveholding white population in its hilly, less fertile lands, in Faulkner's home county, Lafayette, over 40 percent of the population in 1860 were black slaves and close to half of all white families owned slaves. More than just a system of labor, slavery shaped nearly every aspect of social organization, politics, religion, and culture in the world William Faulkner wrote about.

In Faulkner's works readers are treated to only rare glimpses of the experience of slavery from the slave's perspective, and none of Faulkner's slave characters is drawn with great depth. He offered more on white perceptions of slavery, most poignantly in *Go Down, Moses* when young Ike McCaslin probes the horrors his grandfather, Old Carothers, inflicted on his slaves and comes to acknowledge an inherited burden of guilt. Earlier, his father and uncle, Uncle Buck and Uncle Buddy McCaslin, motivated by the same legacy of guilt, repudiate slavery and adopt a bizarre plan by which their slaves work to buy their freedom. Likewise, Goodhue Coldfield is morally disturbed by slavery and rids himself of slave property he received as payment for a debt, though he is careful to make the slaves work to buy their freedom.

Some of Faulkner's early admirers may have exaggerated the author's moral objections to slavery, due in part to the notion, developed most fully in *Go Down, Moses*, that slavery represented a curse upon the South. Faulkner was often ambiguous in his representations of slavery, possibly because he may have felt ambivalent about condemning what was such a fundamental element of Southern society. Nonetheless, his depiction of slavery is frequently at odds with the standard version of happy slaves and paternalistic masters so often nurtured in traditional versions of Southern history and literature.

Faulkner's moral judgment of slavery is sharpest when he deals with it outside the context of Old South society, most powerfully in his short story ''Red Leaves.'' In it an Indian chief has died, and his unnamed slave and body servant is to be buried with him. The story was probably inspired by a local story of a similar dying wish, although this was not Indian custom. The slave in Faulkner's story, acting on an instinctive human will to survive, tries to escape his fate by taking flight into the swamps. Faulkner takes us into the "inscrutable" mind of the slave, a man of forty captured in Africa when he was a boy of fourteen. He recalls his struggle to survive aboard the slave ship coming to America: On the deck above him a "drunken New England captain" is reciting the Bible, while in the hold below the slave manages to grab a live rat and eat it. Now he is again struggling to survive, running for his life through the swamps, hunted by Indians who are puzzled by this desire to escape death, a trait they consider both racial and dishonorable. Faulkner's fictional Indians live outside a culture that values human life for its own sake; in another story Faulkner's Indians contemplate cannibalism as a solution to the surplus slaves they have no use for. However, although he makes his point at the expense of a historically accurate portrayal of the Indians, few can read the story of the doomed slave in "Red Leaves" without feeling revulsion toward any society that has so little regard for another human.

Faulkner made a point of placing slaves at the very founding of the new county whites created as the Indians were removed. They assist in the building of the first courthouse and are an integral part of the economy and social structure. Slavery is typically presented in a morally neutral manner, and few of his white or black characters seem bothered to defend or attack the institution, even as whites prepare to go to war to maintain it.

Absalom, Absalom! not only depicts slavery as a ubiquitous feature of the society but also incorporates a subtle critique of its moral evil. Sutpen is condemned by his critics for his inhuman treatment of others, notably women, whom he regards like breeding animals in his quest to produce a male heir to his would-be dynasty. At the core of slavery is a similar intention to reduce humans to beasts, livestock that can be bought, sold, and treated as the owner pleases. This bestialization of humans is developed in nearly every description of Sutpen's slaves. His band of twenty slaves is described as "wild niggers" or "a herd of wild beasts" who lie huddled under his wagon cover "smelling like a wolfden." He has acquired them in Haiti, and they speak no English, indeed no language any human in Yoknapatawpha can understand or even identify. They are, Faulkner writes, not like any humans black or white but more "like beasts half tamed to walk upright like men, in attitudes wild and reposed." Sutpen uses his slaves to hunt game like a "pack of wild hounds," running deer through the forest for Sutpen to shoot. These wild slaves have no blankets and no beds and "like a sleeping alligator" cover their naked bodies in the mud at night. When the captive French architect tries to flee, Sutpen again uses his slaves like hounds, this time to track and capture the desperate human prey. To further the theme of bestialization, Faulkner describes the brutal exhibitions Sutpen stages for his male friends in the stables behind his mansion. These are bare-knuckled, no-holds-barred fights in which slaves are pitted against one another, surrounded by whites gambling on the outcome, as though the event were a cockfight. Occasionally, Sutpen joins a slave in combat "both naked to the waist and gouging at one another's eyes as if their skins should not only have been the same color but should have been covered with fur too.''

If slavery intended to reduce humans to the level of animals, it was in actual practice a very human relationship between master and slave and very often a contested one in which the slave was rarely altogether powerless. This theme, which has informed much of recent historical scholarship on slavery, is nicely developed in Faulkner's story of Tomey's Turl in *Go Down, Moses*. Turl's persistent habit of running away to his lover, Tennie, a slave on a neighboring plantation, ultimately forces his owners, the McCaslin twins, to buy the object of his desire and bring her home. This comic tale may seem fanciful, but it drew on J. S. Bassett's study of a local plantation, a book Faulkner borrowed and read prior to writing. The book is filled with letters from exasperated overseers telling of incorrigible slaves running off to be with their wives or loved ones and trying, often successfully, to force their owner to return them to Tennessee.

Another of Faulkner's historical sources on slavery was Caroline Barr (Mammie Callie), the family servant who had been the slave of Hugh Barr, a prominent slave owner in Lafayette County. Many former slaves of her generation were being interviewed by the WPA (Works Progress Administration) during the 1930s, and their stories were being reported in the local newspaper. Faulkner must have absorbed some of these other former slave recollections, for the portrait of slavery he sketched frequently complemented their accounts.

When slavery met its ultimate crisis during the Civil War, earlier strategies of running off to bargain for advantage *within* slavery were quickly transformed into flights to freedom and rebellion *against* slavery itself. When Grant's army invaded northern Mississippi in the fall of 1862, Union soldiers did their best to spread word of the coming emancipation. This is what the slave Loosh is referring to at the opening of *The Unvanquished*. Loosh is a rebellious slave who betrays his owners, the Sartoris family, by revealing to the Yankees the location of the buried family silver. As he is preparing to run off to the Union lines, Loosh offers an eloquent defense of his rebellion. ''I don't belong to John Sartoris now,'' he tells Granny Millard. ''I belongs to me and God.'' When Granny asks who gave him the right to give the silver away, Loosh questions the right of his masters to own him: ''Let God ax John Sartoris who the man name that give me to him. Let the man that buried me in the black dark ax that of the man what dug me free.'' The question goes unanswered. Loosh joins a massive flight to freedom north toward the Union lines, in what seems at first to be a mindless, lemminglike rush to disaster. Instead, Faulkner explains, this is something fundamentally human: ''one of those impulses inexplicable yet invincible which appear among races of people at intervals and drive them to pick up and leave all security and familiarity of earth and home and start out, they don't know where, emptyhanded, blind to everything but a hope and a doom.'' This slave exodus was a dramatized interpretation of actual events in northern Mississippi in which slaves rebelled against their masters or just ran off, many to join the Union army. It is a historical moment repressed in the traditional version of Southern history, which dwells on loyal slaves protecting the family silver and rejecting the entreaties of marauding Yankees. The destruction of slavery came from below, from the slaves themselves, with inconsistent help from Union soldiers whom Faulkner casts, in a historically accurate fashion, as reluctant emancipators all too happy to leave the runaway slaves to their former masters. Faulkner was ambivalent but never complacent about slavery and its legacy—and that meant not only to African Americans but to all the South.

FURTHER READING

Berlin, Ira, Joseph P. Reidy, and Leslie S. Rowland, eds. *Freedom: A Documentary History of Emancipation, 1861–1867*. New York: Cambridge University Press, 1982–.

Genovese, Eugene. *Roll, Jordan, Roll: The World the Slaves Made*. New York: Pantheon, 1974.

Kolchin, Peter. *American Slavery, 1619–1877*. New York: Hill and Wang, 1993.

Oakes, James. *The Ruling Race: A History of American Slaveholders*. New York: Knopf, 1982.

Sundquist. *Faulkner: The House Divided*.

Sydnor, Charles. *Slavery in Mississippi*. Gloucester, Mass.: P. Smith, 1965.

Don H. Doyle

SLAVE SHIP (1937), cowritten by Faulkner, is an adventure film about mutiny on the high seas. When novelist-screenwriter Graham Greene reviewed the film, he noted that the presence of Faulkner's name in the film's credits had led him to assume that the movie's course was "set for distinction: but it remains a hot-weather picture" (214). Indeed, the movie is a routine potboiler.

FURTHER READING

Greene, Graham. *The Graham Greene Film Reader: Reviews, Essays, and Interviews*. Ed. David Parkinson. New York: Applause Books, 1995.

Gene D. Phillips

SNOPES. Faulkner worked throughout his career on Snopes material, beginning with the writing of "Father Abraham" in the 1920s, continuing in a series of short stories and novel segments, and culminating in the completion of the *Snopes* trilogy in 1959. The family occupied his thinking more than any other single project in his career. Faulkner seemed amused by his creation of this family, but he took them very seriously. In Virginia in 1957 he observed that a Snopes "will have to cope with his environment or his environment will destroy him" (*FIU* 283).

The Snopes clan is a varied and heterogeneous family. Some are quite devious—Flem, notorious for his cold and heartless dealings; others, such as Wallstreet Panic, are wholly respectable. In nearly every case, however, a

Snopes can be said to resist being typecast or dismissed due to circumstances of origin. As a clan they are skillful manipulators, able to turn what for others would constitute class disadvantage into surprising triumph. Most established families in Yoknapatawpha dislike Snopeses because they are newcomers who demand inclusion. Gavin and Ratliff, throughout the later portions of the trilogy, are zealous in their Snopes-hating and -baiting. But Snopeses are not put off by petty discriminations. In *The Mansion*, for example, Montgomery Ward Snopes knows that outsiders expect a Snopes to be a "son of a bitch." Thus he concludes, "*[W]e'll just show them . . . every Snopes will make it his private and personal aim to have the whole world recognize him as THE son of a bitch's son of a bitch.*"

Critical responses to the Snopes clan provide a telling gauge of the way ideology and literature intersect. Flem Snopes is clearly a product of his time and place, but whether he is the incarnation of evil Ratliff describes, a shrewd capitalist, or a mirror image of prominent citizens depends upon one's conception of Flem's environment and of American capitalism in general. Unlike Faulkner's other major families (Compson or Sartoris, for example), Snopeses do not have a legacy to maintain or lose: They are, throughout the trilogy, in ascendancy.

FURTHER READING

Bassett, John E. "Yoknapatawpha Revised: Demystifying Snopes." *College Literature* 15 (1988): 136–152.

Beck, Warren. *Man in Motion: Faulkner's Trilogy*. Madison: University of Wisconsin Press, 1961.

Urgo. *Faulkner's Apocrypha*.

Watson, James G. *The Snopes Dilemma: Faulkner's Trilogy*. Coral Gables, Fla.: University of Miami Press, 1970.

Joseph R. Urgo

"SNOW," a short story by Faulkner. Efforts to publish "Snow" began in 1942, but the story did not appear until *Uncollected Stories*. The narrator of the story, prompted by his child's question, remembers an experience when he and a companion named Don were traveling together in a Swiss village. A funeral procession ignites their curiosity. The deceased is a man named Britt, a climbing guide who sacrificed his life to save the lives of his bride and his client, a wealthy German. Britt's bride leaves with the German. When Britt's body is retrieved after spring thaw, his well-dressed widow returns for the funeral. The Americans are affected by her lack of fidelity to her husband's sacrifice.

FURTHER READING

Cantrell, Frank. "An Unpublished Faulkner Short Story: 'Snow.' " *Mississippi Quarterly* 26 (1973): 325–330.

Orlofsky, Michael. "Faulkner's Alpine Apprenticeship: 'Mistral' and 'Snow.' " *Iowa Journal of Literary Studies* 5 (1984): 96–105.

Diane Brown Jones

SOLDIERS' PAY, Faulkner's first novel, published in 1926. In January 1925 Faulkner traveled to New Orleans in search of passage to Europe, but his trip was delayed until July. In this period he met Sherwood Anderson, explored the rich cultural and artistic life of the city, and decisively emerged from a diverse apprenticeship in poetry, graphic arts, and prose portraiture to begin one of the world's greatest novel-writing careers. Written between January and May 1925, and published by Boni and Liveright, *Soldiers' Pay* brings "the Lost Generation" home to a small Southern town, Charlestown, Georgia, which resembles in important respects that eventual center of his fictional Mississippi cosmos, the town of Jefferson in a place called Yoknapatawpha County.

The novel is set in April and May 1919—just after the Great War has ended and during the "cruel" mythical season of T. S. Eliot's *The Waste Land* (1922): a season of false renewal, hollow Easter resurrection, and unfulfilled sexual desire. The novel opens with an ironic epigraph taken from an "Old Play (about 19-?)," a fragment of dialogue about shaving between "Achilles" and "Mercury," here cast as sergeant and cadet. The scene is a self-conscious parody of the Joycean "mythical method," a graphic subversion of the heroic mood, and an effective introduction of Joe Gilligan and Julian Lowe, a demobilized soldier and a young air cadet, respectively, whose opportunity for martial glory had been thwarted (as had Faulkner's) by a cruel fate: The Armistice had been declared before they could reach the Western Front. On a train heading south from Buffalo, they vent through drunkenness their mingled frustration and guilty relief, casting themselves, histrionically, as "lost foreigners" in a "foreign land."

Into this overblown scene enters a young aviator, Lieutenant Donald Mahon, who, shot down over Flanders and long presumed dead, now bears a ghastly scar across his brow. He is taken up by an awed Gilligan and Lowe, who are met by a young, beautiful, and "Beardsleyan" war widow, Margaret Powers. Lowe disappears after chapter 1, persuaded by Margaret Powers to return home to his mother; he sends her several semiliterate love letters over the course of the novel. Seeing in Donald the image of her dead husband, Richard Powers, whom she had married on an impulse and who was killed in France before he could receive her letter saying that she did not love him, Margaret decides to escort Donald Mahon home to his father, the Rector Joseph Mahon. With Gilligan she will attempt to prepare the rector for Donald's sudden "resurrection" and impending death and to mediate between Donald Mahon and his fiancée, Cecily Saunders. While attracted by the glamorous idea of being engaged to the dying war hero, Cecily is also repelled by his scar and refuses, finally, to marry him.

Blind, amnesic, and slowly dying, Donald Mahon may be defined principally by his function to structure and overshadow the agitated drama that unfolds around him. In this respect, like his precursors the Shade of Pierrot and the Spirit of Autumn in Faulkner's early Symbolist drama *The Marionettes*, "[w]ithout moving or speaking he dominates the whole scene," a "veiled mirror" that—now inserted into a more realistic and more complex social arrangement—gives a blurred reflection of the fears, fantasies, and desires of a surrounding community of souls. In his dramatic function and partly mythological status, Mahon also resembles Jessie Weston's Fisher King, the slain kings of James Frazer's *The Golden Bough*, and the primal father of Freud's *Totem and Taboo*: Like these figures, Mahon is an essentially "absent" yet strangely potent figure of proscription and authority, presiding over a field of erotic competition and contaminating desire with the remorse evoked by his dying.

The frenetic and comical activity that revolves around Donald Mahon is driven principally by Januarius Jones, a fat, satyrlike, and slightly androgynous Latin teacher. Jones incarnates the principle of a kind of jaded and futile though no less obsessive lust, and he spends his time mainly in pursuit of Mahon's unfaithful fiancée, Cecily Saunders, who, nymphlike, self-centered, and flirtatious, is a precursor of *Sanctuary*'s Temple Drake. Vacillating "furiously" between attraction to and repulsion from both Mahon and Jones, Cecily eventually elopes with George Farr, a young man whose jealous love for Cecily is a constant and unrelieved agony. When Margaret Powers equally proves unconquerable, fated as she is to wed Donald Mahon, Jones finally succeeds in "bedding" the housekeeper, Emmy, who, though displaced by Margaret, remains faithful to the memory of the faunlike young Donald with whom she roamed the moonlit hills and made love in the prewar days of innocence.

By the very force of his mute, impassive being, and by virtue of the emotional and affective intensities with which his figure is invested by those around him, Mahon dominates and distorts the novel's comic itinerary of love. In his capacity of dying, omnipresent, and proscriptive god, he is the fit object of an intense ambivalence of feeling. On the one hand, he is loved and mourned; on the other, he is feared and resented. Of all such mixed transferences of emotion, none is more dominant than that of Margaret Powers, for whom Mahon is an incarnation of Captain Richard Powers, her own murdered husband shot in the face at pointblank range in the trenches of wartime France. In the end Margaret will marry Mahon and so both "undo" and repeat her original emotional betrayal of Richard Powers.

Faulkner's first novel is thus a uniquely modernist fusion of symbol, myth, psychological analysis, and realistic social observation. His characterization of Margaret Powers is particularly noteworthy in all these regards. If she is cast as Persephone in the register of the novel's seasonal and mythical drama (destined as she is to carry Donald Mahon off to the underworld), Margaret is also the occasion of the novel's most extensive foray into psychological realism, the ground of the novel's most convincing exploration and assessment of mental process and motivation. In fact, she becomes Faulkner's first truly extended fictional analysis and representation not only of the female subject but of the psychological subject in general, that is, the subject who harbors an expansive, complex, dynamic inner life. In order to represent the turbulence and complexity of her thoughts and emotions, Faulkner is driven to the kind of experimentation in stream-of-consciousness narration that he would assiduously develop and finally transcend with spectacular effect in *The Sound and the Fury* and *As I Lay Dying*.

With *Soldiers' Pay* Faulkner established himself among the most gifted and promising young writers in America. As the British novelist and critic Arnold Bennett wrote of him on June 26, 1930, on the publication of the British edition of the novel, "Faulkner is the coming man. He has inexhaustible invention, powerful imagination, a wondrous gift of characterization, a finished skill in dialogue; and he writes, generally, like an angel. None of the arrived American stars can surpass him in style when he is at his best" (qtd. in 1974 *FAB* 661).

FURTHER READING

Millgate, Michael. "Starting Out in the Twenties: Reflections on *Soldiers' Pay*." *Mosaic* 7 (1973): 1–14.
Yonce, Margaret J. *Annotations to William Faulkner's* Soldiers' Pay. New York: Garland, 1990.
———. "The Composition of *Soldiers' Pay*." *Mississippi Quarterly* 33 (1980): 291–326.
Zeitlin, Michael. "The Passion of Margaret Powers: A Psychoanalytic Reading of *Soldiers' Pay*." *Mississippi Quarterly* 46 (1993): 351–372.

Michael Zeitlin

SOUND AND THE FURY, THE, a novel by Faulkner, generally regarded as one of the greatest fictional works of the twentieth century. David Minter notes that for fifteen years after Cape and Smith published it in October 1929, little over 3,000 copies were needed to meet the demand for *The Sound and the Fury*. And much of that little demand was spurred by the sensation of *Sanctuary*. Although there were appreciative reviews, scathing remarks dominated the critical discussion; clearly, the author and his publisher had not yet shaped a reading audience for his daring experiment. Such neglect and disparagement must have come all the harder for being in sharp contrast with Faulkner's own judgment about the work. He told Ben Wasson it was the best he had ever written, saying it in his own inimitable fashion: "It's a real son of a bitch (1974 *FAB* 590)."

The novel can be regarded as a Yoknapatawpha document and, as Patrick Samway suggests (Gresset and Polk, *Intertexuality in Faulkner*), should be seen as a palimpsest with *Absalom, Absalom!* and "That Evening Sun," which also follow the Compson family and exhibit Faulkner's profound understanding of the African American culture, the only context in which Faulkner draws out the Compsons' lives. But as André Bleikasten (*Most Splendid Failure*) has reminded us, Faulkner's almost unprecedented psychological penetration and stylistic innovation are not captured under the rubric of Yoknapatawpha alone. It is in the light of all these Faulkner "signatures" that the language with which he described the writing of the novel most reveals its significance. Three remarks in particular lead us into the heart of the novel: first, the comment from his original introduction to the novel, "I wrote this book and learned to read"; next, from his second introduction, "I speak [of the South] in the sense of the indigenous dream"; and third, from his interview with Jean Stein for the Spring 1956 *Paris Review*, "I wrote it five separate times trying to tell the story, to rid myself of the dream" (*The Sound and the Fury*, 2nd Norton Critical Edition 226, 229, 232). (His introductions, incidentally, never appeared with the novel in his lifetime.)

The last of these remarks requires further explanation. As readers know, *The Sound and the Fury* appears in four sections, each with a different narrator, but all in one sense from the same family and all reflecting significant events in the childhoods of a generation of that family. The Compsons are captured at that moment when a generation of children—Candace and her three brothers, Benjy, Quentin, and Jason—are forced to cope one way or another with declining family fortunes, increasing family dysfunction, and outmoded family values challenged by their own experiences. These childhoods and their challenges come into critical focus in the events surrounding their Grandmother Damuddy's death in 1898. Even more specifically Faulkner indicated he was gripped by the image of Caddy's climbing the tree to see into the room where Damuddy's body lies in state, the little girl's muddy drawers exposed to her brothers waiting at the bottom of the tree. The four sections of the novel play out variations on that 1898 scene in the reflections of Quentin in 1910, the year of his suicide, and those of the other narrators registered from Good Friday to Easter of 1928, the novel's present time. Section one, where the word "reflection" should be taken the most literally, is Benjy's "tale told by an idiot" and suggests the source of the title, Macbeth's famous speech upon learning of the death of Lady Macbeth. Section two is Quentin's earlier reflection; section three is given to Jason, back in the present. Section four, a third-person narrative, focuses on Dilsey Gibson, the Compsons' Negro cook, evidently modeled on the Faulkners' own servant, Mammy Callie Barr.

Not only was Faulkner's method of telling the story innovative; it was and remains perhaps the most controversial element in the large body of criticism the novel has elicited. Are readers to understand Faulkner's shift to third person for Dilsey's section as an acknowledgment that a white male author could not do justice to a black female character in the first person? Or is it a sign of an unacknowledged distance between the two, an inability of the author to conceive of black character directly? Is the absence of any narrative from Caddy's point of view an appropriate technique for showing how a patriarchal Southern order writes a Caddy out of her own voice? Or did Faulkner fail to find a way for her to tell her own story? Worse, is this failure a sign of his discomfort with women, with sexuality, the expression of a conflicted personality? Thadious Davis, among others, has raised these and similar questions.

Whatever one's critical stance here, Faulkner's own further comments to Stein are relevant: "It's a tragedy of two lost women: Caddy and her daughter. Dilsey is one of my own favorite characters because she is brave, courageous, generous, gentle and honest. She's much more brave and honest and generous than me" (*LIG* 244–245). It is with Faulkner's reference to Caddy's daughter, also named Quentin, that we get to what Faulkner must have meant by the fifth part. Ten years before his interview with Stein he had written what was intended as yet another introduction, this time explaining the Dilsey section that Malcolm Cowley planned to excerpt to represent *The Sound and the Fury* in his *Portable Faulkner*. What Faulkner wrote—a genealogy in the form of an obituary—is now usually referred to as the "Appendix" and has sometimes been printed with the novel. Whether this should be considered a "fifth" section is debated; but Faulkner seemed to consider it such, and it is here that the story of Caddy's daughter Quentin's situation is given sufficient attention to account for his including her as one of the prominent female figures of the novel.

Faulkner's focus on three women and his comparison of himself with one of them draw us into the South's "indigenous dream" of which Faulkner said he tried to rid himself. Six years earlier, Willa Cather, whose writings Faulkner admired and apparently kept track of, published *A Lost Lady*. There the adjective is ironic, as one suspects that it is to a similar degree in Faulkner's description of Caddy and Quentin. It is not so much that they are lost (for instance, morally, as the community tries to paint them), nor even that they have experienced great loss, though they have, but that they, their value, has been lost by their society. Thus theirs, along with Dilsey's, are the losses that condemn the social order and codes of conduct that "the South" would maintain, the dream that is the indigenous substance that defines it as the South. Whatever its features, obviously patriarchal and white, among others, it is this dream of which Faulkner claims the writing of the novel rid him. The persistence or recurrence of certain of the dream's stereotypes might suggest he could never fully rid himself of it; indeed, he was a Southerner and remained rooted in its soil. But the dramatic change in his work from the fiction that preceded to that which followed *The Sound and the Fury* would suggest he rid himself of it in great measure.

His third comment, that in writing this novel he learned how to read, may indeed explain how he did so. Since he had read extensively before this time, and with a keen memory for what he had read, learning to read must refer to discovering a new dimension in his reading, a way in which he discovered that what he read was indeed about him in some profound and spiritual sense. This would explain the mythic force with which Caddy in the tree suddenly struck him. This was Eden and the Fall and an insight into the New World and the "American Adam." He, his brothers, and their cousin Sallie Murry could be captured as, or at least become material for, the Compson children. All of them were to be measured by their likeness or unlikeness to Dilsey, their companion and caretaker, she with a vision of "de first en de last." In writing the novel he had learned how to read the eternal battles: order and freedom, tradition and creativity. It is such battles Faulkner frames in the "Appendix" by the different escapes from repressive order of Caddy's daughter Quentin, the uncle for whom she was named, and the first Quentin Compson whose journey toward freedom parallels America's own. It does not take much of a stretch to see how the discovery of the truth about oneself, one's family, country, and origins and the embodiment of that truth in one of the century's most extraordinary novels probably qualifies it as "a real son of a bitch."

FURTHER READING

Bleikasten, André. *The Most Splendid Failure: Faulkner's* The Sound and the Fury. Bloomington: Indiana University Press, 1976.

Bloom, Harold, ed. *Modern Critical Interpretations of William Faulkner's* The Sound and the Fury. Philadelphia: Chelsea House, 1998.

Cowan, Michael H., ed. *Twentieth Century Interpretations of* The Sound and the Fury. Englewood Cliffs, N.J.: Prentice-Hall, 1968.

Faulkner, William. *The Sound and the Fury.* 2nd Norton Critical Ed., Ed. David Minter. New York: W. W. Norton, 1994.

Hahn, Stephen, and Arthur F. Kinney, eds. *Approaches to Teaching Faulkner's* The Sound and the Fury. New York: MLA, 1996.

Kinney, Arthur. *Critical Essays on Faulkner: The Compson Family.* Boston: G. K. Hall, 1982.

Matthews, John T. The Sound and the Fury: *Faulkner and the Lost Cause.* New York, Twayne, 1990.

Polk, Noel, ed. *New Essays on* The Sound and the Fury. Cambridge: Cambridge University Press, 1993.

Ross, Stephen M. *Reading Faulkner:* The Sound and the Fury. Jackson: University Press of Mississippi, 1996.

Charles A. Peek

SOUND AND THE FURY, THE, a movie (1959) based on portions of the Faulkner novel and directed by Martin Ritt. As in the novel, Jason Compson resents his sister Caddy for leaving her illegitimate daughter, whom she named Quentin after her deceased brother Quentin, in the care of the Compsons when she left home to lead a wayward life. In the film, however, her brother Quentin does not kill himself in his youth as he does in the novel but instead lives on as a hopeless alcoholic. In another major departure from Faulkner, Jason and Miss Quentin fall in love by the end of the movie. This development required that Jason could not be a blood relative of Miss Quentin, so in the film's scenario he becomes a Compson by adoption. The movie thus negates the tragic denouement of the novel, whereby the Compson clan is irrevocably doomed to die out in the wake of Miss Quentin's flight with a carnival roustabout. By contrast, in the film she and Jason will marry and continue to perpetuate the

Compson family. Although some film reviewers found the outcome of the movie touching, it is clearly no match for the powerful ending of the Faulkner original.

FURTHER READING

Halliwell, Leslie. *Film Guide*. Rev. ed. Ed. John Walker. New York: HarperCollins, 1998.
McGilligan, Pat. "Ritt Large: An Interview with Martin Ritt." *Film Comment* 22.1 (January–February 1986): 38–46.

Gene D. Phillips

SOUTH, THE. In *Absalom, Absalom!* (1936), Canadian Shreve McCannon, lacking the sense of the past Southerners take for granted, asks his Harvard roommate Quentin Compson to "[t]ell about the South." Quentin's story response ends with his repeated attempt to convince himself: "I don't hate it." Juxtapose Faulkner's name with that ill-defined term "the South," and most readers will take Quentin's insistence for Faulkner's own view. Faulkner's own attitudes, no more simple and direct than Quentin's, can be derived from his comments about the South; sifted from the themes of miscegenation, racial discrimination, and Civil War in his fiction; or—according to some critics—reconstituted out of the opinions of fictional characters presumed to be serving as the author's mouthpiece, possibly one of those Southern boys—Charles Mallison (*Intruder in the Dust*), for example—still reliving "the moment just before Pickett's charge at Gettysburg, as if the outcome could be changed."

All these approaches end by echoing Quentin's ambivalence. For example, positing himself in third person, Faulkner ends his essay "Mississippi" (*Holiday*, April 1954): "Loving all of it even while he had to hate some of it because he knows now that you don't love because: you love despite; not for the virtues, but despite the faults."

Faulkner's specific South, whether as personal homeland or mythologized setting, can neither represent the entire Southeast nor the Confederate states. Even critic C. Hugh Holman's three divisions—Delta, Tidewater, and Piedmont, each attached to its author—Faulkner, Glasgow and Wolfe—omit much of the geographical and social South. True, Faulkner's first novel, *Soldiers' Pay*, is ostensibly set in the small town of Charlestown, Georgia (though already feeling more like Oxford, Mississippi); *Mosquitoes* uses Lake Pontchartrain and, like *New Orleans Sketches*, the New Orleans French Quarter; *Pylon* presents rootless midwestern aviators who can barnstorm anywhere but come to New Valois, a.k.a. New Orleans (the story had its origin in real plane crashes at Shushan Airport there). But Faulkner's map of Yoknapatawpha—noting twenty-seven places that had already appeared in his fiction, showing 2,400 square miles, population 6,298 white, 9,313 Negro—shows the focus of Faulkner's South. When he looked at his creation in a June 1953 article in the *Atlantic*, Faulkner attributed this choice of focus to advice from Sherwood Anderson in 1925: "You have to have somewhere to start from; then you begin to learn. . . . Because one place to start from is just as important as any other. You're a country boy; all you know is that little patch up there in Mississippi where you started from'' (*ESPL* 8). Faulkner started from Mississippi: first New Albany, then a few years in Ripley, then at age five to Oxford. He grew up in this county seat and site of Ole Miss where a generation of grandparents still talked about Yankee bullet holes in family bedsteads, about the Civil War and its local, personal cost, though no important battles occurred here. Grant did stop once at Oxford, General Nathan Bedford Forrest's wife lived there, and so did a former member of the Confederate cabinet. The ornaments of folklore and oral memory, however, were used to romanticize rather than galvanize; consequently, there was a public inertia in Oxford resulting less from summer heat and more from poor transportation, weak schools, little capital, the weight of habit, and Jim Crow.

Although Faulkner would travel to Canada, Europe, and other American states, be writer-in-residence at the University of Virginia and a screenwriter in Hollywood, Oxford continued to provide him the locale for the universal. He once wrote in a letter to Malcolm Cowley about *his* South that he just happened to know it and didn't have time in one life to learn another one and write at the same time.

In one interview Faulkner said that, beginning with *Sartoris*, ''I discovered that my own little postage stamp of native soil was worth writing about and that I would never live long enough to exhaust it, and by sublimating the actual into apocryphal I would have complete liberty to use whatever talent I might have to its absolute top'' (*LIG* 255). By the time Faulkner narrowed his South to that microcosm, and Oxford and Lafayette County had been transformed into Jefferson and Yoknapatawpha, the setting was fixed for his best-known fiction, through which time and chronology flowed as if his chunk of Mississippi resembled a tidal pool into which people and events largely from 1865 onward would ebb and flow.

Mississippi eastern upcountry can never serve as a token for the entire and varied South; but because Faulkner's Southern characters possess an excess of both memory and premonition, Yoknapatawpha does in some ways typify a wide swath beyond its stated boundaries, reaching across central Alabama and Georgia into the coastal plain, encompassing the ''black belt'' where slaves and their descendants formed the majority population. On its rich bottom lands along the rivers, large farms (not really plantations) were built on slave labor. Here also lived Faulkner's Compsons, Sartorises, Sutpens, and McCaslins. Poor whites settled the red clay hill country, most of whom never owned slaves but sweated through lives of hard labor themselves, characters like Faulkner's McCallums, Bundrens, Quicks, Workits, and Gowries, surviving hardscrabble on the pine barrens, meadows, and less fertile hills. Throughout the larger South, two thirds of all whites historically belonged to this yeoman group. Add to this Shelby Foote's reminder that there are ''no aristocrats in Mississippi. Those down had been used up, those up had been down'' (Harrington and Abadie, *The South and Faulkner's Yoknapatawpha* 49), and you have something of the South.

Although Faulkner's divisions are not meant to constitute a Southern sociology, his first published story tempted readers to turn symbol into Southern formula. In "A Rose for Emily," the first story set in Yoknapatawpha, the late Miss Emily Grierson is discovered to have slept for years alongside the mummified corpse of her Yankee suitor Homer Barron. Possibly the Southern love for the "Lost Cause" or, alternatively, the seduction of the South by intrusive Yankees may indeed be functioning; but, as Cleanth Brooks finds (*Toward Yoknapatawpha* 384–388), some of the heavily underlined parallels between Miss Emily and the old necrophilic South are overwrought, a warning against too easy an imposition of the literal on the aesthetic and reminder that generalizations about Faulkner's fictional South need testing against his text.

Several such generalizations could be offered as examples:

First, the Varners and Snopeses represent the taking over of the honorable white planter South by climbers and primitive Babbitts. Substituting money for breeding and gentility, the Varners and Snopes of the trilogy exemplify the twentieth-century capitalistic greed overtaking the pastoral virtues and noblesse oblige of the Old South, replacing one evil (slavery) with another. In the texts, however, some of Faulkner's "plain people" possess and act on honor even as the novels put changes in Southern politics and culture into a more national perspective.

Second, the loss of the Civil War was providential and redemptive. As Ike McCaslin argues in section 4 of "The Bear," God loved the South so much that He knew it could "learn nothing save through suffering." It is easy to test this premise against the text's presentation of the region's recent history, particularly where race relations are concerned.

Third, the Fall of the Dark House (of Compson in *The Sound and the Fury* or of Sutpen in *Absalom, Absalom!*) is an analog for the fall of the Old South, after time and history had moved beyond defeated planter families and their values. Cleanth Brooks's warnings against reading into Faulkner's family stories either the tragic House of Atreus or the fall of the Russian Romanovs send us to the text where Faulkner starts from single families to be comprehended within a changing society where family had heretofore been central to the social order. For instance, characters in *Light in August* test and measure themselves within a community they variously endorse or oppose.

Fourth, African Americans represent the good primitives, the white upper class the degenerates. Alternatively, Dilsey is merely a literary vision of Aunt Jemima. Feminist critics take wry note of these fecund, fat, and warm African American servant-matriarchs contrasted with Faulkner's skinny, upper-class, white daughters who can develop into either belles or amazons. But Callie Barr Clark was the real source of Dilsey; Faulkner not only delivered her eulogy and erected her gravestone but also dedicated *Go Down, Moses* to her. Although his expressed affection may seem dated and paternalistic in later decades, the texts show it was obviously genuine.

Finally, certain characters are actually spokesmen for Faulkner. The often cited "The past is never dead. It's not even past" is attributed directly to Faulkner. In the text of *Requiem for a Nun*, however, it is actually part of Gavin Stevens's attempt to use Temple Drake's past in a destructive way, not a philosophic comment on the South and its attachment to history. Faulkner wrote Malcolm Cowley that Stevens spoke not for the author but for how the best of liberal Southerners felt about Negroes.

With such textual referents uppermost in mind, one may turn from the life of Faulkner imagined to the life he actually lived, asking, What are his direct views on the South? In his public statements, he seemed torn between deep affection and furious disapproval. In the mid-1950s, at a time when *A Fable* had moved its setting to World War I Europe and beyond the Southern myth to the Holy Week of Christ, Faulkner frequently stated in interviews that the white Southerners' positions about civil rights were untenable. Over the years he sustained his conviction that even good Southerners had been tainted by slavery and its consequences. Yet, having said that, he could also say, "If I have to make the same choice Robert E. Lee made then I'll make it" (1974 *FAB* 1590). Eleven years old when an actual lynching took place in Oxford, he could write movingly about lynching in "Dry September" yet, in a 1931 letter to the editor, not exactly excuse lynching but not condemn it, either.

These are the inconsistencies of an evolution in his positions about race and the South. In "If I Were a Negro," published in *Ebony* in September 1956, he advocated to blacks Ghandi's passive resistance, "flexibility and forbearance." He early favored the abolishment of segregation but also doubted blacks really wanted social mixing. He began from a Booker T. Washington philosophy that urged self-improvement by African Americans. As time passed, in Lafayette County he was often considered a "nigger lover"; yet to the New York intellectuals he was a white apologist. Some of his public statements—for instance, some foolish remarks occasioned by his concern that Autherine Lucy might be killed while integrating the University of Alabama in 1956—embarrassed public liberals. On the other hand, his condemnation of the murder of Emmett Till was blunt. He was opposed to *forced anything*, including integration forced by even the U.S. government for which he made many goodwill trips. He donated part of his Nobel Prize money to establish a scholarship for black students, was involved in the cause of young Japanese who had survived the Nagasaki bombing, and told the Southern Historical Association in a Memphis speech, "To live anywhere in the world of A.D. 1955 and be against equality because of race or color, is like living in Alaska and being against snow" (*ESPL* 146).

If popular novels like *Gone with the Wind* romanticized plantation life, Faulkner never falsified the moral taint caused by any ownership of one human being by another. As an individual Southerner, he attempted to influence public opinion toward justice and fairness. Especially after receiving the Nobel Prize for Literature in 1950, he seems to have taken seriously his role as a spokesman for a better South than the one in which he grew up. Much of his fiction chronicles one segment of a South that reached back in time to pioneers and original Indian dwellers in Mississippi, through slavery, war, Reconstruction, war again, the Jazz Age, Prohibition, and the passage from an agrarian to a consumer economy. If in all this no one character could be his mouthpiece, Faulkner's own words in "Mississippi" echo Quentin: "Home again, his native land; he was born of it and his bones will sleep in it; loving it even while hating some of it."

FURTHER READING

Cash, W. J. *The Mind of the South.* New York: Vintage, 1941.
Williamson. *William Faulkner and Southern History.*

Doris Betts

SOUTHERN LITERATURE, as generally defined, is writing about and from the South, from its exploration and settlement to the present. Although, to many people, William Faulkner *is* Southern literature, Faulkner's writing developed in part from a long tradition of Southern letters with its own myths and genres.

The South's legends of origins serve to form its identity and differentiate it from the North. As expounded by early writers like Robert Beverley and William Byrd, the warm, fecund South was a new Garden of Eden where humankind could have a second chance. In "The Bear," Ike McCaslin relates this myth to his cousin McCaslin Edmonds and concludes that the cause of the South's Fall, its original sin, was slavery. Another strong tale of origin is the Cavalier myth, still powerful despite its debunking by historians. Since the South, unlike the North, was not settled by largely middle-class Puritans, Southerners like to believe that its settlers were "Cavaliers," down-at-the-heels aristocrats or younger sons looking for opportunity in the New World. The propensity of Faulkner's Sartoris family to name their sons Bayard, evoking knightly chivalry, exemplifies this myth, as well as Southern literature's tendency to look to the medieval romance, as filtered through the novels of Sir Walter Scott, for its models—a tendency that Twain satirized in *A Connecticut Yankee in King Arthur's Court* and other works. As opposed to the increasingly industrialized North, the South relished its identity as agrarian, as exemplified by Thomas Jefferson in *Notes on the State of Virginia* (1785) and the twentieth-century circle of writers around Nashville known as the Agrarians in *I'll Take My Stand* (1930). Not only did Faulkner constantly portray agrarian life in his fiction, but he often mock-humbly downplayed his status as a writer by claiming he was just a farmer.

As the national controversy over slavery intensified in the first half of the nineteenth century, Southern literature responded defensively in three ways. First, Southern poets like Philip Pendleton Cooke or Thomas Holley Chivers avoided the vexations of politics and economics by escaping into a generalized world of beauty, untied to any specific time, place, or issue. Faulkner's early poetry reflects that tradition in that much of it appears to be set in no identifiable place, certainly not the South of his era, and it stresses universal themes such as love and death. Second, some antebellum Southerners, such as Joseph Glover Baldwin, George Washington Harris, and Johnson Jones Hooper, responded to

Northern charges of dirt, sloth, and ignorance by glorying in them for laughs in the "Southwest Humor" tradition of the old Southwest of Georgia and Virginia. These humorists' heirs include Mark Twain and, of course, Faulkner, especially in a tale of greed, trickery, and slapstick comedy like "Spotted Horses." The third way Southerners defended themselves from Northern opprobrium was in the plantation novel, such as John Pendleton Kennedy's *Swallow Barn* (1832), in which a benevolent, patriarchal master cares for happy and childlike slaves. Former slaves like Frederick Douglass and Harriet Jacobs effectively disputed the plantation novel in both their escapes and their slave narratives. Faulkner similarly reacted against the plantation myth by revealing the rapacious cruelty beneath its pleasant veneer through the aspiring plantation master Thomas Sutpen in *Absalom, Absalom!*

In contrast, augmented by anguish over the vanished antebellum plantation and the Lost Cause, nostalgia for a world that had never been was the keynote of the postbellum fiction known as "local color" and produced by writers such as Thomas Nelson Page, Joel Chandler Harris, and Ruth McEnery Stuart. Southern local colorists attempted to preserve a vanishing world and attract urban Northern audiences by emphasizing dialect, rural charm, and folkways. Faulkner's works, of course, use various Southern dialects, evoke the distinctive beauty of different regions of Mississippi, and display folkways such as (in *The Hamlet*) curing an unfortunate individual of his affection for a cow by making him eat it. Faulkner, however, in characters like Miss Rosa Coldfield in *Absalom, Absalom!*, John Sartoris in "An Odor of Verbena," and Miss Jenny Du Pre in *Sartoris*, mocks nostalgia as a euphemism for an unhealthy inability to leave the past and move into the future.

In his skeptical love for the Southern past, Faulkner is most closely associated with such writers of the Southern Renaissance as Allen Tate, Caroline Gordon, Robert Penn Warren, and Katherine Anne Porter. The Southern Renaissance refers to the period between the two world wars when the South experienced a remarkable literary efflorescence or "rebirth." Although critics and historians differ about various nuances of its causes, most agree that the Southern Renaissance occurred when the writers of this generation applied the techniques of international modernism, such as jarring juxtapositions and stream of consciousness, to their ambivalent, yet obsessive, treatment of the Southern past. Faulkner epitomizes this pattern as he probes the personal, familial, and regional past through the startlingly contrasted streams of consciousness in works like *The Sound and the Fury* and *As I Lay Dying*. In his use of stream of consciousness, Faulkner is also elaborating, modernizing, and interiorizing Southern literature's traditional emphasis on the oral, the individual storyteller's distinctive voice.

Faulkner continues to dominate Southern literature through his influence on later writers such as Ellen Douglas, William Styron, and Barry Hannah. Michael Kreyling has recently argued that Faulkner was even postmodern before postmodernism in his reconsideration of the past "under the destabilizing condition of irony" (6).

Faulkner's works are exemplary of the themes and techniques that permeate Southern writing of all eras. In opposition to much canonical American literature that advocates mobility for the renewal or remaking of the self, Southern literature emphasizes place and roots, as abundantly demonstrated in Faulkner's many works about his "little postage stamp of native soil," Yoknapatawpha County, based on Lafayette County, Mississippi. Also unlike much of canonical American literature, in which individual identity is delineated through opposition to society, in Southern literature an individual's identity is inextricably linked with his or her family, in the sense of "blood" or lineage, as illustrated in the conflict of Bascomb versus Compson "blood" in *The Sound and the Fury*, and with the individual's relation to his community, as shown by Joe Christmas's inability to confirm an identity in *Light in August*. Closely related to identity is the concept of honor in which a familial reputation comes before any individual needs or beliefs, a concept Bayard Sartoris successfully manipulates toward healthy change in *The Unvanquished*. As the title and characters of *The Unvanquished* further indicate, stoicism, the ability to confront suffering and defeat honorably, is another important value of Southern literature. In contrast to its internal concern with honor, however, Southern literature is often considered "grotesque" by outsiders, and Faulkner seems to revel in this charge in stories like "A Rose for Emily" with its outlandish display of necrophilia. William Faulkner, while he may not *be* Southern literature, is certainly its genius and avatar.

FURTHER READING

Kreyling, Michael. "Fee, Fie, Faux Faulkner: Parody and Postmodernism in Southern Literature." *Southern Review* 29 (1993): 1–15.
Rubin, Louis, ed. *The History of Southern Literature*. Baton Rouge: Louisiana State University Press, 1985.
————. *The Literary South*. Baton Rouge: Louisiana State University Press, 1979.
Wyatt-Brown, Bertram. *Southern Honor*. New York: Oxford University Press, 1982.

Veronica Makowsky

SOUTHERN RENAISSANCE. *Renaissance* means "rebirth," and it most commonly refers to the renewed interest in Greek and Roman arts and letters in Europe following the Middle Ages. The term was later used to describe the mid-nineteenth-century group of writers, including Emerson, Thoreau, and Hawthorne, who ostensibly displayed the reborn intellectual strength of their Puritan forebears in a New England Renaissance. The "Southern Renaissance" usually refers to the twentieth-century South's great period of literary activity between the two world wars. However, there are individuals like Allen Tate, prominent poet and essayist who is generally regarded as one of the originators of the Southern Renaissance, who believe that there was no great Southern literary tradition before the twentieth century and thus the term is a misnomer. Even if it is not completely accurate, the term *Southern Renaissance* nevertheless reflects the South's aspiration to excel like its European and New England predecessors.

The causes of the Southern Renaissance are equally controversial. Some believe that it was part of the South's attempt to join the industrialized world, a sort of literary version of the economic and commercial "New South" movement. Others posit that it was a way of rising to the challenge of charges of Southern backwardness, like H. L. Mencken's characterization of the South in 1917 as the "Sahara of the Bozarts" (Beaux Arts). Still others argue that the Southern Renaissance was the South's reaction to the crumbling of traditions and standards in the wake of World War I, not unlike the response of writers such as Ernest Hemingway and F. Scott Fitzgerald in the North.

Most, however, tend to agree with some version of Sir Walter Scott's thesis about the historical novel in his "General Preface" to *Waverley, or 'Tis Sixty Years Since* (1892). As his subtitle indicates, Scott believed that a period of sixty years, a span of about two generations, allowed enough distance in time to view past events with some degree of objectivity, yet allowed for direct transmission of insights and emotions from the elderly survivors of the period. This thesis can be applied to the Southern Renaissance in that its beginning was approximately sixty years after the Civil War, and its authors could and did receive recollections from aged relations and acquaintances. As Richard H. King, Lewis P. Simpson, and others have argued, the Southern Renaissance's major task was engaging, through memory and history, the South's painful past of defeat and racial guilt. When the writers of the Southern Renaissance regarded the past with some semblance of Scott's ideal balance of detachment and engagement, and then applied to it the techniques of international modernism, a literary birth occurred.

Most of the authors associated with the Southern Renaissance fall into two groups. The so-called conservative group was associated with the Fugitive poets of Vanderbilt University, many of whom later became the Agrarians of the manifesto *I'll Take My Stand* (1930). As their name and title (from the Confederate hymn "Dixie") suggest, they favored maintaining the agrarian independence of the Southern yeoman in the face of what they considered the cowed wage-slaves of Yankee industrialism. This group and their associates comprise some of the most famous names in Southern literature: Robert Penn Warren, Allen Tate, Caroline Gordon, Katherine Anne Porter, Donald Davidson, John Crowe Ransom, and others. The second group is loosely referred to as liberal and is often associated with sociological studies at the University of North Carolina at Chapel Hill led by Howard Odum. In contrast to the Agrarian adherents, these more liberal writers, such as Lillian Smith and T. S. Stribling, wanted the South to take a more progressive stand, particularly in labor and race relations.

No matter to what group a Southern Renaissance author belonged or was assigned, "anybody who fired off a gun in the region was practically certain to kill an author" (386), as W. J. Cash somewhat hyperbolically claimed in *The Mind of the South* (1941). William Faulkner, of course, was one of these authors and, fortunately for literature, a surviving one. Indeed, his career epitomizes all definitions and groups of the Southern Renaissance. His major works appeared in the decades between the world wars. His career began approximately sixty years after the Civil War, and he incorporated local memories of Oxford, Mississippi, in his fictions about the war, such as *Absalom, Absalom!* and *The Unvanquished.* To do so, he used techniques of international modernism: for example, stream of consciousness in *The Sound and the Fury*, fragmented viewpoint in *As I Lay Dying*, and mythical parallels in *Absalom, Absalom!*

Unlike many of the authors of the Southern Renaissance, though, Faulkner incorporates contradictory stands toward the past and the modern world. Among his representatives of the New South are the vulgarly greedy and commercially astute Snopeses, but they are hardly more unattractive than the fallen, self-indulgent aristocrats who are their foils, such as the Sartoris and Compson families. Faulkner may have bemoaned the post–World War I decline in moral standards through a character like the dissolute Temple Drake in *Sanctuary* and *Requiem for a Nun*, yet her prewar predecessors, like the original Bayard Sartoris of *Sartoris* and Thomas Sutpen of *Absalom, Absalom!*, are no greater models of virtue. Faulkner gloried in tweaking the noses of Yankee critics like Mencken by depicting the often grotesque yet intensely human struggles of a family like the Bundrens in their simultaneously tragic and comic journey to bury their mother in *As I Lay Dying*. Faulkner's attitude toward race is equally protean: He could portray stereotypical "grinnin' and pickin' darkies" in an early work like *Sartoris*, yet take a much more humane approach, for example, when the adolescent white protagonist of *Intruder in the Dust* learns to overcome his racial prejudice. As for so many categories into which one may try to fit Faulkner, he exemplifies the Southern Renaissance, contradicts it, and ultimately transcends it.

FURTHER READING

Bradbury, John M. *Renaissance in the South: A Critical History of the Literature, 1920–1960*. Chapel Hill: University of North Carolina Press, 1963.
Fowler and Abadie, eds. *Faulkner and the Southern Renaissance.*
King, Richard H. *A Southern Renaissance*. New York: Oxford University Press, 1980.
Rubin, Louis D., Jr., and Robert D. Jacobs, eds. *Southern Renascence: The Literature of the Modern South*. Baltimore: Johns Hopkins Press, 1953.
Simpson, Lewis P. "The Southern Recovery of Memory and History." *Sewanee Review* 82.1 (1974): 1–32.

Veronica Makowsky

SPAIN. Faulkner's novels were read and discussed in Spain as early as 1933, only a few years after they were published. During that year two articles about him and the translation of *Sanctuary* were published. The economic and political crises in Spain and the United States appeared so similar to many Spanish writers that when, with the inauguration of the republic, literary works turned to social themes, they began to take their most direct contact with the literary works of the United States (Bravo 13). Various Spanish literary critics recognized and praised the very Faulknerian structural and stylistic techniques, such as the use of the reader-interpreter and suspended narration, which the broader literary world would recognize only years later and for which Faulkner would eventually receive the 1949 Nobel Prize. No articles appeared about Faulkner from 1934 until after the Civil War (1939), a period in which Faulkner received negative criticism in Spain because of the Franco regime and its imposed censorship.

The 1940s, the period of the aftermath of the Civil War and the commencement of the Franco regime, offered little in the way of literary progress: Many writers were in exile; the continuity of the novel was broken; the young authors had no models; and there was severe government censorship of works that did not follow its regulations. It was a period of anguish, hunger, alienation, and rupture that produced a pessimistic, existential, realist novel of disenchantment and desolation. Camilo José Cela's *La familia de Pascual Duarte* (1942), for which he received the Nobel Prize in 1989, is credited with changing the direction of the Spanish novel in that decade. As Bravo notes, Faulkner's *Sanctuary* and Cela's *Pascual Duarte* share affinities of pessimistic tone, worlds in crisis, crumbling values, and human beings swept away by that hecatomb (57).

In the 1940s and early 1950s, in both Madrid and Barcelona, the young intellectuals, the future writers, were reading Faulkner in contraband French or Spanish translations from Latin America and discussing his work, especially the allegedly sordid *Sanctuary*, in their social gatherings. They found a new literary freedom of expression through which reality was authentically and fully expressed. In those groups were Juan Benet, Luis Martín Santos, and Ana María Matute, whose future novels would be influenced by Faulkner's novels. Toward the end of the 1940s and into the 1950s, a slight relaxation in official censorship as well as increasing interest in foreign novels in translation allowed the publication of various novels such as Faulkner's *The Unvanquished* (1951), *The Hamlet* (1953), *As I Lay Dying* (1954), *Soldiers' Pay* (1954), *Go Down, Moses* (1954), and *A Fable* (1955).

The 1950s was the period of social realism in the Spanish novel with plot and characters presented through an external, cinematographic technique. Many of the novels produced in the new direction were influenced by the Italian neorealist novels, documentary films, and the American novelists Faulkner, Hemingway, and Steinbeck. The social novel was a committed discourse of social and political change through a presentation of reality intended for the majority of the people. This testimonial novel set aside any literary experimentation in order to focus on the societal conditions of the struggling, marginalized poor and, in contrast, the more fortunate middle and upper classes who were apparently unaware of the need for change. The novel had to assume the role of the newspaper because the people were unaware of the social problems in their country due to the regime's censorship policies (Goytisolo 63). Chronologically,

Ana María Matute, Luis Martín-Santos, and Juan Benet, all of whose works have affinities with those of Faulkner, belonged to the Generation of 1950 and the social realists; their literary techniques and purposes, however, kept them either on the margin of that group or entirely in other literary styles.

Ana María Matute wrote several of her innovative novels during this period, including the work that many critics believe to be her masterpiece, *Los hijos muertos* (1958). Various points of contact between Matute's and Faulkner's novels have been noted by critics, especially her use of the Cain and Abel theme as found in Faulkner's *The Sound and the Fury*: children of middle-class families in novelistic, enclosed, rural worlds during or in the aftermath of either the American or the Spanish Civil War. Matute is the first post–Civil War novelist whose novels have clear points of contact with those of Faulkner.

Toward the end of the decade, there was a growing disenchantment with the then-current social novel, which appeared to be in a state of stagnation since it no longer reflected a changing and modernizing Spain brought about through growing industrialization and increasing commerce with Europe. With the publication of *Tiempo de silencio* in 1961, Luis Martín-Santos became one of the primary renovators of the contemporary Spanish novel in the 1960s. This work evinced an important and abrupt departure from the then-current objective realism. The novel's world is viewed from both an external and an internal perspective: The first-person narrator/protagonist is operating in an external reality that is internalized in subjective, dreamlike reactions and individual realities. In direct opposition to the language of the social novel, Martín-Santos, like Faulkner, creates a deliberately elaborate, hermetic, artistic discourse.

Martín-Santos was particularly interested in *Light in August*. In an agonized search for self-realization, his protagonist, Pedro, like Faulkner's Joe Christmas in the American South, will be annihilated by the fanaticism of traditional myth, history, religion, and society—in this case, those of the Franco regime. Intrinsic uncertainty in the interpretation of history is also an important focus in the works of both Martín-Santos and Faulkner. The impossibility of finding the historical truth, multiple visions of truth that either complicity or evasion creates, can be found in the novels of both. Both novelists find traditional novelistic form and language incapable of expressing the reality that the individual lives and witnesses. In his novel *Tiempo de silencio*, a character named Matías explains the importance of the American novel and the superiority of its most distinguished creators over the worn-out, exhausted, European techniques that had concluded their literary cycle (66). Pedro, the protagonist, apparently speaking for Martín-Santos, scorns the aesthetic games that come and go and proposes that all American novels come from *Ulysses* "and the [American] Civil War. The Deep South. Now we know that the American novel is superior, and now it influences Europe from which it had its origin" (69).

Juan Benet is not only one of the master innovators of the Spanish novel after Martín-Santos, but he has also exerted the most influence on the young writers. Born in Madrid in 1928, Benet experienced the horror of the Spanish Civil War personally when his father was killed by a firing squad in 1936. The war is a major recurrent image in his fiction. Benet became interested in the works of Faulkner in the 1940s and has repeatedly acknowledged Faulkner's decisive influence in his novels. In response to an interviewer's question about his very cosmopolitan view, Benet said that "any individual who is truly involved with his surroundings, even though they may be in the most remote setting, can achieve that universal understanding . . . for instance, writers who were closely constricted in terms of location, like Thomas Hardy in the nineteenth century, and Faulkner, García Márquez, and Rulfo, in the twentieth century" (Gazarian Gautier 33).

Like Faulkner's Quentin, Caddy, Joe Christmas, and Charles Bon, Benet's characters are struggling against and finally defeated by a changing, but not necessarily better, civilization, one whose logic and reason negate everything that a traditional decadence has led them to believe was true. The Civil War imposes on them an ever-past with no hope or possibility of a future, and this landscape becomes a character that dominates the lives of the people who live within it (Herzberger 47). Benet, like Faulkner, has created a moribund atmosphere that eventually causes complete ruin. In *Volverás a región* (1967) and *Una meditación* (1970), Benet places his characters in the setting of Región, his carefully constructed mythical reality. The area is so described that it takes on great importance in the novel structure and in the action of the characters. There is an obvious similarity to Faulkner's Yoknapatawpha County. It is the protagonist for which many lives will be lost in the Great American tragedy. Región, like Yoknapatawpha, surrounds, hovers, and smothers the inhabitants in its deceptive, morbid tradition.

The experimental novel introduced by Martín-Santos did not gain great acceptance by the Spanish novelists until the late 1960s and the early 1970s, at which time many were writing experimental novels. At the same time, there were realist novels that incorporated some of the new techniques. For example, Juan Marsé's *Si te dicen que caí* (1973) shows many points of contact with Faulkner's novels. Yet although the structure and language appear Faulknerian, the influence apparently came through Latin American writers such as Vargas Llosa and Gabriel García Márquez, who, themselves, had read and were influenced by Faulkner. Marsé believes that realism is based on the way real people talk and act. Marsé's main interest is, like Faulkner's, telling a story.

By the late 1970s, the experimental novel was read by the academics and literary critics but not by the general public, which wanted a more traditional novel. Publishing houses accepted fewer manuscripts from experimental novelists because they could not sell them. The experimental novel did not disappear, however. Amell has pointed out that by the 1980s there were three types of Spanish novels. The first was the novel of little literary value but that sold well and satisfied a certain type of reading public. The second was the experimental novel of great stylistic value such as the work of Juan Benet. This type of novel was read and bought by a small minority of people—mostly other writers and academics. The third type falls between the first two: It integrates a realist narration based on history but takes advantage of both experimental advances and traditional methods. This third novel is of great literary value and reaches a broader spectrum of readers. The works of Antonio Muñoz Molina, Juan Marsé, and Luis Mateo Díez are examples of this third type: the New Spanish Novel (Amell 7–9).

Faulkner's novels still retain their influence in the Spanish literary world of the 1990s. Rosa Montero, award-winning journalist and novelist, explains that the present Spanish writers of her generation were greatly influenced by reading Faulkner, in whose works they found a way of verbalizing and contemplating the world. She points out that this was a general influence, not an influence strictly literary, measurable, or codifiable of the sort academics always are exploring. Her generation grew up in an epoch tremendously influenced by two definite, distinct literary modes: the new Latin American Boom and Faulkner's novels, both of which they read. "We all read Faulkner, we considered him great—and he is—and as a certain identity of cultural sophistication. That early passion had to have left its imprint on us." For Montero, Faulkner's formal literary disruption enlarged her literary horizon as did Proust, Kafka, and the Latin Americans.

Antonio Muñoz Molina also is an award-winning novelist and journalist. In June 1996, at forty years of age, he became the youngest academician to occupy a Chair in the Spanish Royal Academy. Like Faulkner, he comes from a rural society that has a long, oral tradition of storytelling. In his novels, as in Faulkner's *Absalom, Absalom!*, Muñoz Molina wants the reader to reconstruct the story. The fifteen- to thirty-line sentences of his novels are narrated by an unknown first person. According to Conte, Muñoz Molina's novels have resonances of Faulkner's influence in the writing of his splendid prose (7). His first novel (*Beatus Ille*, 1986) is about a poet who was politically involved in the Spanish Civil War. Muñoz Molina explains that the Spanish Civil War has a hold over today's young Spaniards in the same way "William Faulkner wrote about the American Civil War, and he certainly did not experience it personally. . . . Faulkner is very important to me" (Gazarian Gautier 224–225). Muñoz Molina has said that if he could speak to a great writer in the past, he would choose both Cervantes and Faulkner. (Faulkner said that Cervantes's *Don Quixote* was one of his favorite novels, one that he said he read regularly once a year.)

The 1994 publication in Spanish translation of Joseph Blotner's *Faulkner: A Biography* attests to the contemporary influence of William Faulkner in Spain. Conte reminds us that ten years ago there appeared in the United States the "first edition of this great, canonic biography of the eminent North American writer, William Faulkner . . . without doubt, one of the—perhaps—four greatest novelists of this century, whose work, difficult, profound, and fascinating can be placed beside those of Proust, Joyce, and Kafka as one of the giants, the founders, and originators of all the history of universal literature" (11).

See also **Latin America**.

FURTHER READING

Amell, Samuel. "Tradición y Renovación, un Difícil balance en la Novela Actual." *Crítica Hispánica* 14.1–2 (1992): 5–11.

Bravo, María Elena. *Faulkner en España: Perspectivas de la narrativa de postguerra.* Barcelona, Spain: Península, 1985.

Conte, Rafael. "Faulkner: Una biografía." *ABC Cultural 1991–1995: Un lustro de la Cultura Española.* CD-ROM. Telefónica, 1996.

Gazarian Gautier, Marie-Lise. *Interviews with Spanish Writers.* Elmwood Park, Ill.: Dalkey Archive Press, 1991.

Goytisolo, Juan. *Furgón de cola.* Barcelona, Spain: Seix Barral, 1976.

Herzberger, David K. *The Novelistic World of Juan Benet.* Clear Creek, Ind.: American Hispanist, 1976.

June Townsend

SPEECHES. Known throughout his life as a shy and retiring individual, Faulkner did not speak publicly until he became a public personage in the 1950s. Except for the funeral sermon he preached in the parlor of his home for Mammy Caroline Barr in 1940, he gave no formal public speeches until the Nobel Prize Address in 1950, and only seventeen speeches have been published. Fourteen of these are published in James B. Meriwether's *Essays, Speeches & Public Letters by William Faulkner.* They range from the funeral sermon to Faulkner's address to the American Academy of Arts and Letters in May 1962, six weeks before his death. Three others, also edited by Meriwether, have since been published: a speech at Nagano in August 1955, one at the Teatro Municipal in Caracas in 1961, and another in Caracas accepting the Andrés Bello Award, translated back into English from a Spanish translation. Among the most noteworthy of Faulkner's speeches, with the Nobel Prize Address, are two dealing with racial conflict in the South: the 1952 "Address to the Delta Council" and the 1955 "Address to the Southern Historical Association." Both are echoed in Faulkner's public letters of this period.

FURTHER READING

Meriwether, James B. "Faulkner's Speech at Nagano." *Mississippi Quarterly* 35 (1982): 309–311.

———. "Faulkner's Speech at Teatro Municipal, Caracas, in 1961." *Mississippi Quarterly* 27 (1974): 337.

———. "Faulkner's Speech of Acceptance for the Andrés Bello Award, Caracas 1961." *A Faulkner Miscellany,* ed. Meriwether. 164–166.

James G. Watson

SPORT. Any reader familiar with Faulkner's career will recognize at once the importance of sports, games, and play in his work and the range and intensity of Faulkner's personal engagement in sports and games throughout his life. The list of such activities is long: aerobatics, air circuses, barnstorming, baseball, boating, card playing, chess, croquet, fishing, flying, football, fox hunting, golf, horse riding-jumping-racing, hunting, sailing, and tennis. And if the game-sport rubric is broadened to include such folk-play amusements as horse-trading, prankster-trickster activities, and tall-tale telling, the list grows longer.

Faulkner quarterbacking his high school football team is a less familiar image; so, too, that into his twenties he pitched in church league games and all his life was a baseball fan, following even Little League and college as well as professional teams. Whether we envision the younger Faulkner, the avid and competitive golfer and tennis player, or see him, in his thirties and forties, riding and jumping his horses in the mornings and sailing his sailboat in the afternoons, or contemplate his well-known lifelong passion for hunting, we are confronted with the image of the man as *homo ludens* (Man the Player) or *homo agonistes* (Man the Competitor).

Two of his most enduring and passionate preoccupations, flying and riding, when juxtaposed against each other, tell us much about the man and the writer who was concerned with danger, discipline, glory, motion, power, risk, ritual, speed, and triumph. Faulkner the aviator of the 1930s, the careful, disciplined pilot running his own death-haunted, barnstorming air circuses, became in his last years Faulkner the Virginia gentleman riding to the hounds with the Keswick Hunt Club—still, in his sixties, taking riding lessons, training and conditioning himself for the rigors, forms, and rituals of fox hunting, still demanding motion and speed, power and risk, agony and ecstasy, still falling and breaking bones yet exercising ritual mastery on a horse that he named Powerhouse.

As this pattern of lifelong engagement with sport suggests, Faulkner's sporting passions pervade his works. Throughout his novels and short stories, even those not directly concerned with sports and games, sporting and gaming allusions and images are abundant. In *The Town*, for example, there are twenty-three references to hunting, nine references to football, seven references to fishing, and four references to baseball. For the range and significance of sport, game, and play references, images, and themes in Faulkner's fiction, a selective list of some key works must serve: in *A Fable* and *The Reivers*, horse racing and horse lore; in *Flags in the Dust*, hunting, flying, car racing, horse breaking and riding, ballooning; in *Go Down, Moses*, hunting, poker, and folk trading; in *The Hamlet*, football, folk trading, riding and horse lore; in *Pylon*, "All the Dead Pilots," "Death Drag," "With Caution and Dispatch," and other stories, flying, aerobatics, parachuting, wing walking and all the "folklore of speed" centered on those airfields "Created out of the Wasteland" (as the inscription on the airport sign in *Pylon* has it); in "A Courtship," "Lo!," and "Red Leaves," foot races and folk contests; in "A Bear Hunt" and "Race at Morning," hunting.

Three representative works—*Flags in the Dust, Go Down, Moses*, and *The Hamlet*—tell us much about Faulkner and sports. *Flags in the Dust* not only contains, as Faulkner said at the University of Virginia, "the germ of [his] apocrypha" (*FIU* 285), but it also contains the germ, the core imagery of his career-long treatment of sporting matter. The Sartorises may well be the "most playful family in Yoknapatawpha County," as Christian K. Messenger has suggested in the only extensive discussion of Faulkner's uses of sport to date (265). *Flags in the Dust* examines the sporting-and-play spirit in relation to war, both the Civil War and World War I, and, in Messenger's view, "shows play turning from insouciance and defense of honor to desperation and repetitive sensation-seeking" during and after World War I (265). In this reading, the Sartoris code of courage and risk and honor has degenerated into mere recklessness: The Sartoris twins treat life as a pointless game, as sport or play with no purpose other than danger and speed. John, one version of what Messenger calls the "modern ritual sports hero" (or "the Anglo-Saxon college hero, Confederate branch" [267]), recklessly crashes a carnival balloon, goes off to the University of Virginia where he gambles to determine whether he or his brother should be expelled, and finally finds death as a flying ace in the war, thumbing his nose at his twin as he jumps from his plummeting plane. Bayard survives the war, to ride and get thrown by a wild stallion, to race around Yoknapatawpha County in a speeding car, which he finally wrecks, killing his grandfather, and to engage in every form of reckless and destructively playful behavior he can find. He finally achieves the death he quests as a test pilot in a plane crash in Ohio. To be sure, as Faulkner puts it in the closing lines of the novel, regarding "the Player and the game He plays," "perhaps Sartoris is the name of the game itself—a game outmoded . . . and of which the Player Himself is a little wearied." Yet *Flags in the Dust* also suggests the positive or redemptive sporting activity, the paradigm of sport as hunt and quest, sport as an approach to the sacred. This is particularly vivid in the hunting scenes of the MacCallum interlude, in which sport, game, and play continue to provide rituals and sacraments of order and beauty, purpose and value.

In its deployment of sport, game, and play, *The Hamlet* is another exemplary Faulkner novel. Faulkner's folk masterpiece, this novel makes ample use of all the trappings of folk play, horse trading, trickster-pranks, and tale-telling. Yet at the same time it contains, in the story of Labove, Faulkner's definitive portrait of the college athlete: the innocent country boy who does not understand the game of football and sees the football itself as "a trivial contemptible obloid," yet nevertheless plays the game so well that he becomes the school athletic hero. Football enables Labove to get his education, as well as to outfit his family in cleated football shoes and Ole Miss sweaters. In his curious detachment from sport and, simultaneously, his furiously intense participation in the game itself, there is at work a rigorously ascetic sense of sport and play. Labove's mock-epic conduct on and off the football field admirably serves Faulkner's comic purposes, and Labove is a compelling instance of a fictional type that Messenger calls "the school sports hero as satiric emblem" (208). Aside from the humor in Labove's athletic enterprise and his gridironesque pursuit of Eula Varner, some readers may also feel an infinite sadness regarding Labove the athlete, somewhat akin to what many modern sports fans may feel when they gain access to the inner lives of their sports heroes.

Go Down, Moses, in its hunting and wilderness action, images, and themes, provides the most vivid and resonant evidence in Faulkner's work—perhaps in *any* work of fiction—of sport as an approach to the sacred. Faulkner's wilderness and hunting camps are the locus and matrix of "the best game of all, the best of all breathing," as Faulkner puts it at the beginning of "The Bear." In Faulkner's vision of the hieratic Sam Fathers initiating Ike into his "novitiate to the true wilderness" and their sacramental participation in "the yearly pageant-rite of the old bear's furious immortality," we have the only evidence needed that hunting is the mode of sport that Faulkner finds, in Messenger's words, "fullest in its possibilities" (309). Hunting, conducted by the codified rituals at the heart of *Go Down, Moses*, instills humility, endurance, and a sacramental sense of nature and thereby promises the worthy participant spiritual transformation in the arena of sacred space, sacred time. Whether we consider *Go Down, Moses* under the rubric of ancient archetypal patterns of the pursuit of the Sacred Beast ("a divine totem"), patterns of Hunt, Quest, Initiation, and spiritual transformation, as Daniel Hoffman does, or we consider Ike under the rubric of the "ritual sports hero," as Messenger does (9), the recognition is inevitable that hunting holds the center of Faulkner's epiphanic vision of sport. *Go Down, Moses*, then, not only presents, in "The Bear," "the greatest American hunting tale of the twentieth century" (Hoffman 149) but, quite possibly, the greatest hunting tale and the richest vision of the radically spiritual nature of sport in world literature.

Finally, as a related sidelight, Faulkner served a brief stint as a kind of sportswriter for *Sports Illustrated* in the 1950s. In two brief pieces, "Kentucky: May: Saturday" (on the Kentucky Derby) and "An Innocent at Rinkside" (on what was probably the only ice hockey game he ever saw), he was able to convey the multifaceted richness and transforming possibilities of sport. As Robert Hamblin has cogently argued in his essay on Faulkner as sportswriter, sport for Faulkner mirrored all human passion, hope, and folly. The essence of sport, analogous to the essence of art, has to do with a cosmic struggle, "an *agon*— in Faulkner's case, between imagination and fact, dream and reality, individualization and anonymity, survival and annihilation, victory and defeat, the sacred and the profane" (Hamblin 14). Faulkner as sportswriter is concerned that "something is happening to sport in America" that might close off access to sacred space, sacred time. In "An Innocent at Rinkside" he presciently bemoans the fact that sports are being brought indoors, under roofs, and he wonders how long it will be before hunting and fishing will be brought indoors. When that happens, we might conclude, when package tourists hunt deer under domes, when the Big Two-Hearted River flows through astroturf meadows, when the last true sports are desacralized, conducted under radically secular roofs of unreality, under Disneyfied domes of unknowingness, there will be at least one place left to turn for a vision of sacred space, sacred time, for a vision of what sport once promised, what sport once was: Faulkner's fiction.

FURTHER READING

Hamblin, Robert W. *"Homo Agonistes*, or, William Faulkner as Sportswriter." *Aethlon*
    13.2 (1996): 13–22.
Higgs, Robert J. *Laurel & Thorn: The Athlete in American Literature*. Lexington: Uni-
    versity Press of Kentucky, 1981.
Messenger, Christian K. *Sport and the Spirit of Play in American Fiction*. New York:
    Columbia University Press, 1981.

H. R. Stoneback

"SPOTTED HORSES," a short story by Faulkner, has one of the most interesting publication histories of all of William Faulkner's works. It was first published as a separate short story in *Scribner's Magazine* in June 1931, and this
version is reprinted in *Uncollected Stories of William Faulkner*. A revised and
expanded version of "Spotted Horses" appears in the first volume of the *Snopes*
trilogy, *The Hamlet* (1940). There, the original short story is transformed into
a much longer tale called "The Peasants," which comprises the fourth and final
section of the novel. This version, according to Malcolm Cowley, "is nearly
three times as long as the magazine version . . . as well as being three times as
good" (*PF* 322).

Cowley, in editing *The Portable Faulkner*, included yet another version of
"Spotted Horses," one very similar to the version in *The Hamlet*, but this
variant incorporated changes Cowley had suggested to Faulkner, including the
advice that the story end with the judge declaring, "This court's adjourned!
Adjourned!" The piece is retitled "Spotted Horses" and placed by Cowley
under a section heading named *The Peasants*. To make matters even more complicated, "Spotted Horses" also appears in a collection entitled *Three Famous
Short Novels* (Vintage Books, 1963). This tale, then, has the distinction of being
known as a short story, as a major prose section (Book Four) of *The Hamlet*,
and also as a short novel that stands alone.

Critical discussion of "Spotted Horses" has reflected two views: one that
sees it as a humorous tale, the other emphasizing its dramatic message. Cowley
referred to it as the "funniest American story since Mark Twain," and numerous
critics have placed "Spotted Horses" in the American tall-tale tradition. Faulkner, however, saw the story as something more. Donald Houghton argues that
the story dramatizes a conflict between the men, who seem to be more enamored
of Flem Snopes's horses than of their wives, and the women, who are portrayed
as drab farm animals. Houghton quotes Faulkner, who said the horses "symbolized the hope, the aspirations of the masculine part of society that is capable
of doing, of committing, puerile folly for some gewgaw that had drawn him as
juxtaposed to the old practicality of the women" (361–362).

Two fairly recent articles reflect the ongoing debate about whether "Spotted
Horses" is a humorous tale. Dwight Eddins sees it primarily as a humorous tale
that provides a profound analysis of the role humor plays in our lives. He

suggests that "the humor of farce in the story provides a corrective to the routine and dullness of the solid world of duty" (30). Elizabeth D. Rankin finds in "Spotted Horses" a metaphor for the human condition as Faulkner portrays it, not only in *The Hamlet* but throughout the Snopes trilogy. Perhaps the truth lies somewhere in between these two views, that "Spotted Horses" is one of Faulkner's funniest tales while also dramatizing the foibles of human nature.

FURTHER READING

Eddins, Dwight. "Metahumor in 'Spotted Horses.' " *Ariel* 13.1 (1982): 23–31.
Heck, Francis S. "Faulkner's 'Spotted Horses': A Variation of a Rabelaisian Theme." *Arizona Quarterly* 37.2 (1981): 166–172.
Houghton, Donald E. "Whores and Horses in Faulkner's 'Spotted Horses.' " *Midwest Quarterly* 11 (1970): 361–369.
Ramsey, Allen. " 'Spotted Horses' and Spotted Pups." *Faulkner Journal* 2 (Spring 1990): 35–38.
Rankin, Elizabeth D. "Chasing Spotted Horses: The Quest for Human Dignity in Faulkner's Snopes Trilogy." *Faulkner: The Unappeased Imagination*, ed. Carey. 139–156.

Steven P. Schneider

SPRATLING, WILLIAM. *See* **Anderson, Sherwood; New Orleans**.

STALLION ROAD, an unproduced screenplay that Faulkner wrote for Warner Bros. Studio in 1945. Adapted from Stephen Longstreet's novel by the same name, Faulkner's script presents the story of a young veterinarian who must choose between personal profit and public service, as well as between the two women who compete for his love. This latter component, with its strong sexual content that includes adultery and nymphomania, seems to have been one of the principal reasons that Faulkner's script was rejected by the studio.

FURTHER READING

Faulkner, William. *Stallion Road: A Screenplay*. Ed. with intro. by Louis Daniel Brodsky and Robert W. Hamblin. Jackson: University Press of Mississippi, 1989.

Robert W. Hamblin

STEVENS, GAVIN, a major Faulkner character, appears in *Light in August, Go Down, Moses, Intruder in the Dust, Knight's Gambit, Requiem for a Nun, The Town, The Mansion,* and other works. Often alleged to be the voice of Faulkner, County Attorney Stevens is, instead, spokesperson for the good, just, but limited Southern gentleman: limited by upbringing, education, and the history of the South. Witness the irony in the final words of *Go Down, Moses*: " 'Come on,' " Stevens said to the newspaper editor, " 'Let's get back to town. I haven't seen my desk in two days,' " implying that *town* and his *desk* are where his serious business lies—and missing the significance of having spent two days preventing a black man from being ignored as a human being and designated only as Other. Nevertheless, he fails to see that man's human condition, writing him off as "[b]ad son of a bad father." "The past is never dead. It's not even the past," says Stevens to Temple Drake in *Requiem for a Nun*, a remark often attributed to Faulkner. Yet Faulkner's work is rife with characters whose tragedies stem from their inability to see the dynamics of the present working in concert with their past (Reverend Hightower, for example, in *Light in August* and Isaac McCaslin in *Go Down, Moses*). Stevens himself lives out the quotation above as his "serious vocation" exemplifies—"a twenty-two-year-old unfinished translation of the Old Testament back into classic Greek." Clearly not gifted with the vision of the author, Stevens is certainly one of the most caring characters in all of Yoknapatawpha County. As the narrator of *Requiem* summarizes, Stevens is "more like a poet than a lawyer," who champions truth less than he does justice—"justice as he sees it."

FURTHER READING

Toolan, Michael. "Syntactical Styles as a Means of Characterization in Narrative." *Style* 19.1 (1985): 78–93.
Wagner-Martin, Linda, ed. *New Essays on* Go Down, Moses. Cambridge: Cambridge University Press, 1996.

Marion Tangum

STONE, PHIL AVERY (1893–1967), Oxford, Mississippi, lawyer and litterateur who was a lifelong friend and sometime mentor to William Faulkner. When Stone returned to Oxford in 1914 after being graduated from Yale, he adopted Faulkner, four years his junior, as his literary protégé, encouraging the fledgling poet to read the works of Swinburne, Housman, Keats, Eliot, Aiken, Anderson, and others. As their friendship deepened, the two men shared not only their literary interests but also hunting trips into the Mississippi woods and occasional visits to the red-light districts of Clarksdale and Memphis. One of the first individuals to recognize Faulkner's writing potential, Stone personally arranged and financed the publication of Faulkner's first book, *The Marble Faun*, in 1924. In succeeding years, as Faulkner abandoned poetry for prose, Stone's influence declined significantly, although the two friends continued their literary conversations and even swapped tall tales that Faulkner would draw upon in creating his nefarious Snopes clan. Over the years Stone also provided legal assistance to Faulkner, drafting a succession of last wills and testaments for the author.

Beginning in the early 1950s, following Faulkner's winning of the Nobel Prize for Literature and the resultant critical interest in his work, Stone became an important local source for Faulkner scholars, befriending such individuals as Carvel Collins, Robert Coughlan, and James Meriwether on their visits to Oxford and carrying on an extensive correspondence with these and other researchers. Some 100 of these Stone letters are printed in Brodsky and Hamblin's *Faulkner: A Comprehensive Guide to the Brodsky Collection*, Volume II; and they show that while Stone could at times be egotistical, self-serving, irascible, unreliable, and biased on the subject of Faulkner, he nevertheless possessed crucial inside information on Faulkner's life and work, especially with regard to the early years.

Sadly, during this same period the relationship between Stone and Faulkner—especially on Stone's part—became quite strained. Increasingly in his correspondence, Stone is highly critical of his friend, claiming that Faulkner is personally arrogant and greatly overrated as an author. A number of explanations have been advanced to explain Stone's growing negativism: jealousy over Faulkner's artistic and financial successes, resentment over the fact that the student had outgrown the need for a mentor, guilt feelings because he had not repaid a personal loan from Faulkner, even the onrushing dementia that would eventually require institutionalization. However, as the letters reveal, Stone's hugest complaint against Faulkner seems to have resulted from their differing views on the question of race. Over the years Faulkner's views on this subject had become more and more cosmopolitan; Stone's, by contrast, always remained provincial and racist. Typical of Stone's feelings is his comment in a 1957 letter to a publisher who had requested Stone's help in securing some information from Faulkner: "Since he has taken the position he has in turning his back on his own people and his native land," Stone wrote, "I don't care to ask him anything."

Even the volatile issue of race, however, did not completely destroy the friendship of the two men. They appeared together in a 1952 television documentary about Faulkner, and Faulkner dedicated the final two volumes of the *Snopes* trilogy (as he had the first) to Stone. Just three weeks prior to his death Faulkner presented a signed copy of *The Reivers* to Stone and his wife Emily. Stone, in turn, was greatly distressed when he learned of his friend's death; and he served as a pallbearer when Faulkner was buried in Oxford's St. Peter's Cemetery.

FURTHER READING

Hamblin, Robert W. "Introduction." *Faulkner: A Comprehensive Guide to the Brodsky Collection*, ed. Brodsky and Hamblin. Vol. II. xviii–xxiv.
Snell, Susan. *Phil Stone of Oxford: A Vicarious Life*. Athens: University of Georgia Press, 1991.

Robert W. Hamblin

ST. PETER'S EPISCOPAL CHURCH, a historic church located in Oxford, Mississippi. Services were first held for what would become St. Peter's in September of 1840; a clergyman, Andrew Matthews, began serving the little congregation on the Seventh Sunday after Trinity of the following year. The congregation, meeting in the Presbyterian Church and the Court House, petitioned the convention of the Diocese of Mississippi for admission as a parish on May 13, 1851. The church's first resident clergyman was Frederick Augustus

Porter Barnard, later to be Chancellor of the University of Mississippi, for whom the Barnard Observatory, now home to the Center of the Study of Southern Culture, is named. A lot was purchased for $600, the deed dated November 19, 1855; and Richard Upjohn, who designed Trinity Church, New York, designed St. Peter's, built by William Turner and completed except for its tower in 1871. Controversy and a lawsuit for the builder's fee resulted in a subscription by Mrs. Frances Devereux Skipwith, daughter of Bishop Leonidas Polk and wife of St. Peter's Senior Warden; Miss Mary Cox of Philadelphia raised the entire sum, which was actually used to build the rectory. During the War Between the States, when the only services held were the annual visitations of the Bishop, salt was concealed in the north wall; it was still there in 1951. In 1962 Duncan Gray, St. Peter's Rector and Faulkner family friend, played a significant role in the events surrounding the enrollment of James Meredith, Ole Miss's first black student. From the beginning of the church, Thompsons (Compsons in Faulkner's fiction) have been members, as were two Confederate generals: one, Francis A. Shoup, a priest; the other, C. W. Sears, on the Vestry. Mrs. John Faulkner directed the Altar Guild in 1951; Phil Stone served on the Vestry; the altar missal is in memory of Joella Pegues Shegog; Faulkner's daughter Jill and niece Dean were both married in the church; artifacts are in the Mary Buie Museum. Faulkner was a communicant of the church, although he rarely attended services.

Charles A. Peek

STREAM OF CONSCIOUSNESS. Stream-of-consciousness writing creates the illusion of a narrative that presents a character's thoughts, emotions, and impressions unfiltered and unrefined by an intervening narrator. Undoubtedly Faulkner was most directly influenced in his use of this convention by James Joyce in *A Portrait of the Artist as a Young Man* (1916) and *Ulysses* (1922). Stream of consciousness is one of Faulkner's primary narrative methods. He makes complex and varied use of it, especially in his novels written during the 1930s. Stream of consciousness may appear as a few words or sentences, as the narrative medium of an episode, or as the predominant method for an entire book. Unlike Hemingway, who relied on dialogue and external descriptions to narrate his stories, which is essentially a method of implication, Faulkner more aggressively enters into the mind of his characters, not only revealing and presenting their thoughts but often explaining and interpreting them. Stream of consciousness has been traditionally regarded as a method that allows an author to present an unbiased, objective narrative, but recent critics have shown that it enables the writer to manipulate how the reader experiences the text and thus apprehends meaning.

The Sound and the Fury and *As I Lay Dying* are the Faulkner novels most often described as stream-of-consciousness works. *The Sound and the Fury* consists of three chapters of stream-of-consciousness narration and a fourth chapter of more conventional narrative. The first three chapters focus, respectively, on

Benjy, Quentin, and Jason—three brothers in the Compson family. For Benjy, who is mentally retarded, stream of consciousness reveals an absolute lack of comprehension. Because he cannot tell the difference between the present time and the events he remembers from his past, his narrative seems to jump indiscriminately from one point in time to another; and the only clues to the transitions between time periods are evident in the use of italics that signify time shifts (Faulkner at one point wanted to print the opening chapter in different color inks, each color representing a different level of time, but this proved impractical). Quentin is similarly fixated on the past, but he can distinguish past from present. His narrative is more complex than Benjy's, although perhaps more accessible for the reader, since Quentin recognizes and understands the world in a way that Benjy does not. Quentin's chapter presents his present-time perceptions and past-time memories and mixes spoken and recollected dialogue along with Faulkner's intrusions into the deepest levels of Quentin's conscious mind. Although the Jason chapter is more like a spoken narrative than conventional stream of consciousness, he is not speaking to any listener in particular. The effect is of a dramatic monologue. The fact that it conveys an absolutely convincing representation of the state of the mind of a character whom Faulkner once described as the "sanest man I ever knew" helps justify describing it as stream of consciousness.

Unlike the stream of consciousness in *Ulysses*, which presents the contents of the minds of Stephen Dedalus and Leopold Bloom in a seemingly dispassionate manner, Faulkner's stream-of-consciousness narratives are riven with his characters' passions. Moreover, in *As I Lay Dying* they give the illusion of being directed toward an audience, a listener, even if that listener is no one other than the reader. Most of the narrators in *As I Lay Dying* are members of the Bundren family. A few are neighbors or simply strangers whom the family happens to pass during their journey to the burial yard in Jefferson. The individual chapters are unified by a central focus on the Bundrens and their burial journey, but there is no continuity of plot from one chapter to the next—the chapters are not episodes in this sense. Instead, continuity grows from the interrelationships of the characters and from the differing needs that drive Cash, Dewey Dell, Vardaman, and Anse individually toward Jefferson. Some of the chapters, such as those belonging to Anse Bundren (whose narratives show all the elements of oral speech), seem to be spoken-aloud, dramatic monologues, while others do not: Portions of the chapters belonging to Darl and to Dewey Dell read like poetry and convey unconscious thoughts that the characters are probably not capable of expressing. These highly stylized, impressionistic narratives rely heavily on figurative language, and it is evident that some other narrator, an authorial narrator, has intruded, appropriating the voices of the characters and assuming the function of translating their feelings and experiences.

After *As I Lay Dying* Faulkner moves away from first-person stream of consciousness to third-person narratives that present in an intense and often highly stylized manner the contents of the characters' minds. He also begins using stream-of-consciousness narratives in concert with other methods. Most often he uses stream of consciousness to uncover the mind of a character as he does at the beginning of chapter 6 in *Light in August*, which begins with the announcement *"Memory believes before knowing remembers,"* informing the reader that the contents of the chapter, and of the next five chapters, reside in Christmas's mind. The entirety of chapter 5 is a stream-of-consciousness narrative focused on Christmas, though it is not of the same type found in *The Sound and the Fury*. In fact, this chapter exemplifies the difficulty of distinguishing Faulkner's stream-of-consciousness narration from more conventional narration. The chapter is narrated in the third person, but the density and detail of its examination of Christmas's mind move it much closer to stream of consciousness than to conventional narration. Elsewhere in the novel Faulkner uses stream of consciousness at key moments to intrude briefly into a character's thoughts. For example, in the first chapter, which is focused on Lena Grove, the narrative shifts briefly from an external focus on her conscious thoughts, printed in roman type, to her unconscious thoughts, printed in italics: "[Lena] thinks. She thinks of herself as already moving, riding again, thinking *Then it will be as if I were riding for a half mile before I even get into the wagon.*" In chapter 5, focused on Christmas, Faulkner uses an italicized exclamation— *"Something is going to happen. Something is going to happen to me"*—to indicate the fatalism and tension in the character's mind (Faulkner uses the same exclamation, in the same way, to characterize Temple Drake in *Sanctuary* and the Reporter in *Pylon*). At the end of chapter 19, a stream-of-consciousness eulogy characterizes an entire community's state of mind following Joe Christmas's murder.

Absalom, Absalom! uses stream of consciousness in several different forms. The novel is narrated through the mind of Quentin Compson as he listens to other characters talking; the novel tells what Quentin hears, how he reacts, how he interprets what he hears. Virtually the entire narrative consists of a stream of information filtered through his mind. The fifth chapter is an italicized "first-person" stream-of-consciousness narrative focused on Rosa Coldfield as she recalls from a highly subjective point of view her encounters with Thomas Sutpen, the novel's main subject. The end of this chapter reverts to roman type and describes Quentin as he sits listening to Miss Rosa, thus indicating that the chapter has presented Miss Rosa's narrative not as she directly told it but instead as it was received and refined in Quentin's mind. In *Pylon* stream of consciousness is blended with external third-person narration focused on the Reporter. Stream of consciousness also plays an important role in *The Wild Palms/If I Forget Thee, Jerusalem*, especially in the narrative focus on Harry Wilbourne in the "Wild Palms" chapter and the Tall Convict in the "Old Man" chapters.

In some sense, Faulkner creates in many of his novels after *The Sound and the Fury* and *As I Lay Dying* an authorial consciousness that contains and refines all the narrative material that makes up the content of each book. His narrators plunge in and out of the minds of his characters, on occasion seek to represent the consciousness of an entire community, and range back and forth in time. This is certainly the case in *Light in August, Absalom, Absalom!, The Wild Palms, The Hamlet*, and the narrative sections of *Requiem for a Nun*. For Faulkner, then, stream-of-consciousness narrative need not focus on a single character but may instead expand to encompass the consciousness of the entire novel and of its readers as they receive and react to what the novel contains.

See also **Point of View**.

FURTHER READING

Humphrey, Robert. *Stream of Consciousness in the Modern Novel.* Berkeley: University of California Press, 1954.
West, Paul. *The Modern Novel.* 2nd ed. London: Hutchinson, 1963.

Hugh Ruppersburg

STYLISTICS, a speciality of linguistics, concerns itself with the study of patterns of linguistic "choices"—intentional, conscious, or subconscious—in a text or set of texts, which can be seen as characteristic of that text or set of texts, its author, or their authors. These choices can operate on different levels of language simultaneously: the morphological, the lexical, the syntactic, the graphological, the phonological, the semantic, and the pragmatic. On the morphological level, for instance, a choice might consist of a preference for the use of negative prefixes such as *un-*, *dis-*, and *mis-* in a certain text, which creates the internal oppositions of words such as "*un*happiness," "*dis*belief," or "*mis*-trust" that synonyms with the same semantic load but without the negating prefixes—like "sadness" and "doubt"—do not possess. On the pragmatic level, of course, the effect is that an expectation, or at least a consideration, of the positive attribute or state becomes part of the message.

In the texts of Faulkner, such choices often go far beyond the forms that are part of the standard linguistic repertoire—the code—at these various levels of language. To remain within the field of morphology for a moment, his choices include, for instance, the forms *unbelief, unreality*, and *notpeople*, which not only present an explicit negation of an opposite term but have a strong defamiliarizing effect with often far-reaching semantic and pragmatic implications as well. Such effects are also found on other levels of language: for example, on the syntactic level the use of a transitive verb as if it were an intransitive, and on the graphological level, the use of a full stop between attributive clause and attribution. Both of these attributes appear, together with a nonstandard use of the preposition *at*, in the following short passage from the first page of *The Sound and the Fury*: " 'Listen at you, now.' Luster said." Such defamiliarizing features represent a challenge to the linguistic codes rather than a choice from them—the code fighting, as it were, to preserve comprehension, and the author, to accomplish the desired defamiliarization, semantic, and pragmatic effects. In Faulkner's case, editors have often cast themselves in the role of defenders of the codes by "correcting" the author's deviations, naturally to his great dismay. This is not surprising if one considers, on the one hand, the difficulties that readers (editors included) have encountered in Faulkner's texts and, on the other hand, the tremendous effects that such deviations can have, for instance, in creating the personalities of Faulkner's characters such as Benjy Compson.

Stylistic approaches to Faulkner's texts, then, can be distinguished according to the level of language that each has as its main focus or starting point. One example of a study based primarily on the lexical level is Frederik Smith's article on verbal repetition in *As I Lay Dying*, while Bruce Southard's study of the representation of time in *Go Down, Moses* and Michael Toolan's study of the use of progressive verb forms in *Go Down, Moses* are largely syntactic in focus. A pragmatic approach is found in Mark Lencho's study of black English in *The Sound and the Fury*. Important monographs with a wider scope, yet based primarily on the level of syntactics, are Michael Toolan's *The Stylistics of Fiction*, an exhaustive study of *Go Down, Moses*, and Irena Kaluza's discussion of the different types of appended clauses in *The Sound and the Fury*, especially those that characterize the internal monologues of Benjy and Quentin Compson.

The more theoretical study of linguistic choices that serve to present the personality of a character has been taken up by Roger Fowler in his works *Linguistics and the Novel* (Methuen, 1977) and *Linguistic Criticism* (Oxford University Press, 1990). Fowler introduces the concept of *mind-style*, to refer to "any distinctive linguistic presentation of an individual mental self" (*Novel* 103) to be studied as "consistent stylistic choices" that signify "particular, distinctive, orderings of experience" (*Criticism* 9). Mind-style, then, can be seen to comprise aspects of the character's personality as they reveal themselves in this character's conceptualization of the world, expressed in language and including both past and present, as well as the various schemes of anticipation, expectation, desire, dream, hope, and fear that we are wont to call future. Ineke Bockting's monograph on psychostylistics is a study of mind-style and other characterizing techniques in Faulkner's major early works, *The Sound and the Fury, As I Lay Dying, Light in August*, and *Absalom, Absalom!*

FURTHER READING

Bockting. *Character and Personality in the Novels of William Faulkner: A Study in Psychostylistics.*

Kaluza, Irena. *The Functioning of Sentence Structure in the Stream of Consciousness Technique of William Faulkner's* The Sound and the Fury. Kraków, Poland: Kakladem Uniwersytetu Jagiellonskiego, 1967.

Lencho, Mark W. "Dialect Variation in *The Sound and the Fury*: A Study of Faulkner's Use of Black English Dialect." *Mississippi Quarterly Review* 41 (1988): 403–419.

Smith, Frederik N. "Telepathic Diction: Verbal Repetition in *As I Lay Dying*." *Style* 19 (1985): 66–77.

Southard, Bruce. "Syntax and Time in Faulkner's *Go Down, Moses.*" *Language and Style* 14 (1981): 107–115.

Toolan, Michael J. "The Functioning of Progressive Verbal Forms in the Narrative of *Go Down, Moses.*" *Language and Style* 16.2 (1983): 211–230.

——. *The Stylistics of Fiction: A Literary-Linguistic Approach.* London: Routledge, 1990.

Ineke Bockting

SUICIDE. Reckless and potentially self-harming behavior is shown by many of Faulkner's characters, as it was characteristic of Faulkner himself. In a number of cases, such behavior ultimately results in the death of a character. For example, Mr. Compson drinks himself to death after the trouble with his daughter Caddy. Other characters fail to protect themselves adequately from the harmful effects of the actions of others and can thus be said to bring about their own deaths, such as Joanna Burden or Joe Christmas and Popeye. Still others allow themselves to waste away and die, such as Addie Bundren or Ellen Coldfield Sutpen. All of these characters could be called suicidal in some sense.

However, as Gavin J. Fairbairn has argued, one should not talk of suicidal behavior unless this behavior is clearly an "act of intentional and intended wished-for self-destruction." As he puts it, in many cases, "although the risk or even the probability of death is accepted and perhaps willingly embraced, death is usually not aimed at and intended" (112). But the absence of authoritative, omniscient narrators in Faulkner's work means that one often cannot be certain about a character's aims and intentions; even the characters themselves are often unclear or ambiguous about their own motives.

Critics who have written about the question of suicide in Faulkner's work often focus on motivation and personality structure rather than intentions. Elizabeth Kerr, for instance, writes that Bayard Sartoris "was driven to show his reckless courage . . . because of the psychic wound he suffered in the death of his twin brother and because he lacked the inner resources and constructive impulses which might have allowed him to face life without John" (*Yoknapatawpha* 213–214). Richard Gray claims that Eula Varner Snopes killed herself because "evidently" she preferred her daughter Linda "to know her mother to be a suicide rather than an adulteress" (338). However, neither motivation nor personality structure necessarily clarifies the intentions of a character.

In Faulkner's most extensive treatment of suicide, in *The Sound and the Fury*, Quentin Compson prepares himself in such an elaborate way that his intentions seem relatively clear. In addition, Faulkner himself explained: "Quentin is a dying man, he is already out of life, and those things that were important in life don't mean anything to him any more" (*FIU* 18). Yet Quentin's motives are not so simple. Based solely on *The Sound and the Fury*, one might conclude, as Kerr does, that Quentin's suicide "was motivated by Southern gyneolatry and incestuous impulses" (213); but by placing *Absalom, Absalom!* within the time scheme of *The Sound and the Fury*, and by making Quentin its primal narrator, Faulkner suggests a much wider and socially more complex scope of causal factors.

At the end of *Absalom*, when Quentin is asked why it is that he hates the South, he is left panting, "I dont hate it . . . I dont hate it," desperately trying to convince himself. Only months later, as presented in *The Sound and the Fury*, he concludes that his life must be over, using the words "[I]t will be better for me for all of us," thus taking up his own burden with that of family and society.

FURTHER READING

Fairbairn, Gavin J. *Contemplating Suicide: The Language of Self-Harm*. London: Routledge, 1995.

Ineke Bockting

SUTPEN, an important fictional family in the works of Faulkner. Different members of the Sutpen family play a role in the stories "Evangeline," "Wash," "An Odor of Verbena," "The Bear," and "The Old People" and the novel *The Reivers*; and the family name is mentioned in *Requiem for a Nun, The Town*, and the Appendix to *The Sound and the Fury*. By far the most elaborate treatment of the Sutpen family is found in *Absalom, Absalom!*, the story of Thomas Sutpen, his wife Ellen Coldfield Sutpen, their children Henry and Judith Sutpen, his first wife Eulalia Bon, their son Charles Bon, Bon's son Charles Etienne Saint Valery, and Bon's grandson Jim Bond, as well as Clytemnestra (Clytie), the child of Thomas Sutpen by one of his slave women.

Through layers of narration, each with its own preoccupations and prejudices, the reader learns the Sutpen history. Thomas was born in the Virginia mountains in 1807, as a ten-year-old traveled with his desperately poor family into the lowlands of the James River, looking for work, is sent away from the front door of a planter's house by a Negro servant, and realizes that "he would have to do something about it in order to live with himself for the rest of his life."

This experience creates in Thomas Sutpen the need to "have lands and niggers and a fine house to combat them with." His "design" to combat "them" who own the big plantations leads him to marry the daughter of a Haitian slave owner, Eulalia Bon, yet forsake her and their son Charles when he learns of the drop of black blood that makes them unfit to advance his "design." Sutpen moves to Jefferson, where he is not known, to try to create a second, more successful, Sutpen family. He eventually succeeds in establishing a plantation, complete with a house the likes of which had never been seen before, a new wife Ellen Coldfield, the daughter of a local merchant, and two new children, Henry and Judith.

But the injustice done to the first wife and eldest son will not rest. Charles Bon, the rejected mulatto son, comes to haunt his father's home, under cover, first of his friendship with the half brother Henry, and later also of his courtship with the half sister Judith. By threatening to marry Judith, the young man hopes to force his father into acknowledging him as his son. Unwilling to risk his "design" by doing something about the problem himself, Sutpen informs Henry of the secret blood relationship between him and his sister and their friend Charles. Henry kills his half brother to prevent the incest and, what is worse, the miscegenation that marriage would entail. Thus, when one son kills the other and then disappears, and Sutpen fails to create a third family and a third heir, the Sutpen dynasty collapses—basically because Sutpen has put the abstract ideals of his "design" before the concrete needs of his family.

Although most of our knowledge about the Sutpens consists of the conjecture of narrators who are either too closely involved emotionally or too far removed from the original events, the story is real enough. The choice that Sutpen made, at the end of the Civil War—to favor abstract ideals over family concerns— belies the very ideals that the Confederacy had fought for: the preservation of personal relations of family and friendship in the face of Yankee snobbism, industrialization, mechanization, and the market society, with all the associated evils of eroding interpersonal relationships.

FURTHER READING

Kinney, Arthur F., ed. *Critical Essays on William Faulkner: The Sutpen Family*. Boston: G. K. Hall, 1996.
Kuyk, Dirk, Jr. *Sutpen's Design: Interpreting Faulkner's* Absalom, Absalom! Charlottesville: University Press of Virginia, 1990.

Ineke Bockting

T

"TALL MEN, THE," a short story by Faulkner, was first published in the *Saturday Evening Post* on May 31, 1941, and reprinted in *Collected Stories*. The story focuses thematically on conflicts between different sets of social assumptions or "sociologics" involving economics, law, and traditions of individual responsibility and freedom. These issues are represented in the characterization of Anse McCallum and sons (farmers in the hill country of Yoknapatawpha; an earlier generation of which appears in *Flags in the Dust* as MacCallums), the local marshal, and a federal investigator. The investigator arrives to serve a warrant on the sons for failing to register for the first "peacetime" military draft (instituted in 1940, prior to U.S. entry into World War II). While the story is told by an omniscient narrator, who reveals the investigator's inner monologue, the marshal functions as a mediator between the McCallums' "curious" ways and thoughts and the investigator's—thus as an interpreter or "mouthpiece" not unlike Gavin Stevens (and others) elsewhere in Faulkner. Bradford and Howell have provided historical and sociological analyses of this story, which many later commentators find ideologically overburdened and sententious. Publication in the *Saturday Evening Post*, while serving economic motives for Faulkner, can be understood as a political statement about the values of a class of people in his region and a general patriotic endorsement of fealty to then-contested ideals of freedom.

FURTHER READING

Bradford, M. E. "Faulkner's 'Tall Men.' " *South Atlantic Quarterly* 61 (1962): 29–39.
Howell, Elmo. "William Faulkner and the New Deal." *Midwest Quarterly* 5 (1964): 323–332.
———. "William Faulkner and the Plain People of Yoknapatawpha County." *Journal of Mississippi History* 24 (1962): 73–87.

Stephen Hahn

TARNISHED ANGELS, THE, director Douglas Sirk's 1957 film version of Faulkner's novel *Pylon*. The novel centers on a newspaper reporter who is drawn into the lives of daredevil pilot Roger Shumann and his unorthodox "family," whom he meets at a flying circus during Mardi Gras: Laverne, Roger's common-law wife, and Jackie, their illegitimate son. Since the studio's high command feared that the novel's plot was too racy to pass muster with the film industry's censor, screenwriter George Zuckerman eliminated from the script the ménage à trois that is so central to the novel. Roger marries Laverne in the course of the film so that Jackie will have a father; hence, Roger is allowed the kind of regeneration in *Tarnished Angels* that Faulkner denied him in *Pylon*. The movie garnered mixed reviews from the critics, since it rarely rises above the conventions of ordinary melodrama.

FURTHER READING

Degenfelder, Pauline. "Sirk's *Tarnished Angels: Pylon* Revisited." *Literature/Film Quarterly* 5 (1977): 242–251.

Gene D. Phillips

TEXTS. Early on in Faulkner studies, James B. Meriwether began calling attention to the problems of Faulkner's texts. In separate essays on the composition and publication histories of *Sanctuary* and *The Sound and the Fury*, he pointed to specific discrepancies between the texts of the novels as they were published and the texts as Faulkner had written them, typed them himself, and presented them to his publishers for publication. In the late 1950s and early 1960s, Meriwether prepared a new text of *As I Lay Dying* for Random House and worked with Faulkner and Random House on a new text of *Sanctuary*. In 1966 Michael Millgate's *The Achievement of William Faulkner* became the first scholarly study of Faulkner to demonstrate how knowledge of Faulkner's typescripts and manuscripts could illuminate the study of the works.

In 1972 Meriwether formally called for a new complete edition of Faulkner's works, to be edited according to the scholarly principles of the Modern Language Association's Center for Editions of American Authors (CEAA). No such formal scholarly edition has yet appeared, but in 1979 Noel Polk proposed to Random House to edit the original version of *Sanctuary* according to scholarly principles, though without the elaborate apparatus that the CEAA and its successor, the Center for Scholarly Editions, insisted upon for scholarly editions. *Sanctuary: The Original Text*, based on Faulkner's original typescript, was published in 1981. Polk then proposed new editions of *The Sound and the Fury* and *Absalom, Absalom!* Random House agreed, bringing out the former in 1984 and the latter in 1986.

In the meantime, the Library of America had contracted with Random House to publish all of Faulkner's fiction in the Library of America format and asked Polk to prepare the new texts and Joseph Blotner to prepare annotations. The first volume, *Faulkner: Novels 1930–1935*, appeared in 1985; the second, *Faulkner: Novels 1936–1940*, in 1990; and the third, *Faulkner: Novels 1942–1954*, in 1994. The texts of the Random House editions of *The Sound and the Fury* and *Absalom, Absalom!* then appeared in Vintage paperback editions in new typesettings and later were reprinted in facsimile when the Vintage editions gave way to the Vintage International series; except for these two novels, reprinted from the new Random House editions, and *Go Down, Moses*, which was published with a few corrections provided by Polk before the Library of America edition appeared, the Vintage International paperbacks of Faulkner's novels contain texts reproduced from computer disks provided to Vintage International by the Library of America. It remains the Library of America's plan to publish all of Faulkner's fiction, including the stories.

Some of Faulkner's texts, as originally published, varied considerably from the texts Faulkner wrote. The first published text of *Absalom, Absalom!*, for example, was heavily edited by Random House editors who, not having the benefit of fifty years of scholarly study, may not have completely understood what Faulkner was trying to do in the novel and thus edited it heavily, sometimes deleting ten or more lines at a time, altering punctuation, shortening long sentences, identifying deliberately vague pronominal references, and in general, *normalizing* Faulkner's prose. His editors had done the same thing to *Pylon* the previous year (1935) and, in 1939, forced Faulkner to accept a new title, *The Wild Palms*, in place of his own title, *If I Forget Thee, Jerusalem*. Other novels were generally not treated quite so harshly by editors, but many appeared in texts marred by some unwarranted editorial intervention and by carelessness in typesetting and proofreading.

The Library of America/Vintage International editions take as their goal to publish the texts that Faulkner actually wanted in print, insofar as that can be reconstructed from the available evidence. There is a good deal of available evidence, since Faulkner very meticulously saved thousands of pages of his manuscripts and typescripts, from beginning to end of his career, and deposited them in the Alderman Library of the University of Virginia; several thousand other pages have turned up in other collections, most notably the major repositories of Faulkner manuscript materials at the University of Texas, the New York Public Library, the University of Mississippi, Tulane University, and Southeast Missouri State University. In the mid-1980s, Garland Publishers issued *William Faulkner Manuscripts* (Blotner et al., eds.), forty-four volumes of facsimile reproductions of Faulkner's manuscripts and typescripts at the University of Virginia and the New York Public Library. Scholars and readers interested in more information about Faulkner's manuscripts and typescripts and the state of the published texts should look carefully at the introductions to these Garland volumes.

FURTHER READING

Meriwether, James B. "A Proposal for a CEAA Edition of William Faulkner." *Editing Twentieth Century Texts*. Ed. Francess G. Halpenny. Toronto: University of Toronto Press, 1972. 12–27.

Noel Polk

"THAT EVENING SUN," one of Faulkner's best-known short stories, was first published in *American Mercury* in March 1931 and later included in *These 13* and *Collected Stories*. Set around 1898–1899, "That Evening Sun" is narrated by Quentin Compson fifteen years later. Of the Compsons of *The Sound and the Fury*, only Benjy is not present. However, based on the chronology of the novel, Quentin is twenty when he commits suicide and would, thus, be dead when narrating "That Evening Sun." Critics debate whether this discrepancy is an example of Faulkner's inconsistent chronology, an explanation for the ghost-story quality of the narrative, or reason to dissociate the short story from *The Sound and the Fury* and *Absalom, Absalom!*

"That Evening Sun" is presented in six sections, varying reflection and dialogue. Section I points to the difference between the mechanized Jefferson of 1913–1914 and fifteen years before. Quentin recalls Negro women, their bundles "almost as large as cotton bales" balanced atop their heads for the trip between "the white house and the blackened washpot beside a cabin door in Negro Hollow." This recollection, however, leads rapidly to the series of associated memories that are the story's content: of Nancy, who did the Compson laundry, and her husband, Jesus, who, unlike other husbands, would not assist her; of her lateness to work, allegedly because of prostitution, and her accosting a banker and Baptist deacon, Mr. Stovall, for not paying her for his last three visits; of Mr. Stovall's knocking her down in the street, kicking her teeth out; of her being jailed and there failing in a suicide attempt, during which her pregnant condition, later described as a "watermelon," becomes visible; of Jesus, his razor scar, and his threat to "cut down the vine it . . . come off of"; of Nancy's fear of Jesus, Mr. Compson's ordering him off their place, and Mrs. Compson's complaints about the attention Nancy is getting; and of Jason's accusing Nancy—and Candace's teasing Jason—for being "scaired of the dark." During this section, Nancy first utters the expression, "I aint nothing but a nigger," bespeaking both her own separate identity and her misuse by white power structures, as well as introducing the Compson children's early acculturation into racial identity. Section II recounts the time when, Dilsey being ill, Nancy cooks for the Compsons, staying in their house during the nights of her fears. First through dialogue between Dilsey and Nancy in the Compson kitchen, then between Nancy and the children on the way to her cabin, section III recounts how there seems to be no protection for Nancy, how Mrs. Compson "can't have Negroes sleeping in the bedrooms," and how, building a blaze in an already hot cabin, Nancy tells the children about a "queen come walking up to the ditch, where that bad man was hiding." In section IV, Nancy tries desperately to keep the children from going home, making popcorn but burning it, and burns her hand on the lamp globe. Section V presents the arrival of Mr. Compson to take the children home, his belittling the legitimacy of Nancy's fears, and Nancy's resignation to her fate: "Anyway, I got my coffin money saved up with Mr. Lovelady." In section VI, the children return up the lane with their father, who at the end has to silence Candace and Jason's squabbling over whether Jason is "scairder than a nigger." The opening is echoed in Quentin's own last words: "Who will do our washing now, Father?" The ironies on which the story rests may be drawn from the distance between the horrors Nancy endures and the concerns Quentin expresses.

First refused by *Scribner's*, "That Evening Sun" was accepted by *American Mercury*, but only after Faulkner took H. L. Mencken's suggestions to reduce references to the watermelon and vine metaphor for Nancy's pregnancy and change Jesus's name to Jubah. In the versions included in *These 13* and *Collected Stories*, both metaphor and name are restored. Additionally, the *American Mercury* title ended "Go Down," making clear the connection with W. C. Handy's 1914 "St. Louis Blues," which includes the line "I hate to see that evening sun go down" and which Faulkner very likely heard at Oxford dances featuring Handy's band. Faulkner's original manuscript title, "Never done no weeping when you wanted to laugh," similarly has the sound of a blues lyric. Blues and blue notes explain several references to Nancy's making a sound that was "like singing and it wasn't like singing, like the sounds that Negroes make." In any event, the blues provided a pattern of repetition for the story's structure, as well as a motif of call-seeking-response characterizing the failed attempts of several characters to be heard across generational and cultural differences.

FURTHER READING

Johnston, Kenneth G. "The Year of Jubilee: Faulkner's 'That Evening Sun.' " *American Literature* 46 (1974): 93–100.

Kuyk, Dirk, Jr., Betty M. Kuyk, and James A. Miller. "Black Culture in William Faulkner's 'That Evening Sun.' " *Journal of American Studies* 20 (April 1986): 33–50.

Manglaviti, Leo M. J. "Faulkner's 'That Evening Sun' and Mencken's 'Best Editorial Judgment.' " *American Literature* 43 (1972): 649–654.

Pearson, Norman Holmes. "Faulkner's Three 'Evening Suns.' " *Yale University Library Gazette* 29 (October 1954): 61–70.

Toker, Leona. "Rhetoric and Ethical Ambiguities in 'That Evening Sun.' " *Women's Studies* 22 (1993): 429–439.

Charles A. Peek

"THAT WILL BE FINE," a short story by Faulkner, first appeared in the *American Mercury* in July 1935 and was later selected for inclusion in *Collected Stories*. The story is an investigation of the depths of dishonesty, narrated by an ambitious seven-year-old, George, who fantasizes about the gifts of money he will receive on Christmas Day. He relates the sequence of events in which Uncle Rodney, a thief as well as an incorrigible womanizer, is exposed and shot by a vengeful husband. The story works on the tension between the narrator's honest, if naive, ambition and his uncle's thorough dishonesty.

FURTHER READING

Hadley, Charles. "Seeing and Telling: Narrational Functions in the Short Story." *Discourse and Style, II*. By Jean Pierre Petit. Lyons, France: L'Hermes, 1980. 63–68.

Larry Wharton

"THERE WAS A QUEEN," a short story by Faulkner, was first published in *Scribner's* in January 1933 and subsequently appeared in *Doctor Marino and Other Stories* and *Collected Stories*. The story describes to what lengths some individuals will go in order to uphold a family name. The opening and closing of the story are seen through the eyes of Elnora, a black maid who is unaware that her father was Colonel John Sartoris. Nevertheless, Elnora sees herself in league with Mrs. Virginia Du Pre, Colonel Sartoris's ninety-year-old sister, in upholding the Sartoris name. Both are appalled by the manner in which young Bayard's widow, Narcissa Benbow Sartoris, handles the FBI agent who brings the anonymous, obscene letters written to her years before. Mrs. Du Pre dies after hearing that Narcissa travels to Memphis for an assignation with the agent in exchange for the letters.

FURTHER READING

Bradford, Melvin E. "Certain Ladies of Quality: Faulkner's View of Women and the Evidence of 'There Was a Queen.' " *Arlington Quarterly* 1 (1967–1968): 106–134.

Castillo, Phillip. " 'There Was a Queen' and Faulkner's Narcissa Sartoris." *Mississippi Quarterly* 28 (1975): 307–315.

Knieger, Bernard. "Faulkner's 'Mountain Victory,' 'Doctor Martino,' and 'There Was a Queen.' " *Explicator* 30 (1972): Item 45.

Lahey, Michael E. "Narcissa's Love Letters: Illicit Space and the Writing of Female Identity in 'There Was a Queen.' " *Faulkner and Gender*, ed. Kartiganer and Abadie. 160–180.

Young, Daniel T. "Narcissa Benbow's Strange Love/s: William Faulkner." *American Declarations of Love*. Ed. by Ann Massa. New York: St. Martin's Press, 1990. 88–103.

Larry Wharton

THESE 13, Faulkner's first volume of short fiction, represents his initial attempt to create a short story collection with some internal coherence and intertextuality. Hoping to capitalize on *Sanctuary*'s sensational reception, Faulkner signed a contract in May 1931 for a volume tentatively titled "A ROSE FOR EMILY And Other Stories"; in September 1931 it was published as *These 13*, a title that Millgate speculates may refer to Balzac's *Les Trieze* (*Achievement* 260). Faulkner dedicated the work "To Estelle and Alabama," his wife and their infant daughter (named after Faulkner's great-aunt, Alabama Falkner McLean) who died soon after her birth in 1931.

The collection was reviewed favorably in the *New York Times*, though not all reviewers shared this enthusiasm: Granville Hicks, for example, commented in the *Tribune* that Faulkner exhibited more talent as a novelist than as a short story writer. Frederick Karl argues that *These 13* was the by-product of Faulkner's attempt to sell a number of stories as quickly as he could and that Faulkner "was not thinking, primarily, in short fiction terms" but rather writing stories to generate sufficient income to support himself while writing novels (439). While *These 13* contains some of Faulkner's best stories, as a whole it is somewhat uneven; nonetheless, it sold better than any previous Faulkner work except *Sanctuary*.

Faulkner had previously proposed "a collection of short stories of my townspeople" to Horace Liveright. The emphasis on "A Rose for Emily" in the original title of *These 13* suggests the centrality of the village, yet ultimately only the middle section focused on Jefferson and Yoknapatawpha County. The book's three sections (headed only by roman numerals) correspond to the broad categories Faulkner delineated in a letter: "the war, the imaginary town of Jefferson, and a few other settings" (qtd. in Millgate, *Achievement* 260), although the loose final category might be more precisely categorized by the title Faulkner gave to the final section in which they appear in *Collected Stories*: "Beyond." The summer *These 13* appeared, Faulkner remarked that "a book of short stories should be linked together by characters or chronology" (*LIG* 13). While the volume's three groups of stories ostensibly employ neither link, the sections provide a contrapuntal arrangement that anticipates the organizing principle later employed in a more extended and sophisticated fashion in *Collected Stories*. Within each section, as well, Faulkner seems to have given some thought to sequencing stories and to creating juxtapositions.

The first section includes four stories concerning World War I, only one of which—"Ad Astra"—had been published previously; added to this story were the unsold "All the Dead Pilots" and two stories rewritten from an earlier manuscript fragment: "Victory" and "Crevasse." While not the group's strongest story, the heavily ironic "Victory" opens the volume with an overview of the war and its aftermath, chronicling the tainted rise and proud fall of a Scotsman who becomes an officer after heroism during a battle in which he also murders an officer who once reprimanded him. Unable to maintain his elevated economic status and gentlemanly aura in a postwar position, he descends to begging and selling matches when that position is lost. The victors in "Ad Astra" have undergone a similar descent to a condition of stasis, dislocation, and spiritual numbness; in contrast to the American Bland's sorrow and self-pity, the marginalized subadar and the German prisoner understand that the "victorious lose what the vanquished gain." The story's repeated references to victory connect it explicitly with the previous story. "All the Dead Pilots" carries forward the theme of moral and spiritual deadness, contrasting the living death of the war's survivors in their suburban existence with John Sartoris's death in battle before the flame that animated his struggle concerning a French woman with his rival Spoomer expires. "Crevasse" concludes the section with the tale of a patrol whose fall into a crevasse brings them into contact with the skeletons of soldiers buried sitting down after a gas attack; after confronting this horrific image, however, they manage to escape from underground and emerge to rejoin their patrol. All four stories later became part of the fourth section of *Collected Stories*, labeled "The Wasteland."

The middle section, the strongest of the three, contains "Red Leaves," "A Rose for Emily," "A Justice," "Hair," "That Evening Sun," and "Dry September"; all except "A Justice" had been previously published. Four of these six Yoknapatawpha stories were later used in "The Village" section of *Collected Stories* ("Red Leaves" and "A Justice" being shifted to the "Wilderness" section since they chronicle the region's earlier history). Rather than exploiting the obvious links between stories, such as the Indian characters in "Red Leaves" and "A Justice," the use of Quentin Compson as the narrator in "A Justice" and "That Evening Sun," and the appearance of Hawkshaw the barber in "Hair" and "Dry September," Faulkner chose a more contrapuntal structure that juxtaposes the stories focused on the white residents of Jefferson with stories concerned with the Indians from whom the land was acquired and the blacks whose legacy of servitude colors their condition. Millgate notes that "the recurrence of characters, setting, situations, and themes provokes the recollection and hence the continuing coexistence of the earlier story or stories and produces a total effect of progressive enrichment" (*Achievement* 262).

"Red Leaves" opens the section with a portrait of a slaveholding Indian tribe whose decadence is contrasted with the heroic resistance of Doom's slave against the custom that dictates the ritual death of the dead chief's slave; though ultimately caught, he dies nobly. As the codes of the New South take over in "A Rose for Emily," Emily Grierson's struggle against change and death provides a parallel to the slave's attempt to escape the dictates of Indian society. "A Justice," narrated by Quentin Compson rather than the previous story's collective narrator, returns the focus to the days of the Indians, relating not only the origins of Sam Fathers but also Doom's legal maneuvers to keep Herman Basket from illicit liaisons with one slave's wife. In "Hair," passion is more self-controlled: Hawkshaw, the barber, faithfully discharges his debt to his widow's mother by paying the mortgage on her house, although when his obligation is completed, he marries the orphan girl whose hair he has cut since her youth. In contrast, the forces of violence are out of control in "That Evening Sun," which depicts young Quentin's distance from and only partial comprehension of the impending confrontation between Nancy and her angry ex-husband, as well as Mr. Compson's exasperation and ineffectuality. The weather-related violence in "Dry September" is perpetrated by whites whose prejudice is aroused by rumors that a black watchman has raped a fortyish spinster known for her supposed instability and fantasies. While the final stories of the other sections depict an altered awareness following a confrontation of some extreme experience, the conclusion of "Dry September" establishes a more somber mood and suggests that the lynching has only exacerbated the prejudice and hatred.

The final section was created from three previously unsold stories: "Mistral," "Divorce in Naples," and "Carcassonne," all of which feature Americans abroad and concern, according to Millgate, "the enlargement or extension of experience" (*Achievement* 262) in a tragic world. The paired protagonists in the first two stories confront very different types of infidelities, which heighten their awareness of mutability and deceit, while "Carcassonne" concludes the volume with a lyric coda focusing on the world of the imagination. Faulkner later preserved this unit as the final three stories in the concluding section of *Collected Stories*, "Beyond."

FURTHER READING

Showett, H. K. "A Note on Faulkner's Title, *These Thirteen.*" *Notes on Mississippi Writers* 9 (1976): 120–122.
Skei, Hans H. "William Faulkner's Short Story Sending Schedule and His First Short Story Collection, *These 13*: Some Ideas." *Notes on Mississippi Writers* 11 (1979): 64–72.

Robert M. Luscher

"THRIFT," a short story by Faulkner, was published in the *Saturday Evening Post* in September 1930 and included in the *O. Henry Memorial Award Prize Stories* for that year. It also appears in *Uncollected Stories*. The comic plot is based on the stereotype of a Scotsman's frugality. MacWyrglinchbeath serves in the British army for four years. His actions, including refusing leave and declining a promotion, all turn on economic motives. A neighbor at home maintains the soldier's livestock and his accumulating income. MacWyrglinchbeath collects his money to the penny and retrieves his horse and cow. He decides the neighbor can keep the calf born of the cow because the cost of claiming ownership would outweigh the calf's value.

FURTHER READING

Skei, Hans H. "A Forgotten Faulkner Story: 'Thrift.' " *Mississippi Quarterly* 32 (Summer 1979): 453–460.

Diane Brown Jones

TILL, EMMETT, a fourteen-year-old black youth from Chicago, while visiting relatives in Greenwood, Mississippi, in 1955, was abducted and murdered by a group of white supremacists. The atrocity, which received international media attention and became a catalyst for civil rights reform in the South, prompted one of Faulkner's most compelling and passionate statements on racial justice. In a news release written in Rome while en route home following a cultural assignment for the U.S. Department of State, Faulkner emphasized the equal rights of all Americans and concluded: "[I]f we in America have reached that point in our desperate culture when we must murder children, no matter for what reason or what color, we don't deserve to survive, and probably won't" (*ESPL* 223).

Robert W. Hamblin

TODAY WE LIVE (1933) is the only screenplay that Faulkner adapted from one of his own fictional works, a short story entitled "Turn About." The film, which was directed by Howard Hawks, is essentially a tale of romance and heroism during World War I, depicting how the war changes dramatically the relationships of lovers and friends alike. Hawks once said that he found Faulkner, who coauthored five films for him, an obliging collaborator. This was demonstrated by Faulkner's willingness to manufacture, at the request of the studio, a role out of whole cloth for Joan Crawford in the film, in order to take advantage of the star's box office appeal. Movie critics across the land praised the film, which boasts some stunning air and sea battles, as a top-notch action picture.

FURTHER READING

Hogue, Peter. "Hawks and Faulkner: *Today We Live.*" *Literature/Film Quarterly* 9.1 (1981): 51–58.

Gene D. Phillips

TO HAVE AND HAVE NOT (1944), a film directed by Howard Hawks. Faulkner coauthored the screenplay, which was derived from the Ernest Hemingway novel—making this film the only one in cinema history to be the creative product of two Nobel Prize winners. In the movie Humphrey Bogart plays Harry Morgan, a self-styled adventurer in Martinique during World War II. Morgan gets involved in smuggling to safety French Resistance fighters, who are fugitives from the pro-Nazi Vichy government. The critical and popular success of this engrossing wartime melodrama vindicated the confidence that Hawks placed in Faulkner, who cowrote five films for the director. Indeed, this classic film remains one of Hawks's—and Faulkner's—finest motion pictures.

FURTHER READING

Faulkner, William, and Jules Furthman. *To Have and Have Not: A Screenplay.* Ed. Bruce Kawin. Madison: University of Wisconsin Press, 1980.
Phillips, Gene. *Hemingway and Film.* New York: Ungar, 1980.

Gene D. Phillips

"TOMORROW," a short story by Faulkner that first appeared in the *Saturday Evening Post* in November 1940 and, later, in *Knight's Gambit.* The story presents an individual's capacity to love and how this love is threatened by justice and the law. The central action, narrated by Gavin Stevens's nephew, Charles

"Chick" Mallison, involves the one case Stevens claims that he lost even though justice had been on his side. Bookwright, from Frenchman's Bend, is tried for killing Buck Thorpe, who ran off with Bookwright's daughter. The jury is hung by Stonewall Jackson Fentry, who years before had taken in, nursed, and then married a young woman the night before she died in childbirth. For nearly three years Fentry raises the child alone until the young boy is taken by the mother's relatives. The child returns to Frenchman's Bend some years later as the troublemaker Buck Thorpe.

FURTHER READING

Barbera, Jack. "Tomorrow and Tomorrow and Tomorrow." *Southern Quarterly* 19 (1981): 183–197.

Bradford, M. E. "Faulkner's 'Tomorrow' and the Plain People." *Studies in Short Fiction* 2 (1965): 235–240.

Duvall, John N. "Silencing Women in 'The Fire and the Hearth' and 'Tomorrow.' " *College Literature* 16 (1989): 75–82.

Howell, Elmo. "Faulkner's Enveloping Sense of History: A Note on 'Tomorrow.' " *Notes on Contemporary Literature* 3 (1973): 5–6.

Lahey, Michael E. "Trying Emotions: Unpredictable Justice in Faulkner's 'Smoke' and 'Tomorrow.' " *Mississippi Quarterly* 46 (1993): 447–462.

Larry Wharton

TOMORROW (film). As early as 1942, Faulkner envisioned a film adaptation of his 1940 story, writing to Harold Ober that he "will write a picture idea, to sell the story and picture both to a studio" (*SL* 164–165). Although Faulkner never followed through with his plan, the tale did eventually find its way into a visual medium. It first aired on *Playhouse 90*, with the teleplay written by Horton Foote. In 1972, Paul Roebling and Gilbert Pearlman chose "Tomorrow" as their effort to produce films based on American literary classics (Kawin 63).

Dependent once again upon the talents of the Oscar-winning Horton Foote, the screenplay of "Tomorrow" constitutes a close and faithful adaptation of Faulkner's tale. Running 102 minutes, the film nicely manages to encapsulate both Gavin Stevens's gradual insights into human nature and the interior plot featuring the profundity and depth of Jackson Fentry's devotion to the woman and child. While the trial and jury deliberations that frame the film are very brief in comparison to Fentry's marital drama, they nevertheless help to reinforce one of the central themes: Stevens's (referred to as Lawyer Douglas in the film) underestimation of humankind's endless capacity for love, in spite of numerous, almost insurmountable, obstacles. Stevens's narrow assumptions about Fentry and the complexities and mysteries of the human heart in general and then his eventual maturation are visually expressed by the film's outstanding photography by Alan Green.

The employment of strictly black and white photography enhances the metaphorical plea for replacing stereotypical and rash assumptions about people with shades of gray. At the opening of the film, Stevens's voice-over narration (Peter Masterson) is accompanied visually by harsh lighting, and the absence of subtle shadow continues until the entry of Sarah (Olga Bellini) into Fentry's (Robert Duvall) life. As these two bond, the lighting softens, hence visually reinforcing their growing affection.

In turn, the editing by Reva Schlesinger also illuminates the evolution and strengthening of their union. The film opens with rapid-fire sequences, suggesting the impulsive, reckless behavior and thought of those quick to criticize Fentry's actions. With the coupling of Fentry and Sarah, the film gradually moves to incorporate long shots and lengthy scenes, and such a rhythm imposes forced and thoughtful consideration upon the viewer, enabling one to better understand the complexity of the workings of the human heart. At the film's close, the editing resumes its earlier pace. While one juror derides Fentry for his refusal to acquit, we witness a montage of his fond remembrances of raising the boy. Again, Stevens offers his insights in a voice-over, though this time his views have matured, as evidenced by his confession that "I could never have guessed Fentry's capacity to love." The film ends with a long sequence of Fentry's lonely ride back to his farm and Stevens's further expressions of awe and respect for man's ability to "endure, tomorrow and tomorrow and tomorrow."

FURTHER READING

Rollyson, Carl E. "Faulkner into Film: 'Tomorrow' and 'Tomorrow.' " *Mississippi Quarterly* 32 (1979): 437–452.

Kathy G. Willingham

TOTALITARIANISM. In many of his public statements in the 1950s, and in such novels as *A Fable, The Town*, and *The Mansion*, Faulkner expressed great concern over the threat to individual autonomy represented by the rise of totalitarian and militaristic governments around the world. After World War II, Faulkner was increasingly vocal in his challenges to the docility he saw in contemporary individuals, giving particular attention to what he considered as an easy retreat into group identity or ideology. Faulkner held that the health of the community depended not on group allegiance so much as upon the vitality of independent members. He would link a number of American failings, in particular racism, to group thinking, or a failure of individual assessment. Indications of Faulkner's antitotalitarianism may be found in recorded comments made while serving as writer-in-residence at the University of Virginia, in speeches made in the 1950s, such as the Pine Manor graduation speech, and in essays such as "On Fear" and "On Privacy." Political readings of Faulkner's later novels reveal an even stronger antitotalitarian strain, particularly in *A Fable*. In an unpublished preface to this novel, Faulkner made explicit his opposition to the belief that any particular ideology would solve human problems. The preface takes strong issue with the idea that one political system or nation battling another political system or nation might actually end war, establish peace, or provide human happiness. In the preface, Faulkner disavows any faith in "nations or governments or ideologies" as defenders against wars or outside influence. Rather, he implores "simple human beings vulnerable to death and injury" to become fully conscious of their power to confront and overrun the militarists.

FURTHER READING

Faulkner, William. "A Note on *A Fable.*" *A Faulkner Miscellany*, ed. Meriwether. 162–163.

Joseph R. Urgo

"TO THE VOTERS OF OXFORD," an open appeal that Faulkner wrote, paid to have printed in leaflet form, and had distributed to the townspeople of Oxford in 1950. Now called the "Beer Broadside," the leaflet advocates legalized beer sales in Faulkner's hometown by lampooning an earlier printed notice circulated by three Oxford ministers who favored a "dry" community. After offering a humorous point-by-point refutation of the ministers' arguments, Faulkner concludes with a serious call for the separation of church and state: "Yours for a freer Oxford, where publicans can be law abiding publicans six days a week, and Ministers of God can be Ministers of God all seven days in the week, as the Founder of their Ministry commanded them to when He ordered them to keep out of temporal politics in His own words: 'Render unto Caesar the things that are Caesar's and to God the things that are God's.' "

Louis Daniel Brodsky

TOWN, THE, published in 1957 and issued in paperback in 1961, is the second volume of Faulkner's *Snopes* trilogy. The novel was written coterminously with Faulkner's busiest period as a public figure, national spokesperson, and literary authority. He published a series of essays just prior to and during its composition, including "Mississippi" (1954), "On Privacy" (1955), "On Fear" (1956), and "If I Were a Negro" (1956). In addition, Faulkner wrote letters to newspaper editors on a variety of political issues, gave public lectures to such audiences as the Southern Historical Association, the Athens Academy, and the Academy of Arts and Letters, and maintained a demanding travel schedule.

The public role Faulkner had assumed in the 1950s is reflected in the very public quality of *The Town*. In addition to the demands of his personal calendar, Faulkner's home region was in the midst of its most demanding period of social and political tension since the Civil War. The intertwining of writing and politics is underscored by the fact that among the notes and genealogies on Snopes from which Faulkner was working, and on the verso of many typescript pages of *The Town*, are numerous drafts of letters to various individuals and newspapers concerning not only civil rights and Negroes but communism and other social issues and problems. Hence it is clear that ideas of "town," community and politics, and public personae were central to Faulkner's thinking during the writing of the second volume of *Snopes*. Never a social realist, Faulkner's novel of local politics has little to do with the issues he addressed on the verso of the manuscript pages. Rather, the novel is concerned with the cognitive processes by which community issues are understood and acted upon by the private citizen.

The Town, which takes place in the 1920s and 1930s, is divided into twenty-four chapters, narrated alternately (but not in any particular sequence) by three characters: Charles Mallison, Gavin Stevens, and V. K. Ratliff. The narrators engage in an extended dialogue and attempt to come to terms with the integration of Snopeses into Jefferson. Ratliff and Stevens have the most interaction with the Snopeses, while Mallison provides critical commentary, contradicting in particular the more self-serving identification provided by Stevens. It is evident throughout the novel that Stevens and Ratliff have an animosity toward Snopeses far in excess of any rational response; Stevens sees them as acting like "colonies of rats or termites . . . like an invasion of snakes or wildcats." Individual Snopeses appearing in *The Town*, such as Wallstreet, the grocery entrepreneur, disprove such blanket judgments. Nonetheless, as Mallison observes, Gavin becomes obsessed with the danger posed by Snopeses in Jefferson and cannot let go of his initial negative impression, "like something wound up that couldn't even run down, let alone stop."

Erroneous judgment, counterstatement, competing articulations—all such utterances contribute to the "incessant appeaseless voices" of the novel. Faulkner's community knows itself by the words it uses to describe itself and its components. In *The Town* the community is characterized by a continual ideological activity in which narrators attempt to discern what can be known authoritatively and to project that authority publicly. Snopeses, however, threaten to expose those voices as contrived and duplicitous, serving primarily to protect and reinforce such entrenched figures as Stevens and Ratliff. The ongoing discussion about "facts and truth" in the novel illustrates this issue. Facts often get in the way of politics, usually resulting in a suppression of the facts. Gavin's lie to Linda about the identity of her father and Flem's planting whiskey in Montgomery Ward's shop are equally instances in which facts need to be ignored or manufactured to protect community truths.

The central theme of *The Town* transcends its various and sometimes very complicated plot incidents. The novel is concerned above all its details with the immensely complex set of motivations behind any human action or utterance. When Ratliff tells the story of how Flem got his start in Frenchman's Bend, for example, he mystifies events to which he was witness and, in some cases, a participant. The reason he does this is unclear, except that it serves to fuel his own hostility for Flem. The novel's plot revolves around various instances where Stevens and Ratliff (and Flem, in important parallel) attempt to align events to their vision of how things should be. Central events—Eula's affair with Manfred de Spain, Flem's takeover of the bank, Eula's suicide—are discussed and probed. These discussions do not entirely clarify the respective incidents (for example, it is not clear that there has ever been an affair between Eula and de Spain), but they do reveal quite a bit about each narrator's biases and background. And because there is no authorial voice (no one to say "probably true enough" as in *Absalom, Absalom!*), the reader is left with indeterminacy as the primary content of political and intellectual processes.

Faulkner's characterization of Flem Snopes becomes more complex in *The Town* than it was when he introduced him in *The Hamlet*. The revelation of his impotence at the close of the novel adds personal motivation as well as social commentary to his ambitions in Jefferson. The absence of hostility for him on the part of Eula complicates immensely the simplistic and often sophomoric conception of their marriage proffered by Stevens. The way in which Flem is described in key passages ("he knew now that he not only had not the education with which to cope with those who did have education, whom he must outguess and outfigure and despoil, but that he never would have that education now") suggests a certain implicit sympathy born of anxieties shared between Flem and Faulkner. Faulkner's repeated insistence in the 1950s that he was not a literary man in the academic sense of the word mirrors the deficiencies felt by Flem as he sought entry into the monied and pedigreed classes of Jefferson.

Critical reaction to *The Town*, unfortunately, has been unenthusiastic. In part the novel has been a victim of critical biases against the concerns that drive Faulkner's fiction of the 1950s. It is also a very folksy novel, written in an era of more urban and precise focus. The novel serves as an intellectual commentary on the *Snopes* trilogy as a whole, and as such it does not stand impressively as an independent text. It lacks the colorful qualities of *The Hamlet* and the dramatic sense of closure and summation in *The Mansion*. It is also a demanding narrative that is concerned not with major issues of the century but minor, nagging issues of domestic and small-town politics. Early critics, such as Cleanth Brooks (*Yoknapatawpha Country* 216), suggested that the reader might skip the novel and move directly from *The Hamlet* to *The Mansion* in terms of plot. However, such initial frustration with the novel has been overcome, and the indispensable place of the midsection of the *Snopes* trilogy is now secure. Attention has been drawn to the novel's meditation on civic reputation and influence, marriage and family, gender characterizations, narrative method, use of language, and other issues relevant to recent critical debate.

FURTHER READING

Beck, Warren. *Man in Motion: Faulkner's Trilogy*. Madison: University of Wisconsin Press, 1961.

Horton, Merrill. *Annotations to William Faulkner's* The Town. New York: Garland, 1996.

Little, Anne Colclough. "Reconsidering Maggie, Charles, and Gavin in *The Town*." *Mississippi Quarterly* 46 (1993): 463–477.

Moses, Edwin. "Comedy in *The Town*." *Faulkner: The Unappeased Imagination*, ed. Carey. 59–73.

Polk, Noel. "Faulkner and Respectability." *Fifty Years of Yoknapatawpha*, ed. Fowler and Abadie. 110–133.

Towner, Theresa M. " 'It Aint Funny A-Tall': The Transfigured Tales of *The Town*." *Mississippi Quarterly* 44 (1991): 321–335.

Urgo. *Faulkner's Apocrypha*.

Watson, James G. *The Snopes Dilemma: Faulkner's Trilogy*. Coral Gables, Fla.: University of Miami Press, 1968.

Wilson, Raymond J., III. "Imitative Flem Snopes and Faulkner's Causal Sequence in *The Town*." *Twentieth Century Literature* 26 (1980): 432–444.

Joseph R. Urgo

TRANSLATIONS. Almost all works by Faulkner have now been translated, the first one, *Soldiers' Pay* in 1932 in Norway, the last *The Marble Faun* in France in 1992. James Meriwether's compilation of translations in *The Literary Career of William Faulkner* listed twenty-nine countries. Although not included in the list, "Victory" and "Death Drag" were already available in Chinese in 1958, according to H. R. Stoneback. Faulkner's works have since become available in additional languages, including Ukrainian, Lithuanian, Estonian, Georgian, Armenian, Bengali, Burmese, and Catalan. Further translations have appeared in Hungarian, Russian, Rumanian, Japanese, Turkish, Finnish, Swedish, Greek, and Serbo-Croat (Roman and Cyrillic alphabets). Spanish translations were at first more numerous in Latin America, particularly in Argentina where Jorges Luis Borges's translation of *The Wild Palms* was published in 1940. The 1934 publication in Spain of *Sanctuary* was followed, as Myriam Dîaz-Diocaretz has noted, by an "editorial silence" that ended in 1947. Dîaz-Diocaretz suggests as a topic for further study that it is "highly likely that at least some of the Spanish translations of Faulkner's oeuvre came from the French" (37) rather than having been translated directly from English. Translations in German and French continue to flourish, with reprints and retranslations. On the other hand, relatively few more have appeared in Dutch: Petra Gallert indicates "the only frequently reprinted novel is *Sanctuary*" ("Dutch" 386). A number of Italian translations are out of print. The works most often translated are *Sanctuary, The Wild Palms, Light in August, The Unvanquished* (most recently in Chinese in 1994), "A Rose for Emily," and "The Bear" (the only Faulkner work available in Bengali and Burmese).

The lack of an earlier and more significant response in certain countries, such as Turkey, China, Russia, and Japan, can be explained by the difference between Faulkner's culture and language and the political history of these countries. For Turkey, Necla Aytür explains that "in a society where all ties with the past were considered as chains holding it down from progress, Faulkner's preoccupation with the past as a living quality in the present was all but incomprehensible" (36). In China, the cultural revolution slowed down the progress of translations (Stoneback). In Russia, the early publication of three short stories— "That Evening Sun" (1934), "Artist at Home" (1935), and "Victory"

(1936)—was followed by a twenty-year silence. The Russian translation of *Absalom, Absalom!* was not published until 1980. Faulkner's depiction of the post-bellum South found echoes in postwar Japan, where Faulkner's 1950 Nobel Prize induced many translations.

Although Faulkner's translatability is evaluated variously, the Faulknerian text poses a number of challenges. Linguistic problems arise from Faulkner's use of Southern slang, compounds (often coined by him), "negative ultimates" (the prefix "un" and suffix "less"), and swear words that in English are frequently religiously or sexually based. For the profanity, German translators, for example, have to draw on scatological terminology or select words from the animal kingdom. Faulkner's stylistic features pose additional challenges, in particular his frequent lack of punctuation, his repetitions (of phrases or words such as "ditch" in *The Sound and the Fury* and "shucks" in *Sanctuary*), and his use of pronouns without antecedents. Necla Aytür points out that in Turkish, "in which even the invariable *o* that stands for all genders of the third person singular is generally omitted, it is sometimes impossible to guess who is being referred to in a given clause or sentence" (29), as opposed to English, in which there are distinct words for masculine, feminine, and neuter genders of the third-person singular pronoun.

Translators often have the tendency to homogenize and simplify the original, straighten out the grammatical irregularities ("I says," "I hears"), and normalize the punctuation. One of the most telling examples is French translator M.-E. Coindreau's "annexation" of Faulkner's loose sentence into classic French syntax.

The cultural problems are manifold. First, Faulkner's work owes a debt to the tradition of southwestern humor and tall tales. Hence comic aspects are often missed by translators, in particular in France where early readings and commentators focused on the tragic. Also, Faulkner's text develops along numerous intertextual biblical and literary (Shakespearean, for instance) references. Finally, Faulkner's work emerges out of a Mississippian milieu, with local references ranging from farming and hunting to Southern dishes (such as cornbread) and fauna (dogwood, gum). Text-oriented and reader-oriented approaches are practiced by translators.

The most arduous and debated issue concerns the rendering of the variety of Faulkner's dialects. Faulkner distinguishes four dialects in his writing: "The dialect, the diction, of the educated semi-metropolitan white Southerner, the dialect of the backwood Southerner, and the dialect of the Negro—four, the dialect of the Negro who has been influenced by the Northern cities, who has been to Chicago and Detroit" (*FIU* 125). Coindreau's statement that it is "a detail of slight importance" was unfortunately shared by many translators who flattened out Faulkner's text by rendering it in colloquial speech or in the local dialect of their native region; for example, Eberhard Boecker points to Herberth E. Herlitschka's use of the Berlin underworld dialect to translate the language of Popeye and his fellow gangsters (68). Dîaz-Diocaretz laments that in Bruguera's translations of *The Sound and the Fury* "all the characters speak in standard Spanish" (43). Critical examination of these problems has led to re-translations, particularly in Russia, Germany, and France. Such issues give grounds for the study between translation and history and the historical positioning of the translator.

FURTHER READING

Aytür, Necla. "Faulkner in Turkish." *William Faulkner: Prevailing Verities and World Literature*. Ed. Z. T. Wolodymyr and W. M. Aycock. Lubbock: Texas Tech University, 1973. 25–40.

Boecker, Eberhard. *William Faulkner's Later Novels in German*. Tübingen, Germany: Max Niemeyer Verlag, 1973.

Chapdelaine, Annick. "Translating the Comic: A Case Study of *Sanctuaire*." *Faulkner Journal* 8.2 (1993): 67–83.

Dîaz-Diocaretz, Myriam. "Faulkner's Spanish Voice/s." *Faulkner: International Perspectives*, ed. Fowler and Abadie. 30–59.

Gallert, Petra M. "Dutch and Belgian Translations of Faulkner: A Checklist." *Mississippi Quarterly* 37 (1984): 385–388.

———. "German-Language Translations of Faulkner." *Mississippi Quarterly* 35 (1982): 283–300.

———. "Italian Translations of Faulkner." *Mississippi Quarterly* 36 (1983): 329–336.

Kreiswirth, Martin. "Faulkner as Translator: His Versions of Verlaine." *Mississippi Quarterly* 30 (1977): 429–432.

Landor, Mikhail. "William Faulkner: New Translations and Studies." *Soviet Literature* 8 (1968): 180–185.

Ohashi, Kenzaburo. " 'Native Soil' and the World Beyond: William Faulkner and Japanese Novelists." *Faulkner: International Perspectives*, ed. Fowler and Abadie. 257–275.

Stoneback, H. R. "The Hound and the Antelope: Faulkner in China." *Faulkner: International Perspectives*, ed. Fowler and Abadie. 236–256.

Marie Liénard

TULL, in Faulkner's fiction, is the name of a farm family living near Frenchman's Bend. Cora and Vernon Tull are important characters in *As I Lay Dying*. Apart from the members of the Bundren family, they are the most prominent of the novel's fifteen narrators, nine of its fifty-nine chapters being assigned to them. Two daughters, Kate and Eula, are also mentioned. In *The Hamlet*, where they have four daughters, the Tulls have smaller roles to play: Vernon is injured by Eck Snopes's pony, and Cora loses her suit for damages against Eck because he does not have a bill of sale. The Tulls are also mentioned in *The Town* and *The Mansion*. In *As I Lay Dying*, the Tullses' successful marriage, thrift and diligence, and all-too-conventional common sense mark them as foils to the tragic, heroic, and pathetically outrageous Bundrens. Nevertheless, they emerge as interesting characters in their own right. If Addie and Anse Bundren remind one at times of the biblical Job and his wife, the Tulls are a couple out of the book of Proverbs. Cora emulates (and at moments parodies) the model wife of

Proverbs 31, and Vernon, honored for common sense, diligence, and good-heartedness, rejoices in the wife of his youth to the point of seeming henpecked, finally elevating Cora to the status of Lady Wisdom herself. Cora, like Addie a former teacher, could never sink to Addie's level of cruelty, nor love or hate as intensely. She and Vernon represent the safety of conventional wisdom and will never touch the extremes of life reached by the Bundrens. Yet Vernon in particular wins our approval not only by his stalwart diligence but also by tempering his prudence with sympathy for others and by his wonder, and even mild protest, at some of life's outrageous unfairness.

FURTHER READING

Morrison, Gail Moore. "The House That Tull Built." *William Faulkner's* As I Lay Dying: *A Critical Casebook.* Ed. Diane L. Cox. New York: Garland, 1985. 159–178.

Glenn Meeter

"TURNABOUT" (originally, "Turn About"), a short story by Faulkner, first published in the *Saturday Evening Post* on March 5, 1932, and later collected in *Doctor Martino and Other Stories* and *Collected Stories.* A World War I story based partly on accounts Faulkner had heard from combat veterans, "Turnabout" treats the sometimes bitter rivalry between American and British servicemen. An American aviator, Captain Bogard, befriends a young, drunken British sailor, Claude Hope, and then takes the "boy" on a bombing raid over Germany, believing "it would be a shame for his country to be in this mess for four years and him not even to see a gun pointed in his direction." Demonstrating the adage that "turn about is fair play," Hope repays Bogard for the plane ride with a boat ride, which, to the American's great surprise and discomfort, turns out to be an extremely dangerous torpedo attack against a German U-boat. The story ends with a tribute to the courage of both British sailors and American flyers. "Turnabout" became the basis of *Today We Live* (1933), the first film adaptation of a Faulkner work, the script of which was coauthored by Faulkner.

Robert W. Hamblin

TWAIN, MARK (1835–1910), American writer and humorist, author of *The Adventures of Huckleberry Finn* (1884), *The Adventures of Tom Sawyer* (1876), *Life on the Mississippi* (1883), *A Connecticut Yankee in King Arthur's Court* (1889), and other works. Faulkner once said, "Mark Twain was the first truly American writer, and all of us since are his heirs, we descended from him" (*LIG* 137). On another occasion Faulkner listed Twain among "our predecessors who were the masters from whom we learned our craft" (*FIU* 243); and on yet another he said, "[Sherwood Anderson] was the father of my generation of American writers. . . . [Theodore] Dreiser is his older brother and Mark Twain the father of them both" (*LIG* 249–250). It should be noted that such an exalted view of Twain, expressed late in Faulkner's career, contrasts sharply with the opinion Faulkner held as a fledgling writer. In a 1922 essay he wrote for the student newspaper at Ole Miss, Faulkner had called Twain "a hack writer who would not have been considered fourth rate in Europe" (*EPP* 94). As Michael Millgate has pointed out, though, this negative judgment corresponded to the "European" phase of Faulkner's career; after he had matured and discovered, as Twain had, the literary worth of native American materials, his view of Twain altered considerably (*Achievement* 291–292).

Critics have noted a number of parallels between Faulkner's work and Twain's. As demonstrated by such stories as "Spotted Horses," "Mule in the Yard," and "Centaur in Brass," Faulkner very much belongs to the tradition of the southwestern humorists, delighting just as much as Twain in the use of local dialect, folklore, oral storytelling, and the tall tale. As with Twain, however, Faulkner's humor is almost always utilized for serious purposes, whether it be to show the gullibility of the general populace to Snopesism or to present the self-satire of a monstrous Jason Compson. Another theme the two writers share in common is the contrast between nature and civilization. Faulkner's wilderness, like Twain's river, represents an unrealized or lost ideal of freedom and innocence that contrasts sharply with man-made worlds like Jefferson and Twain's river villages. In Ike McCaslin's attempt to negotiate these conflicting values under the tutelage of Sam Fathers, Faulkner is repeating, if expanding, the pattern Twain had employed in the relationship of Huck and Jim. As these characters reveal, a concern for the subject of race represents a third significant bond between Faulkner and Twain. Lucas Beauchamp and Chick Mallison of *Intruder in the Dust* are another pair of Faulkner characters who have reminded readers of Jim and Huck. An additional similarity between the two writers is that both are historical novelists concerned with the presentness of the past. *A Connecticut Yankee* is no more (and no less) about the past than *Absalom, Absalom!*; and *Huckleberry Finn*, in terms of the time differential between its setting and its date of composition, is almost as retrospective a view of American history as "The Bear."

Many of Faulkner's parallels with Twain are undoubtedly coincidental and unconscious, but in at least one instance Faulkner made conscious and deliberate use of a Twain source. In 1940 Faulkner wrote his editor Robert Haas that he planned to do a book that would be "a sort of Huck Finn," tracing the initiatory journey of a young boy about twelve or thirteen years of age (*SL* 123). That book Faulkner would not write for twenty years, and it would be his last: *The Reivers*.

Robert W. Hamblin

"TWO DOLLAR WIFE," a short story by Faulkner, appeared in *College Life* in 1936. A variant existed as early as 1926, and the evolving story bore the titles "The Devil Beats His Wife" and "Christmas Tree." The plot describes the recklessness of a group of college-aged adults who are celebrating New

Year's Eve with drinking, automobile racing, and gambling. Two dollars is the cost of the marriage license Maxwell Johns and Doris Houston purchased somewhat earlier. Both the license, as yet unused, and Doris become the winnings of a dice game. Although Maxwell's rival wins, Maxwell and Doris stand before the justice of the peace. At home, Doris's brother has swallowed a needle that Maxwell stuck in a chair.

Diane Brown Jones

"TWO SOLDIERS," a short story by Faulkner, is the first published of three stories (the others are "Shingles for the Lord" and "Shall Not Perish") relating to the yeoman Grier family. "Two Soldiers" is told by the younger of two sons, nine years old at the time of the action, which takes place close to the time of first publication (*Saturday Evening Post*, March 28, 1942). The two boys, who have lately been preparing the fields and wood supply for winter, listen to radio news of the Japanese attack on Pearl Harbor, and the younger boy reports that the Japanese "was at the Philippines now but General MacArthur was holding um." (The United States surrendered Bataan on April 9, 1942.) Any implied maturation of the narrator needs to be conditioned by this observation. The story has been criticized for what some consider "jingoism" (Ferguson 42), but little note has been made of the close approximation in style to some of Hemingway's stories, such as "My Old Man." Ma and Pa ["Res"] Grier speak in stereotypical ways effective for the purposes of quick characterization in magazine fiction: "But your blood is good as any blood anywhere, and don't you never forget it." Our sense of the narrator's innocence of the world is complicated by his twice drawing a knife on strangers and his use of the word "nigger" (which was deleted in an early reprinting).

Stephen Hahn

TWO SOLDIERS (film), the American Film Institute's thirty-minute film version of Faulkner's short story, premiered on the Arts and Entertainment television network in 1985 and was released by Monterey Home Video in 1992. Starring Huckleberry Fox as the young Grier boy who seeks to follow his older brother Pete into U.S. military service during World War II, the film was scripted by Albert Black and Lily Trayes, produced by Jacob Bertucci, and directed by Christopher LaPalm. The cinematographer was Gregory Matkosky. One of the best film renditions of a Faulkner work, *Two Soldiers* received outstanding reviews by the judges of the New York Filmmakers' Exposition.

Robert W. Hamblin

U

ULYSSES. See **Joyce, James**.

"UNCLE WILLY," a short story by Faulkner, first appeared in the October 1935 issue of *American Mercury* and later in *Collected Stories*. It is actually an initiation story in which the narrator learns the limits and location of responsibility. A fourteen-year-old boy tells the story of Uncle Willy (Hoke Christian), a drug addict, then a hard drinker who dies in his own airplane trying to escape the do-gooders of the town trying to cure him. The young narrator, as with most of the young boys in town, is awed by Uncle Willy's desire to live life as he chooses, free of legal and social restraints. At the story's end, the young narrator feels guilty because of his complicity in Uncle Willy's plan.

FURTHER READING

Polk, Noel, "Faulkner and Respectability." *Fifty Years of Yoknapatawpha*, ed. Fowler and Abadie. 110–133.
Pothier, Jacques. "Of Rats and Uncles: Time Out of Joint in 'Uncle Willy's Jefferson.' " *Faulkner Studies* 12 (1992): 35–52.
Volpe, Edmond L. "Faulkner's 'Uncle Willy': A Childhood Fable." *Mosaic* 12 (1978): 177–181.

Larry Wharton

UNCOLLECTED STORIES OF WILLIAM FAULKNER, edited by Joseph Blotner and published in 1979 by Random House, makes available forty-five stories that had not been included in other collections of Faulkner's short fiction. Part I includes twenty "Stories Revised for Later Books": "Ambuscade," "Retreat," "Raid," "Skirmish at Sartoris," "The Unvanquished," and "Vendee" (*The Unvanquished*); "Fool About a Horse," "Lizards in Jamshyd's Courtyard," "The Hound," and "Spotted Horses" (*The Hamlet*); "Lion," "The Old

People," "A Point of Law," "Gold Is Not Always," "Pantaloon in Black," "Go Down, Moses" "Delta Autumn," and "The Bear" (*Go Down, Moses*); "Race at Morning" (*Big Woods*); and "Hog Pawn" (*The Mansion*). Blotner includes the magazine versions of these stories, not the texts as made part of the respective novels. Twelve stories, included in Part II, "Uncollected Stories," had been published but never collected, some frankly because Faulkner himself did not care much for them. These twelve include "Nympholepsy," "Frankie and Johnny," "The Priest," "Once Aboard the Lugger (I)" and "Once Aboard the Lugger (II)," "Miss Zilphia Gant," "Thrift," "Idyll in the Desert," "Two Dollar Wife," "Afternoon of a Cow," "Mr. Acarius," and "Sepulture South: Gaslight." In Part III, "Unpublished Stories," thirteen stories were published for the first time, many that Faulkner had unsuccessfully marketed for magazines. They are, as are the stories in the previous two sections, ordered according to Blotner's conclusions as to order of composition from earliest to latest: "Adolescence," "Al Jackson," "Don Giovanni," "Peter," "Moonlight," "The Big Shot," "Dull Tale," "A Return," "A Dangerous Man," "Evangeline," "A Portrait of Elmer," "With Caution and Dispatch," and "Snow."

Blotner observes in the introduction to the volume that the range of stories demonstrates Faulkner's talent when it possessed the rough edges of novice attempts and when it reflected the refinement of masterpieces. The texts of the stories that bear connections with novels are especially instructive because they demonstrate Faulkner's vision of how plot and perspective could be altered for the demands of the particular genre. The collection makes available to the reading public stories that would otherwise be inconvenient to obtain or unavailable. Since 1979 critics have identified additional stories that might have merited inclusion in *Uncollected Stories*. These minor objections notwithstanding, Blotner's edition of *Uncollected Stories* offers an immense opportunity for readers of Faulkner to access another dimension of his genius.

FURTHER READING

Brooks, Cleanth. "His Somewhat Lesser Sound and Fury." *Saturday Review* 10 November 1979: 51–53.
Fadiman, Regina K. "Miscellany from the Lumber Room." *Southern Literary Journal* 12.2 (1980): 137–144.

Diane Brown Jones

UNIVERSITY OF MISSISSIPPI. In Faulkner's time, the University of Mississippi (Ole Miss) was largely separate from the town of Oxford, one mile west of the courthouse square and divided from the town by a deep cut for railroad tracks, although in 1930 Faulkner would purchase Rowan Oak and later Bailey's Woods, contiguous with the campus. The first member of his family to attend the university was his grandfather, John Wesley Thompson Falkner, the "Young Colonel," who matriculated when the university reopened at the end of the War Between the States and went on to gain admission to the Mississippi bar in

1869; in time he would serve as a trustee of Ole Miss. The Young Colonel's influence won Faulkner's father, Murry, a job as business manager and secretary at Ole Miss when Faulkner was a youth. The family moved onto the campus, living in the former Delta Psi house, which faced the central part of campus, still called the Old Grove, and the Lyceum, the dominant building still, as well as a statue of a Confederate soldier; Faulkner would use this setting later in *Sanctuary*. The Delta Psi house also looked out on the home of Calvin S. Brown, a professor of English and classics and the author of a book on Mississippi archaeology that Faulkner owned; he was the most influential university professor in Faulkner's life. The Falkner house was extremely ornate with a round tower attached to the front right of the building; after a brief period Faulkner moved out of the back bedroom on the second floor and up into the small tower room where he could read and write in solitude.

Faulkner's formal education was desultory. He never completed high school and so entered Ole Miss as a special student after his return from Canada in late 1918. He never took a full load and apparently attended his classes sporadically; he did not take final examinations. At the end of his first semester, he had earned an A in French, a B in Spanish, and a D in English. In the second semester, he dropped English but earned another A in French and another B in Spanish. The poems he was then writing showed a predominantly French influence, and he spent far more time and energy on his writing than on his classes. His first publication was a poem in the yearbook *Ole Miss*; others followed in the student newspaper *The Mississippian* and the Oxford *Eagle*. One of his poems, given his affectations of dress, behavior, and verse, was parodied by an anonymous student author. In the late spring of 1920 Faulkner won a $10 prize from Professor Brown for the best poem submitted to him that year. He also published his first story, "Landing in Luck," in *The Mississippian*, as well as reviews of Conrad Aiken, Eugene O'Neill, and others.

By the time he was establishing himself as a campus writer, Faulkner was already well known as an artist, with stylized drawings resembling those of Aubrey Beardsley and popular in such Northern magazines as *The Smart Set*. His first published drawings of a couple dancing introduced the "Social Activities" section of the 1916–1917 yearbook. In 1920 his friend Louis Cochran was appointed editor of *Ole Miss* and commissioned five drawings from Faulkner (which he signed adding a "u" to his name), who was also listed as one of six art editors. The pen-and-ink work included a full-page spring scene; a drawing of Harlequin, Pierette, and Mezzetino in the costumes of commedia dell'arte against a background of checkered parquet and candelabra; a couple dancing the Charleston; and a Frenchman flirting with an American officer in the AEF (American Expeditionary Forces) Club. Faulkner also joined the campus theater group, The Marionettes, working with them on the staging of *The Arrival of Kitty* in January 1921 and then serving as stage manager for *Green Stockings*. His one-act play *The Marionettes*, about Pierrot and Marietta, was written in the fall of 1920; he prepared the illustrations and published it himself, lettering, decorating, and binding it by hand.

Faulkner may have been encouraged to attend Ole Miss because his older brother Murry ("Jack") enrolled at the same time as a regular student under the special dispensation given war veterans; Jack completed two years of liberal arts, followed by two years of law before initiating a career in Texas with the FBI. Both brothers joined the Sigma Alpha Epsilon fraternity. Later, Faulkner would be employed on the campus on three separate occasions: to paint the old Geology Building, which with its high and somewhat dangerous architecture resembled the family home at the Delta Psi house; in 1921 to serve as the acting postmaster for the university; and in 1930, after his marriage to Estelle, to work nights stoking the furnace in the power plant where, he later falsely claimed, he had written all of *As I Lay Dying* in six weeks. Of the three jobs, that of postmaster was longest and most notorious. The post office was housed in the University Store building (along with a bookstore, a barbershop, and soda fountain); it no longer exists. There it was Faulkner's job to post mail and packages and to deliver the mail, stored in boxes, to faculty, staff, and students. But he was desultory at this job, according to bitterly complaining patrons; often he lost mail, and frequently he was slow in getting it out or in delivering it. He was, it seemed, always distracted, either reading or playing cards with his friends. It is now thought, however, that he was also deeply engaged at this time in his own private course of study, reading widely in French, Russian, and English literature and even perusing the magazines and newspapers addressed to his customers. After complaints mounted and were unsatisfactorily answered, he was presented on September 2, 1924, with a three-page letter from Postal Inspector Mark Webster of Corinth, charging him on seven counts of misconduct. When he was fired from the post, he told friends the job never interested him anyway, that the "beck and call" of his customers merely distracted him.

In the spring of 1946 Faulkner returned to the Ole Miss classroom at the invitation of a graduate instructor, Margaret Parker, to talk to her English class for a quarter of an hour. He went on the conditions that there be no publicity and that no professors would be present; then he spent an hour discussing what he considered the major influences on his work—the Old Testament, Melville, Dostoevsky, and Conrad—and others of his contemporaries and their work. The following spring, at the invitation this time of Professor A. Wigfall Green, he agreed to return to campus—again on the condition that no faculty would be present and that no students would take notes. This time he taught six sessions, receiving $250.

In 1971, after the death of Faulkner and his wife, the university bought Rowan Oak, Faulkner's home since 1930, which borders the campus and is today maintained by the university as a national historic site.

See also **Postmaster**.

FURTHER READING

Collins, ed. *William Faulkner: Early Prose and Poetry.*
Faulkner, William. *The Marionettes.* Ed. Noel Polk. Charlottesville: Bibliographical Society of the University of Virginia, 1977.

Walton, Gerald. "The Falkners and the University, Mississippi, Post Office." *Faulkner Journal* 5 (1989): 49–50.

―――. "William C. Falkner, Postmaster: Some Correspondence." *Journal of Mississippi History* 51 (1989): 1–15.

Arthur F. Kinney

UNIVERSITY OF VIRGINIA. *See* **Virginia**.

"UNVANQUISHED, THE." *See* **"Riposte in Tertio."**

UNVANQUISHED, THE, Faulkner's tenth novel, published in 1938 as the seventh of his Yoknapatawpha novels, began in 1934 as a series of Civil War short stories centering on Bayard Sartoris and his black companion Ringo. Five of the stories were published in the *Saturday Evening Post* and became, with some revision, the first five chapters of the novel. A sixth, "Skirmish at Sartoris," appeared in *Scribner's* after being rejected by the *Post* under the title "Drusilla" and became the novel's sixth chapter. Six of the novel's seven chapters thus saw publication between September 29, 1934, and December 5, 1936, and were written during the time when Faulkner was heavily involved in his other Civil War novel, *Absalom, Absalom!*, whose central character, Thomas Sutpen, is described in *The Unvanquished* as a rival of John Sartoris. In 1937, having received encouragement from Random House for his proposal to convert the Bayard-Ringo stories into a novel, Faulkner made a number of revisions; notable among them are the inclusion of the scheme of the McCaslin brothers for the emancipation of their slaves through self-purchase ("Retreat") and the haunting picture of crowds of newly freed, displaced slaves thronging the roads. He then added a final chapter, "An Odor of Verbena," after it was rejected for magazine publication by the *Post*.

The novel opens with Bayard Sartoris as a Mississippi boy of twelve in the summer of 1862, and it ends with Bayard as a law student of twenty-four in October 1873. Bayard narrates from the position of an unspecified number of years later. His first five chapters have to do with the war, a time in which Colonel John Sartoris, his father, is largely absent from the plantation—fighting in Virginia and then, after his regiment deposes him, riding with his own irregular cavalry in Mississippi. In his absence, the affairs of the plantation and the home front war are in the charge of Rosa Millard, Sartoris's mother-in-law (his wife having died soon after Bayard's birth), whom both Bayard and Ringo call "Granny." In "Ambuscade" Granny rescues the boys from a Union officer they have tried to shoot, and in succeeding chapters she takes advantage of the gentlemanly behavior of this officer to lead the boys in increasingly daring maneuvers by which they sell Union livestock back to Union troops, with the proceeds going to the local poor and needy. The situation leads to an uncomfortably close association with the freebooter Ab Snopes and finally to Granny's death at the hands of the still-less-scrupulous Grumby. In the fifth chapter Bayard, with the help of Ringo and Uncle Buck McCaslin, tracks down Grumby, kills him, and displays his severed hand over Granny's grave.

In chapter 6 the war is over but is carried on by other means: Sartoris rebuilds his mansion, which was burned by the Yankees, kills two carpetbaggers (the Burdens, previously mentioned in *Light in August*) who are trying to foment a Negro revolution, and sabotages an election that might have installed a former slave as marshal of Jefferson. Meanwhile, the ladies of Jefferson force Sartoris to marry Drusilla, Bayard's cousin who rode with Sartoris's troops for over a year after her fiancé was killed in the war. The last chapter, "Odor of Verbena," begins eight years later: Bayard, home from law school after hearing that his father has been killed by Redmond, a former partner in the railroad he has built, shocks Drusilla and others (including Ringo) by refusing on principle to seek vengeance. Instead, he faces Redmond unarmed; Redmond, after firing two misaimed shots, leaves town. Bayard is now "The Sartoris," inheriting his father's agenda and carrying it forward in a new, more legalistic, age.

Questions about *The Unvanquished* have concerned its relationship to other works involving the Sartorises (*Sartoris/Flags in the Dust*; "There Was a Queen") and to Faulkner's other Civil War novel, *Absalom, Absalom!* The relationship of *The Unvanquished* to Civil War history and to Faulkner's greatgrandfather William C. Falkner is dealt with in Hinkle and McCoy and elsewhere. Some readers, including early reviewers, have welcomed the novel, on the grounds of intelligibility and morality, as a bit of relief from the difficult style and problematized view of Southern history found in works like *Absalom, Absalom!* and *Light in August* and have credited the book's origin in *Saturday Evening Post* stories. Some have blamed the origin in the *Post*, along with Faulkner's own desire to keep the Sartorises "sacrosanct," for the book's apparently more traditional/retrograde view of race relations on the plantation. The novel pictures Ringo as boundlessly enthusiastic for all Sartoris causes, including the exclusion of blacks from voting; and such a characterization is attributed not only to Bayard's smug nostalgia about the Old South but also to Faulkner's. A third, more complicated, view seems in order. Susan Donaldson points out that the novel's last chapter, when Bayard is older, calls into question many of the apparent values of the earlier chapters. Moreover, in "There Was a Queen," Sartoris has a half-black daughter, Elnora—a detail that illustrates that Faulkner does not in fact hold the Sartorises "sacrosanct." It seems, therefore, that we must allow for a separation not only between the beliefs of the earlier and later Bayard but also between Faulkner and his dramatized narrator as well. Future criticism of the novel will have to explore the possibility that the "smug nostalgia" (Taylor 97) of Bayard's narrative is to be read as Bayard's attempt to hide, not merely from the *Post* readership but even from himself, the possibility that Ringo, much like Charles Bon's challenge to the Sutpens in *Absalom, Absalom!*, may be a rival claimant for the title of "The Sartoris."

FURTHER READING

Donaldson, Susan V. "Dismantling the *Saturday Evening Post* Reader: *The Unvan-quished* and Changing 'Horizons of Expectations.' " *Faulkner and Popular Culture*, ed. Fowler and Abadie. 179–195.

Hinkle, James, and Robert McCoy. *Reading Faulkner*: The Unvanquished. Jackson: University Press of Mississippi, 1995.

Kinney, Arthur F. *Critical Essays on William Faulkner: The Sartoris Family*. Boston: G. K. Hall, 1985.

Taylor, Walter. *Faulkner's Search for a South*. 90–98.

Glenn Meeter

V

VARNER, the name of a fictional family in a number of Faulkner's novels and stories. The largest landowners in Frenchman's Bend prior to the arrival of the Snopes clan, Varners make minor appearances in *As I Lay Dying, Light in August, Intruder in the Dust, Knight's Gambit*, and "Shingles for the Lord." The family plays a major role in the *Snopes* trilogy, particularly in *The Hamlet*, where their paternalistic business practices are replaced by Snopes corporatism. Will Varner is introduced as "the chief man of the country," serving as beat supervisor, Justice of the Peace, and election commissioner. His wife, known only as Mrs. Varner, shares her husband's amorality and is upset when news of her daughter's illegitimate pregnancy interrupts her nap. Two of their sixteen children, Jody and Eula, remain at home and play a significant role in ending the Varner dynasty. Jody Varner rents land to Ab Snopes and hires his son, Flem, to tend his store because he fears that Ab will burn his barn (cf. "Barn Burning"). Eula's resistance to male privilege is seen by her refusal to participate in the life prescribed for her by her class and gender. After her marriage to Flem she insists on physical autonomy and passes that independence on to her daughter, Linda Snopes. Eula's effort to live a life of her own definition fails, however, and she commits suicide in *The Town*.

FURTHER READING

Kang, Hee. "Eula Varner Snopes in *The Hamlet*: The Absent Feminine Within Men's Exchange Economy." *Journal of English Language and Literature* 39 (1993): 603–620.

Trouard, Dawn. "Eula's Plot: An Irigararian Reading of Faulkner's *Snopes* Trilogy." *Mississippi Quarterly* 42 (1989): 281–297.

Urgo, Joseph. "Faulkner's Real Estate: Land and Literary Speculation in *The Hamlet*." *Mississippi Quarterly* 48 (1995): 443–457.

Joseph R. Urgo

"VENDÉE," a Faulkner short story published in the *Saturday Evening Post* on December 5, 1936, and revised as the fifth chapter of *The Unvanquished* (1938). As the Civil War ends, teenaged Bayard Sartoris, with the assistance of former slave and playfellow Ringo, avenges the murder of his grandmother Rosa Millard by killing her slayer, the outlaw Grumby. In "Vendée," Bayard Sartoris loses his childhood innocence as he becomes a man, and *The Unvanquished* shifts from a tone of humorous nostalgia to focus on the serious issues of race, gender, and violence during Reconstruction.

FURTHER READING

Meriwether, James B. " 'Vendée': The Short Fiction of William Faulkner." *Proof* 1 (1971): 309.

Veronica Makowsky

VERLAINE, PAUL. *See* **Rimbaud, Arthur.**

"VERSE OLD AND NASCENT: A PILGRIMAGE," an essay by Faulkner published in the April 1925 issue of *The Double Dealer* and later collected by Carvel Collins in *William Faulkner: Early Prose and Poetry*. The earliest of Faulkner's scant autobiographical writings, "Verse" is marred by superficial sexism and a jejune view of writing as a sexual strategy. Yet it illustrates a common pattern in Faulkner's autobiographical revelations—a romantic plot of awakening into enthrallment, pursuit of a path of failure, followed by reorientation on a more productive pathway and a decisive break with the past: "That page is closed to me forever." In addition, "Verse" announces, well before its more evident manifestations, Faulkner's commitment to his native "soil."

Stephen Hahn

"VICTORY," a short story by Faulkner, first appeared in *These 13* (1931) and later in *Collected Stories*. The title is ironic, since the story follows the tragic life of Alec Gray, a young man who, guided by his iron will and determination, leaves home to go to war and never returns. Gray, from a line of Scottish shipwrights, enlists and before he sees action is disciplined and punished. During combat he kills the sergeant-major who disciplined him; in later battles he is twice decorated for heroism. The determination that serves him well in battle and later as he becomes an officer is transposed into a fierce pride after the war, when being an officer offers little reward for a man of no means. His pride becomes destructive as he tries to keep up appearances, even as he is forced to sell matches and live among the homeless.

FURTHER READING

Hook, Andrew. "Faulkner and Sassoon." *Notes and Queries* 41 (1994): 377–378.
Jones, Ann Goodwyn. "Male Fantasies?: Faulkner's War Stories and the Construction of Gender." *Faulkner and Psychology*, ed. Kartiganer and Abadie. 21–55.

Smith, Raleigh W., Jr. "Faulkner's 'Victory': The Plain People of Clydebank." *Mississippi Quarterly* 23 (1970): 241–249.

Larry Wharton

VIRGINIA. In a generally unhappy life, the first half of the 1950s was a particularly miserable time for Bill and Estelle Faulkner. They both were drinking heavily, and Faulkner, now receiving the public recognition that had earlier escaped him, restlessly sought out affairs with younger women. His daughter Jill, now in her late teens, was embarrassed by her parents' behavior. Faulkner was also distressed by the emerging racial crisis in the South. Thus, he was, publicly as well as privately, troubled.

Yet things changed remarkably in the middle of the decade. Jill married an army officer, Paul Summers, in August 1954, after which the couple moved to Charlottesville, Virginia, where Summers entered the Law School. In April 1956, Faulkner was presented with two events that would help make the last six years of his life his most settled and satisfying. First, Jill and Paul Summers gave Faulkner a grandson (and another in 1958); second, he received an offer from Joseph Blotner, his future biographer, and Fred Gwynn, then young members of the English Department at the University of Virginia, to become writer-in-residence there the next spring. Faulkner accepted.

As was the case in those years, Faulkner's public pronouncements often landed him in hot water. Having just arrived in Charlottesville to assume his duties in February 1957, Faulkner was asked by a journalist why he had chosen to spend time in Virginia. Faulkner began by praising the state in conventional terms. Then he added: "I like Virginia, and I like Virginians. Because Virginians are snobs and I like snobs" (*FIU* 12). Though some feathers were ruffled, Faulkner settled in remarkably well.

Over the next two years, he appeared before classes of undergraduates and graduate students to answer questions about his work and other matters, the latter often being questions about race, segregation, civil rights. As Blotner and Gwynn tell it, editing the tapes of some thirty-seven of these sessions was a mammoth task. The published results, *Faulkner in the University* (1959), meant, ironically, that a writer so wedded to the idea of privacy and allegedly heedless of critical opinion ended by speaking extensively about his work. Overall, the book is a record of no little generosity—though not always consistency—on Faulkner's part.

This relative openness undoubtedly derived from Faulkner's sense of well-being in Virginia. As one of his biographers, Joel Williamson, notes, Charlottesville came as a liberation from the close-knit community of Oxford, Mississippi, where he and Estelle had lived practically all their lives and toward which Faulkner, especially, directed great ambivalence. By spending considerable time each year in Virginia—the Faulkners eventually bought a home in Charlottesville—Faulkner was able to fight free of the constricting forces that bound him to his past. The great fictional voice of the presence of the past in the present was thus able to redefine himself a bit by escaping the past.

It helped, of course, that Faulkner was treated as an eminent, world-class writer rather than resented for his racial views or mocked for his incomprehensible "dirty" books. He seemed to find genuine enjoyment in talking with students and faculty about his work. Moreover, he was surrounded by a family that extended into the future rather than reaching backward in time. He adored his grandchildren and a daughter who had a life of her own, and he felt the freedom of not being as financially strapped as he once had been. Jill thought her father "less remote and self-centered" (Williamson 338) in the Charlottesville years. Estelle had stopped drinking, and some of Faulkner's restlessness seemed to have been quelled. A marriage that had often been hell for both of them now became something approaching a consolation.

Faulkner, of course, was far from immune to the traditional Southern respect, bordering on reverence, for Virginia. As the "birthplace of Presidents" and the locus classicus of Southern aristocracy, Virginia allowed Faulkner to escape the somewhat rougher-hewn ambience of the lower South. In short, being in Virginia signaled a rise in status. Indeed, questions about the desegregation crisis evoked from Faulkner a hope, even plea, for Virginia to do the statesmanlike thing and "take the lead in this" (*FIU* 214). If this happened, he argued, the Deep South—Arkansas and Mississippi, Alabama and Georgia—might follow suit and avoid more violence and disruption. Unhappily, in this regard Faulkner's respect for the Old Dominion was not to be rewarded.

During his time in Charlottesville, Faulkner also made ample use of the Albemarle County country clubs for horseback riding and hobnobbing with the local gentry. Formal photographs of the period show him in riding habit, looking every bit what Williamson calls the "gentleman rider," a new persona to add to the series of self-images he had constructed over the years and a reflection of his affinity with the more stylish, relaxed way of life in the upper South. But there was a strong measure of stubbornness bordering on self-destructiveness in Faulkner. He was simply too small and too inept as a rider to command a horse. Over the years he had suffered numerous falls from horses, and in Virginia, there were several more. The results were injuries to his spine and back, accompanied by excruciating pain. The pain in turn led to a downward spiral of heavy drinking and ingestion of pain killers.

The beginning of the end came in December 1961, when Faulkner suffered a bad fall in Virginia, then another in early January 1962, and then another in Oxford later in the month. In mid-June, still in Mississippi, he was again thrown from his horse. His heavy drinking, combined with pain killers, led his nephew Jimmy Faulkner and Estelle to commit him to the sanatorium in Byhalia, Mississippi (just south of Memphis), on July 5. The next day he suffered a heart attack and died.

Richard H. King

"VISION IN SPRING," a poetry sequence that Faulkner wrote, assembled, and hand-bound in 1921 and presented to Estelle Franklin, his future wife. Most critics, including Judith Sensibar and Richard Gray, refer to "Vision in Spring" as an apprentice work. The narrator of the fourteen poems, a figure named Pierrot, emerges inconsistently, never assuming a coherent persona. Sensibar argues that the varying faces of Pierrot allow Faulkner to experiment with identity and perspective. Gray, however, views the "persona of Pierrot as not so much fragmented as lost at several moments in the sequence" (94). Since "Vision in Spring" is clearly an early experimental work, the effect of Pierrot probably lies somewhere between these two poles: Faulkner is indeed experimenting with identity, but he often fails to meet this objective throughout the poems. According to Sensibar, the major literary influences on "Vision in Spring" include Keats, Swinburne, Tennyson, the Symbolists, Conrad Aiken, and Eliot. The questions that Pierrot poses in "The World and Pierrot: A Nocturne" obviously mimic Eliot's lines in Prufrock: "Who am I, thinks Pierrot, who am I / To stretch my soul out rigid across the sky? / Who am I to chip the silence with footsteps, / Then see the silence fill my steps again?"

FURTHER READING

Sensibar, Judith. "Introduction." *Vision in Spring*. By William Faulkner. Austin: University of Texas Press, 1984.

Rebecca Rowley

VISUAL ARTS. Faulkner's fiction offers a startling number of vividly visual scenes, as when Ike McCaslin and the dog Lion confront Old Ben in "The Bear" or when the Sutpen house burns at the end of *Absalom, Absalom!* Faulkner's ability to portray crucial scenes in intensely visual terms can be explained at least in part by his early interest in drawing and painting. Indifferent to most subjects in school, he showed an early passion for drawing and at the age of fourteen won a drawing contest. A few years later, when he was beginning to write poetry as a part-time student and employee at the University of Mississippi (1919–1924), he was also drawing pen-and-ink sketches. His most significant production of this early period was a play, *The Marionettes*, which he produced during the fall of 1920 in at least six hand-lettered and illustrated copies in volumes he bound by hand and presented to friends. His illustrations in *The Marionettes* reflect the strong influence of Aubrey Beardsley's illustrations for Oscar Wilde's play *Salome*. Faulkner's illustrations are less brooding and grotesque than Beardsley's, but the influence is clear. One drawing, for example, portrays a woman gazing at the silhouette of a male figure on a hillside; in the background a nude woman stands in a pond, gesturing vaguely toward the sky. In another, a woman dressed in an erotic costume that prominently exposes her breasts sits between two peacocks. Other illustrations convey with considerable skill and sophistication the dreamy, fanciful nature of the play.

Between 1917 and 1922, Faulkner also produced a series of illustrations that appeared in the University of Mississippi yearbook *Ole Miss* and campus newspaper *The Mississippian*. Many of these highly stylized and even atmospheric drawings were reflective of the flapper era of the 1920s, but the Beardsley influence remains, along with flashes of German expressionism. Joseph Blotner compares these drawings to the illustrations in H. L. Mencken's magazine *The Smart Set*, which helped set the tone for depictions of popular culture in the 1920s (1984 *FAB* 77). The drawings vary in content and style. Men and women in stylish dress are portrayed in angular and elongated exaggeration, often in moments of stylized and frenetic motion. One drawing shows a fashionably dressed couple struggling in a stiff breeze. Another shows a geometrically entangled man and woman dancing what appears to be the Charleston. In both illustrations the background is barely suggested by a carefully placed detail: a tree or a road. Other drawings are more ornate. A Beardsleyesque picture captioned ''Social Activities'' shows an apparently grief-torn man kneeling next to a dancing couple at a party; all three figures are highlighted against a dark background and candelabra. The drawing suggests an allegory of passion and heartbreak. An illustration for a dramatic program for the Marionettes theater group shows a Pierrot figure kneeling in grief or thought.

In addition to *Marionettes*, Faulkner produced a series of handmade volumes during the 1920s. They include *The Lilacs* (1920), *Vision in Spring* (1921), *Mayday* (1926), *Helen: A Courtship* (1926), and *The Wishing Tree* (1927). *Vision in Spring* and *The Wishing Tree* were typed; the three others were lettered by hand. He provided pen-and-ink as well as water color illustrations for some of these volumes, which he bound by hand and presented to family, close friends, or women with whom he was romantically involved (he gave *Vision of Spring* to Estelle Oldham Franklin, whom he later married, and *Mayday* and *Helen: A Courtship* to Helen Baird). Although these volumes are mainly interesting for what they reveal of his developing sensibility as a writer, they show that he invested much time and energy in producing these handcrafted books. Their visual appearance clearly had artistic value for him, and Noel Polk has noted that this concern for the printed appearance of his books continued well into his later career (Introduction to *Marionettes* ix–x).

As the 1920s progressed, Faulkner focused increasingly on his writing, but it is clear that the visual arts gripped his imagination at this early stage and never wholly released their hold. On his trip to Paris in 1925, he visited the Luxembourg Galleries and the Louvre, as well as exhibits of impressionist and cubist paintings, and one can argue that the concepts and methods of modern art had a significant impact on his written work. The most obvious influence was probably Aubrey Beardsley, who, as one critic has suggested, provided Faulkner with a window into the decadent arts movement of the late 1890s. A number of critics have noted Beardsley's influence on characterization in Faulkner's first novel, *Soldiers' Pay*, especially in the characters of Margaret Powers and the satyrlike Januarius Jones. Faulkner clearly felt an affinity with Beardsley's eroticized depictions of women—in their sexual beauty and their predatory menace. He openly calls attention to this influence in three novels, most notably in *Light in August*, where the following passage describes Joanna Burden at the height of her sexual passion with Joe Christmas: "Now and then she appointed trysts beneath certain shrubs about the grounds, where he would find her naked, or with her clothing half torn to ribbons upon her, in the wild throes of nymphomania, her body gleaming in the slow shifting from one to another of such formally erotic attitudes and gestures as a Beardsley of the time of Petronius might have drawn."

Faulkner's attention in his fiction to such elements as the quality of light, to flowers and shrubbery (perhaps an influence of the Impressionists), and to motion is likely a consequence of his early interest in painting and drawing.

FURTHER READING

Bross, Addison C. "*Soldiers' Pay* and the Art of Aubrey Beardsley." *American Quarterly* 19 (1967): 3–23.

Hönnighausen, Lothar. "Faulkner's Graphic Work in Historical Context." *Faulkner: International Perspectives*, ed. Fowler and Abadie. 139–173.

———. *William Faulkner: The Art of Stylization in His Early Graphic and Literary Work*.

Reid, Panthea. "The Scene of Writing and the Shape of Language When 'Matisse and Picasso Yet Painted.' " *Faulkner and the Artist*, ed. Kartiganer and Abadie. 82–110.

Hugh Ruppersburg

VISUAL RECORD. There is a vast record of Faulkner and his environs in photography, water color, acrylic, oil, montage, and sculpture. Portraits of Faulkner have been done by William C. Baggett, Jr., Murray Lloyd Goldsborough, John Sokol, and Faulkner's mother, Maud. The Goldsborough portrait, acquired by the University of Mississippi in 1965, was chosen to adorn the Faulkner commemorative stamp issued by the U.S. Postal Service in 1987. Most prominent among photographers have been J. R. Cofield and his son Jack, of Oxford, whose photos of Faulkner, many posed, cover the years 1930 to 1962 (see Cofield, *William Faulkner: The Cofield Collection*, 1978); and Martin J. Dain, whose photographs of Faulkner, Oxford, and Lafayette County appear in *Faulkner's County: Yoknapatawpha* (1964) and *Faulkner's World* (1997). Additional miscellaneous photos of Faulkner were taken by Bern Keating, Hubert A. Lowman, and Ed Meek; Keating's shots of Faulkner at the Mississippi Delta Council meeting in 1952 have added historical value. Other photographers who turned their attention to Faulkner's surroundings include Milly Moorhead, Thomas S. Rankin, and William Eggleston, the last of whom provided the photographs to accompany Willie Morris's text in *Faulkner's Mississippi* (1990). Eudora Welty's photographs of Mississippi (*Photographs*, University Press of Mississippi, 1990), as well as her thousands of negatives deposited in the Mississippi

State Archives in Jackson, would also be particularly interesting to Faulkner readers. Work of still others from the photographic collection of the Archives appears in *Mississippi Observed* (University Press of Mississippi, 1994).

Among other art forms, the most notable have been sculptures, paintings, prints, and murals. Leon Koury sculpted a likeness of Faulkner's head for the University of Mississippi in 1965; that work is now on display, along with the Goldsborough portrait, in the John Williams Library on the Ole Miss campus. More recently, in conjunction with the Faulkner Centennial, William Beckwith created a life-size bronze statute of Faulkner that now occupies a prominent place on the Oxford town square. Beckwith, a nationally recognized sculptor who lives in Taylor, Mississippi, had earlier created a twenty-four inch statue of Temple Drake. The Faulkner Centennial also inspired the creation of a Faulkner mural for Southeast Missouri State University's Center for Faulkner Studies by Southeast art professor Grant Lund. John McCrady (1911–1968), perhaps the South's best-known regionalist painter, Glennray Tutor, who became an Oxford resident in the early 1970s, and William Dunlap have produced Faulkner-related paintings that have been reproduced on posters for the annual Faulkner and Yoknapatawpha Conference and the New Albany Tallahatchie River Festival.

Charles A. Peek and Robert W. Hamblin

VITELLI, POPEYE, a major character in *Sanctuary*, is one of Faulkner's most reprehensible villains. Although we learn in *Requiem for a Nun* that Popeye has a surname, in *Sanctuary* he is simply Popeye, a "monstrous" presence. With his bulging eyes, parchment pallor, diminutive stature, black suits, and lethal .45, he is a caricature of the 1920s gangster, based on a Memphis underworld figure Faulkner had heard of. Yet this nightmarish gnome, who commits two murders and a vicious corncob rape of Temple, is often compared to a "sick child" who sulks and whimpers. As he passively awaits execution (ironically for the wrong murder), he seems not quite to know what is happening. Even when the hangman is poised to spring the trap, Popeye is concerned that the noose has mussed his hair. In the final chapter, one added during Faulkner's revision, we get a putative biography of Popeye that complicates our response considerably. Popeye was a sickly baby born to an unwed mother, with a streak of insanity in her heredity, and a syphilitic strikebreaker who passed his venereal disease on to both mother and child. Popeye was lucky to survive, although a doctor says Popeye will never be sexually functioning, will be allergic to alcohol, and most tellingly, "will never be any older than he is now." The physician makes this prognosis when Popeye is five. So the novel's figure of cosmic evil is essentially a five-year-old whose adult crimes are merely an extension of his childhood mutilations of lovebirds and a kitten. The final chapter offers an "explanation" that explains nothing, hardly creating sympathy or making sense out of his bizarre actions. Thus Popeye becomes the ultimate horror since there is no explanation for him.

FURTHER READING

Adamowski, T. H. "Faulkner's Popeye: The Other as Self." *Twentieth Century Interpretations of* Sanctuary: *A Collection of Critical Essays*. Ed. J. Douglas Canfield. Englewood Cliffs, N.J.: Prentice, 1982. 32–48.

Cantwell, Robert. "Faulkner's Popeye." *Nation* 15 February 1958: 140ff.

Heller, Terry. "Mirrored Worlds and the Gothic in Faulkner's *Sanctuary*." *Mississippi Quarterly* 42 (1989): 247–259.

Rossky, William. "The Pattern of Nightmare in *Sanctuary*: or, Miss Reba's Dogs." *Twentieth Century Interpretations of Sanctuary*, ed. Canfield. 70–78.

Schafer, William J. "Faulkner's *Sanctuary*: The Blackness of Fairytale." *Durham University Journal* 83 (1991): 217–222.

David L. Vanderwerken

W

WAR BIRDS, a screenplay that Faulkner wrote in 1933 at MGM. It was based on *Diary of an Unknown Aviator,* a book derived from the diary of John McGavock Grider, a pilot killed in World War I. Faulkner combined material from the Grider book with elements from three of his fictional works: his novel *Flags in the Dust* and two 1931 short stories closely related to the novel: "All the Dead Pilots" and "Ad Astra." All three works involve the Sartoris twins, John and Bayard, who, like the real Grider, saw action as aviators in World War I. For whatever reason, *War Birds* never found a place on MGM's production schedule.

Gene D. Phillips

WARNER BROS. PICTURES, INC. *See* **Hollywood**.

WARREN, ROBERT PENN (1905–1989), American poet, novelist, and critic. Faulkner and Warren had little personal contact during their lifetimes. Faulkner's opinion of Warren was cautiously positive. In a 1946 letter to Lambert Davis, an editor at Harcourt Brace who had sent him a review copy of Warren's *All the King's Men,* Faulkner wrote, "The Cass Mastern story is a beautiful and moving piece. The rest of it I would throw away" (*SL* 239) (the Cass Mastern episode does seem to bear the influence of Faulkner's *Absalom, Absalom!*). When Faulkner and Warren had dinner together in 1953, arranged by their Random House editor Albert Erskine, Faulkner indicated that he had read at least one of Warren's short stories as well as the novel *At Heaven's Gate.* However, in an interview several years later in Nagano, Japan, Faulkner claimed that the only Warren novel he had read was *All the King's Men* (*LIG* 11). Throughout his career Warren regarded Faulkner as one of the great modern American novelists and enthusiastically promoted his name. In a 1946 review for *The New Republic* of Malcolm Cowley's *The Portable Faulkner,* Warren ranked Faulkner "beside the masters of our own past literature" and predicted that Faulkner "as much as any writer of our place and time" could be confident of his place in literary history. The review, which identified a number of themes in Faulkner's work, helped renew interest in his fiction and was a significant early influence on Faulkner criticism. Two decades later Warren edited and wrote an introduction for an anthology of criticism about Faulkner (*Faulkner: A Collection of Critical Essays*, 1966). The anthology *American Literature: The Makers and the Making* (1973), which Warren coedited with Cleanth Brooks and R.W.B. Lewis, prominently features Faulkner and places several of his novels on a short list of works that all students of American literature are advised to read. As a leading proponent of the New Criticism, Warren was among a group of critics and writers who helped to shape the modern American literary canon and who played a major role in advancing Faulkner's literary reputation.

FURTHER READING

Warren, Robert Penn. "Cowley's Faulkner." *New Republic* 12 August 1946: 176–180; 26 August 1946: 234–237.

Hugh Ruppersburg

"WAS," the opening chapter of Faulkner's *Go Down, Moses* (1942) and one of only two pieces in the novel not published in earlier form. Set in 1859, it is a comical tale about Buck and Buddy McCaslin's attempt to recapture Tomey's Turl, a slave who has run away to Hubert Beauchamp's neighboring plantation to be with his sweetheart Tennie. Buck embarks upon a ritualized hunt to recapture the fugitive; through a series of misadventures, however, Buck himself becomes the prey when Hubert's sister, Sophonsiba, traps him into a marriage engagement after he loses a card game. Buck is freed from his predicament when Buddy, a better poker player, arrives and raises the stakes in another poker hand; as part of the agreement, though, the McCaslins must purchase Tennie. The story's comic tone, in which moral questions are never raised, together with the title, makes the narrative seem little more than an anecdote of an idyllic, antebellum past before war made everything more serious; but an introductory passage about Isaac McCaslin, who was not born at the time of the story, and the hunting metaphors in the story serve as portents of the hunting and wilderness themes developed later in the novel. Underlying the story also are weighty themes of miscegenation, incest, and ownership that become increasingly more obvious and profound as the novel progresses.

FURTHER READING

Bradford, Melvin E. "All the Daughters of Eve: 'Was' and the Unity of *Go Down, Moses*." *Arlington Quarterly* 1.1 (1967): 28–37.
Salmon, Webb. "Faulkner's *Go Down, Moses*." *Explicator* 46.4 (1988): 29–32.

Walker, David. "Out of the Old Time: 'Was' and *Go Down, Moses.*" *Journal of Narrative Technique* 9 (1979): 1–11.

John B. Padgett

"**WASH**," one of Faulkner's finest short stories, first appeared in *Harper's Magazine* in February 1934. It was reprinted in *Doctor Martino and Other Stories* (1934) and as the first story in "The Middle Ground" section of *Collected Stories*. A considerably reworked version of the story became a major segment of *Absalom, Absalom!*

The plot of "Wash" is centered on the murder of Thomas Sutpen by Wash Jones, his poor-white tenant. The story balances action and meditation, violence and epiphany. Sutpen, returned to his ruined plantation after the Civil War, has an affair with Jones's teenaged granddaughter Milly. When Milly gives birth to Sutpen's daughter, Wash is outraged by the arrogant indifference of Sutpen, who expresses greater concern for his mare that foaled a colt the same day. The shock of discovery, the disillusionment with his great hero, the brave, gallant "Kernel," destroys Wash's life in an instant. He murders Sutpen with a scythe. When the sheriff and his men come for Wash, he murders his granddaughter and her baby, sets fire to his house, emerges from the flames and charges suicidally, with lifted scythe, toward the raised guns of the sheriff's posse.

"Wash" has sometimes been overlooked as one of Faulkner's best tales, undoubtedly because of its relation to *Absalom, Absalom!*; however, with its focus on the epiphany of Wash Jones, the story is much more than just an earlier version of a key episode in the novel. When it has been considered as a separate entity, it has been praised for its handling of the basic theme of the discovery of evil, for its skillful presentation of disillusionment and loss of innocence, and for its commentary on an important thematic concern in Faulkner, the dangers of the abstraction of social status and class.

It has also been suggested, by way of critical reservation, that the lyrical power of Jones's meditative disillusionment with Sutpen is incongruous for such a crude character—that given his speech and actions, there is a forced poetic quality in his renunciation of Sutpen. The poetry in the interior monologue of such a character, however, recognizes that all human beings *feel* lyrically and poetically. A memorable, poetic, and epiphanic line captures what Jones thinks or feels: "Better that all who remain of us be blasted from the face of earth than that another Wash Jones should see his whole life shredded from him and shrivel away like a dried shuck thrown onto the fire."

Critical commentary has also been concerned with the substantial differences of both detail and presentation that are found in "Wash" and in the novelistic reshaping of the same material. For example, Sutpen's concern with his design, with fathering a son, which is crucial in *Absalom, Absalom!*, is only implicitly present in the short story. And the Sutpen of "Wash" is a much more diminished, ruined man, after the war, than the Sutpen of the novel. The telling of the events, too, is quite different: In the short story, events are facts presented by an omniscient narrator, whereas in the novel the presentation of "fact" and "truth" reverberates and oscillates in the telling and retelling by a sequence of narrators who were not present at the events. On its own, "Wash" is a compelling, self-contained story concerned, not with the design and demise of Sutpen, not with the intricacy of narration and the difficulty of reclaiming the past, but with the moving epiphany and powerful tragedy of Wash Jones.

FURTHER READING

Brodsky, Louis Daniel. "The Textual Development of William Faulkner's 'Wash': An Examination of Manuscripts in the Brodsky Collection." *Studies in Bibliography* 37 (1984): 248–281.

Stewart, Jack F. "Apotheosis and Apocalypse in Faulkner's 'Wash.'" *Studies in Short Fiction* 6 (1969): 586–600.

Tuso, Joseph F. "Faulkner's Wash." *Explicator* 27 (1968): item 17.

H. R. Stoneback

WASSON, BEN (1899–1982), lawyer, author, editor, and literary agent who was a lifelong friend of Faulkner. A native of Greenville, Mississippi, Wasson first met Faulkner in 1916 when Ben came to Oxford to enroll in the University of Mississippi. The two young men quickly became friends, sharing a mutual interest in literature, music, art, and social activities. Early in his novelistic career Faulkner engaged Wasson, who had recently published a novel, *The Devil Beats His Wife* (1929), and who was then living in New York, as his literary agent; and it was Wasson who ensured the publication of *Sartoris* by cutting the manuscript by a third. It was also Wasson to whom Faulkner delivered the manuscript of *The Sound and the Fury* with the comment, "Read this, Bud. It's a real son-of-a-bitch" (1974 *FAB* 590). In later years, though Faulkner terminated his business relationship with Wasson, the two men remained close friends, spending time together not only in New York and Mississippi but also in Hollywood, where both men worked for a movie studio. Wasson was one of the small number of intimate friends invited by the Faulkner family to attend the private funeral service for Faulkner. Wasson's book of reminiscences, *Count No 'Count: Flashbacks to Faulkner*, was published in 1983.

Louis Daniel Brodsky

"WEEKEND REVISITED." *See* **"Mr. Acarius."**

WILBOURNE, HARRY, is the central male character in the "Wild Palms" narrative of Faulkner's novel *The Wild Palms/If I Forget Thee, Jerusalem*. A medical internist in the last stages of his residency in New Orleans, Harry falls in love with sculptress Charlotte Rittenmeyer, a married woman with two children. They run away together, hoping to live a life free of bourgeois conventionality, their attempt impeded first by financial worries, then by Charlotte's unexpected pregnancy, which leads to a failed effort at abortion, Charlotte's subsequent slow death, and Harry's long-term imprisonment. In their brief time together Harry struggles to prove himself worthy of Charlotte's love. A twenty-seven-old virgin when he first meets Charlotte, he is emotionally and temperamentally the less daring of the two. Habituated to penury, he finds himself plagued throughout their relationship by anxieties about money and by an overly punctilious sense of propriety and respectability. His struggle to surmount these feelings reaches its tragic climax in the attempted abortion, when he is unable to control the trembling of his hands and therefore botches the operation. The scenes depicting Harry's subsequent life comprise a moving meditation on the nature of grief and memory. Harry is tempted toward suicide, but realizing that Charlotte will continue to exist only if he lives to remember her, he decides, in one of Faulkner's most famous formulations, that *"between grief and nothing [he] will take grief."* Wilbourne bears a number of similarities to the Tall Convict, the central character of the "Old Man" sections of the novel, including beginning in a quasi-monastic existence, free of involvement with women; entering into a complicated, stress-filled relationship with a woman, centering on a pregnancy; and concluding as an inmate in Mississippi's Parchman Prison. At the heart of these parallels, though, is a deep-seated opposition between the Tall Convict's desire for security and peace and Harry's struggle to overcome similar desires.

FURTHER READING

McHaney, Thomas L. *William Faulkner's* The Wild Palms: *A Study*. Jackson: University Press of Mississippi, 1975.

Rhodes, Pamela, and Richard Godden. *"The Wild Palms*: Degraded Culture, Devalued Texts." *Intertextuality in Faulkner*, ed. Gresset and Polk. 87–113.

Zender, Karl F. "Money and Matter in *Pylon* and *The Wild Palms*." *Faulkner Journal* 1.2 (1986): 17–29.

Karl F. Zender

WILDE, META CARPENTER. *See* **Carpenter, Meta Doherty**.

WILD PALMS, THE, the eleventh of Faulkner's novels, now usually called by its original title, *If I Forget Thee, Jerusalem*, was first published in early 1939, not long after the appearance of *The Unvanquished*. One of Faulkner's most daring structural experiments, the novel interweaves two seemingly unconnected narratives: "Wild Palms," the account of an adulterous, ultimately fatal love affair between Charlotte Rittenmeyer and Harry Wilbourne; and "Old Man," the comic account of a nameless convict's struggle against outrageous obstacles to rescue a pregnant woman from the Mississippi River flood of 1927.

The "contrapuntal quality" of the novel, as Faulkner termed it (*FIU* 171), at first puzzled readers, leading to an odd textual history in which "Old Man" was sometimes published separately and the two sections were once published in sequence, rather than as alternating chapters. Thanks to the labors of many critics—most notably Thomas McHaney—the integrity of the work is now well recognized and understood, as consisting of an elaborate series of thematic, imagistic, characterological, and structural parallels and oppositions. Central to these are two paradoxical quests: Charlotte and Harry's for freedom from bourgeois conventionality and (as he is called throughout) the Tall Convict's for a return to the quasi-monastic peace and security of the prison.

A pregnancy impedes each quest. A pregnant woman's coming to term in the middle of the flood subsequently involves the Tall Convict, against his will, in a sort of parody of domestic life and impedes his return to prison. The story of Charlotte and Harry, which Faulkner always insisted was the main narrative of the novel, confronts a similar frustration, but one resulting in a tragic rather than a comic resolution.

Having run away from Charlotte's husband and children, the two lovers try to create (primarily at Charlotte's insistence) a life that will be "all honeymoon, always." Frustrated first by dwindling finances, this effort entails a restless movement from Chicago to a cabin in the Wisconsin woods to a mining camp in Utah. It confronts its ultimate obstacle in Charlotte's unexpected pregnancy. Harry, only a few months short of completing his medical internship when he meets Charlotte, botches an attempt at an abortion in which he only reluctantly engages. Toxemia sets in, Charlotte dies a slow and agonizing death, and Harry is sentenced to fifty years in prison—a term to be served, in a final irony, in the same Parchman Prison to which the Tall Convict has finally gratefully succeeded in returning.

The Wild Palms was the subject of a number of sympathetic and insightful readings in the 1960s and 1970s, most notably Cleanth Brooks's analysis of the novel in relation to the traditions of romantic and chivalric love (*Toward Yoknapatawpha*) and McHaney's book-length study (*A Study*), which not only demonstrates (as noted above) the structural integrity of the work but also traces artistic affiliations with the works of Hemingway and Anderson and explores intellectual indebtednesses to Schopenhauer and Nietzsche. In general, though, it is fair to say that *The Wild Palms*, like the other "non–Yoknapatawpha" novels, received less study and esteem in the 1960s and 1970s than did the greatest of the novels set in Yoknapatawpha County. This circumstance, however, has changed in recent years, in large part because the novel has proven remarkably responsive to feminist and cultural materialist/New Historicist readings. Feminist critics have found in Charlotte Rittenmeyer a rewarding character for study, discovering in Faulkner's treatment of her "a respect . . . that is absent from his treatments of other sexually active and assertive and intelligent women" (Anne Jones, " 'Kotex Age' " 145). They have argued against negative earlier appraisals of her character (most of which valorize traditional communal and family values) and have demonstrated that she is the site of one of Faulkner's most sustained and thoughtful explorations of the nature of artistic creativity and of the artistic temperament. Similarly, cultural materialist studies have discovered in *The Wild Palms* an intricate meditation on American popular and consumer culture and on the economic dislocations produced by the Great Depression.

Another reason for the high level of current interest in *The Wild Palms* is the biographical revelations that have come into print over the last twenty years—most notably Meta Carpenter Wilde and Orin Borsten's *A Loving Gentleman: The Love Story of William Faulkner and Meta Carpenter* (1976). In 1952, Faulkner wrote a letter in which he said that he had written *The Wild Palms* "in order to try to stave off what I thought was heartbreak" (*SL* 338). The cause of the heartbreak was the apparent termination of his affair with Meta Carpenter, whom he had met and fallen in love with in Hollywood in 1935. Awareness of this background lends resonance to the Charlotte Rittenmeyer–Harry Wilbourne portion of the novel, particularly to the agonizing scenes of Charlotte's illness and death and to Harry's dedication of his subsequent life to grief and to memory. Other aspects of Faulkner's biography—for example, his early infatuation with Helen Baird, his unhappy marriage, and his financial difficulties in the mid-1930s—also contribute to an understanding of the novel.

The title of *The Wild Palms* was not Faulkner's choice. He reluctantly abandoned his original title, *If I Forget Thee, Jerusalem*, when one of his editors argued that it might arouse anti-Semitic feeling (1974 *FAB* 1002). The loss was unfortunate, not only because it led to the illogicality of a novel entitled *The Wild Palms* containing a subnarrative entitled "Wild Palms" but because it deprived the book's title of a rich variety of allusive meanings. The source of the original title, Psalm 137, laments the Jewish exile into Babylon. The verse from which the title is taken—"If I forget thee, O Jerusalem, let my right hand forget her cunning"—resonates against both the botched abortion and the idea of Charlotte Rittenmeyer (and of Meta Carpenter, Helen Baird, and perhaps Estelle Oldham) as the lost "Jerusalem" for which *The Wild Palms* is an elegiac song of mourning; it also intimates a larger insight on Faulkner's part into the relationship between artistic creativity and the experience of loss and between memory and the life of the body. It is therefore good that the original title has been restored in the most recent edition of the novel.

FURTHER READING

Eldred, Joyce Carey. "Faulkner's Still Life: Art and Abortion in *The Wild Palms*." *Faulkner Journal* 4.1–2 (1988–1989): 139–158.

Jones, Anne Goodwyn. " 'The Kotex Age': Women, Popular Culture, and *The Wild Palms*." *Faulkner and Popular Culture*, ed. Fowler and Abadie. 142–162.

McHaney, Thomas L. *William Faulkner's* The Wild Palms: *A Study*. Jackson: University Press of Mississippi, 1975.

Karl F. Zender

WILLIAMS, JOAN (1928–   ), Memphis-born author of *The Morning and the Evening* (1961), *Old Powder Man* (1966), *The Wintering* (1971), and other works. *The Wintering*, the story of a young woman and a famous writer, is a fictionalized account of Williams's relationship with William Faulkner. The two met in Oxford in 1949 when he was fifty-two, she twenty-one. Her story "Rain Later," published in August 1949, had won a *Mademoiselle* fiction award. Meeting her and reading her story evoked in Faulkner a sense of his own youth and a desire to be for Joan "whatever you want me to be to you" (1974 *FAB* 1313). She had yet to finish college, not graduating from Bard until the following June. They met in Memphis, at her parents' home and more privately; at Bard; in Holly Springs; in New York, where they would take in a show together; or at Saxe Commins's residence in Princeton—wherever their two lives allowed. Upon graduation, Williams worked first at the Doubleday Bookshop in New Orleans, then for *Look* in New York. Faulkner monitored her efforts as a budding writer, suggesting authors for her to read (Housman, Malraux, Bergson), critiquing her stories, sketching scenes for her to develop, and sharing with her scenes from *Requiem for a Nun*, on which he had hopes she would collaborate. These hopes came to nothing, however; and though they became lovers, his mentoring ceased being anything more than occasionally opening doors of publishers' offices for her. At one point Faulkner gave Williams the handwritten manuscript of *The Sound and the Fury*, which she declined to keep. By 1953, aware that besides Estelle there were other women in Faulkner's life (Meta Carpenter Rebner, Else Jonsson), Joan began to break away from the relationship, which she had never found totally comfortable. The mutual anguish over their breakup was apparently assuaged by Faulkner's meeting Jean Stein and Joan's meeting Ezra Bowen, the son of Catherine Drinker Bowen, whom she would later marry and then divorce. Some critics feel that the Gavin Stevens and Linda Snopes relationship in *The Town* mirrors that of Faulkner and Williams.

FURTHER READING

Williams, Joan. "Twenty Will Not Come Again." *Atlantic* May 1980: 58–65.

Charles A. Peek

WISEMAN, EVA, a character in *Mosquitoes*, is notable as Faulkner's portrait of a lesbian artist. One of the strongest members of the yacht party, decisive, practical, and forthright, she rejects artistic posturing and empty analysis. Faulkner reveals something of her erotic life but more of her art. She is a published poet, whose *Satyricon in Starlight*, summed up as the "syphilis book" by the Major, stimulates some of the most animated debate among the *Nausikaa*'s more sophisticated readers. Faulkner would later republish the quoted poems, under his own name, in *A Green Bough*. For Faulkner's critics, Eva Wiseman is, all in all, one of the most interesting artist-figures in his early work.

FURTHER READING

Altman, Meryl. "The Bug That Dare Not Speak Its Name: Sex, Art, Faulkner's Worst Novel, and the Critics." *Faulkner Journal* 9.1–2 (1993–1994): 43–68.

Michel, Frann. "William Faulkner as a Lesbian Author." *Faulkner Journal* 4.1–2 (1988–1989): 5–20.

Wittenberg, Judith Bryant. "Configuration of the Female and Textual Politics in *Mosquitoes*." *Faulkner Studies* 1.1 (1991): 1–19.

Pamela E. Knights

WISHING TREE, THE, a typed and hand-bound gift booklet, is Faulkner's story for children. Early in 1927, Faulkner presented one copy (dated "5-february-1927") to Victoria Franklin for her eighth birthday and a slightly longer version, *The Wishing-Tree*, to Margaret Brown, leaving each child with the impression that he had written the story especially for her. He made further copies for friends' children in time for Christmas 1948. The discovery that no gift was exclusively personal caused some consternation in later years. The tale reached a wider readership in 1967 when the "Victoria" version was published in the *Saturday Evening Post* on April 8 and, in book form, illustrated by Don Bolognese, by Random House on April 11. In the story a young girl, Dulcie, in the company of her black maid Alice and other assorted companions, journeys in search of the Wishing Tree. After magical and comic adventures, they meet good St. Francis and learn how to wish unselfishly. The tale has elements of the fairy story, the quest narrative, *Alice in Wonderland*, and *The Blue Bird*; and critics have appreciated Faulkner's considerable skill as a writer for a young audience. In general, readers find the story most interesting for aspects that Faulkner takes up again in his fiction for adults. Here, he lays out his world of whites and blacks, children, adults, and rival social groups, in a mixture of lyricism, comedy, and satire. He derives considerable humor from two war veterans: an aged white man who fought in the Civil War and Alice's renegade husband, Exodus, returned from Europe. Although Random House, sensitive to stereotyping, edited the heavily marked black dialect, some critics suggest that Exodus and Alice are strong figures, akin to more complex African American characters such as Caspey, Jesus, and Nancy. For others, *The Wishing Tree* anticipates *The Sound and the Fury*, above all as a story in which St. Francis presides over a narrative of wishing and desire, conducted in a dream space of flower-scented mists and waters. The reassuring ending, however, is all its own.

FURTHER READING

Gidley, Mick. "William Faulkner and Children." *Signal: Approaches to Children's Books* 3 (1970): 91–102.

Hargrove, Nancy D. "Faulkner's *The Wishing Tree* as Children's Literature." *The Image of the Child*. Ed. Sylvia Patterson Iskander. Battle Creek, Mich.: Children's Literature Association, 1991. 132–140.

Zorzi, Rosella Mamoli. "The Artist as Magician: The Power of the Word in *The Wishing Tree*." *The Artist and His Masks: William Faulkner's Metafiction*. Ed. Agostino Lombardo. Rome, Italy: Bulzoni, 1991. 109–116.

Pamela E. Knights

"WITH CAUTION AND DISPATCH," a Faulkner short story, composed in 1932 or 1933 but not published until *Uncollected Stories* (1979). In the story American John Sartoris is a member of a British squadron preparing to fly to France in March 1918. A failed loop maneuver forces Sartoris to crash-land. Later, in another plane, Sartoris tries to rejoin his squadron. Flying low, under rain clouds, just above the water of the Channel, he crashes on a ship. Flight Commander Britt provides yet another plane, and Sartoris crashes at the field in France. He arrives, finally, with neither caution nor dispatch.

FURTHER READING

Sederberg, Nancy Belcher. " 'With Caution and Dispatch': 'Deliberate Speed, Majestic Instancy.' " *Critical Essays on William Faulkner: The Sartoris Family*. Ed. Arthur F. Kinney. Boston: G. K. Hall, 1985. 190–203.

Diane Brown Jones

WOMEN. Faulkner's creation of women characters is central to his art; indeed, of all the characters in his Yoknapatawpha landscape, his women characters are the ones who most endure. His many famous women characters, such as Caddy Compson, Temple Drake, Lena Grove, Joanne Burden, and Addie Bundren, inhabit a permanent place in the American twentieth-century literary pantheon.

Readers hotly debate Faulkner's women characters. Some critics, such as Linda Wagner and Cleanth Brooks, believe that Faulkner is sympathetic to his women characters, whereas others, such as Leslie Fiedler and Irving Howe, believe that Faulkner is a misogynist. Faulkner, himself, made statements that pointed to his misogyny, yet at other times, he stated that he thought women were *wonderful* and more interesting to write about than men. Sally Page's groundbreaking work *Faulkner's Women: Characterization and Meaning* sees Faulkner's women characters as part of a dialectic "which is forever unresolved in Faulkner's fiction" (173). Indeed, the lack of dialectic resolution of the women characters in Faulkner's fiction appears to be one of the few consistencies found in the literary criticism about this topic.

This dialectic has caused critics to both praise and condemn Faulkner's creations. In *Love and Death in the American Novel* (Criterion, 1960), Leslie Fiedler writes that no other writer creates more pejorative stereotypes of women. He believes that only in Faulkner's last books does he show respect for any female character not past menopause. Fiedler places Faulkner's women into two stereotypical categories: the insatiable daughters of the aristocracy and the mindless daughters of peasants.

Joseph Blotner, Faulkner's biographer, finds striking similarities between Faulkner's women characters and the real women in Faulkner's life. He notes similarities between Estelle Faulkner and Cecily Saunders, Belle Mitchell, and Temple Drake; between Helen Baird and Charlotte Rittenmeyer; and between Joan Williams and Linda Snopes Kohl. In *What Else But Love?: The Ordeal of Race in Faulkner and Morrison*, Philip Weinstein writes that Faulkner models

Dilsey and Nancy after his own mammy, Mammy Callie Barr, who lived on his land until she died. She introduced Faulkner to his culture's central neurosis: its unresolved racism. Since Faulkner spent so many of his early years with her, he could not dismiss her as less than human, yet to him she would always remain as *other*: black and woman. Weinstein asserts that Faulkner's women characters suffer the fallout from his mythic Yoknapatawpha story. In telling the story of the disenfranchised white son's lost homeland, a story both patriarchal and Oedipal, Faulkner deems that women, along with blacks, must bear the brunt of the white Southern male's loss of power.

Faulkner critics often analyze Faulkner's women characters in terms of archetypal, mythic, and/or psychological methods, motivated by Faulkner's own comments and by the current popularities of literary criticism. Mimi Reisel Gladstein, in *The Indestructible Woman in Faulkner, Hemingway, and Steinbeck* (UMI Research Press, 1986) echoes feminist critics who find American literature lacking in strong, multidimensional women characters; nevertheless, she believes that the *indestructible* woman is the primary archetype that permeates Faulkner's fiction. She believes that Faulkner defines his women characters as the *other, the primitive*, those who have been the least affected by contemporary life, and therefore the characters most capable of enduring that life. Faulkner, Gladstein continues, places his women characters into a category that includes the Negro, the Indian, the peasants, and the primitives (7). He does this because of his inability to come to terms with the *otherness* of women. In addition, he equates women characters with matter, especially with that matter that connotes their sexuality. Many indestructible women characters are developed using earth imagery, such as Lena Grove, the pregnant woman in *Light in August*, whose name, actions, movements, and odor suggest Mother Earth; Caddy, the daughter of the Compson family in *The Sound and the Fury*, associated with both trees and water in symbolic and natural terms; and Temple Drake of *Sanctuary*, Addie Bundren of *As I Lay Dying*, and Eula Varner of the Snopes trilogy, all of whom share identification with nature, the earth, and the sexuality of the world. Other myths found in Faulkner's fiction include the Demeter/Persephone myth as a pattern for female continuity that appears in *The Sound and the Fury*, the *Snopes* trilogy, and *Requiem for a Nun*.

Faulkner's indestructible women are also characterized as the old undefeated spinster aunt and the seemingly fragile but steel-spined Southern woman in the personae of Miss Habersham, Granny Rosa Millard, and Miss Jenny Du Pre, all of whom evolve out of Faulkner's subjective masculinism, his inability to see woman as anything but the *other*. It is difficult to piece together a coherent criticism of Faulkner's female characters because of the multiple ambiguities found among them, but the indestructible woman appears throughout his work, even though these characters are often presented and viewed by a subjective male voice. Ultimately, according to Gladstein, women play the part of the indestructible character because of Faulkner's belief in their ability to prevail and endure.

Other critics have used alternate categories to identify Faulkner's women characters. Doreen Fowler, in the introduction to *Faulkner and Women: Faulkner and Yoknapatawpha, 1985* (Fowler and Abadie), states that his characters fall into one of two categories: introspective women in Faulkner's fiction who resemble their male counterparts, celebrating masculinity, such as Addie Bundren, Joanna Burden, Drusilla Hawk, and Charlotte Rittenmeyer; or the elderly women safely past the age of sexual desirability. Linda Snopes Kohl may be the one exception (viii).

Mothers also occupy a powerful place in Faulkner's fiction. His own mother exerted a powerful influence on Faulkner, and his women characters, not surprisingly, exert maternal power, according to Deborah Clarke in her work *Robbing the Mother: Women in Faulkner*, but the relative importance of the roles of the women varies. Clarke writes that while the female characters are usually silenced, exiled, or killed, the psychological impact of women's bodies remains. The bodies of Caddy Compson and Addie Bundren control the plots of their texts. Temple Drake's and Eula Varner's sexuality "mocks and destroys male illusions of potency and power and thus forces a realization that the nature of humanity rests on respecting women's bodies." Lena Grove and Joanna Burden operate within literal and symbolic discourse, and in *Absalom, Absalom!*, Faulkner casts the mother as the "notmother, as maternal creativity transcends the boundaries of bodies, of language, and of race" (153). The duality of Faulkner's women characters can be found in the character of Caddy, moving between sister, mother, virgin, and whore; Addie Bundren as mother, adulterer, dead body, and speaking voice; Temple Drake as both feminine sexuality and boyish body; Eula Varner who embodies both virginity and fertility; Lena Grove as asexual earth mother; Joanna Burden as sexually repressed nymphomaniac; and others (126).

This female power is echoed by Minrose Gwin in *The Feminine and Faulkner: Reading (Beyond) Sexual Difference*, where she states that Faulkner, even though a product of his own misogynistic culture, in his greatest works creates female characters who in "powerful and creative ways, disrupt and sometimes even destroy patriarchal structures" (4). For example, Caddy Compson, Rosa Coldfield, Charlotte Rittenmeyer, and others are active disruptive subjects in their narratives. Caddy becomes the other of language of which the deconstructionists speak. She pursues a way out of male discourse and "remains the difference within his text, the difference that deconstructs phallic authority" (55). According to Gwin, Caddy's voice "speaks the tragic results of the cultural objectification of real people and the disastrous effects of a system of barter which makes women commodities" (56). Gwin asserts that Caddy's voice is a voice to which feminist readers are particularly attuned because it is a voice that struggles within a text in a culture that seeks to silence her.

Because Faulkner's women characters operate in a patriarchal society that is disintegrating around them, they often appear as stereotypical characters the patriarchy attempts to conquer while not being engulfed itself. In Faulkner's fiction, man continues to be the subject and woman is the object, or the other; therefore, the inadequate realization of Faulkner's female characters may point to his inability to come to terms with the otherness of woman. After all, Faulkner suffered from the tensions of Faulkner as the writer and Faulkner as the product of a Southern upbringing during the early years of the twentieth century.

In sum, Faulkner created women characters that reveal the range of humanity. His women characters function as the *other*; they prevail and endure; they are often portrayed mythically; and they are seen as incomprehensible through the subjective lenses of the male characters as well as the author himself. Despite the variety of critical analyses, Faulkner's women characters will continue to live within the twentieth-century literary canon, for in few other authors' writings can one find so many complex women literary characters.

See also **Feminist Approaches**.

FURTHER READING

Clarke. *Robbing the Mother: Women in Faulkner.*
Fowler and Abadie, eds. *Faulkner and Women.*
Gwin. *The Feminine in Faulkner.*
Page. *Faulkner's Women: Characterization and Meaning.*
Williams. *Faulkner's Women: The Myth and the Muse.*

Bonnie Davis

WORLD WAR I, for William Faulkner, along with the Civil War, always remained the Great War of his imagination. The protracted and bloody fighting in Europe and the Middle East, 1914–1918, introduced the world to modern, mass, impersonal warfare, with devastating consequences on all sides, leading many to question the meaning of peace gained at such cost. Such disillusion seemed stronger still, in contrast with the romantic idealism with which many had entered the war. Although Faulkner had no direct experience of the conflict, he published his first work during the war and wrote his first novels in its aftermath, and as for most writers of his generation, it made a profound and lasting impact on his life and his art. In the early war years, as he recalled in 1953, his own dreams were of heroism in the air: to get to France "and become glorious and beribboned too" (*FR* x). After the United States entered the struggle in 1917, he still hoped to participate, but when he was at last in training as a Royal Air Force (RAF) cadet in Canada, the end of hostilities on November 11, 1918, frustrated his prospects of seeing active military combat. Like Cadet Lowe in *Soldiers' Pay*, he found "they had stopped the war on him."

Yet Faulkner continued to draw from World War I powerful materials to transform imaginatively into fictions in both his life and his writing. Although he later took pains to put an end to the myth that he had seen active service, and to the other legends that accrued to his war years, he fabulated out of the war stories that clung to him for a lifetime. In his art, he completed most of the explicit "war" stories before the early 1930s, but in more pervasive ways,

World War I preoccupied his imagination for the greater part of his career. It enters his poetry, his drawings, and his fiction, sometimes stylized in terms of a fin de siècle aesthetic, sometimes in contemporarily realistic tones. A wounded pilot is the primary voice in the early poem "The Lilacs"; and aviators and the experience of war are at the heart of Faulkner's first story, "Landing in Luck," his first novel, *Soldiers' Pay*, and his first major venture into Yoknapatawpha, *Sartoris/Flags in the Dust*. His first two screenplays, *Today We Live* and *The Road to Glory*, deal with the war. World War I also holds a special place in *Collected Stories*, where Faulkner gathered together in "The Wasteland" section five of his short fictions—"Ad Astra," "Victory," "Crevasse," "Turnabout," "All the Dead Pilots"—and a related story, "Honor," in "The Middle Ground." The war is the frame for some of his lighter; satirical, or more bizarre writing, stories such as "Thrift," "With Caution and Dispatch," and "The Leg"; but even after World War II, it provided the foundation of his most ambitious task, *A Fable*, his would-be magnum opus. Late in his life, he looked back again, reflecting on the significance and consequences of the experience, in public interviews with students, scholars, and readers all over the world.

Faulkner's fiction represents the war from the viewpoint of the front and from home, encompassing the experiences of soldiers and civilians; it recounts tales of military action but also dwells extensively on the repercussions of the conflict, especially in the postwar years. Damaged survivors—the wounded, the cynical, the living dead—haunt his narratives from "The Lilacs" onward. His perspective ranges from the wryly satirical to the tragic, often a mixture of the two. Even when writing for children, in *The Wishing Tree* in 1927, he uses his two veterans, one white, one black, to state matters in the simplest terms. The two men share the certainty that, in the black man's words, "I never seed a soldier yet that ever won anything in a war. But, then, whitefolks' wars is always run funny." Faulkner sharpened this kind of perception in other stories: in his treatment, for example, of the existential bewilderment of a multinational group of aviators in "Ad Astra"; or in his panoramic vision of twentieth-century power structures in *A Fable*. But if, for the ordinary person, all wars have much in common, *The Wishing Tree* also suggests that different wars have their own character. Although neither veteran knows the name of the war he fought, each can define his experience in terms that echo through Faulkner's other fictions. For the old white man, his war, the Civil War, was the one fought "right down in my pappy's pasture"; for the younger black man, the war was the one "across the water." For Faulkner, too, the Civil War represented the stories of family, history, and heritage, written into places and to people close to home, whereas World War I was a foreign war, distant, alien, at times exotic. In his fiction, the European conflict always remains a strange and incomprehensible experience for Southern country men and boys. In *Flags in the Dust*, Buddy's "Yankee" war service is never mentioned in the Confederate MacCallum household. When he does speak, it is a story he can hardly tell: "a vague, dreamy sort of tale, without beginning or end . . . an imminent but incomprehensible nightmare."

Whether in the chatter around the tennis court, in Caspey's hyperbole, or in young Bayard's compulsive retelling of his brother's death, World War I is remote, confusing, a contrast with the luminous heroics in the parallel tales of the Civil War.

In the figure of the aviator, Faulkner found an image that concentrated much of the chivalric glamour he drew from stories of the Southern cause. But even this image loses its dazzle, and the need for it is satirized in characters such as Lowe in *Soldiers' Pay* and, more seriously, in the legends of Johnny Sartoris. The stories of World War I, then, contain some of the most disturbing and uncomfortable of Faulkner's writing. Critics have long been interested in these narratives, comparing Faulkner positively with writers such as Hemingway and Dos Passos (who came closer to combat) in giving voice to a "lost" generation. Those who have traced his response generally outline a pattern of change in his characters, from eager fascination to disillusion and rootlessness, marked by a sense of extreme disruption and shock. Early critics were often engaged with issues of metaphysical conflict and of the mythic dimensions of the fictions that locate the characters in a postwar Waste Land. Attention has moved in more recent years to such concerns as Faulkner's wider literary deployment of World War I, as metaphor and as master narrative, and to an interest in the construction of gender and social groups within these fictions, in the all-male worlds of the military and in those who do not fit there: the noncombatants, the feminine men, the powerless, the nonwhites, the women beyond its boundaries. Such inquiries open up speculation into the cultural and psychoanalytic interrelations between war and writing, violence and civilization, power and language. Or as Horace Benbow muses in *Flags in the Dust*: "Perhaps this is the reason for wars . . . The meaning of peace."

FURTHER READING

Bradford, M. E. "The Anomaly of Faulkner's World War I Stories." *Mississippi Quarterly* 36 (1983): 243–261.
Hönnighausen, Lothar. "The Military as Metaphor." *Faulkner Journal* 2.2 (1987): 12–22.
Jones, Anne Goodwyn. "Male Fantasies?: Faulkner's War Stories and the Construction of Gender." *Faulkner and Psychology*, ed. Kartiganer and Abadie. 21–55.
MacMillan, Duane J. "Fictional Facts and Factual Fiction: William Faulkner and World War I." *Faulkner Journal* 2.2 (1987): 47–54.
Nordanberg. *Cataclysm as Catalyst: The Theme of War in William Faulkner's Fiction.*

Pamela E. Knights

WORLD WAR II (1939–1945), while having far less impact upon Faulkner than either the American Civil War or World War I, nevertheless played a significant role in his life and works. In early 1942 Faulkner sought a commission in the U.S. Navy "to get a little nearer the gunfire, which I intend to try to do" (*SL* 149); failing in that attempt (just as he had failed to see action in

World War I), he spent most of the remaining war years in Hollywood, where he became a part of Warner Bros. Pictures' civilian "war industry" by writing movie scripts in support of the Allied cause. His work on such projects as *The De Gaulle Story*, "The Life and Death of a Bomber," *Air Force, Battle Cry, God Is My Co-Pilot*, and *To Have and Have Not* (for which he helped transform Hemingway's Great Depression novel into a Free French propaganda statement) allowed Faulkner not only to participate vicariously in the conflict but also to feel that he was making a genuine contribution to the war effort. Interestingly, writing about the war seems also to have rekindled his earlier fantasies about actual combat experience. In a 1943 letter to his nephew Jimmy, a combat pilot, Faulkner lied: "I would have liked for you to have had my dog tag, R.A.F., but I lost it in Europe, in Germany. I think the Gestapo has it; I am very likely on their records right now as a dead British flying officer spy" (*SL* 170).

While Faulkner's treatment of World War II finds expression primarily in his movie scripts, he occasionally visits the subject in his fiction. In "Delta Autumn" (1942) Uncle Ike McCaslin voices his belief that "when the time comes," America "will cope with one Austrian paper-hanger" (i.e., Hitler); and this patriotic theme is developed in three stories of the same period: "The Tall Men" (1941), "Two Soldiers" (1942), and "Shall Not Perish" (1943). In his later fiction the war continues to be a definite, if minor, presence: Chick Mallison volunteers for war at the end of *Knight's Gambit* and returns home as a former bombardier and prisoner of war in *The Mansion*; the Reverend J. C. Goodyhay of *The Mansion* is an ex-marine who was decorated for valor in the Pacific; and the Marshall Plan is alluded to in *A Fable*. In addition, references to the atomic bomb appear in some of Faulkner's speeches, including the Nobel Prize acceptance speech.

FURTHER READING

Carothers, James B. " 'I Ain't a Soldier Now': Faulkner's World War II Veterans." *Faulkner Journal* 2 (1987): 67–74.

Robert W. Hamblin

Y

YOKNAPATAWPHA, the name that Faulkner adopted for his imaginary county, was borrowed from the river (later shortened to Yocona) that flows through the southern portion of Lafayette County. Contrary to Faulkner's usual rendition, according to the most common translation of *Yoknapatawpha*, "Yokna" means "land" and "patawpha" means "split," "split apart," "ploughed," "furrowed," or "tilled." This was the definition Faulkner's contemporaries would have found in Cushman's *History of the Choctaw, Chickasaw, and Natchez Indians* (1899) or in Byington's *Dictionary of the Choctaw Language* (1915)—the Chocktaw and Chickasaw languages being virtually the same. Most people in Lafayette County understood the word translated to "land divided" or "split land," but there seems to have been no definitive agreement on exactly what that meant.

Additional meanings to this cryptic word are offered by a more recent authority on the Chickasaw language (Munro and Willmond). "Yaakni" (a phonetic variation of "yokna"), this dictionary explains, could mean "ground, earth; land, property" but also "country; the earth, the world." This same source notes that "patafa" means "to be ripped; to be cut open for disemboweling." Faulkner himself seemed only vaguely aware of what his imaginary county's name might actually mean. More than once he told people it meant "water runs slow through flat land," a translation repeated so often it has taken on an authority of its own. Faulkner's apparent misunderstanding is puzzling because he clearly had done research (probably in Byington's 1915 dictionary) on the names he used for his Indians. Also the meaning of the word was well known among those contemporaries who knew local history. Whether he understood it or not, the word was full of meaning for the world he explored in his fiction.

FURTHER READING

Byington, Cyrus. *A Dictionary of the Choctaw Language*. Ed. John R. Swanton and
     Henry S. Halbert. Washington, D.C.: Government Printing Office, 1915.
Cushman, H. B. *History of the Choctaw, Chickasaw, and Natchez Indians*. Ed. Angie
     Debo. 1899. Greenville, Tex.: Headlight Printing House, 1962.
Munro, Pamela, and Catherine Willmond. *Chickasaw: An Analytical Dictionary*. Nor-
     man: University of Oklahoma Press, 1994.

Don H. Doyle

Selected Bibliography

BOOKS BY FAULKNER

Absalom, Absalom! New York: Random House, 1936.

As I Lay Dying. New York: Jonathan Cape and Harrison Smith, 1930.

Battle Cry, ed. Louis Daniel Brodsky and Robert W. Hamblin. Jackson: University Press of Mississippi, 1985.

Big Woods. New York: Random House, 1955.

Collected Stories. New York: Random House, 1950.

Country Lawyer and Other Stories for the Screen, ed. Louis Daniel Brodsky and Robert W. Hamblin. Jackson: University Press of Mississippi, 1987.

The De Gaulle Story, ed. Louis Daniel Brodsky and Robert W. Hamblin. Jackson: University Press of Mississippi, 1984.

Doctor Martino and Other Stories. New York: Harrison Smith and Robert Haas, 1934.

Essays, Speeches & Public Letters by William Faulkner, ed. James B. Meriwether. New York: Random House, 1966.

A Fable. New York: Random House, 1954.

Flags in the Dust, ed. Douglas Day. New York: Random House, 1973.

Go Down, Moses. New York: Random House, 1942.

A Green Bough. New York: Harrison Smith and Robert Haas, 1933.

The Hamlet. New York: Random House, 1940.

Helen: A Courtship. New Orleans, La., and Oxford, Miss.: Tulane University and Yoknapatawpha Press, 1981.

Idyll in the Desert. New York: Random House, 1931.

Intruder in the Dust. New York: Random House, 1948.

Knight's Gambit. New York: Random House, 1949.

Light in August. New York: Harrison Smith and Robert Haas, 1932.

The Mansion. New York: Random House, 1959.

The Marble Faun. Boston: Four Seas Company, 1924.

The Marionettes: A Play in One Act, ed. Noel Polk. [Charlottesville]: Bibliographical Society of the University of Virginia and the University Press of Virginia, 1975.

Mayday. [Notre Dame, Ind.]: University of Notre Dame Press, 1977.

Mississippi Poems. Oxford, Miss.: Yoknapatawpha Press, 1979.

Miss Zilphia Gant. [Dallas]: Book Club of Texas, 1932.

Mosquitoes. New York: Boni and Liveright, 1927.

New Orleans Sketches, ed. Carvel Collins. New York: Random House, 1968.

Notes on a Horsethief. Greenville, Miss.: Levee Press, 1951.

The Portable Faulkner, ed. Malcolm Cowley. New York: Viking Press, 1946.

Pylon. New York: Harrison Smith and Robert Haas, 1935.

The Reivers. New York: Random House, 1962.

Requiem for a Nun. New York: Random House, 1951.

Sanctuary. New York: Jonathan Cape and Harrison Smith, 1931.

Sanctuary: The Original Text, ed. Noel Polk. New York: Random House, 1981.

Sartoris. New York: Harcourt, Brace, and Company, 1929.

Soldiers' Pay. New York: Boni and Liveright, 1926.

The Sound and the Fury. New York: Jonathan Cape and Harrison Smith, 1929.

Stallion Road, ed. Louis Daniel Brodsky and Robert W. Hamblin. Jackson: University Press of Mississippi, 1989.

These 13. New York: Jonathan Cape and Harrison Smith, 1931.

The Town. New York: Random House, 1957.

Uncollected Stories, ed. Joseph L. Blotner. New York: Random House, 1979.

The Unvanquished. New York: Random House, 1938.

The Wild Palms. New York: Random House, 1939.

William Faulkner: Early Prose and Poetry, ed. Carvel Collins. Boston: Little, Brown, 1962.

The Wishing Tree. New York: Random House, 1967.

BIBLIOGRAPHICAL SOURCES

Bassett, John E. *Faulkner: An Annotated Checklist of Recent Criticism.* Kent, Ohio: Kent State University Press, 1983.

———. *Faulkner in the Eighties: An Annotated Critical Bibliography.* Metuchen, N.J.: Scarecrow, 1991.

———. *William Faulkner: An Annotated Checklist of Criticism.* New York: David Lewis, 1972.

Blotner, Joseph. *William Faulkner's Library: A Catalogue.* Charlottesville: University Press of Virginia, 1964.

Blotner, Joseph, Thomas L. McHaney, Michael Millgate, Noel Polk, and James B. Meriwether, eds. *William Faulkner Manuscripts.* 44 vols. New York: Garland Publishers, 1985–1987.

Bonner, Thomas, Jr., comp. *William Faulkner: The William B. Wisdom Collection: A Descriptive Catalogue.* New Orleans, La.: Tulane University Libraries, 1980.

Brodsky, Louis D., and Robert W. Hamblin, eds. *Faulkner: A Comprehensive Guide to the Brodsky Collection.* 5 vols. Jackson: University Press of Mississippi, 1982–1988.

Capps, Jack L., ed. *The Faulkner Concordances.* 34 vols. Ann Arbor, Mich.: UMI Research Press/The Faulkner Concordance Advisory Board, 1977–1990.

Cox, Leland, ed. *William Faulkner: Biographical and Reference Guide: A Guide to His Life and Career.* Detroit, Mich.: Gale Research, 1982.

Howard, Peter. *William Faulkner: The Carl Petersen Collection.* Berkeley, Calif.: Serendipity Press, 1991.

Kawin, Bruce, ed. *Faulkner's MGM Screenplays*. Knoxville: University of Tennessee Press, 1982.

Massey, Linton, comp. *William Faulkner: "Man Working," 1919–1962: A Catalogue of the William Faulkner Collections at the University of Virginia*. Charlottesville: Bibliographical Society of the University of Virginia, 1968.

McHaney, Thomas. *William Faulkner: A Reference Guide*. Boston: G. K. Hall, 1976.

Meriwether, James B. *The Literary Career of William Faulkner: A Bibliographic Study*. Columbia: University of South Carolina Press, 1972.

———. *The Merrill Checklist of William Faulkner*. Columbus, Ohio: Merrill, 1970.

———, ed. *A Faulkner Miscellany*. Jackson: University Press of Mississippi, 1974.

Petersen, Carl. *Each in Its Ordered Place: A Faulkner Collector's Notebook*. Ann Arbor, Mich.: Ardis, 1975.

———. *On the Track of the Dixie Limited: Further Notes of a Faulkner Collector*. La Grange, Ill.: Colophon Book Shop, 1979.

Ricks, Beatrice. *William Faulkner: A Reference Guide*. Metuchen, N.J.: Scarecrow, 1981.

Sensibar, Judith. *Faulkner's Poetry: A Bibliographic Guide to Texts and Criticism*. Ann Arbor, Mich.: UMI Research Press, 1988.

Sweeney, Patricia. *William Faulkner's Women Characters: An Annotated Bibliography of Criticism, 1930–1983*. Santa Barbara, Calif.: ABC-Clio, 1985.

BIOGRAPHICAL SOURCES

Bezzerides, A. I. *William Faulkner: A Life on Paper*. Ed. Ann Abadie. Jackson: University Press of Mississippi, 1980.

Blotner, Joseph. *Faulkner: A Biography*. 2 vols. New York: Random House, 1974. One-vol. rev. ed., 1984.

———, ed. *Selected Letters of William Faulkner*. New York: Random House, 1977.

Brodsky, Louis Daniel. *William Faulkner: Life Glimpses*. Austin: University of Texas Press, 1990.

Brodsky, Louis Daniel, and Robert W. Hamblin, eds. *Faulkner: A Comprehensive Guide to the Brodsky Collection*. Vol. II: *The Letters*. Jackson: University Press of Mississippi, 1984.

Cofield, Jack. *William Faulkner: The Cofield Collection*. Oxford, Miss.: Yoknapatawpha Press, 1978.

Coughlan, Robert. *The Private World of William Faulkner*. New York: Harper, 1954.

Cowley, Malcolm. *The Faulkner-Cowley File: Letters and Memories, 1944–1962*. New York: Viking Press, 1966.

Cullen, John B., and Floyd C. Watkins. *Old Times in the Faulkner Country*. Chapel Hill: University of North Carolina Press, 1961.

Dain, Martin J. *Faulkner's County: Yoknapatawpha*. New York: Random House, 1964.

———. *Faulkner's World: The Photographs of Martin J. Dain*. Ed. with intro. by Thomas S. Rankin. Jackson: University Press of Mississippi, 1997.

Falkner, Murry C. *The Falkners of Mississippi: A Memoir*. Baton Rouge: Louisiana State University Press, 1967.

Fant, Joseph L., and Robert Ashley, eds. *Faulkner at West Point*. New York: Random House, 1964.

Faulkner, Jim. *Across the Creek: Faulkner Family Stories*. Jackson: University Press of Mississippi, 1986.

Faulkner, John. *My Brother Bill: An Affectionate Reminiscence.* New York: Trident, 1963.

Franklin, Malcolm A. *Bitterweeds: Life with William Faulkner at Rowan Oak.* Irving, Tex.: Society for the Study of Traditional Culture, 1977.

Gray, Richard. *The Life of William Faulkner: A Critical Biography.* Oxford, England: Blackwell, 1994.

Gresset, Michel. *A Faulkner Chronology.* Jackson: University Press of Mississippi, 1985.

Gwynn, Frederick L., and Joseph Blotner, eds. *Faulkner in the University: Class Conferences at the University of Virginia, 1957–1958.* Charlottesville: University of Virginia Press, 1959.

Haynes, Jane Isbell. *William Faulkner: His Lafayette County Heritage.* Columbia, S.C.: Seajay Press, 1992.

———. *William Faulkner: His Tippah County Heritage.* Columbia, S.C.: Seajay Press, 1985.

Jelliffe, Robert A., ed. *Faulkner at Nagano.* Tokyo, Japan: Kenkyusha, 1956.

Karl, Frederick. *William Faulkner, American Writer: A Biography.* New York: Eidenfield and Nicolson, 1989.

Lawrence, John, and Dan Hise. *Faulkner's Rowan Oak.* Jackson: University Press of Mississippi, 1995.

Meriwether, James B., and Michael Millgate, eds. *Lion in the Garden: Interviews with William Faulkner, 1926–1962.* New York: Random House, 1968.

Minter, David. *William Faulkner: His Life and Work.* Baltimore, Md.: Johns Hopkins University Press, 1980.

Morris, Willie. *Faulkner's Mississippi.* Birmingham, Ala.: Oxmoor House, 1990.

Oates, Stephen B. *William Faulkner: The Man and the Artist.* New York: Harper and Row, 1987.

Raimbault, R. N. *Faulkner.* Paris, France: Editions Universitaires, 1963.

Richardson, H. Edward. *William Faulkner: The Journey to Self-Discovery.* Columbia: University of Missouri Press, 1969.

Snell, Susan. *Phil Stone of Oxford: A Vicarious Life.* Athens: University of Georgia Press, 1991.

Taylor, Herman E. *Faulkner's Oxford: Recollections and Reflections.* Nashville, Tenn.: Rutledge Hill Press, 1990.

Wasson, Ben. *Count No 'Count: Flashbacks to Faulkner.* Jackson: University Press of Mississippi, 1983.

Watson, James G., ed. *Thinking of Home: William Faulkner's Letters to His Mother and Father, 1918–1925.* New York: Norton, 1992.

Webb, James W., and A. Wigfall Green, eds. *William Faulkner of Oxford.* Baton Rouge: Louisiana State University Press, 1965.

Wells, Dean Faulkner. *The Ghosts of Rowan Oak: William Faulkner's Ghost Stories for Children.* Oxford, Miss.: Yoknapatawpha Press, 1980.

Wilde, Meta Carpenter, and Orin Borsten. *A Loving Gentleman: The Love Story of William Faulkner and Meta Carpenter.* New York: Simon and Schuster, 1976.

Williamson, Joel. *William Faulkner and Southern History.* New York: Oxford University Press, 1993.

Wittenberg, Judith Bryant. *Faulkner: The Transfiguration of Biography.* Lincoln: University of Nebraska Press, 1979.

Wolff, Sally, with Floyd C. Watkins, eds. *Talking about William Faulkner: Interviews with Jimmy Faulkner and Others*. Baton Rouge: Louisiana State University Press, 1996.

GENERAL STUDIES

Adams, Richard P. *Faulkner: Myth and Motion*. Princeton, N.J.: Princeton University Press, 1968.

Backman, Melvin. *Faulkner: The Major Years: A Critical Study*. Bloomington: Indiana University Press, 1966.

Barth, J. Robert, ed. *Religious Perspectives in Faulkner's Fiction: Yoknapatawpha and Beyond*. Notre Dame, Ind.: University of Notre Dame Press, 1972.

Bassett, John Earl. *Vision and Revisions: Essays on Faulkner*. West Cornwall, Conn.: Locust Hill Press, 1989.

Beck, Warren. *Faulkner: Essays*. Madison: University of Wisconsin Press, 1976.

Bleikasten, André. *The Ink of Melancholy: Faulkner's Novels from* The Sound and the Fury *to* Light in August. Bloomington: Indiana University Press, 1990.

Bloom, Harold, ed. *Modern Critical Views: William Faulkner*. New York: Chelsea House, 1986.

Bockting, Ineke. *Character and Personality in the Novels of William Faulkner: A Study in Psychostylistics*. Lanham, Md.: University Press of America, 1995.

Brooks, Cleanth. *On the Prejudices, Predilections, and Firm Beliefs of William Faulkner*. Baton Rouge: Louisiana State University Press, 1987.

———. *William Faulkner: First Encounters*. New Haven, Conn.: Yale University Press, 1983.

———. *William Faulkner: The Yoknapatawpha Country*. New Haven, Conn.: Yale University Press, 1963.

———. *William Faulkner: Toward Yoknapatawpha and Beyond*. New Haven, Conn.: Yale University Press, 1978.

Broughton, Panthea Reid. *William Faulkner: The Abstract and the Actual*. Baton Rouge: Louisiana State University Press, 1974.

Brown, Calvin S. *A Glossary of Faulkner's South*. New Haven, Conn.: Yale University Press, 1976.

Brylowski, Walter. *Faulkner's Olympian Laugh: Myth in the Novels*. Detroit, Mich.: Wayne State University Press, 1968.

Campbell, Harry M., and Ruel E. Foster. *William Faulkner: A Critical Appraisal*. Norman: Oklahoma University Press, 1951.

Carey, Glenn O., ed. *Faulkner: The Unappeased Imagination: A Collection of Critical Essays*. Troy, N.Y.: Whitston, 1980.

Carothers, James B. *William Faulkner's Short Stories*. Ann Arbor, Mich.: UMI Research Press, 1985.

Chabrier, Gwendolyn. *Faulkner's Families: A Southern Saga*. New York: Gordian, 1993.

Chappell, Charles. *Detective Dupin Reads William Faulkner: Solutions to Six Yoknapatawpha Mysteries*. San Francisco: International Scholars Publications, 1997.

Clarke, Deborah. *Robbing the Mother: Women in Faulkner*. Jackson: University Press of Mississippi, 1994.

Coffee, James M. *Faulkner's Un-Christlike Christians: Biblical Allusions in the Novels*. Ann Arbor, Mich.: UMI Research Press, 1983.

Coindreau, Maurice E. *The Time of William Faulkner: A French View of Modern American Fiction*. Ed. and trans. George M. Reeves. Columbia: South Carolina University Press, 1971.

Coy, Javier, and Michel Gresset, eds. *Faulkner and History*. Salamanca, Spain: Universidad de Salamanca, 1986.

Dabney, Lewis M. *The Indians of Yoknapatawpha: A Study in Literature and History*. Baton Rouge: Louisiana State University Press, 1973.

Davis, Thadious M. *Faulkner's "Negro": Art and the Southern Context*. Baton Rouge: Louisiana State University Press, 1983.

Dowling, David. *William Faulkner*. New York: St. Martin's Press, 1989.

Duvall, John N. *Faulkner's Marginal Couple: Invisible, Outlaw, and Unspeakable Communities*. Austin: University of Texas Press, 1990.

Emerson, O. B. *Faulkner's Early Literary Reputation in America*. Ann Arbor, Mich.: UMI Research Press, 1984.

Everett, Walter K. *Faulkner's Art and Characters*. Woodbury, N.Y.: Barron's Educational Series, 1969.

Fayen, Tonya T. *In Search of the Latin American Faulkner*. Lanham, Md.: University Press of America, 1995.

Ferguson, James. *Faulkner's Short Fiction*. Knoxville: University of Tennessee Press, 1991.

Ford, Dan, ed. *Heir and Prototype: Original and Derived Characterizations in Faulkner*. Conway: University of Central Arkansas Press, 1988.

Fowler, Doreen. *Faulkner's Changing Vision: From Outrage to Affirmation*. Ann Arbor, Mich.: UMI Research Press, 1983.

———. *Faulkner: The Return of the Repressed*. Charlottesville: University Press of Virginia, 1997.

Fowler, Doreen, and Ann J. Abadie, eds. *"A Cosmos of My Own": Faulkner and Yoknapatawpha, 1980*. Jackson: University Press of Mississippi, 1981.

———. *Faulkner and Humor: Faulkner and Yoknapatawpha, 1984*. Jackson: University Press of Mississippi, 1986.

———. *Faulkner and Popular Culture: Faulkner and Yoknapatawpha, 1988*. Jackson: University Press of Mississippi, 1990.

———. *Faulkner and Race: Faulkner and Yoknapatawpha, 1986*. Jackson: University Press of Mississippi, 1987.

———. *Faulkner and Religion: Faulkner and Yoknapatawpha, 1989*. Jackson: University Press of Mississippi, 1991.

———. *Faulkner and the Craft of Fiction: Faulkner and Yoknapatawpha, 1987*. Jackson: University Press of Mississippi, 1989.

———. *Faulkner and the Southern Renaissance: Faulkner and Yoknapatawpha, 1981*. Jackson: University Press of Mississippi, 1982.

———. *Faulkner and Women: Faulkner and Yoknapatawpha, 1985*. Jackson: University Press of Mississippi, 1986.

———. *Faulkner: International Perspectives: Faulkner and Yoknapatawpha, 1982*. Jackson: University Press of Mississippi, 1984.

———. *Fifty Years of Yoknapatawpha: Faulkner and Yoknapatawpha, 1979*. Jackson: University Press of Mississippi, 1980.

———. *New Directions in Faulkner Studies: Faulkner and Yoknapatawpha, 1983*. Jackson: University Press of Mississippi, 1984.

Friedman, Allen Warren. *William Faulkner*. New York: Ungar, 1984.

Godden, Richard. *Fictions of Labor: William Faulkner and the South's Long Revolution*. Cambridge: Cambridge University Press, 1997.

Gold, Joseph. *William Faulkner: A Study in Humanism: From Metaphor to Discourse*. Norman: Oklahoma University Press, 1966.

Gresset, Michel. *Fascination: Faulkner's Fiction, 1919–1936*. Durham, N.C.: Duke University Press, 1989.

Gresset, Michel, and Noel Polk, eds. *Intertextuality in Faulkner*. Jackson: University Press of Mississippi, 1985.

Gresset, Michel, and Patrick Samway, eds. *Faulkner and Idealism: Perspectives from Paris*. Jackson: University Press of Mississippi, 1983.

Grimwood, Michael. *Heart in Conflict: Faulkner's Struggles with Vocation*. Athens: University of Georgia Press, 1987.

Gutting, Gabriele. *The Function of Geographical and Historical Facts in William Faulkner's Fictional Picture of the Deep South*. New York: Lang, 1992.

Gwin, Minrose. *The Feminine in Faulkner: Reading (Beyond) Sexual Difference*. Knoxville: University of Tennessee Press, 1990.

Harrington, Evans, and Ann J. Abadie, eds. *Faulkner and the Short Story: Faulkner and Yoknapatawpha, 1990*. Jackson: University Press of Mississippi, 1992.

———. *Faulkner, Modernism, and Film: Faulkner and Yoknapatawpha, 1978*. Jackson: University Press of Mississippi, 1979.

———. *The Maker and the Myth: Faulkner and Yoknapatawpha, 1977*. Jackson: University Press of Mississippi, 1978.

———. *The South and Faulkner's Yoknapatawpha: The Actual and the Apocryphal: Faulkner and Yoknapatawpha, 1976*. Jackson: University Press of Mississippi, 1977.

Harrington, Gary. *Faulkner's Fables of Creativity: The Non-Yoknapatawpha Novels*. Athens: University of Georgia Press, 1990.

Hines, Thomas S. *William Faulkner and the Tangible Past: The Architecture of Yoknapatawpha*. Berkeley: University of California Press, 1996.

Hoffman, Daniel. *Faulkner's Country Matters: Folklore and Fable in Yoknapatawpha*. Baton Rouge: Louisiana State University Press, 1989.

Hoffman, Frederick J. *William Faulkner*. 2nd ed. New York: Twayne, 1966.

Hoffman, Frederick J., and Olga W. Vickery, eds. *William Faulkner: Three Decades of Criticism*. East Lansing: Michigan State University Press, 1960.

———. *William Faulkner: Two Decades of Criticism*. East Lansing: Michigan State College Press, 1951.

Holmes, Edward M. *Faulkner's Twice-Told Tales: His Re-Use of Materials*. The Hague, Holland: Mouton, 1966.

Hönnighausen, Lothar. *Faulkner: Masks and Metaphors*. Jackson: University Press of Mississippi, 1997.

———. *William Faulkner: The Art of Stylization in His Early Graphic and Literary Work*. Cambridge, England: Cambridge University Press, 1987.

———, ed. *Faulkner's Discourse: An International Symposium*. Tübingen, Germany: Max Niemeyer Verlag, 1989.

Howe, Irving. *William Faulkner: A Critical Study*. Rev. ed. New York: Vintage Books, 1962.

Hunt, John W. *William Faulkner: Art in Theological Tension.* Syracuse, New York: Syracuse University Press, 1965.

Hunter, Edwin R. *William Faulkner: Narrative Practice and Prose Style.* Washington, D.C.: Windhover, 1973.

Inge, M. Thomas, ed. *William Faulkner: The Contemporary Reviews.* Cambridge, England: Cambridge University Press, 1995.

Irwin, John T. *Doubling and Incest/Repetition and Revenge: A Speculative Reading of Faulkner.* Exp. ed. Baltimore, Md.: Johns Hopkins University Press, 1996.

Jehlen, Myra. *Class and Character in Faulkner's South.* New York: Columbia University Press, 1976.

Jenkins, Lee Clinton. *Faulkner and Black-White Relations: A Psychoanalytic Approach.* New York: Columbia University Press, 1981.

Jones, Diane Brown. *A Reader's Guide to the Short Stories of William Faulkner.* New York: G. K. Hall, 1994.

Kartiganer, Donald M. *The Fragile Thread: The Meaning of Form in Faulkner's Novels.* Amherst: University of Massachusetts Press, 1979.

Kartiganer, Donald M., and Ann J. Abadie, eds. *Faulkner and Gender: Faulkner and Yoknapatawpha, 1994.* Jackson: University Press of Mississippi, 1996.

———. *Faulkner and Ideology: Faulkner and Yoknapatawpha, 1992.* Jackson: University Press of Mississippi, 1995.

———. *Faulkner and Psychology: Faulkner and Yoknapatawpha, 1991.* Jackson: University Press of Mississippi, 1994.

———. *Faulkner and the Artist: Faulkner and Yoknapatawpha, 1993.* Jackson: University Press of Mississippi, 1996.

———. *Faulkner in Cultural Context: Faulkner and Yoknapatawpha, 1995.* Jackson: University Press of Mississippi, 1997.

Kawin, Bruce. *Faulkner and Film.* New York: Ungar, 1977.

Kerr, Elizabeth M. *William Faulkner's Gothic Domain.* Port Washington, N.Y.: Kennikat Press, 1979.

———. *William Faulkner's Yoknapatawpha: "A Kind of Keystone in the Universe."* New York: Fordham University Press, 1976.

———. *Yoknapatawpha: Faulkner's "Little Postage Stamp of Native Soil."* Rev. ed. New York: Fordham University Press, 1976.

Kinney, Arthur F. *Faulkner's Narrative Poetics: Style as Vision.* Amherst: University of Massachusetts Press, 1978.

Kirk, Robert W., and Marvin Klotz. *Faulkner's People.* Berkeley: University of California Press, 1963.

Kreiswirth, Martin. *William Faulkner: The Making of a Novelist.* Athens: University of Georgia Press, 1983.

LaLonde, Christopher A. *William Faulkner and the Rites of Passage.* Macon, Ga.: Mercer University Press, 1995.

Leary, Lewis. *William Faulkner of Yoknapatawpha County.* New York: Crowell, 1973.

Lee, Robert, ed. *William Faulkner: The Yoknapatawpha Fiction.* New York: St. Martin's Press, 1990.

Levins, Lynn Gartrell. *Faulkner's Heroic Design: The Yoknapatawpha Novels.* Athens: University of Georgia Press, 1976.

Lockyer, Judith. *Ordered by Words: Language and Narration in the Novels of William Faulkner.* Carbondale: Southern Illinois University Press, 1991.

Longley, John L., Jr. *The Tragic Mask: A Study of Faulkner's Heroes*. Chapel Hill: North Carolina University Press, 1963.

Malin, Irving. *William Faulkner: An Interpretation*. Stanford, Calif.: Stanford University Press, 1957.

Matthews, John T. *The Play of Faulkner's Language*. Ithaca, N.Y.: Cornell University Press, 1982.

Millgate, Michael. *The Achievement of William Faulkner*. New York: Random House, 1966.

————. *Faulkner's Place*. Athens: University of Georgia Press, 1997.

Miner, Ward L. *The World of William Faulkner*. Durham, N.C.: Duke University Press, 1952.

Moreland, Richard C. *Faulkner and Modernism: Rereading and Rewriting*. Madison: University of Wisconsin Press, 1990.

————. *Faulkner's Modernism Under Revision*. Madison: University of Wisconsin Press, 1990.

Morris, Welsey, and Barbara Alverson Morris. *Reading Faulkner*. Madison: University of Wisconsin Press, 1990.

Mortimer, Gail L. *Faulkner's Rhetoric of Loss: A Study in Perception and Meaning*. Austin: University of Texas Press, 1983.

Nilon, Charles H. *Faulkner and the Negro*. New York: Citadel Press, 1965.

Nordanberg, Thomas. *Cataclysm as Catalyst: The Theme of War in William Faulkner's Fiction*. Uppsala, Sweden: Almqvist, 1983.

O'Connor, William Van. *The Tangled Fire of William Faulkner*. Minneapolis: University of Minnesota Press, 1954.

Ohashi, Kenzaburo, and Kiyoyuki Ono, comps. *Faulkner Studies in Japan*. Ed. Thomas L. McHaney. Athens: University of Georgia Press, 1985.

Page, Sally. *Faulkner's Women: Characterization and Meaning*. Deland, Fla.: Everett/Edward, 1972.

Parker, Robert Dale. *Faulkner and the Novelistic Imagination*. Urbana: University of Illinois Press, 1985.

Peavy, Charles. *Go Slow Now: Faulkner and the Race Question*. Eugene: University of Oregon Press, 1971.

Peters, Erskine. *William Faulkner: The Yoknapatawpha World and Black Being*. Darby, Pa.: Norwood, 1983.

Phillips, Gene D. *Fiction, Film, and Faulkner: The Art of Adaptation*. Knoxville: University of Tennessee Press, 1988.

Polk, Noel. *Children of the Dark House: Text and Context in Faulkner*. Jackson: University Press of Mississippi, 1996.

Powers, Lyall H. *Faulkner's Yoknapatawpha Comedy*. Ann Arbor: University of Michigan Press, 1980.

Putzel, Max. *Genius of Place: William Faulkner's Triumphant Beginnings*. Baton Rouge: Louisiana State University Press, 1985.

Reed, Joseph W., Jr. *Faulkner's Narrative*. New Haven, Conn.: Yale University Press, 1973.

Richardson, Kenneth E. *Force and Faith in the Novels of William Faulkner*. The Hague, Holland: Mouton, 1967.

Roberts, Diane. *Faulkner and Southern Womanhood*. Athens: University of Georgia Press, 1994.

Rollyson, Carl E. *Uses of the Past in the Novels of William Faulkner*. Ann Arbor, Mich.: UMI Research Press, 1984.

Ross, Stephen M. *Fiction's Inexhaustible Voice: Speech and Writing in Faulkner*. Athens: University of Georgia Press, 1983.

Runyan, Harry. *A Faulkner Glossary*. New York: Citadel, 1964.

Ruppersburg, Hugh M. *Voice and Eye in Faulkner's Fiction*. Athens: University of Georgia Press, 1983.

Ruzicka, William T. *Faulkner's Fictive Architecture: The Meaning of Place in the Yoknapatawpha Novels*. Ann Arbor, Mich.: UMI Research Press, 1987.

Schwartz, Lawrence H. *Creating Faulkner's Reputation: The Politics of Modern Literary Criticism*. Knoxville: University of Tennessee Press, 1988.

Sensibar, Judith L. *The Origins of Faulkner's Art*. Austin: University of Texas Press, 1984.

Singal, Daniel J. *William Faulkner: The Making of a Modernist*. Chapel Hill: University of North Carolina Press, 1997.

Slatoff, Walter J. *Quest for Failure: A Study of William Faulkner*. Ithaca, N.Y.: Cornell University Press, 1960.

Snead, James A. *Figures of Division: William Faulkner's Major Novels*. New York: Methuen, 1986.

Stonum, Gary Lee. *Faulkner's Career: An Internal Literary History*. Ithaca, N.Y.: Cornell University Press, 1979.

Sundquist, Eric. *Faulkner: The House Divided*. Baltimore, Md.: Johns Hopkins University Press, 1983.

Swiggart, Peter. *The Art of Faulkner's Novels*. Austin: University of Texas Press, 1962.

Swisher, Clarice, ed. *Readings on William Faulkner*. San Diego, Calif.: Greenhaven Press, 1997.

Taylor, Walter. *Faulkner's Search for a South*. Urbana: University of Illinois Press, 1983.

Thompson, Lawrance. *William Faulkner*. New York: Barnes and Noble, 1963.

Tuck, Dorothy. *Crowell's Handbook of Faulkner*. New York: Crowell, 1964.

Urgo, Joseph R. *Faulkner's Apocrypha*: A Fable, Snopes, *and the Spirit of Human Rebellion*. Jackson: University Press of Mississippi, 1989.

Vanderwerken, David L. *Faulkner's Literary Children: Patterns of Development*. New York: Peter Lang, 1997.

Vickery, Olga W. *The Novels of William Faulkner: A Critical Interpretation*. 3rd ed. Baton Rouge: Louisiana State University Press, 1995.

Visser, Irene. *Compassion in Faulkner's Fiction*. Lewiston, N.Y.: Edwin Mellen, 1996.

Volpe, Edmond L. *A Reader's Guide to William Faulkner*. New York: Noonday, 1964.

Wadlington, Warwick. *Reading Faulknerian Tragedy*. Ithaca, N.Y.: Cornell University Press, 1987.

Waggoner, Hyatt H. *William Faulkner: From Jefferson to the World*. Lexington: University of Kentucky Press, 1959.

Wagner, Linda W., ed. *William Faulkner: Four Decades of Criticism*. East Lansing: Michigan State University Press, 1973.

Warren, Robert Penn, ed. *Faulkner: A Collection of Critical Essays*. Englewood Cliffs, N.J.: Prentice-Hall, 1966.

Watson, James G. *William Faulkner, Letters and Fictions*. Austin: University of Texas Press, 1987.

Watson, Jay. *Forensic Fictions: The Lawyer Figure in Faulkner*. Athens: University of Georgia Press, 1993.

Weinstein, Philip. *Faulkner's Subject: A Cosmos No One Owns*. New York: Cambridge University Press, 1992.

———. *What Else But Love: The Ordeal of Race in Faulkner and Morrison*. New York: Columbia University Press, 1996.

———, ed. *The Cambridge Companion to William Faulkner*. New York: Cambridge University Press, 1995.

Williams, David. *Faulkner's Women: The Myth and the Muse*. Montreal, Can.: McGill-Queen's University Press, 1977.

Wright, Austin M. *Recalcitrance, Faulkner, and the Professors: A Critical Fiction*. Iowa City: University of Iowa Press, 1990.

Zacharasiewicz, Waldemar, ed. *Faulkner, His Contemporaries, and His Posterity*. Tübingen, Germany: Francke, 1993.

Zender, Karl F. *The Crossing of the Ways: William Faulkner, the South, and the Modern World*. New Brunswick, N.J.: Rutgers University Press, 1989.

Index

Italic page numbers indicate location of main entries.

Absalom, Absalom!, *1–4*, 15, 37–38, 40–
41, 59, 61, 63, 65, 73, 76, 80, 86–88,
93, 99–100, 104, 118, 121, 133, 136,
140, 146–47, 157–58, 161, 169, 176–
79, 181–82, 187, 189, 191, 193, 195,
204, 206, 211, 220, 237–38, 248, 250,
252, 255–56, 266, 270, 274–75, 289,
291–92, 296–97, 301–2, 306, 320, 331,
340, 346–47, 349, 354, 360, 364, 366,
369, 372, 376, 387–91, 394–96, 407,
409, 412, 418–19, 425, 430, 432, 441
"Absolution, An," 137. *See also* "Fire
and the Hearth"
"Ace, The," 25
"Ad Astra," *4–5*, 25, 48, 83, 182, 399,
430, 443
Addie, 278
Addresses. *See* Speeches
"Adolescence," *6*, 415
African American, *6–9*, 15, 32, 36, 65,
131, 147, 158, 167, 193, 205, 237, 261–
62, 269–70, 283, 301, 310, 322–23,
326, 351, 353–56, 360, 366–67, 438.
See also *Go Down, Moses; Intruder in
the Dust*; Race; Slavery
"Afternoon of a Cow," *9–10*, 79, 166,
415

Agnes Mabel Becky, 258
Agrarian(s), 52, 68, 96 107, 146, 155,
185, 196, 322, 344, 368, 371
Aiken, Conrad, 62, 102, 143, 202, 257,
383, 416
Air Force, *10*, 445
Ailanthia. *See* "Elly"
Alcoholism *10–12*, 87, 133, 295, 358,
414, 423–24; Compson, 66, 87, 147,
363, 390; drug addiction, 42, 242; Sut-
pen, 66. *See also* "Mr. Acarius"
Alice, 438
Alienation, estrangement, 3, 44, 51, 71,
102, 113, 210, 306, 373, 444; absence,
presence, 8, 166, 181, 241, 359; aliens,
269; isolation, 332
"Al Jackson," *12*, 16, 122, 132, 415
Allen, Bobbie, 183, 230; Allen, Paula
Gunn, 197
Allison, Howard Judge, 39
"All the Dead Pilots," *12–13*, 25, 83,
219–20, 399, 430, 443
"Ambuscade," *13*, 414, 418
American Adam, 187, 301, 362. *See also*
Eden
The American Dream, 23; national narra-
tive, 33. *See* "On Fear"

American Mercury, 65, 104, 155–56, 165, 181, 287, 396–97, 414
American Renaissance, *13–16*, 135. *See also* Emerson, Ralph Waldo; Hawthorne, Nathaniel; Melville, Herman; Thoreau, Henry David; Whitman, Walt
Ames, Dalton, *16*
Andersch, Alfred, 145
Anderson, Sherwood, 12, *16–17*, 20, 22, 107, 122, 132, 143–44, 153, 227, 257, 268, 272, 285, 358, 364, 383, 411, 435; Elizabeth Prall, 268; *Sherwood Anderson and other Famous Creoles*, 17, 269, 272
Angelo, 297
Apocrypha, *17–18*, 21, 41, 69, 133, 168, 208, 261, 293, 304, 365, 378
"Appendix, Compson, 1699–1945," 8, *18–19*, 24, 79, 87, 135, 147, 160, 194, 237, 296, 362–63
L'Apres-Midi d'un Faune, 10, *19*, 140, 232, 261. See Also *Marble Faun, The*
"Aria Con Amore," 261
Art. *See* Visual Arts
"Artist at Home," *19–20*, 408
Artist, figure of, 20, 22, 37, 58–60, 94, 96, 169, 246, 257, 281–82, 286, 288–89, 298, 327, 329, 383, 423, 435, 437
As I Lay Dying, 15, *20–23*, 38, 41, 51, 55, 63, 65, 68, 77, 115, 133, 142, 144, 146, 153, 157–58, 177, 187, 189–90, 194, 196, 204, 208, 247, 266, 276, 290–91, 303, 311, 320, 339, 341, 360, 369, 372–73, 385–87, 389, 394, 410, 417, 421; Tandis que j'agonise, 79. *See also* Bundren
Athletics. *See* Sport
Atlantic Monthly, The, 118, 272, 288, 348, 364
"Aubade," 261
Automobile, *23–25*, 109, 182, 317–18, 342, 346–48, 413
Aviation, 7, 8, 11, *25–26*, 93, 95, 124, 128, 133, 134, 236, 241, 268, 270, 305–6, 346, 348, 358, 377–79, 411, 414, 430, 439, 442–45; Flying Faulkners, 122
Awards: *Ellery Queen Mystery Magazine*

Second Prize, 118, 295; French Legion of Honor, 269; *Mademoiselle*'s Forty Best Stories, 57; National Book, 81, 118; National Institute Gold Medal 49; Nobel, 19, 38, 80–82, 129, 133–34, 140, 146, 203, 257, 271, 287, 294, 348, 367, 373, 383, 402, 409; O'Henry, 83, 89, 401; Order of Andres Bello, 281–82, 377; Pulitzer, 118, 317

Bacall, Lauren, 11
Backhouse, Lt. Cousin Philip, 262
Backus, Melisandra, 217
Baird, Helen, *27*, 61, 132, 169, 268–69, 329, 426, 436, 439
Baldwin, James, 8, 193
Balzac, Honoré de, *27–28*, 101, 138, 166–67, 398
"Barn Burning," *28–29*, 75, 82, 99, 135, 166, 224, 296, 421
Barn Burning, *29–30*
Barnes, Djuna, 194, 285
Barnett, Ned, *30–31*, 336
Barr, Caroline, 8, *31*, 138, 147, 149, 312, 336–37, 355, 361, 366, 377, 440
Barr Films, 34
Barron, Homer, *31–32*, 163, 331–35, 366
Basket, Herman, 90, 193, 213, 400
Basket, John, 36
Basso, Hamilton, 268
Battle Cry, 25, *32*, 96, 140, 178, 445
Baudelaire, 10, 327
Beach, Sylvia, 286; Shakespeare and Co., 286
"Bear, The," 7, *32–34*, 43, 98–100, 112–13, 115, 121, 135, 149, 151, 171, 190–91, 194–95, 197, 204, 215, 232, 276, 292, 301, 366, 368, 380, 391, 408, 412, 415, 425
Bear, The, *34–36*
Beard, Mrs. Will, 164
Beardsley, Aubrey, 247, 358, 416, 425–26
"Bear Hunt, A," *36*, 43–44, 81, 213, 378
Beauchamp, *36–37*, 114, 251; Henry, 150; Hubert, 431; Lucas, 24, 31, 34, 36, 76,

100, 104, 115, 120, 137–38, 149–50, 156, 199–201, 212, 240, 251, 283, 289, 308, 412; Molly (Mollie), 31, 36–37, 41, 115, 138, 148, 150, 182; Natalie, 289; Samuel Worsham "Butch," 211; Sophonsiba (*see also* McCaslin), 150, 431. *See also* Edmonds; *Go Down, Moses*; *Intruder in the Dust*; McCaslin; Priest

Belief, faith, 70, 87, 148, 242, 319, 325, 328, 338, 351

Bellow, Saul, 112

Benbow, *37–38*; Belle (Mitchell), 37, 253–54, 345, 439; Cassius Q., 37, 314; Horace, 24, 37, 106, 118, 143–44, 181–82, 207, 223, 246, 253–54, 303, 342–46, 444; Judge, 37; Narcissa (*see also* Sartoris), 37, 118, 162, 223, 303, 342–43, 345–46, 398

Benet, Juan, 373–75

Bennet, Arnold, 50, 360

Bergson, Henri, *38–39*, 254–55, 437; *Creative Evolution*, 38; *Two Sources of Morality and Religion*, 39

Berry, Louis, 315–16

"Beyond," *39*, 84, 105

Bezzerides, Albert I., 11–12, 29, *39–40*, 47

Bible, 1, 12, 33–34, *40–42*, 49, 99–100, 206, 262, 316, 320, 322, 354, 409; Abraham, 148; Adam, 111–113; Apocalypse, 148; Bethesda, 154; Cain/Abel, 374; Cana (water/wine), 321; David, 41, 274; Esau, 4; Exodus, 322; Genesis, 112, 135, 174; Gethsemane, 173; Good Shepherd, 154; Israel, 323; Jesus' birth, 322; Jesus' Passion, 69, 229, 321, 323; Jesus' Temptation in the Wilderness, 120; Job, 149, 410; Job. 1:21, 41; John, 154, 228, 321; John. 19, 229; John the Baptist, 154, 229; Jordan, 311; Joseph, 153, 229; Lazarus, 154; Luke, 16:21, 40; Mary, 153, 164, 231; Meek shall inherit the earth, 233; New Testament, 255; Nicodemus, 229; Old Testament, 49, 149, 217, 383, 417; Pharisee, 229; Pharoah, 148, 219; Pontius Pilate, 152, 229; Promised Land, 41; Proverbs, 41, 410; Psalm 137, 41, 436; Rachel, 148; Render unto Caesar, 405; Revelation, 41, 322, 351; 2 Samuel 13, 1; Solomon, 274; Suffering Servant, 242; Yahweh, 229

"Big Shot, The," 1, *42*, 110, 415. *See also* "Dull Tale"

Big Sleep, The, *42–43*, 179, 295

Big Woods, 36, *43–45*, 81, 87, 191, 213, 250, 310, 415

Bilbo's Mississippi, 131

Bildungsroman, 65, 102, 211–12, 317–19; coming-of-age, 28, 251, 292, 317; developmental stages, 71, 117, 246, 256; initiation, 15, 32, 35, 44, 65, 88, 102, 113, 151, 191, 210, 318, 380, 412, 414; rite of passage, 67. *See also* Childhood

Biographies, *45–48*

"Black Music," *48*, 59, 84, 104–5, 261

Blair, Harrison, 139; Blair, John, 20; Mrs. Harrison Blair, 139

Bland, Gerald, 4, 16, *48*, 399

Bleikasten, André, 141, 177, 293, 360

Blotner, Joseph Leo, 12, 46, *48–49*, 82, 85, 97, 124, 132, 139, 160, 202–3, 226, 252, 293, 299, 302, 326, 376, 394, 414–15, 423, 426, 439

Blount, Dr. Gavin, 42, 110, 327

Boccaccio, 233

Bogard, Captain, 411

Bogart, Humphrey, 42, 402

Boggan, 321

Bon, Charles, 3, 118, 121, 302, 375, 391–92, 419; Charles Etienne St. Valery, 391; Eulalia (*see also* Sutpen), 182, 391

Bond, Jim, 211, 391

Boni and Liveright (Horace), 285, 345, 358, 399

Book Club of Texas, 252

Bookwright, 403

Bootlegging, bootlegger 10–11, 217, 223, 229, 270, 276, 283, 321, 342; alcohol smuggler, 280. *See also* Prohibition

Boozer, William, 246

Borges, Jorge Luis, 220, 408

Bowman, Mr., 92

Boyd, Don, 97; Boyd, Howard, 51; Mrs.
   Boyd, 51
Bradford, Roark, 268
Breckenridge, Hugh Henry, 57
Breit, Harvey, 288
British influences and reception, *49–51*,
   234, 267, 417. *See also individual au-*
   thors
Britt, Flight Commander, 357, 439
"Brooch, The," *51–52*
Brooks, Calvin, 140
Brooks, Cleanth, 50, *52–54*, 59, 170, 180,
   185, 203–4, 299, 326, 330, 333, 366,
   407, 431, 435, 439
Brown, Calvin, 416; Charles Brockden,
   111–12, 156; Clarence, 201; Joe, 24,
   54, 164, 229–30; Joe C., 15
Brown vs. Board of Education, 310
Brzewski, Corporal, 321. *See also* Corpo-
   ral
Buchanan, James (President), 335
Bud, Uncle, 343
Built Environment, 47–48, 74, 125, 130,
   157, 268, 285–86, 347, 349, 354, 384,
   416–17. *See also* College Hill Presby-
   terian Church, Rowan Oak, St. Peter's
   Episcopal Church
Bunch, Byron, *54*, 153, 164, 172, 229–
   31, 258
Bunden, Bud, 6; Bunden, Juliet, 6
Bundren, 41, *55*, 63, 65, 365, 372, 386,
   410–11; Addie, 55, 77, 79, 93, 137,
   153, 158, 195, 208, 390, 411, 439–41;
   Anse, 55, 78, 157, 189, 386; Cash, 55,
   386; Darl, 55, 136, 142–44, 183, 210,
   247, 259, 303, 386; Dewey Dell, 55,
   136, 190, 386; Jewel, 55, 77, 182, 210;
   Mrs., 55; Vardaman, 55, 93, 153, 386.
   See also *As I Lay Dying*
Burch, Lucas, 56, 164, 228
Burden, *55–56*, 63–64, 314, 419; Nathan-
   iel, 56
Burden, Joanna, 24, 55, *56*, 70, 154, 164,
   177, 210, 229, 231, 291, 314, 321,
   328, 390, 427, 439, 441
Butler, Lelia, *56–57*, 93, 123
Butler, Maud. *See* Falkner, Maud Butler

"By the People," *57*, 244
Byron, Lord (George Gordon), 330

Callicoat, David. *See* Ikkemotubbe
Calvo, Lino Novás, 220
Camus, Albert, *58–59*, 140, 241
Cantwell, Robert, 281
Cape & Smith, 341, 360
Capote, Truman, 157, 294
Carcassonne, *59*, 171
"Carcassonne," *59–60*, 82, 84, 93, 140,
   184, 261, 401
Carl, 103, 181
Carl Petersen Collection, 85, 226
Carpenter, Meta Doherty, *61*, 133, 180,
   226, 329, 436–37
Carter, Hodding, *61–62*, 104. *See also*
   Silver, James Wesley
Carvel Collins Collection, 85. *See also*
   Collins, Carvel
Caspey, 438, 444
Cather, Willa, *62–65*, 70, 90, 362
Cavalier, chevalier, chivalry, 4, 57, 193,
   316, 322, 330, 368; Roland, 171; Sam-
   urai, 265
Cela, Camilo José, 373
"Centaur in Brass," *65*, 81, 83, 412
Cerf, Bennett, 11, 281, 297
Cervantes, 189, 376
Chandler, Raymond, 42, 100, 342
Chaucer, 131, 233
Chekov, Anton, 337
Chestnutt, Charles Waddell, 6, 224
Childhood, 3, 22, 46, *65–67*, 117, 144,
   195, 319, 322, 361, 402. *See also* Bild-
   ungsroman
China, *67–69*, 408
Christian, Hoke (Uncle Willy), 414
Christianity, 39, 42, *69–70*, 71, 96, 120,
   198, 231, 262, 269–70, 321; Christ,
   Christ-like, 79, 89, 119, 148, 153–54,
   228, 230, 241, 266, 321
Christmas, Joe, 24, 41, 50, 54–56, 65–67,
   69, *70–71*, 76, 78, 80, 115, 135, 137,
   143–44, 153, 173, 177, 182–83, 195–
   96, 210, 229–31, 239, 269, 291, 301,
   303–4, 308, 320–21, 370, 374–75, 387,
   390, 427

Civil Rights, 103, 226, 293–94, 308–09, 312–13, 315, 352, 367, 401, 423. *See also* Dixiecrats; Politics; Race

Civil War, 13, 28, 33, 41, 49–50, *71–75*, 77–78, 83, 105, 107, 120, 136, 175, 177, 195, 206, 238, 249, 259, 262, 275, 311, 314, 322, 327–28, 339, 346–47, 350, 353, 355, 364–66, 371–72, 374–76, 379, 392, 405, 418–19, 422, 432, 438, 442–44; battle sites: Gettysburg, 364; Shiloh, 72; Officers: Beauregard, 126; Nathan Bedford Forrest, 262, 313, 365; Ulysses Grant, 73–74, 355, 365; Robert E. Lee, 86, 367; Picket, 86, 364; Sherman, 73, 86; Whiskey Smith, 74; Van Dorn, 73; War Between the States, 85, 335, 385, 415. *See also* Union

Class: 50, 53, 71, *75–77*, 82, 98, 184, 186, 196, 224, 248–49, 267, 332–35, 343–44, 357, 366, 373, 393, 421, 432; Aristocracy, 3, 75, 295, 312, 333, 347, 365, 424, 439; Black Bourgeosie, 8; bourgeosie, 244, 333, 339–40, 433; equalization, 167; establishment, 320; faux nobility, 196; gentility, 105; gentry, 337, 366; hillbilly, 206; marginalized, 373; masses, 312; masters, 175–76, 206, 238, 353; middle class, 257; paternalism, 421; patriarchy, 209, 361, 440–41; peasantry, 439; planter elite, white planter, 312, 366; poor white, white trash, 84, 190, 206, 240, 259, 347, 365, 432; poverty vs. power, 196; privilege, 159–60, 188; rednecks, 206, 239–40; underclass, 318; yeomen, 249, 365, 371, 413. *See also* Economics; Historical Materialism; Marxism, New Historicism

Clemens, Samuel. *See* Twain, Mark

Clergy, *77–79*, 172, 228, 323

"The Cobbler," 270

Cofield, J. R., Jack, 427. *See also* Visual Record

Coindreau, Maurice-Edgar, 20, 58, *79–80*, 140–41, 409

Coldfield, Ellen, 86, 157, 182, 266, 390–91; Coldfield, Goodhue, 40, 73, 320,

353; Coldfield Rosa, 2, 136, 143, 157, 177, 182, 255–56, 291, 331, 369, 387, 441. *See also* Sutpen

Collected Stories of William Faulkner, 4, 13, 19, 25, 28, 36, 39, 51, 59, 65, *80–84*, 89, 91, 95, 103, 105, 108, 116, 135, 139, 155, 165, 181, 213, 225, 232, 253, 259–60, 262, 287, 315, 331, 350–51, 393, 396–97, 399–401, 411, 414, 422, 432, 443

Collections, *84–85*

Collectivism, 83, 112, 120, 122, 160, 186; anonymity, 380; authority, authoritarian(ism), 69, 89; compulsion, force, 228, 367; conformity, 187; masses, 234; mobs, gangs, 108, 122, 187, 201, 239, 306, 343. *See also* Totalitarianism

College Hill Presbyterian Church, *85–86*, 130

College Life, 412

Collier's magazine, 148, 289

Collins, Carvel, 21, 47, 269, 287, 383, 422; Wilkie, 99. *See also* Carvel Collins Collection

Comedie humaine, La, 27, 101

Comedy, comic, 39, 138, 150, 190, 231, 260, 262, 283, 314, 319, 342, 344, 350–51, 354, 359, 372, 401, 409, 431, 435, 438

Commins, Saxe, *86–87*, 134, 149, 227, 276, 281, 437

Compson, 18, 64–66, 69, 75, *87–88*, 94, 102, 118, 136, 147, 157, 182, 205, 210, 237–38, 242, 297, 303, 321, 347, 357, 360–61, 365–66, 370, 372, 385; Benjy, 19, 117, 136, 143–44, 147–48, 174–76, 195, 207, 237, 246, 258, 270, 301, 321, 336, 351, 361, 386, 389, 396; Candace, Caddy, 16, 18, 19, 48, 64, 117, 136, 171, 174–75, 186, 205, 270, 301, 303, 321, 329, 346, 361–63, 375, 390, 396, 439–41; Caroline (Bascomb), 40, 75, 136–37, 351, 396; Damuddy, 174, 361; Jason Richmond Sr. (III, Mr.), 136, 185, 187, 292, 390, 396, 400; Jason IV, 18–19, 24, 41, 64, 75, 124, 136–37, 147, 157, 182, 186, 190, 210, 237, 301, 303, 351, 361, 363,

386, 396–97, 412; Jason Lycurgus II (General), 87, 193, 256; Quentin (female), 18, 24, 147, 175, 182, 237, 362–63; Quentin (male), 1, 2, 16, 19, 37, 41, 48, 64, 66–67, 76, 93, 106, 115, 121, 135–36, 142–44, 147, 157–58, 175, 177, 181–82, 185–86, 189, 195, 203, 207, 211, 213, 232, 237–38, 250, 252, 255, 269, 275, 292, 302–3, 321, 346, 349, 361, 363–64, 368, 375, 386–87, 389–91, 396–97, 400; Quentin Maclachlan, 18, 363; Quentin Maclachlan II (Governor), 87

Compson Appendix. *See* "Appendix, Compson, 1699–1945"

Community, 53, 113, 139, 167, 185–86, 205, 216–17, 219, 222, 224–25, 230–31, 238, 244, 262, 266, 289–90, 321, 324, 331–33, 351, 362, 366, 388, 405–6, 435

Comyn, 4–5

Condillac, 246

Confederacy, Confederates, 39, 56, 71–73, 84, 86, 105, 125–26, 131, 159, 172, 21, 259, 262, 311–12, 328, 334, 364–65, 370, 379, 385, 392, 416; Dixie, 371. *See also* Civil War

Conferences: Faulkner and Yoknapatawpha, 23, 47, 124, 128, 171, 303, 428; China, 68; International Faulkner Symposium (Colloquium), 147, 204

Conrad, Joseph, 49, *88–89*, 138, 186, 189, 194, 290, 316, 417

Contempo, 161, 280

Cooper, Minnie, 76, *89*, 108, 331, 400

Cooper, James Fenimore, 112–14

Cop, 270

Copernicus, 141

Corncob, 342

Corporal, *89*, 119–21, 338. See *Fable, A*

Corrected Texts. *See* Texts

Cosmopolitan magazine, 155

Cosmos, 27, 101, 205; Little Postage Stamp of Native Soil, 131, 208, 272, 347, 365, 370

Cotton, 40, 73, 176, 206, 253, 266, 277, 353, 396

Cotton, Ernest, 184

Coughlan, Robert, 45, 281, 383

Country Lawyer, 89

"Country Mice," 270

"Courthouse, The," 135, 324

"Courtship, A," 83, *90*, 378

Cousin Melisandre, 262

Cowley, Malcolm, 17–18, 45, 81, *90–91*, 133, 164, 179, 226, 235–36, 276–77, 281, 296, 348, 362, 365, 367, 381, 430; Faulkner-Cowley File, The, 226, 297

Craig, Gordon, 247

Crane, Hart, 107, 235; Joan St. C., 245, 298

Crawfishford, 213

"Crevasse," 83, *91*, 399–400, 443

Crump, Lucas, 192

Cummings, E. E., 235, 284

Dain, Martin, 352, 427. *See also* Visual Record

"Damned Don't Cry, The," *92*

"Damon and Pythias," 270

"Dangerous Man, A," *92*, 415

Danny, 287

Dante, 190, 255

"Danzas Venezuela," *92–93*

Dark House, 1, 158, 228, 306, 366

Darwin, Charles, 39, 142, 153, 188, 254

David, 258

Davidson, Donald, 371

Davy, 225

Deacon, 66

Death, 20–21, 39, 49, 58, 60, 80, 84, 91, *93–94*, 102, 106, 113, 115, 122, 129, 134–35, 148, 153–54, 163, 172–73, 182, 185, 199, 210, 215, 225, 229, 236, 248, 278, 284, 287, 300, 305–6, 311, 315, 317–18, 325, 327–29, 333, 347, 349–50, 354, 357–59, 361, 368, 377, 384, 390–91, 399–400, 405, 417, 424, 434–35, 443

"Death Drag," 83, *95*, 105, 182, 296, 408

Deconstruction, *95–96*

De Gaulle Story, The, 32, *96–97*, 101, 140, 178, 445

DeLoria,Vine, Jr., 197

"Delta Autumn," 7, 36, 44, *97–98*, 115, 149, 151, 204, 279, 296, 415, 445
Delta Council, Address to, 377, 427
Delta Democrat-Times, 61
Depression, Great Depression, 22, 95, 159, 228, 233, 304; New Deal, 175; Roosevelt, Franklin Delano (President), 96, 333; Wall Street Panic, 20; WPA, 351, 355, 436, 445
de Spain, *98–99*, Major, 28, 35–36, 44, 75, 82, 176, 191, 232, 276, 350; Manfred, 99, 183, 406–7
Detective stories 84, *99–101*, 105, 177, 216, 241, 289, 295, 342. See also *Intruder in the Dust*; Knight's Gambit
Dickens, Charles, 49, *101–2*, 138, 322, 333
Dickinson, Emily, *102*, 260
"Diana," 102
Dietician, 71, 229
Díez, Luis Mateo, 376
Dilsey. *See* Gibson, Dilsey
Dispossession, dislocation, displacement, exclusion, exile, ostracism, outcast, 7, 18, 33, 41, 44, 84, 105, 143, 155, 159–61, 172, 196, 231, 236, 244, 373, 399, 422, 441; thresholds, 3, 29, 42, 187, 391
"Divorce in Naples," 84, *103*, 181, 297, 401
Dixiecrats, *103–4*. See also *Intruder in the Dust*
Dr. Martino and Other Stories, 39, 48, 81, 95, *104–5*, 116, 139, 181, 184, 216, 225, 259, 398, 411, 432
"Doctor Martino"/"Dr. Martino," *105–6*
Dodge, Granby, 216
Don, 357
"Don Giovanni," *106*, 261, 415
Doom, D'Homme, 44, 90, 193, 213, 315–16, 400. *See also* Ikkemetubbe
Dos Passos, John, 79, 90, 220, 235, 248, 284, 290, 348, 444
Dostoevsky, Fyodor, 119, 138, 144, 186, 189, 337–38, 417. *See also* Russia
Double Dealer, The, 11, *106–7*, 132, 144, 268–69, 300, 422

Douglas, Ellen, 369
Doyle, Arthur Conan, 99, 105, 216, 295
Drake, Temple, 41–42, 92, *107*, 132, 136, 144, 190, 223, 242, 270, 303, 324–25, 342–45, 359, 372, 382, 387, 428, 439–41; Judge, 342–43
Dream, fantasy, vision, 10, 16, 48, 59, 60, 66, 89, 115, 117, 127, 144, 148, 173, 207–8, 229, 247, 253, 262, 270, 274–75, 278–79, 327, 342, 347–48, 351, 359, 361–62, 400, 425, 443, 445
Dreiser, Theodore, 411
Drums Along the Mohawk, 179
"Dry September," 76, 79, 83, 89, *108–10*, 135–36, 165, 169, 204, 240, 331, 367, 400–401
Dulcie, 438
"Dull Tale," 42, *110*, 415
Dunbar, Paul Lawrence, 6
DuPre, Jenny Aunt, Miss (Virginia Sartoris), 211, 346, 369, 398, 440

Early Prose and Poetry, 173
Easter, Holy (Passion) Week, 69, 87, 119–20, 147–48, 182, 208, 229, 321, 351, 358, 361
Ebony magazine, 192, 309, 367
Economics: 29, 44, 87, 150, 165, 167–68, 176, 244, 254, 265, 297, 314, 354, 368, 371–72, 393; capital, 244; dirt farmer, 55; labor, work, jobs, 65, 156, 159, 162–63, 173,77, 182, 265–66, 284, 311, 317, 351–55; landlord, 176; mechanization, industrialization, technology, 26, 33, 35, 43–45, 99, 151, 219, 221, 249, 306, 323, 333, 340, 371, 374, 392; money, 22, 103, 151, 234, 281, 295–96, 305–6, 351–52, 397; ownership, 47, 98, 115, 125, 138, 176, 251, 326, 421, 431; sharecropper, sharecropping, 28, 137, 176, 347; trade, commerce, exchange, barter, swapping, buying, selling, 22, 73, 167 183, 190, 193, 232, 247, 260, 311, 316, 354, 396, 410. *See also* Class; Historical Materialism
Eden, 44, *111–14*, 149, 155, 347, 362, 368

Edmonds, *114–15*, 251; McCaslin, Cass, 33, 36, 40–41, 112, 114–15, 121, 128, 149, 171, 215, 251, 279, 368; Roth, Carothers, 36, 97, 114–15, 137, 148, 150, 156, 182; Zack, 31, 114–15, 150. *See also* Beauchamp; *Go Down, Moses*; McCaslin; Priest

Einstein, 2

Eisenhower, Dwight David (President), 288

Ek, 270

Ellery Queen's Mystery Magazine, 118, 216, 295. *See also* Awards

Eliot, Thomas Stearns, 49, 59, 62, 83, *115–16*, 131, 153–54, 162, 207–8, 236, 255–56, 262, 284, 299, 306, 330, 358, 383

Ellison, Ralph, 6, 9

"Elly," 83, 105, *116*

Elmer, 93, 103, 106, *116–18*, 133, 140, 144–45, 207, 286–87, 297, 302. *See also* "Portrait of Elmer, A"

Elnora, 125, 398, 419

Emancipation, 73, 125, 175, 238

Emerson, Ralph Waldo, 14–15, 235, 258, 370

Emmy, 359

Emotion(s), desire(s), feelings, 1, 3, 6, 27–29, 37, 51, 54, 84, 93, 106–9, 116–17, 130–33, 137, 139, 142, 158, 169, 187, 200, 236, 241–42, 244, 246–47, 252, 256–57, 266, 272, 283–84, 300, 308, 325, 330, 337, 348, 353, 358–59, 364, 368, 384, 389, 434, 436–37

Erdrich, Louise, 197–98

Ernest, Mister, 45, 310

"Error in Chemistry, An," *118*, 145, 216

Erskine, Albert, 52, 430

Essays, Speeches, & Public Letters, 58, 164, 192, 199, 215, 226, 228, 252, 264, 272, 280, 288, 377

Eunice, 34, 251

"Evangeline," 1, 42, *118*, 391, 415

Ewell, Walter, 35

Ewing, April ("Lalear"), 155; Ewing, Ira Jr., 155; Ewing, Voyd, 155, 181

Existential(ism) 58, 93, 140, 147, 188, 283, 348, 373, 443; absurd(ity), 58, 83,

287, 344; Kierkegaard, 162; l'etranger, 271. *See also* Alienation; Camus, Albert; Sartre, Jean-Paul

Exodus, 438

Fable, A, 12, 14, 25, 36, 40, 69–70, 86, 89, 96, *119–122*, 129, 134, 140, 145–46, 182, 184, 186, 204, 227, 247, 271, 281, 286, 288, 293, 321, 336, 338, 367, 373, 378, 404, 443, 445

Fairchild, Dawson, *122*, 257

"Faith or Fear." *See* "Pine Manor Commencement Address"

Falkner. *See also under Faulkner entries*

Falkner, Alabama (McLean), 286, 398

Falkner, Dean Swift, 25, 61, 93, *122*, 306

Falkner, John Wesley Thompson, 11, *123*, 124, 415

Falkner, Mary Holland (Auntee), 123

Falkner, Maud Butler, 10, 122, *123*, 132, 227, 285–86, 323, 427, 441

Falkner, Murry Charles, Jr., 45, 122, *123*, 298, 417

Falkner, Murry Cuthbert, 40, 123, *124*, 162, 298, 320, 416

Falkner, Murry Cuthbert, II ("Chooky"), *124*

Falkner, Sallie Murry, *124–25*, 362

Falkner, William Clark, 31, 73, 123, *125–27*, 314, 320, 347, 419

Falkner, Willie Medora Aunt, 10

Farmer, Cecilia, 94, 324

Farr, George, 359

Father Abraham, 20, *127*, 166, 243, 345, 356

Fathers, Sam, 33, 35, 43, 66–67, 113, *127–28*, 151–52, 171, 193, 195–97, 213, 276, 278–79, 301, 380, 400, 412

Faulkner. *See also under Falkner entries*

Faulkner, Alabama, 130, 228, 398

Faulkner, Dean (Wells), 385

Faulkner, James Murry ("Jimmy"), 3, 29, 47, *128–29*, 424, 445

Faulkner, Jill, 14, 23, 61, *129*, 130, 134, 288, 336, 385, 423; Jill Faulkner Summers Archive, 226

Faulkner, John Wesley Thompson, III,

25, 45, 124, 128, *129*, 134, 162; Mrs. 385

Faulkner, Lida Estelle Oldham, 11–12, 31, 40, 46–47, 61, 86–87, 92, 123, 129, *130*, 131–32, 134, 228, 261, 320, 336, 398, 417, 423–24, 426, 436–37, 439

Faulkner, Lucille Ramey, 128

Faulkner, William, *130–34*; physical stature, 26, 236, 424; self-estimate, 2, 62, 98, 131–32, 169, 227, 286, 326, 328, 341, 345, 349, 360, 363, 422, 433. *See also* Sport; University of Mississippi

Faulkner Reader, The, 94, *134–35*,

Feminist approaches, 98, 107, 122, *135–37*, 144, 181, 254, 293, 329, 366, 435, 440–41. *See also* Gender; Women

Ferber, Edna, 288

"Fire and the Hearth, The," 115, *137–38*, 150, 251, 283, 289

Fitzgerald, F. Scott, 90, 235, 284, 290, 294, 371; Fitzgerald, Edward, 232

Flags in the Dust, 31, 93, 106, 118, *125*, 127, 133, *144–45*, 162, 207, 253–54, 265, 269, 341, 345–47, 378–79, 393, 419, 430, 443–44. *See also* Sartoris

Flaubert, Gustave, *138–39*

Flint, Joel (Signor Canova), 118, 217

Flowers, Paul, 11

"Fool About a Horse," *139*, 414

Foote, Horton, 29, 278, 296; Foote, Shelby, 131, 365, 403

Fortinbras, Brother, 78

Forum, 331, 333

Four Seas Company, 245

"Fox Hunt," 105, *139*

France, 131, *139–41*, 234, 267, 408–10, 417; French Resistance, 402. *See also* individual authors

"Frankie and Johnny," *141*, 261, 269, 415

Franklin, Cornell, 130; Malcolm, 130, 337; Victoria (Fielden Johnson), 47, 130, 337, 438

Frazer, James Sir, 152, 208, 228–29, 254, 262, 321, 359. See also *Golden Bough, The*

French Architect, 354

French Symbolists, 19, 327, 359; European Symbolists, 247

Frenchman's Bend, 20, 57, 83, 127, 165–67, 182, 187, 313, 403, 406, 421

Frost, Mark, 257; Robert, 284–85, 299

Freud, Sigmund, 88, 116, 120, 131, *141–44*, 153, 254–55, 300–304, 332, 359; Family Romance, 22. *See also* Jung; Psychoanalytic Approaches

Fuentes, Carlos, 220–21

Fugitive (Vanderbilt) Poets, 52, 96, 371. *See also* Agrarian

Fukunaga, Takchiko, 204

Gaines, Ernest, 6

Games. *See* Sport

Gant, Zilphia, 252–53, 331; Mrs., 252–53

Gardner, Erle Stanley, 216

Garland Publishers, 395

Gauldres, Captain, 183, 217–18

Gender, 53, 72, 75, 87, 115, 117, 137, 143–44, 167, 181, 187, 197, 209–10, 243, 257, 267, 304, 331, 344, 407, 421–22, 444. *See also* Feminist Approaches; Masculinity; Women

George: "Divorce in Naples," 103; "The Leg," 225; "That Will Be Fine," 397

German Prisoner, 83, 399

Germany, *145–47*, 408–10, 426. *See also* individual authors

Ghost, haunting, 3, 71, 136–37, 158, 396, 418, 443

Gibson, Dilsey, 8, 18, 31, 41, 53, 64, 76, 136–37, *147–48*, 157, 160, 182, 210, 242, 291, 301, 320, 351, 361–62, 366, 396, 440

Gillespie, 22, 55

Gilligan, Joe, 358

Glasgow, Ellen, 364

"Go Down, Moses," 36, *148*, 382–83, 415

Go Down, Moses, 31–34, 36, 40–41, 43, 65, 76, 81–82, 87, 94, 97–98, 114, 127, 133, 135, 137–38, *148–152*, 156, 161, 180, 191, 193, 200, 208, 211, 216, 224, 232, 250–51, 271, 275–76, 278–79, 283, 289, 292, 308, 327, 346,

353, 355, 366, 373, 378, 380, 389, 395, 415, 431

God, figures of God, 45, 79, 102, 112, 119, 151, 153, 184, 227, 253, 256, 266, 320–21, 355, 366, 379, 405

God Is My Co-Pilot, 445

Golden Book, 17

Golden Bough, The, *152–54*, 208, 228, 255, 262, 321, 359

"Golden Land," *155*, 181

"Gold Is Not Always," 137, *156*, 415. *See also* "Fire in the Hearth"

Goodyhay, Joe (J. C.), 41, 78–79, 352, 445

Goodwin, Lee, 238, 342–43

Gordon, *156*; Caroline, 369, 371; Charles, 327; Randolph, 327

Gothic, 3, 15, 50, *156–58*, 188

Gowrie, 239, 365; Vincent, 199

Graham, Eustace, 24

Gray, Alexander, 91, 422; Gray, Duncan, 385

Great Migration, *158–61*, 355

Great White Father, 233

Green Bough, A, *161–62*, 185, 214, 252, 299, 437

Greene, Graham, 50, 356

Greenfield Farm, 31, 129, *162–63*

Gresset, Michel, 141, 162, 204, 246

Grier, 82, 413; Pete, 413; Res, 351

Grierson, Emily, 31, 75, 83, 102, 136, 158, *163*, 296, 331–35, 366, 400

Grimm, Percy, 108, 187, 229–30, 239, 320

Grinnup, Lonnie, 216–17

Grove, Lena, 41, 54, 56, 69, 115, 153, *163–64*, 171–72, 182, 215, 228–31, 258, 291, 301, 320, 387, 439–41

Grumby, 73, 328, 419, 422

"Guest's Impression of New England, A," *164*

Haas, Robert K., 149, 227, 309, 412

Habersham, Eunice Miss, 100, 182, 199, 201, 211, 440

"Hair," *165*, 257, 400

Hait, Mannie, 260

Hall, Donald, 288, 299

Hamlet, The, 10, 21, 28, 41, 80–81, 99, 105, 127, 135, 139, 153, *165–68*, 183–84, 189–90, 216, 221, 223, 227, 232, 234, 243, 266, 269–70, 292, 296, 301, 311, 338–40, 346, 369, 373, 378–79, 381–82, 388, 407, 410, 414, 421. *See also* Snopes Trilogy

Hammett, Dashiell, 100, 342

"Hand Upon the Waters," 216

Handy, W. C., 6, 131–32, 397

Hannah, Barry, 269

Harcourt, Brace and Company, 345, 430

Hardy, Thomas, 375

Harlem Renaissance, 235, 301

Harris, George Washington, 189–90, 368; Joel Chandler, 369

Harriss, Max, 183, 217

Harper's, 28, 39, 104–05, 139, 184, 206, 216, 232, 265, 280, 294, 309, 349, 432

Harry Ransom Humanities Research Center, 85

Harvard University, 66, 250, 291, 364

Hawk, Drusilla, 182, 274–75, 311, 328, 352–53, 419, 441. *See also* Sartoris

Hawks, Howard, 10, 32, 42, 61, 134, 179–80, 219, 329, 402

Hawkshaw (Stribling, Henry), 83, 89, 108, 165, 240, 400

Hawthorne, Nathaniel, 14–15, 112, 131, 202, 235, 246, 255, 370. *See also* American Renaissance

Heat, 21, 109, *168–69*, 254. *See also* Nature

Heisenberg, 2

Helen: A Courtship, 27, 47, *169–70*, 252, 426

Hellman, Lillian, 257

Hemingway, Ernest, 79, 90, 107, 131, 140, 145–46, *170–72*, 235, 237, 272, 281, 284, 294, 342, 346, 348, 371, 373, 385, 402, 413, 435, 444–45

Heppleton, Joan, 253–54, 345

Herbie, 106

Hervey, Henry C., 92

Higginbotham, Ellwood, 239

Hightower, Gail, 41, 54, 77–78, 115, 120, 133, 136, 164, *172–73*, 177, 182, 228–

31, 291, 320, 349; Gail (grandfather), 172, 248; Mrs., 172, 320, 323, 383

"Hill, The," 162, *173*, 247, 272

Hillyer, Robert, 288

Hines, Euphues Doc, 54, 78, 210, 229–30, 247, 320; Janitor, 71; Milly, 66, 78; Mrs., 172

Historical materialism, *173–77*; New Historical, 249. *See also* Marxist Approaches

History, 2, 24, 34, 51, 71, 82, 97, 111, 113, 149, 151–52, 160, 169, *177–78*, 186–88, 197, 204, 209, 219–20, 224–25, 232, 242, 248, 255, 262, 267, 306, 314–17, 322, 324–25, 335, 337, 339–40, 347, 350, 353, 356, 367–71, 374, 382, 400, 408, 410, 412, 419, 427; Southern Historical Society, Address to, 352, 367, 377, 405

Hodge, Elmer, 106, 116, 143–44, 207, 286, 297, 303; Jo-Addie, 117, 297–98

Hogan, Linda, 117

Hogganbeck, Boon, 24, 35, 43, 196, 232, 251, 276, 278, 318–19; David, 90, 193; Everbe Corinthia, 24, 183, 211, 318; Lucius, 36

"Hog Pawn," *178*, 415

Holiday magazine, 252, 364

Holland, Anselm, 216

Hollowell, Lee, 6

Hollywood, 1, 25, 61, 83, 119, 133, 155, *178–80*, 200, 296, 365, 433, 436, 445

Holmes, Jack, 305

Holtzman Collection, 85

Homer, 131

Homosexuality, *180–81*; gay literature, 103; homoerotic, 113, 250; homosocial, 184; lesbian, 161, 437

"Honor," 105, *181–82*, 443

Hope, Claude, 411

Horse, 12, 26, 128, 134, 138–39, *182–84*, 191, 215–16, 223, 229, 266, 317–18, 328, 336, 378, 381, 401, 424

"Hound, The," 81, 104–5, 166, *184*, 414

House, Darrel, 192

Housman, A. E., 93, 162, *184–85*, 255, 383, 437

Houston, Doris, 413; Houston, Jack, 105, 166, 168, 182–84, 245; Houston, Sam, 130

Howes, Anne, 20; Howes, Roger, 19

Hughes, Richard, 50

Hule, 259

Humanism, 16, 67, 69–70, 147, *185–88*, 284, 340

Humor, 39, 143, 154, *188–90*, 250, 262, 277, 281, 319, 321, 346, 369, 381–82, 409, 422, 438

Hunting, 43, 98–99, 128–29, 151, 181, *191*, 195, 197, 251, 279, 295, 310, 336, 354, 377–80, 383, 409, 431. *See also* "A Bear Hunt"; *Big Woods*; *Go Down, Moses*

Hurston, Zora Neal, 70

Huxley, Aldous, 257

"Hymn," 261

"Idyll in the Desert," 130, *192*, 415

If I Forget Thee, Jerusalem, 41, 61, 106, 144, 227, 286, 292, 328, 387, 395, 433–34, 436. See also *The Wild Palms*

"If I Were a Negro," *192–93*, 367, 405. *See also* Race

Ikkemotubbe, 18, 90, 128, *193–94*, 196, 213, 233, 278; Doom, D'Homme, 44, 90, 193, 213, 315–16, 400

I'll Take My Stand, 344, 368, 371. *See also* Agrarians; Fugitive Poets

Imagery, description, word play, 22, 30, 35–36, 41, 80, 108–110, 128, 135–37, 154, 156, 162, 176, 183, 195, 198, 208, 215, 233, 247–48, 254–55, 258, 269, 277–79, 295, 301, 306, 316, 321, 324–25, 327, 329, 335, 337–38, 343, 347–50, 354–55, 380, 386, 388, 396–97, 406, 409, 426, 432

Impressionism, 140, *194–95*, 270, 426–27

Incest, 3, 33, 117, 149–50, 158, 251, 257, 262, 345–46, 390, 392, 431

Indians *195–99*, 315, 353, 367, 400, 440, 446; Chickasaw, 33, 42, 44, 82–83, 128, 193, 233, 278, 315–16, 446; Choctaw, 195, 233, 259, 446. See also *Big Woods*; "Red Leaves," individual stories

Individual, individualism, individuality, 3,

15–16, 50, 53, 65, 67, 83, 96, 120, 179–80, 186, 194, 199–200, 205, 217, 248, 254, 267, 281, 289, 293, 309–10, 320, 326, 332, 370, 380, 393, 402, 404; individuation, 209; nonconformist, 146; outlaws, 235
Influences and Reception, pollen of ideas, 209. *See also* African American; Britain; China; France; Germany; Indians; Japan; Nagano; Latin America; Russia; Spain; Translations; individual authors
Inheritance, legacy, 32–34, 36, 43, 98, 114–15, 149, 151, 233, 251, 274–75, 347, 353, 357
"Innocent at Rinkside, An," *199*, 215, 380
Inoue, Mitsuharu, 204
Intruder in the Dust (novel), 24, 36, 41, 62, 67, 76, 86, 100, 104, 121, 129, 133, 146, 160, 182, 188, *199–201*, 204, 211–12, 217, 224, 240, 249–50, 295, 308, 339, 364, 372, 382, 412, 421
Intruder in the Dust (film), 179, *201*, 296
Issetibeha, 43, 193, 278, 315–16

Jackson, Andrew (President), 16, 233
James, Henry, 81, 194, *202–3*; James, William, 254
Japan, 14, 63, 134, 179, *203–5*, 264–65, 294, 367. *See also individual authors*
Jazz Age, 368; flapper era, 426. *See also* Lost Generation
"Jealousy," 270
Jeffers, Robinson, 255
Jefferson, Yoknapatawpha county seat, 21, 24, 31, 37, 41, 54–56, 65, 70–72, 77, 79 83, 89, 94, 99, 105, 108, 127, 151, 157, 163–66, 172, 182, 215, 222–23, 229–31, 242, 249, 253–54, 257, 291, 301, 311, 314, 325, 331–32, 342, 344, 346, 350, 352, 358, 365, 386, 391, 396, 399–400, 406–07, 412, 419
Jefferson, Thomas (President), 368
Jesus, *205–6*, 396, 400, 438
Jiggs, 305
Jobaker, 278
Johns, Maxwell, 413

Johnson, Andrew (President), 312; Johnson, James Weldon, 6; Johnson, Uwe, 146
Jones, Januarius, 359, 426; Milly, 182, 206, 432
Jones, Wash, 66, 83, 104–5, 184, 188, *206*, 432–33
Joyce, James, 49, 70, 106, 115–16, 131, 144, 153, 186, 189, 194, *206–9*, 236, 255–57, 286, 290, 299–301, 306, 338, 358, 374, 376, 385
Jubal, 259
Julio's Sister, 64
Jung, Carl G., *209–213*. *See also* Freud; Psychoanalytic Approaches
"Justice, A," 44, 83, 128, 135, 193, 195, *213*, 296, 400

Kafka, Franz, 70, 221, 376
Kant, Immanuel, 187
Kazin, Alfred, 248, 270. *See also* New York Critics
Keats, John, 33–34, 36, 38, 49, 94, 131, 197, *214–15*, 246, 330, 383; nympholeptic encounter, 214
Kennedy, John (President), 294; Watt, 24
"Kentucky: May: Saturday," 199, *215–16*, 380
King, Louise, 106
"The Kingdom of God," 270
Kit, 12
Klopfer, Donald, 281
Knight's Gambit, 81–82, 100, 105, 118, 204, *216–17*, 223, 249, 295, 324, 382, 402, 421, 445
"Knight's Gambit," story, 37, 182–83, *218*
Koeppen, Wolfgang, 145
Kohl, Linda Snopes, 24, 182, 186–87, 245, 338, 340, 390, 406, 421, 437, 439, 441. *See also* Snopes
Kreymbourg, Alfred, 247

Labove, 166, 379
Lafarge, Oliver, 268
Lafayette County, 9, 17, 47, 59, 74, 131,

162, 190, 239, 312–13, 335, 353, 355, 365, 367, 370, 427, 446
Lafe, 55
Lamar, L.Q.C., 313; Ruby, 342–45
Land of the Pharaohs, 179, *219*, 295–96
"Landing in Luck," 416, 443
Langgässer, Elizabeth, 145
Laroche, Captain, 329
Latin America, 51, 80, 92–93, 134, *219–22*, 281, 294, 373, 376–77, 408. *See also individual authors*
Law, 30, 89, 99–101, 200, 216–17, *222–25*, 233–39, 244, 253, 255–56, 267, 275, 281, 309–10, 312, 315, 324–25, 342–43, 382–83, 393, 400, 402–3, 414, 417–19, 421, 433. *See also* Stevens, Gavin; *Intruder in the Dust*; *Knight's Gambit*
Lawrence, D. H., 153, 301
Lee, Harper, 224
"Leg, The," 84, 104–5, *225*, 443
Legate, Will, 97
Letter, A, 92
Letter to Grandmamma, A, 92
Letters, 47, 132, 159, *226–27*, 261, *285–86*, 298, 308, 383–84, 405, 445
"Letter to the North, A," *228*. *See also* Race
Levine, 26
Lewis, Sinclair, 86
"Liar, The," 270
Library of America, 394–95
"Life and Death of a Bomber, The," *228*, 445
Life magazine, 45, 119, 228, 281, 309
Light in August, 8, 12, 24, 40–41, 54–56, 63, 65, 69–70, 73, 76, 78, 80, 108, 115, 130, 133, 135–37, 143–44, 146–47, 153–54, 161, 163, 172, 177, 187, 195–96, 204, 210, 217, 224, *228–31*, 239, 258, 270, 275, 290–91, 296, 301, 303–4, 308, 314, 320–21, 323, 346, 349, 366, 370, 374, 382–83, 387–89, 408, 419, 421, 427, 440; Lumière d'août, 79
Lilacs, The, 25, 93, *232*, 299, 426, 443
Lillabulero, 280

Lincoln, Abraham (President), 175, 312
Linscott, Robert, 18
Lion 33, 151, 232, 276, 414, 425
"Lion," 33, 32, 99, 151, *232*, 276, 414, 425
Lion in the Garden, 47
Littlejohn, Mrs., 139
"Lizards in Jamshyd's Courtyard," 166, *232*, 414
Llosa, Mario Vargas, 221, 375
"Lo!," 83, 195, *232–34*, 378
Long Hot Summer, The, *234*, 296
"Longshoreman, The," 269
Longstreet, Augustus Baldwin, 190; Longstreet, Stephen, 382
Loos, Anita, 62, 268
Loosh, 326, 355
Lost Cause, 74, 172, 322, 366, 369; religion of the confederacy, 39
Lost Generation, 25, 225, *234–37*, 286, 358, 444
Louis Daniel Brodsky Collection, 46–47, 85, 93, 226–27, 232, 252, 281, 288, 383
Lovelady, Mr., 396
"Love Song," 255
Lowe, Julian Cadet, 358, 442, 444
Luster, *237–38*
Lynching, 24, 74, 108, 169, 187, 199, 201, *238–40*, 283, 309, 313, 367, 401

MacWyrglinchbeath, Wully (Mac), 401
Maddow, Ben, 201
Mademoiselle, 57, 437
Magdalen," 270
Mahon, Donald, 236, *241*, 300, 358–59; Mahon, Rev. Joseph, 77, 358
Mailer, Norman, 294
Malamud, Bernard, 70
Mallard Collection, 85
Mallarmé, Stephané, 19, 246, 327
Mallea, Eduardo, 220
Mallison, Charles "Chick," 26, 36, 65, 76, 100, 104, 118, 121, 129, 178, 199–201, 211–212, 216–18, 223–24, 240, 295, 309, 364, 402–3, 406, 412, 445
Malraux, André, 140, *241–42*, 437

Mann, Thomas, 119, 145, 153

Mannie, 150, 283, 327

Mannigoe, Nancy, 70, 205, *242–43*, 324–25, 345, 396–97, 400, 438, 440

Mansion, The, 24, 26, 41, 49, 57, 78, 87, 99, 129, 146, 165, 178, 182, 184, 217, 223–24, *243–45*, 250, 265, 339–40, 352, 357, 382, 404, 407, 410, 415, 445. *See also* Snopes Trilogy

Marble Faun, The, 14, 93, 123, 132, 161–62, 241, *245–47*, 252, 258, 295, 349, 383, 408

Marionettes, The, 93, *247–48*, 299, 359, 425–26; Harlequin, 416; Marietta, 247, 416; Mezetino, 416; Pierette, 416; Pierrot, 37, 359, 416, 426; Spirit of Autumn, 359. *See also* "Pantaloon in Black"

Márquez, Gabriel García, 221, 375

Marsé, Juan, 375–76

Martin-Santos, Luis, 373–75

Marxist approaches, 98, *248–49*, 293; Marxism, 24, 267. *See also* Historical materialism

Masculinity, male(s) 16, 32, 48, 51, 90, 106, 113, 151, 160, 182–84, 210–12, 235, 249, 272, 304, 354, 381, 390, 440–42, 444. *See also* Gender; Feminist Approaches

Matute, Ana María, 373–74

Maurier, Mrs. Patricia, 122, 156

Mayday, 27, 47, 93, 287, 426

Mays, Will, 89, 108, 240, 400

Max, 66

McAlmon, Robert, 284

McCallum (s), *249*, 365, 379; Anse, 393; Buddy, 249, 443; Rafe, 182

McCannon, Shrevlin, 2, 41, 158, 177, *250*, 255, 275, 292, 364

McCaslin, 114, 127, 148–49, 162, 191, 211, *250–51*, 347, 365; Amodeus (Uncle Buddy), 33, 76, 149–50, 251, 353, 418–19, 431; Isaac (Uncle Ike), 15, 33, 35–36, 40–41, 43–44, 65–67, 94, 97–99, 102, 112–114, 120–21, 128, 149, 171, 187, 191, 211, 215, 251, 275, 278–79, 301, 353, 366, 368, 380, 383, 412, 425, 431, 445; Lucius Quintus Caroth-

ers, 32–33, 36, 41, 97, 114–15, 121, 125, 148–49, 151, 193, 200, 210–11, 251, 353; Ned 31, 40, 183, 211–12, 251, 318; Sophonsiba (Mrs. Theophilus, nee Beauchamp), 150, 431; Tennie (Beauchamp), 36, 150, 355; Theophilus (Uncle Buck), 33, 76, 149–50, 251, 353, 418–19, 431; Thomasina (Tomey), 251; Turl (Tomey's), 34, 36, 65, 76, 150, 211, 251, 355, 431. *See also* Beauchamp; Edmonds; *Go Down, Moses*; Priest

McCullers, Carson, 157

McEachern, 71, 166, 183, 321; Simon, 229, 320

McGee, Willie, 309

McHaney, Thomas, 170, 435

McLendon, 76, 108, 136

Meadowfill, Essie, 178; Mrs. Meadowfill, 178; Meadowfill, Otis, 178, 244

Melville, Herman, 14–15, 81, 112, 143, 235, 302, 417. *See also* American Renaissance

Mencken, H. L., 106, 320–21, 371–72, 397, 426

Memphis, Tennessee, 10–11, 77–78, 107, 126, 132, 160, 190, 216–17, 222, 251, 309, 318–19, 324, 326–27, 341–42, 344, 352, 367, 383, 398, 424, 428, 436–37; Memphis *Commercial Appeal*, 309

Meredith, James, 385, 408

Meriwether, James, 68, 383, 394. *See also* Essays, Speeches, & Public Letters

Metro-Goldwyn-Mayer (MGM), 179, 430

Midgleston, Wilfrid, 48

Migration. *See* Great Migration

Millard, Rosa Granny, 74, 212, 310–11, 326, 328, 355, 418–19, 422, 440. *See also* Sartoris family

Millay, Edna St. Vincent, 190

Miller, Henry, 285

Millgate, Michael, 15, 84, 167, 326, 341, 394, 398, 400–401, 412

Milton, John, 190

"Mirrors of Chartres Street," 268

Miscegenation, 1, 33, 97, 125, 146, 149, 175, 251, 257, 259, 364, 392, 398, 431

Mississippi, 17, 25, 43, 57, 67, 72, 79, 86, 89, 97, 125–28, 130, 133, 152, 168, 180, 206, 214, 233, 239, 252, 259, 268–69, 285, 312, 314, 324, 324, 326, 353, 355, 365, 367, 369, 415, 418, 424, 427, 433; Batesville, 191; Byhalia, 134, 424; Clarksdale, 383; Columbus, 123; Corinth, 73; Greenville, 61–62, 433; Greenwood, 401; Holly Springs, 73, 313, 437; Jackson, 342; New Albany, 126, 131, 162, 365, 428; Oxford, 47, 59, 61, 69, 72, 74, 85, 87, 123–25, 128–34, 140, 153, 158–59, 162–63, 169, 172, 201, 226, 236, 239, 247, 252, 257, 261, 269, 272, 287, 294, 308, 313, 335–36, 364–65, 367, 372, 383–84, 397, 405, 415, 423–24, 427–28, 433, 437; Oxford Eagle, 336, 416; Parchman, 434; Pascagoula, 27, 269; Pontotoc, 25, 122, 126; Ripley, 124–27, 131, 315, 365; Taylor, 428; Tunica, 61

"Mississippi," 3, 31, 252, 364, 368, 405

"Mississippi Hills," 93

Mississippi Poems, 170, 252

Mississippi River, Old Man, 44, 90, 277–78, 412, 434. *See also* Old Man

Mississippi Quarterly, 141, 226, 300

Mississippian, The, 173, 232, 247, 261, 272, 327, 412, 416, 426

"Miss Zilphia Gant," 79, 252–53, 415

"Mistral," 1, 42, 84, 253, 401

Mitchell, 253–54; Belle (Benbow), 37, 253–54, 345, 439; Harry, 253–54; Little Belle, 253–54, 342

Modern Library, 341

Modernism, 50–51, 110, 143–44, 153, 200, 203, 206, 208, 228, 254–56, 262, 267, 284–86, 290, 299, 306, 321, 339, 359, 369–70

Mohrt, Michel, 79

Moketubbe, 315–16

Molina, Antonio Muñoz, 376

Momaday, N. Scott, 197

Monaghan, 5, 182

"Monk," 216, 223

Monroe, James (President), 233

Monson, Myrtle, 203

de Montaigne, Michel, 300

de Montigny, Paul, 116

"Moonlight," 256–57, 415

Morris, Willie, 134, 427

Morrison, Toni, 6

Moseley, 41, 55

Mosquitoes, 17, 27, 59, 63, 106, 115, 118, 122, 132, 144–46, 156, 161, 181, 189, 207, 236, 255, 257–58, 269, 286, 302, 364, 437

"Mountain Victory," 83, 105, 259–60, "Mr. Acarius," 260, 415

Mulatto Mistress, 97

"Mule in the Yard," 81, 83, 260, 412

Mules, 26, 40, 73, 129, 162, 183, 310, 312, 324, 328

Mulligan, Robert, 29

Murray, Albert, 6

Murry, Dr. John Young, 125

Music, 6, 41, 80, 194, 205, 208, 247, 260–62, 281, 288, 320, 322, 333, 397, 433

"My Grandmother Millard and General Bedford Forrest and the Battle of Harrykin Creek," 262

Myrtle, 298

Myth, 3, 17, 20–21, 13, 75, 111–12, 115–16, 133, 135, 137, 151, 153, 155, 167, 169, 177, 186, 191, 195–96, 232, 241, 248, 254, 262–63, 325, 332, 335, 33839, 358–59, 364, 367–68; Achilles, 358; Agamemnon, 21; Demeter-Persephone-Kore, 21, 359, 440; Dionysus, 231, 321; Electra, 163, 332; Fisher King, 359; House of Atreus, 366; Isis, 164, 231; Mercury, 358; Odyssey, 21, 255; Oedipus, 99, 143, 255, 302–03, 440; Orestes, 2; Pan, 48; Ulysses, 207–08; West, 155. *See also* Apocrypha; Eden; Golden Bough; Religion

Nagano, 47, 138, 203, 264–65, 377, 430

"Naiad's Song," 261

Nakagami, Kenji, 205

National Endowment for the Humanities, 11, 29

Native Americans. *See* Indians

Nature, 94, 98, 113, 133, 149, 152, 167, 171, 184, 191, 196, 198, 219, 258, 265–

67, 300, 330, 337, 380, 412, 440; dirt, dust, earth, ground, land, 1, 28, 33, 112, 162–63, 169, 178, 196, 214, 219, 221, 265–66, 301, 362, 365, 422, 446. *See also* Heat

Nebraska, 155. *See also* Cather, Willa

New Criticism, 8, 52, 257, 267, 330, 431. *See also* Brooks, Cleanth

New Historicism, 28, 96, 249, *267*, 435

New Orleans, 10, 12–13, 16–17, 25, 27, 46, 61, 106–07, 118, 132, 140, 143–44, 153, 169, 193, 217, 226–27, 257, 259, *268–69*, 272, 280, 285, 288, 298, 300, 302, 304, 316, 328, 358, 364, 433, 437

New Orleans Sketches, 46, 82, 107, 141, 269, *269–70*, 288, 300, 364

New Republic, 19

New York Critics, 248, *270–71*

New York *Herald Tribune*, 2, 81

New York Public Library, 85, 226–27, 395

Nietzsche, Frederick, 254, 262, 435

Nin, Anaïs, 285

Nobel Prize Acceptance Speech, 18–19, 38, 82, 120–21, 129, 135, 142, 185–86, 190, 264, *271*, 281, 295, 297, 377, 445

"Nocturne," 261

"Note on Sherwood Anderson, A," 17, 272

"Nympholepsy," 162, 173, 214, *272–73*, 299, 415

Ober, Harold, 403

O'Connor, Flannery, 70, 157

"Ode on a Grecian Urn," 33–34, 36, 49, 94, 197, 214–15, 246, 330; urn motif, 38, 162. *See also* Keats, John

Odelthrop, Monk, 216, 223

"Odor of Verbena, An," 37, 127, 135, 183, *274–76*, 315, 369, 391, 418–19

Oe, Kenzaburo, 205

Old Ben, 33, 35–36, 151, 191, 197, 232, *276*, 301, 425

Old Frenchman's Place, 166, 342–43

Old General, 119–21, 338

Oldham, Estelle (*See* Faulkner, Lida Estelle Oldham); Lemuel, 14, 298

Old Het, 260

Old Man, 29, 135, 224, *276–78*, 387, 434

Old Man, 29, *278*

"Old People, The," 43, 98–99, 150–51, 193, 195, *278–80*, 391, 414–15

Ole Miss, 63, 124–25, 130, 158, 285, 365, 379, 385, 412, 415–17, 428; yearbook, 261, 416, 426. *See also* University of Mississippi

Omlie, Vernon C., 25

Omnibus Film, 163

"Once Aboard the Lugger," 82, *280*, 415

Onetti, Juan Carlos, 220

O'Neill, Eugene, 86, 247, 416

"On Fear: The South in Labor," *280*, 404–5

"On Privacy," 265, *280–81*, 294, 404–5

Ord, Matt, 305

Order of Andrés Bello, The, *281–82*, 377

"Out of Nazareth," 270, 272

Owens, Louis, 198

"Pantaloon in Black," 6, 149–50, *283–84*, 301, 327, 415

Pap, 342–43

Paris, 116, 140, 172, 193, 207, 235–36, *284–87*, 297, 316, 324, 426; Luxembourg Gardens, 133, 140, 285–86, 324

Paris Review, 361

Parker, Margaret, 417

Parks, Joe, 162

Partisan Review, 270

Partridge, Bellamy, 89

Pascal, Blaise, 289

Patton, Nelse, 239

Peabody, Dr. Lucius, 39, 41

"Pennsylvania Station," 287

People-to-People Partnership, *287–88*, 294, 299

"Percy Grimm," 135

Perversion, beastiality, grotesque, necrophilia, 32, 155, 157–58, 166, 190, 254, 301, 332–33, 342, 346, 366, 428

Pete, 242, 280

"Peter," *288*, 415
Pettibone, 66
Pine Manor Commencement Address, *288–89*, 404
Pitavy, François, 141
Poe, Edgar Allan, 3, 93, 99–100, 105, 156, 162, 216, 255, *289*
Poetry, 14–15, 59, 102, 161, 185–86, 255, 266, 269, 272, 327–28, 330, 383, 432, 437. *See also* Early Prose and Poetry; *Green Bough, A*; *Helen: A Courtship*; *Lilacs*; *Marble Faun, The*; *Mississippi Poems*; "Vision in Spring"; individual poets
"Point of Law, A," 137, *289*, 415
Point of View, 64, 88, 104, 146–47, 158, 166, 177, 182, 185, 194, 204, 207, 216, 220–21, 225, 243–44, 246, 250, 255, 258, 269, 283, 287, *290–92*, 306, 314, 317–19, 331–32, 338, 343, 350, 361, 372, 374, 376, 385–87, 390, 393, 407, 415, 433
Politics, 57, 97, 217, 222–24, 233, 270, 289, *293–94*, 309–11, 314, 322–23, 338, 352–53, 366, 368, 372, 393, 404–08; cold war, 33, 120, 171, 297; communism, 245, 299, 405; facism, 32; Gestapo, 445; Nazi, 146, 230; political novel, 121; populist, 96. *See also* Dixiecrats
Polk, Noel, 242, 341, 394–95, 426
Pope, Alexander, 233
Popeye. *See* Vitelli, Popeye
Popular Culture, *294–96*, 306, 435–36
Portable Faulkner, The, 17–18, 81, 90, 133–34, 179, 226, 276, 281, *296–97*, 315, 326, 348, 362, 381, 430. *See also* Cowley, Malcolm
Porter, Kathryn Anne, 188, 285, 369, 371
"Portrait," 107
"Portrait of Elmer, A" *297–98*, 415. *See also* Elmer
Postmaster, 124, 132, *298–99*, 417
Pound, Ezra, 107, 162, 203, 236, 284, 288, *299–300*
Powers, Margaret, *300*, 358–59, 426; Powers, Richard 358–59

Priest, 114, 251; Boss (L.Q.C.), 24, 41, 212, 251, 292, 317–19; Lucius, 24, 65, 67, 183, 187, 211–12, 251, 317–19; L.Q.C. , 251; Maury, 237. *See also* Beauchamp; Edmonds; McCaslin; Reivers, The
"Priest, The," 269, *300*, 415
Primitivism, 153–54, 196, *300–301*, 440
Princeton University, 79, 85
Pritchell, 118
Pritchett, V. S., 50
Privacy, 219, 280–91, 293–94, 309, 423; solitude, 113. *See also* "On Privacy"
Prohibition, 12, 107, 268, 285, 338, 368; moonshine, 150. *See also* Bootlegging
Prostitute, brothels, red light districts, 10–11, 103, 141, 223, 230, 242, 288, 295, 306, 318–19, 324–25, 341–42, 345, 383, 396; Jezebel, 71
Proust, Marcel, 348, 376
Provincetown Playwrights, 247
Provine, Lucius, 36
Psychoanalytic approaches, 21, 241, *301–4*, 444. *See also* Freud, Sigmund; Jung, Carl G.
Pylon, 5, 25, 58, 106, 132, 146, 161, 204, 269, 290, 296, *304–7*, 364, 378, 387, 394–95
Pynchon, Thomas, 294

Queen, Ellery, 295
Quick, 365; Ben, 234; Solon, 351
Quincannon, Captain, 10

R.A.F. (Royal Flying Corps), 25, 63–64, 227, 236 306, 442, 445
Race, 3, 7–8, 34, 50, 53, 55, 61–62, 71, 75, 87, 90, 97–98, 104, 109, 113, 115, 133–34, 137, 146, 149, 152, 168, 174, 187, 196, 200–201, 212, 224, 230–31, 243, 245, 259, 267, 270, 275, 278, 280, 283–84, 288, 293, *308–10*, 318, 320, 323, 331, 339, 351–52, 364, 366–67, 371–72, 384, 391, 396, 404, 412, 419, 422–24, 440; black/white 36, 65, 77, 89, 133, 137–38, 150–51, 192, 209–11, 229–30, 238–40, 242, 259, 327,

364, 382, 396–97, 405, 438; Black
Belt, 365; Black Codes, coding, 71,
312; ethnic, 113, 175, 233; equal justice, 343; integration, (de)segregation,
18, 62, 74, 103, 228, 265, 280, 309,
352, 423–24; Jim Crow, 62, 159, 228,
365; Ku Klux Klan, 238, 313;
NAACP, 192, 228, 239; ''nigger/ni-
gra,'' 3, 70, 151, 175–76, 200, 205,
210–12, 229–30, 259, 314, 325, 354,
367, 396, 413; non–white, 444; pater-
nalism, 148, 192, 240, 308, 353, 366;
White Man's Burden, 56; white supremacy, 4, 8, 201, 238, 401. *See also*
African American; Civil Rights; Great
Migration; Hodding Carter; ''If I Were
a Negro''; Lynching; Miscegenation;
James Wesley Silver, ''Letter to the
North, A''
''Race at Morning,'' 43–44, *310*, 378, 15
''Raid,'' *310–11*, 414
Railroad, trains, 24, 33, 44, 99, 124, 126,
192, 287, 314, 342, 358, 415, 419
Raimbault, René-Noël, 79, 140
Ramey, Myrtle, 252
Randolph, Lewis, 327
Random House, 1, 86, 127, 148–49, 179,
192, 227, 243, 281, 297, 394–95, 414,
418, 430, 438
Ransom, John Crow, 107, 321, 371
Rape, 89, 108, 190, 341–42, 400, 428
Ratliff, Vladimir Kyrlytch, 28, 36, 53, 57,
139, 166, 171, 187, 232, 244, *311*,
357, 406
Realism, 120, 138, 166, 173, 207, 248,
330, 359, 373–75, 406; local color,
369; magical, 198, 220; mimesis, 121,
223; naturalism, 248
Reconstruction, 7, 56, 238, *311–15*, 352,
367, 422; Forty Acres and a Mule, 312;
Freedman's Bureau, 313
Red, 190
''Red Leaves,'' 43, 83, 127, 193, 195,
296, *315–17*, 353–54, 378, 400
Red Ozier Press, 127
Redmond, Ben, 212, 274–75, 314–15,
419

Reed, Susan, 256–57
Reivers, The: A Reminiscence (novel), 31,
36, 39, 41, 67, 131, 133, 147, 159, 182–
83, 189, 194, 211–12, 237, 250–51,
271, 292, 296, *317–19*, 378, 384, 391,
412; Les Larrons, 79
Reivers, The, (film), *319*
Religion, 60, 87, 120, 238, 256, 261–62,
268, 312, 314, *320–22*, 353, 374, 409;
Anglican, 323; Baptist, 163, 320–21,
323, 396; Calvinist, 55, 69, 71, 111,
231, 269, 320–21, 323; (Roman) Catholic, 171, 269, 322; Civil, 323; Comparative, 152, 254; Episcopal(ian), 69, 77,
132, 320, 322–23, 384–85; Evangelical,
320, 322; Faith/Works, 351; Gnostic, 69–
70; Judaism, 322; Judeo-Christian, 39,
70; mass, 172; Methodist, 69, 86, 125,
320–21, 323; Mormons, 40; Original
Sin, 322; prayers, 125; Presbyterian, 66,
71, 78, 85–86, 172, 320–22, 384; Protestant, 231; Puritan(ism), 22, 56, 71, 80,
320–22, 368, 370; Sacral, Sacramental,
sacred, 33, 380; St. Francis, 438; Spiritual Narrative, 33; Unitarian, 316;
YMCA, 320–21. *See also* Religion,
Southern
Religion, Southern, *322–23*
Reporter, The, 304–6, 387
Requiem for a Nun, 39, 41, 43, 58, 70, 72,
74, 87, 92, 94, 107, 115, 134–35, 143,
146, 177, 194, 204, 224, 242, 261, 266,
271, 292, 297, 311, 323, *323–26*, 344,
367, 372, 382–83, 388, 391, 428, 437,
440; Requiem pour une nonne, 79
''Retreat,'' *326*, 414, 418
''Return, A,'' *326–27*, 415
Rice, Elmer, 288
Rider, 6, 150, 283–84, 301, *327*
Rimbaud, Arthur, *327–28*
Ringo (Marengo), 13, 85, 183, 211–12,
275, 311, 314, 326, 328–29, 418–19,
422
''Riposte in Tertio,'' *328*
Rittenmeyer, Charlotte, 27, 40, 61, 247,
328–29, 433–34, 439, 441; Francis
(Rat), 328

Ritual(s), 33, 35, 191, 195, 238–39, 261, 310, 315, 317–18, 323, 334, 378, 380, 431

Rivers, Reba Miss, 24, 318–19, 342–44

Road to Glory, The, 61, 179, *329*, 443

Robyn, Patricia, 27, 156

Rogers, 182

Romanticism, 19, 50, 74, 100, 125, 214, 248, 300, *330–31*, 422; elegiac, elegy, 252, 436; pastoral, 246, 257; Genteel Tradition, 90

"Rose for Emily, A," 31, 67, 75, 79, 83, 100, 102, 135–36, 158, 163, 185, 189, 203, 224, 291, 296, *331–33*, 366, 370, 398–400, 408

Rose for Emily, A, 333–35

"Rose of Lebanon," 326–27. *See also* "Return, A"

Rousseau, Jean-Jacques, 300

Rowan Oak, 36, 40, 47, 62, 85, 128, 130, 133, 153, 162, 228, *335–37*, 415, 417; Shegog Place, 31

Rulfo, Juan, 220, 375

Runner, The, 89, 121

Russia, *337–40*, 408–60, 417. *See also under individual authors*

Salinger, J. D., 49, 294

Sanctuary (novel), 20, 24, 37, 38, 41, 58, 65, 79, 100, 104, 106–7, 115, 118, 133, 140, 144, 153, 157, 161, 180–82, 190, 204, 207–8, 220, 222–23, 228, 238, 241, 262, 286, 296, 319, 324, 325–26, 339, *341–44*, 346, 359–60, 372–73, 387, 394, 398–99, 408–9, 416, 428, 440

Sanctuary (Film), 324, *344–45*

Sander, Aleck, 100, 199, 201, 211, 254

Sarah, 404

Sartoris, 5, 12, 24–25, 37, 40, 46, 77, 311, 320, 330, 341, *345–47*, 348, 365, 369, 419, 433, 443

Sartoris family, 13, 39, 41, 76, 120, 310, 328, *347–48*, 355, 357, 365, 368, 372, 378–79, 419; Bayard II (old), 13, 41, 183, 211–12, 262, 274–75, 310–11, 314–15, 328, 346, 370, 372, 379, 418–19, 422; Bayard III (young), 5, 24–25, 37, 162, 171, 210, 236–37, 249, 266, 326, 345–46, 348, 372, 379, 390, 398, 430, 444; Benbow, 37; Drusilla (Hawk), 182, 274–75, 311, 328, 352–53, 419, 441; Granny (*see also* Millard, Rosa), 74, 212, 310–11, 326, 328, 355, 418–19, 422, 440; John (Col.), 41, 55–56, 125, 163, 182, 210, 274–75, 314, 326, 332, 346–48, 352, 355, 369, 398, 418–19; John II (young Col.), 24, 347; John(ny), 5, 12, 25–26, 236, 345–46, 348, 379, 390, 399, 430, 438, 444; Narcissa (*see also* Benbow), 37, 118, 162, 223, 303, 342–43, 345–46, 398

Sartre, Jean-Paul, 58, 140, *348–49*

Saturday Evening Post, 13, 32–33, 36, 43, 104, 216, 226, 232, 259–60, 274, 310, 315, 326, 328, 351, 393, 401–2, 411, 413, 418–19, 422, 438

Saunders, Cecily, 130, 358–59, 439

Saxon, Lyle, 268

Schopenhauer, 329, 435

Schulberg, Budd , 86

Schwartz, Delmore, 270

Scot, clan, 46, 51, 85, 91, 125, 131, 317, 399, 401, 422

Scott, Walter Sir, 156, 330, 368, 371

Scribner's, 51, 89, 95, 104, 108, 139, 216, 226, 260, 280, 352, 381, 397–98, 418

Selected Stories, 68

"Sepulture South: Gaslight," 93, *349*, 415

Sewanee Review, 90

Shakespeare, William, 62, 138, 143–44, 162, 186, 189, 255, 302, *349–50*, 409; *Hamlet*, 99, 283; *Henry IV*, 78; *Macbeth*, 361

"Shall Not Perish," 82, *350*, 413, 445

Shaw, Irwin, 86

Shegog, Reverend, 41, 69, 238, 322, *351*

Shelley, Percy Bysshe, 162, 214, 330

Shenton, Edward, 43

"Shingles for the Lord," *351–52*, 413, 421

Sholohov, 339

Shuman, Dr. Carl, 305; Shuman, Jackie, 305, 394; Shuman, Laverne, 305, 328, 394; Shuman, Roger, 26, 305, 394

Sienkiewicz, Henryk, 134

Silko, Leslie Marmon, 196

Silver, James Wesley, *352. See also* Carter, Hodding, Sr.

Simms, William Gilmore, 156

Skeet, 256

"Skirmish at Sartoris," 37, 56, 274, *352–53*, 414, 418

Slavery, 44, 50, 55–56, 71–73, 76, 83, 86, 127, 151, 154, 159, 175–76, 193, 195, 220, 238, 251, 259, 308–16, 339, 347, 352–53, *353–56*, 365–68, 400, 418–19, 431. *See also* Civil War; Class; Confederacy; Race

Slave Ship, 356

Smith, Harrison (Hal), 161, 242; Smith, Lilian, 371

"Smoke," 81, 105, 216, 223

Snopes, 65, 114, 127, 157, 167, 190, 216, 292, 301, 311, 352, *356–57*, 366, 372, 383, 405–6, 412, 421; Ab, 28, 73, 75–76, 112, 139, 166, 176, 183, 187, 224, 244–45, 248–49, 260, 296, 418, 421; Byron, 144, 345; Clarence Eggleston, 57, 244, 343; Eck, 187, 410; Eula Varner, 99, 125, 166, 182–83, 186, 190, 232, 340, 379, 390, 406–07, 421, 440–41; Flem, 24, 65, 76, 139, 162, 166, 182–83, 187, 189, 210, 223–24, 232, 234, 244–45, 270, 311, 320, 338, 356–57, 381, 406–7, 421; Ike, 10, 166, 190, 208, 246, 301; Linda (*see also* Kohl, Linda Snopes), 24, 182, 186–87, 245, 338, 340, 390, 406, 421, 437, 439, 441; Lump, 190; Mink, 65, 79, 166–68, 182–84, 187, 224, 244–45, 340; Montgomery Ward, 210, 224, 357, 406; Orestes, 178, 352; Sarty (Colonel Sartoris), 28; Trilogy (see also *The Hamlet; The Mansion; The Town*), 39, 133, 165, 186, 223, 243, 271, 293, 311, 340, 356, 366, 382, 384, 405, 407, 421, 440; Virgil, 342; Wallstreet Panic, 356, 406

"Snow," 42, *357–58*, 415

Soldiers' Pay, 6, 17, 25, 63, 77, 93, 132, 144, 146, 159, 161, 203–4, 207–8, 236, 241, 268, 285, 291, 320, *358–60*, 364, 373, 408, 426, 442–43

Sometimes Wakeup, 193

"Song, A," 261

Sound and the Fury, The (novel), 1–2, 8, 16, 18–20, 24, 31, 38, 40–41, 48, 52, 64–65, 68–69, 75–76, 80–81, 87–88, 106, 115, 117–21, 133, 135–36, 142, 144, 145–47, 153, 157, 159, 161, 174, 177, 180–81, 185–86, 189–90, 193, 195, 203–4, 207–8, 210, 237, 242, 250, 255, 258, 270, 287, 290–91, 296–97, 301, 303, 308, 320–22, 339–41, 348–49, 351, 360, *360–63*, 366, 369–70, 372, 374, 385, 387–91, 394–95, 409–10, 433, 437–38, 440 ; La Bruit et la fureur, 79

Sound and the Fury, The (film), 296, *363–64*

South, The, 2–4, 8, 32, 36, 40–42, 56, 69, 71–72, 75, 77, 87–88, 96–97, 106, 118, 120, 135, 147, 151–52, 156, 163–64, 169, 175–78, 181, 189, 195, 203–5, 217, 221, 224–25, 228–29, 231, 238–39, 249–50, 252, 255, 258, 265, 274, 280, 283–84, 289, 293, 295, 308–15, 320–21, 323, 332–33, 337–40, 344, 346–47, 351–52, 353, 356, 358, 361–62, *364–68*, 371–72, 374, 382, 390, 396, 409–10, 419, 423–24, 440, 442–44 ; New South, 75, 400–401; solid South, 103. *See also* Great Migration

Southerner, The, 179, 296

Southeast Missouri State University, 85, 226, 395, 428

Southern literature, 40, 59, 107, 132, 135, 175, 225, 289, 330, 339, *368–70*; Southern Gothic, 157. *See also* Fugitive Poets; Southern Renaissance; individual authors

Southern Renaissance, 369, *370–72. See also* Southern Literature

Spain, *372–77*, 408, 410. *See also* individual authors

Speeches, 14, *377. See also by title*
Spenser, Edmund, 30
Spillane, Mickey, 39
Spoomer, 12–13, 399
Sport, 11, 49, 191, 215, 301, 318, 342, 377–81, 413, 417, 431. *See also* "Kentucky: May: Saturday"; "An Innocent at Rinkside"
Sports Illustrated, 199, 215, 380
"Spotted Horses," 20, 55, 82, 99, 127, 135, 166, 183, 223, 369, *381–82*, 412, 414
Spratling, William, 268–69, 285, 288
Stallion Road, 179, *382*
Stamper, Pat, 139, 183, 190
Stefan, 89
Stein, Gertrude, 235, 255, 284–85; Stein, Jean, 69, 134, 143, 361–62, 437
Steinbeck, John, 288, 301, 348, 373
Stevens, Bucky, 324; Gowan, 24, 324–25, 342
Stevens, Gavin, 7, 37, 62, 70, 104, 118, 121, 143, 148, 151–52, 183, 187, 200–201, 216–18, 223–24, 242, 244–45, 295, 308, 324–26, 357, *382–83*, 393, 402–4, 406–7, 437
Stone, Emily, 384; James (General), 191; Rosie (Miss), 125
Stone, Phil Avery, 13–14, 45, 131, 134, 140, 144, 191, 232, 235, 242, 244–45, 285, 298–99, 302, 313, *383–84*, 385
Stoneback, H. R., 408
Story, oral traditions, story-telling, tall tale, 19, 31, 53, 57, 72, 90, 97, 104, 116, 180, 189–90, 195, 232, 250, 253, 262, 270, 275, 291–92, 303, 311, 350, 365, 375, 383, 386, 409, 412, 443; trickster figure, roverman, 6, 232–33
Stovall, Mr., 396
St. Peter's Cemetery, 124–25, 130
St. Peters Episcopal Church, *384–85*
Stream of consciousness, 84, 116, 146, 194, 198, 204, 207, 255, 290–91, 338, 340, 360, 369, 372, *385–88*
Stribling, T. S., 371
Strother, Simon, 31
Styron, William, 134, 369
Stylistics, *388–90*

Subader, Tha, 4–5, 83, 399
Suicide, 1, 64, 66, 75, 87, 130, 160, 182, 185–86, 203, 229, 250, 320, 327, 335, 346, 350, *390–91*, 396, 421
"Sunset," 270
Supreme Commander, 89
Sutpen, 365–66, *391–92*, 425; Clytemnestra (Clytie), 391; Ellen (Coldfield), 86, 157, 182, 266, 390–91; Eulalia (nee Bon), 182, 391; Henry, 118, 121, 211, 302, 391–92; Judith, 1, 72, 94, 118, 391–92; Raby, 118; Thomas, 29, 41–42, 50, 52, 59, 65–67, 76–77, 83, 86, 88, 102, 104–5, 112, 114, 121, 125, 157, 169, 176, 182, 184, 187–88, 193, 195, 206, 210–11, 221, 250, 256, 274–75, 292, 301, 316, 335, 347, 354, 372, 387, 391–92, 418–19, 432. See also *Absalom, Absalom!*
Sutter's Gold, 179
Sutterfield, Rev. Tobe Rev. (Tooleyman), 321
Swift, Graham, 51
Swinburne, Algernon, 10, 49, 62, 93, 131, 299, 383
"Symphony, A," 261
Symons, Arthur, 247

T. P., 238
Talliaferro, Ernest, 106, 117, 144, 258
Tall Convict, 210, 387, 434–35
"Tall Men, The," 82, 249, *393*, 445
Tarnished Angels, The, 296, *394*. See also *Pylon*
Tate, Allen, 107, 289, 369–71
Taylor, Jeremy, 134; Taylor, J. J., 278
Tennyson, Alfred Lord, 78, 349
Texts, *394–95*; intertextuality, textual criticism, history, 18–19, 20–21, 28, 36, 43, 57, 59–60, 65, 80–81, 84, 88, 97, 110, 114, 117–18, 127, 137, 139, 141, 149–50, 156, 162, 165–66, 184, 213, 227, 232, 237, 243–44, 246, 249–50, 252–54, 257–58, 267, 269–70, 276, 280, 286, 296–97, 310–11, 326–28, 341–42, 345–46, 352, 358, 360, 362, 381, 388–89, 391, 396–97, 401, 405,

407, 410, 412, 414–15, 418, 426, 432–
    36. *See also* Translations
"That Evening Sun," 79, 83, 87, 135,
    146–47, 204–5, 242, 261, 324, 360,
    396–97, 400, 408
"That Will Be Fine," 146, *397–98*
"There Was a Queen," 37–38, 79, 105,
    125, 146, 275, *398*, 419
Theroux, Paul, 112
These 13, 4, 12, 59, 80–83, 91, 103–4,
    108, 130, 165, 213, 253, 315, 331, 396–
    97, *398–401*, 422; Treize histoires, 79
Thoreau, Henry David, 14–15, 114, 235,
    370
Thorpe, Buck, 403; Thomas Bangs, 190
Three Baskets, 315–16
Three Famous Short Novels, 381
"Thrift," 82, *401*, 415, 443
Thurmond, R. J., 126–27, 314
Till, Emmett, 309, 367, *401–2*
Time magazine, 281
Times-Picayune (New Orleans), 132, 268–
    70, 272, 285, 300
de Tocqueville, Alexis, 320
Today We Live, 25, 179, 295, 329, *402*,
    411, 443
To Have and Have Not, 179, 295, *402*,
    445
'Toinette, 13
Tolstoy, Leo, 138, 337
Tommy, 24, 342
Tom-Tom, 65
"Tomorrow," 29, 216, 349, *402–3*
Tomorrow, 29, 296, *403–4*
Totalitarianism, *404–5*. *See also* Collec-
    tivism
"To the Voters of Oxford," *405*
Town, The, 36, 41, 65, 81, 86–87, 99,
    129, 146, 165, 187, 194, 217, 223–24,
    243, 249–50, 260, 340, 378, 382, 391,
    404, *405–8*, 410, 421, 437. *See also*
    Snopes Trilogy
Tragedy, tragic, 22, 39, 50, 56, 65, 82,
    84, 138, 231, 241–43, 270, 333–34,
    340, 347, 350, 362–63, 372, 375, 383,
    401, 409–10, 422, 433–35, 441, 443
Translations, *408–10*
Trueblood, Ernest V., 9

Truman, Harry S. (President), 103–4, 200
Tulane University, 85, 170, 252, 395
Tull, *410–11*; Cora, 223, 320, 410–11;
    Eula, 410; Kate, 410; Vernon, 55, 410–
    11
Turgenev, 337
"Turnabout," 25, 105, 135, 402, *411*,
    443
Twain, Mark, 7, 15, 99, 112, 189–90,
    224, 318, 368–69, 381, *411–12*
Twentieth Century-Fox, 1, 179
"Two Dollar Wife," *412–13*, 415
"Two Soldiers," 79, *413*, 445
Two Soldiers, 413

Uncle Rodney, 397
"Uncle Willy," 55, *414*
Uncollected Stories of William Faulkner,
    6, 9, 12, 42, 57, 82, 92, 97, 106, 110,
    118, 139, 141, 148, 156, 178, 184,
    192, 232, 252, 256, 260, 272, 280, 288–
    89, 297, 300, 310, 326, 349, 352, 357,
    381, 401, *414–15*, 439
Underworld, demimonde, gangsters, rack-
    eteers, 10, 66, 321, 325, 341–42, 345–
    46, 409, 428. See also *Requiem for a
    Nun*; *Sanctuary*
"Une Ballade des Femmes Perdues," 63,
    232, 261
"Une Ballade d'une Vache Perdue," 261
Union, Yankee, 13, 56, 71, 73–74, 84,
    86, 105, 126, 189, 311, 326, 328, 355–
    56, 365, 371–72, 392, 418; Battle
    Hymn of the Republic, 41. *See also*
    Civil War
Universal Studios, 179
Universality, universal, 69–70, 147, 247,
    263, 315, 325–26, 376
University of Alabama, 367
University of Michigan, 85
University of Mississippi, 85, 122–24,
    128, 140, 162, 209, 232, 272, 274,
    298, 337, 342, 352, 385, 395, *415–18*,
    425–28, 433. *See also* Ole Miss
University of North Carolina (Chapel
    Hill), 371
University of Texas, 85, 226, 395
University of Virginia, 47–49, 85, 129,

143, 191, 202, 226, 243, 294–95, 342, 365, 378–79, 395, 404, 423; Faulkner in the University, 32, 48, 423. *See also* Virginia

"Unvanquished, The," 328, 414. *See also* "Riposte in Tertio"

Unvanquished, The, 13, 28, 40–43, 55–56, 68, 71–75, 77–78, 80–82, 85–87, 125, 127, 135, 146, 211–12, 216, 220, 248, 250–51, 262, 274, 296, 310, 314–15, 326, 328, 336, 352, 355, 370, 372–73, 408, 414, *418–20*, 422, 434

Updike, John, 22

Van Dyming, Mrs., 48

Varner, 366, *421*; Clara, 234; Eula (*see also* Snopes), 99, 125, 166, 182–83, 186, 190, 232, 340, 379, 390, 406–7, 421, 440–41; Jody, 421; Mrs., 421; Will, 57, 166–67, 187, 232, 234, 244, 421

Vatch, 259

"Vendée," 414, *422*

Verlaine, Paul, 10, 327. *See also* Arthur Rimbaud

"Verse Old and Nascent: A Pilgrimage," 214, *422*

Versh, 238

Vice(s), evil, immorality, sin, transgression, villainy, 3, 12, 21–22, 30, 44, 50, 57, 77–78, 83, 101, 107, 112, 134, 139, 148, 150, 155, 166–67, 187, 193, 228–29, 287, 317, 325–26, 342–43, 351, 356–57, 369, 372, 397–99, 401, 411, 421, 432. *See also* Perversion; Prostitution

"Victory," 83, 399, 408, *422–23*, 443; victory and defeat, 5, 78, 158, 178, 215

Vidal, Francois, 259

Vidal, Gore, 29

Viking Press, 296

Vintage Books, 395

Virgil, 255

Virginia, *423–24*

Virtue(s), codes of ethics, duty, heroism, values, redemption, 3, 12, 17, 19, 21–23, 26, 28–29, 31, 36, 43, 45, 67–69,

76–77, 82–83, 106–7, 111–13, 120, 122, 135, 148, 155, 165, 187, 197, 206, 215–16, 218, 242, 244, 249, 265, 272, 274–75, 287, 322, 350, 362, 364, 370, 379, 382–83, 393, 400, 402–4, 411, 414, 419, 422

"Vision in Spring," *425*, 426

Visual Arts, 336, *425–27*; artistic movements, 132, 286; Cezanne, 140, 286; Chavannes, 286; Degas, Edgar, 194, 286; graphic arts, 358; impressionistic painters, 88; Manet, Edouard, 194, 286; Matisse, 286; Monet, Claude, 194; painting, 129; Picasso, 153, 286; Renoir, Pierre Auguste, 194; Rodin, 286. *See also* Impressionism

Visual record, 349, 424, *427–28*

Vitelli, Popeye, 24, 42, 50, 65, 110, 144, 157, 181, 210, 341–44, 390, 409, *428–29*

de Vitry, Soeur Blonde Chevalier, 193, 316

Walker, Margaret, 7

Wallis, Hal, 12

War Birds, 25, *430*

Warner Bros., 10, 32, 40, 89, 92, 179, 228, 382, 445; Jack Warner, 96

Warren, Captain, 95

Warren, Robert Penn, 49, 52, 107, 224, 293, 369, *430–31*

"Was," 76, 149–50, 296, *431–32*

"Wash," 1, 28, 83, 104–5, 135, 206, 296, 391, *432–33*

Washington, Booker T., 367

Wasson, Ben, 11, 46, 61, 261, 345, 360, *433*

Wasteland, Waste Land, 60, 81, 83, 91, 105, 241, 306, 344, 358, 443–44

"Wealthy Jew," 269

Weddel, Francis Chief, 233; Saucier, 259

Welty, Eudora, 157, 188, 427

Werner, Peter, 29

West, American, frontier, pioneer, 22, 67, 112, 155–56, 189, 164, 301, 320, 324; Daniel Boone, 112; Promised Land, 41; Vanishing American, 197

West, Nathanael, 284

Weston, Jessie, 359
Wharton, Edith, 284
"White Beeches," 130
White Rose of Memphis, The, 126
White Springs, Elliot, 5
Whitfield, Rev. (Nevard), 21–22, 55, 77, 352
Whitman, Walt, 14–15, 235, 294
Whittington, Shawn, 29
Wilbourne, Harry, 40, 106, 143–44, 171, 227, 247, 328–29, 387, *433–34*, 435–36
Wild Palms, The, 27, 40–41, 62, 80–81, 132, 135, 146, 153, 170, 178–79, 204, 210, 220, 247, 269, 276, 278, 281, 292, 296, 328, 387–88, 395, 408, 433, *434–36*; Les Palmiers sauvages, 79. See also *If I Forget Thee, Jerusalem*
Wilde, Meta Carpenter. *See* Carpenter
Wilde, Oscar, 49, 246, 257, 286, 425
Wilder, Thornton, 107, 235
Wilderness, 33, 35, 43–45, 97–99, 111, 113, 120, 151, 157, 191, 197–98, 251, 276, 278–79, 301, 324, 350, 380, 412, 431
Wilets, Bernard, 34
Wiley, Ash (Old Man Ash), 36
Wilkins, George, 156, 289
William B. Wisdom Collection, 85
William Faulkner: Early Prose and Poetry, 422
William Faulkner: A Life on Paper, 40, 47
Williams, Joan, 38, 94, 133, 227, 242, *436–37*, 439; Williams, Tennessee, 157, 269; Williams, William Carlos, 288, 299
Winbush, Fonzo, 342
Wiseman, Eva, 161, *437–38*
Wishing Tree, 79, 426, *438*, 443
"With Caution and Dispatch," 415, *439*, 443
Wolfe, Thomas, 145, 235, 294, 364

Women, 23, 38, 56, 71, 73–74, 76, 89, 92, 97, 106–7, 135, 158, 182–83, 205, 209–11, 231, 240, 245, 252–54, 260, 270, 311, 325, 328–29, 340, 343, 354, 359, 362, 381, 426–27, 435–36, *439–42*, 444; feminine cycle, 321; feminine ideal, 156; feminine propriety, 166; New Woman, 300; sexism, 224, 235. *See also* Feminism
Woolf, Virginia, 194
"A Word to Young Writers," 14
Wordsworth, William, 255, 331
Workit, 365
World War I, 4, 12, 25, 38, 55, 69, 91, 95, 120, 123, 159, 171, 181–82, 225, 233–35, 238, 250, 268, 286, 300, 321–23, 329, 346, 348, 358, 367, 369–72, 379, 399, 402, 411, 430, *442–44*, 445
World War II, 26, 49, 79, 83, 98, 114–15, 123, 146–47, 159, 217, 228, 249, 270, 297, 299, 308, 322, 330, 340, 348, 350, 369, 393, 402, 404, 413, 443, *444–45*
Worsham, Doctor, 77–78; Miss, 151–52
Wright, Richard, 6, 9, 283
Wyatt, 334
Wylie, Elinor, 62

Yale University, 58, 85, 235, 383
Yáñez, Agustín, 220
Yeats, William Butler, 62, 254, 299
Yoknapatawpha, 7–8 17, 20, 25, 28, 36, 41, 52, 55, 59, 66, 71–72, 74, 77, 79, 81–82, 86–87, 98–101, 120, 131, 133, 139, 148–49, 186, 191, 193, 195, 205–6, 216–17, 222–24, 236, 245, 249, 257, 265, 275, 278, 292, 296–97, 304, 313–16, 326–27, 339, 345–47, 350, 354, 357–58, 360–61, 364–66, 370, 375, 378, 383, 393, 399–400, 418, 435, 439–40, 443, *446–47*
Yoknapatawpha Press, 252

About the Contributors

GARRY R. ALKIRE teaches in the Department of Language and Arts at Western Nebraska Community College in Scottsbluff, Nebraska.

DORIS BETTS, Alumni Distinguished Professor of English at the University of North Carolina at Chapel Hill, is the author of nine books of fiction, the most recent being *The Sharp Teeth of Love*.

INEKE BOCKTING has taught courses in American Literature and Culture at the Universities of Amsterdam, The Netherlands; Tromsø, Norway; and Orléans, France. She is the author of *Character and Personality in the Novels of William Faulkner: A Study in Psychostylistics*.

LOUIS DANIEL BRODSKY is a poet, book collector, and scholar who lives in St. Louis. He is the author of *William Faulkner: Life Glimpses* and coeditor of the multivolume *Faulkner: A Comprehensive Guide to the Brodsky Collection*.

ARTHUR A. BROWN is Assistant Professor of English at the University of Evansville. He has published critical essays on Poe, Henry James, and Faulkner in *Nineteenth-Century Literature, Studies in Short Fiction, Colby Quarterly*, and *Mississippi Quarterly*.

CAROLINE CARVILL is Associate Professor of American Literature at Rose-Hulman Institute of Technology. Her research interests include modern Southern writers and women's studies.

BONNIE DAVIS is the Director of Humanities Programming for the International Education Consortium, housed at the University of Missouri at St. Louis. A recipient of a National Council of Teachers of English writing award, she is currently doing research in the areas of cultural awareness and the literary canon.

DON H. DOYLE is Professor of History at Vanderbilt University and the author of a number of studies of Southern history, including a forthcoming book on the history of Lafayette County, Mississippi.

JOHN N. DUVALL, Associate Professor of English at Purdue University, is the author of *Faulkner's Marginal Couple: Invisible, Outlaw, and Unspeakable Communities* and numerous essays on twentieth-century American fiction.

CHARLES FORT holds the Reynolds Chair in Poetry at the University of Nebraska at Kearney. The recipient of a Randall Jarrell Poetry prize and other awards, he has authored two books: *The Town Clock Burning* and *Darvil*.

MARK FRISCH has published articles and a book on U.S. and Latin American literature. He is an Associate Professor at Duquesne University in the Department of Modern Languages and Literatures.

IKUKO FUJIHIRA is Professor of American Literature at Tokyo Gakugei University. Her research interests include three Nobel laureates, William Faulkner, Toni Morrison, and Kenzaburo Oe; and her recent book *The Patchwork Quilt in Carnival Colors: Toni Morrison's Novels* won the 1997 American Studies Association of Japan Award.

RICHARD GODDEN teaches American Literature at the University of Keele. He is the author of *Breathing Exercises: An Argument, Fictions of Capital*, and *Fictions of Labor: William Faulkner and the South's Long Revolution*.

STEPHEN HAHN is Professor of English and Associate Provost at William Paterson University. He is coeditor of *Approaches to Teaching Faulkner's* The Sound and the Fury, published by the Modern Language Association.

ROBERT W. HAMBLIN is Professor of English and Director of the Center for Faulkner Studies at Southeast Missouri State University. Coeditor of *Faulkner: A Comprehensive Guide to the Brodsky Collection* and editor of *Teaching Faulkner*, he has published criticism, personal essays, poetry, and fiction in a number of books and periodicals.

VIRGINIA V. JAMES HLAVSA, who taught at Queens College of New York, is the author of *Faulkner and the Thoroughly Modern Novel*. She also served as editor of *Women's Studies* for a special issue on Faulkner. Her poems have appeared in journals such as *Commonweal* and *The Dalhousie Review* and in two books, *Waking October Leaves* and *Squinnied for a Sign*.

W. KENNETH HOLDITCH is Research Professor Emeritus of American Literature at the University of New Orleans. Editor of the *Tennessee Williams Journal*, he gives literary walking tours of the French Quarter and has published extensively on Williams, Faulkner, and other Southern authors.

M. THOMAS INGE is the Robert Emory Blackwell Professor of English and

Humanities at Randolph-Macon College. He has authored and edited numerous books and articles on Southern literature, American humor, and popular culture.

DIANE BROWN JONES, the author of *A Reader's Guide to the Short Stories of William Faulkner*, is Lecturer in the Department of English at North Carolina State University.

RICHARD H. KING teaches American and Canadian Studies at the University of Nottingham, United Kingdom. He is the author of *A Southern Renaissance, Civil Rights and the Idea of Freedom*, and other works.

ARTHUR F. KINNEY is Thomas W. Copeland Professor of Literary History at the University of Massachusetts, Amherst, and Adjunct Professor of English at New York University. He is the author of *Faulkner's Narrative Poetics: Style as Vision* and Go Down, Moses: *The Miscegenation of Time*, editor of four volumes on Faulkner's families, and coeditor of *Bear, Man, and God* and *Approaches to Teaching Faulkner's* The Sound and the Fury.

PAMELA E. KNIGHTS lectures in English and American Literature at the University of Durham, England. She has published numerous articles on Faulkner, Edith Wharton, and others and is currently working on Kate Chopin.

TATYANA E. KOMAROVSKAYA, Professor and Chair of Russian and Foreign Literature at the Belarusian State Pedagogical University, Minsk, is the author of *Irving Stone's Works, The Representation of the Past in the American Historical Novel of the 20th Century*, and other works on modern American literature.

MICHAEL E. LAHEY received his Ph.D. in English from the University of Alberta in Edmonton, Canada, where he conducted his dissertation under an interdisciplinary committee of professors of English and Law. He has published articles on Faulkner in *Women's Studies, Journal of the Short Story in English, Mississippi Quarterly*, and the annual Faulkner and Yoknapatawpha Conference collections, *Faulkner and the Artist* and *Faulkner and Gender*.

CHERYL LESTER is Associate Professor of English, American Studies, and African American Studies at the University of Kansas at Lawrence. She is presently completing a book on Faulkner and the Great Migration.

MARIE LIÉNARD, who holds a Ph.D. from Cornell University and previously taught at Bard College, is a Professor at École Polytechnique, France. She has published critical articles and reviews and is currently working on two book manuscripts: *Mauriac and Faulkner: Poetics of Heat* and *Desire and Metaphor in Faulkner's Writings*.

ROBERT M. LUSCHER is Associate Professor and Chair of the Department of English at the University of Nebraska at Kearney. Among his publications are *John Updike: A Study of the Short Fiction* and essays on Updike, Ernest Gaines, J. D. Salinger, Emily Dickinson, and others.

VERONICA MAKOWSKY is Professor of English at the University of Connecticut. She is the author of *Caroline Gordon: A Biography, Susan Glaspell's Century of American Women*, and articles on Faulkner, Walker Percy, Kaye Gibbons, Eudora Welty, and Margaret Atwood, among others.

GLENN MEETER, Professor of English at Northern Illinois University, is the author of a novel, *Letters to Barbara*, and short stories appearing in *Atlantic Monthly, Redbook, Epoch*, and *The Literary Review*. His Faulkner essays have been presented at the annual Faulkner and Yoknapatawpha Conference and published in *Mississippi Quarterly* and other publications.

JOHN B. PADGETT is a doctoral candidate at the University of Mississippi. He teaches in the English Department and designed and manages several web sites at the university, including "William Faulkner on the Web" and the English Department's "Mississippi Writers Page."

CHARLES A. PEEK is Professor of English and Director of the Prairie Institute at the University of Nebraska at Kearney. The associate editor of *Teaching Faulkner*, he has published essays on Faulkner in the *Faulkner Journal* and the MLA volume *Approaches to Teaching Faulkner's* The Sound and the Fury.

GENE D. PHILLIPS is Professor of English at Loyola University in Chicago, where he teaches literature and film history. He is the author of *Fiction, Film, and Faulkner; Hemingway and Film; Fiction, Film, and F. Scott Fitzgerald*; and *Conrad and Cinema*.

SANFORD PINSKER, who is Shadek Professor of Humanities at Franklin and Marshall College, writes widely about American literature and culture.

NOEL POLK is Professor of English at the University of Southern Mississippi. His many publications on Faulkner include *Faulkner's* Requiem for a Nun: *A Critical Study* and *Children of the Dark House: Text and Context in Faulkner*.

GLENN REED is a faculty member in the English Department at Northern Arizona University in Flagstaff. His scholarly interests include Southern literature, the novel, and the Gothic influence on American literature. His most recent publication is a critical edition of William Gilmore Simms's *Martin Faber*.

REBECCA ROWLEY teaches English and American literature at Clovis Community College in New Mexico. Her scholarly interests, in addition to Faulkner, are Flannery O'Connor and British Romantic and Victorian writers.

HUGH RUPPERSBURG is Professor of English and Associate Dean of Arts and Sciences at the University of Georgia. He is the author of *Voice and Eye in Faulkner's Fiction, Robert Penn Warren and the American Imagination*, and

Reading Faulkner: Light in August, and he has edited two anthologies of writing from the state of Georgia.

STEVEN P. SCHNEIDER, Associate Professor of English at the University of Nebraska at Kearney, is the author of *A. R. Ammons and the Poetics of Widening Scope* and editor of a collection of essays entitled *Complexities of Motion: New Essays on A. R. Ammons's Long Poems*. His own poetry has appeared in *Prairie Schooner, Literary Review, Beloit Poetry Journal*, and other journals.

DARCY SCHULTZ, a member of the Department of English at the University of Nebraska at Kearney, is a doctoral student at the University of Nebraska at Lincoln.

DEAN SHACKELFORD is Assistant Professor of English at Southeast Missouri State University. He has published essays on Faulkner, Flannery O'Connor, Tennessee Williams, Harper Lee, and others.

MERRILL M. SKAGGS, Baldwin Professor of Humanities at Drew University, is author of *The Folk of Southern Fiction* and *After the World Broke in Two: The Later Novels of Willa Cather*, as well as numerous essays.

H. R. STONEBACK is Professor of English at the State University of New York at New Paltz. Both scholar and poet, he has published widely on Faulkner, Hemingway, and other writers.

MARION TANGUM is Associate Professor of English and Associate Vice President for Research at Southwest Texas State University. She has published treatments of Faulkner, Zora Neale Hurston, and Larry McMurtry and is currently working on Toni Morrison's *Jazz*.

TERRELL L. TEBBETTS is Brown Professor of English at Lyon College in Batesville, Arkansas.

JUNE TOWNSEND is Associate Professor of Spanish and Chair of the Department of Modern Languages at Wilmington (Ohio) College. A specialist in nineteenth- and twentieth-century Peninsular literature, her dissertation was entitled ''William Faulkner and the Spanish Post–Civil War Novel: Luis Martin Santos.''

JOSEPH R. URGO is Professor and Chair of the Department of English and Humanities at Bryant College in Smithfield, Rhode Island. He is the author of *Willa Cather and the Myth of American Migration; Novel Frames: Race, Sex, and History in American Culture*; and *Faulkner's Apocrypha*: A Fable, Snopes, *and the Spirit of Human Rebellion*.

DAVID L. VANDERWERKEN is Professor of English at Texas Christian University. He is the author of *Faulkner's Literary Children: Patterns of Development*, in addition to a number of journal articles and reviews on Faulkner.

GERALD W. WALTON is Provost and Professor of English at the University of Mississippi. His research interests include Faulkner, Katherine Anne Porter, and the history of Ole Miss.

JAMES G. WATSON is Professor of English at the University of Tulsa. He is the author of *The Snopes Dilemma* and *William Faulkner, Letters and Fictions* and editor of *Thinking of Home: William Faulkner's Letters to His Mother and Father, 1918–1925*.

LARRY WHARTON teaches late nineteenth-century American fiction, American Studies, and fiction writing at the University of Alabama at Birmingham.

ARTHUR WILHELM, a retired French and English teacher who lives in Atlanta and France, completed his doctoral dissertation on Maurice Coindreau under the direction of Thomas McHaney.

KATHY G. WILLINGHAM received her doctorate from Texas Tech University and presently teaches at Clovis Community College in New Mexico. She has authored notes and articles on Faulkner, Hemingway, and O'Neill and has presented papers at both national and international conferences.

JUERGEN C. WOLTER is Professor of English at Bergische Universität in Wuppertal, Germany. He has published extensively on American drama and literature.

MICHAEL ZEITLIN is Associate Professor of English at the University of British Columbia. He has presented papers at the annual Faulkner and Yoknapatawpha conferences and published essays on Faulkner in *Mississippi Quarterly, The Faulkner Journal, The Canadian Review of American Studies*, and other publications.

KARL F. ZENDER is Professor of English at the University of California at Davis. He is the author of *The Crossing of the Ways: William Faulkner, the South, and the Modern World* and other works on Faulkner, as well as critical studies of Shakespeare, Ben Jonson, and Theodore Dreiser.

ISBN 0-313-29851-3

90000>

EAN

9 780313 298516

HARDCOVER BAR CODE